Youth Baseball:

A Complete Handbook

Youth Baseball:

A Complete Handbook

Edited by: **Michael A. Clark, Ph.D.**
Tom Smith, M.S.
Thomas George, Ph.D.
Jill Elliott, M.S.

Youth Sports Institute
Michigan State University
Vern Seefeldt, Ph.D., Director

COOPER
PUBLISHING
GROUP

Library of Congress Cataloging in Publication Data:

Clark, Michael A., 1945
    Youth Baseball: A Complete Handbook

Cover Design: Gary Schmitt

Executive Editor: I. L. Cooper

Production Manager: Joanne Cooper

Project Coordinator: Jan Edmondson

Copy Editor: Kathy Childers

Library of Congress Catalog Card number: 88-43255
ISBN: 1-884125-01-8

Printed in the United States of America by Cooper Publishing Group, 701 Congressional Blvd., Suite 340, Carmel, IN 46032.

10 9 8 7 6 5 4 3 2 1

YOUTH COACHING SERIES

The Youth Coaching Series of books were written to provide comprehensive guides for coaches, parents, and players participating in youth soccer, baseball, football, softball, and basketball.

Developed by the Youth Sports Institute of Michigan State University, these books meet the guidelines established for youth coaches by the National Association for Sport and Physical Education.

Books in the Series:

Youth Baseball
A Complete Handbook (ISBN: 1-884125-01-8)
Skills and Strategies
Rules of Play
Effective Coaching
Training and Conditioning

Youth Basketball
A Complete Handbook (ISBN: 15183)
Organizing for the Season (ISBN: 15185)
Rules of Play (ISBN: 15186)
Individual Basketball Techniques (ISBN: 15187)
Basic Strategies (ISBN: 15188)
Methods for Effective Coaching (ISBN: 15189)
Sports Medicine and Training (ISBN: 15190)

Youth Football
A Complete Handbook (ISBN: 15191)
Skills and Strategies (ISBN: 15192)
Effective Coaching (ISBN: 15193)
Conditioning and Training (ISBN: 15194)
Rules of Play (ISBN: 15195)

Youth Soccer
A Complete Handbook (ISBN: 14837)
Organizing for the Season (ISBN: 15201)
Methods for Effective Coaching (ISBN: 15202)
Rules of Play (ISBN: 15203)
Individual Techniques for Soccer Field Players (ISBN: 15204)
Individual Techniques for Soccer Goalkeepers (ISBN: 15205)
Basic Strategies of Soccer (ISBN: 15206)
Sports Medicine and Training (ISBN: 15207)

Youth Softball
A Complete Handbook (ISBN: 15200)
Skills and Strategies (ISBN: 16417)
Rules of Play (ISBN: 16418)
Effective Coaching (ISBN: 16420)
Conditioning and Training (ISBN: 16419)

Also available: Program for Athletic Coaches Education (PACE), a program specifically designed by the Youth Sports Institute for interscholastic coaches. (ISBN: 14827)

For information on discounts for youth sports groups or to order books in the Youth Coaching Series contact:

Cooper Publishing Group
701 Congressional Blvd., Suite 340
Carmel, IN 46032
(317) 573-6420

Contents

Introduction

Youth Baseball is intended for coaches of players from 6 to 18 years of age. Those of us involved in its writing believe it is important to teach young athletes the skills and essential strategies of the game. Not only will such learning improve their ability to play the game, it also will provide them with an appreciation and enjoyment of the game known as "America's pastime." Moreover, we believe that the most successful coaches are the best teachers; we have prepared the various materials with the idea of providing you with the information necessary to improve your ability to teach the game. Thus, we have considered everything from the role of the baseball coach to dealing with injuries.

Everything from basic skills, to advanced strategies, to the essentials of sport science have been incorporated. This material, contained in twenty-six chapters, has been broken into six sections of varying length. Each section is organized around one of the key topics related to being an effective baseball coach, so that you can quickly find the essential information on each topic. Within these sections, each chapter contains illustrations and descriptive material designed to assist you in understanding both specific skills and related scientific concepts. In an Appendix to the text, we have provided an extensive set of drills for teaching baseball's essential skills and strategies. Complementing these drills is a matrix identifying each drill, the skill taught, the athletes involved, and the appropriate age for its use.

The book supplies the youth coach with much of the information needed to deal effectively with teaching essential baseball skills. Chapters 1 through 7 cover the mechanics of throwing, catching, fielding, pitching, hitting, and base running. For each of these topics essential coaching points are identified as either key elements or common errors. Next come chapters 8 to 11 which describe commonly used defensive and offensive strategies, rules, and terms used in the game. The following fifteen chapters deal with such concerns as seasonal and daily planning, working effectively with players and parents, and health issues relating to youthful athletes—all subjects generally not covered in coaching books. Taken together, these twenty-six chapters meet the goals proposed in the National Association for Sport and Physical Education publication, *Guidelines for Coaching Education: Youth Sports.*

Those people chosen to prepare material for this book are all knowledgeable, experienced teachers and coaches. These qualities join with their interest in the scientific study of sport to produce a book at once practical but thorough. And, though working with the coach in mind, the authors' real goal is to make baseball an enjoyable and positive experience for everyone concerned, especially the athletes. All of us hope that our efforts help you in working with all boys and girls so that their baseball skills improve, they have fun playing, they learn to be part of a team, and they heighten their self-esteem.

Mike Clark
Youth Sports Institute
Michigan State University

Thomas George
Department of PE
University of Michigan

Jill Elliott
Coach
Waverly High School
Lansing, Michigan

Tom Smith
Baseball Coach
Michigan State University

Vern Seefeldt, Director
Youth Sports Institute
Michigan State University

Acknowledgments

We would like to take this opportunity to thank the following people for their help in preparing this book: Randy Bass and Steve Elliott, who provided photographic skills; Eileen Northrup, editorial assistant, whose patient help in typing and revising the manuscript was invaluable as was her skill in translating rough sketches into finished illustrations; Tom George and Glenna DeJong, who provided initial work on many of the illustrations; and Keith Chapin and Bob Benham, who assisted with various photo sessions. Finally, we offer a deeply felt thank you to all the youth baseball players and coaches from the mid-Michigan area who worked with us as we tried to capture the essence of baseball skills on film. This was a challenging task, and their patience and support helped immensely.

Section I
Baseball Skills and Strategies

1
Throwing

Jill Elliott, M.S.

QUESTIONS TO CONSIDER
- What are the four phases of throwing?
- Throwing accuracy is determined by what factors?
- What is the significance of the follow-through?
- What is indicated by an ipsilateral throwing pattern?
- Most mechanical errors occur in what phase of throwing?

INTRODUCTION

The purpose of throwing in baseball is to get the ball from one point to another as efficiently as possible. Although an easy toss is sometimes effective, the majority of throws require force and accuracy. Throwing a baseball with force and accuracy can be reduced to four basic components or phases:

1. the preparatory phase
2. the propulsive phase
3. the release phase
4. the follow-through

Slight variations of the throw may occur depending on the distance and speed requirements. Throwing variations include:

1. the snap throw
2. the sidearm throw
3. the underhand toss

This chapter focuses on understanding the basic components of throwing to teach throwing efficiency. Following the description of the basic throw is a description of throwing variations for specific game situations.

THROWING FUNDAMENTALS
Preparatory Phase

The Grip

The preparatory phase starts with gripping the baseball. The grip involves spreading two or three fingers across the seams with the thumb in opposition around the ball (see Figure 1-1). The baseball should be thrown with two fingers and the thumb in contact with the ball. However, players with smaller hands may have to use three fingers to control the ball when they apply force in the throwing motion. When gripping the baseball, it is important to use the fingers and thumb only. The ball should not contact the palm of the hand (see Figure 1-2). However, younger players may not be able to grip the ball properly without contacting the ball with the palm of the hand.

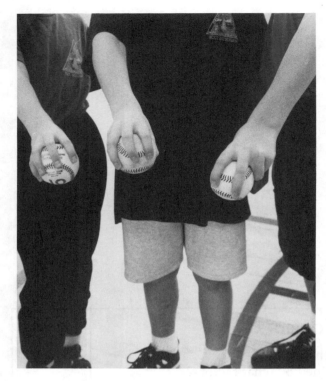

Figure 1-1. Gripping the ball with 2, 3 or 4 fingers, as needed for control.

Figure 1-2. Gripping the ball with the fingers and thumb only, no contact with the palm of hand.

The Pivot

An important part of the preparatory phase involves getting the body into a position to propel the ball efficiently. Place the body in the correct position by pivoting (or stepping) on the throwing-side foot until the foot is perpendicular to the intended path of the ball (see Figure 1-3). The pivot turns the body sideways with the glove side toward the intended target. The purpose of the pivot and perpendicular body position is to:

1. place the body in a position to use the muscles involved in hip and trunk rotation effectively
2. create more distance through which the arm can move and so generate greater force on the ball

Figure 1-3. The throwing-side foot is perpendicular to the path of the ball.

The Throwing Arm

As the pivot is completed, the throwing arm action begins. Initially, the throwing arm moves in a downward and backward direction until it is almost fully extended behind the body (see Figure 1-4). The hand remains on top of the ball throughout this extension movement. The throwing arm then moves in an upward direction until the elbow is behind and above the shoulder. The upper arm is near horizontal, the lower arm is near vertical and the hand is now to the "inside" of the ball (see Figure 1-5). Here, the position of the ball is held relatively constant until the propulsive action of the shoulder is initiated.

The Glove Side

As the ball is taken out of the glove and the throwing arm is extending back, the glove arm extends toward the target. As the glove arm extends, the glove-side foot strides toward the target. Throwing with the glove-side foot striding toward the target is also known as throwing *contralaterally*. When the glove-side foot contacts the ground, the fingers of the glove and the toes of the foot point toward the target and the glove-side knee bends to absorb the impact of the stride. As the glove-side foot fully contacts the ground the propulsive phase begins.

Figure 1-5. Upper arm horizontal, lower arm vertical, hand "inside" ball.

Propulsive Phase

The propulsive phase begins as the glove-side foot fully contacts the ground and ends as the ball is released from the hand. The glove-side foot contact initiates a series of force-producing joint actions which begins with the larger joints and moves sequentially to the smaller joints. Although this joint sequence is more detailed than the action described here, it is important to understand the general concept as it relates to throwing forcefully.

Hip and Trunk Rotation

The first action to occur is hip rotation. The hips rotate to bring the throwing-side hip toward the target. As hip rotation reaches its greatest velocity, the trunk, which until now has been "riding along" with the hips, begins to contribute to the force production. The trunk begins its rotational contribution at a greater velocity than the velocity of the hips.

Shoulder Action

As the hips and trunk rotate, a relaxed shoulder allows the throwing arm to lag behind until its turn to make a contribution to the force production. The arm lag enables the lower arm to incline backward from its previous near

Figure 1-4. Downward and backward movement of the throwing arm.

vertical position (see Figure 1-6). This backward incline is a position not possible to duplicate slowly or manually. The arm lag stretches the shoulder muscles, enabling a more forceful contraction of these muscles to bring the arm through at the greatest velocity. The forceful contraction of the shoulder muscles brings the upper arm forward and rotates it slightly inward. This action of the shoulder is known as "medial rotation" or "rotation to the middle."

Glove Side

Because all of the action thus far has been of a rotating nature, "opposite" actions of the glove side of the body will also contribute to the total rotational velocity. These actions are pulling the previously extended glove to the glove-side shoulder as the throwing side rotates forward, and forcefully extending the previously bent knee of the glove-side leg as the ball is released (see Figure 1-7). Both of these actions create an equal but opposite forward movement on the throwing side.

Arm and Wrist Action

The final contributors to the joint sequence are elbow extension and wrist flexion (see Figure 1-7 again). Neither, however, is completely extended or flexed until just after the ball has been released. When all of the joint actions are complete, the ball is released at an initial velocity equal to the velocity of the hand. Therefore, the greater the velocity of the hand, created by the joint sequence, the greater the velocity of the ball. The entire propulsive phase takes less than 0.16 seconds for a skilled thrower to complete (Atwater 1968).

In summary, the force-producing joint sequence occurs as follows: hip rotation, trunk rotation, shoulder medial rotation, elbow extension and wrist flexion. Facilitating the "opposite" actions are the glove pull and the glove-side knee extension.

Release

If the force production phase is consistent, the path of the ball or throwing accuracy is determined by

1. the path of the ball prior to release
2. the exact point of release

Figure 1-6. Throwing arm "lag."

Figure 1-7. Actions of the glove side. The glove is pulled to the body. *Note:* The glove-side knee is more extended than in Figure 1-6.

If the path of the ball goes from right to left prior to release, the ball will go to the left of the target. Likewise, if the path of the ball goes from left to right prior to release, the ball will go to the right of the target. Therefore, if an individual is consistently missing to the right or left of the target, it would be wise to check the path of the arm prior to release.

If the path of the ball prior to release is directly in line with the target, and the force production phase is consistent, the height of the throw is determined by the release point. A high throw will result from an early release, whereas a low throw will result from a late release. Either one of these trajectories may be desirable depending on the game situation. A low throw, for example, increases the chance of tagging a sliding base runner. A shoulder-high throw allows a baseperson to stretch for the ball, increasing the chance of "forcing out" a base runner.

Follow-Through

The follow-through occurs immediately after releasing the ball. The purpose of the follow-through is to

1. prevent any interruption of the joint sequence prior to release
2. avoid injury by safely reducing the force produced in the propulsive phase

The follow-through is a direct result of the propulsive action phase:

- The wrist continues to flex.
- The lower arm faces down, or *pronates*.
- The upper arm continues to rotate inward.
- The shoulder brings the path of the arm downward to the non-throwing side of the body.
- The throwing-side leg comes forward to help maintain balance.

As young athletes work on developing the correct mechanics of the throw, they even may be encouraged to exaggerate the follow-through as beginners often tend to stop it short (see Figure 1-8).

Although the follow-through does not have any direct effect on the ball, it is important to note because it may provide insight into possible errors in the throwing pattern. For example, a follow-through in which the inside of the forearm faces up, or *supinates*, may be an indication of future elbow injury:

Figure 1-8. The follow-through.

- Forearm supination is in direct opposition to the inward rotation of the upper arm and usually results in undue strain on the elbow joint.
- Forearm supination is common and is detectable by observing the position of the forearm in the follow-through (see Figure 1-9 a and b).

Correct pronation of the forearm may require a great deal of concentration and practice to achieve; however, the threat of injury is great enough to make it worth the coach's and athlete's time to develop the proper form.

Key Elements:
- Focus the eyes on the target.
- Pivot on the throwing foot to turn the body sideways to the target, glove side to the target.
- Move the throwing arm through a backward and downward extension, then an upward preparatory action.
- Take a contralateral stride with the glove-side foot, the toes pointing to the target.
- Allow a summation of forces through the proper joint sequence: hip, trunk, shoulder, elbow, wrist.
- Release.
- Follow through.

Figure 1-9a. Supination of throwing-side forearm.

Figure 1-9b. Pronation of throwing-side forearm.

Common Errors:

- An ipsilateral throwing pattern (throwing-side foot strides to the target) may occur in early stages of throwing.
- An inconsistent release point problem improves with correct practice and feedback from the coach.
- Forearm supination, not pronation, can result in elbow injury due to conflict with inward rotation of the upper arm.
- Improper joint sequence reduces the total force production. Errors include: (1) only the shoulders turn sideways to the target while the hips stay square to the target, (2) the elbow stays below the shoulder at release of the ball and the wrist flexes without the elbow extending (tucked elbow), or (3) elbow extension without inward medial rotation ("pushing" the ball).
- Little or no follow-through (1) minimizes the force applied to the ball prior to release, or (2) increases the chance for injury by abruptly stopping the body parts.

PROGRESSIONS FOR TEACHING THROWING

The *contralateral* throwing pattern (see Figure 1-6) is the most advanced throwing pattern. Most individuals will progress through several specific throwing patterns before acquiring a contralateral pattern. A group of beginning players may exhibit a variety of throwing patterns. As a coach it is important to understand that the throwing pattern executed by an individual is not an indication of throwing potential; rather, it is an indication of past experience. For example, it is likely that an individual who strides toward the target with the glove-side foot, or contralaterally, has had more experience throwing than an individual who strides with the throwing-side foot, or *ipsilaterally*. An ipsilateral throwing pattern does not indicate that the thrower is uncoordinated; it indicates that he or she has had less previous throwing experience. Understanding this can reduce frustration and anxiety for both the coach and the player.

When teaching an individual to throw correctly, establish learning priorities and emphasize one phase of the skill at a time. The following are suggested progressions for teaching the various components of throwing.

Preparatory Phase

Contralateral Stride

Learning any skill first requires an understanding of what is involved in performing that skill. Footprints in the dirt of the infield or tape on the floor of a gym can be used to help the individual gain an understanding of the footwork involved in throwing correctly (see Figure 1-10). Initially, the player (1) stands sideways to the target, glove side in front, then (2) steps toward the target, placing the glove-side foot into a footprint already on the ground.

The length of the stride is unimportant at this stage. It should be long enough for the player to feel body movement but short enough to be comfortable. Other than realizing these considerations, the coach need not be too concerned about the stride; it will develop quite naturally as the athlete continues to practice correct technique.

The Pivot

Once the player understands how the contralateral step "feels," the pivot can be introduced. Without a ball, the player

1. faces the target
2. pivots (or steps) on a footprint with the throwing-side foot
3. strides to a footprint with the glove-side foot
4. completes the throwing motion

When the player can execute the pattern without looking at the footprints it is time to add a ball and a target. The player

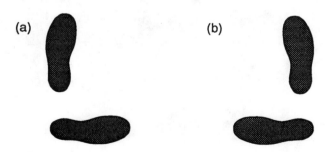

Figure 1-10. Footprints in the dirt showing the contralateral stride: (a) right-handed thrower and (b) left-handed thrower.

1. focuses the eyes on the target
2. pivots on the throwing-side foot
3. strides with the glove-side foot
4. throws to the target

Once the contralateral pattern has been established the players must repeat the motion until the pattern becomes a habit. Any time a breakdown in the pattern occurs, simply go back to the footprints.

Propulsive Phase

The proper joint sequence can occur only with a contralateral stride. With this in mind, delay a focus on force production until the correct stride has become a habit. If the player has to stop and think before striding correctly, an internalization of the correct stride has yet to take place. Players cannot successfully produce force without an automatic contralateral stride. Also, players cannot successfully internalize the contralateral stride if they focus on accuracy and force production while they are learning the movement pattern.

Throwing Arm Motion

Correct execution of the throwing motion is the key to force production and injury prevention. To focus exclusively on the throwing motion, the player begins on one knee. Although the player does not stride, the contralateral "feeling" is reinforced with the throwing-side knee down and the glove-side knee up and in front of the body. In this position, the ball is held just above the ear with the elbow above and in front of the shoulder and the wrist extended (see Figure 1-11). From this position the player simply executes elbow extension, wrist flexion and release to a target several feet away.

When the pattern from elbow extension to release is understood, the throwing arm is then placed in its initial propulsive position. Still on one knee, the player begins with the elbow behind and above the shoulder and the glove extended to the target (see Figure 1-12). From here, the player executes shoulder rotation, elbow extension, wrist flexion and follow-through. The glove is pulled to the glove side simultaneously with the propulsive throwing action. While executing the throwing motion in this position, the player must be aware of (1) the

Figure 1-11. On one knee, the player focuses on elbow extension and wrist flexion.

Figure 1-12. On one knee, the player executes the throwing motion from the "propulsive position."

elbow position in relation to the shoulder and, (2) the elbow leading the wrist to the target. Progressing further, the player, still on one knee, executes the entire throwing motion: The arm moves down and back, then moves up, forward and finishes with the follow-through (see Figure 1-13).

Rotation

Although the sequential rotation of the hips, trunk, and shoulders play a significant role in force production, the force of throwing usually occurs quite naturally if the stride, rotation and release are done properly. Telling a player to "throw as hard as you can" to a specific but large target (such as an area of the backstop) is usually effective in developing proper joint sequence. Also, throwing back and forth in groups of two and gradually increasing the distance requirements will help develop throwing strength and efficiency.

Coaches should be aware that most mechanical errors in throwing occur in the propulsive phase. A player who "looks uncoordinated" when throwing is usually erring in the joint sequence. As a coach, understanding this sequence is extremely important for error correction.

Release

Getting the "feel" of various release points can be accomplished by attempting to hit various targets (high and low). The targets provide the individual with immediate feedback; the focus should be on the feel of each release in relation to each target. As the release points change with the force produced players should not sacrifice force production for accuracy. However, they may also find it helpful to be aware

Figure 1-13. On one knee, the player executes the entire throwing motion.

of varying amounts of force in relation to the release points. A consistently accurate throw takes constant correct repetition, often over a period of years, and a lot of PATIENCE.

Safety Considerations

When a player executes a forceful throw, even an object that weighs as little as a baseball can exert a stressful force on the muscles of the shoulder and elbow. Therefore, to prevent injury, there should be a gradual emphasis on velocity and distance. Early practices should involve "easy" throwing only.

To avoid injuries to other players, keep all throwing paths clear. Observers must stand behind and away from the throwers and keep their eyes on the balls in flight. Throwing practice should NOT take place near crowds or spectators. If someone may be hit with a thrown ball, warn them immediately: "Look out!", or "Cover up!"

THROWING VARIATIONS

Several situations in baseball require a throw other than the overhand throw. If a potential play on a base runner is close to the fielder but cannot be made unassisted, other types of throws may be used to quickly release the ball. The following is a description of three other types of throws and possible situations for their use. The throws are

1. the snap throw
2. the sidearm throw
3. the underhand toss

The Snap Throw

The snap throw uses only the shoulder rotation, elbow extension and wrist flexion portion of the overhand throw. The ball is initially held above the shoulder approximately even with the ear. The elbow is to the side at a 90 degree angle and the upper arm is parallel to the ground (see Figure 1-14). In this position, the ball is clearly visible to the receiver. A quick rotation of the shoulder, extension of the elbow and flexion of the wrist combine to "snap" the ball forward. The arm finishes approximately parallel to the ground following the release of the ball (see Figure 1-15).

Figure 1-14. The initial snap throw position.

Figure 1-15. The snap throw follow-through.

The snap throw is used in situations where a quick, short, direct throw is necessary. For example, the snap throw is used in a "rundown" (see Chapter 8, Defensive Strategies). The ball is held in the initial snap throw position, is in clear view of the receiver, and is quickly released as dictated by the action of the runner. Similarly, a catcher retrieving a wild pitch with a runner coming home may also use a snap throw to return the ball to the pitcher covering the plate.

The Sidearm Throw

The sidearm throw is used by infielders who need to throw quickly to a base after fielding a batted ball. The shortstop, for example, may use the sidearm throw to get the ball quickly to second base to "force out" the runner coming from first base. The sidearm throw is quicker than the overhand throw because the throwing arm travels less distance prior to releasing the ball. Less distance traveled by the throwing arm prior to release also means less force produced behind the ball, making the sidearm throw less effective over longer distances. The sidearm throw is useful as a middle distance throw.

A right-handed infielder throwing to the left (for example, shortstop to second base) fields the ground ball and in a continuous motion brings the ball to the throwing side. The hands separate, the throwing elbow leads the throwing arm back a short distance more, then the throwing elbow leads the throwing arm forward and extends the arm out to the side. As the hands separate, the fielder takes a short step toward the target with the left foot. The ball is released so that it will hit the receiver about chest high and the arm follows through to the target (see Figure 1-16 a - c). This is also the technique used for the left-handed fielder throwing to the right (for example, left-handed first baseperson throwing to second base).

A right-handed fielder throwing to the right (for example, second baseperson to second base) anticipates the sidearm throw and fields the ball with the throwing foot further behind the glove foot than normal. With the hips now more open to the target, the fielder

1. fields the ground ball
2. in a continuous motion brings the ball to the throwing side
3. simultaneously pivots on the throwing foot

The hands separate, the throwing elbow continues back and then leads the throwing arm forward and extends the arm to the side. Depending on the distance the ball has to be thrown and the strength of the fielder's arm, a short step with the left foot prior to the forward motion of the arm may be desirable. The ball is released so that it will hit the receiver about chest high and the arm follows through to the target. This is also the technique used by the left-handed fielder throwing to the left.

(a)

(b)

(c)

Figure 1-16a-c. The side arm throw.

The Underhand Toss

The underhand toss is used when the ball is fielded close to the base and the fielder must throw to another player for the out. For example, the first baseperson may toss the ball underhand to the pitcher when the first baseperson fields the ball away from first base and the pitcher covers the base.

The player fields the ball and then steps to the target with the glove foot. As the glove foot steps to the target, the hands separate and the throwing arm drops down and back then moves forward (see Figure 1-17). Throughout the arm motion, the elbow is extended and the wrist is stiff to create a pendulum motion of the tossing arm. The ball is released so that it will hit the receiver about chest high and the arm follows through to the target. Also, the throwing leg comes through with the throwing arm to ensure a smooth continuous motion (see Figure 1-18).

REFERENCES

Atwater, A. E. (1968). *DGWS Softball Guide, 1968-1970*. Reston, VA: AAHPERD.

Figure 1-17. The underhand toss pendulum motion.

Figure 1-18. The underhand toss follow-through.

2
Catching and Catching/Throwing as a Combined Skill

Jill Elliott, M.S.

QUESTIONS TO CONSIDER

- What are three fundamental rules of catching?
- When the eyes follow the ball to the glove, what part of the ball should be focused upon?
- What are two advantages of catching with two hands?
- Why do the arms give with the ball?
- How many rules can a beginner focus on at one time?
- Why is it important to teach catching and throwing as a combined skill?
- What are the four steps involved in speed throwing?
- Name three game situations where the speed throw can be used specifically.
- How can goals be set so that everyone has an equal opportunity to experience success?
- What are safety considerations while practicing speed throwing?

INTRODUCTION: CATCHING

Every time a baseball is thrown or batted, a player on the defensive team must catch the ball. Often, several players must catch the ball to make the play successful. If no one player catches the ball, the play cannot be successful. Without the opportunity for defensive success through proper catching fundamentals the game becomes very frustrating.

In general, there are three fundamental rules of catching:

- The rule of the eyes
- The rule of the hands
- The rule of the glove

Whether it is a thrown ball, a batted ball, a ground ball, or a fly ball, these rules always apply. The following is an explanation of the three rules of catching.

The Rule of the Eyes

The eyes must follow the center of the ball directly into the glove. If the ball to be caught is high, the eyes look up. If the ball to be caught is low, the eyes look down. If the ball to be caught is to the right, the eyes go right, and so on (see Figures 2-1 and 2-2). The action of the eyes must occur with all catches—it must become a habit! Often with what is perceived to be a "simple"

Figure 2-1. The rule of the eyes: Ball is low, eyes are low.

Figure 2-2. The rule of the eyes: Ball to left, eyes following ball.

catch, a player will discontinue watching the ball before it enters the glove. If neglecting to follow the ball with the eyes during a simple catch becomes a habit, the eyes will not follow the ball into the glove during a more difficult catch. When the eyes do not follow the ball into the glove, the catch is left to chance, and chance is not a desirable part of defensive play.

The Rule of the Hands

The ball should be caught with two hands, in front and near the center of the body whenever possible (see Figure 2-3). Both arms are slightly extended as the ball approaches, the throwing hand immediately covers the ball as it enters the glove, and both arms "give" to absorb the force of the ball. Catching the ball with two hands minimizes "bobbles," and equally important, reduces the time needed to transfer the ball to the throwing hand. Giving with the force of the ball is especially important as the speed of the ball increases.

When the ball cannot be caught near the center of the body, two options are available. The first option is to move the feet so that the ball lines up with the center of the body. If there is not enough time to move the feet, a second option is to extend the glove to the ball and keep the throwing hand as close to the glove as possible (see Figure 2-4). Here, the throwing hand is not in a position to help secure the ball. However, it is in a position to (1) help recover a bobble, and (2) permit an efficient transfer of the ball from the glove to the throwing hand.

The Rule of the Glove

In general, the fingers of the glove point in the direction the glove has to move to make the catch (see Figures 2-5 and 2-6). If the glove starts at the waist, a ball caught above the waist would require the glove to move up; in which case, the fingers of the glove would point up. Using two hands, all fingers point up with the thumbs together. A ball below the waist requires the fingers to point down with the little fingers together.

A ball at the waist can be caught by (1) catching the ball with the glove fingers in an upward direction and bending the knees (such as catching a thrown ball for a force out), or

Figure 2-3. The rule of the hands: Hands in front, near center of body; arms extended ready to "give" with ball.

Figure 2-5. The rule of the glove: Glove fingers point up to a ball over the head.

Figure 2-4. The rule of the hands: Glove extended to ball; throwing hand close.

Figure 2-6. The rule of the glove: Glove fingers point down to a ball well below the waist.

(2) catching the ball with the glove fingers in a downward direction and elevating the shoulders (such as fielding a batted ball). In all cases, the eyes follow the ball into the glove, and the throwing hand is as close to the glove hand as possible.

Key Elements:
- The eyes follow the center of the ball into the glove.
- Both hands are involved in every catch.
- The arms "give" to absorb the force of the ball.
- The fingers of the glove point in the direction the glove must move to catch the ball.

Common Errors:
- The eyes lose sight of the ball before it enters the glove.
- The eyes look down when the ball is high or look up when the ball is low (see Figure 2-7).

Figure 2-7. ERROR: Eyes lose contact with the ball before it enters the glove.

- The throwing hand is down at the side or behind the body which (1) reduces the chance of recovering a bobble and (2) makes the transfer of the ball to the throwing hand more time consuming.
- The arms move toward the ball as it is being caught rather than giving with the ball. This increases the probability of (1) the ball popping out of the glove and (2) the player experiencing pain in the catching hand.
- The fingers of the glove are down with a throw above the waist. In this situation the ball can go off the heel of the glove and into the face.

DEVELOPMENTAL PROGRESSIONS

Learning how to catch a ball with a glove can be a very difficult task for beginning players. Therefore, the coach must understand that the beginner cannot work on all three rules of catching at one time. The rules of catching must be prioritized and emphasized one at a time.

Eye Contact

Because the ball cannot be caught consistently if it is not seen, the rule of the eyes should be the first priority. At this stage, the success of the player is determined by the action of the eyes, rather than catching the ball. Once the eyes have been trained to follow the ball into the glove consistently, the rule of the hands becomes the second priority.

Two Hands

Most beginners will instinctively want to keep the glove fingers down when catching the ball. Therefore, the rule of the hands is more easily emphasized when balls are rolled, bounced, or thrown waist high or below. The player watching the ball into the glove concentrates on (1) extending the arms to the ball, (2) immediately covering the ball with the throwing hand, and (3) giving with the force of the ball.

Glove Control

When the first two rules become a habit, the rule of the glove becomes the third priority. Throw balls to a variety of locations and have the player concentrate on pointing the fingers of the glove in the correct direction. As the fingers of the glove automatically move in the correct direction, the player can concentrate on incorporating all three rules of catching.

Although only one rule of catching is emphasized at a time, skilled demonstrations throughout the learning process provide players with a model to imitate. In many cases, the other rules of catching can be learned and reinforced through imitation without a conscious focus. Also, it is important to provide enough practice so that players obey the rules of catching with every catch and the glove becomes no more than an extension of the hand.

Catching Lead-Up Progressions

1. The player practices catching a large, soft ball without a glove.
2. The player progresses to a baseball.
3. The player practices catching the baseball with a mitten on the glove hand.
4. The player progresses to catching the baseball with a 6-by-6 inch pillow glued or sewn into a regular fielder's glove.
5. The player advances to a regular glove and practices catching:
   - a ping-pong ball or a plastic golf ball
   - a baseball size or tennis ball

INTRODUCTION: CATCHING AND THROWING

Very rarely does a baseball player have the luxury of throwing the ball without having to catch it first. For this reason it is important to consider throwing and catching together all in one motion. Whether fielding a ground ball, line drive, or fly ball, there is often an opportunity to make another play. The efficiency with which a ball can be received and delivered is directly related to the success of making these plays. The purpose of this combined skill called speed throwing is to teach players to make the transition quickly from catching to throwing.

SPEED THROWING FUNDAMENTALS

All of the fundamentals of catching and throwing are involved in speed throwing. Therefore, the learner should be able to catch and throw proficiently before speed throwing is introduced.

The key to speed throwing is to begin to throw the ball as it is being caught. Speed throwing can be broken down into the following four steps.

Step 1

The ball is caught with two hands in front of the body as the glove-side foot steps to the ball (see Figure 2-8).

Step 2

The ball is transferred immediately to the throwing hand and "cradled" with the glove hand as both hands are brought to the throwing shoulder. Simultaneously, the throwing-side foot steps in a *forward* direction but behind the glove-side foot and perpendicular to the intended path of the ball (see Figure 2-9).

Step 3

The weight completely transfers onto the throwing-side foot and the hands separate. As the hands separate, the glove (or glove-side elbow for short, quick throws) points to the tar-

Figure 2-8. Speed throwing, Step 1: Glove-side foot steps to the ball.

Figure 2-9. Speed throwing, Step 2: Throwing-side foot steps forward but behind and perpendicular to the glove-side foot.

Figure 2-10. Speed throwing, Step 4: Glove-side foot strides to target as throwing arm begins motion.

get and the throwing arm begins to move back to the throwing position.

Note that the movement of the throwing arm depends on the requirements of the throw. A shorter, quicker throw requires the throwing arm to go directly to the throwing position. A long throw requires a full preparatory motion.

Step 4

The glove-side foot strides to the target, the throwing arm begins to propel the ball forward and the glove-side elbow pulls to the glove side (see Figure 2-10).

The "speed throw" can also be executed when the target is not in the same direction as that of the ball being received. If the glove-side foot steps to the ball and the throwing-side foot steps perpendicular to the target, the body will always be in a position to make a forceful throw. For example, if the second baseperson has to catch a throw coming from the third base area and then has to quickly throw the ball to first base, the second baseperson

1. steps to the throw from third base with the glove-side foot
2. steps "forward" (behind the glove foot in relation to first base) and perpendicular to first base with the throwing-side foot
3. steps to first base with the glove-side foot and completes the throw (see Figures 2-11 and 2-12).

(See also Chapter 4, Position Play, "Second Base," "Turning the Double Play.")

Note: Catching and then throwing the ball in this manner also allows the ball to be kept in full view of the next receiver. Whether fielding a ball off the bat, running the ball in from the outfield, chasing a runner in a rundown or attempting to turn a double play, the ball should always be in a position to be seen by the receiver!

Key Elements:

- The glove-side foot steps *TO* the ball as the ball is caught with two hands in front of the body.

Figure 2-11. Step to the ball with the glove-side foot.

Figure 2-12. Step perpendicular to the target with the throwing-side foot.

- The ball is transferred to the throwing hand and is cradled with the glove hand as both hands are brought to the throwing shoulder.
- Simultaneous with the transfer of the ball to the throwing hand, the throwing-side foot steps forward, but behind the glove-side foot and perpendicular to the target.
- The throwing arm begins to move to the throwing position.
- Simultaneous with the action of the throwing arm, the glove-side foot steps to the target and the throw is completed.
- As skill improves and the movement is understood, players should develop a rhythm of
  1. step, catch
  2. step behind
  3. step and throw

Common Errors:

- The initial step to the ball with the glove-side foot occurs before the ball is caught, reducing the ability to adjust to the ball's path when necessary.
- The initial step to the ball with the glove-side foot occurs after the ball is caught, eliminating the effect of momentum into the ball and increasing the time required to throw the ball following the catch.
- The throwing hand does not stay as close as possible to the glove hand as the ball is caught, resulting in an inefficient transfer of the ball from the glove hand to the throwing hand. The total time prior to release is increased.
- After the initial step with the glove-side foot, the throwing-side foot steps parallel to the target rather than perpendicular. As a result, the hips stay square to the target and cannot contribute to the force production (see Figure 2-13).
- The throwing-side foot's step behind the front foot moves in a backward direction, carrying the body's momentum in the opposite direction of the throw.

Progressions for Teaching Speed Throwing

Because catching and throwing proficiency are prerequisites of the speed throw, the suc-

Figure 2-13. ERROR: Throwing-side foot stepping parallel to the target.

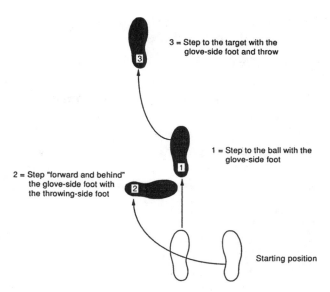

3 = Step to the target with the glove-side foot and throw

1 = Step to the ball with the glove-side foot

2 = Step "forward and behind" the glove-side foot with the throwing-side foot

Starting position

Figure 2-14. Footprints in the dirt: Speed throwing.

cess of this skill lies first in the footwork. The footwork can be practiced in a small amount of space without a ball. It can be practiced individually or as a group. Once the player understands the verbal cues "step as you catch," "step behind," and "step and throw," this skill can also be practiced at home.

Foot Movement Without the Ball

Initially, the footwork is practiced without a ball. Footprints are placed in the dirt or on the floor and individuals simply follow the footprints (see Figure 2-14). When the correct steps become automatic, the individual is ready to practice with a ball.

Foot Movement With the Ball

The ball is thrown to the individual who steps *TO* the ball as the ball is caught. The ball is returned to the thrower and the process is repeated. When practicing the step to the ball, the goal is to catch the ball as the glove-side foot contacts the ground. Accurate throws are essential to correctly practice the step to the ball.

Once the individual has successfully timed the step *TO* the ball several times in a row, the step forward and behind with the throwing foot, commonly called a "crow hop," is added. The individual steps to the ball with the glove-side foot and steps behind with the throwing-side foot then stops and repeats the process.

When the individual is successful at stepping to the ball with the glove-side foot and then stepping behind the glove-side foot with the throwing-side foot, the final stride to the target with the glove-side foot is added. With the weight of the body on the throwing-side foot as a result of the crow hop, the final stride to the target with the glove foot comes quite naturally. At this point, the individual practices

1. stepping to the ball with the glove-side foot as the ball is caught
2. transferring the ball to the throwing hand and cradling the ball with the glove hand during the "crow hop"

3. stepping to the target with the glove-side foot as the ball is thrown

Speed Throwing With a Partner

When the steps of the speed throw are clearly understood and can be repeated automatically, the players begin to focus on decreasing the time it takes to execute the steps. Getting in groups of two and forming two parallel lines, the players play catch incorporating the speed throw. The sequence is as follows:

1. Player A throws the ball
2. Player B receives the ball, executing the speed throw back to Player A
3. Player A receives the ball, executing the speed throw back to Player B, and so on.

Note: As Player A receives the ball and executes the speed throw (Number 3 above), Player B, who has moved forward as a result of the speed throw, must take a step back to the original location and then prepare to step to the returning throw.

Success is now dependent upon

- an accurate throw
- a clean catch and a quick transfer of the ball to the throwing hand
- the correct footwork to result in a forceful return throw.

Counting the number of successful catches and throws in a given amount of time provides feedback on the player's speed throwing efficiency. When counting the number of catches and throws in a given amount of time, daily goals can be set relative to the skill level. Each group can have a different goal, and the goals can change as the skills of the groups change. Each group's goal should be to equal or exceed a specific number of catches per time interval rather than to surpass another group's number of catches. Setting goals in such a manner is essential for each player to have an opportunity to experience success.

Example: Group 1 consists of two highly skilled players. Group 1 may try to execute the speed throw 40 times in 60 seconds. Group 2 consists of two players of lower skill and 40 catches in 60 seconds is not possible. Group 2's goal may be to execute the speed throw 30 times in 60 seconds. If Group 1 executes 40 and Group

2 executes 30, both have been successful in reaching their goal and are rewarded equally. The next goal is 41 speed throws in 60 seconds for Group 1 and 31 speed throws in 60 seconds for Group 2. If, on the next day, the players from Group 1 and Group 2 exchange partners, the goal for both new groups may be to execute the speed throw 35 times in 60 seconds.

Speed Throwing to Targets in Various Directions

For speed throwing during baseball games, players must be able to receive a ball from one direction and then throw it to a target in another direction. This can be practiced by placing a player at each base. The player at home plate throws to the player at first base, who throws to the player at second base, who throws to the player at third base, who throws to the player at home plate. The ball goes around the bases several times, with each player concentrating on stepping to the ball with the catch and then correctly stepping behind and throwing the ball to the next base.

Next, the direction of the ball is reversed. The ball goes from home to third to second to first to home. Finally, the ball can be thrown diagonally across the infield. For example, the ball goes from first to third to second to home to third to first to second to home to second to first, and so on. Speed throwing around the bases can also be timed with goals set to equal or beat a specific number of catches per time interval. Goals should be flexible and specific to the skill level of the players. Efficiency in catching and throwing to targets in various directions will help prepare a player for the many diverse situations that may occur in a baseball game (see Figure 2-15).

SAFETY CONSIDERATIONS

When speed throwing is practiced for a specific time interval, the initial time interval must be small and gradually increase over a period of weeks because this drill places great demand on the entire body. As the legs get tired, the demand on the arm increases and can result in long-term injury if proper precautions are not taken. A gradual increase of the time interval, however, can provide specific conditioning; for example, Week 1, 15 seconds three times a day; Week 2, 30 seconds two times a day; and Week 3, 60 seconds one time a day.

Remember that all throwing paths should be kept clear. Individual groups of two should be well spaced, and observers should keep their eyes on the balls at all times. Players should be instructed NEVER to turn their back on a thrown ball or cross in front of another player who is receiving a ball.

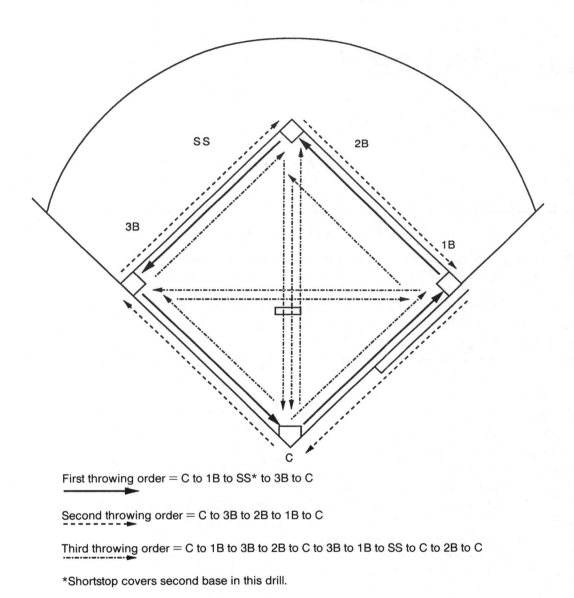

First throwing order = C to 1B to SS* to 3B to C

Second throwing order = C to 3B to 2B to 1B to C

Third throwing order = C to 1B to 3B to 2B to C to 3B to 1B to SS to C to 2B to C

*Shortstop covers second base in this drill.

Figure 2-15. Drill to practice speed throwing around the bases to various targets.

3
Playing Defense

Jill Elliott, M.S.

QUESTIONS TO CONSIDER

- What are four basic components common to most fielding techniques?
- Why should the fielder field the short hop as close to the ground as possible?
- What safety factors should be considered when practicing fielding?
- How should an infielder field a ball that has to be charged?
- What should the fielder do if he or she is not confident that a fly ball can be caught successfully?

INTRODUCTION

The purpose of fielding is to catch a batted ball and quickly and efficiently throw the ball to prevent the opposition's advancement on the bases. To complicate matters, the batted ball is usually hit with the intention of getting it by the fielder. On any given pitch, the ball could be hit on the ground or in the air, easy or hard, to the infield or to the outfield. The fielder is not in control of the batted ball; because of this uncontrollable factor, the fielder must be in the proper position and ready for anything.

It is essential to have a systematic approach to efficiently fielding the ball. The following is a description of such an approach for the various types of batted balls that may have to be fielded. As with catching and throwing, there are four basic components common to most fielding techniques that should be understood before attempting to learn about specific techniques. These components are

- the ready position of the fielder
- the approach to the ball
- the catch of the ball
- the throw to complete the play

FOUR COMPONENTS OF FIELDING

The Ready Position

To allow quick and efficient movement to the ball, each fielder must assume the ready position prior to the release of the pitch. The ready position:

- The feet are approximately shoulder-width apart.
- The glove-side foot is even with or slightly in front of the throwing-side foot.
- The weight is evenly distributed over the balls of the feet.
- The knees are bent.

- The backside is down to keep the center of gravity fairly low to the ground and centered over the base of support.
- The shoulders are square to the batter with the trunk forward of vertical.
- The arms are relaxed and in front of the body with both hands low and facing the batter.
- The elbows are slightly bent.
- The head is up.
- The eyes are focused on the hitter's strike zone. Most importantly, the fielder is balanced and ready (see Figure 3-1).

When to assume the ready position is usually a matter of individual preference. In general, however, the longer the ready position is held, the more likely that the weight will shift back over the heels and inhibit movement to the ball. A long ready position also increases the chance of a fielder being distracted prior to the pitch. Therefore, it is recommended that the ready position be assumed sometime between the pitcher's step on the pitching plate and the start of the pitching delivery.

The Approach

The fielder's movement to the ball is called the approach. The approach is dependent upon the path of the ball in relation to the ready position of the fielder. A more detailed discussion of the approach will be presented later in this chapter. In general the ball should be approached so that it can be fielded on the centerline of the body whenever possible. The movement of the body should be toward the ball. Efficient movement to the ball requires the weight to be shifted from one foot to another in such a way that balance is always maintained.

The Catch

After successfully completing the approach, the subsequent catch and throw is identical to speed throwing. The glove is open to the ball with the fingers pointing in the appropriate direction, and the eyes are focused on the center of the ball until the ball has been secured. The approach is timed so that the glove-side foot steps to the ball as it is being fielded. If the ball is fielded along the centerline of the body, the throwing hand immediately covers the ball as it enters the glove and both arms "give" to absorb the force of the ball (see Figure 3-2).

As the arms give, the ball is transferred to the throwing hand and cradled with the glove hand and both hands continue to the throwing-

Figure 3-1. Fielding ready position.

Figure 3-2. Catching a ground ball from the ready position.

side of the body. If the ball cannot be fielded in the center of the body, the throwing hand must remain as close to the glove hand as possible so that a quick transfer of the ball can still be achieved.

When fielding a "short hop," the fielder should catch the ball as close to the ground as possible (see Figure 3-3). This will reduce the various angles the ball might take coming off the ground and help avoid possible injuries such as the ball hitting the chin. The head must stay down in order to (1) allow the eyes to continue to follow the ball until it is secured, and (2) keep the glove from pulling up too early.

The Throw

As the ball is brought to the throwing side of the body, the weight completely transfers onto the glove-side foot. The throwing-side foot then steps in a forward direction (crow hop), behind the glove-side foot and perpendicular to the target (see Figure 3-4). The weight completely transfers onto the throwing foot, the hands separate, and the throwing arm begins its preparatory motion. The glove-side foot strides to the target, and the throw is completed (see Figure 3-5).

INFIELD GROUND BALLS

The infielder must be prepared to field any of four basic ground ball possibilities:

1. The ball has been hit directly to the fielder.
2. The ball has to be "charged" by the fielder.
3. The ball has been hit to the glove side of the fielder or forehand.
4. The ball has been hit to the throwing side of the fielder or backhand.

Figure 3-4. The crow hop.

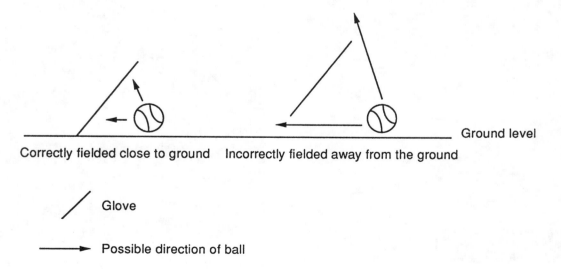

Correctly fielded close to ground   Incorrectly fielded away from the ground

Ground level

Glove

Possible direction of ball

Figure 3-3. Fielding the short hop.

Figure 3-5. The throw; glove-side foot striding to target.

The ready position, the body movement once the ball has been caught, and all of the basic fundamentals of catching and throwing remain the same for each ground ball possibility. The approach, however, is dependent on the location of the ground ball and therefore varies with each possibility. The remainder of this section will focus on the different approaches to the four ground ball situations.

Ground Balls—Direct

Any ground ball that can be fielded along the centerline of the body is a direct ground ball and should be fielded along the centerline whenever possible. From the ready position, one or more steps are taken toward the ball. The steps are alternated and timed so the glove-side foot steps in the direction of the ball as the ball is about to enter the glove. This step causes the body to momentarily resume the ready position. Resuming the ready position maximizes balance by providing a larger base of support and allows the ball to be fielded along the centerline of the body. If the ball is hit hard and there is no time for a step in the direction of the ball, the body weight simply shifts over the

glove-side foot as the ball is fielded. The step in the direction of the ball or the weight shift over the glove foot will quickly free the throwing-side foot for the subsequent crow hop.

Similar to catching, with a ground ball below the waist the glove fingers point down, the eyes focus on the center of the ball until the ball is secured, the ball is caught with two hands in front of the body, and the arms give to absorb the force of the ball. As with speed throwing, once the ball is secured

1. the hands then bring the ball to the body
2. the throwing-side foot steps forward yet behind the glove foot (crow hop)
3. the glove-side foot strides to the target
4. the throw is completed

Key Elements:
- The player assumes the ready position.
- The eyes focus on the center of the ball until it is secured with the throwing hand.
- The body weight shifts over the glove-side foot as the ball is being fielded.
- The ball is fielded with two hands in front of the body and the arms give to absorb the force of the ball.
- The player executes the crow hop: (1) the throwing foot steps or hops "behind" the glove foot; (2) the glove foot strides to the target; and (3) the throw is completed.

Common Errors:
- The eyes focus 2 to 3 feet in front of the reception leaving the catch to chance.
- The head raises up. This not only causes the eyes to lose sight of the ball, but it also pulls the shoulders and glove up and gives the ball a chance to get under the glove.
- The throwing-side foot steps as the ball enters the glove, preventing an efficient crow hop.
- The throwing hand is away from the glove or is behind the body as the ball enters the glove.

Progressions for Teaching Beginners

The direct ground ball is the simplest type of ground ball to be fielded in a baseball game. Therefore, an individual must assess the fundamentals for fielding the direct ground ball before other, more complicated, fielding skills can be successfully learned.

Relation to Speed Throwing

The first goal of the coach is to get the player to understand what is required to properly field a direct ground ball. If the player is skilled enough to have already learned the speed throw, simply suggest "step (or shift) as you field the ball, crow hop and throw." Because the footwork has previously been learned, the focus can be on the eyes following the ball into the glove and the hands out in front and working together. If this is done effectively, the player goes from a somewhat choppy execution to a smoother, automatic execution.

Footprints/Invisible Ball

For lower-skilled players who lack the requisites for the speed throw, the footwork for the ground ball can provide a base for future learning of the speed throw. Using footprints in the dirt or on the floor, the player starts in a ready position and, without having to field a ball, follows a laid-out pattern of footprints. Because the beginner may not be able to coordinate the initial step to the ball with the glove-side foot, that step can be temporarily eliminated. Verbal cues such as "field the ball, step behind, step and throw" may aid the fielder. Following the footprints without a ball should be repeated several times initially, and again each day at the beginning of fielding practice.

Stationary Ball

Once the fielders can duplicate the steps without following footprints, use a stationary ball. Place the ball directly in front of the fielder's body and instruct the fielder to "field the ball, step behind, step and throw." Check to be sure that the ball is picked up with two hands and the eyes are on the ball until the ball is secured.

Rolling the Ball

Now roll the ball slowly to the player from about 10 feet away. The steps should be very slow and deliberate at first. The coach can help the process with verbal cues such as "two hands out in front, eyes on the ball, field the ball, step behind, step and throw" as the player executes the skill. The speed and the distance of the rolled ball can be gradually increased.

Moving to the Ball

Next, the players need to understand that they have to move to the ball. Now the ball is rolled to various locations so the player has to move to get in front of the ball. At this point, the coach can begin to fungo hit, starting with slow ground balls and gradually increasing to faster ground balls. A variety of games and drills may be used to reinforce these fundamentals. Eventually the timed step to the ball as it's fielded can be introduced, although many times it begins to show up naturally.

Safety Considerations

The individuals should be spaced well apart and throwing paths should be kept clear. The ground condition should be checked prior to fielding practice and potential "bad hop" areas should be avoided. Also, the skill level of the individual should be considered when determining the speed of the ground balls to be fielded. Individuals should not be expected to learn at the same rate. When fungo hitting, the player catching for the batter should be placed well away from the bat and be instructed to "let the ball go" if it is missed and deflected near the batter. Close supervision is necessary if the players are fungo hitting to each other.

Ground Balls—Charging

Many steps are needed to charge a bunt or slow-rolling ground ball. Because time is used moving to the ball, a clean catch and a quick throw are essential. To insure fielding efficiency when charging a ground ball, a player should use a two-handed pick-up. Using two hands

- makes it easier to pick up a ball with excessive spin
- puts the body in a more balanced position to make a forceful and accurate throw
- reduces the temptation to lift the head before the ball is secured

Basic Technique

From the ready position, the infielder runs as hard as possible to the ball. As the fielder runs to the ball, the body and the hands stay low to the ground (see Figure 3-6). Just prior to fielding the ball, the feet momentarily reset into the ready position. The feet can be quickly reset with a jump into the ready position (see Figure 3-7). The ball is fielded along the centerline of the body with the throwing hand picking up the ball and the glove hand wrapping around the ball to secure it in the throwing hand. Though both hands are used, their roles are reversed. Both hands take the ball to the throwing side of the body as the crow hop is executed, and the throw is completed.

Note: As skill and timing increase, the jump into the ready position has the throwing-side foot contact the ground first and the glove-side foot contact the ground as the ball is being fielded. The weight is smoothly transferred to the glove-side foot in order to free the throwing-side foot for the crow hop and throw.

The right-handed first baseperson charging the ball and making a throw to first base must remember that the most efficient way to crow hop is to open the hips to the first base foul line (throw with the hips facing the first base foul line). The left-handed first baseperson should close the hips or turn the back to the first base foul line. The right-handed third baseperson throwing to third base should open the hips toward the infield.

Figure 3-7. The fielder resets the feet as the ball is fielded.

Advanced Technique

Advanced infielders with strong throwing arms can further reduce the time needed to charge and throw a ball. As the ball is approached, the feet are set in a position around the ball so that an efficient weight transfer can take place toward the target. The feet may be set such that the throwing-side foot is perpendicular to the target and the glove-side foot points toward the target. With the ball secured, the body weight simply transfers to the throwing-side foot as the ball is taken to the throwing position, then transfers to the glove-side foot as the ball is thrown (see Figures 3-8 and 3-9). A three-quarter-arm or sidearm throw may be used to decrease throwing time.

Note: A short step to the target with the glove foot may be necessary if the foot cannot initially be pointed toward the target (see Chapter 1, Throwing, "The Sidearm Throw").

The first baseperson or third baseperson charging a ball and throwing to a base behind themselves should position the feet around the ball so that

1. the throwing-side foot is in front of the ball and perpendicular to the base
2. the glove-side foot is behind the ball and pointing toward the base

Figure 3-6. The fielder stays low when charging the ball.

Figure 3-8. Foot placement around the ball.

Figure 3-9. Weight transfer to the throwing-side foot.

After the ball is fielded, the weight is transferred to the throwing-side foot as the ball is taken to the throwing position. The weight is then transferred to the glove-side foot and the ball is thrown. A short step with the glove-side foot prior to the weight shift may be necessary to completely open the hips to the base.

Key Elements:
- The player assumes the ready position.
- The player charges the ball hard, body position low.

- The feet momentarily take the ready position stance as the pickup point is approached.
- The head is down and the eyes focus on the moving ball.
- The throwing hand fields the ball, and the glove hand wraps around the ball.
- The ball is quickly taken to the throwing position.
- The player crow hops (or shifts weight) and throws.

Common Errors:
- The eyes lose focus early, often resulting in the ball being bobbled or missed.
- The pickup is attempted with only one hand—the throwing hand or the glove hand. This technique is unreliable even among highly skilled individuals.
- The charge and pickup occur off-balance, resulting in rushed, erratic throws.
- The fielder takes the "long way around" to throw to a target behind (as in a right-handed first baseperson turning toward the infield to throw to first base). This action may
  1. increase the time necessary to field and throw the ball
  2. impair the accuracy of the throw because the target is not immediately visible
  3. hide the ball from the receiver to make a more difficult catch.

Suggestions for Teaching

Stationary Ball/Slowly Rolled Ball

Charging the ball correctly can be learned by placing a stationary ball 15 to 20 feet in front of the player. The player then has to

1. charge the ball hard
2. quickly reset the feet in the ready position
3. correctly field the ball—catch with the throwing hand, secure the ball in the throwing hand with glove hand
4. keep the head down with the eyes following the ball into the hands
5. crow hop and throw.

Once the technique is achieved using a stationary ball, the ball may then be hit or rolled slowly, requiring the player to charge and adjust to the moving ball.

Base Runners

Many times charging the ball is performed correctly in a practice situation, but problems often occur in a game situation when the need for speed is emphasized. Therefore, to fully prepare an infielder must practice charging the ball in simulated game situations prior to actual game conditions. This can easily be accomplished in practice by using base runners when rolling or hitting slow ground balls.

Initially, there is a runner at home plate only (the batter) and the play is to be made at first base. From there, runners can be placed at first base, first and second base, second and third base, and so on. Sufficient practice helps reduce the panic that sometimes occurs during game situations.

Ground Balls—Forehand

Basically two types of ground balls require a forehand catch:

1. those hit hard and close to the glove-side leaving no time to get in front of the ball.
2. those hit a bit slower, and several feet away

The close, hard-hit ball will be addressed first.

Pivot

From the ready position, the feet pivot so that the hips and shoulders are square to the path of the ball. If necessary, the glove-side foot may take a short step as the throwing-side foot pivots to slightly extend the fielder's reach. The glove remains low to the ground as it is moved to the location of the ball. The throwing hand stays as close to the glove hand as possible and the eyes follow the ball into the glove.

The weight is placed on the glove-side foot as the ball is fielded. The throwing-side foot steps (or hops) perpendicular to the target as the ball is transferred to the throwing hand. Then the ball is taken to the throwing position, the glove-side foot strides toward the target, and the throw is completed (see Figures 3-10 to 3-12).

Crossover

The ground ball hit several feet away requires that the initial step be taken with the

Figure 3-10. Forehand pivot to field a ground ball.

Figure 3-11. A hop with the throwing-side foot perpendicular to the target.

Figure 3-12. Stride and throw.

Figure 3-13. Forehand crossover step to the path of the ball.

throwing-side foot. From the ready position, the throwing-side foot crosses in front of the glove-side foot and the glove-side foot pivots so that the hips and shoulders are square with the path of the ball. The crossover step allows a large and more powerful initial step to be taken toward the ball (see Figure 3-13). If the ball is hit fairly hard, fielding range can be increased by angling the crossover step about 45 degrees back from the original position.

The body maintains a low position throughout the approach and the arms are used to gain needed velocity. The steps to the ball are coordinated so that the ball is fielded as the weight moves over the glove-side foot. In this position, the throwing-side foot steps or hops perpendicular to the target and the throw is completed.

Key Elements:
- The player assumes the ready position.
- The glove-side foot pivots or short steps; the throwing-side foot pivots; or the player makes a crossover step with the throwing-side foot to square the body with the intended point of pickup.
- The eyes follow the ball into the glove.

- The throwing hand is as close to the glove as possible.
- The weight shifts to the glove-side foot as the ball is fielded.
- The throwing-side foot steps behind the glove foot in a crow hop and the throw is completed.

Common Errors:
- The body does not square to the ball, which results in: (1) the eyes losing sight of the ball, (2) the ball being fielded off-balance, and (3) an inefficient throw.
- The throwing hand is behind the body rather than as close to the glove as possible, increasing the time needed to transfer and throw the ball.
- The glove is held high when moving to the ball and results in a less efficient downward motion to catch the low ball.

Ground Balls—Backhand

Similar to the forehand, two types of ground balls require a backhand catch: (1) balls hit hard and close to the throwing side; and (2) balls hit slow and several feet away. The close, hard hit ball will be addressed first.

Pivot

From the ready position the feet pivot to square the hips and shoulders with the path of the ball. If necessary, the throwing-side foot may take a short step as the glove-side foot pivots to slightly extend the fielder's reach. The weight shifts to the throwing-side foot and the glove slides (staying low) to the location of the ball. The throwing hand remains as close to the glove as possible and the eyes follow the ball into the glove (see Figure 3-14). The ball is efficiently transferred to the throwing hand, with the glove wrist remaining stiff and the glove arm moving upward and turning inward to meet the throwing hand.

Often, when the ball is hit hard enough to allow only a pivot on the throwing-side foot, a player has plenty of time to transfer the weight to the glove-side foot, then complete the crow hop and throw. If there is no time for a weight transfer and crow hop, the body pivots on the throwing-side foot until the foot is perpendicular to the target. The glove-side foot strides toward the target and the throw is completed.

Crossover

Ground balls requiring a longer reach are fielded with an initial crossover step with the glove-side foot. The throwing-side foot pivots as the glove-side foot crosses over so that the hips and shoulders are square with the path of the ball (see Figure 3-15). If the ball is hit fairly hard, the crossover step is angled back about 45 degrees from the original position in order to increase fielding range. The body position remains low throughout the approach and the arms are used to gain velocity. The glove moves to the ball along the ground and remains open with the thumb down. The throwing hand remains as close to the glove as possible, and the eyes focus on the center of the ball.

The steps to the ball are coordinated so that weight is moving over the glove-side foot as the ball is fielded. The throwing-side foot then continues through the catch and plants behind the glove-side foot (in relation to target). With the weight on the throwing-side

Figure 3-14. Backhand pivot to the ball.

Figure 3-15. Backhand crossover step to the ball.

foot, the glove-side foot strides toward the target and the throw is completed (see Figure 3-16 a and b). If the throw is long and a crow hop following the plant of the throwing foot is required, the fielder must carefully evaluate the situation; just holding the ball may be best in a critical game situation.

Figure 3-16a. The throwing-side foot continues through the catch.

Figure 3-16b. The weight shifts to the throwing-side and the glove-side foot strides toward the target.

Key Elements:
- The player assumes the ready position.
- The throwing-side foot pivots or short steps; the glove-side foot pivots; or the player makes

a crossover step with the glove-side foot to square the body with the ball.
- The body and glove stay low during the approach.
- The eyes follow the ball into the glove.
- The weight moves over the glove-side foot as the ball is fielded.
- The throwing hand is as close to the glove as possible; the glove wrist remains stiff and the glove arm moves upward and turns inward to meet the throwing hand.
- The throwing-side foot continues through the catch and pivots perpendicular to the target.
- The glove-side foot strides toward the target to complete the throw.

Common Errors:
- During the approach, the glove is placed at or above waist level before moving downward resulting in (1) lost time getting to the ball, and (2) the glove moving in the wrong direction in the event of a high bounce.
- The player "swats" at the ball instead of "giving" with the ball.
- The wrist of the glove arm circles around to transfer the ball to the throwing hand resulting in (1) lost time, and (2) the ball circling around and out of the glove.

Suggestions for Teaching

The forehand and backhand techniques are advanced techniques and should be introduced only when the player has become proficient at approaching ground balls and fielding them along the midline of the body. The first priority of learning to field with the forehand or backhand technique is to develop proper judgment of balls hit to the side of the body. A very efficient way for all players to develop judgment is through the use of a ball and a wall. Each player starts out 2 to 3 feet away in a side orientation to the wall. To practice the forehand, the throwing side is closest to the wall; for the backhand, the glove side is closest to the wall. Without a glove, the player tosses the ball to the wall just above the ground and attempts to catch it with the "glove hand" only. The player should focus on giving with the ball as the ball is caught, then quickly transferring the ball to the throwing hand, and again tossing the ball to the wall. As skill increases, the speed of the ball and the distance from the wall can be increased. Counting the number of tosses and catches in 30 seconds can provide feedback on backhand and forehand efficiency. This exercise is initially quite difficult, but improvement usually occurs rapidly.

A variation of this drill using a glove requires the player to face the wall, 5 to 15 feet away and to throw the ball to either side. The player focuses on

- footwork
- reception
- efficiency of transferring the ball to the throwing hand

These drills can be done during practice (instead of players waiting in line to bat) or at home; and they can be used throughout a career to keep forehand and backhand skills sharp.

OUTFIELD GROUND BALLS

Fielding a ground ball in the outfield differs slightly from fielding a ball in the infield. One reason for this difference is time. The forehand and backhand are used sparingly in the outfield because outfielders have more time to get in front of the ball. A second reason is a successfully fielded ground ball does not always require an immediate throw—the ball could be run into the infield. However, often a quick and long throw is required, in which case efficiency and accuracy are essential. A third reason is the outfield is the last line of defense. A ball that gets past the outfielder can be disastrous, so outfielders must take extra precautions to keep the ball in front of them.

The following is a description of various outfield fielding techniques. Included are

- ground balls hit direct
- ground balls requiring a charge
- balls hit to forehand or backhand

Ground Balls—Direct

Moving to the Ball

The outfielder picks up the flight of the ball as it comes off of the bat. Once the out-

fielder determines the flight of the ball, he or she quickly moves to field the ball. If the ball is hit directly to the outfielder, he or she moves straight to the ball. If the ball is hit slightly to the right or left of the outfielder, the outfielder uses a 'drop step' to begin movement to the ball. A drop step is a short step with the ball-side foot that puts the outfielder in a position to arc to the ball. The arc should place the outfielder directly in line with the ball (see Figure 3-17). With the shoulders square to the path of the ball, the fielder now moves straight to the ball.

Fielding the Ball

As the ball nears, the throwing-side knee drops to the ground and the glove-side knee bends to 90 degrees with the foot perpendicular to the path of the ball. The glove is open and both hands are in front covering the space between the legs (see Figure 3-18). The head and eyes follow the ball into the glove and the throwing hand immediately covers the ball.

Returning the Ball to the Infield

The ball is transferred to the throwing hand as the fielder either (1) crow hops into the throw or (2) runs the ball to the infield. If a

Figure 3-17. Outfield arc to the path of the ball (drop step, arc).

Figure 3-18. Fielding a ground ball in the outfield.

Figure 3-19. Adjustments for a long outfield throw.

long throw is required, the outfielder should reach near complete extension of the throwing arm during the back swing and near complete extension at release. Also, the glove-side shoulder should drop to increase the length of the throwing arm lever and help increase the distance of the throw (see Figure 3-19).

If the outfielder chooses to run the ball to the infield, the ball is carried in a position near the ear, ready to throw if necessary. If a throw does become necessary, the outfielder executes a crow hop and completes the throw.

Key Elements:

- The player assumes the ready position; the glove can be about waist level.
- The player moves toward the ball with the shoulders square to the path of the ball; the right foot drop steps with a ball hit to the right of the fielder, or the left foot drop steps with a ball hit to the left of the fielder.
- The throwing-side knee drops as the ball nears, the glove-side knee bends and the foot is perpendicular to the path of the ball.
- Both hands are in front, covering the space between the legs.
- The head is down and the eyes follow the ball into the glove.
- The ball is fielded and thrown or run into the infield.

Common Errors:

- Running directly to the ball hit to either side of the outfielder, requiring a less reliable forehand or backhand catch rather than using a drop step and arcing to the ball.
- Incorrectly timing the drop of the glove-side knee. Adjusting to the speed of the ground ball comes through practice.
- Dropping to the glove-side knee rather than the throwing-side knee, interfering with a smooth transition into the throwing motion.
- Attempting to throw the ball from the outfield using the shorter infield throwing motion, thus putting undue strain on the throwing arm and producing less force to apply to the ball.
- Running the ball to the infield and, if necessary, throwing with the weight moving over throwing-side foot rather than the glove-side

foot. This results in a less than forceful and often inaccurate throw.

Suggestions for Teaching

Stationary Ball

To learn correct fielding technique, the outfielder initially works with a stationary ball. The ball is placed in the outfield grass, with the player one step behind. The player takes a step to the ball with the glove-side foot and the throwing-side knee drops to the ground. The glove-side knee is bent, both hands are in front and the head is down with the eyes on the ball. The pickup is made; the outfielder quickly comes up with the weight over the glove-side foot, executes a crow hop and completes the throw. When one step to the ball becomes comfortable, the fielder starts progressively further back from the stationary ball. The drop step and arc can be practiced by starting behind and to one side of the stationary ball. A drop step is taken and the arc is made so that the fielder is in a position to drop to one knee and field the ball in the center of the body.

Moving Ball

Once the technique is learned, the outfielder must work on timing his or her approach to various speeds of ground balls. Timing can be learned by first rolling the ball to the outfielder from only a few feet away. As the outfielder becomes comfortable with fielding a moving ball, the distance over which the ball is rolled and the speed at which the ball is rolled are gradually increased. As the fielder becomes consistently successful with the rolled ball, the ball may then be hit to the outfielder, with the hitter starting fairly close to the fielder and gradually working back to home plate. At this stage, repetition, variety in speed and direction, and constructive feedback are all essential for continued improvement.

Ground Balls—Charging

Charging a ground ball is differentiated from fielding a direct ground ball because charging requires a quick and strong throw to a specific base. Charging a ball is an advanced skill and is used conservatively (for situations such as a winning run on second base, ground ball to

right field). An outfielder has a greater chance of missing a charge ball because there is little room for adjustments to bad hops or misjudgments.

From the ready position, the fielder runs hard to the ball. The approach is coordinated so that the weight is on the glove-side foot as the ball is fielded. The back of the glove fingers are on the ground, just outside of the glove-side foot. The head is down, the eyes are focused on the center of the ball and the throwing hand is as close to the catch as possible (see Figure 3-20). Once the catch has been made, the throwing-side foot continues to step forward and plant perpendicular to the target (see Figures 3-21 and 3-22). If the momentum of the fielder does not allow the foot to plant perpendicular to the target on the step forward, the fielder follows the forward step with a skip on the throwing foot to plant the foot perpendicular to the target. The skip can help the fielder regain body control and add momentum to the throw, especially if the throw is a long throw. The glove-side foot then strides to the target and the throw is completed.

Key Elements:
- The fielder must charge the ball hard.
- The eyes focus on the center of the ball all the way into the glove.

Figure 3-20. Charging the ball to prevent a game winning run.

Figure 3-21. Forward step into the throw home.

Figure 3-22. Throwing-side foot plants perpendicular to the target.

- The player fields the ball with the back of the glove fingers on the ground just outside the glove-side foot and the throwing hand as close to the catch as possible.
- The weight is on the glove-side foot as the ball is caught.
- The throwing-side foot continues forward to

plant perpendicular to the target or skips to plant perpendicular to the target to place the body in an efficient throwing position.
- The glove-side foot strides to the target and the throw is completed.

Common Errors:
- Attempting to field the ball in the center of the body (1) takes more time to field and throw the ball, or (2) creates an unbalanced position because the fielder is charging hard.
- The eyes move up to check the runner before the ball has been caught.
- The ball is fielded with the fingertips of the glove and falls out on the way to the throwing hand.
- The fielder inefficiently transfers his or her weight after the pickup by taking too many steps.
- A fielder uses this technique when it's not absolutely necessary.

Ground Balls—Forehand and Backhand

In the outfield, balls that are hit to the extreme right or left of the fielder are the only balls that require a forehand or backhand catch. Anytime an outfielder moves laterally to field a ball, he or she should employ a crossover step in order to quickly and efficiently begin movement to the ball (see Figure 3-23). The cross-

Figure 3-23. Outfielder's crossover step.

over step is taken to properly align the outfielder's pursuit with the path of the ball. Many times outfielders instinctively run directly to the ball, but if the ball is hit hard or is a good distance away from the fielder, he or she will not be able to field it.

Taking the proper pursuit angle to the ball will allow the outfielder to reach the path of the ball before it passes by (see Figure 3-24). The angle of pursuit taken depends on the speed of the ball, the speed of the outfielder, and the distance between the outfielder's starting position and the ball's path. A fielder can attain an understanding of these angles by practicing the fielding of ground balls at various speeds and distances. Keep in mind that ground balls in the outfield should be approached at full speed with the ball being fielded in the center of the body whenever possible.

Key Elements:

- A crossover step initiates the movement to the ball.
- The speed of the ball, the speed of the outfielder and the distance of the ball from the outfielder dictate the outfielder's path to the ball.
- The eyes focus on the center of the ball until it enters the glove.
- The glove-side foot plants as the ball is fielded.
- The outfielder takes as few steps as possible in order to maintain momentum, and crow hops and throws to the appropriate location or runs the ball into the infield.

Common Errors:

- The outfielder uses a forehand or backhand catch when there is plenty of time to get in front of the ball.
- The outfielder does not take the appropriate angle to the ball, resulting in an inefficient pursuit.
- The outfielder does not plant the feet hard enough to quickly change the body's momentum into the throw. Too many steps are taken after the catch is made.

FLY BALLS (POP-UPS)

Catching a fly ball is basically the same for the infielder and the outfielder; the only difference is the distance the ball travels before it is caught and the distance the ball has to be thrown after it is caught. Therefore, this discussion will address all types of fly balls, regardless of position. The types of fly balls included are those hit

- in front of or slightly behind the fielder
- over a fielder's head
- in the sun
- near a fence

Fly Balls: In Front of Or Slightly Behind the Fielder

Similar to fielding ground balls, the flight of the fly ball is picked up immediately off of the bat, and the initial step takes place as soon as the flight of the ball is determined. From the

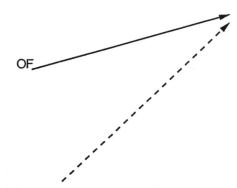

More efficient, correct angle of pursuit

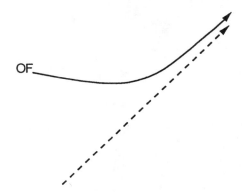

Time-consuming incorrect angle of pursuit

Figure 3-24. Correct and incorrect angles of pursuit.

ready position, the player quickly moves to the expected spot of the catch and waits for the ball. If the ball carries to the fielder or is directly in front of the fielder, a stationary or straight-in approach is used. If the ball is slightly behind or to either side of the fielder, the fielder can use a drop step to move directly in line with the ball. The fielder should run to the spot of the catch on his or her toes in order to keep the eyes level and clearly focused on the ball. With the body positioned under the ball, the hands move up and in front of the head. The arms extend to the ball and give as the ball is caught slightly on the throwing-side of the body (see Figure 3-25).

Moving Into the Catch

When a throw will be required following a catch, the outfielder moves to a position behind the expected point of the catch. As the ball approaches, several quick steps are taken into the catch. The steps are alternated and timed so the weight is moving to the glove-side foot as the ball is caught. The hands move up and in front of the head, the arms slightly extend to the ball, and the ball is caught on the throwing side of the body (see Figure 3-26).

With the weight on the glove-side foot and the ball secured, the eyes move to the target and the ball transfers to the throwing hand as

Figure 3-26. Weight moving to the glove-side foot.

the throwing-side foot steps ahead of the glove foot (see Figures 3-27 a and b). The step ahead of the glove foot is also known as a "travel step." The travel step creates more momentum into the throw than does the crow hop, as long as the throwing-side foot is planted perpendicular to the target. If the throwing-side foot plants parallel rather than perpendicular to the target, the subsequent loss of hip rotation negates the added momentum. Following the travel step, the glove-side foot strides to the target and the throw is completed (see Figure 3-27 c).

Key Elements:

- The fielder assumes the ready position.
- As soon as the ball's flight is determined the fielder makes the initial movement to the ball via straight-in or drop step approach.
- The movement to the ball is hard and players should run on the toes to keep the eyes level.
- The fielder moves to a position at or behind the expected spot of the catch and waits for the ball.
- Both arms extend to the ball as it approaches and give with the ball as it is caught slightly on the throwing side of the body.
- When an immediate throw is required following the catch, the fielder moves into the

Figure 3-25. Catching a fly ball.

(a)

(b)

(c)

Figure 3-27a-c. The travel step, stride and throw.

catch: (1) the weight moves to the glove-side foot as the ball is caught; (2) the throwing-side foot steps ahead of the glove-side foot, perpendicular to the target; and (3) the glove-side foot strides to the target and the throw is completed.

Common Errors:

- Running to the ball flat-footed causes one's vision of the ball to be "blurred."
- The fielder "drifts" with the ball rather than running hard and waiting for the ball.
- The arms extend too early and directly in front of the eyes, blocking the fielder's vision.
- The arms extend too late, causing the glove to move in the opposite direction of the ball at the time of the catch. The arms must "give" with the catch.
- The eyes remain straight ahead or look down with the glove high—a poor and dangerous technique.
- The throwing hand is not involved in the catch, resulting in a less reliable catch and wasted transfer time on the throw.
- No room is left to step into the ball when a throw is to follow.
- The throwing-side foot plants parallel to the target on the travel step, eliminating hip rotation during the throw.

Progressions for Teaching

Fly Ball Judgment

Before focusing on movement to the fly ball, the fielder must learn to judge the ball's flight. The flight of the ball should start small and increase gradually according to the fielder's success at catching. This can be done by initially throwing short, low fly balls and progressing to throwing longer and higher fly balls. Each fielder should be evaluated individually, and thrown or tossed fly balls in accordance with his or her ability. Low, short fly balls for higher-skilled fielders are not challenging; long, high fly balls for lower-skilled players do not facilitate success.

Movement to the Ball

As the fielders become proficient at judging fly balls, correct footwork must be learned for efficient movement to the ball. Correct footwork can be learned by temporarily eliminating the ball. The player visualizes a situation in his or her mind and physically and verbally goes through the correct execution: for example, "fly ball slightly back and to the left, glove-side foot drop step, run hard to the spot of the catch, catch the ball." When the player feels comfortable with the proper footwork, a ball may be used. Fly balls may be thrown to the right, left or center, short or long, high or low. The objective is to combine quick, correct judgment with proper footwork. The next progression requires the player to set up behind the ball, and move into the catch to make a throw.

Game-Simulated Fly Balls

As the fielder's skill progresses, fungo hitting becomes the next step. Again, fly balls should start short and low and gradually increase to higher and longer fly balls hit to the player's right or left. Eventually, the coach can hit fungoes from home plate with fielders at all positions in order to simulate specific game situations.

Fly Balls: Over a Fielder's Head

Once the flight of the ball has been determined to be over the fielder's head, the fielder has to get to the end of the ball's flight as quickly as possible. To initiate movement to the ball, the fielder drops the ball-side foot back while pivoting on the opposite foot (see Figure 3-28). The opposite foot then crosses over the ball-side foot so that the fielder is directly in line with the ball. Because the ball commonly "tails" to the

Figure 3-28. Fielder's drop step to go back on a fly ball.

foul line, the fielder usually drops the foot closest to the foul line when the ball is hit *directly* overhead. The drop step occurs with the left foot for fielders on the right side of the field and with the right foot for fielders on the left side of the field.

If the initial steps are determined to be in the "wrong" direction, the fielder has two options to correct the direction.

- *Option 1.* Plant the foot on the side of the desired direction and pivot and drop back with the other foot (see Figure 3-29 a and b). The eyes stay focused on the ball at all times.
- *Option 2.* Continue running back and, at the moment a necessary change in direction becomes obvious, quickly turn the head to the side of the ball and change the direction of the run. The eyes lose sight of the ball for an instant but immediately regain focus with the completion of the head turn. With practice, option 2 becomes more efficient.

If possible, the fielder should begin to turn toward the infield as the point of catch nears and wait for the ball. If this is not possible, while the player is still running the arms and

(a)

throwing-side foot continues "through" the catch and plants perpendicular to the target as quickly as possible. More than one step may be necessary to change one's momentum. Once the throwing-side foot has been planted, the glove-side foot strides toward the target and the throw is completed. If the play requires a long throw, an extra crow hop may also be necessary.

Key Elements:
- The fielder takes a drop step to the side of the ball.
- The opposite foot crosses over so that the player is in a direct line to the ball.
- The arms extend to the ball just prior to the catch.
- The eyes follow the ball into the glove.
- The throwing-side foot is planted as soon as possible.
- An extra crow hop is taken for a long throw.
- The glove-side foot strides to the target to complete the throw.

(b)

Figure 3-29 a and b. Plant and pivot to change direction, Option 1.

hands fully extend to the ball just prior to the catch. The eyes follow the ball over the shoulder and into the glove (see Figure 3-30). When a quick throw is required following a catch, the

Figure 3-30. Arms extending to the ball for an over the shoulder catch.

Common Errors:

- The arms extend to the ball too soon, which slows the fielder's movement to the ball.
- The arms never extend to the ball or they lower too soon when the fielder assumes the ball cannot be caught in the air.
- The fielder turns the wrong direction and does not immediately correct the movement.
- Back pedaling significantly slows momentum and often results in a loss of balance.

Fly Balls: In the Sun

Fielders should always be aware of the position of the sun in relation to their position on the field. When a player is looking toward the sun while pursuing a fly ball he or she raises the glove to a position that will shade the eyes (see Figure 3-31). The ball can then be followed through the sun area by viewing it on one side of the glove. As the ball nears the fielder, both hands move to catch the ball. For safety rea-sons, when a fielder loses sight of a ball and cannot relocate it, it is best to "cover up" rather than attempt a chance catch.

Fly Balls: Near a Fence

If the fielder is in a position to attempt to catch a ball hit high and near a fence, the fielder must first be aware of the initial distance away from the fence. With the hit, the fielder moves immediately to the fence and extends the throwing arm to locate the fence. Once the fence is located, the fielder moves from the fence to catch the ball. If there is not enough time to get to the fence first, the fielder uses the extended throwing arm to help cushion any contact with the fence (see Figure 3-32). If the fielder has to jump to catch the ball, the throwing arm is used to facilitate the jump. When the fence is on the glove-side of the fielder, the glove arm extends to locate the fence, then moves up to catch the ball.

Figure 3-31. Shading the eyes with the glove.

Figure 3-32. Extending the arm to the fence.

4
Position Play

Jill Elliott, M.S.
Tom Smith, M.S.
Steve Simensky, M.A.
Michael A. Clark, Ph.D.

QUESTIONS TO CONSIDER

- What is the correct position of the backup fielder in relation to the play being backed up?
- What is the advantage of letting the ball come to the glove versus reaching for the ball when attempting to tag a runner?
- How is a force play related to speed throwing?
- When a fly ball is hit between an outfielder and an infielder, which player has priority to make the catch?
- Why is communication among fielders important?

INTRODUCTION

In addition to being proficient at the basic skills of fielding, throwing, and catching, each defensive player must also know the techniques and responsibilities unique to a specific position. Defensive success is achieved through a combination of the correct execution of basic skills and the correct execution of techniques and responsibilities specific to position play.

Basic techniques and responsibilities for each position are described in this chapter. The positions are discussed in the following order:

1. pitcher
2. catcher
3. first base
4. second base
5. third base
6. shortstop
7. left field
8. center field
9. right field

PITCHER

Responsibilities

Fielding

The pitcher also must be prepared to act as a fielder at numerous times during the game. This is why the pitcher should always communicate with the infielders about who will be covering which base in each instance. For example, with a runner on first base with less than two outs, the pitcher must know who will be covering second base in case a ball is hit straight back to the mound. In short, the pitcher must be aware of the situation: the number of outs, the infielders' positions, and the likely defensive options.

As described in the section on the delivery (see Chapter 5, Pitching), the pitcher should be in a position to field the ball after the pitch. The pitcher "chicken wings" the glove hand so that it ends up near the head as protection in case of a line drive; the body is balanced on both legs with the knees flexed. If a ball hit up the middle is fielded, then the pitcher steps toward the base to make the throw. Only in extreme cases should a pitcher be running when throwing to a base; even in Major League Baseball errors often occur as pitchers on the run throw wildly on the easiest plays.

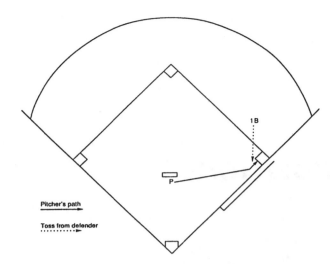

Figure 4-1. Pitcher's path to cover first base.

Covering First Base

Perhaps the most common situation involving the pitcher as a fielder is a ball hit between first and second base. This situation requires a great deal of coordination and practice as both infielders tend to go for the ball and the pitcher has to cover first base. All players involved in this play should practice their roles so that either infielder can make a throw to the pitcher who is in a predictable location.

To get into the proper position, the pitcher must follow an exact path to the base. When a ball is hit to the right side of the infield, the pitcher runs directly to a spot approximately 10 feet in front of the base and then turns toward first base to run parallel to the baseline (see Figure 4-1). The toss from the infielder ideally is caught about 3 feet in front of the base, and the base is touched with the right foot. Because other base runners may be trying to advance, the pitcher must then turn back toward the infield and be prepared to throw to any base.

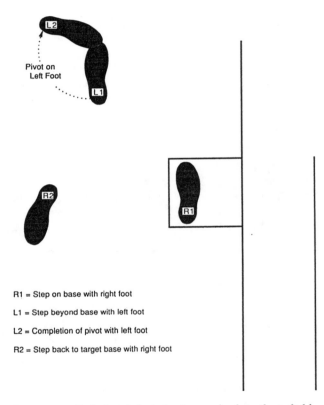

R1 = Step on base with right foot

L1 = Step beyond base with left foot

L2 = Completion of pivot with left foot

R2 = Step back to target base with right foot

- *The left-handed pitcher* touches first with the right foot, plants the left foot and turns toward the target base (see Figure 4-2).
- *The right-handed pitcher* touches first, continues an extra stride past the bag, plants the right foot and turns to the target (see Figure 4-3).

This additional step should be taken on a curved path in toward the center of the field, as this decreases the likelihood of interfering with the runner. In any event, the quickest, most ef-

Figure 4-2. Left-handed pitcher's turn back to the infield.

ficient move for all pitchers is a pivot inwards toward the glove side.

Only through practice do all these moves become coordinated. Drills also give the infielders an opportunity to learn how much ground they can cover and when they can make the putouts unassisted by the pitcher.

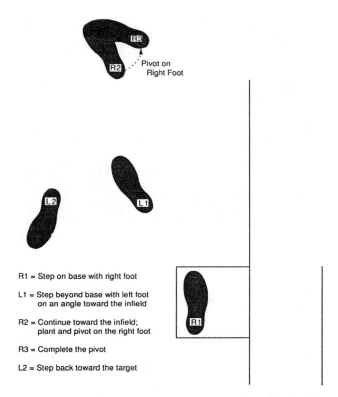

R1 = Step on base with right foot

L1 = Step beyond base with left foot on an angle toward the infield

R2 = Continue toward the infield; plant and pivot on the right foot

R3 = Complete the pivot

L2 = Step back toward the target

Figure 4-3. Right-handed pitcher's turn back to the infield.

Starting Double Plays

With a runner on first and less than two outs, the pitcher must communicate with the middle infielders and learn who will be covering second base on a ball hit back to the pitcher. If such a play develops, the pitcher starts the double play by pivoting on the glove-side foot to turn toward second base. A step and throw, not a running motion, is used to make the throw, which leads the infielder slightly to the bag.

Backing Up Bases

Besides fielding batted balls and covering first base, a pitcher also backs up throws from the outfield. With runners on base and a ball hit into the outfield, the pitcher anticipates where the throw is likely to go and moves to stand behind the target base in line with the outfielder. The proper distance back of the base varies, but a good rule of thumb is one-third or more of the distance between bases (20 feet or so on bases set 60 feet apart, 30 feet or more on those set 90 feet apart). If a player in the backup position stands closer to the base, then a high or deflected throw may be impossible to catch. These guidelines apply to all bases, but in some cases the pitcher cannot tell whether to back up third base or home plate and so should stand between the bases in foul territory and watch the play unfold. If receiving the ball and having to throw, the pitcher turns on the glove-side foot and steps toward the base.

Covering Home Plate

With runners in scoring position, the pitcher must cover home plate on any wild pitch or passed ball. In these situations the pitcher should run in the direction of the ball, pointing at it and calling, "There!" to the catcher (see Figure 4-4 a). These actions help the catcher locate the ball. Once the catcher finds the ball, the pitcher runs directly to the plate holding the glove near chest height and open toward the catcher. This presents a good target for the catcher while allowing the pitcher to react quickly to throws that might be off line (see Figure 4-4 b). If getting to home before the throw, the pitcher gets into position straddling the plate and facing the catcher; otherwise the pitcher gets the feet properly positioned and continues to provide a good target by holding the glove open toward the catcher (see Figure 4-4 c); otherwise, the pitcher gets the feet properly positioned and continues to provide a good target by holding the glove open toward the catcher. This is especially important because a defensive player is not allowed to block a runner's path to *any* base unless the defender has possession of the ball. Once having the ball in the glove, the pitcher turns to open the hips toward the third base line and makes a sweep tag of the runner. The move is accomplished by pivoting on the left foot to bring the body roughly parallel to the baseline (see Figure 4-4 d). This action minimizes the likelihood of collision or injury.

CATCHER

Responsibilities

Receiving the Pitch

The first responsibility of a catcher is to receive the pitch from the pitcher. A catcher's stance varies with the game situation. When the bases are empty, the catcher uses a crouched or down position. With runners on base, the catcher uses a semicrouched position or up position.

Figure 4-4a. Pitcher helping catcher locate wild pitch or passed ball.

Figure 4-4b. Pitcher presenting target to catcher.

Figure 4-4c. Pitcher straddling plate to receive ball from catcher.

Figure 4-4d. Pitcher's move into position for a sweep tag.

Crouched Position

In the crouched position, the catcher squats down with

- the feet approximately shoulder width apart
- the glove-side foot even with or slightly in front of the throwing-side foot

- the weight distributed on the balls of the feet
- the glove-side arm extended in front of the body and slightly flexed
- the glove open wide, producing a large target
- the throwing hand positioned behind the back or behind the leg in order to protect it from a foul tip or a wild pitch (see Figure 4-5).

Figure 4-5. The catcher's crouch position.

- the back is approximately parallel to the ground (see Figure 4-6)
- the throwing hand is loosely clenched
- the throwing hand is placed behind the glove so that the hand is protected, yet in position to quickly transfer the ball (see Figure 4-7)

Figure 4-6. The semicrouched position, side view.

The target is positioned along the centerline of the catcher, so that the stance location changes slightly with the desired pitch location. For example, on an inside pitch the catcher's midline should be lined up with the inside edge of the plate. Similarly, on an outside pitch, the catcher's midline should be lined up with the outside edge of the plate.

Semicrouched Position

With runners on base, the catcher must be prepared to make a throw following each pitch. The semicrouch position allows the catcher to quickly execute a throw. The catcher starts in the down position. As the pitcher prepares to deliver the pitch, the catcher widens his or her stance by moving the glove-side foot out and raising the hips. In the semicrouch position

- the glove-side foot is slightly in front of the throwing foot
- the hips are up

Figure 4-7. Front view of the semicrouch. Notice the position of the hands.

Throwing

If the situation requires a throw to a base, upon receiving the pitch the catcher shifts the weight over the glove-side foot and simultaneously leans forward in order to rise to a standing position. In a continuous motion, the catcher executes a crow hop to plant the throwing-side foot perpendicular to the target (see Figure 4-8). If the throw is to be made to first base or third base and the batter is on the side of the throw, the crow hop must place the catcher in front of the batter. During the crow hop, the ball is transferred to the throwing hand as both hands move toward the throwing shoulder. The throwing elbow is placed shoulder high and leads the throwing hand back, stretching the shoulder muscles. The glove-side foot strides toward the target, and the elbow leads the throwing hand forward to quickly complete the joint sequence and release the ball (see Figure 4-8 a-c).

If the catcher has a strong throwing arm, he or she may execute a quick "jump pivot" upon receiving the pitch. The jump pivot consists of placing the throwing-side foot perpendicular to the target and the glove-side foot toward the target. The pivot must be executed as the catcher is standing up to complete the throw; otherwise, valuable time is lost. With the jump pivot, the body weight lands on the throwing-side foot and quickly transfers to the

(b)

(c)

Figure 4-8 a-c. Sequence of a catcher using the crow hop to throw to a base.

glove-side foot during the throw. The throwing action of the arm is the same as with the crow hop, but quicker (see Figure 4-9 a-c).

Blocking Pitches

Occasionally, pitches hit the ground before they get to the catcher. With runners on base, the catcher must be prepared to block a pitch and keep the ball in front of the body. Assum-

(a)

(a)

(c)

Figure 4-9 a-c. Sequence of the jump pivot throw by a catcher.

(b)

ing the catching stance as close to home plate as possible allows the catcher to block a pitch closer to the ground and reduces the effect of a "bad bounce."

Blocking Pitches—Center

On low pitches directly in front of the catcher, he or she drops down to the knees, and then slides into the pitch. The head is down and the eyes focus on the ball while the shoulders remain square to the pitcher. The back is slightly curved forward in order to deflect the ball downward, and the glove is placed between the knees and open (see Figure 4-10). After the ball has been blocked, the catcher immediately moves to recover the ball. The catcher positions his or her feet so that a crow hop can be easily executed if throwing to a base is necessary. The catcher fields the ball and immediately looks for a play.

Blocking Pitches—Left

When a pitch is pitched to the ground on the left side of the catcher, he or she takes a quick step with the left foot and moves the body to the left by pushing off with the right foot. The right knee is placed on the ground, followed by the left knee. The hands fill the space between the knees, with the glove open to the ball and contacting the ground. As the catcher moves toward the ball, the left shoulder is turned inward to deflect the ball forward. The head is down, and the eyes focus upon the ball with the arms tight to the sides of the body (see Figure 4-11). The initial step must place the catcher in such a position that the ball may be blocked along the centerline of the body. A pitch slightly to the left of the catcher requires a less forceful step than a pitch farther to the left. After the ball has been blocked, the catcher jumps up, recovers the ball and prepares to throw. When recovering the ball, the feet are positioned so that a crow hop can be easily executed if a throw is necessary (see Figure 4-12).

Blocking Pitches—Right

When the ball is pitched to the ground on the right of the catcher, he or she takes a quick step with the right foot and pushes off with the left foot. The catcher then drops to the left knee, followed by the right knee. The hands fill the space between the knees, with the glove open to the ball and in contact with the ground. The right shoulder turns inward to deflect the ball forward, and the head positions downward with the eyes focused upon the ball (see Figure

Figure 4-10. Proper position to block pitches in front of the catcher.

Figure 4-11. Position for blocking pitches to the catcher's left.

Figure 4-12. Recovering from blocking the ball; in position to crow hop and throw.

4-13). As with the ball to the left, the initial step must place the catcher in a position to block the ball along the midline of the body. After the ball has been blocked, the catcher jumps to her or his feet, quickly picks up the ball and prepares to throw.

Retrieving Wild Pitches and Passed Balls

If a pitch gets by the catcher and there are runners on base, the catcher must get to the ball quickly and efficiently. The moment the ball has passed the catcher, he or she executes a drop step to the side the ball passed and uses the ball-side arm to help keep the umpire clear of the path to the ball. A passed ball on the left requires a drop step with the left foot and a clearing motion with the left arm; a passed ball on the right requires a drop step with the right foot and a clearing motion with the right arm (see Figure 4-14).

Figure 4-13. Blocking pitches to the right.

Figure 4-14. Catcher making a drop step and clearing the umpire with the arm to pursue a ball to the right.

Following the initial drop step, the catcher stays low and moves directly to the ball. As the catcher prepares to field the ball, the feet are positioned so that the throwing-side foot is planted just beyond the ball and perpendicular to home plate (see Figure 4-15). The ball is picked up with the throwing hand and is secured with the glove. As soon as the ball is secured, the catcher "shows" the ball to the pitcher and then shifts the weight to the glove-side foot and "snaps" (see Chapter 1, Throwing, "The Snap Throw") the ball to the pitcher (see Figure 4-16). The throw must be controlled and not rushed.

Figure 4-15. Catcher recovering the ball and ready to throw.

Figure 4-16. Catcher making a snap throw to the pitcher.

Fielding

The catcher's basic fielding responsibilities include:

1. fielding bunts or weakly hit ground balls in the area around home plate
2. calling the position of a throw when a bunt is fielded by another infielder
3. catching any pop-ups in the home plate area
4. forcing or tagging out runners attempting to score
5. backing up first base when there are no runners on base.

A description of each of these responsibilities and techniques for execution is provided below.

Fielding the Bunt

On a bunt, the catcher moves to the ball and positions the feet around the ball (throwing-side foot perpendicular to the target) so that the ball is fielded with two hands near the midline of the body (see Figure 4-17). The catcher then (1) executes a crow hop to help gain momentum into the throw, or (2) executes a weight shift from the throwing-side foot to the glove-side foot. The option chosen usually depends on the strength of the throwing arm and the skill of the catcher. Figures 4-18 and 4-19 show the catcher's weight shift to the glove-side foot and the crow hop. It is extremely important that the catcher communicate with the other infielders. Immediately calling for the ball eliminates uncertainty and possible collisions.

Figure 4-18. Weight shift to the throwing side.

Figure 4-19. Crow hop position for throw.

Calling the Throw

In a bunt situation, the catcher is the only player involved who can see the entire playing area. Therefore, if another infielder has a better opportunity to field a ball, the catcher is responsible for telling the other players. As soon as the catcher knows that another player will field the ball, the catcher must focus on the action of the runners. If, for example, the runner on first base did not get a good "jump" on the bunt, the catcher must see this and yell, "Two!"

Figure 4-17. Fielding a bunt.

The player fielding the ball should then respond and throw to second base.

Catching Pop-Ups

Because the catcher is positioned close to the batter, the catcher cannot always immediately pick up the flight of a pop-up hit around the home plate area. Other fielders can help the catcher by yelling "up" or "back" or any other helpful word and simultaneously pointing to the location of the ball. When the ball is popped up, the catcher removes the mask with the throwing hand and focuses on the flight of the ball. When the flight of the ball is determined, the mask is thrown in the opposite direction (see Figure 4-20 a and b). Waiting to throw the mask eliminates the possibility of tripping over the mask while attempting to catch the ball. The spin of a ball that has been popped up near or behind home plate usually causes the ball to carry toward the infield. If the catcher turns her or his back to the infield to make the catch, the ball will carry toward the catcher. The ball is caught with two hands, above the head. Immediately following the catch, the catcher looks to the infield to prevent any base runners from advancing.

If the pop-up is hit so that the catcher and an infielder call for the catch simultaneously, the infielder has priority. Again, because of the spin, the ball carries toward the infield and is easier for the infielder to catch.

(b)

Figure 4-20 a and b. Locating the ball and discarding the mask.

Making Tag Plays at Home Plate

Unless the runner is forced to go home, the catcher must tag the runner with the ball in order to get the runner out. To do this safely and efficiently, the catcher initially moves to the front edge of home plate and gives a target for the throw (see Figure 4-21). As the ball approaches home plate, the catcher must determine whether it will arrive on time to tag the runner. If the ball will not arrive on time to tag the runner, the catcher must remain out of the runner's way. If the ball will arrive on time to tag the runner, the catcher moves to block the plate.

As the ball arrives, the catcher takes a short step with the left foot to line it up with the third base foul line (see Figure 4-22). If the position of the left foot is anything but parallel to the path of the runner (the third base foul line), contact between the catcher and the runner may result in injury to the knee. As the throw is caught, the shoulders square to the runner. The ball is held with the throwing hand and both are protected with the glove. The glove and ball are placed on the ground in front of the foot to tag the sliding runner. If the runner attempts to slide around the tag, the catcher slides the ball and glove along the ground toward the runner. With other runners on base,

(a)

Figure 4-21. Catcher in position to receive ball for a tag play.

the catcher must make the tag and then immediately check the runners and prepare to throw.

Assisting Force Plays at Home Plate

A force play at home plate occurs when runners are on all three bases—when the bases are loaded. When the ball is hit, the catcher immediately moves to the front of the plate. The weight is evenly distributed over both feet and the shoulders are square to the fielder making the throw. A chest-high target is provided for the fielder. As soon as the path of the throw is known, the catcher quickly adjusts the throwing-side foot to the front edge of home plate and steps toward the ball with the glove-side foot (see Figure 4-23). If the throw is off target, the catcher must move away from the plate and catch the ball so that the other base runners may not advance further.

If there are less than two outs, the catcher

1. steps toward the ball with the glove-side foot in order to make the catch
2. immediately executes a crow hop
3. throws to first base in an attempt to complete a double play (as in the speed throw) (see Figures 4-23 to 4-25).

Figure 4-22. The catcher's step into position to make tag.

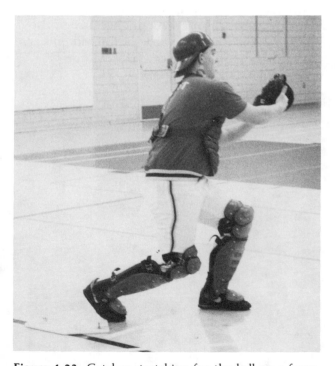

Figure 4-23. Catcher stretching for the ball on a force play.

Figure 4-24. Crow hop from stretch position.

Figure 4-25. Throw to first to complete the double play.

Although the double play throw can go to any base, the throw to first base is generally more successful. The runner moving toward first base has to wait for the pitch, hit the ball, and follow through with the swing before ini-

tiating the run. The runners moving toward second base or third base may initiate their run on the release of the pitch and therefore are less likely to be forced out in an attempted double play.

Backing Up

When no runners are on base, the catcher plays an important role in backing up first base. When a throw is made from the second base position or the second base side of the shortstop, the catcher runs to a point behind first base, directly in line with the fielder (see Chapter 9, Defensive Strategies). When the throw is made from the third base or shortstop position, the right fielder is the primary backup. The catcher, however, should be in a position to field any balls that deflect off the first baseperson's glove or off the runner toward the home plate side of first base.

FIRST BASE

Ready Position Location

The first baseperson's usual starting position is some 6 to 8 feet off the foul line and 3 to 15 feet behind the base. This is quite a large area in which to position oneself, and within it each athlete must find a spot to stand that permits good defensive coverage. Generally this spot should be close enough to the line to protect against ground balls hit between the player and the base but far enough over and back to help cover the second base line. However, because the first baseperson's prime responsibility is making force outs by catching throws from infielders, the initial placement also should be near enough to the base to allow for getting there before these throws are made. Infielders should not be expected to throw to moving targets or open bases, and the first baseperson should determine in practice where to start in each situation.

A number of factors may cause adjustments in this positioning. As suggested, many of these situations are best worked out in practice, but two merit special consideration: bunts and holding base runners. Bunt situations usually require a starting position well in toward home. This position should be close enough to allow the player to field a soft bunt but far enough back to give some protection against hits resulting from unexpected offensive moves. Situations generally dictate that runners at first should be held close to the base. Often holding the runner close requires the first baseperson to be in the infield with the right foot against the bag; other times, the first baseperson simply being nearby keeps the runner close. Holding runners on base is discussed under "Tag Plays—Pickoff Attempts by the Pitcher" in this chapter.

Fielding Batted Balls

The first baseperson is responsible for fielding ground balls, fly balls and bunts hit to

1. fielding bunts, ground balls and fly balls hit to the first base area
2. receiving throws to first base for force plays and tag plays
3. backing up other players
4. acting as a cutoff person for throws from the outfield to home plate

Each of these responsibilities and techniques for execution are described in the following sections.

Fielding Batted Balls

The first baseperson is responsible for fielding ground balls, fly balls and bunts hit to the first base area (see Figure 4-26). This area, however, does not have exact boundaries and will expand as the athlete becomes more experienced and mature. Therefore, communication with other fielders is essential. When a ground ball is hit or bunted toward the first base area, fielding the ball is the primary responsibility of the first baseperson. Once the ball has been fielded, the first baseperson must decide whether to make the play unassisted or rely on the second baseperson or pitcher to take the throw. When the play can be made with either option, it is best to touch the base or tag the runner. A slow ground ball hit to the right side (fielder's right) of first base is best fielded by the first baseperson, with the second baseperson or pitcher covering first base. The first baseperson can get to this ball quicker and, therefore, make the play more easily.

The first baseperson has priority on fly balls hit in front of first base, extending to the pitcher's mound. The second baseperson, how-

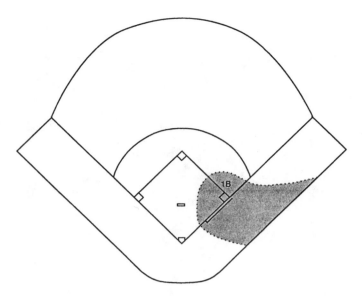

Figure 4-26. Area to be covered by the defender at first base.

ever, has priority on fly balls behind first base and on fly balls that are called for simultaneously. If "called off," the first baseperson must cover first base.

Receiving Throws at First Base

Force Plays

When the ball is hit to another infielder, the first baseperson sprints to the base, turns toward the infield, and looks to receive the throw. The receiving ready position at the base consists of the heels of both feet placed near the front edge of the base, and the shoulders square to the throw. The feet are about shoulder width apart and the weight is evenly distributed over both feet (see Figure 4-27).

After the flight of the throw has been determined, the throwing-side foot is placed on the front edge of the base and the glove-side foot stretches toward the ball (see Figure 4-28). If the ball is thrown to the right of the base, the throwing-side foot adjusts to the right side of the base. If the ball is thrown to the left of the base, the throwing-side foot adjusts to the left side of the base. If the first baseperson stretches with the glove-side foot before the flight of the throw has been determined, adjustments to poor throws will be difficult. Also, touching the base by placing the outside of the throwing-side foot against the base reduces the potential

Figure 4-27. Receiving the throw at first.

of losing contact with the base when a long stretch is required.

If the ball is thrown too low, the first baseperson must decide whether (1) to stretch in order to catch the ball on the short hop, or (2) to widen the feet in order to field the throw as if it were a ground ball. If the ball cannot be caught while maintaining contact with the base, the first baseperson must leave the base and catch the ball. A younger or inexperienced athlete may become preoccupied with keeping a foot on the base, so practice with varied throws to first base is essential. If the throw is toward the home plate side of first base, the first baseperson may "sweep" the ball across the baseline to tag the runner out.

Tag Plays—Pickoff Attempts by the Pitcher

With a runner at first or runners at first and third, the first baseperson moves to the home plate side of the bag and puts the right foot against the base. The left foot is near the foul line so the athlete's body roughly parallels the foul line (see Figure 4-29). Keeping the right foot against the base minimizes the likelihood of injury caused by a sliding runner.

When the pitcher attempts a pick off at first, the throw is taken and in one sweeping

Figure 4-28. Moving the feet into position to tag the base.

Figure 4-29. Defender at first holding the runner close.

motion the ball and glove are laid in front of the base. This move may involve a pivot on the right foot. A right-handed person playing first generally will expose the back of the glove to a sliding runner, thus affording some protection to the ball; a left-handed player however, may need to practice making the tag while protecting the hand. The ball and glove are kept in contact with the runner in case of an overslide or missed base, but the defender must remain aware of any other runners on base. Once the umpire has made the call, the first baseperson promptly returns the ball to the pitcher; sometimes a fake throw may be made in order to fool a careless runner into leaving the base before the pitcher has received the ball.

An alternative position with runners at first and second or with the bases loaded has the first baseperson closer to the base but not in the pickoff position. The defender takes a spot between the base and the runner, a step or two behind the baseline (see Figure 4-30). From here the fielder may react to any batted balls while still keeping the runner close; this can be done even more effectively if the first baseperson occasionally slaps the mitt with the bare hand. This sound reminds the runner that the defender is at hand, and often the runner will shorten the lead as a result.

Tag Plays—Pickoff Attempts from the Catcher

If a runner on first base takes a big lead or is slow in returning to the base, the catcher may throw to first base in order to pick off the runner. This play is not a force play because the runner may choose to run to second base. Therefore, the first baseperson must move efficiently to catch the throw and tag the runner.

The attempted pickoff play at first base may begin with a sign from either the catcher or first baseperson. As the ball crosses the plate the first baseperson pivots on the right foot, looks toward the catcher for the throw and listens for the runner (see Figure 4-31). The ball is caught and taken to the ground directly in front of the base using a sweeping motion. (See Figure 4-32 a and b.) When making a tag at any base, it is important to let the ball come to the glove. The ball will travel at a greater speed than the fielder can move the ball and glove. This also emphasizes the significance of forceful accurate throws. If the runner cannot be heard or seen, the first baseperson must listen for directions from other fielders and immediately prepare to throw the ball to second base.

Backing Up

Although the pitcher traditionally backs up home plate, sometimes it is best for the first baseperson to assume this role. Many times

Figure 4-30. Position used by the defender at first with runners at first and second or bases loaded.

Figure 4-31. Position at first base to receive a pickoff throw from the catcher.

(a)

(b)

Figure 4-32 a and b. Tagging the runner on an attempted pickoff with an outside pivot and sweep tag.

beginning pitchers are not ready to assume multiple responsibilities; therefore, when there will not be a play at first base and a runner has a chance to score, the first baseperson may back up home plate. The first baseperson must also be aware of potential problems at other bases and back up those plays whenever necessary.

Cutting Off Throws

On an outfield throw to home plate from center or right field and more than one runner on base, the first baseperson (or pitcher) moves to a cutoff position. The cutoff position is assumed directly between the origin of the throw and home plate, generally even with the mound; however, throws from center field actually may be taken behind the mound so as to avoid bad bounces (see Figure 4-33). Adjustments are made in relation to the origin and strength of the throw; a throw from deep in the outfield or a weak throw will require the cutoff person to be further from home plate. A common error is to be positioned too close to home plate, which blocks the catcher's view of the throw and limits the catcher's ability to react to the play.

In the cutoff position, the arms are raised overhead in order to give a clear target for the throw. The cutoff person listens for directions from the catcher. In general, the only time the ball is cut off is when the catcher yells "cut" or if the throw is off target. Otherwise, the ball goes through to the catcher. Besides cutting off throws from the outfield, the first baseperson may also trail the batter/runner to second on doubles to the left side, thus providing coverage at second in case the base is unguarded (see Chapter 8, Defensive Strategies).

Figure 4-33. Defender from first in cutoff position.

SECOND BASE

Ready Position Location

The ready position for the second baseperson is generally located slightly more than halfway to second from first and 10 to 15 feet behind the base path (see Figure 4-34). This general location varies, however, depending upon the hitting tendencies of the batter, the game situation, and the ability of the second baseperson. For example, a second baseperson with strong forehand fielding ability but weak backhand fielding ability would be more effective playing slightly closer to second base, especially if the batter tends to hit the ball up the middle. In a bunt situation, however, the second baseperson should move slightly closer to first base. A runner on first and less than two outs might find the second baseperson moving in a few steps to cut down the distance on a possible double play. A runner on third base might require the second baseperson to position him or herself on or in front of the base path in order to allow time to make a throw to home plate.

Fielding Responsibilities

The second baseperson's basic fielding responsibilities include:

1. fielding all ground balls and fly balls hit in the second base area
2. covering first and second base
3. handling force plays at second base, including the double play
4. making tag plays at second base
5. making tag plays at first base
6. relaying the ball from right field and right-center field to the infield

A description of the techniques for executing these responsibilities is provided in the following sections.

Fielding Batted Balls

The second baseperson has primary responsibility for fielding all ground balls and fly balls hit to the second base area (see Figure 4-34). As with all positions, this area has no definite boundaries. For instance, note that the second baseperson must take fly balls hit behind first base because the first baseperson may have a difficult time going back and locating

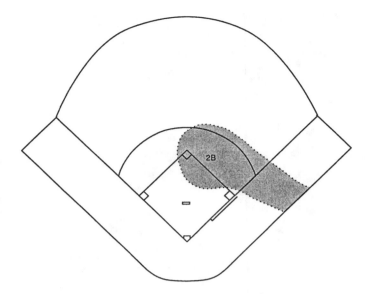

Figure 4-34. Area to be covered by the defender at second base.

the ball. Obviously communication with other fielders is essential. On fly balls, the second baseperson has priority over the pitcher and first baseperson. If all three call for the ball, the pitcher and first baseperson must allow the second baseperson to make the catch. Outfielders, however, have priority over the second baseperson. If the right fielder and the second baseperson both call for the ball, the second baseperson must allow the right fielder to make the catch. The second baseperson must also be prepared to back up any ground ball or line drive hit to the pitcher or the first baseperson.

Covering Bases

Generally, if the ball is hit to the right side of the field, the second baseperson may cover first base. Similarly, if the ball is hit to the left side of the field, the second baseperson covers second base. More specifically, the second baseperson covers first base any time the first baseperson attempts to field a ball. For example, a bunt situation may require the first baseperson to charge the ball even if it is fielded by the pitcher. Therefore, the second baseperson must cover first base and receive the throw (see the section "First Base").

The second baseperson covers second base on any ball hit to third base, shortstop, left field or to the left side of center field. For example, on a ball hit to left field, the shortstop moves into position for a possible relay, and the second baseperson covers second base. In a situation where a base runner is on first base and there are less than two outs, the second baseperson must be prepared to cover either first or second base. If the ball is bunted, the second baseperson covers first base. If the ball is hit to the left side of the field, the second baseperson covers second base for the force out.

Force Plays at Second Base

Turning the Double Play

There are several methods used to turn a double play at second base. Each has its advantages and disadvantages. The simplest method for teaching youth baseball players to initiate a double play is to speed throw across the base. (See Chapter 2, Catching and Catching/Throwing as a Combined Skill.) Speed throwing across the base allows the player two options.

Option 1: The player's first option is to
1. step on the base with the glove-side foot as the ball is caught
2. step across the base with the throwing foot perpendicular to the target
3. step toward the target with the glove-side foot in order to complete the throw (see Figure 4-35 a-c).

(b)

(a)

(c)

Figure 4-35 a-c. Turning the double play, Option 1.

Option 2: The player's second option is to
1. step across the base with the throwing-side foot as the ball is caught
2. drag the glove-side foot across the base and plant it pointed to the target
3. step toward the target with the glove-side foot and complete the throw (see Figure 4-36 a and b).

(a)

(b)

Figure 4-36 a and b. Turning the double play, Option 2.

With either option the defender should slow down a bit upon nearing the base. As soon as the ball is hit, the second baseperson breaks as fast as possible for the base but slows a step

or two before arriving there. This allows the player to control the pivot on the double play.

In any case, it is essential to plant the throwing-side foot away from the base in order to keep the fielder clear of the runner's path. A player who is proficient at speed throwing quickly learns how to turn a double play. If a double play attempt is not realistic for the skill of the second baseperson or if the force out at second base is the only play to be made, the second baseperson receives the throw using the same techniques as those described for the first baseperson (see the section "First Base").

Tag Plays at Second Base

With a runner at first intending to steal and a right handed batter, the second baseperson covers second. When making a tag at second base, the second baseperson must position the body so that the shoulders are square to the throw and the ball is caught in the center of the body. Body position varies with the origin of the throw. When positioning for the throw, it is important to leave the first base side of second base open (see Figure 4-37). A sliding runner may injure a player's foot if it is positioned

Figure 4-37. Tagging the runner at second.

on the first base side of second base. The ball is caught with two hands, and the glove is placed on the first base side of second base. Adjustments are made in relation to the path of the runner. The glove should give as the runner is tagged in order to reduce the force of impact.

Force Plays at First Base

In most situations involving a bunt, the second baseperson has responsibility for covering first base and making the force out. Once the ball is thrown, the player breaks for first and assumes a position like a first baseperson in a similar circumstance (see above). This involves weight shifts, stretches and handling wild throws, so the second baseperson needs as much practice as possible in making such plays.

Tag Plays at First Base

Occasionally, the second baseperson takes a throw at first and has to tag a runner. Usually this happens in a bunt situation with a runner at first. If the ball is not bunted but the first baseman charges, the runner may be slow in returning to first. If the second baseperson and catcher see this and communicate, the second baseperson positions him or herself with the feet straddling the base, the shoulders square to the catcher (see Figure 4-38). The ball is caught and placed on the ground in front of the base with the back of the glove to the runner, and adjustments are made in relation to the path of the runner.

Making Relays

Generally, when the ball is hit to right field or to right-center field, the second baseperson positions him or herself in the outfield in order to receive the throw and relay the ball to the infield. The location of the relay position depends upon the outfielder's throwing ability, the location of the ball and the intended target (base) of the relay. A weak throwing arm and a long hit would require the relay location to be fairly deep into the outfield. A potential play at third base would require the relay person to be positioned in line with the outfielder and third base.

Once in the appropriate location, the relay person faces the outfielder with the arms overhead in order to give a clear target (see Figure

Figure 4-38. The defender from second covering first on a tag play.

4-39). As the ball approaches, the glove-side foot begins to step toward the intended target, while the shoulders remain square to the ball (see Figure 4-40). As the ball is caught the relay person executes a crow hop and rotates the shoulders parallel to the intended target. Simultaneously, the ball is taken to the throwing position. The glove-side foot strides toward the target and the ball is thrown.

If the intended target is a short distance away and the relay person has a strong throwing arm, the outfielder's throw is received as the weight moves over the throwing-side foot. As the ball is caught, the throwing-side foot quickly pivots perpendicular to the target and the glove-side foot strides forward in order to complete the throw. Eliminating the crow hop saves time but reduces momentum into the throw, therefore, the relay person using this method must have a strong throwing arm.

Figure 4-39. Relay position.

Figure 4-40. Dropping the glove-side foot toward the intended target.

THIRD BASE

Ready Position Location

As with other positions, the third base person may change the ready position depending upon the game situation. Whether the hitter "pulls" the ball or is a bunter, the inning and the game score all affect the player's position. However, there are some guidelines: The third base person should begin 5 feet or so from the line and nearly the same distance behind the base. Adjustments can be made as needed, but in general the third baseperson should be able to touch the glove to the foul line with one or one and a half crossover steps. The third baseperson could be positioned farther away from the foul line for a left-handed batter known to "pull" the ball and closer to the foul line for a right-handed batter who "pulls." Similarly, a fast player known to bunt or a bunt situation brings the third baseperson in closer, some 8 to 10 feet in front of the base.

Fielding Responsibilities

The third baseperson's basic fielding responsibilities include

1. fielding all fly balls, ground balls, and bunts hit to the third base area
2. covering third base on balls hit to other fielders
3. making force plays at third base
4. making tag plays at third base

A description of these responsibilities and techniques for execution is provided in the following sections.

Fielding Batted Balls

The third baseperson is responsible for fielding all fly balls, ground balls, and bunts hit to the third base area (see Figure 4-41). Because the third base area does not have exact boundaries, communication with other fielders is essential. The third baseperson has priority on fly balls hit between the player's ready position and the pitcher's mound. The shortstop has priority on fly balls behind third base. The third baseperson must also back up any ground balls hit to the third base side of the pitcher, and

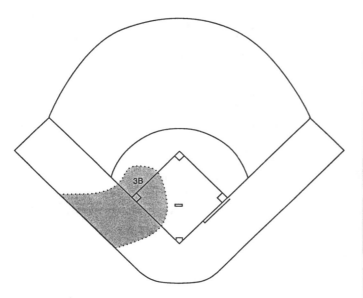

Figure 4-41. Area to be covered by the defender at third base.

field any slow-hit ground balls to the shortstop area.

Covering Bases

The third baseperson must cover third base unless he or she is attempting to field the ball. Even if there are no runners on base, automatic coverage is wise. If the ball is hit to the pitcher, the third baseperson first backs up the play, and then immediately covers third base. If a fly ball is hit to right field, the third baseperson immediately covers third base. Defensive success is greater when the other fielders know the bases are covered. Once positioned at third base, the third baseperson prepares for either a force play or a tag play.

Force Plays at Third Base

The technique of receiving the throw at third base is similar to that used at first base, with the exception of feet placement. The throws must be taken at the corners of the base as opposed to the infield edge of the base. The third baseperson should straddle the corner of the base closest to the throw (see Figure 4-42). The shoulders are square to the fielder making the throw. The feet adjust to the flight of the ball (see Figure 4-43). Immediately following the catch, the third baseperson must check other runners and prepare to throw.

Figure 4-42. Straddling the bag in preparation for a force play at third.

Figure 4-43. Adjusting to the ball and touching the base on a force out at third.

Tag Plays at Third Base

From the Field

On tag plays at third base, the third baseperson straddles the base with the shoulders square to the throw (see Figure 4-44). The feet must be kept clear of the runner's side of the base in order to avoid injury. Upon catching the ball, the glove is placed on the ground in front of the base so that the runner slides into the tag. As the runner contacts the glove, the arm and hands should give with the force of the slide. Immediately following the tag, the third baseperson must check any other runners and be prepared to throw.

On Steals

The third baseperson may receive a throw from the catcher in order to tag a runner attempting to steal third base. In this case, the third baseperson focuses on the action of the

Figure 4-44. Position for a tag play at third.

runner and sprints to the base. The third baseperson straddles the base and looks for the throw from the catcher. The third baseperson may want to stop short of straddling the base to save a step; however, the runner must not be allowed to slide safely to the unprotected side of the base.

On Pickoffs

Occasionally the pitcher or catcher may try to pick off a runner at third. Because of the risk involved in this play—any missed throw will almost surely result in a run—communication is important so that all the defensive players know what is going to happen. Generally the third baseperson should break to the base at the last possible moment, and the pitcher should expect to throw to the base rather than to the defender who will still be moving into position. This puts a great deal of pressure on both players, but especially on the third baseperson who quickly must get square to the ball, make the catch, and get the tag down while moving. This is a difficult play, and most often it is used as a fake with runners on first and third. The idea is to make the runner at first believe a steal is possible or to distract that runner's attention; the pitcher fakes the move to third, quickly turns toward first, and may be able to pick off the runner there.

Making Relays

In certain instances the third baseperson has responsibilities for cutoffs and relays. With a runner at second and a single hit to left field, the third baseperson moves to a position on line between the left fielder and catcher, and 25 to 30 feet from the catcher. This gets the players close enough to communicate well and also gives the third baseperson a good view of the runner rounding first.

Backing Up Throws

Unless involved in a play at the base, the third baseperson is responsible for backing up throws to second from right or center field. However, with a runner at second who tags up on a fly and tries to advance to third, the third baseperson covers the bag while the shortstop backs up second and the pitcher backs up third.

SHORTSTOP

Ready Position Location

The ready position for the shortstop is generally located halfway between second and third base, 10 to 15 feet behind the base path (see Figure 4-45). This general location varies, however, in relation to the hitting tendencies of the batter, the game situation, and the ability of the shortstop. For example, if a batter tends to hit up the middle, the shortstop would move a few steps toward second base. If a right-handed batter tends to pull the ball, the shortstop would move a few steps toward third base. In a situation where a runner must be prevented from scoring, the shortstop would move a few steps toward home plate in order to reduce the time and distance required for the throw home. In general, the deeper the position, the greater the fielding "range"; the more shallow the position, the more certain the throw.

Fielding Responsibilities

The shortstop's basic fielding responsibilities include:

1. fielding all ground balls and fly balls hit to the shortstop area
2. covering second and third base
3. making force plays at second base
4. making tag plays at second base
5. making tag plays at third base
6. acting as a relay on throws from left and center field.

A description of these responsibilities and techniques for execution is provided in the following sections.

Fielding Batted Balls

The shortstop is responsible for fielding all ground balls and fly balls hit to the shortstop area (see Figure 4-45). The shortstop is the leader of the infield and, consequently, has priority on all ground balls and fly balls hit in his or her general area. For example, if a ball is hit on the ground up the middle of the infield, and the shortstop and the second baseperson both have an equal chance of fielding the ball, the shortstop has priority and fields the ball while the

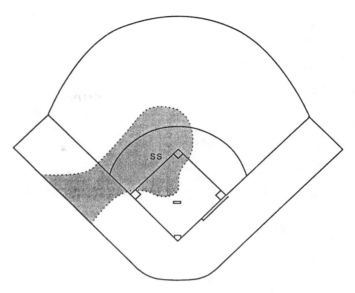

Figure 4-45. Area covered by the shortstop.

second baseperson backs up the play. If a fly ball is simultaneously called for by the shortstop, third baseperson, and pitcher, the shortstop should make the catch. Outfielders, however, have priority over the shortstop. If a fly ball is called for by the left fielder and the shortstop, the shortstop must allow the left fielder to make the catch. Also, the shortstop must back up ground balls hit to the third baseperson or to the pitcher.

Covering Bases

Generally, any time the ball is hit to the right side of the field, the shortstop covers second base. If a batter bunts the ball, with no runners on base or with a runner on first base, the shortstop covers second base.

Anytime a play is to be made at third base and the third baseperson is involved in fielding the ball, the shortstop covers third base. For example, with runners on first and second base, the shortstop would cover third base if the third baseperson is fielding a bunted ball. Similarly, if a ball is hit to the third baseperson and there is a runner on third base, the shortstop must cover third base in order to help hold the runner while the throw is made to first base. If the shortstop does not cover third base in this situation, the runner may get a big lead and either run home on the throw to first base, or distract the third baseperson and allow the batter to safely reach first base.

Force Plays at Second Base

Turning the Double Play

The simplest method for teaching youth baseball players to turn a double play is to speed throw across the base (see Chapter 2, Catching and Catching/Throwing as a Combined Skill). However, the shortstop must approach the base differently when a ball is fielded behind the base path rather than fielded in front of the base path.

If a ball is initially fielded behind the base path, the shortstop moves to the base in line with the fielder and

1. steps on the base with the glove-side foot as the ball is caught
2. steps across the base and plants the throwing-side foot perpendicular to the first baseperson
3. steps toward first base with the glove-side foot in order to complete the throw (see Figure 4-46)

For safety reasons, the step across the base with the throwing-side foot (Step 2) should take the shortstop out of the base path. An alternative to stepping on the base with the glove-side foot is to step across the base with the glove-side foot and drag the throwing-side foot over the base before planting for the throw to first base (see the "Second Base" section, "Turning the Double Play").

If a ball is initially fielded in front of the base path, the shortstop moves to the inside corner of the base and

1. touches the inside edge of the base with the glove-side foot
2. steps away from the base with the throwing-side foot, planting it perpendicular to the first baseperson
3. steps toward first base with the glove-side foot and completes the throw (see Figure 4-47)

As with the second baseperson, the shortstop should begin with a quick break to the base but slow down a step or two before arriving there. Thus, the body is under control and the throw is made more easily and accurately.

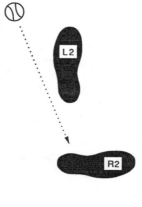

Between steps L1 and R2, the shortstop pivots in the air so that R2 lands perpendicular to the target line.

Figure 4-46. Sequence of footprints showing the shortstop turning the double play after fielding the ball behind the base line.

A shortstop who understands the speed throw quickly learns how to turn the double play with a throw from either side of the base path. If the force out at second base is the only play to be made, the shortstop receives the throw using the same technique as that described for the first baseperson.

Tag Plays at Second Base

From the Outfield

When receiving a throw from the outfield, the shortstop straddles the base, squares the shoulders to the throw, and catches the ball along the midline of the body. To prevent injury, the first base side of second base must be left open for the runner. The shortstop keeps the glove low and allows the ball to come to the glove. In one continuous motion, the ball is caught, the glove is moved to the runner's side of the base, and the tag is made.

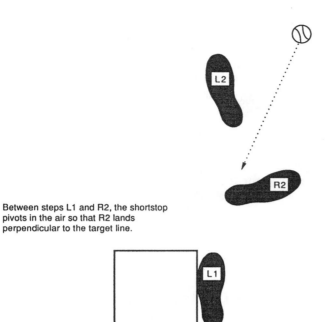

Between steps L1 and R2, the shortstop pivots in the air so that R2 lands perpendicular to the target line.

Figure 4-47. Sequence of footprints showing how to turn the double play after fielding the ball near to or in front of the base line.

From the Catcher

With a left-handed batter and a runner on first base attempting to steal second base, the shortstop moves toward second base as soon as the ball crosses the strike zone. Upon approaching the base, the shortstop

1. straddles the base
2. plants the left foot next to the inside corner of the base in preparation for the throw (see Figures 4-48 and 4-49)

Note that setting up on the inside corner of the base is quickest, but it often leaves the back edge of the base open for the runner. If the catcher's throw is on target, the shortstop keeps the glove low and allows the ball to come to the glove. As the ball is caught, the glove continues toward the ground on the runner's side of the base. Adjustments are made in relation to the path of the runner. If the catcher's throw is off target, the shortstop must move to

Figure 4-48. Straddling the base to take the throw from the catcher.

Figure 4-49. Taking the throw from the catcher with the foot against the base.

catch the ball and attempt to tag the runner as quickly as possible.

Tag Plays at Third Base

If there is a runner at second and the third baseperson plays in anticipating a bunt, the shortstop covers third base. Often this means that the shortstop must be ready to tag the runner. In any case the shortstop must arrive at third base ahead of the runner and quickly straddle the base, facing the infield (see Figure 4-50). If the throw is on target, the glove is kept low and the shortstop allows the ball to come to the glove. As the catch is made, the glove is placed on the ground on the runner's side of the base. If the throw is off target, the shortstop must move to catch the ball and tag the runner as quickly as possible.

If covering third base in a force out situation, the shortstop moves like the third baseperson. The shortstop takes the throw by straddling the corner of the base nearest the throw. The shoulders are square to the thrower, and if necessary, the feet adjust to the flight of the

Figure 4-50. Shortstop covering third base on a tag play.

ball. Following the catch, the shortstop checks any remaining runners and prepares to throw.

Making Relays

When the ball is hit deep to left or center field, the shortstop positions him or herself in the outfield in order to receive the throw and relay the ball to the infield. The location of the relay depends upon the outfielder's throwing ability, the location of the ball, and the intended target. The shortstop relay is identical to the second baseperson's relay (see the "Second Base" section, "Making Relays").

LEFT FIELD

Ready Position Location

The general location of the ready position for the left fielder is in the middle of the left field area (see Figure 4-51). This may put the left fielder behind the shortstop, although the outfielder may wish to move a bit to one side for an unobstructed view of the batter. As for depth, the left fielder is even with or a bit closer than the center fielder (see the "Center Fielder" section, "Ready Position Location").

The left fielder's ready position may be adjusted in relation to the hitting tendencies of the batter, the game situation, the field conditions, and ability to move back or to the side. Obviously, a left fielder would play further back and closer to the foul line for a batter that consistently hits "deep" and "down the line." However, if that same batter were at the plate with the game-winning run on third base and less than two outs, the left fielder would continue to play close to the line but shallow enough to catch the ball in the air and throw the runner out at home plate. Field conditions will also dictate the depth of play. For example, long thick grass has a slowing effect on ground balls; thus, the left fielder may play shallower than if the ground was hard and dry.

Fielding Responsibilities

The left fielder's basic fielding responsibilities include

1. fielding all ground balls and fly balls hit to the left field area

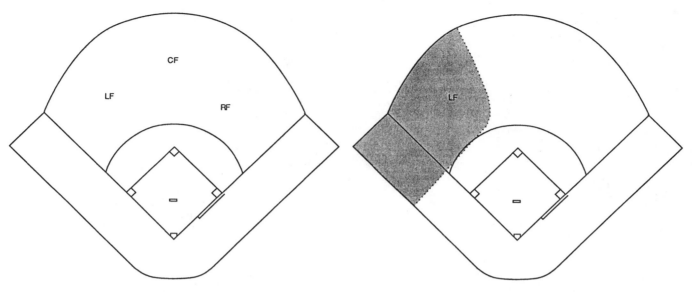

Figure 4-51. Normal playing position for the outfielders.

Figure 4-52. Area covered by the left fielder.

2. backing up the third baseperson, shortstop and center fielder
3. backing up and covering third base in rundowns and other situations
4. making accurate throws to the relay/cutoff person

A description of each of these responsibilities and techniques for execution is provided in the following sections.

Fielding Batted Balls

The left fielder is responsible for fielding all ground balls and fly balls hit to the left field area (see Figure 4-52). As with the infield, there are no exact boundaries in the outfield; therefore, communication is essential. On fly balls, the left fielder has priority over all infielders. However, the center fielder has priority over the left fielder. If the left fielder and shortstop simultaneously call for a fly ball, the shortstop must allow the left fielder to make the catch. If the left fielder and the center fielder simultaneously call for a fly ball, the left fielder must allow the center fielder to make the catch. If a fly ball is hit foul, and the left fielder catches the ball, the batter is out. If, however, there is a runner on base, the runner has the option to tag the base then advance immediately following the catch. The left fielder must be aware of this possibility and be prepared to throw the ball to the appropriate base.

In addition to fielding, the left fielder must back up all ground balls and fly balls hit to the center fielder. The left fielder should be positioned far enough behind the center fielder to be able to react to a missed ball. The left fielder must also back up any ground balls or fly balls hit to the shortstop or third baseperson. A successful catch by other fielders should never be assumed!

Backing Up Infield Plays

The left fielder is responsible for backing up batted balls at the third base and shortstop positions. In these situations the outfielder's initial move toward a hit continues until the left fielder is close enough to handle the ball if need be but far enough behind the play to have time to react. Further, the player coming in may become better positioned to play the ball, and once communicating this to the infielder, the left fielder gains priority and continues on for the catch.

The left fielder also must back up third base on throws from right field or the infield. When backing up throws, the left fielder comes in at an angle toward the third base side fence or out of play line, and once there, continues toward the base (see Figure 4-53). The player should be far enough behind third base to allow time to react to an overthrown or deflected ball. Also, if for any reason third base is not cov-

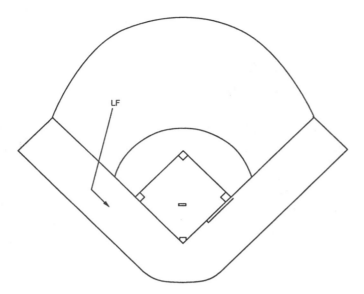

Figure 4-53. Movement by the left fielder to back up infield plays at third base.

ered by an infielder, the left fielder should cover the base.

The most common instances of a left fielder having responsibilities to cover third base are on rundown plays or when the third baseperson is in cutoff position. In the case of rundowns, the left fielder must recognize the start of such a play and immediately run to a position on the foul line near the base. The outfielder may be in either a backup position or have primary responsibility at the base. In the second event, the fielder continues on to the base and takes position like an infielder: feet straddling the bag, shoulders square to the target and fielder prepared to make a tag or continue the rundown. The left fielder takes the same position when covering for a third baseperson in the cutoff position. These plays demand skills not often used by an outfielder, and so they must be practiced along with other elements of outfield play.

The left fielder is also in the best position to back up throws to second base from first base. Thus, when a ground ball is hit to the right side and a throw to second is possible, the left fielder should move into position on line with the throw. Similarly, the left fielder should back up second base on all throws from the right field area. If the throw is missed or deflected, the left fielder should be in a position to

prevent the base runners from advancing further.

Throwing to the Relay Person

When retrieving a ball that has been hit beyond the outfielder, the first priority of the fielder is to gain possession of the ball. Therefore, as the outfielder moves toward the ball, his or her eyes must remain focused on the ball. As the outfielder retrieves the ball, he or she should listen for the location of the relay person. If the ball has stopped rolling, it may be fielded by planting the throwing-side foot just beyond the ball. After fielding the ball, the weight immediately transfers to the glove-side foot and the eyes focus on the relay person (see Figures 4-54 and 4-55). The outfielder executes a crow hop and throws the ball to the relay person as quickly and as accurately as possible. If the ball is still rolling when the outfielder fields it, he or she must stop the body's momentum, execute a crow hop and throw as soon as possible.

CENTER FIELD

Ready Position Location

The center fielder generally plays directly behind second base, in the middle of the outfield (see Figure 4-51). The depth of play depends on the size of the infield. A good rule of thumb locates the center fielder from two to

Figure 4-54. Retrieving a ball hit beyond the outfielder.

Figure 4-55. Weight transfer to throw.

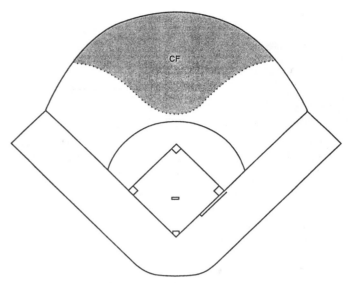

Figure 4-56. Area to be covered by the center fielder.

two and a half times the distance from home to second. With bases 60 feet apart, this would place the center fielder about 200 feet from the plate; with bases at 90 feet, the player would be around 300 feet deep. However, as with left field, the exact ready position location is dependent upon hitting tendencies of the batter, the game situation, the field conditions, and the center fielder's ability.

Fielding Responsibilities

The center fielder's basic fielding responsibilities include

1. fielding all ground balls and fly balls hit to the center field area
2. backing up fielding plays by the right and left fielders and second baseperson
3. backing up throws to second by the catcher or pitcher
4. coordinating all outfield play

Fielding Batted Balls

The center fielder is responsible for fielding all ground balls and fly balls hit to the center field area (see Figure 4-56). Because the center fielder is the leader of the outfield, this player has priority on all ground balls and fly balls hit to the center field area. If a ground ball is hit between left field and center field, the center fielder generally moves directly to the ball and the left fielder backs up the play. If the center

fielder, left fielder, and shortstop simultaneously call for a fly ball, the shortstop and left fielder must allow the center fielder to catch the ball.

Backing Up Plays

The center fielder is also responsible for backing up all ground balls and fly balls hit to the left fielder, right fielder, second baseperson, and shortstop. If the ball is hit to left field and the left fielder misses the ball, the center fielder must be in a position to field the ball. The left fielder must then look for the action of the base runners and let the center fielder know what to do with the ball once it is fielded.

The center fielder also backs up balls hit to shortstop or second base positions. In these situations, the outfielder's moves toward the ball continue until close enough to handle the ball if need be but far enough behind the play to have time to react to any misplay. The advancing center fielder may be more likely to reach the ball and, after communicating this to the infielder, have priority for the play.

Backing Up Throws to Second Base

The center fielder is responsible for backing up certain throws to second base. If the ball is being thrown to second base by the pitcher or catcher, the center fielder moves directly toward second base. The center fielder must be positioned far enough behind second base to allow time to react to a missed or deflected ball. In addition, the center fielder must cover second base if no infielders are able to do so.

Coordinating Outfield Play

The center fielder directs all outfield play. This includes positioning the players, communicating about backup and cutoff situations, indicating responsibility for fly balls and directing possible plays on base runners. In both primary and backup responsibilities, the center fielder covers the most territory in the outfield. All this requires the outfield to work together in practice, with the center fielder developing the skills needed for the position.

RIGHT FIELD

Ready Position Location

Because the majority of hitters are right handed, the ready position for the right fielder is generally located in shallow right field (see Figure 4-51). This puts the fielder more nearly behind the second baseperson and 50 feet or more closer to the plate than the center fielder. However, for left-handed batters, the right fielder moves back and into a position at the center of right field area and 200 to 300 feet form home plate, depending upon field size. The right fielder also adjusts the ready position to specific game situations.

Fielding Responsibilities

The right fielder's fielding responsibilities include:

1. fielding all ground balls and fly balls hit to the right field area
2. backing up the first and second basepersons and center fielder on all defensive plays
3. backing up all infield throws to first base
4. making accurate throws to the relay person (see the "Left Field" section, "Throwing to the Relay Person")

A description of these responsibilities is provided in the following section.

Fielding Batted Balls

The right fielder is responsible for fielding all ground balls and fly balls hit to the right field area (see Figure 4-57). Because the right

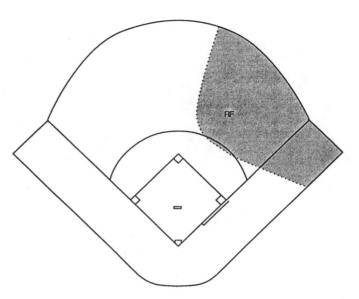

Figure 4-57. Area covered by the right fielder.

fielder often is positioned in shallow right field, communication with the second baseperson is critical. The right fielder has priority over the second baseperson on fly balls. The right fielder must also be prepared for the right-handed batter with a "slow" bat. If such a batter hits the ball to right field, the ball will generally "tail" toward the foul line. If the ball hits the ground in front of the right fielder, it will generally bounce toward the foul line. An awareness of this possibility can help the right fielder move to the correct position to field the ball. The "tailing" of balls hit to the outfield is also true of the left-handed batters hitting to left field.

Backing Up Batted Balls

The right fielder is also responsible for backing up all ground balls and fly balls hit to the first baseperson, second baseperson, and center fielder. The center fielder generally fields balls hit between center and right field, while the right fielder backs up the play. Again, the right fielder must be positioned far enough behind the play to allow him or her time to react to a missed or deflected ball.

Backing Up Infield Throws to First Base

The right fielder must back up first base on every infield throw to first base. Also, the pitcher and catcher can relax and more easily throw to first base on pickoffs knowing that the right fielder will be there to back up the throw. As with all other backups, the right fielder must be lined up with the origin of the throw and with first base and be far enough behind the base to be able to react to a missed or deflected ball. If for some reason first base is not covered by an infielder, the right fielder should move in to cover the base.

Backing Up Outfield Throws to Second Base

Anytime the left fielder throws the ball to second base, the right fielder must back up the throw even if the left fielder is only returning the ball to the infield. It must become a habit—backing up is a critical role of *all* outfielders!

CONCLUSION

Baseball presents the coach and player with a difficult challenge. Baseball is a team game, but the individual athlete generally performs at great distance from any teammates. Thus, while the youthful baseball player can—and often does—develop skills through practice in isolation, the athlete also must understand the concept of being part of a group working toward team goals.

For instance, no matter how much skill or range an outfielder might have in fielding fly balls, each catch represents only one out and may not keep an opponent from scoring. But having learned the essentials of team play, the outfielder knows how and when to aggressively throw the ball to the infield; the infielder receiving the throw understands how to pivot and make the relay while another player simultaneously is calling where the ball should be thrown; still another team member is in position to back up the play. Clearly each individual has to perform a complex set of tasks and the team's success depends upon each defender working smoothly in unison with all the others.

The coach's task is to provide time and practice settings for every ballplayer to develop physical and mental skills. Athletes should be given the opportunity to learn the requirements of their positions, and so individual position drills—like fielding ground balls for infielders—are important. But players also have to work in settings that involve their position with those around them, and such drills as having the middle infielders turn double plays become necessary. And finally, the entire team must work as a unit; thus, time must be set aside for working on relays, cutoffs and backing up bases. No one drill or practice can accomplish all of this; nevertheless, such plays are crucial to everyone's mastery of baseball. Only through careful planning on the part of the responsible adult can young baseball players become complete defensive athletes.

SUGGESTED READINGS

Howard, E. (1966). *Catching*. New York: Viking Press.
Ledbetter, V. (1964). *Coaching Baseball*. Dubuque, IA: Wm. C. Brown.
McDougald, G. & McMane, F. (1980). *Baseball: The Sports Playbook*. Garden City, NY: Doubleday.

5
Pitching

Steve Simensky, M.A.

QUESTIONS TO CONSIDER

- What are the components of the delivery?
- How is pitching from the set position different from the full windup?
- What is the most effective pitch in baseball?
- When should young pitchers begin to throw breaking balls?
- How many innings should younger athletes pitch?
- How does the balk rule effect the pickoff moves of pitchers?
- What types of pickoff moves are effective at the various bases?
- What is the pitcher's responsibility in backing up defensive plays?
- What does the pitcher do when a ball eludes the catcher?

INTRODUCTION

Careful observation of Major League Baseball pitchers reveals that each player has a unique way of throwing a baseball. Yet, the results of these different styles of pitching are very similar—good control and high velocity. This is because all successful pitchers use good pitching fundamentals, in spite of idiosyncrasies such as height of the leg kick and the gyrations of the delivery. To be a successful baseball pitcher, one must learn the fundamentals of pitching and practice them.

This chapter addresses the fundamentals of pitching in three sections. Section one deals with each step of the pitching delivery, including the windup and set positions. Section two describes the various pitches and their respec-

tive grips. Section three describes the pitcher as a pickoff artist and fielder.

THE DELIVERY
The Full Windup

The "windup" refers to the position the pitcher takes prior to delivering the baseball. During the windup, the front foot is in contact with the pitching rubber and the shoulders of the pitcher are parallel to home plate. The pitcher, holding the ball either in front of the body or behind the back, will then take a step back, place the back foot in front of, yet parallel to the side of the rubber, kick the front leg, and throw the ball toward the plate. While it is relatively easy to perform the windup delivery, it is very difficult to perform it correctly. This is why each of the major steps of this skill will be identified and discussed separately.

The Stance

The purpose of the stance is to allow the pitcher optimal balance while taking the sign from the catcher. Just as proper technique in getting out of the blocks is important to the sprinter, the proper stance in the windup position is important to the overall effectiveness of the pitcher. The stance is the basis from which originates the power of the windup and the velocity of the pitch.

The pitcher begins the stance with both feet on the pitching rubber or with the throwing-side (dominant) leg on the rubber and the glove-side leg behind the rubber (see Figure 5-1 a and b). The ball may be held either behind the back or in front of the body. Despite the posi-

Figure 5-1b. Pitcher beginning with the throwing-side leg on the rubber and the glove-side leg behind.

Figure 5-1a. Pitcher beginning with both feet on the rubber.

tion chosen by the pitcher, one thing should be made certain. The pitcher should have the pitching hand touching the ball at all times during the stance. It is easier for the pitcher to change grips on the ball when the hand is already in contact with the ball; the pitcher should not have to dig into the glove with the throwing hand in search of the proper seams. Also, having the ball already in hand allows the pitcher to throw to any base to prevent runners from advancing.

Pitchers and coaches often wonder where on the rubber the pitcher should stand. Generally speaking, most pitchers should stand to their pitching-hand side of the rubber. Thus, a left-handed pitcher should be on the left side of the rubber, and a right-handed pitcher, to the right-hand side. The reason for this positioning is that the delivered ball will be seen by the batter as coming in at a greater angle; this makes it more difficult for a batter to hit the ball than when it appears to be coming head on.

The Pump

After accepting the sign with a slight nod of the head, the pitcher begins to place the body in position to generate momentum for the delivery toward home plate. The delivery of the baseball requires a lot of force and the rocking motion or "pump" of the pitcher is the initial phase in the generation of this power.

The pitcher begins the rocking motion with a small step directly backwards with the glove-side foot (see Figure 5-2). (A common mistake made by many young pitchers is to take a step off to the side of the mound instead of straight backwards. This side step directs the pitcher diagonally away from the batter instead of directly toward home plate. As the step forward occurs, the pitcher must either continue to move diagonally or make the motion in two parts—move diagonally to the rubber and turn to go straight toward home. In any case, these moves significantly decrease the amount of momentum and power that can be transferred to the ball.) This small step backwards allows the dominant side foot to be placed parallel to the rubber for the push off (see Figure 5-3).

Figure 5-3. Throwing-side foot parallel to the rubber.

Figure 5-2. Step backward to start the pump.

As the pitcher is shifting the body weight backwards toward second base, the hands meet in front of the body and may be either raised over the head or remain around the torso area (see Figure 5-4). The preferred style is to have the hands raised over the head because this action facilitates the rocking motion necessary for power production in delivering the ball. Only after the hands have been joined should one attempt to change the grip of the ball in order to conceal it from the batter. Advanced players should try to pinch the heel of the throwing hand to the heel of the glove when raising the hands over the head so that the hitter cannot see the grip on the ball and learn what kind of pitch will be thrown.

The Kick

After the dominant leg has been placed in front of the rubber, the kick phase of the wind-up begins. In the kick phase, the glove-side leg swings up and around, rotating the body so that the glove-side shoulder and hip are directly aligned toward the plate (see Figure 5-5). A common mistake is to over-rotate the leg and shoulder, causing the body to turn toward second base. Such an exaggerated rotation may

Figure 5-4. Hands together in pump position.

Figure 5-5. Pitcher's leg kick.

cause any number of mechanical problems for the pitcher, but most of such problems derive from the pitcher's resulting inability to uncoil sufficiently during the rest of the delivery. Known as "throwing across the body," this movement reduces the distance over which the pitcher can generate force and results in a loss of ball velocity. Remember, fatigue sets in rapidly for pitchers, and any inefficient movements that cause extraordinary stress on the body may result in costly mistakes, especially late in the game.

As the glove-side leg kicks up and the body rotates, the front hip is lifted slightly higher than the rear. The toes of the raised foot point to the ground so that the pitcher can land balanced on the ball of the foot. These movements further add to the coiling effect and help create an explosive move toward home plate (see Figure 5-6).

At this point, the shoulder, hip and foot on the glove side point directly at home plate and

Figure 5-6. Coiling of the pitcher's body. Notice the position of the glove-side foot.

are essentially perpendicular to the rubber. The pitcher should be able to balance on the push off leg in this position; having a slight bend in the leg facilitates such balance. Leaning too far back or forward in this kick position causes a loss of balance and an inadequate delivery (see Figure 5-7 a and b), so an excellent drill for younger pitchers is having them balance in this position for 10 to 15 seconds at a time.

The Arm Motion

In continuing the delivery, the hands drop from above the head to the waist where they separate. This allows the ball hand to reach down toward the ground and then back toward second base in a circular motion (see Figure 5-8 a-d). The pitching hand should be on top of the ball throughout this motion which ends with the ball raised well above the head and the elbow held high (see Figure 5-8 a-d).

Two common mistakes in the pitcher's arm motion need attention. One mistake is not taking the ball from the glove fast enough to coordinate with the body's momentum forward.

Figure 5-7b. Leaning too far forward in the wind up.

This puts undue stress on the shoulder and elbow and results in high balls. The other mistake is not keeping the hand on top of the ball, which causes an inadequate elevation of the elbow. The elbow should be well above the shoulder on all conventional pitches to the plate. There are two reasons for this. First, it increases accuracy. The pitcher in later innings may become tired and wild as the elbow falls parallel to or below the shoulder. Secondly, dropping the elbow this way aids the hitter in ball perception. A hitter who sees a ball traveling parallel to the ground and nearly level with the eyes, as when the elbow is dropped parallel to the shoulder, will have an easier time seeing the ball than a hitter facing a ball coming down from above.

The Delivery and Stride

The pitcher's body weight and the ball should explode simultaneously toward the batter. As the back leg forcefully pushes off of the front of the rubber, the front leg swings around

Figure 5-7a. Leaning too far back in the wind up.

(a)

(b)

(c)

(d)

Figure 5-8 a-d. Sequence of pitcher's arm motion in basic delivery.

toward the plate (see Figure 5-9). Although much of the power that is needed for any pitch is generated by the legs, the rotation of the torso also aids in ball velocity. This rotation results from the glove-hand elbow pulling across the body and down toward the front knee as the ball is released.

Although forceful, the stride is also a very delicate motion. It determines where the ball will be thrown. As the torso and front leg rotate towards the plate, the knee of the front leg begins to drop down toward the ground (see Figure 5-10). The ball of the front foot should make contact with the ground first—the heel of the foot touching first will result in high balls (see Figure 5-11). While the pitcher uses a long stride forward, the throwing arm moves forward and releases the ball when the hand is approximately 12 inches in front of the head (see Figure 5-12). The glove-hand remains near the pitcher's head in a "chicken wing" fashion as the ball is released. This is necessary in case a ball is lined back toward the pitcher, who

Figure 5-10. Front leg dropping toward ground.

Figure 5-9. Push off by pivot foot and uncoiling of body.

Figure 5-11. Ball of front foot contacting ground first.

Figure 5-12. Throwing arm at release.

must field the ball or protect himself (see Figure 5-13). Throughout this whole motion, the body is kept low and driving toward the batter.

The Follow-Through

Proper follow-through aids the speed and control of the ball, while helping absorb the shock resulting from the whip of the arm in delivering the ball. After the ball is delivered, the whole body continues low toward the plate. The body should bend at the waist as the throwing arm swings across the body and past the outside of the glove-side knee (see Figure 5-14 a and b). A common error finds the pitcher's throwing arm between the legs, as opposed to outside the front knee (see Figure 5-15). When this happens, the ability to dissipate the force of the pitching motion is lost. Strain is put on the arm or speed simply is not built up in the first place.

After the ball is delivered the pitcher's weight transfers from the back leg to the front leg. The push off leg swings around the body

Figure 5-13. Glove in "chicken wing" position at follow-through.

to touch down approximately 15 to 25 inches across from and parallel to the front foot (see Figure 5-16). Landing with the feet in a wide parallel position ensures that the pitcher lands with proper balance in case a fielding play must be made. Because the follow-through results in large body rotation, the pitcher may actually lose sight of the plate for a while. This will have no effect on the flight of the ball, as it should already be on its way toward the batter. However, the pitcher must regain sight of the ball as soon as possible.

Key Elements:
- The pitcher assumes a balanced stance; the pitcher's hand is in contact with the ball while taking the sign.
- The pitcher takes a short step directly backwards with glove-hand side leg.
- Ball and glove raise overhead while the front foot slides in front of the rubber.
- The body turns so that the glove-side shoulder, knee, hip, and foot are perpendicular to the batter with the toe pointing down toward the ground while both hands descend to the pitcher's waist.
- The throwing hand separates from the glove and stretches down and back toward second

(a)

Figure 5-15. ERROR: Follow-through with throwing arm between legs.

(b)

Figure 5-14 a and b. Follow-through with bend at waist and throwing arm outside glove-side knee.

Figure 5-16. Push off or pivot leg following through.

base while the dominant leg pushes off the rubber.

- The elbow is above the shoulder and 12 inches in front of the head as the planted foot touches the ground and hand releases the ball.
- The body continues forward, while the glove-side arm swings across the body and past the front knee ("chicken wing") followed by pitching hand.

- The push off leg lands 15 to 25 inches across from and parallel to the front leg as the pitcher assumes a fielding position.

Common Errors:
- Back step of the pump goes to the side.
- Leg and shoulders over-rotate during the kick.

- Leaning too far forward or back in kick results in an off-balance position.
- Hand is not on top of ball.
- Elbow is even with or below shoulder at delivery.
- Stride is off to one side rather than toward home.
- Stride is too long or too short.
- Follow-through ends with arm between legs.
- Body is not square to the plate and thus is off-balance at end of follow-through.
- Glove is not in position to field the ball.

Set Position

The set position is mandatory with runners on base because it allows the pitcher to check any runners and make pickoff moves to all bases. In this delivery, the pitcher takes the sign with the throwing-hand-side leg already positioned against the rubber. The front foot should be slightly to the side of the back foot (see Figure 5-17). This position is better than having the feet parallel because it reduces the amount of time needed to deliver the ball to home plate and so prevents base runners from getting good

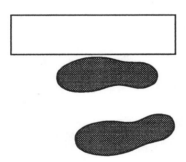

Figure 5-17a. Proper positioning of the feet in the set position by a right-handed pitcher.

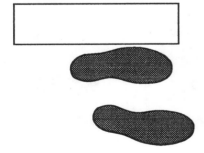

Figure 5-17b. Proper positioning of the feet in the set position by a left-handed pitcher.

jumps. Further, the pitching motion from the set must be as efficient as possible, because most bases are stolen on the pitcher, not the catcher.

Keeping the potential base stealer in mind, a right-handed pitcher must minimize the leg kick as much as possible in the set position, because most base stealers break toward the next base as soon as the pitcher makes the first move to home plate. A left-handed pitcher has an obvious advantage by facing the runner at first. This position allows a higher leg kick and gives more time to decide whether to pick off the runner. Pickoffs will be covered later in this chapter.

Once the throwing hand and ball are taken from the glove, the motion of the set position is very similar to the full windup. Correct arm motion, stride, and follow-through are equally as important when pitching from the set as from the windup position.

GRIPS

Older pitchers should learn to use different grips on the ball, relying on the physics of a spinning ball in relation to the swirling air to cause the ball to move up, down and sideways in its path to home plate. However, it is equally important that preteen players absolutely refrain from throwing **any** pitches that result in the snapping of the arm or wrist in a lateral motion. More simply put, preteens should not try to throw any form of breaking ball. The rationale for this is fourfold.

First and most importantly, numerous studies have shown that because preteens' bones, muscles, tendons, and ligaments are still developing, any motion causing undue stress on the arm can result in irreparable damage. This predisposition of young arms and shoulders to suffer from overuse is true even for fastball pitchers. Consequently, each preteen pitcher should be limited to 50 pitches per game and two games per week, for a total of 100 pitches in competition.

Secondly, preteens who begin to throw different types of breaking balls tend to neglect the fastball. The fastball is the most important pitch in baseball and is relied upon heavily in advanced leagues. By neglecting the fast ball, young pitchers will be unprepared for upper-level play. There are many different fastballs with different motions, and if preteens master them, they will be more successful in advanced leagues.

Thirdly, a pitcher who learns to throw a breaking ball accurately down at 45 feet will have a lot of difficulty throwing it at 60 feet, 6 inches. This brings us to the fourth point. Many young pitchers do not learn to throw breaking balls properly and use makeshift curveballs that work well at shorter distances. However, once they have moved back to 60 feet, 6 inches, they pitch ineffectively and so have to learn the proper technique. This is more difficult and time consuming than initially learning the correct procedure.

Deciding when a developing athlete should begin throwing breaking balls, including the curve, is difficult for the coach. There can be no specific age because children mature physically at different chronological ages. Rather, the coach must look at pitching hopefuls individually and evaluate the relative maturity of each. Generally pitchers of any age who appear "filled out" or adult-like in their musculature (see Figure 5-18 a-d) may begin working on break-

ing balls. Similarly, any young pitchers who look long, thin, even "childlike" (see Figure 5-19 a-d) should not be allowed to throw curves, no matter what their chronological age. These guidelines can be followed safely by any coach because they represent a conservative approach to the decision. However, if the coach wishes a definitive evaluation of a pitcher's biological maturity, then a physician should be consulted.

Developing a full repertoire of pitches, having confidence in them, and knowing when to throw them is important for success in pitching. Therefore, this section will deal first with fastballs, then breaking balls and finally the change-up. However, it is the coach's responsibility to teach only those pitches appropriate to the age of the athletes.

Fastballs

Across-the-Seams

A fastball gripped across the seams is sometimes referred to as a "true fastball." The across-the-seams fastball is a favorite of pitchers who throw very hard because it can appear to rise on its way to the plate. In fact the ball remains

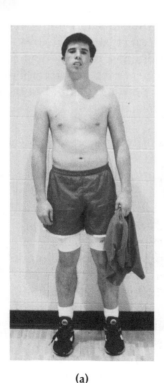 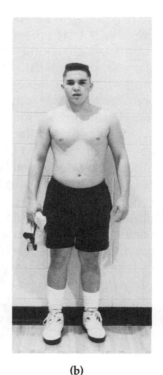 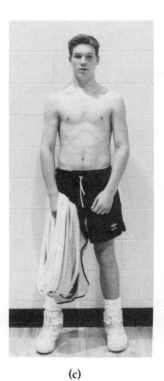 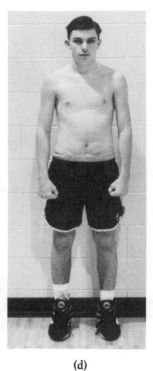

| (a) | (b) | (c) | (d) |

Figure 5-18 a-d. Athletes who exhibit adult-like musculature and are ready to throw breaking balls.

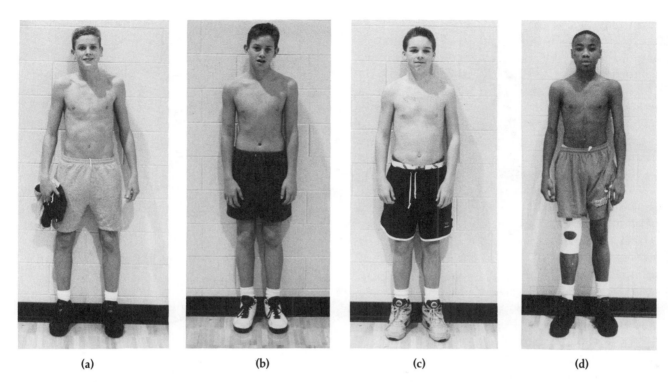

(a)   (b)   (c)   (d)

Figure 5-19 a-d. Long, thin athletes who should not be allowed to throw breaking balls.

relatively straight and drops little as it comes to the plate. The four seams spinning rapidly end-over-end produce better bite into the air and make the pitch a good choice for hard throwers. Because the ball has very little movement on it, the pitcher must make certain to throw it hard or place it in a position that make it difficult to hit.

The grip of the ball involves placing the index and middle finger across the center of the **U** part made by the seams (see Figure 5-20a). The fingers are placed relatively close together; the ball should remain on the fingers. Ideally, there should be a space between the ball and the palm of the hand (see Figure 5-20b), but the hands of young pitchers may require that the fingers and palm touch the ball. The thumb should be positioned on the underside of the ball, bisecting the seam below (see Figure 5-20c). Only the *side of the thumb*, and not the inside surface, should contact the ball. A grip involving the palm or the fat part of the thumb causes undue friction upon release and results in a loss of speed and rotation.

The across-the-seams fastball should have three pressure points: the first knuckles of the index and middle fingers and the side of the knuckle of the thumb (see Figure 5-21). This pressure of the fingers across the **U** of the baseball and the thumb underneath should allow the pitcher to get a good grip on the ball. When the pitch is thrown, the two top fingers pull down on the center of the ball, letting the bottom of the ball leave the hand first. The thumb releases as soon as possible, thus permitting the index and middle fingers to impart the rotation to the ball (see Figure 5-22).

With-the-Seams

A with-the-seams fastball normally has more movement than an across-the-seams fastball. This results from only two seams rotating backwards as opposed to the four-seam movement in the across-the-seams fastball. This two-seam movement makes the ball more subject to differences in air pressure. A two-seamer can also have more movement on it if a pitcher puts pressure on either of the top fingers, causing the pitch to have some lateral spin and not spin perfectly backwards.

The with-the-seams fastball is normally gripped along the two seams that make the **U** of the ball (see Figure 5-23 a). A cut fastball can be thrown by shifting the fingers to one side of

Figure 5-20a. Across-the-seams fastball grip. Notice placement of index and middle fingers.

Figure 5-20b. Across-the-seams fastball grip, side view showing space between ball and palm.

Figure 5-20c. Across-the-seams fastball grip, thumb on underside of ball.

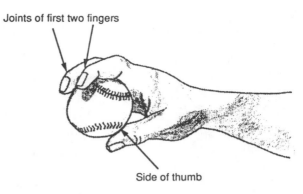

Figure 5-21. Pressure points on an across-the-seams fastball.

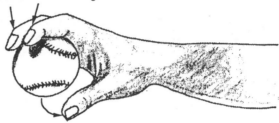

Figure 5-22. Releasing an across-the-seams fastball.

the with-the-seams fastball grip and turning the ball slightly so the middle finger contacts more of the seam (see Figure 5-23 b). In either case, the pressure points, the pull of the fingers, the push of the thumb and the resulting spin are similar to those elements of an across-the-seams fastball.

Curveball

Spin, the prerequisite to causing a pitch to curve, can be applied to a ball in a number of ways. Unfortunately, many of the means used to apply spin have been found to damage the arms of younger pitchers. First attempts at throwing breaking balls often involve the player moving the arm in a plane nearly parallel to the ground and throwing a roundhouse curve (see Figure 5-24 a-d). This brings the arm across the body in a whip-like motion that makes it nearly impossible to release safely the energy of the delivery.

Another common practice has the pitcher

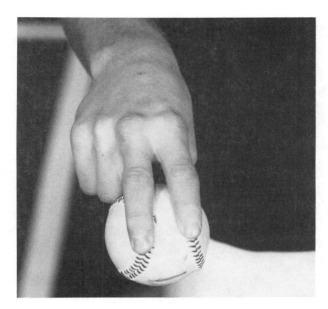

Figure 5-23a. With-the-seams fastball grip, along the "**U**."

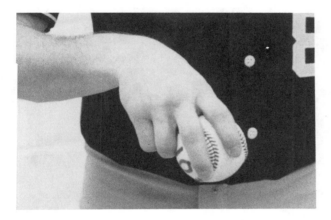

Figure 5-23b. "Cut" fastball grip.

attempting to throw a curve by rotating the hand at release so the palm turns toward the body, even to the point of facing up (see Figure 5-25). Such supination of the arm again directly opposes the movements needed to dissipate energy built up during the force-producing phase of the pitch. In either case, a great deal of stress is placed on various parts of the arm, and repeated use of these deliveries likely will result in a sore elbow, shoulder, or both. The pain may be located in any of several spots (see Figure 5-26), but they all can be avoided if the coach and player understand what really must happen to successfully and painlessly throw a curve.

The traditional curveball grip is similar to that used for a with-the-seams fastball. The ball normally gets tucked a little closer to the palm of the hand than in the fastball, but the ball should not be touching the palm. Rather than placing both fingers over the seams of the **U**, the pitcher slides them toward the outside seam of the ball (see Figure 5-27). The middle finger should be slightly off to the outside of its seam, and the index finger should be right next to the middle finger. One or the other of these fingers provides the pressure point that causes the spin on the ball, and because they are on the outside of the ball, the diagonal spin will cause a right-handed pitcher's curve to break down and away from a right-handed batter. The more pressure applied, the greater the spin and potentially the more break on the pitch. Thus, the pitcher strives to put as much spin as possible on the ball by really pressing hard with the fingers at the point of release. *Remember:* It is the amount of pressure caused by the contact of the fingers that determines how much spin is put on the ball.

The arm motion essential to producing this forward spin is similar to that of any other pitch (see "The Delivery" section, "Arm Motion"). Starting with the correct circular motion, the arm and hand begin behind the head, travel directly over the head or a bit off to the side, and reach straight out toward the catcher when passing the head. The elbow may be slightly bent and *well above the shoulder*; this causes the curve to break diagonally down, appearing to "drop right off the table." Experienced pitchers may so exaggerate this motion that they drop the glove-side shoulder below the throwing one (see Figure 5-28). Most pitchers even bend the upper body to the glove side in an unconscious attempt to keep the hand, elbow and both shoulders on a common plane and so increase the ball's movement while easing the pressure on the arm.

At release, the sensation of throwing a curve may be one of the arm coming straight down on top of the ball, much like pulling down an old-fashioned window shade; but more to the point, the fingers press down as though quickly snapping off a light switch. It is this pressure exerted on the outside of the ball that gives the curve its characteristic forward and

(a)

(b)

(c)

(d)

Figure 5-24 a-d. Sequence showing a "roundhouse" curve delivery.

Figure 5-25. Curve thrown by supinating the arm.

downward spin. However, after the release, the wrist must be allowed to pronate (see Figure 5-29) so the arm's muscles and joints can properly relax into the follow-through. If the wrist is kept stiff or forced to turn inward, a great deal of strain is placed on the elbow and shoulder. (Some coaches and players may feel that pronating the wrist produces the "screwball," a pitch that moves away from the pitcher's glove side. However, high-speed photographic work done by researchers at Michigan State Univer-

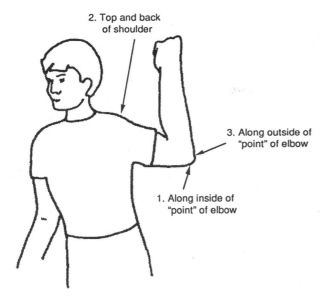

Figure 5-26. Common points of injuries resulting from incorrect mechanics used to throw a curve.

Figure 5-27. Curve ball grip.

Figure 5-28. A pitcher using the "high arm" position to throw the curve.

Figure 5-29. Arm pronating following release of curve.

sity clearly shows that the wrist must also pronate on a well-thrown curve.) The hand and arm then continue on into the follow-through position common to all pitches.

Although little is changed in the arm and hand motions when throwing the curve, some adjustments in body motion should be made. As suggested previously, players may drop the glove-side shoulder in an effort to keep the throwing arm well above the shoulder. This high arm position at the point of release can also be accomplished by opening the hips slightly and so striding more to the glove side (see Figure 5-30 a and b). The stride should be shortened a bit also. The correct length for the stride is easily determined: if it is too short, the ball will land several feet short of the plate; if it is too long, the curve will break too high and "hang."

Besides the stride, the young pitcher may also have trouble timing the release of the ball. The pitcher just learning to throw breaking balls must experiment with the pattern of the release points for both the fastball and curve. But generally the release point for the curve is a little farther in front of that of the fastball.

Throwing the curveball properly is one of the most difficult tasks that a pitcher faces. The athlete must change the finger grip, the pressure point, the stride, and the release. However, if these are mastered, the pitcher can throw what many players consider to be the most difficult pitch to hit in baseball.

Slider

The Classic Slider

The slider is similar to the curveball in that it is a breaking ball. However, the motion of the two balls is very different. Where the curveball breaks from high to low, the slider breaks from side to side.

The grips for the curveball and slider are essentially the same except that for the slider the ball fits deeper into the palm (see Figure 5-31). The middle finger is placed along the outer seam of the **U** with the index finger right next to the middle one. However, the arm and hand move quite differently. To throw the slider, the wrist remains stiff and the ball simply slides off the middle finger (see Figure 5-32). While this is a very simple pitch to learn, it places a lot of stress upon the elbow and should be used with caution.

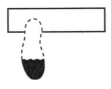

Figure 5-30a. Normal fastball stride.

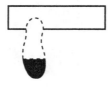

Figure 5-30b. Stride used for the high arm curve ball. *Note:* The stride is shorter and the left foot lands more to the side and so opens the hips more.

Figure 5-31. Gripping the slider.

Figure 5-32. Release of the slider.

The slider is very effective because it is a step slower than a cut fastball but has much more lateral movement. The batter, anticipating a fastball, is very vulnerable to the slider. Thrown relatively hard, the slider has the initial appearance of a fast pitch, and the batter prepares to swing at a straight fastball. However, as the ball nears the plate and breaks at the last possible moment, the lateral motion takes over to deceive the hitter.

The Slurve

The slurve is a combination of the slider and curve. It is held and thrown like a slider, but the pitcher pulls down on it slightly like a curveball. The pull on the slurve causes the ball to break both down and laterally. While it can be very difficult to throw the slurve, it can be a formidable addition to the pitcher's arsenal. The slurve is very effective against hitters who pull away from the plate too soon, such as a batter who likes to pull the ball or one who is afraid of getting hit. When pitcher and batter have the same dominant arms (left-hander vs. left-hander or right-hander vs. right-hander), the slurve appears to be heading toward the batter and then dips down and away. The hitter may bail out on the pitch and then see that it drops over the outside corner of the plate. Pull hitters are especially vulnerable to the slurve because they try to get their big power swings started early.

The Change-Up

The OK Change-Up

The change-up is one of the least used pitches because many pitchers are afraid that hitters will eventually guess this pitch correctly and knock it out of the park. However, when used in conjunction with the other pitches, the change-up is one of the most effective pitches.

The OK change-up refers to the grip. With all change-ups, the ball is tucked deep into the hand so that it is touching the palm. The bottom of the **U** rests along the curve between the thumb and forefinger (see Figure 5-33). The index and middle finger are then wrapped around the curved part of the **U** on one side. The thumb should be placed on the other leg of the **U**. The tips of the thumb and forefingers are near each other in a position similar to the "OK" sign made with the fingers. The other fingers should slide around the ball.

When the pitcher throws the OK change-up, the middle, ring and fifth finger are stuck up into the air. The ball is allowed to roll off these fingers as it is released, and the hand is slightly turned over toward the thumb (see

Figure 5-33. "OK" change-up grip.

Figure 5-34). This action makes the ball slow down and spin, causing the ball to drop as it approaches the plate. The most effective change-up is thrown low, preventing hitters from getting a good look at the ball.

The Classic Change-Up

The classic change-up is gripped a bit differently from the OK change-up, but it has a similar effect. The curved part of the **U** is tucked deep into the palm of the hand, and the fifth finger and thumb wrap around the lower part of the ball (see Figure 5-35). The index, middle and ring fingers stick straight up as the ball is released so that it rolls off them (see Figure 5-36).

Remember that no matter which change-up the pitcher learns to throw, the actual changing of the grip on the ball should be done in the glove. Because there is no other pitch gripped quite like it, the change-up is easily detected by a wary hitter. To disguise this pitch, the pitcher must minimize the amount of movement made

Figure 5-35. Classic change-up grip.

Figure 5-34. Release of the "OK" change-up.

Figure 5-36. Release of the classic change-up.

in the glove. Also, during the pitching motion, the pitcher should keep down on the ball the three fingers that will eventually be stuck up into the air. Only a split second before releasing the ball should these fingers pop up off the ball, for if they appear even briefly, these fingers will allow the batter to correctly assume that a change-up is coming.

While the change-up is difficult to master, it provides pitchers with an excellent complement to the fastball. Additionally, because the two pitches are thrown with the same motion, the change-up gives young pitchers an off-speed pitch that does not stress their arms like breaking balls. For advanced players, the change is an important addition to their pitching options. In either case, the use of an off-speed pitch that does not break in any significant fashion allows the pitcher to keep the hitter off-balance at the plate. The first few milliseconds when the fastball and change-up look the same are all it takes to confuse a batter.

PICKOFFS AND FIELDING

Pickoffs to First Base

Keeping runners close to first base is an art, especially for left-handed throwers. Whereas right-handed pitchers must be quick to the plate to keep runners from getting a good jump to second base, the left-hander must be able to disguise the move to first.

When attempting to pick off runners, the left-handed pitcher must keep in mind two important rules for throwing to first and avoiding a balk. First, if the right leg or foot crosses an imaginary straight line extending along the back side of the pitching rubber toward first base, the pitcher must throw home. A throw to first would be called a balk; all runners would be awarded a base and a ball would be added to the batter's count. Secondly, in making the throw, the left-hander's right foot must land behind another imaginary line running at a 45 degree angle from the back side of the pitching rubber toward the first base foul line; if the pitcher's foot comes down on the home plate side of this line when a throw to first is made, then a balk has been committed. Figure 5-37 illustrates these two lines and shows the area within which a left-handed pitcher's foot must land. As a re-

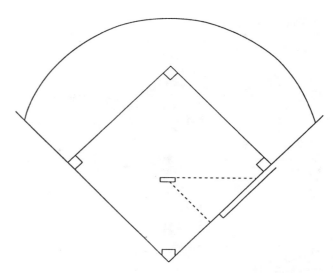

Figure 5-37. Imaginary lines defining where a left-handed pitcher must step to avoid a balk call.

sult of these rules, the left-handed pitcher must practice the pickoff move until finding the right balance between a successful pickoff move and a balk.

For a left-handed thrower, the delivery home must appear identical to the move to first base in order to keep the runner off-balance. The body action should be similar, from the pumping of the hands to the parting of ball and glove. The leg kick should be nearly parallel to the rubber so that the runner does not know whether the pitcher will throw home or to first base, and the kick ought to look the same in both cases. Often left-handers try to disguise the pickoff move by looking toward the catcher before throwing to first base. However, it is important to mix up the pattern of glances between home and target base before throwing the ball.

For a right-handed pitcher quickness is the key to picking off runners. The pitcher should take the sign from the catcher with most of the weight on the right leg so that a move to first can be made at any moment. When attempting a pickoff, a right-handed pitcher does not have to step off the rubber before throwing—rather, the pitcher performs a pivot and hop off the right foot and "short arms" the ball to first base (see Figure 5-38 a and b). This action is very different from the long, circular motion used to throw home; it is much more like the motion made by an infielder throwing to first. The arm

(a)

(b)

Figure 5-38. Hop and pivot pick off attempt.

simply follows a straight-back, straight-forward pattern. To help minimize the amount of movement in this short arm throw, right-handed pitchers should come to the set position very high, near the top of the chest as a part of their normal delivery from the set position (see Figure 5-39).

All pitchers must keep in mind one rule about holding runners close to first base. After taking the sign and moving through the pump, the pitcher must bring the arms to a complete stop (often referred to as "come set") before the ball can be delivered home. If there is no noticeable stopping of the arms and the pitcher delivers the ball home, a balk may be called for a "quick pitch." A come set position does not have to be used in order to throw the ball to first base, however.

Figure 5-39. High set position.

Mixing up pickoff moves to first base is as important to the pitcher's success as is disguising the moves. There are four points at which a pitcher may throw to first and so keep the runner guessing. The first move is simply "freezing" the runner. The pitcher reaches the come set position and remains there for 3 to 5 seconds. By staying in this position for such a long time, the pitcher freezes the runner in the lead-off position and prevents a quick start toward second base. The pitcher may then throw to first or deliver the pitch home. The second through fourth moves have to do with throwing to first base at different phases of the pitcher's stance. A throw to first can occur

1. while the pitcher is taking the sign
2. at the moment when the glove and throwing hands meet
3. in the come set position.

Much practice should be given to all of these variations so that they become second nature to the pitcher. Picking off runners usually occurs during stressful parts of the games, and if the pitcher has difficulty in using any of these variations, it may result in a costly error or lack of concentration on pitches that are delivered to home plate.

Pickoffs to Second Base

There are two types of pickoff moves to second base. One involves a continuation on the leg kick and the second, involves a spin move. The first has the pitcher kick the leg up as if to deliver home but not stopping it at the parallel line extending from the rubber. The kick leg continues past this imaginary line and the pitcher completes a 180 degree turn toward second base. While this move rarely fools a runner, it can be successfully used when the pitcher feels the runner likely will attempt to steal third base. In such a case, the pitcher may not even look at the base runner before initiating this move.

The second pickoff is similar to a right-hander's move to first in that it involves a jump and turn. However, in the move to second base, a complete 180 degree turn is needed. The pitcher must jump and in midair complete this half turn; to do this correctly, the pitcher must jump off both legs and spin toward his or her glove side. The throw should be short armed to whomever is covering the bag.

In disguising the pickoff move toward second base, a pitcher should alter the pattern of looking back at the runner before the pitch or pickoff move is enacted. If a pitcher never looks back at the runner, the runner will easily steal third base as soon as the pitcher begins the pitching motion. In fact, once the runner detects any consistent pattern of glances from the pitcher, the runner will be off and the pitcher must suffer the consequences.

CONCLUSION

The previous discussion of pitching is little more than an introduction to the key element of baseball. At first glance, it appears that pitching is little more than throwing and that any athlete can pitch. As described in Chapters 2 and 4, the mechanics of throwing and pitching are very similar. However, the pitcher generally must be able to throw with more speed and accuracy and has to maintain these characteristics after throwing many more times than even the most active of fielders. Further, the pitcher must learn to use various grips, to throw from the set position, and to play defense at close range. But perhaps most importantly, the pitcher must want to pitch—to be at the center of the action. This mental element of pitching is key to the success and well-being of the young pitcher, and the coach has the responsibility to assist each pitching-hopeful in learning to deal with the pressures of the position. Many books have been written on pitching, and some of the better ones are noted below. The youth coach is advised to seek additional help from the wealth of information available.

ADDITIONAL READINGS

Allman, F.L., Jr. (1978). *Care and Conditioning of the Pitching Arm for Little League Baseball.* Winter Park, FL: Anna Publishing.

Jordan, P. (1977). *Sports Illustrated Pitching.* Philadelphia: J.B. Lippincott.

Palmer, J. (1975). *Pitching with Jim Palmer.* New York: Atheneum.

Seaver, T. (1984). *The Art of Pitching.* New York: Hearst Books.

Stone, S. with Anglum, N. (1991). *Teach Yourself to Win: Cy Young Winner Steve Stone Tells What It Takes to Make Success a Habit.* Chicago: Bonus Books.

Wolff, R. (1986). *The Psychology of Winning Baseball.* Englewood Cliffs, NJ: Prentice Hall.

6
Hitting and Bunting

Michael A. Clark, Ph.D.

QUESTIONS TO CONSIDER

- What is the single most important element in becoming a successful hitter?
- What are the three commonly used grips, and which is best for young players?
- How do the wrists affect the velocity of the bat?
- How can successful hitting be defined so that any young hitter can be a success?
- What sequence can be used to teach hitting?
- What considerations are common to all types of bunting?
- Why should the barrel of the bat always be above handle when bunting?
- Why must successful bunters "catch" the ball with the bat and not push it?
- What sequence can be followed to teach bunting?
- What role does visualization play in learning to be a good hitter or bunter?

INTRODUCTION

While defense and pitching keep teams in many baseball games, offensive play scores the runs needed to win them. Fortunately, young athletes always seem to be willing to work on their offensive skills—especially hitting—and so they often can become competent offensive players with good coaching. Proper mechanics and techniques are as important to success in this area as in other baseball skills, and this chapter will provide information about the fundamentals so key to success in four offensive areas:

- hitting
- bunting
- base running
- sliding

HITTING

Ted Williams once observed that hitting a baseball is the hardest thing to do in all of sports. Consider the size and shape of bat and ball, the movements of both, the break on a pitch, the numerous distractions in the environment and the small room for error. Clearly getting a hit is chancy at best, and even top professional batters are successful little more than 30% of the time. Thus Williams, the last Major League Baseball player to hit over .400 for a season, is probably correct in his assessment. The conclusion young athletes should reach is that they need to work long hours on the fundamental skills involved, and coaches should recognize that the batter doing everything exactly as practiced will not guarantee a hit. Both ball players and coaches should keep these points in mind so that they maintain their perspective and confidence when perfect swings produce outs.

Fundamentals

The elements leading to success in hitting are numerous, but the following list serves as an outline of the things to be considered in teaching young athletes to be good hitters: bat selection, grip, stance, body and arm position, swing mechanics and follow-through.

Bat Selection

A young athlete often gets in the first swings with a bat that is much too long and heavy. As a result the barrel drops down, the swing is slow and the follow-through throws the youngster off-balance. The ball may be missed completely, or if contact is made, it often produces soft pop-ups that drop a few feet in front of the hitter. These events can be discouraging, but they may be avoided by helping the young ball player find the right bat.

For a variety of reasons, aluminum is the material of choice in youth baseball bats. These bats range from 24 to 36 inches in length, and their weights run from 20 to 31 ounces. While there is a rough relationship between length and weight, variations occur, and it is the coach's responsibility to help members of the team find a bat that suits them. This is especially critical because the bat may be the single most expensive piece of equipment required to play baseball.

To check the fit between player and bat, the coach has the athlete use the lower hand to grip the bat at its end. The player then extends the arm while trying to hold the bat parallel to the ground (see Figure 6-1 a). If this cannot be done with ease or if the barrel of the bat droops towards the ground (see Figure 6-1 b), then it is too heavy for the youngster, and a lighter bat is in order. This has the additional benefit of getting the youngster to choose one that can be swung more quickly; because bat speed affects so much about a hit ball, this can be an advantage.

Grip

The grip is important because it connects the athlete to the bat. Besides the human ele-

Figure 6-1a. Player holding bat to check for correct weight.

Figure 6-1b. Bat too heavy for player.

ments of the grip, there are three important variables

- the rubber grips applied to aluminum bats
- batting gloves worn by athletes
- materials applied such as resin or pine tar

These accessories are designed to improve

the athlete's hold on the bat, but each must be considered carefully. The synthetic grip applied to the bat has a long life and provides a comfortable, yet tacky surface. However, it can become torn or slippery with use or brittle over time. If any of these things occurs, the grip should be replaced; most larger sporting goods stores provide this service. One or two batting gloves may be worn by the player, but they should be properly fitted and not allow the bat to move in the player's hands. If one glove is worn, it should be on the bottom hand. Resin is intended to keep moisture from affecting the player's grip, but a cotton towel can accomplish much the same end. Pine tar generally should not be used on metal bats because it may cause the rubber grip material to deteriorate much more rapidly than normal.

When most young athletes pick up a bat, they generally use an approximation of the correct grip. However, some will not, and all will benefit from the coach's checking how they hold the bat:

- place the bat at the base of the fingers rather than in the palms (see Figure 6-2)
- keep the hands are together
- line up the second set of knuckles on both hands
- or rotate the knuckles of the top hand slightly toward the front (see Figure 6-3)
- make the grip firm but not tight

This combination produces a comfortable, flexible, controlled grip that a hitter can use confidently at any level. However, the coach should regularly check each athlete's grip, especially if the players are younger, hitting weakly, or in a slump.

- The hands may be held against the bat's knob in the "full" or "power" grip (see Figure 6-4).
- Or the hands can be moved up several inches into the "choke" position (see Figure 6-5).

The power grip allows a full swing with more power and leverage. It is used when the batter is ahead in the count, when a fly ball is needed, or whenever power is required. Swings with the full grip tend to be a bit longer, slower, and more difficult to control. The choke grip provides better bat control and so is used to hit the ball to a particular place, to counter a pitcher

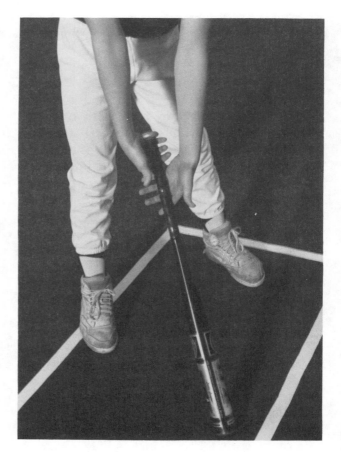

Figure 6-2. Gripping the bat at the base of the fingers.

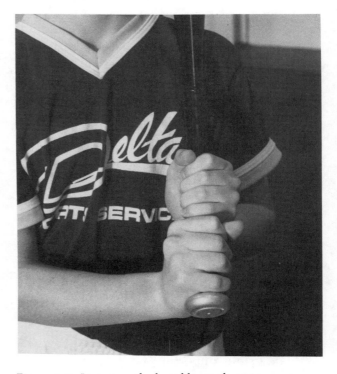

Figure 6-3. Lining up the knuckles in the grip.

Figure 6-4. Full grip.

who is overpowering the hitter, or to prepare for any pitch if the batter has two strikes. Because all these situations arise regularly, each athlete should practice both grips and learn when to use them. Some athletes settle on a position between these two extremes; this is known as the "modified" grip (see Figure 6-6).

Often a player performs well in practice but becomes very anxious about hitting in games. This translates into tension in the hands, arms, and shoulders which in turn causes poor swings. The most common means of dealing with this tension is having the player flex the fingers on the bat. This slight opening and closing of the hands allows the muscles to relax, but the grip will naturally tighten once the swing begins.

Key Elements:

● The bat is gripped at the base of the fingers.
● The second knuckles are in alignment.
● The grip is firm but not tight.

Common Errors:

● The bat is held in the palms.
● The hands are split apart on the bat.

Figure 6-5. Choke grip.

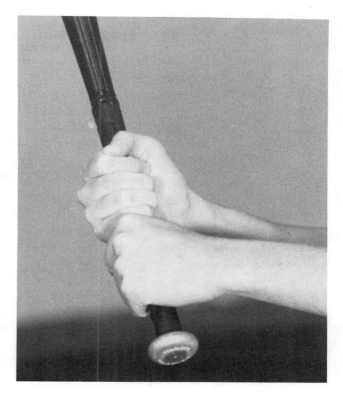

Figure 6-6. Modified grip.

● The hands are rotated toward the body so that the bottom knuckles are nearly in a line.

Stance

Two elements of the stance must be considered:

1. where in the batter's box to stand
2. how to position the feet

The younger player generally needs help with both, and the coach must to be ready with suggestions. However, once changes are made, the athlete may complain about feeling uncomfortable, so the coach should have players practice the stance just as they would any other skill. Much can be accomplished by the player working with some sort of substitute plate and going over the entire process of getting into the stance. In fact, this makes a great rainy day practice activity which can be further enhanced by having the athletes use a full-length mirror to observe themselves.

Players should begin by placing their front foot nearly even with the front of the plate and the back foot about shoulder width away (see Figure 6-7). This position is close enough to the plate to allow the bat to get to any ball thrown for a strike; a good starting point can be found by having the player bend slightly at the waist and reach the bat out until the barrel end just touches the outside front corner of the plate (see Figure 6-8). This assures good plate coverage without getting the batter too close to the plate to swing comfortably (see Figure 6-9). The coach may evaluate the position simply by having the player reach out with the bat, or the athlete can do a self-check with a mirror.

Many really young players will want to use an "open" stance (see Figure 6-10) because they see the ball better in this position and think they are more likely to hit it. However, as these youngsters gain confidence in their hitting, they should be encouraged to close up the stance because an open stance tends to limit the power of the swing. At the other extreme is the "closed" stance (see Figure 6-11). This position partially obscures the batter's vision of the pitcher and so allows little time to react to the ball; this stance should be discouraged for safety reasons if for none other. Between these two stances is the "square" stance (see Figure 6-12).

Figure 6-7. Placement of the feet relative to the plate.

This represents a compromise of sorts, but it makes it somewhat difficult to fully involve the large muscles of the body. To make it easier for the developing hitter to involve the large muscles of the legs and trunk, the front foot is moved a bit closer to the plate in a slightly closed position. If at the same time this front foot is pointed ever so slightly toward the pitcher, the hips will be free to pivot open during the swing to generate much more power (see Figures 6-13 and 6-14). This stance provides a comfortable and balanced position from which to begin the swing, and it should be practiced regularly.

As the level of play improves, the hitter may want to change some element of this positioning; however, any changes should still al-

Figure 6-10. Open stance.

Figure 6-8. Gauging the stance by using the bat to touch the outside corner of the plate.

Figure 6-9. Plate coverage from a properly located stance.

Figure 6-11. Closed stance.

Figure 6-12. Square stance.

Figure 6-14. Opening of the hips.

Figure 6-13. Pointing the front foot slightly toward the pitcher.

low good plate coverage without causing a loss of power. Good balance is the key to successful hitting; a sound stance provides good balance.

Body and Arm Position

Beginning with a firm base created by feet approximately shoulder width apart, the body flexes slightly at the waist and knees. If this is done by bending first at the waist and then at the knees, the weight spreads on the balls of the feet. The athlete then shifts the weight slightly to the back foot to establish a 40 to 60% bias toward the rear. The hips should be level and turned slightly inward by having the front foot closer to the plate.

The arms are away from the body with the elbows bent. The hands are even with the back shoulder, approximately at chest height, and some 6 to 10 inches from the body. The bat forms about a 45 degree angle with the ground. Shoulders are level and may follow the hips into a partially closed position (see Figure 6-15).

Head and Eyes

The head is erect and turned toward the pitcher; the eyes remain level and focused on

Figure 6-15. Body and arm position in the initial stance.

Figure 6-16. Erect head turned toward pitcher, eyes level and focused on point of release.

the potential location of the release (see Figure 6-16). The coach can help the athlete discover the correct head position by having the batter get in the box, assume the stance, and cover the eye closest to the pitcher. The player then turns the head until the pitcher just comes into view, and if the head has moved but kept the eyes level, the head is in the proper position.

Key Elements:

- The hitter's weight is on the balls of the feet, with approximately 60% on the back foot.
- The stance is taken close enough to the plate to allow coverage of the outside edge.
- The front foot is even with the front of the plate.
- The front foot is slightly closer to the plate with the toes turned a bit toward pitcher.
- The body is slightly bent at the waist, and the knees are flexed.
- The hips and shoulders are level and slightly closed.
- The hands are held chest high and even with the back shoulder.

- The bat is approximately 45 degrees to horizontal.
- The eyes are level and focused on ball.

Common Errors:

- The stance is taken too close to the plate.
- The stance is taken too far back in the batter's box.
- The player points the front foot toward either third base or first base.
- The batter holds the body very upright or stiff.
- The hitter crouches excessively.
- The player carries the hands too low.
- The hands are too close to the body with the elbows extended from the sides in an exaggerated manner.
- The batter keeps the elbows too close to body.
- The bat is held straight up.
- The bat is allowed to drop nearly horizontal.
- The player tilts the shoulders.

Before even trying to hit the ball, every young athlete should learn two skills:

1. to become comfortable at the plate while having a ball thrown at them
2. to practice finding and following the pitch

A simple drill to accomplish both has the batter take a properly aligned stance and simply watch the ball as a number of pitches are thrown. Throughout the drill, the head remains still in relationship to the body's midline, and the eyes remain level with one another. As the player's eyes pick up the center of the ball and watch it all the way back to the catcher's mitt, the head swivels on the neck. This allows the eyes to move downward and back in unison to track the ball. If they do not or if the head cocks to the side, the batter loses sight of the ball or sees it only with peripheral vision. In either case, the player will have a difficult time making contact. By concentrating on following the ball to the catcher, the hitter not only practices proper focus and head movement but also develops the habit of focusing attention at the plate (see Figure 6-17 a-c).

The coach can also use this drill to check on the grip and any bat movement prior to swinging. The grip should be firm but not tense, and the bat still. A slight opening and closing of the hands will relieve tension. Some bat motion also may be used to relax the batter. However, extra movement should be minimized and

(b)

(a)

(c)

Figure 6-17 a, b and c. Sequence of the head turning to follow the ball from release to catcher's glove.

only serve to relax tension or "trigger" the swing.

Mechanics of the Swing

The correct stance and focus prepare the batter for success, but still more needs to be done to get hits. Because even relatively young pitchers can throw fastballs that get to the plate in less than one second, a hitter cannot rely on good reaction time alone. Rather, both the speed of the swing and its proper initiation are important. The faster the swing, the more time available for evaluating the pitch's location and spin, and the longer the batter can wait to start the swing. As a youthful player becomes stronger, bat speed naturally will improve and consequently so will many other aspects of hitting. However, at any particular point of the career, a good hitter tries to maintain a constant bat speed and responds to different speed pitches by changing when the swing starts. Thus, the same swing should work for any pitch in any situation. The successful athlete concentrates on starting the swing in a habitual manner and using a consistent speed.

Weight Shift

The swing begins by shifting still more weight to the back foot. This causes the hips and shoulders to close a bit more and coil around the body's centerline. At the same time the hands extend back toward the catcher in position to aggressively drive forward. The back leg bends slightly, and the hips and shoulders remain parallel to one another. The eyes remain focused on the flight of the ball (see Figure 6-18). These actions stretch the muscles used in hitting and prepare them for the vigorous contraction that results in a powerful swing. While the degree of coiling and stretching may vary depending on the hitter's purpose or the pitcher's speed, the goal remains the same: a controlled explosion of muscular force that drives the ball for a hit.

Stride

With the weight shifted and the body coiled, the front foot is free to take a small stride forward. After this 4 to 6 inch step, the foot lands gently so that the head and body are not jarred out of line, and the muscles remain ready to

Figure 6-18. Backward weight shift and extension of the hands. Notice eyes are focused on the ball.

transfer the weight forward into contact with the ball. The foot should be placed at an angle approximately 45 degrees to the plate (see Figures 6-19 and 6-20). All this allows the body and head to remain steady while providing a bit more time to evaluate the pitch.

The stride also begins a sequence of movements that result in the swing, contact, and follow-through. This complicated series of events occurs in a very short period of time and may be very difficult to analyze. However, the coach must understand the various parts in order to help the athlete properly execute them.

Rotation

If a swing is to have the maximum power, the decision to swing needs to be made at about the same time the stride foot contacts the ground. The weight shift forward onto the front foot begins a dramatic hip rotation, which upon reaching its highest speed causes the trunk of the body to turn toward the pitch at an even greater rate. The shoulders now begin to rotate forward at a still greater speed and continue to do so until they come parallel to the hips. All this spinning body mass produces a tremendous increase in the force—especially because the arms and hands have remained back and are just beginning to move (see Figure 6-21).

Figure 6-19. Start of stride.

Figure 6-21. Rotation of body; arms and hands have remained back.

Figure 6-20. Front foot at 45° to the plate.

Arms and Hands

The front elbow begins the swing as it starts the extension to the ball. This brings the bat into the hitting area knob first (again see Figure 6-21). As the elbows approach full ex-

tension, the wrists are still in a cocked position (see Figure 6-22). This allows the bat to come forward into the hitting zone by the shortest path, so it provides the quickest possible swing (see Figure 6-23).

Now the wrists must quickly snap forward to bring the bat to the ball (see Figure 6-24). This move, sometimes called "rolling the wrists over," causes the barrel of the bat to move a great distance in a very short time and greatly increases the momentum of the swing (see Figures 6-25 and 6-26). Keeping the hands back in the cocked position as long as possible gives the hitter a bit more time to adjust to any late motion of the ball.

Because of the speed and force involved in the swing, the player may be concerned about letting go of the bat. Generally the hands react to the forces by tightening the grip, so the bat seldom flies out of the hands. This strengthened hold has the additional advantage of improving the player's bat control. However, from time to time the top hand lets go of the bat, and even more rarely the bat flies from the hands. The coach must prepare hitters—and defensive players—for this possibility by insisting that ALL players watch for bats and balls flying through the air, whether in games or during practices.

Figure 6-22. Elbows nearing full extension; wrists still cocked.

Figure 6-24. Wrists rolling over.

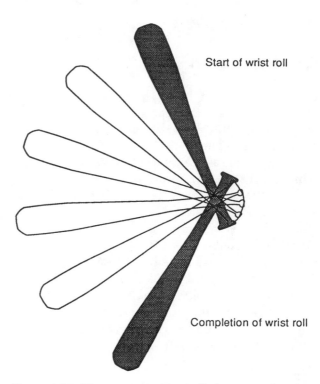

Start of wrist roll

Completion of wrist roll

Figure 6-25. Diagram comparing roll of wrists with movement of the bat.

Figure 6-23. Bat entering hitting zone with the wrists cocked.

Front Leg

As the arms and wrists near full extension and just before contact with the ball, the front leg extends (stiffens). This forceful extension of the knee causes the front side of the hitter's body to turn to the back. This in turn increases

Figure 6-26. Completion of wrist movement.

Figure 6-27. Front leg extension. Notice the movement of the batter's back foot.

the force with which the backside comes around—in fact, the back foot may actually leave the ground as the batter "hits against the front leg" (see Figure 6-27).

The previous sequence of movements—hip, trunk, and shoulder rotation, elbow extension, and wrist snap—generates much force to the swing. The extension of the front knee concludes the power generation portion of the swing, and the resulting turn of the body gives the hitter that last little bit of power to really drive the ball. If the head, and consequently the midline of the body, remains relatively still throughout this motion, then the batter will not only hit the ball hard, but the ball is likely to be hit on a line in fair territory.

Head and Eyes

During this complicated series of movements, the batter strives to keep the head fixed in relationship to the midline of the body. When the hitter is in the correct stance, the head is turned a bit so the back eye just sees the pitcher. The eyes are on the point from which the ball will probably come, and as soon as it appears, the batter focuses on its center. In completing the swing, the head may turn on the neck to allow the eyes to follow the ball, and the body ro-

tates around the midline. But throughout, the head and midline remain fixed in a vertical position, and the eyes stay level with one another. This allows the head and eyes to "stay on the ball" (compare Figures 6-15 and 6-27).

Follow-Through

The swing begins with the batter's weight on the balls of the feet and a bit biased toward the back foot; it shifts almost entirely to the rear and comes forward to be completely on the front foot. All this movement happens in approximately four-tenths of a second and involves nearly every part of the body. If the batter is to keep the swing in sequence and at the same time avoid injury, then the athlete needs some means of dissipating the force of the swing. The follow-through is the natural consequence of these actions. The wrists are rolled over, the arms and shoulders continue their rotation, and the body comes open to the pitcher (see Figure 6-28).

While the follow-through obviously cannot affect the flight of the ball, it provides important clues to the observant coach. For example, the location of the hands tells something about the swing path: if they finish near shoulder height, then the swing likely is upward and may result in fly ball outs. If the hands finish down below the waist, then the swing may have

Figure 6-28. Follow-through of the swing.

a jerky, chopping motion that results in a loss of power. Similarly, if the follow-through is incomplete and stops before full extension, then the mechanics of the swing have broken down, and the power will be much less than expected.

Contact

If the swing is executed correctly, the contact phase finds the batter in a position essentially like Figure 6-24, and the ball is projected off the bat toward the outfield. However, pitchers make every effort to keep the swing from happening this way; therefore, the batter must recognize and control three elements that affect the flight of the ball

1. the swing path
2. where the bat and ball meet
3. when the bat and ball meet

Swing Path

As previously suggested, if the swing goes up and the bat strikes the center of the ball, the ball tends to rebound along a similar path and become a fly ball. If the bat travels downward and strikes the ball's center, the ball deflects downward with a bit of top spin and is a line drive or grounder. Finally and least likely, if the swing is parallel to the ground and connects with the center of the ball, the ball starts out as a line drive near waist level.

In general, most younger baseball players should try to hit the ball with a slightly downward swing. With the hands starting at chest height and the arms extending into the hitting zone to bring the bat knob first to the ball, a downward swing is the natural result. Such a swing produces many more line drives and well-hit ground balls, but more importantly it clearly results from the proper execution of the outlined mechanics. (In fact, the coach can tell much about a player's swing by watching the flight of the ball off the bat.)

As a baseball player matures there may come a time when different swing paths are appropriate. For instance, many power hitters use an upward swing to lift the ball over the fence. Or there may be times when a sacrifice fly is all that is needed, and the batter decides to swing upwards to increase the likelihood of hitting an outfield fly. However, these are somewhat advanced considerations which primarily affect play at the upper levels. Younger hitters often have enough difficulty in just hitting the ball, so they should be expected to work on a single swing path until they become able to regularly make good contact. Thus, they are best served by following the proper mechanics and using a slightly downwards swing.

Where Bat and Ball Meet

Because both the bat and ball have rounded shapes, contact between them must occur very near their centers if forces are to be transferred linearly. If the bat strikes nearer the bottom of the ball, a pop-up results; if nearer the top, a slow-rolling ground ball results. Either of these actions may result from an otherwise perfectly executed swing. More often than not, a player who regularly pops up or weakly grounds out is not focusing on the center of the ball. Recognizing this, the coach should pay attention to the entirety of the swing in helping the athlete overcome these tendencies. Repetition of swings is the best solution, and proper use of a batting tee, as outlined below, may help both the coach and the hitter.

When Bat and Ball Meet

Clearly the bat and ball should meet when the batter is generating the most power. Most of the time this will occur at a point in front of the plate (see Figure 6-29). This point of contact also minimizes the chance of the hitter being fooled by any movement on the ball. An additional advantage is that the batter is not required to keep the weight back and delay the swing. Thus, making contact in front of the plate probably means that the arms and wrists are fully extended and that the body is fully rotated. Maximum power is generated, and the ball flies away at top speed. Consequently, the young player will benefit most from trying to make contact before the ball gets to home plate.

The age and experience of the athletes involved make a difference in the capabilities of the hitter and, consequently, the expectations of the coach. The hitter eventually must learn to handle pitches near the corners of the plate as pitchers improve their control; and the need may arise for the batter to advance the runner by "hitting to the right side." In the former instance, minor changes in the stride allow the hitter to deal with pitches inside or outside, and flexing at the knees gets the bat to balls down in the strike zone. Hitting to the right side is a challenge for right-handed hitters, and it can only be done by making contact with the barrel of the bat angled to the right (see Figure 6-30). Clearly this involves several possible actions: a stride angled toward the outside of the plate, the arms and wrists not extending, a "late" swing, or a combination of these. In any case the right handed batter will sacrifice some power in order to advance runners by hitting to the right side.

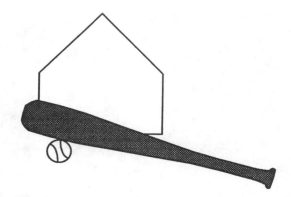

Figure 6-30. Diagram showing bat position to allow a right-handed hitter to hit the ball to right field.

Key Elements:
- Eyes focus on ball.
- Initial weight transfers to back foot with partial closing of body position.
- A 4 to 6 inch stride lands 45 degrees to plate.
- Proper sequence of rotation is hips, trunk, shoulders.
- Elbows extend, wrists roll over.
- Front knee stiffens.
- Bat and ball contact center-to-center.
- Body follows through.

Common Errors:
- Weight does not transfer.
- Head moves with shoulders.
- Shoulders and hips move together in stiff-appearing swing.
- No stride is taken, or stride is too long.
- Body and/or head move toward pitch with stride.
- Hands drop down from chest height.
- Arms extend or wrists flex too early in swing.
- Front knee remains bent.
- Follow-through is non-existent or weak.

At every level of play, the batter will be challenged to perform a difficult task. Use a round bat to hit a moving spherical ball that probably is also breaking in two additional planes. Such challenges can be overcome only through practice. The athlete must work to develop a mechanically sound swing, one that follows a slightly downward path to meet the ball near its center slightly in front of the plate.

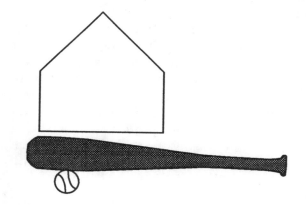

Figure 6-29. Diagram of ideal contact between bat and ball—in front of the plate.

Sequence for Teaching Hitting

In order to teach hitting to young players, the coach must recognize that it is a difficult skill to master and that the athletes will progress at different rates. But more importantly, the good coach realizes that success is relative. If being successful means getting on base after hitting the ball, then batters fail much more often than they succeed, even in Major League Baseball. As suggested previously, a 30% success rate, or hitting .300, is outstanding at any level of play; but this also means that even great hitters make outs twice as often as they get hits. Equating success in hitting with getting on base also causes problems because even young players recognize that a poor swing may result in a hit while a good one can produce an out. These events—which everyone knows regularly happen at the plate—practically guarantee that a batter's confidence is an uncertain thing. Therefore, since self-confidence and motivation are keys to the development of young athletes, the coach and players must work together to redefine success in more personal and meaningful terms.

A beginning player may be asked to consider as successful any turn at bat that includes the ball being hit. A bit more experienced athlete may think of success as any swing that is mechanically correct and contacts the ball. Still later, success for the batter might be swinging hard with good fundamentals. Clearly the pattern is established. Redefining success in such a personalized way allows each hitter to develop confidence by setting a personal goal and reaching it. This challenges the coach to understand the elements of good hitting and to have a plan for teaching them in proper sequence.

Initial Instruction

Every season should begin with the coach and players focusing attention on the basics of a good swing: bat selection, grip, elements of the stance, and mechanics of the swing. The coach should take the time to evaluate every athlete's ability to perform each of these skills, so that coach and player alike have an idea of areas that need work and what can already be done well. Moreover, this evaluation gives the coach an opportunity to work with each player to define success personally and to set meaningful individual goals jointly.

The coach starts this process by having each player hold a bat that the players has used previously to see whether a different one is appropriate (see Figure 6-1). Then the coach checks the athlete's grip and helps the hitter decide if a change is necessary (see Figures 6-2 to 6-6). The coach, asking the batter to simulate standing at the plate, considers the athlete's stance and makes any needed adjustments (see "Stance" in this chapter). Once the player can assume a good stance the player takes a few practice swings, and the coach evaluates the mechanics involved and again makes changes as needed (see "Mechanics of the Swing" in this chapter). Once the youngster has been evaluated by the coach, the player should know how to execute a good swing. But more importantly, all athletes should know what they need to work on to be successful in their own terms.

Much of this early season appraisal can be done indoors, where variations in weather are not a factor in performance. Also, after the hitters have been through the evaluation process, they can accomplish much by simply going through the motions and checking their own performance. If available, a full-length mirror is useful for this process of self-evaluation.

Incorporating the Ball

To this point, the athlete has only dealt with half the equation—the bat. Now the ball must be considered. As previously suggested, making solid contact between two round, moving objects is a difficult task, one which involves a great deal of eye-hand coordination. In fact, it is so challenging that even professional ball players spend time hitting balls off batting tees, and that is how young athletes should begin each season's efforts.

The tee puts the ball in a set, visible position that allows the hitter to work on the fundamentals of the swing while maintaining good head position and eye contact with the ball. However, the design of most tees means that the batter may be fooled into taking a poor hitting position. Many tees have a base piece shaped like home plate and an upright support for the ball roughly in the middle of the base. Quite naturally, a young hitter looks at the base, sees a plate, and takes the stance in relation to it (see Figure 6-31), but this unnatural ball position means that it will be hit very early in the swing, near the middle of the body. In this situation, either the arms will not be fully extended or the player will compensate by standing very upright—even to the point of leaning backward (see Figure 6-32). Consequently, poor technique could result from using this type of batting tee.

To have an athlete correctly hit from a tee, the coach should do one of three things.

1. Use a tee that allows the upright to be placed in various relationships to the base.
2. Use the tee in conjunction with another home plate shape.
3. Use a tee that does not have a base shaped like home plate.

In every case, the goal is to have the batter take a position that will allow the full extension of the arms and wrists while meeting the ball well in front of the body (see Figure 6-33). The plate/tee combination used in this figure has an upright that can be moved relative to the plate. However, much the same thing can be accomplished by using a second plate shape in conjunction with a nonadjustable plate/tee. A rub-

Figure 6-32. Location of contact resulting from incorrect use of a tee. Notice the poor extension.

Figure 6-31. Incorrect positioning relative to a batting tee.

Figure 6-33. Correct use of a tee.

ber "throw down" plate can be used as the second plate, or a reasonable substitute can be cut from an old automobile floor mat or carpet scrap. In any case, athletes are asked to position themselves with respect to this second shape while the one with a tee is set in front.

Note: Using a tee thusly, a right-handed batter tends to hit to the left side of the field while a left-handed hitter is more apt to hit to the right. In other words, the player likely pulls the ball. The coach should not be concerned by this, as the purpose of tee work is to groove the mechanics of the swing. Further, the physics of hitting off a tee are different from hitting a moving ball; and as the player makes this transition, batted balls will tend to be hit to other areas of the field.

Once taking the stance, the batter strides, swings and hits the ball. The head stays still, eyes focused on the ball. Repeated swings make the batter aware of the correct head position. The coach pays particular attention to the head and eyes at this stage, but the stride should also be noted as a very young batter may try to stride with the back foot. Moving the rear foot severely limits many parts of the swing, so the coach should not allow an athlete to continue the progression until this has been corrected.

A Moving Ball

A ball placed on a tee presents a stationary target—hardly the normal situation in baseball. Rather, the batter must be able to locate and hit a moving object. To accomplish this, the hitter's eyes must be focused on the ball as it moves from the pitcher's hand to the plate, and the head and eyes must make coordinated movements to track the ball the whole way. This ability to see and follow the ball's flight is an essential skill. If everything else is done perfectly but the eyes fail to trace the ball's path, the athlete will seldom hit the ball. But if all the other mechanics are performed poorly while good eye contact is maintained, the batter may hit the ball more often than not.

The coach can help the players realize the correct movements by having them think of the head and hands going in opposite directions. The head begins turned a bit toward the front shoulder and swivels to follow the ball to the rear; the hands start back, and as the swing is made, they move forward. Or if a swing is not made, the chin moves from front to rear shoulder as the head turns to allow the eyes to follow the ball into the catcher's mitt. The following techniques can be used to teach the athletes how the head and eyes are coordinated in the swing.

Having the players imagine themselves performing these skills—using visualization—is a good starting point. The athletes begin by gripping bats and taking their stances. The coach then describes the situation, and the players use their imaginations to initiate the proper bodily movements:

- "The pitcher winds and releases the ball." Head and eyes are forward.
- "The ball is on its way. Now it is nearly to the plate." Head turns to follow ball.
- "You decide to swing." Head is down with eyes focused on point just in front of body; swing begins.
- "The pitch is a ball; you let it go." Head turns on neck as eyes remain level and focused on the ball to watch it into the catcher's mitt.

Some players may become confused by all the different instructions dealing with head movements. Possibly the simplest way for the coach to sum up things is, "Turn it, don't tilt it." In other words, the head swivels on the neck to allow both eyes to remain level while following the ball. It is alright to turn the head to follow the ball, but the head remains set over the midline of the body throughout the swing. The head does not tilt or cock to either side (see Figure 6-34).

This activity is followed by having a batter positioned at the plate and the coach moving the ball through a pitching motion and carrying it into the hitting zone. The hitter traces the path of the ball and at the proper moment swings to meet the ball. (*Note:* This should be an easy swing intended to indicate where contact should be made.) The ball may also be moved out of the strike zone so that the batter has to follow it to the catcher.

The coach next has the player follow the ball as it is actually pitched from a short distance. As proper head and eye coordination are mastered, the batter will hit the ball more con-

Figure 6-34. Head position in swing, neither tilted nor cocked.

Figure 6-35. Set up for soft toss. *Note:* The tosser is only a bit in front of the plate and some 6 to 10 feet from it, and both players are wearing eye protection.

sistently. The coach can then move back and throw faster.

While the outlined drills are intended to develop the player's feel for the movements involved, they do not necessarily improve the athlete's sense of pitch location or develop the needed eye-hand coordination. To accomplish these skills, the following may prove useful:

1. Commonly available plastic balls and over-sized bats
   - Initially, use slower pitches from shorter distances.
   - As skill improves reduce the ball size and progress to a regular-sized bat.
2. A ball with a hole drilled through it and a rope attached
   - Suspend the ball above the batter; move the ball for the batter to hit.
3. "Soft toss" (see Figure 6-35). The batter takes a normal stance, with respect to the plate, while the tosser kneels 6 to 10 feet on the opposite side of the plate and slightly in front of it. The tosser aims waist-high tosses at the batter's front knee but are intended to drop short. The distance between the tosser and plate varies depending on the ball and bat combination being used: plastic golf balls and dowel may have the tosser closer while bats and balls require more room be-

tween hitter and tosser. *(Remember, eye protection for both athletes is important.)* Use the following progression.
   - Batter swings a 30-to 36-inch-long piece of 1-inch dowel or broom handle with adhesive tape knob while the tosser uses plastic golf balls.
   - Batter uses dowel or broom handle to hit tennis balls.
   - Batter swings regular bat at tennis balls.
   - Batter uses bat to hit baseballs.

Caution: **The soft toss drill presents the possibility of eye injury—especially when soft plastic or tennis balls are used. If you decide to incorporate this drill, make eye protection MANDATORY for all participants. The tosser may be placed behind a protective screen or, alternatively, may wear a catcher's mask or safety goggles. The hitter should always wear goggles.**

4. Pitching machine with variable speeds
5. Balls with one half painted in a highly visible color
   - Use painted balls in conjunction with any hitting drill.
   - Have the batter observe which color strikes the bat; this can only be done with good eye contact.

All the previous drills provide the necessary repetition and variety to keep the players' attention while helping them improve their eye contact and coordination. Further, these drills involve other elements of the swing without having to consciously attend to them. Successes with these drills represent real pluses, for now the athletes should be ready for full-speed batting practice.

Batting practice is an important element in the game of baseball. However, it presents a real challenge to the youth coach, who could easily fall into the habit of letting most of the players stand around and watch one or two hitters. To avoid this, the coach must enlist as much adult help as possible and set up a variety of hitting stations. A typical arrangement might find a pair of athletes doing some peer coaching as they use a tee to work on form hitting. Another twosome may take turns swinging at a suspended ball, while a third is playing soft toss. The next player is hitting off a tee with a coach watching, and the "on deck" batter is using visualization to time swings at the pitcher's deliveries. Finally a batter is hitting balls thrown by either a pitching machine or coach. Remaining players are given defensive assignments, in order to turn batting practice into effective defensive practice as well; runners may be put on base to make things still more realistic.

Slumps and Correcting Errors

All the suggested drills and practices come with no guarantees. Batting is a complex skill, and every part of it needs to be practiced regularly. Slumps occur at every level of baseball, and escaping them requires special strategies on the part of every successful coach and player.

Whether a slump is mental or physical in origin, it usually is best dealt with by returning to the tee and working on the mechanics of the swing. This allows the player to attend to a single element of the swing without having to worry about adjusting to a moving ball. Similarly, the coach can focus more easily on potential problem areas in this controlled setting. The following comments represent both a review of the swing's key components and an outline of how to aid a slumping batter.

Stride

The stride starts the swing. The batter takes the stance in proper relationship to the tee, and while in the ready position, the coach marks the midline of the body. This can be done by drawing a line in the batter's box, putting a bat down, or taping the floor if inside (see Figure 6-36). The sequence of stride, swing and

Figure 6-36. Using a bat to mark the midline of the body in the stride.

contact is followed by a check of the relative position of body midline and mark. If the swing mechanics are performed correctly, then the body and mark remain nearly aligned (see Figure 6-37). An overstride or incorrect weight transfer puts the body midline well ahead of the mark, while leaning back or not shifting the weight results in the body behind or tilted away from the mark.

While evaluating a player's stride, the coach also should check the hand movement. The stance begins with the hands held away from the body at chest height, and any tendency to drop them with the start of the swing will result in poor timing and maladjustment to the pitch. The batter must begin the swing by moving the hands toward the ball and not down to the waist.

Body Rotation

The coach checks proper body rotation by having the athlete take a position at the tee and

Figure 6-37. Completion of the stride with the midline marked.

attempt to hit the ball as hard as possible. This forces the batter to use the entire body, and proper rotation almost always results. However, a player may so exaggerate the swing that the body midline and head slide forward while rotating too far forward—even to the point of being turned away from the flight of the ball. The coach's reminder to the player to "keep the head down and in" often solves this problem, but a fair amount of time may be spent on tee hitting before the batter becomes completely comfortable with a full body rotation and firm head position. Once becoming aware of how the body parts feel in full rotation, the hitter may develop a more powerful swing by learning to concentrate on the hips pulling the shoulders through.

Arm and Wrist Extension

Remembering the proper relationship between stance and tee (review Figure 6-33), the coach should ask the athlete to swing from a position that requires full extension of the arms and wrists. Continuing to use correct mechanics, the player should pay special attention to arms and wrists: hands held away from the body near the chest. The swing starts by "driving the knob of the bat towards the ball," and finishes by "throwing the barrel of the bat at the ball" to produce a slightly downward arc. Using this description, the coach can help the batter create a mental image of the correct action; once having this in mind, the player should be better able to evaluate his or her own performance.

Hitting off the Front Knee

Much power is lost if the hitter fails to fully extend the front knee. Often this occurs as a result of the batter striving to overcontrol the bat; the player may also fall into the habit of taking less than full swings to guide or slap the ball and thus end up hitting off a bent front knee. In any case, the coach should ask the athlete to focus on fully extending the front knee and driving the ball.

Full Swing

Once coach and player together have worked through the elements of the swing, the athlete becomes responsible for continuing to work with the tee to improve the timing, smoothness, and speed of the swing. After hitting successfully from the tee, the player is ready to return to the regular batting practice routine. But even now, the number of repetitions remains important. The more one swings correctly, the more confidence one gains, and the more successful one is likely to be. Equally important as the amount of practice are the attitudes of player and coach. Both must be patient in working on improving the swing, and both need a positive approach toward evaluating the hitter's performance. This is especially true if the athlete is expected to hit in a game situation before being fully prepared. In such a case, everyone involved must be willing to accept a properly executed swing as a successful turn at bat.

Correcting Errors

Hitting is a complex skill, and errors may appear at any time and in any combination.

Consequently, whether deep in a slump or needing to correct a minor mechanical flaw, a batter must receive consistent help. If two flaws have crept into the swing, one at a time must be chosen for elimination. Similarly, if two adults are working with the athlete, their efforts must complement one another. Otherwise, confusing messages are sent, and the batter may try to change two things at once. This generally proves unsuccessful, and the player becomes frustrated and anxious. An environment is thus created that practically guarantees failure. Only by focusing the athlete on one aspect of the problem can the coach create change in an efficient manner.

Finally, the time to correct errors is during practices. Only in such a controlled setting can the coach bring about change through close attention to mechanics and numerous repetitions. In game settings there are simply too many distractions and too little time. Reminders like "head down" or "throw the barrel" may get the player's attention and be productive, but more complex instructions during games may distract the hitter from a difficult task.

Evaluating Success

Each swing, each turn at bat, each hitter must be evaluated individually. The emphasis in every instance is on the batters performing the proper mechanics to the best of their ability.

Excellent defensive plays and perfect pitches result in outs, and no batter can avoid them. On the other hand, outs may result because the hitter is not ready for a pitch or swings poorly; these mental and mechanical errors can be controlled by the player and should be considered failures. Older, more experienced players may be able to judge their own performance, but more likely the coach will have to help in this process. In either case, the emphasis should be on the hitter's successful execution of actions within their own control. When this is done and a good hit results, the batter must strive to duplicate that performance each succeeding trip to the plate. Such an effort makes the athlete more consistent and so improves the chances of success.

A player has a number of aids in working for consistent performance. Self-evaluation, coaches' evaluations and practice can lead to success. But three additional aids merit mention: a video camera, a mirror, and a good imagination. If a video camera is available, then every athlete should be filmed at every step: at the tee, in batting practice, in game situations, while playing soft toss, when hitting well, when slumping. In this way the player and coach have a variety of swings to look at and so are more likely to see good performances and recognize bad ones. Knowing what a good swing looks like, the hitter uses a mirror to watch his or her own performance and become used to making self-evaluations. This in turn allows batters to internalize the elements of the swing to the point they are able to imagine themselves making perfect swings and getting hits. Such use of visualization is a powerful tool in creating good hitters.

BUNTING

Although not an essential offensive skill at every level of the game, bunting gives the batter another option and provides the coach with a strategic weapon. Bunting can be used to get a runner on base or to advance those already there. A competent bunter with excellent speed puts tremendous pressure on the defense. Generally, as the level of play improves, bunting becomes more common and useful.

There are really only two general types of bunts: the sacrifice and the hit. Variations occur within each type, and as the athletes practice both sorts of bunts, each one will find an approach to bunting that works personally. Also each batter may be more competent at performing one kind of bunt. Consequently, the coach must recognize that sacrificing and bunting for hits represent two distinctly different skills and that all players may not be equally proficient in both. Thus, the coach must evaluate each hitter's skills so that the athletes are not asked to do something beyond their ability. (See Chapter 9, Offensive Strategies.)

While there are differences in bunting skills, there also are some similarities. No matter what the game situation or the kind of bunt to be made, the athlete should be consistent in stance, grip, and bat position. The hitter will also need to adjust to different pitches in order to make proper contact between bat and ball. These common elements are considered first. Specific directions on sacrificing and bunting for hits follow.

General Considerations

Stance

To avoid tipping off the play, a hitter should use the same stance whether the play calls for swinging away or bunting. The weight is evenly balanced on both feet, about shoulder width apart. The body flexes at the knees and waist, and the arms are comfortably away from the trunk. Hands are held away from the body near chest height. The positioning of the stance is the only change involved. The player moves to the inside front corner of the batter's box. This move essentially locates the athlete in fair territory, and the bunt is much more likely to be fair. Also, by being closer to the pitcher, the hitter will be confronted by less break on pitches, and the defense will be given less time to react to the play.

Grip

Because bat control is the key to success in bunting, a hitter should begin with either a modified or choke grip. This allows the bat to be comfortably balanced in the hands, and so it is more easily controlled. The lower hand provides the real strength and control of the grip while the upper hand guides and softens the bat movement. As the bunt play develops, the athlete slides the top hand up near the middle of the bat. The fingers clinch loosely to form a sort of shelf for the bat, and the thumb tucks in safely behind the bat (see Figure 6-38). By resting lightly in the upper hand, the bat is free to "give" on contact with the ball.

Bat Position

Generally the bat should be held near the top of the strike zone. Because any pitch higher should be a ball, the player need not attempt to bunt any pitches over the bat. Such positioning also puts the bat in proper relationship to the pitches to be bunted. By starting above the ball, the bat travels slightly downward and contacts the ball at or slightly above its midpoint; this increases the likelihood of bunting the ball on the ground. To further improve the chances of

success, the hitter should have the barrel of the bat higher than the handle (see Figure 6-39). This second point is especially important for younger athletes who often let the barrel drop down and so tend to pop the ball up.

Adjusting to Pitches

With the single exception of a squeeze play (see Chapter 9, Offensive Strategies), the player should try to bunt only pitches that are strikes.

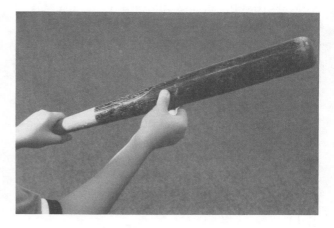

Figure 6-38. Gripping the bat to bunt the ball.

Figure 6-39. Positioning of the bat in bunting. Notice the barrel is above the handle.

However, each pitch is different, so every attempted bunt is different. Jabbing or pushing the bat at the ball will result in any number of mistakes: pop-ups, foul balls, soft line drives at infielders. Consequently, the necessary adjustments cannot be accomplished by simply moving the bat to the ball. Rather, the entire body must be involved when adjusting to the approaching ball. If the pitch is down, the knees flex more to provide the correct movement. If the pitch is inside or outside, the body's weight is shifted in the desired direction. In any case, the relative positions of arms, bat and head do not change (see Figure 6-40 a and b). Coaches sometimes teach this skill by having the athlete think of the bat, hands and head forming a triangle that does not change shape when moving to the ball.

Contact of Bat and Ball

Ball and bat ideally meet well in front of the plate. While beginning bunters may be satisfied with just accomplishing this action, the direction of the bunt can be controlled and so make it more effective. This placement of the bunt is accomplished by using the firm lower hand to position the barrel of the bat. If the

(b)

Figure 6-40 a and b. Adjusting to inside and outside pitches without changing the relative positions of arms, bat and head.

bottom hand is moved with respect to the body while the upper hand maintains position, then the barrel of the bat is moved. Thus, a right-handed batter bringing the bottom hand in to the body turns the barrel in the direction of third base, resulting in a bunt on the left side of the infield. Likewise, if the same hitter moves the lower hand away and so turns the barrel toward first base, the bunt goes to the right side of the infield. (Left-handed hitters make similar adjustments, with mirror image results.)

As with any hit, the bat should meet the ball from slightly above, and the center of the bat should be on line with or a bit higher than the center of the ball. The point is to keep from popping the ball up. Such a soft fly ball almost always results in an easy double play for the defense.

When contact is made, the hands and arms move slightly back to the body and so absorb some of the pitch's energy. This sensation of "catching" the ball deadens the rebound of the ball and increases the bunt's effectiveness. This

(a)

softening of the rebound is especially important when sacrifice bunting. As pitchers become stronger and fielders quicker, the successful bunter must become more skillful. However, the goal remains the same: to get the ball on the ground in a spot where it cannot be fielded or where two or more defensive players will have to communicate to successfully get an out.

Finally, after making contact, the player must drop the bat and run. While these points will be considered in more detail below, it can be said that the bunter usually shifts the weight to the front foot upon contacting the ball. This means that the back foot makes a crossover step to first base. At the same time, the athlete should drop—not throw—the bat on the left, or third base side, of the body. This keeps the bat from interfering with the sprint to first base.

The Sacrifice

Squaring Around

The theory of the sacrifice bunt is that the defense will have to make a play on the batter at first base while any other base runners have the opportunity to advance. There are various forms of this play, which will be discussed in Chapter 9 on Offensive Strategies, but generally the coach calls for a sacrifice bunt when a single run will win a ball game. The batter is expected to make an out; they are "sacrificing" themselves in order for a runner on base to move nearer to home. Clearly this is a pressure situation, and the hitter will have to perform to the best of his or her ability. The traditional way to do this is by "squaring around" to bunt.

Although some coaches have the sacrifice bunter start out facing the pitcher, more often the hitter has to move into position from the normal stance. Beginning near the inside front corner of the box, the athlete pivots on the *back* foot through nearly 90 degrees to the outside. (While this gives up a bit of the advantage gained by moving forward in the box, it guarantees that the batter will not be called out for contacting the ball while outside the batter's box.) The body comes square to the pitcher as the feet are parallel to one another, shoulder width apart and pointing to the infield. The knees and waist flex to keep the bunter on bal-

ance. While this is happening, the top hand slides up the bat to assume the bunting grip. The barrel end of the bat is higher than the handle and near the chest (see Figure 6-41 a and b). Often the knees end up being bent much more than in a normal hitting stance. Any adjustment to the location of the pitch occurs before the ball gets to the plate, and the batter must be especially mindful of contacting the top half of the ball to get the bunt on the ground.

At contact, the hands and arms "give" as

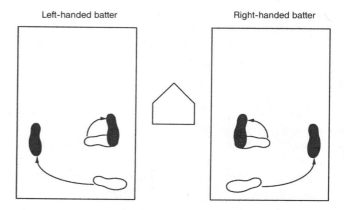

Figure 6-41a. Moving into position for squared around bunting.

Figure 6-41b. The batter in squared around bunting position.

the bat "catches" the ball. Also, the bunt should not go directly back to the pitcher; to be most effective, it should be directed to the right side of the infield. Once certain that the ball is fairly bunted, the hitter completes the play by dropping the bat to the left and hustling for first base. The bunter's objective is to force the defenders to concentrate on the play at first.

Key Elements:
- Begin in the regular batting stance, but move to the inside front corner of the batter's box.
- As windup begins, pivot on the back foot to bring the body around square to face the pitcher.
- During the pivot, slide the top hand near middle of the bat.
- Extends the bat in front of the body with the barrel near the top of the strike zone and higher than the handle.
- Focus eyes on the ball.
- Make any needed adjustments to the pitch location with the entire body.
- Make contact in front of the plate. Move the bat slightly downward to the ball with the center of the bat hitting near the center of the ball.
- Let the arms and hands "give" with the pitch to deaden the ball.
- Use the position of the lower hand relative to the body to provide the placement of the bunted ball.
- To start to first, shift weight to the right foot and cross over with the left.
- Drop the bat to the left, or third base side, of play.

Common Errors:
- Making the pivot after the windup begins.
- Ending the pivot on the front foot with the back foot fully outside the batter's box—resulting in an out if contact is made.
- Dropping the barrel end of the bat below the handle.
- Wrapping the thumb around the bat in a position where the thumb can be injured.
- Hitting the bottom of the ball with the bat, causing a pop-up.
- Making the adjustment to the pitch by jabbing the bat at the ball.

- Hurrying through the bunting sequence in order to start running.

Pivoting to Bunt

Many coaches have come to feel that squaring around to sacrifice puts the hitter in an unnatural and potentially dangerous position. Fully facing the pitcher has the batter at the disadvantage of having to view the pitch from an unusual position; further, the batter has more difficulty in avoiding being hit by inside pitches. Some hitters have in fact injured their backs in just such a situation. These considerations have lead to the alternative of pivoting the body on both feet to get into bunting position.

Taking the normal stance near the inside front corner of the box and waiting until the pitcher begins the windup, the batter separates the hands and pivots on the balls of the feet. The UPPER body turns toward the front as the feet simply turn to point at the mound. At first the player may feel a bit off-balance in such a position, but this can be counteracted by bringing the back foot a few inches closer to the plate, thus providing a slightly broader base. The same situation develops if the front foot is placed a bit farther from the plate. The method used is a matter of choice, and players should experiment with all three possibilities and decide for themselves which to use. In any case the feet are staggered, the back knee is flexed more than the front, and the upper body leans a bit forward to put the weight on the front foot. The chest and shoulders are square to the pitcher (see Figure 6-42 a and b). After the pivot, the bunt becomes exactly like the squared around sacrifice.

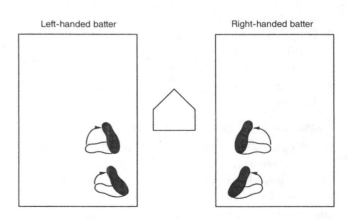

Figure 6-42a. Moving into position for pivot bunting.

Figure 6-42b. The batter in pivot bunting position.

Key Elements:

- Pivot on balls of the feet.
- If necessary, improve balance by moving back foot closer to or front foot further from plate. Adjustment is a matter of only inches.
- Flex the back knee more than the front. The upper body leans a bit forward to put more weight on the front foot.
- Continue the actual bunt execution as in the squared around stance.

Common Errors:

- Poor balance results from the feet being too close together or from inadequate practice in adjusting position.
- Initial position is too far away from plate.
- Bunter pivots after pitcher delivers ball and so has too little time to adjust to pitch.
- The "Squaring Around" section lists **Common Errors.**

Sequence for Teaching Sacrifice Bunts

Begin with the batter in position, either squared around or pivoted. The coach helps the bunter get the body, hands and bat in proper position and then asks the player to duplicate the positioning. Once batters can assume the correct position, the coach slowly tosses the ball from 5 to 10 feet away and the athlete focuses on "catching the ball with the bat." If the top half of the ball is hit and if the arms and hands "give" on contact, the ball will fall to the ground (see Figure 6-43).

As with other elements of batting, the athlete can accomplish much by watching themselves in a mirror as they imagine a ball being thrown to them. In this setting, the player performs the skills numerous times to learn through both repetition and visualization. A player not "giving" or having difficulty in "catching" the ball on the bat may be helped by using a glove on the top hand. The player first takes the stance with a glove on and simply catches the ball as the coach pitches it from in close. Once comfortable doing this, the athlete grips a bat with the lower hand and lays the barrel in the glove. The coach again throws softly from a short distance, and the hitter literally "catches" bat and ball together. To be successful the bunter has to "give" almost perfectly.

Next the beginner works on adjusting to pitches. Starting from the squared around or pivoted position, the batter works to move to soft pitches in various locations. The bunter uses a glove on the top hand as above, while the coach focuses on the head, hands and bat moving as a unit.

Figure 6-43. Learning the sacrifice bunt. Notice how the ball drops softly to the ground.

Once all these skills have been mastered, the athlete repeats the sequence but begins from the normal batting stance. The coach reminds the players why sacrifice bunting is important. The play is designed to advance runners, not to get a hit; and "showing bunt" early is reasonable, even desirable. Therefore, the squaring around or pivot move can occur early—even before the pitcher initiates the windup. Once the timing is correct, three additional skills must be learned: sliding the top hand up the bat, forming the proper grip, and extending the bat into the strike zone with the barrel uppermost. Practice with a mirror or a partner begins the process; trying to bunt easy pitches from a short distance follows.

Having mastered all the previous skills, the batter works on placing the ball to various parts of the infield. Moving the lower hand with respect to the body accomplishes this, but such movement must occur before the ball arrives in the hitting area. Having the hitter practice moving the lower hand without having to hit a ball is a good starting point. Then bunting for placement against easy pitching can be tried. Throughout, the emphasis is on making the hand adjustment before contacting the ball.

Finally the athlete is ready to make sacrifice bunting a part of full-speed batting practice. Since it is difficult to do with a suspended ball or off a tee, bunting practice is limited to attempting to hit thrown balls. However, the coach should ask the player to bunt at various points during the turn at bat. In other words, the coach avoids the habit of having every batter follow the same sequence—start with three bunts, end with a "good" sacrifice, and so on. Instead, the coach should describe a situation—"Runner at second with no one out; tie game." for example—and ask the hitter to attempt to bunt the runner along.

Bunting for a Hit

In general, a player should attempt to bunt for a hit when the defenders at first or third are playing deep, when the pitcher is a poor fielder, or when the pitcher has an exaggerated follow-through off to the side. If having particularly good speed, the batter can attempt to push the ball past the pitcher toward the gap between first and second bases. Each of these situations exploits the element of surprise, because the batter must wait until the last possible moment to begin the bunt. Bunting for a hit requires the bunter to be moving when the ball is contacted.

The most basic forms of bunting for a hit are the "push" for right-handed batters and the "drag" bunt for left-handers. In the first case, the player seemingly pushes the ball at the hole between first and second base. In the second case, the left-handed batter drags the ball along with the body on the break to first base. Starting out so much closer to first, a left-handed batter has an advantage and should exploit it by becoming a skilled bunter. A right-handed batter can also benefit from bunting, and there are times when the coach may expect any player to bunt to keep the opponents guessing. Clearly, bunting for a hit has real uses; every developing hitter needs to work on it. However, just as surely, bunting for a hit requires such precise timing that it presents a formidable challenge to the developing baseball player. Therefore, it should be attempted only after the athlete has mastered the previously outlined mechanics of bunting to advance a runner.

Push Bunting for the Right-Handed Hitter

Rather than moving up in the batter's box as when sacrificing, the player assumes the normal hitting stance and position. As the ball nears the plate, the hitter steps backward with the right foot and then shifts the weight to the front foot. This motion puts the body in position to get a good running start. The hands simultaneously slide up the handle and separate. The bottom hand moves about 4 inches or so, and the right hand, an additional 6 to 10 inches. The arms extend the bat in front of the body with the barrel higher than the handle, and the eyes focus on the ball. Depending on the situation, the bat is angled to one side or the other of the infield (see Figure 6-44 a-c).

For the briefest time prior to contact, the bat is stationary; and at the moment of contact, the arms "give" with the ball's force to allow the hitter further control of the bunt. The ball is not really pushed; rather the batter's weight, already moving towards first base, provides enough momentum to get the ball beyond the

(a)

(c)

Figure 6-44 a-c. Sequence showing push bunting by a right-handed batter.

pitcher. Thus, the ball appears to be "pushed" toward the infield.

Unlike when sacrificing, the player need not bunt a particular pitch. Instead, the experienced batter looks for a pitch from the middle of the plate out. Any inside or high pitch should be disregarded because such pitches are difficult to bunt on the ground fairly.

Drag Bunting for the Left-Handed Batter

The preliminaries for the left-hander are similar. Assume normal stance and location (although bringing the stance a bit closer may help plate coverage) and wait until the ball nears the plate. The hitter then takes a short jab step with the front foot and moves the hands up the bat—4 inches or so for the bottom hand and another 6 to 10 inches for the top one. The left foot begins a crossover step, and the weight shifts to the front foot. The eyes focus on the

(b)

ball while the arms extend the bat—barrel above handle—in front of the body. The bat may be angled to direct the ball. Contact occurs about halfway through the crossover step (see Figure 6-45 a-c). Following this, the stride continues on towards first base, so it is especially important for the left-handed batter to drop the bat on the third base side of the play.

As with all other bunts, the bat is stationary and the player's arms give with the contact. However, the ball often appears to be dragged down the first base line as the entire play moves in that direction, and so the play is called a "drag bunt."

The player intends to get a hit and can choose the perfect pitch. For the left-hander, the best pitch to bunt is one that is low on the inside half of the plate. Any pitch away from the batter almost certainly will be bunted foul, and a pitch up in the strike zone probably will be popped up.

Key Elements:

● Batter begins in a normal stance and location, although a left-handed hitter may move a bit closer to the plate.

(b)

(a)

(c)

Figure 6-45 a-c. Sequence showing drag bunting by a left-handed batter.

- Eyes focus on the ball, and head is held as still as possible.
- Bat is stationary at the moment of contact.
- When contact occurs, weight is on the front foot, and the back foot immediately strides toward first base.

Common Errors:

- The hitter gives away the play by changing the position in the batter's box or moving the back foot too soon.
- The first move is directed at first base. A right-handed hitter will be jammed by an inside pitch while a left-hander will have practically no plate coverage.
- Eyes or head turn toward first base rather than concentrating on the ball.
- Bat is moving at contact.

Sequence for Teaching Bunting for a Hit

As suggested previously, only after the batter has become skilled in the essentials of sacrifice bunting should bunting for a hit be tried. Because the play requires the hitter to be moving while attempting to bunt, it demands a fair degree of coordination. The essential new skill to be developed is the correct movement of the feet. As with other hitting skills, the athlete should follow a progression from executing the moves, through slow-speed drills, to full-speed bunting. Executing the moves first goes from using visualization to seeing oneself accomplishing the bunt, to performing the correct motions while imaging a pitch being thrown, to watching in a mirror while doing the motions of bunting for a hit. The point is for the athlete to become comfortable waiting as long as possible to move the bat and shift the body weight and to then continue on to first base.

After using visualization, the athlete attempts to bunt slower pitches from a machine or batting-practice pitcher. Special attention is paid to timing the move and bunting only pitches that are suited to the purpose. (If necessary, the developing bunter may benefit from putting a glove on the top hand and going through the motions of bunting to catch the ball in the glove.) The player gradually works up to bunting full-speed pitches. In many respects, bunting for a hit is the most challenging of batting skills, and it may require a great deal of practice.

Slap Bunting

A seldom-used ploy in modern times is the slap bunt, in earlier eras known as "the butcher boy." The name is somewhat deceiving because the play is neither a bunt nor a slap at the ball. Rather, it might be better known as a swinging bunt—although that phrase often is used to describe a hard, full swing that barely tops the ball and produces a slow roller. In any case, the play of interest starts out looking like a bunt but ends up taking advantage of defensive plays that create openings in the infield.

More specifically the batter, often with a runner on base, moves into the pivot bunt position and "reads" the defense. If the middle infielders fail to respond, the hitter may continue to bunt. However, if the defense scrambles to cover both the bunt and bases, then the batter slides the hands together near the top of the rubberized grip, cocks the bat near the inside shoulder, and shifts the weight to the front foot (see Figure 6-46). The eyes focus on the ball, and when it arrives, the player forcefully

Figure 6-46. Repositioned grip used for slap bunting.

extends the front knee to drive the ball into an unprotected part of the infield.

The keys to success in swinging or slap bunting are simple.

- Make the move look like a bunt so the defense moves.
- Take the bat back only to the shoulder.
- Use a short, controlled swing.

A great deal of practice is needed before a young baseball player can use this play. However, it provides an effective response to teams who defense the bunt aggressively. The swinging or slap bunt also can be used by slumping players to regain some confidence, and by hitters having trouble seeing the ball who may try the play because it puts them in good position to watch the ball all the way to the bat.

CONCLUSION

Batting is a complex of skills that must be mastered in sequence. The mechanics outlined earlier in this chapter—grip, stance, hand and arm movement, stride, and so on—represent the essentials of good hitting. However, the two biggest factors in determining success in hitting and bunting are eye contact and body balance. Young players who learn to focus their attention on the ball while in a comfortable, balanced stance will be much more likely to hit the ball. The coach must give each athlete the necessary time and practice to learn these skills. Remember, the player's repetition of the skills combines with positive feedback from the coach to make success possible. There are no short cuts; the time must be spent by athlete and coach alike if the player is to become a good hitter with a variety of skills at hand.

ADDITIONAL READINGS

Boggs, W. & Brisson, D. (1990). *The Techniques of Modern Hitting.* New York: Putnam.
Hriniak, W. with Horenstein, H. & Starr, M. (1988). *A Hitting Clinic: The Walt Hriniak Way.* New York: Harper & Row.
Lau, C. (1980). *The Art of Hitting .300.* New York: Hawthorn Books.
Lau, C. with Glossbrenner, A. (1984). *The Winning Hitter: How to Play Championship Baseball.* New York: Hearst Books.
Pecci, S. (1991). *Building a Better Hitter.* Dubuque, IA: Wm. C. Brown.
Williams, T. (1982). *The Science of Hitting.* New York: Simon & Schuster.
Wolff, R. (1986). *The Psychology of Winning Baseball.* Englewood Cliffs, NJ: Prentice Hall.

7
Base Running

Michael A. Clark, Ph.D.

QUESTIONS TO CONSIDER

- While running from home to first base, when should the runner be in foul territory?
- Why should the runner follow a curved path when advancing to more than one base?
- What circumstances determine the length of the lead at each base?
- What can a runner reasonably expect to do when completing a steal?
- Name the various types of slides. When is each used?
- What sequence of skills can be used to teach base running and sliding?

INTRODUCTION

Base running determines a team's success because every run not scored by a home run must be scored by someone running the bases in jeopardy of being tagged out. While the players' speed makes a difference, the coach's attitude toward running has a greater role in the team's base running accomplishments . Running is not simply getting from one base to the next as quickly as possible, nor is it just stealing bases. Rather, it involves a variety of skills that require practice and mental preparation. Much of the work in base running can be done as part of team conditioning drills or within the context of defensive drills and batting practice. Nevertheless, base running must be a regular, conscious part of baseball practices.

As suggested, speed is an asset in base running; however, the player's mental state is at least as important. Hustling on every play, being aware of the defense, knowing the pitcher and game situation, having a good sense of one's own ability, paying attention to the coach, these ingredients make the average—or even the slow—base runners into challenging opponents. The coach has three responsibilities in helping young athletes become good runners

1. teach them the skills necessary to run the bases efficiently and safely
2. develop their confidence in performing these skills
3. foster the aggressive exploitation of these talents.

Clearly the goal is to create an atmosphere of success surrounding each player's turn on the bases.

This chapter begins with a discussion of the techniques involved in the essential base running plays

- running through first base
- rounding bases
- advancing more than one base on a hit

- leading off
- stealing
- sliding

These comments will be followed by a discussion of the mental aspect of base running. Although most suggestions for practice can be found in the chapter on drills, some observations will be made about a possible sequence for teaching base running skills and some ideas will be provided about how to work on base running within the context of other activities.

RUNNING

There is much more to running than simply putting the head down and going somewhere quickly. Proper form makes a difference in the athlete's overall speed. The coach should evaluate each player's style and make adjustments when inefficient patterns are detected. No matter the starting point, the runner begins low and gradually becomes more upright as speed builds. The runner's weight, balanced on the balls of the feet, is well forward throughout the sprint. The arms swing freely at the sides and are not allowed to cross over the chest. The elbows bend at right angles, and the hands are loosely clinched (see Figure 7-1). The initial steps usually are short and choppy, but as the player's speed increases, the stride lengthens. If viewed on video tape or in photographs, the athlete's body forms a straight line from back foot through head when fully extended.

Several common weaknesses can be observed in the running styles of younger players. Often they run without using their arms. Having them concentrate on lifting the hands to the shoulders while running will help these athletes improve their speed. Beginning players often begin to run with the arm and leg acting in unison, that is, the right arm comes up as the right leg extends. This limits extension and throws the body off-balance. Instead, the right arm should come forward as the left leg pushes off; the left arm and right leg work similarly.

Running to First

Getting out of the batter's box quickly can mean the difference between being safe or out. If the player follows through correctly, part of

Figure 7-1. Proper relation of various body parts when running to first base.

the battle has been won, because then the weight is fully on the front foot. Consequently, the back foot is free to stride to first while the loaded muscles of the front leg explosively push off. A left-handed batter naturally follows through toward first base and merely needs a crossover step to be off. However, right-handed batters are moved toward third base in their follow-through, so they consciously must drive toward first base. As the initial step occurs, hitters must also drop the bat behind themselves and turn the eyes to first base (see Figure 7-2).

Starting with short, quick steps, the runner gradually lengthens the stride while heading for first base. After four or five steps, the player attempts to locate the ball with a quick glance (see Figure 7-3). If the ball cannot be seen, the batter must assume that the catcher or pitcher is fielding the ball behind them. In this case, the athlete must cover the last half of the base line by running in the marked lane in foul territory. This guarantees that the runner will not be called out for interfering with the throw if hit with the ball.

If an infielder is playing the ball, the runner continues straight on for the base. Ideally the left foot hits the front *outside* corner of the bag (see Figure 7-4). This minimizes the time and

Figure 7-2. Dropping the bat and looking to first base.

Figure 7-3. A quick glance locates the ball after a few steps down the line.

distance needed to reach the base, as well as the likelihood of colliding with the defender covering first. A forward body lean like that of a track athlete crossing the finish line is desirable, but the base runner should not jump or lunge at the base; this may result in injury when the player's foot lands awkwardly with a great deal of weight on it. Upon crossing the bag, the runner should peek over the right shoulder to see if the defender has misplayed the ball (see Figure 7-5). The runner similarly must listen for instructions from the base coach and be prepared to turn toward second. In any case, the runner concentrates on continuing at full speed for several more steps.

If making a move toward second base, the runner must remember that a tag play is possible—even if only a single step has been taken. Consequently, both athlete and coach must attend to the play, and the runner must be prepared for quick, decisive moves.

Some beginning athletes will have seen professional ballplayers slide into first base on close plays and may be tempted to emulate them. These young people should be told that sliding slows down the runner and should be used only if the defender is attempting a tag play.

Many younger or inexperienced players tend to stop on the base. To help them develop the correct habits, the coach should have these

Figure 7-4. The left foot hitting the outside front corner of first base.

Figure 7-5. Runner looking over right shoulder after having touched first base.

athletes practice the entire sequence after imagining themselves hitting the ball. Further, the coach should tell them to imagine running all the way to a base located two to three strides beyond first base. This focuses their attention beyond the real base and usually results in a good, quick sprint all the way through first. In fact, the coach may go so far as to put a dummy base cut from cardboard or rubber at the grass and have the players touch both it and the real base.

Key Elements:

- Make the initial step to first with the back foot.
- Follow a straight path toward first.
- After several steps down the line, check the location of the play.
- Run in foul territory if play is behind runner.
- Hit outside front corner of the base with the left foot.
- Lean like a sprinter at the base.
- Immediately after crossing the base, look over the right shoulder to find the ball.
- Continue running hard well beyond first base.
- Be prepared to react to defensive misplays and coach's instructions.

Common Errors:

- Taking too many short, choppy steps at start.
- Running inside the foul line with play behind runner.
- Slowing down before the base or stopping at the base.
- Jumping or lunging at the base.
- Not paying attention to misplays or coach's directions.

Turning Toward Second

The third possible play to confront the batter involves a ball hit to the outfield. If the initial glance finds the ball going to the outfield, the runner should *always* assume that an extra base can be taken. This involves rounding first base aggressively, and, to that end, a different path should be followed on the sprint to first base. Starting between 10 and 20 feet from the base, the runner arcs to the right some 4 to 8 feet (see Figure 7-6). This **S** curve is made at full speed with the player intending to hit the *inside*, front corner of first base with the left

Figure 7-6. Starting the turn toward second.

foot (see Figure 7-7). The runner, after first being certain of touching the base, focuses on the developing outfield play (see Figure 7-8). The player's next step is a crossover with the right leg that puts the right foot directly on line to second base. Leaning a bit into the center of the field helps the athlete complete the turn at full speed.

Having thus rounded the base and located the play, the runner—with the base coach's help—decides whether to continue on at full speed to second base or to stop and return to first. Going ahead to second clearly requires that the runner and coach are knowledgeable of the runner's speed and the defender's arm. The game situation also affects this decision; however, once the decision is made the offensive player goes hard at the base and must expect to slide at the end of the play (see "Sliding," in this chapter). If instead of going to second the runner decides to stop at first, the player plants the right foot, pivots on the left, and returns to first (see Figure 7-9). Once having decided to return to first, the runner does not

Figure 7-7. Touching the inside front corner of first base as part of the turn to second.

Figure 7-9. Returning to first base.

Figure 7-8. Checking outfield play after touching first.

Figure 7-10. The runner continues to watch the defensive play.

simply pivot and jog back to the base. Rather, the runner's attention still should be on the defensive play (see Figure 7-10). Outfielders misplay ground balls, cutoff people fail to get into position or do not catch the ball, and relay people attempt to throw out runners. While the latter case may be directed at the runner

rounding the base and thus presents different problems, the other situations are opportunities to be exploited by aggressive base runners and teams.

One final coaching point: if at all hesitant after rounding first, the player should return to the base. Usually there is not enough time for the runner to stop and start again and still be safe at second. The base coach should be prepared to help the athlete decide whether to continue to second as soon as first base is assured. Confusion, uncertainty or unclear signals result in outs.

Advancing Beyond First

If the ball is hit into the gaps between outfielders or bobbled by an outfielder, the runner continues to second base or further. If second can be easily reached but there clearly is no hope of reaching third, the player gradually slows by taking shorter steps in approaching the base. However, it is much more likely that the runner will have to slide at second. Sliding stops the athlete almost instantly; and because it allows the base runner to go full speed until the last possible moment, sliding increases the chances of safely reaching second.

Additional bases may be available if the player has hit the ball particularly well. In that case, each base is turned with the same sort of curved path used at first (see Figure 7-11). Upon nearing second, the runner checks the third base coach for help in deciding what to do (see Figure 7-12). The coach may stop the player at second, bring the player to third, or wave the player home (see "Signs and Strategy"). In any case, the runner touches the *inside* corner of second base, preferably with the left foot. (However, the player should not break stride solely

Figure 7-12. Nearing second base, the runner checks the third base coach.

to use the left foot.) The following step after touching the base is a crossover that puts the runner on line to the next base, if third or home is the goal. Again, it is important for the athlete to expect to slide at the last base attempted.

Key Elements:
- Gradually curve to the right 4 to 8 feet, beginning 10 to 20 feet before base.
- Hit the *inside* front corner with the left foot. However, do not break stride merely to use the left foot.
- Lean slightly toward the middle of the infield.
- After touching first base, use a crossover step by the right leg to align the body with the next base.
- After being certain the base has been touched, locate play in the outfield; listen for help from the first base coach.
- Quickly decide whether to continue. Run hard for second, or plant the right foot and pivot on the left to return to first.
- Use a curving path, a left foot tag of the base and a crossover step whenever rounding a base.
- Expect to slide at the last base attempted.

Common Errors:
- Failing to use a curved path. Either the runner slows or turns dangerously far beyond the base.
- Hitting the middle or outside of the bag. The foot may slip, or the defender may be in the way.
- Breaking stride to touch base. If the left foot is not set up correctly, use the right.

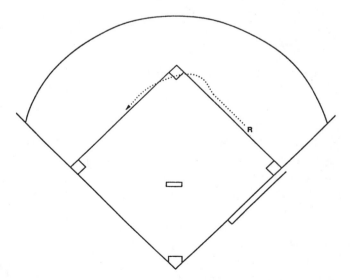

Figure 7-11. The path to be followed when rounding second for third.

- Failing to watch defensive play. Balls elude outfielders, relay throws get past infielders and cutoff people make plays on runners—all present opportunities for aggressive runners and teams.
- Hesitating by player or coach about whether to run. In such situations, DON'T GO!

Leading Off

First Base

As the pitcher looks at the catcher for the sign, the runner establishes the lead with a step-slide-step motion. The leadoff may begin with a walking step or two down the line, but eventually the base runner must take a position square to the base line between first and second. Once in this stance the runner centers the weight on the balls of the feet, which are spread shoulder width apart. The body bends at knees and waist. The arms hang loosely at the sides with the hands loosely clinched. The eyes focus on the pitcher throughout the leadoff (see Figure 7-13).

Note: To minimize possible injuries to the hands, players should be taught to loosely hold something while running the bases. Some athletes may choose to pick up infield dirt while others will want to carry batting gloves. Either will do, but the point is to keep the hands busy so they are not the first thing to hit the ground or base in a slide.

From this position, the shuffle lead begins. The right foot steps directly at second base and finishes comfortably wider than the shoulders; the left foot closes to about half the width of the shoulders (see Figure 7-14 a and b). The runner never crosses the feet nor is ever off-balance. Rather, the player is prepared to move in either direction at any time. The process repeats until the runner is in position—close enough to get back to first if a pickoff is attempted, but far enough to make stealing second a possibility. This distance can be learned only through practice, and it will change over time and with the capabilities of the pitcher and catcher.

A good base runner may want to see the pitcher's pickoff move or to learn how long a lead is possible. This player may use the "one-way lead." In the one-way lead most of the me-

Figure 7-13. The runner leading off at first base.

Figure 7-14a. Starting the shuffle lead by stepping toward second with the right foot.

Figure 7-14b. Closing up the left foot to half the shoulders width.

chanics of leading off are the same, but the player goes a bit farther toward second and keeps the body weight on the left leg. This weight shift has the runner constantly leaning back to first, and so makes it easier to get back safely if a throw is made.

The decision to get back to first is made with the pitcher's first move. If a right-handed pitcher's front shoulder moves toward home or a left-hander's front foot passes behind the left leg, the runner can safely assume that a pitch is being thrown. If the pitcher throws home, the base runner extends the lead with the same step-slide-step sequence used before. This continues to the point where the athlete can just get back to the base ahead of a pickoff throw from the catcher.

However, if a right-handed pitcher turns the shoulders to first or a left-handed pitcher's front foot does not cross behind the back leg, the runner should be prepared to return to first. The player also should get back if the pitcher steps off the rubber, and clearly the runner must react quickly if the pitcher throws to first base. In these situations the athlete pivots on the left foot and takes a crossover step with the right (see Figure 7-15). The runner focuses on the base and does not watch the attempted pick-off; this helps avoid injury in case of a wild throw.

Upon returning to first base, the runner touches the inside back corner of the base with the left foot, if possible; the right leg then takes a drop step toward right field and ends in foul territory (see Figure 7-16). This makes a tag more difficult while putting the runner in good position to sprint for second if the ball gets past the defender. Some players will want to dive headfirst back to the bag; however, head first sliding exposes the player to the risk of potentially serious injury (please see the caution noted in "Head-First Slide"). They also should intend to touch the inside back corner of the base; in doing so, these runners should turn the head toward the outfield to reduce the possibility of injury (see Figure 7-17).

Figure 7-16. Touching first with the left foot and drop stepping away from the defender with the right foot.

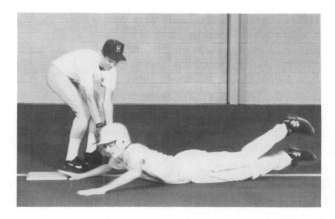

Figure 7-17. Turning the head toward the outfield to reduce the chance of injury.

Figure 7-15. Left foot pivot and right crossover step to return to first.

Any time the base runner must return to first, the same left pivot and right crossover moves occur. However, if having to advance to second, the player pivots on the right and crosses over with the left leg (see Figure 7-18 a and b). These pivot, crossover moves are faster than any other possible combination of foot movements. All team members should practice these moves until they become automatic.

Figure 7-18a. Starting for second by pivoting on the right foot.

Figure 7-18b. Crossing over with the left to continue toward second.

Key Elements:

- Focus attention on the pitcher.
- To minimize the possibility of hand injuries, carry something—dirt, batting gloves—while running bases.
- Balance weight on balls of feet, feet shoulder width apart, body flexed at knees and waist.
- Step with the right foot, slide the left, and continue in getting a lead.
- To return to first, pivot on the left foot and crossover with the right. Touch the inside back corner with the left foot and drop step the right into foul territory.
- To move toward second, pivot on the right foot and crossover with the left.
- Watch the pitcher's first move to decide whether to return or advance.

Common Errors:

- Feet cross during lead.
- Base runner bounces or jumps when leading off; head should remain steady to aid vision.

- Runner is indecisive in response to pitcher's action.
- Runner watches play develop while returning to base.

Second Base

Leading off at second is much like leading from first. The actual mechanics are very similar, with the only real differences coming in the length and positioning of the lead.

Because no one defensive player has responsibility for holding the runner close to second, the offensive player can extend the lead. However, this extension should be delayed until just before the pitcher is ready to deliver the ball so that all defenders are in their normal fielding positions. The initial lead, taken during the pitcher's look in to the catcher, need only be a step or two longer; the real change comes with the secondary lead made on the pitcher's delivery. With the pitch, the runner can move to a point almost even with the shortstop. While taking the lead, the player must remain alert to either middle infielder moving to cover second; because the coaches are quite some distance away, they can provide little help. Also, the runner's longer secondary lead makes him or her a tempting target for pickoff plays, so the runner must pay attention to the ball while returning to second.

The other change in the lead from second has to do with where the runner begins. Instead of starting on the straight line between bases, the athlete moves 4 to 6 feet behind the base line. This places the runner in a good position to follow the desired curved path in rounding third (see Figure 7-19).

Third Base

A runner leading off third base is confronted with some special problems. Chief among these is the possibility of being hit by a ball pulled down the line by a right-handed hitter. Not only could this result in an out if the runner is hit while in fair territory, but an injury might also occur. To avoid both of these situations, the base runner stands a foot or two in foul ground and places a bit more weight on the left or rear foot. This position puts the player out of range of all but the most determined pull hitter, and the weight shift from quickly

Figure 7-19. Taking the lead from second behind the base line.

Figure 7-20. The lead from third.

Figure 7-21. Completing the lead from third in position to start home quickly.

Figure 7-22a. Left foot pivot to start back to third.

Figure 7-22b. Right foot crossover to continue to third.

pushing off the left foot gives the runner the chance to avoid being hit.

Starting outside the base line and with a 60% weight bias toward the left foot, the runner moves as far from the base as the defensive player (see Figure 7-20). The right foot is closest home, and the feet are the usual shoulder width apart. As the pitcher's motion toward home begins, the left foot slides closer to the right, and a series of normal walking steps moves the runner 10 to 15 feet down the line in foul territory. The player crouches somewhat by bending at waist and knees while striving to carry a bit more weight on the left or rear foot. Ideally, the right foot takes the last step as the pitch crosses the plate; this puts the runner in position to push off with the left foot to react quickly to a passed ball or wild pitch (see Figure 7-21).

However, the pitch routinely ends up in the catcher's mitt—the runner pivots on the left foot and crosses over with the right leg to retrace the steps to third (see Figure 7-22 a and b). This move puts the player at or inside the base line where the catcher will have difficulty seeing any defender moving to cover third. Also, by watching the defensive player at third, the base runner can see if a play is being made and can tell how aggressive to be in getting back. (see Figure 7-23).

Often when a runner is at third, the ball is hit on the ground. If attempting to score, the runner at third pushes off hard with the left

Figure 7-23. Checking the defender while going back to third.

Figure 7-24. Correct tag up position at third.

foot and uses the momentum to get home as quickly as possible. However, other times the coach may wish the runner to stay at third when the player is not being forced to run. The coach must communicate this play to the athlete (see "Strategy").

When the batter hits the ball in the air, the base runner at third immediately starts back to the base. If the runner sees the ball in the outfield before getting back to the base, the player plants the left foot, pushes off hard, and sprints for home. However, if the runner returns to third base before knowing the outcome of the play, he or she places the left foot sideways against the front of the bag and waits for the coach's command to "GO!" The athlete's attention is toward home; the runner **does not** watch the outfield play (see Figure 7-24). Once the coach gives the word, the runner pushes off the base and hustles home.

STEALING BASES

In youth baseball, all runners are expected to attempt to steal bases when given the proper sign, but some players will be aggressive enough to attempt steals on their own. In either case, the coach and athletes must work together to improve the players' chances of success. Coach

and player alike must realize that stealing bases is less a matter of speed and more a question of preparation. Athletes should be taught to watch each pitcher's moves—both to first base and home plate—while the coach looks for any trick pickoff moves or gimmick plays used by the opponents. Each player and coach must know the athlete's speed, and the coach should have a sense of each hitter's likely success in advancing the runners. Finally, both coach and players should evaluate the steal in terms of the game situation and alternative plays. Once the decision to run has been made, there is no room for either the coach or athletes to second-guess the play. If everyone involved has weighed the options and practiced the play, then attempting the steal is the right thing to do.

Stealing Second

Knowing the pitcher's moves, the base runner has a sense of how big a lead to take and when to break for second base. The steal obviously begins with the runner leading off as previously described, but once the shuffle lead begins, the runner does not stop moving until forced to by the pitcher. Even at some distance from the base, the player continues to step-slide-step, albeit with shorter steps than usual.

This movement is continuous and fluid, and the weight stays balanced on the balls of the feet. When the pitcher commits to home, the runner pivots on the right foot and begins the crossover step (review Figure 7-18 a and b). Make this initial step with the left foot a strong one. To get the weight moving forward toward second, the athlete accompanies this step with an aggressive swing of the left arm.

Having made several strides toward second, the base runner takes a quick look at the play (see Figure 7-25). If the catcher has the ball, the runner expects to slide into second. If the ball has eluded the catcher, the player rounds second and considers going to third. (The third base coach should help with this decision.) Finally, if the batter has hit the ball, the base runner may have to return to first because of a line drive or fly ball, or the player may be able to advance farther on a base hit. Otherwise, the runner again prepares to slide at second base.

The last possibility for the potential base stealer and first base coach to consider is the pickoff move. If the pitcher's heel moves away from the rubber or if the shoulder turns toward first, the player immediately stops the shuffle lead and returns to first (see "Leading Off," "First Base"). The coach helps the player

by focusing on the pitcher's front shoulder and calls "Back!" when the shoulder is turned toward first base. The coach also assists the runner by watching for wild throws and the return throw to the pitcher.

Stealing Third

As noted previously, the lead from second base can be somewhat longer, and because so many batters are right handed, the chances of the catcher's possible throw to third being blocked are much greater. These situations make stealing third much easier than stealing second. However, the coach must weigh these considerations against the possible loss of a run if the player is thrown out. Ultimately, the decision rests on the coach's philosophy as much as anything else.

The actual procedure in stealing third base is much like that of stealing second. The runner actually goes a bit farther when leading off. The player has an easier time deciding when to return to the base because the most effective pickoff moves require the pitcher to pivot completely around. The main concern is that one of the middle infielders will move behind the runner to cover second, and the third base coach can help watch for this. A good base runner can continue the shuffle lead and so be quite some distance from second and going almost full speed when the pitch is thrown. Once the move has been made, the player may quickly glance in the direction of home to see what is happening, but the runner almost always must slide at third.

Stealing Home

Very few youth baseball players steal home; the move is a difficult one which requires experience and timing. It should only be attempted by a runner with good speed and sliding skills only when a right-handed batter is at the plate. Having a right-handed batter at the plate is important to success in stealing home. The runner at third is at least partially hidden from the catcher by the hitter; this gives the catcher an incomplete view of the developing play. Thus, the base stealer will be more likely to surprise the catcher and also will be running faster when finally seen. The hitter must be a disciplined

Figure 7-25. Checking play at the plate while stealing second.

athlete who checks signs and follows them well. The particular game situation should be considered as well.

When all these options have been considered and the decision to steal is made, the runner leads from third as previously described. The runner starts outside the base line with a 60% weight bias toward the left foot and the right foot closest to home and moves as far from the base as the defender. If the pitcher uses the full windup and pays little attention to the base runner, then the runner keys on the pitcher's motion toward home. When the pitcher begins to pivot, the base stealer pushes off on the left foot to start the sprint home; this necessitates a slight pivot to the right which can be aided by throwing the left arm in the direction of the plate (see Figure 7-26). As much of the distance home as possible should be covered in foul territory, and the runner should expect to slide. The batter must be aware of the possible attempt to steal and get out of the way at the last possible instant.

There is a degree of risk in stealing home. From the coach's standpoint, there is the chance of losing a run that might otherwise be scored. For the athlete, the play involves some possibility of injury. Consequently, stealing home

Figure 7-26. Aiding the pivot toward home with the left arm.

should be practiced before the player attempts it during a game. The coach also must have a sign for the batter that indicates when the play is coming. This will keep the hitter from swinging at the ball and increasing the risk to the base runner. However, the batter must remain in the box until the last possible moment and then perform a drop step with the left leg to immediately clear the area.

SLIDING

As suggested in many of the previous comments, sliding is an essential element in the game of baseball. The ability to slide allows the athlete to sprint as hard as possible for a base with little risk of overrunning it, for the slide brings the runner to a stop very quickly. With the base as the target of the slide, it almost always gets touched and the player's momentum is expended near it. Thus, the experienced runner can not only use the slide as a means of beating the ball to the base, but also as a means of avoiding being out even if a defensive ballplayer is attempting a tag. Finally, with two—or sometimes more—speeding athletes approaching the same base, a correctly performed slide allows the runner to come to a controlled stop, minimizing the possibility of colliding with a defender.

Younger players must learn very early on that the slide does not involve jumping at the base. Sliding also requires careful timing. The move must be made near enough to the base so that the player does not stop short of the bag, but not so close as to make injuries likely as a result of hard contact with a firmly fixed base. Base runners should also learn to avoid injury by clinching their hands or by holding something in their hands and by keeping their arms and head up, away from the play. Finally, beginning sliders should quickly learn that once having decided to slide they must not change their minds—complete the slide no matter what happens.

To enjoy the benefits of sliding while minimizing the risks, an offensive ballplayer has to practice the move regularly. In this way, the runner not only learns when and how to slide, but the types of slides. How to slide can be taught in controlled settings that allow the athlete to develop a great deal of confidence and skill. The need to slide is often assumed at the very outset of a play, but the decision must be finalized when within 25 or 30 feet of the base. At that point, the athlete also must settle on which sort of slide to attempt. The options are

1. the bent leg or "figure 4"
2. the pop up
3. the hook slide
4. the head first slide

It should be noted that all manufacturers of bases include with their products a warning something like the following:

> **Be advised that sliding into a baseball or softball base represents a clear and present danger. Injury may occur. Sporting events are dangerous in nature and participants assume all risks therein. All players should be informed of the risks inherent in this activity. (Beacon Products Co.)**

Bent-Leg or "Figure 4" Slide

The most basic technique is the bent leg or "figure 4" slide. It is the most commonly used and leads directly to the more popular pop-up slide and such variations as the fade away and hook slides. Every baseball player should master the bent-leg slide before attempting any of the others.

Having decided to slide well before nearing the base, the runner continues at full speed until reaching the point to begin the slide. This point will vary with the speed, size and skill of the athlete. A slower, smaller, less experienced person will begin to slide closer to the base, while a faster, larger, more skilled one should start sliding farther away. However, most youth baseball players should begin to move down within 10 to 12 feet of the base.

The player may initiate the slide by lifting either foot and tucking it behind the opposite knee. (This move crosses the legs like the number 4, hence the name.) The athlete necessarily falls to the ground on the calf, thigh and hip of the bent leg, and the momentum of the run up causes the player to slide to the base. (Note that neither the bottom foot or heel should be allowed to drag along the ground.) To accom-

plish this, the runner will have to either turn the body slightly onto the bent leg or will have to bend the ankle inwards a bit. At the same time, the top leg extends toward the base and keeps the foot 6 inches or more off the ground; the top knee and ankle are flexed slightly to help cushion the shock of hitting the bag.

As the leg extends, the arms are thrown up and back, and the chin is brought down to the chest. The arm action helps the player get lower, faster; and tucking the chin keeps the head from hitting the ground while providing a good view of the developing play. Throughout the slide, the body is kept low to the ground. This helps minimize injuries by spreading the weight more evenly, while presenting an opponent with a more difficult target to tag (see Figure 7-27). The *heel* of the top leg touches the base first, and the various leg joints flex to absorb contact (see Figure 7-28).

Figure 7-27. Keeping the body low to the ground when sliding.

Figure 7-28. Touching the base with the heel of the top leg.

Often the coach can evaluate a slide by checking where the runner has gotten dirty. A player with dirt on the back outside of the calf, thigh and hip of the down leg is sliding correctly (see Figure 7-29). However, an athlete who finishes a slide with dirt on the knees or complete side of the pants is going about it incorrectly. If just one knee or the side is dirty, then the runner is rolling over on contact, and this should be corrected. If a runner is afraid to slide, they often will fall to the knees rather than tucking one leg under; this results in both lower legs and knees getting dirty. Such a situation requires immediate attention because the player is risking serious injury. Finally, an athlete with dirt well up on the jersey is staying too low and probably is stopping short of the base.

A "fade away" slide is simply a bent knee slide that is aimed about an arm's length to the side of a base. This approach is used when the defender is set up for the tag on one side of the base. By starting out heading straight for the base, the runner slides and appears to fade away from the base. This is accomplished with a bent-knee slide begun a step or so later than usual because there is no risk of injury from hitting the base, and a step to the side away from the opponent's tag. The sliding player will go a bit beyond the bag but will be in position to touch it by reaching out the hand on the side closest to the base (see Figure 7-30).

Key Elements:

- Slide begins 10 to 12 feet from base.
- Takeoff foot tucks behind opposite knee to form legs into a figure 4 shape.
- Calf, thigh and hip of underneath leg contact the ground.
- Top leg extends toward base. The leg is slightly flexed at knee and ankle and the foot is held at least 6 inches off ground.
- Runner throws back arms, clinches hands and tucks chin to chest.
- Body stays low along ground.
- Heel of top foot touches base, and knee and ankle further flex to take up shock.
- Runner uses "fade away" slide if the defensive player is clearly to one side awaiting a tag play.

Common Errors:

- Failing to decide to slide until almost at base. MANY SLIDING INJURIES RESULT FROM STARTING THE SLIDE TOO CLOSE TO THE BASE! It is far better to slide too early or not at all than to begin too near the base.
- Sliding too early or slowing down before sliding. Player stops short of base.
- Sliding too late. Knee or ankle may jam into base, potentially injuring the player.
- Holding extended leg stiff at either knee or ankle. This has similar injury potential.
- Not lifting contact foot well off the ground.
- Holding hands down behind player. Finger or wrist injuries may result.
- Not placing head on chest. Back of head is likely to hit ground.
- Not keeping body low to ground. Poorly balanced weight can cause injuries, and upright posture presents better target for tag.

Figure 7-29. Dirt on the pants indicating proper sliding technique.

Figure 7-30. The end of the fade away slide.

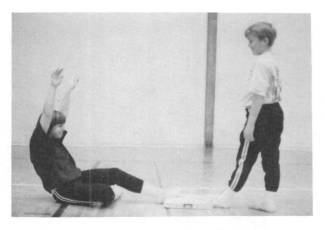

Figure 7-31. Approaching the base when attempting a pop up slide.

Pop-Up Slide

The pop-up slide is essentially a bent-leg slide with the upper body in a more upright position. It is used by aggressive base runners who are always looking to advance as many bases as possible. Rather than finishing the slide laying on the ground, the player's motion ends with them seeming to "pop up" into a standing position at the base. The slide involves a complicated set of movements to reach this end, and it demands good body control and balance by the player. Consequently, the pop-up slide should only be attempted after mastery of the basic figure 4 slide.

In the pop-up slide the run up, takeoff, and contact points are all the same as in the bent leg slide. (However, it is best if the runner bends the left leg to form the 4, as this allows the athlete to complete the slide facing the next base. This reduces the time needed to get started running if advancement is possible.) The arms are not thrown up and back; rather they extend above the head; coupling this with pulling the chin to the chest causes the player to approach the base in nearly a sitting position (see Figure 7-31). The body's center of gravity is forward, over the upper legs. This aids in the next series of movements.

As the *instep* of the top foot touches the base, the bent leg begins the pop-up. The lower leg muscles contract to push against the ground and so extend the down leg. The push of the leg combines with the upper body's momentum to start the player up. The action is completed by the athlete forcefully swinging the arms for-

ward and around behind the body (see Figure 7-32). The player ends up standing with one foot on the base and the other trailing about a step behind. From this position the athlete can easily turn for the next base, if the play allows. To accomplish this, a runner sliding with the left leg down merely needs to push off the base to run. But a player sliding on the right leg will have to pivot on the left foot and take a cross-over step to face the next base.

Key Elements:
- Runner uses same initial mechanics as in the bent-leg slide, preferably with the left leg down.
- Runner approaches base in sitting position.
- At contact of top foot's *instep*, the bent leg stiffens; the upper body's momentum continues forward and is assisted by swinging arms forward and down.
- Runner squares to next base and advances, if possible.

Common Errors:
- Runner completely stops before standing up.
- Player puts hands down to push off, rather than using the down leg.
- Runner slows down before sliding or slides too soon and loses momentum to bag.

Hook Slide

Like the fade away slide, the hook slide carries the runner to one side of the base in an effort to avoid an opponent's attempted tag. As

Figure 7-32. Swinging the arms to pop up at the base.

Figure 7-33. The start of the hook slide. Notice the flexed left knee.

Figure 7-34. Nearing the base in the hook slide.

before, the player early on watches the defender's position to decide on which side of the base to slide—usually the outfield side. The runner then aims the play 2 to 3 feet to the side opposite the opponent.

Running at full speed to the takeoff point, the player leans back and a bit on the side away from the base. (As before, throwing the hands above the head assists the action. The chin also should be on the chest for safety.) Thus, the upper leg rather than the calf becomes the point of contact, and because most such plays require the athlete to slide to the base's outfield side, the right hip is down. *Both* legs extend toward the base with the toes pointed, but it is especially important that the right (or down) foot be well off the ground so that the heel does not dig in and cause an injury.

Initially, the player's body is nearly prone as in the bent-leg slide, but turned away from the base. While keeping the chin down, the player's head rolls slightly left so that the eyes can focus on the base. The left leg is raised off the ground, and as the slide continues on the outside of the right upper leg, the left knee flexes to bend the leg away from the body with the inside of the leg down (see Figure 7-33). The right knee gradually flexes both to slow the slide and absorb some of the shock of contact with the base, but the right leg is kept well away from the bag. As the player nears the base, the left foot is raised somewhat, and the ankle flexes down to point the toes away from the front of the leg (see Figure 7-34). The inner part of the lower left leg makes first contact

with the base; the front of the foot then "hooks" the base, as the rest of the runner's body continues past the base. The athlete comes to a stop in a "scissors" position (see Figure 7-35).

This series of movements carries the runner away from the base while presenting the defensive player with little more than a foot to attempt to tag. The hook slide can be an effective means of getting to a base, but it presents some potential for injury. Only older, more experienced athletes should attempt to use it, and only after they have become skilled in the other sliding techniques.

Key Elements:
- Run at full speed, aim slide 2 to 3 feet to side of base.
- Lean back and onto side away from base; throwing the arms up and back helps. Chin is on chest.

Figure 7-35. The scissors position at the end of the hook slide.

- Slide on outside of right upper leg.
- Extend both legs with toes pointed.
- Focus on base.
- Bend the left leg away from body with left knee flexed. Inside of lower left leg is down, toward the ground.
- Flex the right knee; the right leg is away from the base.
- Flex the left ankle to point toes away from the front of leg.
- Touch bag first with the inner lower-left leg. The "shoelaces" of the left foot next "hook" the base.
- Finish with legs in the full "scissors" position.

Common Errors:

- Sliding too late. Player may be moving too fast when base is contacted and knee injury may result.
- Turning too far to side. Player may actually end up sliding on stomach.
- Failing to keep heel of right foot from dragging on ground. The heel may dig in and cause injury.
- Holding right knee extended stiffly. This is a common source of injury.
- Bending left knee, but still holding it stiff. A stiff knee cannot give on contact.
- Not bending left ankle to point toes down and away from front of leg. Toes may jam and left ankle will have to absorb full impact of contact.

Head-First Slide

Head first sliding presents the possibility of serious injury as it exposes the player's head to contact. Several instances of paralysis have resulted from sliding players either striking the ground with their heads or colliding with the legs of a defender. Other injuries have also resulted. The coach would be well advised to weigh these risks when considering whether to teach this technique.

This technique is the fastest way to get to a base while sliding. The legs continue to drive full speed toward the base, so there is little lost momentum. Moreover, the slide is a natural response to quick plays—especially pickoff attempts at first base—and some players may find themselves using the head-first slide in a game before having tried it in practice. Other athletes may be reluctant to try the slide out of fear, but they should overcome this with practice.

Carrying so much more speed into the slide, the runner begins the head-first slide further from the base—at least one stride further, 14 to 16 feet away. The player pushes hard with either foot to take off; this drives the body forward toward the base. Simultaneously, the head and shoulders lower, and the arms assist by swinging aggressively at the bag (see Figure 7-36).

The chest and stomach are the primary points of contact with the ground, although the upper portion of the hips may get dirty as well. The head, shoulders, knees and lower legs

Figure 7-36. The start of the head first slide.

are held up off the ground; the knees may bend to help keep the feet from dragging. The arms extend to the base. The elbows flex to "give" with contact. The wrists are bent back so that the heels of the palms touch the base. The fingers are clinched loosely but do not touch the palms. The heels of the hands should just brush across the top of the base and be carried across the bag with the body's momentum. Near the base, the player turns the head away from the play for safety reasons but should strive to keep the base in view (see Figure 7-37).

As with other slides, the coach can assess the runner's performance by checking the dirt on the uniform. In this case, the athlete should have dirt on the chest, stomach and possibly upper hips (see Figure 7-38). If the player has dirt on the legs—especially at the knees—then they are slowing down too quickly and may be ending the slide short of the base. If the arms or palms are dirty, the slider probably is dragging them and running a risk of injury.

Key Elements:

- Begin slide a stride further from base—14 to 16 feet.
- Push hard at takeoff.
- Lower the head and shoulders to the base; swing the arms up and to base.
- Hit the ground with the chest, stomach and hips.
- Flex the elbows, bend the hands back at the wrists and clench the fingers loosely.
- Contact the hands with the *top* of the base: heels of hands touch first and momentum carries the slider across base.

Figure 7-38. Dirt on the player indicating proper head first sliding technique.

- Head turns away from play.

Common Errors:

- Sliding too close to base. Runner hits the base with the body or actually lands on the base; either way, injury is possible.
- Dropping the head as it turns and dragging the chin on ground or base.
- Holding the elbows, wrists or fingers stiffly; the joints can potentially jam on contact.
- Pointing the fingers at the base; jams or breaks can occur.
- Hitting the side rather than top of the base with the hands; hand and wrist injuries are likely.
- Not turning the head away from play; runner may be hit in the face.

Figure 7-37. Turning the head away when nearing the base sliding head first.

Sequence for Teaching Base Running and Sliding

Running is something that young people do all the time, and the coach may assume that simply telling them to run hard for a base is sufficient—but, such is not the case. For a variety of reasons, base running is not like the running in other settings, either athletic or playful. Baseball players must practice the required techniques many times before they come naturally. The best way to teach base running skills is to set up game-like situations in practice and have the players respond to them over and over. Thus, the players will learn *why* as well as *how* to run through first base or follow a curved path around second to third. Much the same can be said about teaching sliding, but the coach likely will have much more preparation to do before asking the athletes to perform these skills at game speed. The following suggestions may be useful in helping the entire team become skilled base runners and sliders.

Often what initially appears an easy bit of base running technique can be broken down into a number of still simpler skills that lead quite naturally one to another. These, in turn, build into more sophisticated skills. Every step along the way, the players perform many repetitions of the correct skill. Such an approach might be outlined this way:

1. Perform the desired skill in its simplest form.
2. If some special footwork or body motion is needed, go through it as slowly as necessary to use correct technique.
3. Gradually increase the speed to game level.
4. Have a coach or other adult put the ball in play to simulate game play further.
5. Add a base coach.
6. Involve defensive players.

The first four steps probably are best done in specific drill situations, but the last two stages eventually can be made part of regular fielding or batting practice—if the coach has enough adult assistance. Finally, the coach must recognize that the athletes will often need to see the skill performed correctly, and they will need feedback about their own performances. The coach should be prepared to demonstrate the skill, or have someone available who can do it.

Video also can play a role both in showing the players the proper technique and in letting them see themselves in action.

Consider how this might be applied to running through first base. Have the players begin on the third base side of home plate and run as hard as possible for first. They should concentrate on touching the outside front edge of the base while going well toward the outfield grass. Another useful technique involves placing a second target well beyond first base and asking the players to touch both. Once everyone can run through first this way, the athletes grip a bat, take a stance and swing at an imaginary pitch; they then drop the bat and use the proper footwork to start for first. The players go as slowly as necessary to perform the correct motions, then increase the speed until they really sprint for first.

The coach next asks the players to turn their heads and find the play after having taken several steps out of the batter's box. The coach rolls balls at various infield positions to make this more realistic. The runners then work on looking to their right after crossing first. In this case, the coach throws balls past the base to simulate game conditions; this naturally leads to the players making the turn and going to second. Next, the coach throws balls into the outfield as the players run to first. They find the ball, follow the correct curved path around first and go for second. At some point, a coach is positioned at first base, and the players respond to instructions. Finally, defensive players are placed in the field, and the runners react to the developing play.

Obviously, the athletes have learned to run through first, but they also have practiced each individual element of the skill in a variety of settings. Having learned to react to these options, they will be much more likely to perform correctly in games. The same sort of progression can be followed with taking extra bases, leading off, stealing or sliding. After reducing each of these complex tasks to its simplest bits and ordering them all logically, the coach can have the players practice each part in turn. This combines with many repetitions to develop and reinforce the proper techniques.

The exact order for teaching base running skills will differ with each local situation, including any special base running rules in use. However, sliding normally should be practiced relatively early in the season. Following the outlined approach, a sequence for teaching this skill might go something like this.

1. *The players should first learn to fall.* Begin by having the players work on the bent-leg slide. They should start in an upright position and fall by simply tucking one ankle behind the opposite knee, throwing their arms back, and landing on the bent leg's calf, thigh and hip. Some athletes will feel quite comfortable doing this, and they may even have settled on a takeoff leg. These people should not necessarily be asked to change, but if they show no preference or if they are just beginning to slide, the players should try to takeoff with the left leg. (See Appendix A, "Finding Your Sliding Leg.") The left-leg takeoff presents some real advantages in the pop-up slide or when the athlete needs to advance more than one base. As young baseball players spend the first years of their lives learning to stand and move without falling, some may be reluctant to fall to start the slide. These athletes will benefit from practicing sliding with an adult on either side supporting them as they go down (see Figure 7-39).

2. *The players progress to walking a few steps, tucking one ankle behind the opposite knee, throwing their arms back, and falling.* This should be done on a relatively soft surface such as gymnastic mats. Some sliders may still express fear, and the coaches again can help them by partially supporting their weight as they walk through the drill. Next comes running and sliding across a slippery material at a loose base. The players should be given specific instructions, such as: "Run four steps, take off and slide." This causes them to concentrate on the run up and takeoff, so they are less likely to worry about hurting themselves when falling. It is also useful to mark a take-off point for the players.

    Note: Two possible slide-practice materials are (1) a very large piece of cardboard and (2) a large plastic tarp sprayed with silicone water repellent. Either is slippery enough to allow the players to easily slide some distance. These aids can be used in the

Figure 7-39. Coaches supporting a player just learning how to slide.

outfield grass with teammates sitting on the corners. The loose base should be a rubber throw-down or a base cut from an old automobile floor mat or carpet. Do not use a real base, unless an old strap-held one is available and make sure the stakes have been removed.

3. *After these steps have been mastered, the athletes move to the infield and begin sliding at real bases.* Again they begin practicing at shorter distances and slower speeds and gradually work up to sprinting from one base to the next. At this point, the crossover step can be introduced as the runners begin in a lead off position and imagine themselves stealing second. The coach, or a pitcher, can be throwing from the mound to help the players gauge their leads and practice timing the break for second. Eventually, a defender is added at first and pickoff moves come into play.

4. *As soon as one of the base runners dives back to first, the coach begins the above progression over with the head-first slide.* (Consider the previously mentioned warning relating to sliding head first.) However, if everyone comfortably expects to slide and not hurt themselves, they should master the head-first slide relatively quickly.

Once the players successfully perform a head-first slide on the infield, they can resume working in simulated game conditions.

5. *The next step involves sliding while a play is being made.* A middle infielder covers second, and the runners practice sliding into the base. The fade away slide can be worked in fairly easily; in fact, some athletes will probably discover it for themselves. Because the fade away slide is merely a variation of the basic bent-leg slide, the fade away likely can be learned from little more than a brief description and perhaps a demonstration.

6. *Once players have mastered the basic slides, the coach can introduce the pop-up slide.* At some point sliding has to be done during fielding or batting practice, and almost certainly situations will arise in which the pop-up slide is appropriate. Because the pop-up slide involves some new techniques (pushing down with the lower leg while throwing the arms forward and down), the pop-up slide requires the coach and players to return to the beginning sequence:

   a. The athletes walk through the mechanics of the slide.
   b. They do it following a short run up on a soft, slippery surface.
   c. They perform the slide on the infield with a short run up and no other play happening.
   d. They gradually increase the speed and length of the run up.
   e. They attempt the pop-up after a full sprint from first.
   f. They pop up at second and continue to third.
   g. They use the slide in game-like situations.

If the players have mastered everything leading up to this point, the pop-up slide can be learned rapidly.

However, the athletes will progress through each of these activities at different rates. Do not expect them to all attain the same skill level, simultaneously. Similarly, individual players will learn some skills faster than others. The coach must allow for such variations and should not expect players to progress from one skill to the next until each has been mastered in turn.

CONCLUSION

Notice that by focusing on just two points, running hard through first and sliding, essentially every base running skill has been developed. Somewhere in one or the other sequence, everything was covered: getting to first, rounding the base, leading off, stealing, sliding and advancing more than one base. The unsettling thing for the beginning coach is the obvious amount of time involved in teaching the skills this way. Unfortunately, there is no short cut; it is important that each athlete progress as far as possible through the sequence. The players' safety demands it and playing the game properly requires it. Good initial instruction will save time later on, and both seasonal and daily plans are essential. But both coach and athletes must be willing to spend the necessary time if the players are to become good, safe base runners.

ADDITIONAL READING

McDougald, G. & McMane, F. (1977). *Baseball: The Sports Playbook.* Garden City, NY: Doubleday.

8
Defensive Strategies

Michael A. Clark, Ph.D.

QUESTIONS TO CONSIDER

- What should be the basic defensive goal for most youth baseball coaches?
- What defensive plays should be practiced most?
- Why should essentially all outfield throws be directed at second base?
- How should run down plays be initiated, implemented and concluded?
- What positions should each player assume in backup, relay, and cutoff situations?
- How can the defense deal with opponents on base at first and third?
- What is the role of signs in defensive baseball?

INTRODUCTION

As players progress through the various levels of youth baseball, defensive play becomes more sophisticated. But even in Major League Baseball, the goal remains the same: allow opponents the minimum number of outs by avoiding errors and making all the routine plays. This chapter contains observations about general defensive guidelines, suggestions for strategies to follow, descriptions of typical game situations, and comments on defensive signaling. A variety of diagrams are included to show how to set up for particular plays. References are made to previous chapters on defensive play and to the drills included in the appendix. From among these possibilities, the coach will have to choose those appropriate to the particular level of play and players' experience; similarly, the coach must plan some sort of logical sequence for working through the drills and situations.

ELEVEN GENERAL DEFENSIVE GUIDELINES

1. **Involve every ball player in every play of each game.** Although this is difficult to accomplish at the lower levels of baseball, it is possibly the most important single element in successful team defense. This presents the coach with some real challenges. How to get the athletes on the field to concentrate, and how to involve the players on the bench. Involving all the players in defense is more easily accomplished in games if they have been made part of every defensive drill and practice session. As soon as players begin to take different positions on the field, they should start trying to work as a unit. Consequently, each player in each position should know how to field and throw the ball, how and when to cover bases, how to back up plays and where to

go for relays and cutoffs. All of these moves should be practiced until they become automatic.

By literally learning to cover all the bases, a defensive team can hold opponents to the minimum number of bases. Knowing where teammates will be gives the player making a relay throw an advantage. An athlete develops a sense of "team" by being but one person in a play that might require the involvement of four or more others. Both the players on the field and those on the bench are forced to concentrate on the game if they are expected to know the number of outs, the batter's count, and possible defensive plays. In the initial stages of learning, this information and the potential strategies that emanate require a great deal of time, but the effort will be rewarded. Besides making the team better defensively, practicing these elements makes everyone feel a part of the team. Finally, there will be fewer discipline and motivation problems if every player feels a part of every play.

2. **Get the 3 outs as soon as possible by minimizing errors and concentrating on correctly making the "routine" plays.** It takes just three outs to complete a defensive inning and 21 or less for a typical youth league game.

Teams should spend the most time on the simplest plays: fielding ground balls and throwing to first and catching fly balls. These routine plays win games. Gimmick plays seldom work, and incredible catches are rare. At the lower levels it is almost impossible to turn the double play in the classic sense. Practice with the middle infielders on taking the toss at second and making the throw to first in practice, but do not expect to get more than the lead runner. Have the shortstop going into the hole behind third attempt a play at third—especially if a force out there is possible. Ask the person covering first to come off the base and check for runners trying to advance. Get infielders into the habit of looking for tag plays or the possibility of doubling someone off after a caught line drive. Practice relays and cutoffs. But expect most outs to come on forces at first

and caught fly balls. These plays are called "routine" because they happen all the time at every level and produce the majority of outs.

3. **As the players gain experience and confidence, have them expect to complete the more complex plays.**

4. **With two outs, have infielders either touch a base for an unassisted force out, or make the throw to first.**

5. **If it is late in the game and the winning run is at third with less than two outs, have both the infield and outfield in for a possible play at the plate.** Infielders can be about even with the base lines, and outfielders should come in about halfway.

6. **In other situations, bring the infield in only if allowing another run critically affects the game.** There are so many scoring opportunities in youth baseball games that the coach must carefully consider whether having the infield play in presents a real advantage. Cutting down the distance between these defenders and the hitter may make a play at the plate easier, but it also makes it much simpler for the batter to drive the ball through the infield. And the defensive team may have scoring chances left.

7. **Have the outfielders generally direct all throws to second base to keep the runners split or hold the runner at first.** This increases the likelihood of getting a force out at second base, turning a double play, or keeping a runner out of scoring position.

8. **Expect the shortstop to cover second base on everything hit up the middle or to the right side.** The pitcher and middle infielders must communicate about the base coverage every time a runner is at first with less than two outs. The pitcher must know who will be taking the throw at second if a double play is to be attempted.

9. **In steal situations, send the shortstop to second unless the batter is a right-handed hitter known to pull the ball.** The shortstop has a better angle on the throw as throws from the catcher will tend to move to the third base side of second. However, if the batter is a right-handed pull hitter or if the pitcher throws a lot of off-speed

pitches, the player at second base should cover the bag.

10. **Have the pitcher back up all throws from the outfield.**

11. **Keep track of where each opponent hits the ball and note the use of any specific offensive plays.** At higher levels of play, this record kept by the coach, another adult, or a player should help the coach position the defense and keep the team from being caught off guard.

STRATEGIES FOR SPECIFIC SITUATIONS

Beside these general guidelines, there are a series of strategies that every baseball coach and player should expect to use when on defense. Knowledge of these basic defensive strategies is also useful when confronted with them on offense. Since they apply to situations that arise all the time, these tactics can be seen at nearly every level of play. The strategies focus on seven areas:

- pitching
- cutoffs
- relays
- rundowns
- first and third situations and related double steals
- pickoffs
- bunts

Each of these will be discussed in the following sections. However, the coach will again have to decide which particular elements are essential, because the developmental level of the players or rules modifications may make some of them inappropriate.

As with any other part of the game, these strategies will have to be practiced. While working with the athletes on the physical skills involved, the coach also should expect to help them realize the reasoning behind the plays. It is not enough for the players to know *what* to do, they must also realize *why* something needs doing. Only in this way will they come to recognize the importance of moving to a certain spot or making a particular throw. Once young baseball players begin to understand these strat-

egies, they will begin to develop an appreciation of the game.

Pitching

Once pitchers have mastered the mechanics of their position, the coach and athletes can begin working on the essential strategies for dealing with batters in game situations. Again, the players' skill level must be considered, but the following are generally useful.

1. *Begin with a positive attitude.*

The pitcher takes the mound having confidence in one particular pitch and feeling capable of throwing it for a strike on the first delivery. After completing the warm-up throws and being directed by the umpire to begin, the athlete's procedure should go like this:

a. Assume the pitcher's position.
b. Concentrate on the catcher's target.
c. Take a deep breath to fully relax.
d. Visualize a strike.
e. Throw the pitch with confidence.

In short, the pitcher begins focused on the first hitter, the first pitch. If this attitude persists, the player will be successful consistently.

2. *Make the opening pitch a good strike.*

The lead-off hitter is at least as nervous as the pitcher at the start; therefore, the batter likely either will not swing or swing poorly at the first pitch. Thus, a good strike—not so good as to be easily hit, but not too "fine" either— will get the pitcher "ahead in the count." On succeeding pitches, the batter will be a bit more defensive and the umpire will have become accustomed to seeing the pitcher throw strikes.

3. *Keep the ball low in the strike zone.*

Pitchers will be more successful because low pitches result in more ground balls and fewer line drives or fly balls. Batters have a difficult time fully extending the arms on these pitches and seldom drive them with great velocity. However, the catcher's job is made more difficult, as more pitches may be in the dirt.

4. *Work the edges of the strike zone.*

Stay away from the middle of the plate unless the count is 3-0 (three balls and no strikes) and the opponents are known to take pitches. Older pitchers should begin trying to throw strikes in particular spots—especially the inside and outside corners near knee height. They should practice throwing to these spots while warming up.

5. *Change speeds.*

As soon as possible, young athletes should learn this skill. Keeping batters off-balance is the key to success in pitching, and nothing accomplishes this quite like the pitcher's having control of at least two pitches with different speeds—a fastball and change-up are adequate to the task.

Changing the pitch speed is usually most effective if pitchers are ahead in the count, but other considerations include:

- the hitter—free swingers are especially vulnerable to off-speed pitches
- hitter's position in the batting order—hitters further down tend to wait for slower pitches
- base runners—change-ups handicap the catcher in steal situations
- the batter's attitude—if the batter is frustrated, change speeds and keep the hitter guessing.

6. *Avoid falling into a pitching pattern.*

Once able to change speeds, pitchers must vary their patterns. For example, many young players get into the habit of throwing change-ups whenever the batter gets two quick strikes, or they may always throw a fastball on the first pitch. Varying the pattern keeps the hitter off-balance.

7. *Make each delivery look the same to avoid tipping off the pitches.*

Good opponents will watch for indicators that might reveal whether a fastball, curve or change-up is being thrown. Using the same delivery for all pitches counteracts the tendency to "telegraph" the pitch to be thrown.

8. *When well ahead in the count, 0-2 or 1-2, make the next pitch a "borderline" one.*

These pitches around the margins of the strike zone are sometimes referred to as "waste pitches." However, no pitch should be considered wasted by either coach or players. Rather,

pitchers should attempt to throw these pitches just close enough to the plate that they might be called a strike. Such pitches are likely on—or just off—the corners of the plate. The goal is to tempt the batter into swinging at something that cannot be hit well.

9. *When attempting to throw the ball up in the strike zone, keep the ball well up—even to the point of being out of the strike zone—and make it a fastball.*

Many hitters find high pitches attractive; they see them better and expect to hit them better. In many instances this is true, if the pitch is from waist to chest height. However, if the delivery is shoulder high or above, then the pitch likely will be missed or popped-up. This applies to fastballs; high breaking balls tend to be very easy to hit well—avoid them.

10. *Quickly adapt to the umpire's strike zone and make good pitches at its edges.*

In each game, pitchers must contend with three strike zones: the one described in the rule book, the one the umpire is calling, and the one in which the pitcher can safely throw strikes. These may, or may not, be the same; and every player who wants to pitch must learn to deal with this bit of uncertainty. Since the strike zone defines which pitches the batter should try to hit, good pitchers are those who quickly identify and adapt to the umpire's strike zone.

11. *Study hitters to find their strengths and weaknesses.*

Until a batter's abilities are known, it is usually best to pitch low and away and change speeds. However, once known, the hitter's strengths and weaknesses can be turned to advantage. Pitchers should throw at the weak spots while exploiting the strengths by throwing pitches that are almost—but not quite—there.

12. *Pitch for outs, not strike outs.*

Even at the lowest levels of play, pitchers seldom win games by consistently striking out the opponents. Rather, games are won by pitchers who can move the ball around in the strike zone, change speeds well, and keep the defense involved in the game.

These pitching strategies do not guarantee success, nor can they all be applied at the beginning levels of the game. After individually evaluating each team, player and situation, the coach must decide which tactics are appropriate and work on them accordingly. Moreover, the coach also must have in mind some sequence for teaching them.

Cutoffs

Cutoff plays are designed to deal with very specific situations:

- balls hit into the outfield with a runner in scoring position
- a trailing runner who may attempt to advance beyond first base

When the ball is hit to center or right field, the defender at first moves into cutoff position; when the ball goes to left field, the player at third base assumes the cutoff responsibility. In either case, the player generally assumes a position even with the mound and on a line between the fielder making the play and the plate (see Figure 8-1 a and b). However, this is only an approximation as the person in cutoff position will have to make allowances for the strength of the outfielder's arm and so may have to be from 40 to 70 or more feet from the plate. Also, note how each base is covered—no matter who is in cutoff position.

Note: When assuming the cutoff position, the player may choose to stand on the mound. This helps the player avoid either tripping over the mound or having to play bad hops off it.

Outfielders should use the cutoff person as the target. Thus, their goal is to throw the ball all the way to the cutoff and to have it get there at chest height. As the ball approaches the cutoff position, the defender considers the throw; if it is well off line or likely to bounce several times, the player immediately intercepts it. Otherwise, the cutoff person waits for the catcher's decision. If there is a chance to get the runner at home, the catcher simply says nothing, and the ball is allowed through to the plate. However, if the throw will arrive too late to get the runner or is off line, the catcher shouts "Cut!" and the cutoff person catches it. In this case, the person in cutoff position should look for a possible play on the trailing base runner, although the catcher may help by calling out

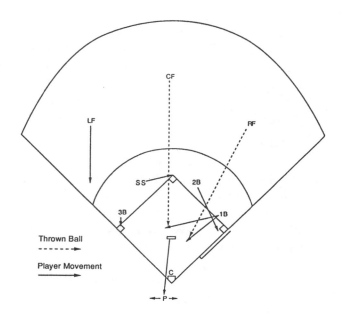

Figure 8-1a. Ball hit to right field or center field, first base cutoff position.

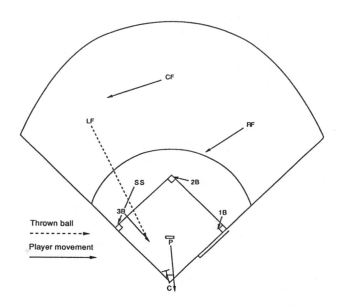

Figure 8-1b. Ball hit to left field; third base cutoff position.

the location of a possible play, as in "Cut . . . Two!" As examples of how these plays might develop, consider the following:

1. Cutoff play splits the base runners.

With less than two outs, runners are at first and second when the batter grounds the ball up the middle and into center. The center fielder charges the ball as the lead runner continues past third in an effort to score. Anticipating a play at the plate, the pitcher sprints into backup position there as the defender from first base takes up a cutoff position on the mound. Sensing the outfielder's throw will not beat the runner to the plate, the catcher shouts out "Cut!" The player in cutoff position takes the throw and turns to check the batter/runner who has rounded first. Because the defender from second has moved over to cover first, the opponent returns to first as the other base runner holds at third. The runners have been "split." The batter/runner has not been allowed to advance beyond first. One less person is in scoring position, and there remains a double play opportunity. Even better, if the batter/ runner had gone too far around first, an out may have resulted.

2. Cutoff play tags the batter/runner.

Again, there are less than two outs and a runner at second; the batter singles to left field. The runner rounds third and attempts to score; seeing this, the defender at third base moves into cutoff position. After retrieving the ball, the left fielder makes a throw to the plate. The catcher realizes the throw is coming in off line and immediately checks the batter/runner's actions. Seeing that opponent turning for second, the catcher shouts, "Cut!" and the cutoff person catches the ball. The middle infielder covering second takes the throw from the cutoff and tags the sliding opponent. In this case the cutoff play resulted in an out, but even if it had not, the fact that the defense made the play well might cause future runners to hold at first.

Key Elements:

- Once the ball is in the outfield and there is the chance of a play at home, the appropriate defender quickly moves into cutoff position. (Plays in center or right find the player from first in position; balls in left field cause the player from third to take the cutoff.)
- The cutoff position is on line with the throw and 40 to 70 feet from home plate. (On plays to straight away center, the cutoff player may be on the mound.)
- Outfielders aim their throws at the cutoff person's chest.
- A throw already bouncing or off line is immediately cutoff.

- The catcher shouts "Cut!" if the throw will be too late, and the cutoff person looks for a possible play on the base runners.

Common Errors:

- The cutoff person is not on line between the outfielder and home plate.
- The cutoff person takes a position too close to the plate. This not only blocks the catcher's view of the play, it also gives the cutoff player little opportunity to make a play on the trailing base runners.
- The cutoff person assumes a position too far from home. This forces the catcher to make the decision to cut the ball too early in the play; few runners will be gotten out at home in this situation.
- The outfielder's throw is too high for the cutoff player to handle.
- The catcher hesitates in making the decision to have the ball cut off and so fails to give the cutoff player adequate time to make the play.

Relays

Relays are intended to get a ball played into the outfield back to the infield as quickly as possible. The idea is that two short throws can be accomplished quicker and more accurately than a single long one. This in turn gives the defense a better chance of stopping any base runners.

These plays get their name from an infielder moving toward an outfield play, taking a throw from the outfielder, and "relaying" the ball on to another infielder covering a base (most often second base). Relays are much like cutoffs in that the player assumes a position on line between the outfielder and a possible play on an opposing base runner; in fact, the play is sometimes called a "double cutoff." However, relays involve more players than does the cutoff and so require better communication among teammates. The coach must keep this in mind: adequate practice time must be given to relays because essentially the entire team is involved in them and beginning players generally do not talk enough to make relays successful.

A typical relay begins with a well-hit ball going to the side of an outfielder. The defender nearest the ball retrieves it and prepares to throw; any other outfielder coming into the area provides backup coverage and tells the player where to throw. The outfielder aims the throw at the relay person's glove-side shoulder.

Meanwhile, one of the middle infielders runs well into the outfield, holds both arms above the head, and calls "Relay!" (How far into the outfield is determined by the strength of the outfielder's arm, the beginning location of the throw and the final target of the relay.) While waiting for the throw, the relay person steps toward the outfielder with the throwing-side leg. By making this move and planting the foot perpendicular to the path of the expected throw, the player turns the body a bit to the in-field and essentially starts the pivot to throw. The athlete then catches the ball near shoulder height, completes the pivot, and throws as di-rected.

If the ball is particularly well hit or if the outfielder making the throw has a strong or er-ratic arm, the other middle infielder trails the play into the outfield and assumes a backup po-sition. Otherwise, this athlete covers second base by straddling the bag open to the relay. In either case, the infielder checks the base run-ners and decides what play should be made. By calling out "Home!" "Two!" or "No play!" the player communicates this decision, and the re-lay person takes appropriate action.

In most cases, the player at second base moves into relay position if the ball is hit to right center field or around to the right side. The shortstop moves out on everything to the left (see Figures 8-2 a and b). However, if one of these athletes—usually the shortstop—has a significantly better arm, then that person should take the relay position whenever time allows.

Many of these options are illustrated at the conclusion of this chapter among the dia-grams of typical defensive situations. The coach should study these and see how they relate to the various drills suggested in Appendix A. Again, cutoffs and relays need be practiced as a *team*, with each person learning to communicate or listen as needed.

Key Elements:

- Outfielders must learn to field the ball while listening for the infielder's call of "Relay!"

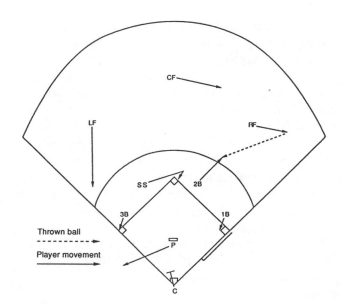

Figure 8-2a. Relay of ball hit to right field.

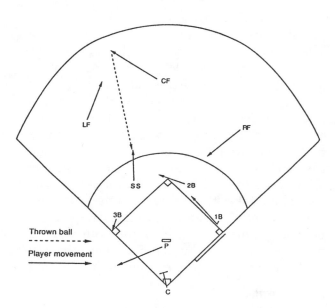

Figure 8-2b. Relay of ball hit to center or left field.

Outfielders also assist one another by com-municating where the relay person is located.

- The person in relay position must know the strength and accuracy of each outfielder's arm.
- Outfielders aim their throws at the relay per-son's glove-side shoulder.
- The relay person positions the body in good throwing position even while waiting to make the catch.

- The player in relay position listens for the other middle infielder to indicate if and where to throw. If there is any confusion or doubt, the relay person should turn to the infield, scan the play, and make the decision.

Common Errors:

- The outfielder tries to locate the relay person before picking up the ball. More often than not, the outfielder will bobble the ball and extra bases will be available to the opponents. The player must look the ball into the glove on every play.
- The outfielder tries to pick up the ball with just the glove while still running. The results are similar to the above.
- The outfielder's throw is too high for the relay player to handle.
- The relay person assumes a position too far out or not far enough out. Ideally the two throws should be nearly equal in length.
- The person in relay position turns to make the throw before catching the ball.
- The players involved talk either too much or too little.

Rundowns

Rundowns, sometimes called "pickles," involve a runner caught between bases and at least two, but preferably four or more, defensive players. As with so much of defensive baseball, the whole team may become involved in such plays, especially if more than one runner is on base.

A rundown sometimes starts with a defender realizing that an offensive player has gone too far around a base. In this case, the defender begins the rundown by sprinting directly at the base runner; sometimes the defensive player may find that the runner freezes and so can be tagged out. However, it is more likely that the opponent will take off for one base or another; because ideally the runner is gotten out or at least kept from advancing a base, the defender immediately gets the ball to a teammate covering the base ahead of the runner. Figure 8-3 a, shows a diagram of a typical rundown play involving a runner caught between first and second.

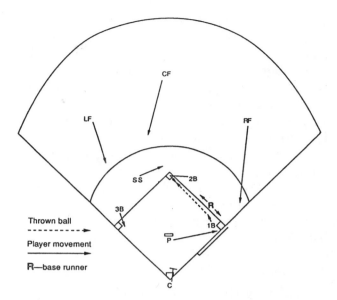

Figure 8-3a. Player positions at beginning of run down between first and second bases. (Runner picked off first base, commonly.)

1. The Chaser

This player begins to chase the runner back to the base last touched. In making this move, the "chaser" sprints hard at the runner while holding the ball high in throwing position. Fake throws are to be avoided, as they may distract a teammate or cause the ball to come loose; if either occurs, the runner has a better chance of escaping the rundown.

2. The Tagger

The defender covering the base—the "tagger"—takes position in front of the bag and a bit to one side of the immediate baseline. This gives the chaser a good target and the tagger a better view of the throw. In fact both the chaser and tagger should be on the same side of the runner, because this decreases the chance of a throw hitting the offensive player and allowing them to reach base safely. Further, if the defenders move to the infield side of the play, any ball that does get away likely will be tracked down more quickly and so minimize the damage.

3. The Rundown Play

The chaser drives the runner back toward the base, and the tagger may move to cut down the distance between the two. When the offensive player is 10 to 12 feet away and moving at full speed, the tagger breaks toward the runner. This is the signal for the chaser to get the ball to the tagger; the throw should be quick, chest-height, and a bit to the glove side. (The tagger may also shout "Now!" or the chaser simply may throw as soon as the runner turns the back to sprint for the base.) The runner, moving so quickly, is unlikely to be able to change directions and elude the tag, and the ideal rundown play results: one throw, one out. However, if the runner does manage to reverse direction, the tagger becomes a chaser, and the backup players get involved.

4. The Backups

As the play develops, defenders move into backup positions at each base involved. Initially the backup position is well behind the base, for the players concerned must have time to react to the ball; however, as the play develops, the backup people can move to and then beyond the base. This gives the chaser, formerly the tagger, someone to throw the ball to at the base ahead of the runner. As before, the ball should be gotten in front as quickly as possible. The sequence of chase-throw-tag repeats until the play ends with an out—or the offensive player finds a base.

After giving up the ball each chaser follows the throw and moves into the backup position at the base toward which they are moving (see Figure 8-3 b). However, these people, and any other defenders without the ball, must move well to the outside of the play. This allows them to avoid obstructing the runner.

Any additional base runners present a final complicating factor. In such a case, one of the defensive players must assume responsibility for watching the other runners and communicating their actions. Most probably this should be the pitcher.

Key Elements:

- A chaser, a tagger and at least two backup players are involved.
- As quickly as possible, the ball moves ahead of the runner. This drives the opponent back to the bag last touched.
- The chaser sprints at the base runner while

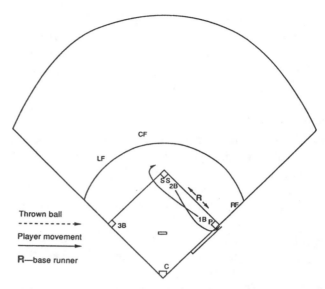

Figure 8-3b. Continuation of run down play with chasers moving into backup positions.

holding the ball high, in good throwing position.
- The chaser and tagger move to the inside of the base line.
- The chaser's throw is quick, chest-high and a bit on the glove side; it is made when the runner turns the back, when the tagger breaks toward the runner, or when the tagger calls, "Now!"
- The throw is a snap or "short arm" style throw, not a hard one.
- After throwing, the chaser follows the throw and takes a backup position at the proper base.
- If failing to complete the play within a step or two, the tagger gets the ball to the backup person who has stepped forward to cover the base ahead of the runner.
- Someone, preferably the pitcher, is responsible for watching any additional base runners.

Common Errors:

- The ball does not move out in front of the runner, or the runner is chased forward around the bases.
- The defenders do not run at full speed, thus the runner has time to change directions when the throws are made.
- The chaser and tagger do not get off to one side of the play; this allows the runner to get

directly between them and interfere with the throw.

- The tagger gets the ball at or behind the base.
- The chaser fails to move into backup position after making the throw.
- Backups are too close to the play.

First and Third Situations/Double Steals

A troublesome, yet very common, situation in youth baseball finds runners at first and third. This puts tremendous pressure on the defense, and how they respond may determine the outcome of the game. What makes this particular circumstance so difficult are the length of the throws involved, the possibility of two runners moving at the same time, and the number of possible options. Watchfulness and communication are essential to the defense's dealing successfully with this challenge.

The defenders on the mound, behind the plate, and covering second base have key roles in stopping the offense.

- In the set position, the pitcher must listen for a middle infielder calling "Step off!"
- The catcher has to constantly check both runners.
- The player covering second must be ready to throw home even as preparing to make a tag or start a rundown.

These actions represent the essentials of dealing with the two most common offensive strategies used in first and third situations: starting one runner and having the other delay or sending both runners simultaneously. Considering all the possibilities, there are six different defensive plays that can be used in the first-third situation.

Play 1.

As the pitcher is in the set position and using the various tricks to hold the runners close, one of the middle infielders—preferably the one at second base—is watching the runner at first. If that player makes any sort of move to second, the infielder calls out, "Step off!" and the pitcher immediately moves the push off foot back and away from the rubber. Turning to locate the runner, the pitcher decides whether to throw. Meanwhile, the defender at second—presenting

a good target to the pitcher by holding the glove chest-high—runs on a line toward the pitcher until reaching the baseline. The pitcher may then throw to the infielder, who may then tag the runner coming down the line from first. However, it is more likely that the infielder will have to throw home, because the lead runner should break from third on the pitcher's throw. The defender at third watches the runner in order to communicate any motion; the catcher steps to the front of the plate to prepare for the tag play.

Play 2.

The pitcher holds the runners close and delivers to the plate. The runner starts from first, and the catcher throws through to second. The usual steal coverage occurs, and the middle infielder taking the throw must not only prepare to make the tag but to check the runner leading off third. If the player on third heads home with the catcher's release, the middle infielder steps in front of second base and makes a return throw to the catcher without attempting to tag the runner advancing from first base (see Figure 8-4).

Play 3.

A second possibility is much like the previous situation, but both runners break simul-

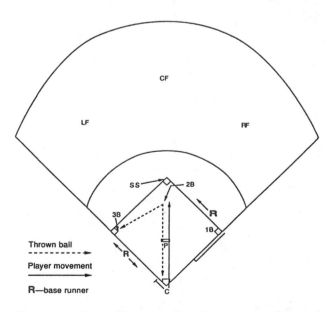

Figure 8-4. Second base cutoff with runners on first and third.

taneously. The defender covering second must see this happening and cut well in front of the bag as soon as possible. This not only gets the ball under control sooner, it also gives the middle infielder a much shorter and quicker throw back to the catcher.

Play 4.

Another option has the catcher seemingly throwing through as the runner breaks from first, but the pitcher rather than second base is the target. (The catcher must sell the play by making the throw look exactly like one to second base.) The pitcher cuts off the ball and immediately checks the runner at third. If that player is headed home, the pitcher throws back to the catcher. If the runner is "hung up" halfway home, the pitcher runs directly toward the opponent to force a decision about which way to go. The pitcher then can easily throw the ball to either base. If the runner at third picks up the play and is going back, the pitcher throws to third base. If the lead runner is not moving, the pitcher spins and *fakes* a throw toward second in an effort to cause some movement. If throwing to a base in any of these situations, the pitcher continues to that base to cover it in case of a possible rundown; however, once a position player arrives, the pitcher should give up the base and move into backup position. For the coverage by the other players, see Figure 8-5.

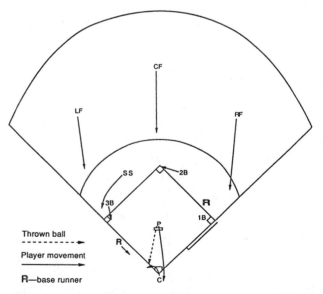

Thrown ball - - - - - - →
Player movement ———→
R—base runner

Figure 8-5. Coverages with runners on first and third and double steal being attempted.

Note: Fake throws have to look as much as possible like real ones. If wanting players to use plays involving fake throws, the coach must allow time in practice for working on them. Too many young players tend to make fakes by simply holding the ball in plain view and waving it in the direction of the throw. Instead, they must learn to use both the arm and body to "sell" the fake. Fake catches are like fake throws. They must look realistic, and to accomplish this, they have to be practiced.

Play 5.

This play is a logical follow-up to the previous one, as the catcher *fakes* the throw and the pitcher *fakes* cutting off the throw. If the lead runner stays put, the catcher quickly checks the opponent at first. That runner may have been going and will now be caught partway between bases; in that case, the catcher runs directly toward second and throws to the infielder covering the base. If the lead runner breaks for home with the fake, the catcher immediately begins the rundown from the chase position. Finally, if the runner at third simply strays off a bit too far and is slow getting back, the catcher makes a throw on the inside of the base to the defender at third. Generally, the base coverage is similar to those shown in Figure 8-4; however, the pitcher covers home if the catcher makes the play at second, and the player at first base must cover home or first—whichever base is part of a rundown.

Play 6.

As before, the pitcher holds the runners close, delivers the pitch, and *fakes* taking the catcher's throw. However, the catcher simply looks the runner back to third and throws through to second only if the runner at third remains there. If the lead runner does move home, the catcher fakes the throw and initiates the rundown. The coverage for the remaining defenders is a bit different. As before, the player at first has to be prepared for a rundown at either first or home. However, the person at second moves 8 to 10 feet in front of the base and on line with the catcher's possible throw; from this position, the defender can either cut off a throw and return the ball home if the lead runner breaks, or let the ball go through to the bag if the runner stays. The shortstop covers second base, but in the eventuality of a run-down, the player should be ready to move wherever needed. The defender at third breaks to the inside corner of the bag and communicates any movement by the lead runner. Outfielders back up the base in front of them.

Just reading over these six plays should convince the coach of the need to practice them often. They are complex, and each involves several options. They require a great deal of communication, and essentially every player gets involved in each one. For all these reasons, the coach cannot expect the players to be able to use all six plays until they have a good deal of experience. Rather, the plays should be put in gradually—quite probably in the outlined sequence—so that the team has the opportunity to master one before having to learn another.

Pickoffs

Pickoff plays usually involve the pitcher's effort to get out runners who have stretched their lead a bit too far off first base. This basic play was covered in Chapter 5, Pitching, but a pitcher should also be aware of some strategies to use in other situations.

With a base runner on at second, the pitcher has three options.

Option 1.

The pitcher holds the runner close with a series of looks as the shortstop bluffs a move toward second. If seeing "daylight" between the shortstop and the runner—in other words, if the shortstop gets a step closer to the base— the pitcher turns and throws to second.

Option 2.

The catcher gives a sign to the pitcher and shortstop which begins a "count" play. Once the pitcher comes set, both defenders silently count, "One thousand one . . . one thousand two . . . one thousand three." On three, the shortstop sprints to the bag and the pitcher turns to throw.

Option 3.

The last option is similar, except the catcher's sign tells the pitcher to turn and throw immediately after coming set.

With a single runner at third, the coach may decide to have the pitcher work from the set position and so hold the opponent close. If the pitcher chooses to throw to the base, the initial move must be a step back off the rubber, and the pitcher may "short arm" the ball to the bag. This is the basic pickoff move to third, but of more use may well be a set play for first and third situations:

1. The pitcher checks the runners, pauses and steps back.
2. The pitcher fakes the throw to third.
3. The pitcher extends the follow-through to spin around and check the opponent at first.

Not only the pitcher but also the catcher should be prepared to attempt pickoffs of runners. The catcher watches for opponents who have gone too far off base or who are slow in getting back. If seeing a runner on first base guilty of either one, the catcher gives a sign to the defenders at first and in right field to alert them that a throw will be coming on the next pitch. Immediately upon receiving the delivery, the catcher makes a jump pivot and attempts to pickoff the runner. Although a similar play can be tried at second base, it is much more difficult to get the runner there. At third, a sign generally is not used; the catcher simply throws to the defender covering the inside of the base.

Bunts

Bunt plays, like many of the other plays discussed, involve the entire defense. Three different situations must be considered.

1. Runner on First.

With an opponent at first, the defense should look to force out the runner going to second while being certain to get the batter going to first. The catcher attempts to field all bunts within reach and otherwise calls the play before moving to cover third. The pitcher charges from the mound, and the defenders at first and third move in to cover the areas between the baseline and the mound. The shortstop takes second base, and the player at second moves over to take the throw at first. The outfielders move in to back up the bases in front of them.

2. Runners at First and Second.

A bunt coming with opposing players at first and second again presents the defense with the choice of trying to force the lead runner or settling for an out at first. The additional runner forces the defense to cover third, and there are two different ways to accomplish this. If the player from third charges to field the bunt, the shortstop sprints to cover the base. Otherwise the defender at third stays back, and the pitcher has to cover more territory. In either case, the catcher covers any bunts within reach or directs the defense as needed. The players at first and second and in the outfield cover as in the previous play.

The coach should decide ahead of time which player will take third base. The considerations involved are the fielding ability of the pitcher, the range of the defender at third, and the speed of the shortstop. Currently, most teams cover with the shortstop, whenever possible. However, offensive teams may try to take advantage of this rotation with the swinging bunt.

3. Runner at Third.

A runner at third with less than two outs involves the possibility of a "squeeze play," which has the batter bunting the ball in an effort to bring in a single run. There are two versions of this play:

- the safety squeeze: the runner moves on the bunt
- the suicide: the runner starts with the release of the pitch.

With the exception of the catcher, the defenders cover the play much as they would a bunt coming with a single runner at first. After calling out "Bunt!" upon seeing the play develop, the catcher remains at the plate and the pitcher has much more ground to cover.

If having an opportunity to react to the squeeze play, the pitcher should try to throw a fastball high and outside—no matter on which side the batter is standing. This causes the hitter to reach for the ball, which can result in the batter popping the ball up or hitting it while out of the batter's box. In either case, the squeeze play is nullified.

Finally, two general strategies apply to bunt situations:

1. *Whenever a runner is on base and a bunt seems likely, the pitcher attempts a pickoff.* The batter may react to the pitcher's move and give away the intended bunt by moving the hands on the bat or even squaring around. Noticing this, an observant coach or catcher will signal for the proper coverage.
2. *If a bunt is a strong possibility, then the infielders at first and third play in—at least even with their bases.* This also is an effective means of dealing with a batter known to bunt for hits.

Additional figures showing these and other defensive plays appear in a supplement at the end of the chapter.

SIGNS

Throughout this chapter, the need for communication among coach and players is stressed. In some cases the use of signs is suggested specifically; at other points, options for dealing with particular defensive situations clearly imply the need for signs. Occasionally, verbal cues may be used, but these work only if the people concerned are relatively close together as in cutoff and relay plays. Such spoken signs are best limited to a single word (such as "cut," "now," or "bunt") or short phrases (like "cut . . . two," "no play," or "step off"). Longer oral directions take too much time, are easily misunderstood and may go unheard. Consequently, the majority of baseball signs have traditionally been visual. Further, signs generally involve a sequence of communication—essentially a sign and countersign—between people.

Between Pitcher and Catcher

The catcher and pitcher are the most regular users of signs. Simply put, the catcher must have a sign for each pitch thrown by the pitcher, and the pitcher must have some means of either agreeing with the sign or changing it. To call for particular pitches, the catcher assumes the crouched position, puts the bare hand between the legs, and holds down one or more fingers. (The catcher keeps the legs fairly close together while doing this so the opposing team's base coaches are unable to steal the signs.) At the lower levels of play, the catcher probably would show one finger for a fastball and two for a change-up and the pitcher could accept the sign by either nodding the head or simply beginning the windup. However, if wanting to throw a different pitch, a younger pitcher might shake the head to ask the catcher for another sign.

As everyone involved becomes more skilled, the catcher will need more signs and may wish to indicate the preferred location as well. (For example, one finger shown and pointed in toward the batter would call for a fastball on the inside; three fingers held closer to the right leg would indicate a change-up on the outside.) Similarly, the pitcher may want to be able to respond by changing the pitch; this usually is done with some motion of the gloved hand. (The pitcher might respond to two fingers by brushing the glove once on the leg. This might "add one" so that the catcher's sign becomes three, a change-up; the brushing motion can also be used to subtract one and so turn the sign into one, a fastball. Clearly the players and coach settle on this before the game.)

The catcher also may have to give signs differently whenever a runner is at second. From this position, an opposing player can see the signs as easily as the pitcher, and an intelligent athlete may be able to relay information to the batter about what sort of pitch to expect. The pitcher and catcher can counteract this by agreeing ahead of time on some means of indicating which sign to use out of a sequence. For example, suppose the catcher shows three signs in the following order: one finger (fastball), two fingers (curve), three fingers (change). By touching the chest protector, the catcher indicates that the second sign is "live" and so expects a curve. Or the catcher might adjust the mask to show that the third sign is the correct one, and the pitcher should throw a change-up. Such ploys can be effective in dealing with opponents suspected of stealing signs. However, there clearly is great potential for miscommunication, and all involved—the coach and everyone who pitches or catches—must practice this strategy. Further, whenever the need to switch signs arises, the coach should have the catcher and pitcher talk over the indicators and changes.

Position Players and the Catcher's Signs

At the upper levels of youth baseball, a right-handed hitter will be more likely to hit a good fastball to the right side while pulling breaking balls to the left. A left-handed batter would be expected to do the opposite. Therefore, the middle infielders also should pay attention to the catcher's signs, as knowing the pitch helps them decide how to cover second base in steal situations. Once this decision is made, preferably by the shortstop, it is communicated between the players with another sign: Holding the glove in front of the face, the shortstop signals coverage by opening the mouth ("You") if the defender at second base will be responsible or keeping it closed ("Me") if the shortstop will take the base.

Because it clearly may help the outfielders to know what pitch will be thrown, this information should be communicated to them by one of the middle infielders. By briefly putting the hand behind the back and holding it open or closed to indicate breaking ball or fastball, the infielder relays this information to the outfielders.

Pickoffs

In certain situations, the coach may wish to call for the pitcher to attempt some sort of pickoff play. The most common sign for this has the coach touch the nose ("pickoff") and then some part of the face to indicate the play (usually right cheek for a straight pickoff attempt at first, chin for whichever option is being used at second, and left cheek for the fake throw to third). Although the pitcher should be watching for these signs from the coach, the catcher still should relay them to the pitcher as a precaution. This is done exactly like signaling a pitch: The catcher, in the crouch position, puts the bare hand between the leg and shows a clinched fist with the thumb sticking out. This warns the pitcher that a pickoff play has been called.

If seeing a base runner leading too far off first, the catcher may decide to attempt a pickoff play. However, the player covering first (and the right fielder) should be ready for the throw, so a sign is needed. One way for the catcher to do this is to put the bare hand up to the opposite shoulder. This lets the defenders know that the next delivery will be followed by a throw to first, if the catcher handles the pitch cleanly. If the player at first initiates this play by giving the same sign, the catcher should acknowledge the sign by returning it and so warning the right fielder as well. (Note that this play is used only with a runner at first, so there is no confusion between this sign and the one the catcher uses to change signs when a runner is at second.)

Bunts

When the need arises for the defense to protect against the bunt, it usually is so obvious that everyone knows what is at hand. Therefore, bunt coverage is relatively easy and straightforward to communicate. The catcher simply steps in front of the plate, reminds the infielders of the number of outs, and tells them to expect a bunt. The catcher then calls the coverage, "Bunt 1!", "Bunt 3!" or whichever option is being used. Because the outfielders' backup responsibilities on bunt plays are always the same, the middle infielders merely need to call out "Bunt!" to remind them to cover the bases.

Some Final Thoughts

Giving and receiving signs is as much a part of baseball as throwing or hitting, and like those skills, it must be practiced. A missed sign can result in anything from not getting an out, to giving up a run, to losing a ball game. But most importantly, a missed sign can result in injury. For example, if the shortstop fails to cover second on a pickoff play, the pitcher may turn to throw only to find no one there; and in suddenly trying to stop the throwing motion, the pitcher may strain the arm. Clearly this is not only undesirable, but it could have been avoided if adequate time had been given to practicing the various plays and the signs that go with them.

CONCLUSION

After reading all the preceding material, the youth baseball coach likely will have one of two responses: "The game is so complicated that I'll never be able to teach or coach it," or "I'm going to expect my team to learn every single one of these plays." Neither one is appropriate. Baseball is a simple, enjoyable game; it becomes something else only when adults intend to make it so.

Coaches should keep in mind the ability and experience levels of both their team and the opponents. While one cannot expect beginning players to use any one of three different bunt coverages, a coach should teach older athletes various ways of dealing with defensive situations. Moreover, the team and coach should practice all the plays and related signs before using them in games. Remember the four basics of successful defensive baseball:

1. Get every player involved in every play.
2. Practice the routine plays, and get three outs as quickly as possible each inning.
3. Apply only those strategies appropriate to your team.
4. Practice everything—including signs—over and over before using them in games.

ADDITIONAL READINGS

Allen, A. (1960). *Coach's Guide to Defensive Baseball*. Englewood Cliffs, NJ: Prentice Hall.
Bethel, D. (1980). *Inside Baseball*. Chicago: Contemporary Books.
Dugan, K. (1980). *Secrets of Coaching Championship Baseball*. West Nyack, NY: Parker Publishing.
Editors of Sports Illustrated. (1960). *The Sports Illustrated Book of Baseball*. Philadelphia: J.B. Lippincott.
Ledbetter, V. (1964). *Coaching Baseball*. Dubuque, IA: Wm. C. Brown.
Weaver, E. with Pluto, T. (1984). *Weaver on Strategy*. New York: Macmillan.

Supplement 8-1.
Preferred Defensive Coverages for Typical Situations

Good defensive coverages are simple and logical. Positioning that naturally makes sense to the fielder decreases the time needed to make the play while increasing the probability of good execution. The following discussion and diagrams indicate each player's responsibilities for various common plays. Those not included are logical extensions of ones shown, and the coach should be able to position the players after a bit of practice and experience.

However, since these suggestions reflect average athletes making typical plays, the coach may need to change some coverages because of personnel. For example, a particular shortstop may not be able to make relay throws as well as the person at second base, and the coach may wish to have that player handle most relay assignments. Or the person put at third base may not be able to handle cutoff throws, and the coach may prefer to have the player from first base take all such plays. If such adjustments are necessary, they should be as simple as possible and should appear logical to the defenders involved.

This section opens with a diagram showing depths of play commonly used in baseball. Following this is a look at ground balls to infielders, and by the end of the diagrams, various infield and outfield plays are covered. The coach must remember to use these as guides, not rules. The judgment of coach and athletes remains important.

Depth of play in various situations

See Figure 8-1s for some indication of general playing depth of the various fielders. 1's show the "normal" position for players; these spots should be taken most of the time. They allow the players plenty of time to react to the ball and get into back up position. Infielders should play in part way—at position 2—whenever the double play is to be attempted. By starting a bit closer to the plate, the infielders will get to the ball more quickly and so have a better chance of completing the double play. Infield position 3 should be taken only if a runner at third base must be kept from scoring. Being

on the base lines or even closer, the infielders have little time to react to balls hit to either side; however, a hit directly at an infielder will result in a play at the plate or the runner being looked back to third. Even more rarely taken is outfield position 3 which has the outfielders in almost half way from their usual spots. This defensive alignment is used only with the winning run at third base with less than two outs, as a long fly ball will score the opponent anyway. The defenders play close enough to practically guarantee throwing out the runner trying to score. The outfielders have little time to react to the ball, but they really have no choice.

Situation: No runners on base, infield ground ball.

Defensive play: Make the out as efficiently as possible.

The defender in the area of the ball with the easiest throw to first has primary responsibility for fielding the ball. At least two players should be moving to field any batted ball. In the case of a ground ball on the infield, one of the defenders probably will be moving toward first base. For example, a ball hit toward the hole between shortstop and third base will have the defenders at third and short on the move. The player from third, moving to the right field side, should make the play if at all possible, because the athlete's momentum is somewhat toward first base and the throw will be more easily made. On the other hand, the shortstop would have to stop, plant the foot, and throw quickly; this is not an impossible play, but it is difficult. Similarly, balls hit up the middle are better played by the shortstop, and ones hit between first and second bases likely should be taken by the defender at second who throws to the pitcher covering first. Balls hit between home plate and the mound present particular problems, but the general idea applies: The player moving toward first base usually should expect to make the play. Otherwise, responsibilities are as follows:

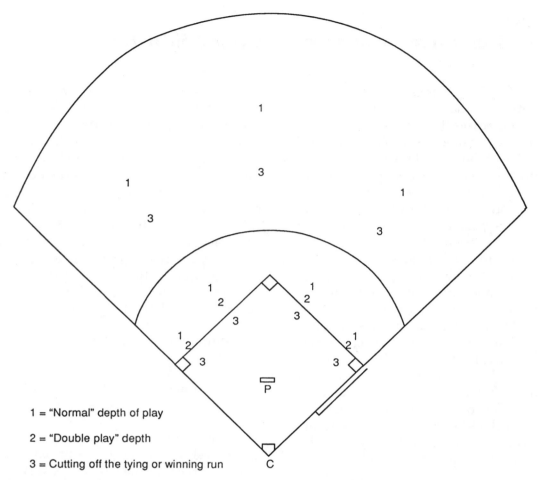

1 = "Normal" depth of play

2 = "Double play" depth

3 = Cutting off the tying or winning run

Figure 8-1s. Depth of play.

Position	Responsibilities
Pitcher (P)	Cover first base, if ball is hit to right side of infield. Stay clear of any throws (lie on the ground, if necessary) and prepare for any misplays.
Catcher (C)	Back up the infield side of first play, direct throws.
First base (1B)	Cover first base.
Second base (2B)	Cover first base and communicate with pitcher, if defender at first plays ball. Cover second base on balls hit to left side.
Third base (3B)	Cover third base.
Shortstop (SS)	Back up the defender at third, if ball is hit into that area. Cover second base, if ball is hit to right side of the infield.
Left field (LF)	Back up plays on left side of infield. Back up throws to left side of second base.
Center field (CF)	Back up balls hit to the middle of the infield. Back up throws to the right side of second base.
Right field (RF)	Back up balls hit to the right side of the infield. Back up throws from infielders to first base.

Even without a play at second or third base, these bases should be covered and backed up. Such efforts will save runs and get outs over the course of a season; however, these coverages will occur only if they are practiced regularly and the coach expects the players to perform them.

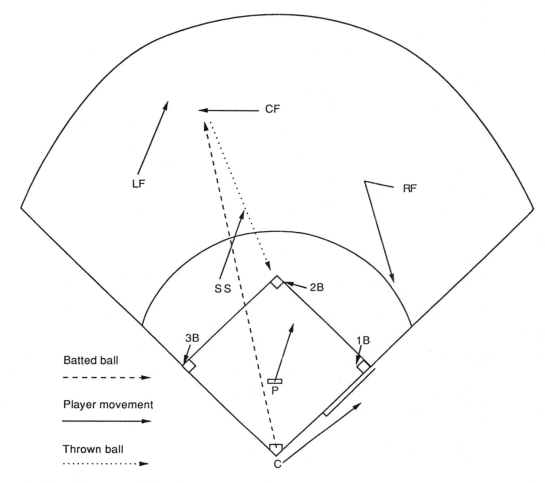

Figure 8-2s. Single to left-center field with no runners on base.

Situation: No one on base, single to left or center field.

Defensive play: Limit the batter to first. Look for batter/runner rounding base too far.

Position	Responsibilities
P	Back up throw to second base.
C	Back up infield side of first base, watch runner rounding first.
1B	Cover first base; watch runner rounding base.
2B	Cover second base; be aware of possible relay to first.
3B	Cover third base.
SS	Move to the hit, communicate with the left and center fielders, move into cutoff position.
LF	Field ball and make throw on line through shortstop to second base, or back up center fielder.
CF	Field ball and make throw, or back up left fielder.
RF	Back up outfield side of first base.

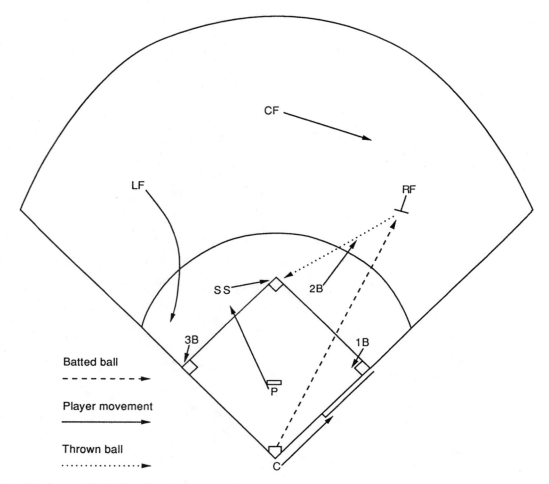

Figure 8-3s. Single to right field with no runners on base.

Batted ball
- - - - - - - ▶

Player movement
——————▶

Thrown ball
· · · · · · · · ▶

Situation: No one on base, single to right field.

Defensive play: Hold the runner to one base. Throw ahead of the runner—to second base—and look for a possible play if runner goes too far around first. (If the right fielder is playing in, the ball is hit sharply, and the runner is slow, then the right fielder may have a chance to force out the batter at first. This seldom happens in baseball; however, it remains a possibility, and the outfielder should be aware of the play and practice it.)

Position   Responsibilities

P   Back up throw to second base.
C   Move to back up any possible throw to first base.
1B   Cover first base, watch runner rounding base.
2B   Moves out to relay position.
3B   Cover third base.
SS   Cover second base.
LF   Back up possible play at third base.
CF   Back up right fielder.
RF   Fields ball and makes indicated throw.

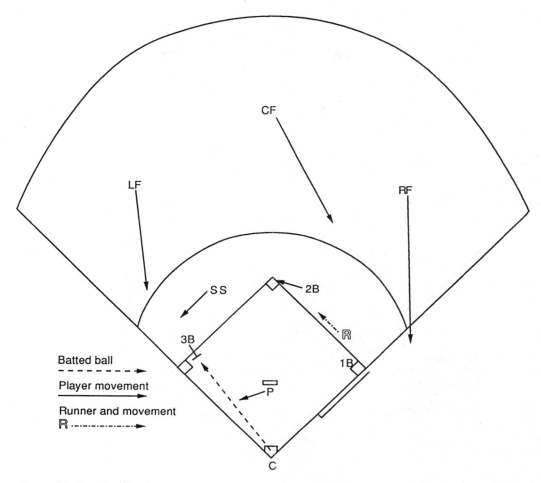

Figure 8-4s. Ground ball to third with a runner on first; less than two out.

Situation: Runner on first base and less than two outs, ground ball to third.

Defensive play: (1) Look for the double play. (*Note:* In any double play situation, the fielders generally should realize that the play requires fielding the ball cleanly. Any bobbling of the ball should cause them to go to first base for the force out. The exception to this involves a ball hit to the middle infielders, as they generally have a chance to recover and still get the force at second base.) (2) At least get the force out at first base.

Position   Responsibilities

P   React to ball being deflected into the pitching area, move to cover home plate.

C   Help direct throw to first base or second base as needed; back up infield side of first base.

1B   Cover first base.

2B   Cover second base and turn double play, if possible.

3B   Field the ball. Anticipate double play attempt at second base; if not, throw to first base.

SS   Move to back play, then cover third base on throw.

LF   Back up play fielding play at third and any subsequent throws to third base.

CF   Back up right field side of second base.

RF   Back up outfield side of first base.

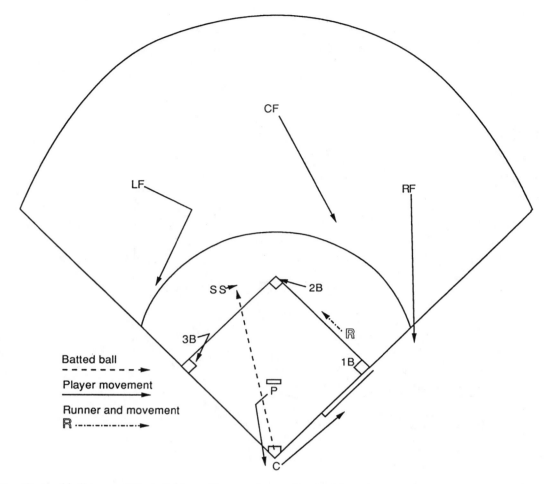

Figure 8-5s. Ground ball to a middle infielder with a runner on first and less than two outs.

Situation: Runner on first base and less than two outs, ground ball to short or second.

Defensive play: (1) Look for the double play. (2) Make the force out on the lead runner at second base. (3) Get the force at first base.

Position	Responsibilities
P	React to ball, move to cover plate.
C	Back up infield side of first base.
1B	Cover first base.
2B	Field ball and start double play, or cover second base and turn double play, as needed.
3B	Cover third base after initial move to any ball hit to left side.
SS	Field ball and start double play, or cover second base and turn double play, as needed.
LF	Back up fielding play by shortstop or throw from second, as needed. Then move to back up possible later throws to third base.
CF	Back up second base.
RF	Back up outfield side of first base.

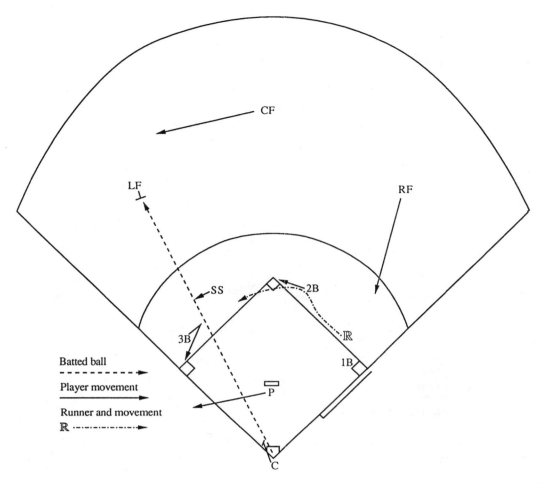

Figure 8-6s. Single to left field with a runner on first.

Situation: Runner on first base, single to left.

Defensive play: Hold the runner and batter to one base each. Out fielder throws to third base *only* if the runner tries to advance and a *sure* out is possible. Otherwise, *all* throws go to the shortstop in relay position.

Position	Responsibilities
P	Back up possible throw to third base.
C	Cover home plate.
1B	Cover first base.
2B	Cover second base.
3B	Cover third base, communicate with shortstop.
SS	Move into relay position, listen for instructions.
LF	Field ball throw to shortstop.
CF	Back up left fielder.
RF	Back up plays on right side of infield.

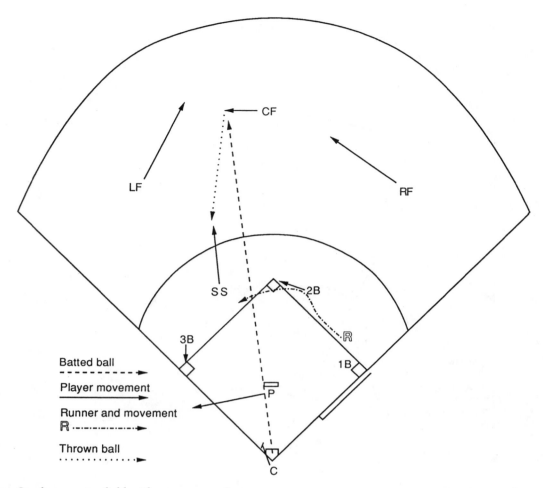

Figure 8-7s. Single to center field with a runner on first.

Situation: Runner on first base, single to center.

Defensive play: Limit the runner batter to one base. Fielder throws to third *only* if the runner is advancing and a *sure* out will result. Otherwise, the throw *always* goes to the shortstop.

Position	Responsibilities
P	Back up possible throw to third.
C	Cover home plate.
1B	Cover first base.
2B	Cover second base.
3B	Cover third base; communicate with shortstop.
SS	Move out into relay position, listen for instructions.
LF	Back up center fielder.
CF	Throw on a line to the shortstop in relay position.
RF	Move to back up center fielder.

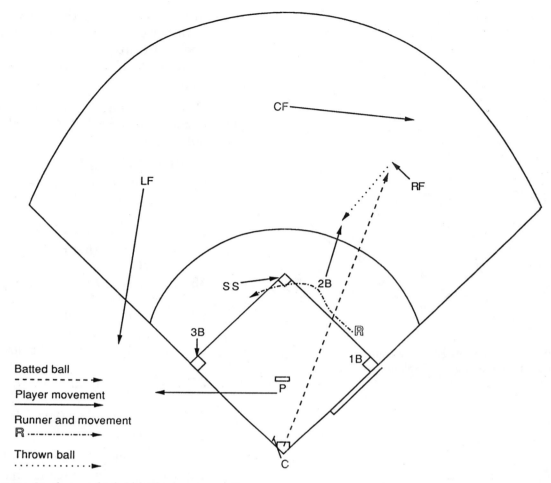

Figure 8-8s. Single to right field with a runner on first.

Batted ball	----➤
Player movement	──➤
Runner and movement	ℝ ·-·-·-·-➤
Thrown ball	·········➤

Situation: Runner on first base, single to right.

Defensive play: Limit the runner to second base and the batter to first base. Right fielder throws along the double relay line formed by second coming out and the shortstop moving to second base. The middle infielders let the ball go through if the defender at third does not shout "Cut;" however, this should occur only if the runner is trying to advance and a *certain* out is possible.

Position	Responsibilities
P	Back up possible throw to third base.
C	Cover home plate.
1B	Cover first base.
2B	Move out for possible relay, direct right fielder as needed.
3B	Cover third base.
SS	Cover second in double relay position.
LF	Back up third base.
CF	Back up right fielder.
RF	Make play on ball, throw on line through double relay toward third base.

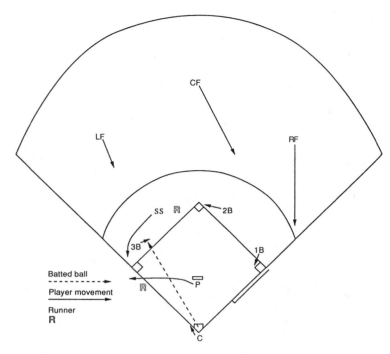

Figure 8-9s a. A runner at second or runners at second and third with less than two outs, a ground ball hit to third base.

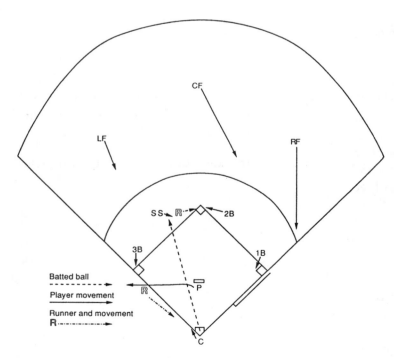

Figure 8-9s b. A runner at second or runners at second and third with less than two outs, a ground ball hit to shortstop.

Situation: With less than two outs and a runner on second or runners at second and third bases, a ground ball is hit to the left side (third base or shortstop).

Defensive play: Keep any base runners from advancing, while getting the force out at first base.

Position	Responsibilities
P	Move to ball, prepare for a deflected ball in area; back up third.
C	Cover home plate.
1B	Cover first base.
2B	Cover second base.
3B	React to ball; make play or cover third base as required.
SS	Move to ball; field it or cover third base as needed.
LF	Back up ground balls on left side.
CF	Back up throws to second base.
RF	Back up outfield side of first base.

The infielders need to "look back" the runners. This means that after playing the ball, the defender checks the lead runner and makes certain that the opponent is not trying to move up a base. Often, inexperienced runners may try to advance or may simply "freeze" too far off base. In these cases, the defender with the ball starts a run down play. If third starts this play, the shortstop covers third base, and the run down play continues as discussed above.

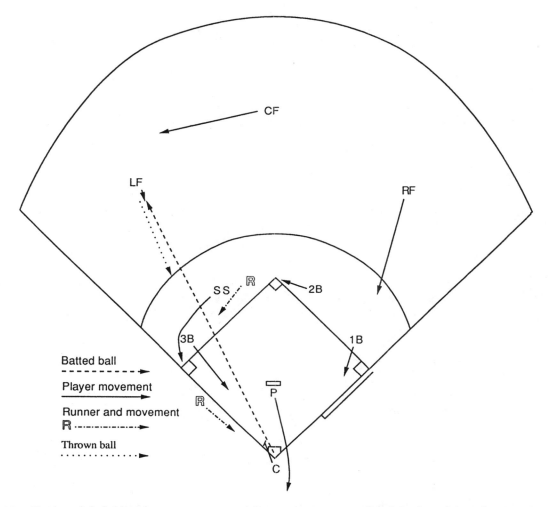

Figure 8-10s. Single to left field with a runner on second or runners at second and third, with less than two outs.

Situation: Runner on second or second and third bases, single to left; less than two outs.

Defensive play: Throw out runner from second at home, prepare for possible cutoff play on batter/runner.

Position	Responsibilities
P	Back up throw to home plate.
C	Cover home plate, check runners, call cutoffs and relays.
1B	Cover first base, watch batter/runner.
2B	Cover second base.
3B	Move into cutoff position, listen for "Cut," and be prepared for play on batter.
SS	Cover third base.
LF	Field ball and throw home on line through cutoff player.
CF	Back up left fielder.
RF	Prepare to back up play second or first base.

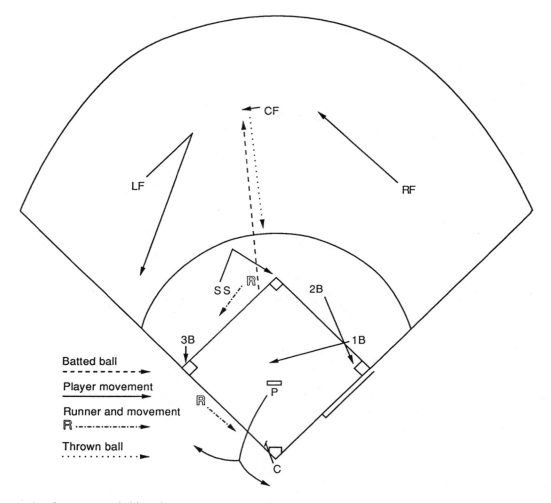

Figure 8-11s. Single to center field with a runner on second or runners at second and third, with less than two outs.

Situation: Runner on second or second and third bases, single to center; less than two outs.

Defensive play: Throw out runner from second at home, prepare for possible cutoff play on batter/runner.

Position Responsibilities

Position	Responsibilities
P	Back up throw to home; anticipate possible need to back up third.
C	Cover home plate, check runners, call cutoffs and relays.
1B	Take cutoff position. Listen for call of "Cut."
2B	Cover first base.
3B	Cover third base.
SS	React to ball, move to relay the ball if it is hit deep, cover second base.
LF	Back up center, then move to back up third base.
CF	Field ball and throw home on line through relay and cutoff people.
RF	Back up center field.

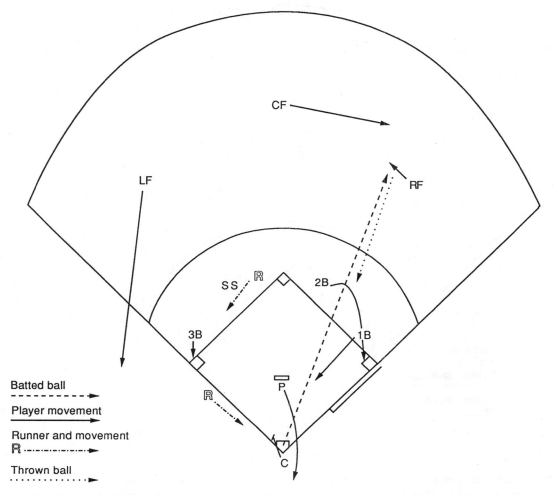

Figure 8-12s. Single to right field with a runner on second or runners at second and third, with less than two outs.

Situation: Runner on second or second and third bases, single to right; less than two outs.

Defensive play: Throw out runner from second at home; hold batter/runner to first base or prepare for possible cutoff play on batter/runner.

Position	Responsibilities
P	Back up throw to home.
C	Cover home plate, check runners, call cutoffs and relays.
1B	Take cutoff position. Listen for call of "Cut."
2B	React to ball; move to relay the ball, if it goes deep; cover first base.
3B	Cover third base.
SS	Cover second base.
LF	Back up third base in foul territory.
CF	Back up right fielder and help with throws.
RF	Field ball; throw to cutoff, if normal depth or closer; hit relay, if ball is hit deeper.

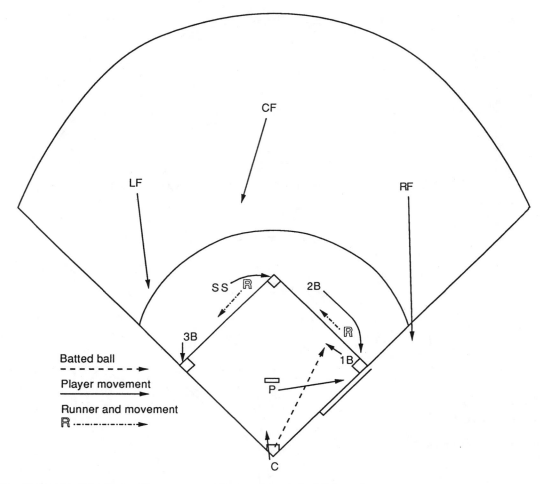

Figure 8-13s. Ground ball to first with runners on first and second with less than two outs.

Situation: Runners on first and second bases with less than two outs, ground ball to first base.

Defensive options: There appear to be three possibilities: (1) Make a force play on the runner going to third base, (2) throw to second to start the double play, or (3) get the batter/runner out at first base. The first of these options is difficult to accomplish, as the runner usually gets a good jump off second base, so it seldom is used; however, in certain situations, this option may be the necessary choice. Nevertheless, the best play is the second one, as it splits the runners and keeps the double play alive. Splitting the runners means keeping the runners at first and third bases, rather than allowing the trail runner to move to second base. Not only does this keep a second opponent from scoring position, it also maintains the possibility of a double play.

Position	Responsibilities
P	React to ball; move to cover or back up first base, as needed.
C	Stay near home plate, call the throw.
1B	Field the ball; throw to second base to start the double play or make a play on the batter coming down to first base.
2B	Back up fielding play; may need to cover first base for completion of the double play.
3B	Cover third base.
SS	Cover second base. Complete double play, be prepared for lead runner attempting to score.
LF	Back up third base.
CF	Back up throws to second.
RF	Back up initial fielding play at first base, then cover return throw on double play.

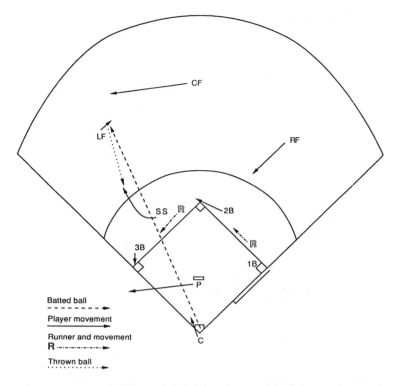

Figure 8-14s a. Ball hit to left field with runners on first and second with less than two outs.

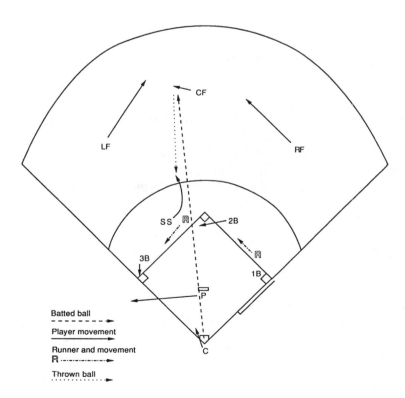

Figure 8-14s b. Ball hit to center field with runners on first and second with less than two outs.

Situation: Runners on first and second bases with less than two outs, fly ball to left or center.

Defensive play: Minimize advancement of runners; split the runners if necessary.

Position	Responsibilities
P	Back up third.
C	Cover home plate, check runners, call cutoffs and relays.
1B	Cover first base.
2B	Cover second base.
3B	Cover third base, watch runners, communicate with shortstop.
SS	React to ball, move to relay the ball if it is hit deep. Ball may go to third, if the lead runner advances but can be thrown out. If not, the shortstop may elect to run the ball back into the infield or throw to second base to hold the runners.
LF	Field ball; throw to third base or relay person, as needed. Or back up center fielder.
CF	Back up left fielder; or field ball and throw to relay person.
RF	Back up second base; back up center fielder.

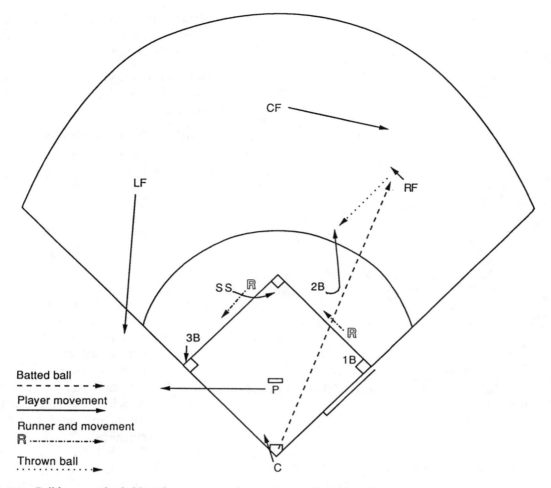

Figure 8-15s. Ball hit to right field with runners on first and second and less than two outs.

Situation: Runners on first and second bases with less than two outs, fly ball to right field.

Defensive play: Minimize advancement; split the runners, if possible.

Position	Responsibilities
P	Back up third base.
C	Cover home plate, check runners, call cutoffs and relays.
1B	Cover first base.
2B	React to ball, move to relay the ball if it is hit deep. Ball may go to third, if the lead runner advances but can be thrown out. If not, this relay/cut off player may elect to run the ball back into the infield or throw to second base to hold the runners.
3B	Cover third base.
SS	Cover second on line in tandem relay position.
LF	Back up third base.
CF	Back up right fielder.
RF	Field ball; make throw through relay to second base.

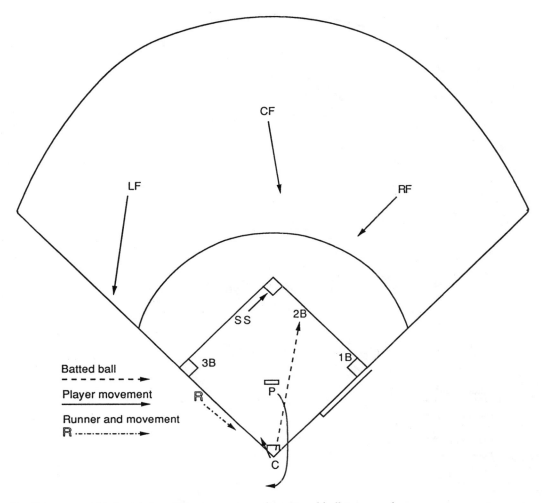

Figure 8-16s. Runner on third with less than two outs and a ground ball to second.

Situation: Runner on third base with less than two outs, a ground ball to second.

Defensive options: (1) If the run is of little importance, get the out at first base. (2) However, if the run must be stopped, the infielders play in (see Figure 8-1s) and throw home if the runner breaks on contact. Occasionally the runner may take a large lead but not go. This gives the defense an opportunity (3) to throw the runner out returning to third base or (4) to start a run down. (5) Most commonly, however, the infielder looks the runner back and throws to first base, and the defender at first is prepared to throw home after completing the force out.

Position	Responsibilities
P	React to ball, but stay clear of any throws. Once the ball passes by, move to back up home.
C	Cover the plate; watch runner and call throws.
1B	Cover first base, and be prepared to throw home.
2B	Field ball. Be prepared to (1) throw home, if the runner breaks on contact or has a large lead; (2) look the runner back; (3) initiate a run down play, if the runner is stopped some distance off base; (4) throw to third base, if the runner stops well off base; or (5) throw to first base.
3B	Cover between third base line and pitcher.
SS	Cover second base.
LF	Back up possible play at third base.
CF	Back up middle of field.
RF	Back up play at second and back up outfield.

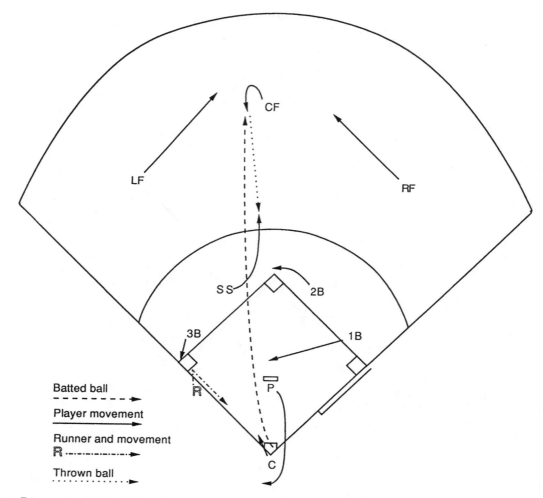

Batted ball - - - - - - - - - ➤

Player movement ―――――――➤

Runner and movement
R ·-·-·-·-·-·-·-➤

Thrown ball ·············➤

Figure 8-17s. Runner on third with less than two outs and a fly ball to center field.

Situation: Runner on third base with less than two outs, fly ball to center field.

Defensive play: Throw out runner trying to score.

Position	Responsibilities
P	Back up home plate.
C	Cover home plate.
1B	Cutoff position on line between center fielder and home plate.
2B	React to ball then cover second base in case of dropped ball.
3B	Cover third base; watch runner for correct tag up.
SS	React to ball; direct outfielders; get into relay position, if ball goes deep.
LF	Back up center fielder.
CF	Make catch on throwing arm side while moving in toward home; throw on line to plate.
RF	Back up center fielder.

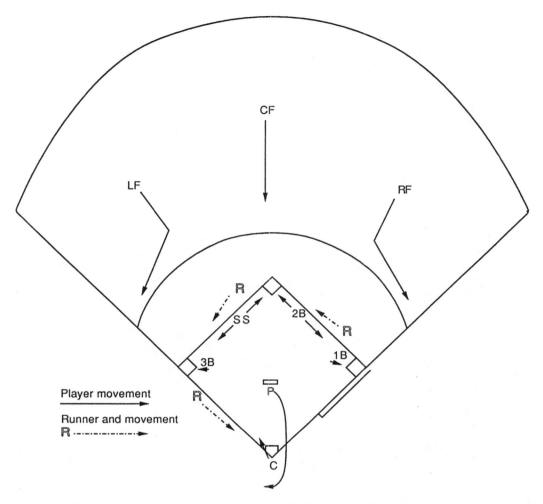

Figure 8-18s. Bases loaded with less than two outs and a ground ball to an infielder.

Situation: Bases loaded with less than two outs, ground ball to an infielder.

Defensive options: (1) If the run is critical, infielders play in for the force out at the plate, and the catcher may follow the force out with an attempt to double up the batter going to first. (2) If the run is not important, the defense plays back and attempts the double play. (3) No matter what get one out.

Position	Responsibilities
P	React to ball and throw home; otherwise, back up home plate.
C	Take throw and tag base. Immediately clear area and look to first base for a double play; check other runners.
1B	React to hit; cover first base.
2B	React to ball. Cover second base if ball is hit to left side; cover first base if ball is hit to defender there.
3B	React to hit. Cover third base.
SS	React to ball. Cover second base, if ball is hit to pitcher or right side; cover third base if that player fields ball.
LF	Back up play on left side and possible throws to third base.
CF	Back up middle infielders.
RF	Back up plays on right side and then outfield side of first base.

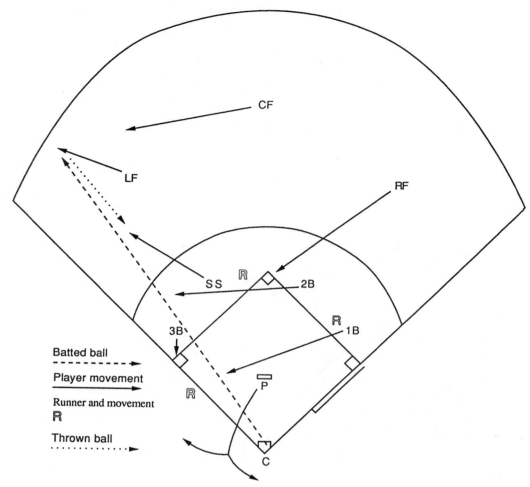

Figure 8-19s. An extra base hit to left field with the bases loaded.

Situation: Bases loaded, extra base hit to left field.

Defensive play: Minimize the number of runs allowed while trying to get an out if a runner rounds base too far.

Position   Responsibilities

P   Move to third base line and back up third or home as required by developing play.

C   Cover the plate, watch runners, direct throws.

1B   Move into cutoff position.

2B   Move into second position in tandem relay.

3B   Cover third base.

SS   Move into relay position on direct line between out fielder and home plate.

LF   Field ball, listen for call of throw, make throw home along line of relay people.

CF   Call throw and back up left fielder.

RF   Back up second base.

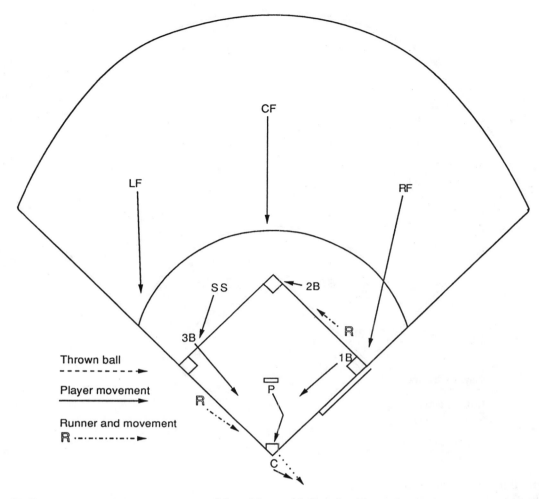

Figure 8-20s. Runner attempting to score on a wild pitch/passed ball with additional runner or runners on base.

Situation: Runner attempting to score on a wild pitch/passed ball, an additional runner or runners on base.

Defensive play: Try for an out at home while holding any other runners to only one base.

Position	Responsibilities
P	Help catcher locate ball, cover home plate.
C	Retrieve pitch, make throw to pitcher at plate.
1B	Move in to back up throw getting away from pitcher to right side.
2B	Cover second base.
3B	Move in to back up throw getting away to left side.
SS	Cover third base.
LF	Back up third base.
CF	Back up second base.
RF	Move in to cover first base. (Crucial if play occurs on a walk.)

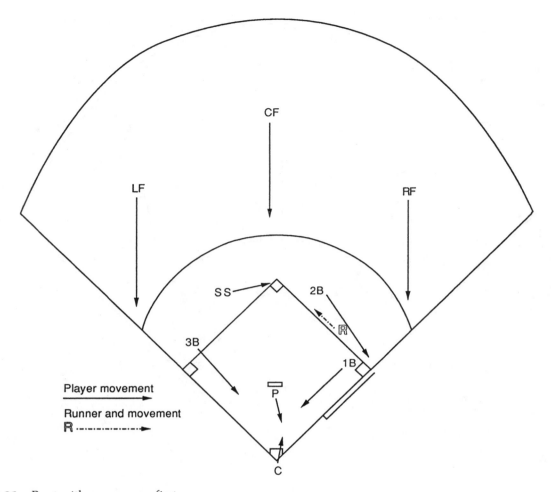

Figure 8-21s. Bunt with a runner on first.

Situation: Runner on first base, bunt.

Defensive options: (1) Force out the runner at second base. (2) Otherwise, be sure to get the out at first base.

Position	Responsibilities
P	Move to field bunt.
C	Field the bunt if possible; if not, call play, move to cover third base.
1B	Cover the area between first base line and pitcher.
2B	Cover first base.
3B	Cover the area between third base line and pitcher.
SS	Cover second base.
LF	Back up any possible play at third.
CF	Back up second base.
RF	Back up first base.

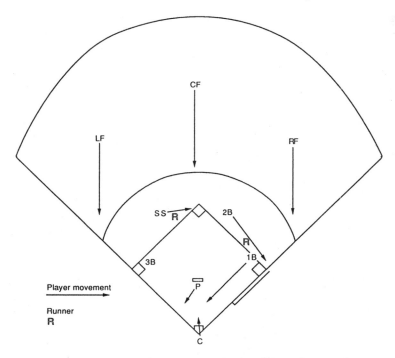

Figure 8-22s a. Bunt with runners on first and second, normal coverage.

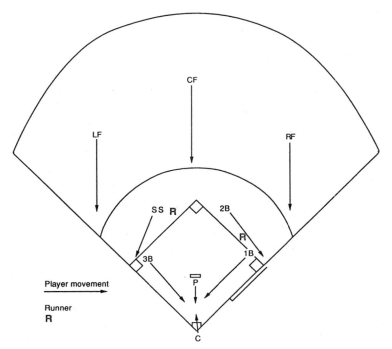

Figure 8-22s b. Bunt with runners on first and second, "rotation" coverage.

Situation: Runners on first and second bases, bunt.

Defensive options: (1) Force out the runner at third base. (2) If not possible, get an out, probably at first base.

Position	Responsibilities
P	Move to cover area between third base line and mound.
C	Field bunt if possible; if not, call play and move to cover home.
1B	Cover between first base line and pitcher.
2B	Cover first base.
3B	Cover third base or make fielding play in area between third base line and pitcher, as determined by coach.
SS	Cover second or third base as determined by coach. (The coach must decide in advance whether to use the rotation play that sends the shortstop to cover third and has the defender from third charging. This decision must be communicated to all defensive players.)
LF	Back up third base.
CF	Back up second base.
RF	Back up first base.

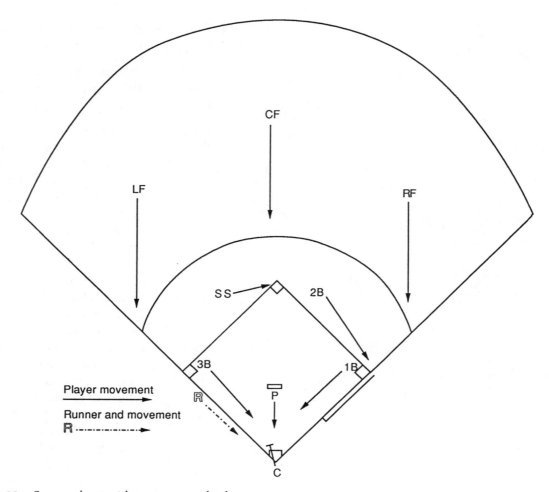

Figure 8-23s. Squeeze bunt with a runner on third.

Situation: Runner on third base, squeeze bunt.

Defensive options: Fielders get to ball as quickly as possible to start (1) tag play on runner at plate or (2) throw to first base for the force out.

Position	Responsibilities
P	Field ball.
C	Upon noticing batter trying to bunt, calls out play and positions self for tag play at home.
1B	Charge to field ball.
2B	Cover first base.
3B	Charge with runner, field ball.
SS	Cover second base.
LF	Back up third base in case of possible run down.
CF	Back up second base.
RF	Back up first base.

9
Offensive Strategies

Michael A. Clark, Ph.D.

QUESTIONS TO CONSIDER

- What should be the basic approach toward offense in youth baseball?
- What considerations go into making up the batting order?
- How many different ways can the batter get to first base?
- How can the "run and hit" and "run and bunt" plays be used to advance runners?
- How can bunts be used to get the offense going?
- When are steals worth the risk?
- How does taking the extra base affect play?
- What role do base coaches play in baseball?
- How are signs involved in offensive play?

INTRODUCTION

While much of baseball is fun and enjoyable, offense is the part most young athletes—and their fans—like best. This is especially so if the coach and team take an aggressive, attacking approach to the game. Playing this way, the team is always on the move and causing things to happen. Besides putting tremendous pressure on the opponents and forcing them into defensive mistakes, an attacking offensive team is more enjoyable to play on and more fun to watch. In short, the more aggressive the style of play, the more successful is the team.

An aggressive style of offensive baseball makes use of the skills previously described in Chapters 6, Hitting and Bunting, and 7, Base Running; the coach must consider the level of mastery displayed by the athletes when deciding which of the suggested strategies to use.

Thus, at the lower levels, offense may consist of little more than hitting and running. However, as the players become more skilled, other options become available to them and the coach. This chapter opens with some general thoughts on offensive play, followed by a look at considerations a coach should make when setting the batting order. Next come observations on hitting, bunting, and other means of getting to first base. Comments on stealing and taking extra bases, the role of pinch hitters and runners, and an outline of situational options follow. The chapter concludes with comments on base coaching and signs.

When reading this material and deciding which strategies to use, the coach should keep in mind several important points:

- First, consider that local rules modifications may disallow certain of the suggested strategies. For example, bunting and stealing are often not part of the game for younger athletes.

- Secondly, remember that the level of competitiveness affects the strategies chosen. Thus, in games involving inexperienced players or mismatched opponents, repeated steals or run-and-bunt plays might not be appropriate.
- Thirdly, work within the limits established by the skills and experience of the athletes. For example, do not expect beginning players to execute the run-and-hit, but plan on older athletes being able to handle breaking pitches.
- Next, teach and use aggressive offensive skills. In this context, aggressive means that the coach and players are assertive, that they take the initiative; it *does not* suggest that young athletes are taught skills or strategies that might recklessly endanger themselves or others.
- Finally, repeatedly practice every desired tactic well in advance of expecting the players to use it in a game. Players become nervous and frustrated if asked to do something not previously done, and they are likely to fail at their first attempts.

GENERAL OFFENSIVE GUIDELINES

1. *If using a designated hitter, rotate the assignment among team members.* This allows all athletes to develop more complete skills.
2. *Remember that in youth baseball, big offensive innings with lots of runs scored are common.* Consider this before committing to a strategy of playing for only one or two runs—unless of course one run will win the ball game.
3. *Do not rely on home runs.* In youth baseball, they come too seldom and cannot be coached. Rather, count on good hitting and base running as consistent producers of runs.
4. *After the opponents commit an error or fail to throw out a base stealer, consider putting on the steal sign or attempting some other play.* Opponents often react to errors or failed plays by letting their concentration slip. This tendency can be used to the offense's advantage.
5. *Study opposing pitchers.* This may reveal an opponent's favorite pitches, any particular pattern of pitches, and pickoff moves. Coach

and players alike can find such knowledge useful in selecting a hitting or offensive strategy to use.

6. *Have every player run hard on every offensive play, whether hitting, bunting, or base running.* This not only puts tremendous pressure on the opponents, but it also allows the offensive player to take advantage of any errors or other opportunities to advance an extra base or two.
7. *Remember that the more things the defense has to do well in order to get an out, the more risk the offense can take.* If the ball has to be caught, thrown accurately and quickly, and a tag made, then the offensive player has a good chance of being safe. And if a double play is needed, the likelihood of the defense being effective is not very great. Generally, coaches tend to be much more conservative than either the players or opponents deserve.
8. *Do not expect to have every piece of strategy in place at the beginning of the season.* Usually pre-season practices do not allow enough time to get everything "game-ready," so decide which plays are absolutely essential, put them in first, and expect to add to them during the season.
9. *Keep signs simple, and make spoken commands clear and unmistakable.* The coach's signals to moving base runners involve big arm movements. Strategic signs to hitters and runners are simple actions that the coach is unlikely to do without thinking. Spoken directions are one or two words long and cannot be mistaken for other commands. (For example, "Go" and "No" sound nearly identical when shouted. Use the first one, but rather than "No" call out "Stop" or "Stay" instead.) Remember, *a player wearing a helmet has difficulty hearing instructions.*

DETERMINING THE BATTING ORDER

At the lower levels of play, the particular batting order makes little difference. Players and coach alike properly focus on skill development, and every athlete should have a chance to hit the ball and run the bases as much as possible. (*Note:* Having all team members bat is a very common rule modification found in tee ball and other entry-level play. See Chapter 10 for other common rule changes.) However, as the players become more experienced and the games become more competitive, the coach must weigh the team members' abilities. This allows the coach to arrive at a batting order that gives each player a chance to be successful while helping the team. Thus, the lineup puts the available players in position for the strongest possible order from lead-off to ninth hitter.

Often it is helpful to think of the batting order as being broken into thirds. Over the course of a game and throughout a season, the first third of the order will have more turns at bat. Consequently, the top three spots are filled by players who are consistent hitters and have good on-base percentages. Also the fastest players usually appear at the top of the batting order, as speed on the bases does more to disrupt a defense than anything else. The next three batters usually will be hitting with teammates on base, so this middle third of the order is made up of players capable of delivering extra base hits. The bottom of the lineup generally includes batters with only partially developed skills, but the wise coach neither overlooks nor "throws away" this last third of the order. The performance of these three hitters often makes a difference in close games, so these players may become important factors in the team's success. Therefore, these positions often are filled by batters who can "work" a pitcher for a walk, who are good bunters, or who have good speed. More specifically, the following describes the ideal characteristics of the person filling each spot in the order.

Lead-off

The lead-off hitter has the best on-base percentage and runs well—even to the point of being the best base stealer on the team. The athlete has a "good eye," typically does not swing at pitches out of the strike zone, and may walk often. When all else fails, the player can bunt for a base hit.

Number Two

Also having a good on-base ratio, the number two batter is patient and has excellent bat control. The player executes the run-and-hit and run-and-bunt well and is willing to sacrifice bunt. Further, this athlete has enough speed to be an effective lead-off hitter in case the first batter fails to get on base. A left-handed batter may be particularly suited to this spot.

Number Three

Possessing a combination of speed and power, the number three player has the highest batting average on the team. The hitter can drive in runs and occasionally gets extra base hits. (This is also a good spot for a left-handed batter.)

Number Four or "Cleanup"

The number four hitter's primary responsibility is driving in runs; consequently, the player in this spot should be the best power hitter on the team. This athlete regularly produces extra base hits and occasionally gets a home run. (However, if this person also has the best batting average, then the third spot would be a better choice, because as a third place batter the player will get a few more turns at the plate.)

Number Five

Having essentially the same role as the cleanup batter, the number five hitter is a power player who simply produces a bit less often.

Number Six

This is another power spot, but relatively few teams will have three hitters of this sort. Consequently, many times this position is filled by a player with characteristics like those of the second batter, but whose on-base percentage is a bit lower or whose speed is inconsistent.

Numbers Seven to Nine

Again, positions seven through nine are critical to the team's success. The available people likely will not have fully developed batting skills, but they still should be able to do something to help the team. Generally, players in these spots are patient hitters who seldom try to pull the ball. They willingly take walks, execute run-and-hit or run-and-bunt plays, bunt for hits or move runners along with a sacrifice. These athletes have good speed and can make things happen when they get on base. In some ways, the ninth place hitter is almost a second leadoff batter, so the person in this spot should have the most speed of the three.

The above ideas are summarized in Table 9-1. However, these points simply provide suggestions—an effective batting order results only from thorough knowledge of the players and much experimentation. Seldom should a coach expect to establish an order at the beginning of the season and have it intact at the close—without even considering the possibility of injuries.

Note: If fortunate enough to have several left-handed batters, the coach should consider spacing them throughout the lineup. This causes the defensive players to adjust constantly and so makes them uncomfortable. It also keeps the opposing coach from gaining a significant advantage by putting in a left-handed pitcher.

GETTING TO FIRST BASE

Getting to first base is the start of sophisticated offensive strategy, and there are many different ways to accomplish this. (In fact, there are so many means of advancing a batter to first that listing them all is a typical sports trivia

Table 9-1. Characteristics of players filling various spots in the batting order.

Position	Ideal Characteristics
1	Best on-base percentage; runs well. Knows strike zone and seldom swings at bad pitches, walks a lot.
2	Good on base average. Good bat control; can run-and-hit, run-and-bunt, will sacrifice. A second lead-off hitter. Good spot for a left-handed batter.
3	Highest batting average. Combines speed and power. Also a place to use a left-handed hitter.
4	"Cleanup" batter. Best power on team; often delivers extra base hits.
5	Similar to number four hitter, but less consistent producer.
6	Third power spot; however, more likely to be similar to number two hitter.
7 and 8	Patient hitters willing to get on base however they can. Will advance runners and have good speed themselves.
9	Similar to those batting in the previous two spots; however, has more speed and can be another leadoff type hitter.

question.) However, most baseball coaches and players should focus on hits, bunts and walks because these are directly controlled by the athlete. Other possible ways of reaching base remain, and they will be considered for reasons of either safety or general knowledge.

Hitting Strategies

Offensive strategic play begins at the plate. Some of this strategy involves only the batter during each individual turn at the plate, while other strategies require input from the coach. Some tactics relate directly to the one-on-one confrontation between hitter and pitcher while others are more a part of the broader competition between offense and defense. Some gambits are simple enough that beginning players can master them, while others should only be attempted by especially skillful or experienced athletes. But no matter what level of play is involved, the coach and—to the extent of their abilities—players can benefit from learning and using the strategic elements of hitting. These components of getting to first base will be considered, beginning with the batter's level of concentration and working through such points as the variety of strike zones, the count, the opposing pitcher and breaking pitches, and the game situation.

Concentration or "Focus"

The most essential strategy in good hitting is concentration, or "focus," at the plate. Often the younger athlete is not fully attentive to the upcoming pitch. This may result from any number of reasons. The player may be concerned with missing a previous good pitch, or may be upset about the umpire's call. The coach may distract the batter by pointing out some needed mechanical adjustment. Someone may shout the player's name from the stands. In fact, many things might divert the batter's attention, but the result will generally be the same: the athlete faces the next pitch without fully concentrating on it and so is easily fooled—a strike or a weak hit surely results.

To deal with distractions, the hitter must learn to focus attention on each pitch—even to the point of stepping out of the batter's box between pitches to refocus. This, like other aspects of the game, is a skill that can be developed. The coach may use batting practice as a time for players to learn to hit in spite of distractions, be it a poor call by the umpire or noises in the crowd. (As previously mentioned, the coach should avoid talking to hitters about mechanical changes during a turn at bat.) Distractions may be simulated by teammates, and the batter can learn to focus attention on the pitcher's deliveries. To be successful, the hitter must attend to each pitch in turn and expect to hit every one well, and this can only be accomplished by anticipating good pitches in hittable locations. Focus, or concentration, is key.

Strike Zones

To begin, batters—like pitchers—must learn the strike zone. This is a complex bit of knowledge; for as mentioned in the previous chapter on defensive strategy, each of three people involved establishes a potentially different strike zone:

- The hitter's body combines with the plate to determine a strike zone based on the rule book.
- The umpire expands or shrinks this zone based on any number of considerations.
- The pitcher usually attempts to throw the ball only within certain areas of the umpire's zone.

However, *the key is the umpire's zone*, as this determines which pitches the batter will be expected to try to hit.

The younger athlete should be learning to deal with the variations in the strike zone by concentrating on making good contact with pitches in the umpire's strike zone. In practice and later in games, the player may experiment with different grips, different positions in the batter's box and "going with the pitch." For example, with two strikes a hitter may choke up a bit and concentrate on making contact in an effort to put the ball in play while avoiding a strike out. Similarly, an athlete may stand further back in the box if the pitcher has control of a good fastball, or the batter might step toward the pitcher to hit slower pitches with good movement. Finally, the developing hitter may work on driving outside pitches to the opposite field and pulling inside ones.

The older, more experienced athlete should

develop two additional skills related to the idea of strike zones.

1. *As soon as possible during each game, the player strives to discover what the umpire considers a strike and adjust accordingly.* This can be done by paying close attention to each turn at bat—the athlete's own as well as teammates'. From these observations, the player will learn what sort of pitches the opposing pitcher is throwing for called strikes. The coach similarly studies the pitcher's deliveries and the umpire's calls, and coach and players together discuss their findings at various points throughout the game. Thus, each potential batter steps to the plate knowing what pitches to expect.
2. *Every batter also works to develop a fourth zone for pitches: a "hitting" zone, not a strike zone.* This hitting zone, made up of pitch locations where the athlete can confidently put bat on ball, allows the proficient youth baseball player to simplify the strategy of batting: get ahead in the count, and hit the best possible pitch. With practice, the player becomes able to determine quickly whether a pitch will be in a good location. This allows the athlete to swing confidently and expect positive results.

The Count

Early in the baseball experience, a youth player should concentrate on getting a good swing at the best possible pitch, no matter when it comes. So one might go after the first pitch, if it is hittable; or the athlete may not swing at all, if none of the pitches are manageable. However, at the upper levels of play, the successful batter learns to hit pitches based on the count as well as the location. "Ahead in the count," having no strikes or only one, the athlete concentrates on swinging only at a good pitch in the hitting zone. In other words, the batter, rather than the umpire or pitcher, is responsible for the decision to swing. Each player may choose to swing at a different sort of pitch, but it will always be a pitch the athlete feels capable of hitting well.

With two strikes, the batter must become a bit defensive. Often called "protecting the plate," this situation requires the batter to necessarily focus on the pitcher's and the umpire's zones—especially the points of overlap. This allows the player to react to any pitch that possibly might be called a strike. However, even in this situation, the batter is not completely helpless and may choose one of two approaches.

1. The player uses a choke grip and shortens the swing with the goal of simply making contact with the ball. Thus, the ball is put in play, and the defense is under pressure to perform in order to get an out.
2. The batter attempts to foul off close, even marginal pitches until the pitcher finally throws the ball in the hitting zone.

The older, stronger, more experienced hitter usually has better knowledge, bat control and reactions. These allow the player to avoid changing much while using this strategy. Because the grip and swing are not altered much, the player should be able to hit the ball well.

Thoughts on hitting at various points in the count are summarized in Table 9-2.

The Pitcher

As previously suggested, the players and coach work together to determine the pitcher's strike zone, but other elements of the pitcher's performance merit study as well. For example, the pitcher may be known to rely almost exclusively on a particular pitch. This may be a fastball a bit ahead of most batters' ability to react, or it may be a newly learned off-speed pitch. Similarly, the pitcher may throw pitches only in certain locations: fastballs may always be up in the strike zone or breaking balls may only be on the outside part of the plate. Finally, some pitchers allow themselves to fall into patterns of pitches, such as always throwing a change up with two strikes on the hitter. All these bits of knowledge help the hitter prepare for a turn at bat, and they should be collected and used.

Breaking Pitches

At some point every youth pitcher will experiment with breaking balls; and as suggested previously, pitchers successfully mastering a curve may develop a reputation for throwing it in particular situations. Therefore, the batter will need a strategy for dealing with such deliveries. Of course, batting practice allows the player to see breaking pitches before having to

Table 9-2. Hitting strategies related to specific counts on the batter.

Count (Balls-strikes)	Strategy
0-0	Concentrate on hitting a pitch in the "hitting zone." This is one that the hitter feels confident of hitting well, one that the player knows can result in a base hit.
1-0, 0-1, 1-1, 2-1	Again, look for a pitch in the "hitting zone."
2-0	Become more selective; limit the "hitting zone" to just those pitches that the batter is practically certain of driving for hits.
3-0, 3-1	Swing only at the "perfect" pitch, the one that the batter prefers to hit over all possible others.
0-2, 1-2, 2-2	Be ready to swing at any pitch. Know the umpire's strike zone and go after pitches that may be within it—even to the point of swinging at ones a bit beyond it or breaking balls that start out in it. Know the pitcher's patterns and strengths and look for pitches in these spots. Make contact, and foul off close pitches, if possible. Extend the count, or put the ball in play.
3-2	Be prepared to swing. Knowledge of the strike zone and pitcher help, but the goal is to foul off close pitches until eventually getting one near the "hitting zone."

hit them in game situations and so face them with some confidence. Also, because breaking balls generally work by disrupting a batter's timing of the swing, there are some similarities in dealing with them that can be developed through practice. However, the three general breaking balls are just different enough to present the hitter with slightly different challenges.

The Curveball

The primary problem with the curveball lies in the break. When first confronted by curves, a youth baseball player often jumps out of the box only to have the ball break over the plate and be called a strike. The athlete must begin by simply seeing enough curves to learn that the ball will bend away before hitting the batter. Even after learning this, a young player often attempts to "catch up" to the break by making off-balance, lunging swings at curves. Only more practice helps the athlete learn the best means of hitting a curve: overcome the fear of being hit, time the slower speed, keep the hands back and hold the weight shift as long as possible, use a quick swing and stride a bit toward the pitch.

The Slider

Sliders similarly disrupt the hitter's timing, but their smaller break means that the batter generally does not first react by trying to jump out of the way. Rather, the hitter can concentrate on timing the swing while holding up the weight shift and forward movement of the hands. Maintaining swing speed is important, but adjusting the stride usually is unnecessary. Again, batting practice is the time to develop these skills.

The Change-Up

Initially looking like a fastball, the straight change up presents special problems. Because it does appear to be a fastball, the batter almost always shifts the weight too early and ends up "hitting off the front foot." Such efforts result in weak hits—especially if the hitter also tries to slow the swing to make contact after recognizing the pitch. Extensive practice will allow the hitter to choose between two possible responses. (1) If the batter feels off-balance as a result of being fooled, the player may attempt to stop the swing. (2) The batter may feel comfortable enough to allow the weight shift to continue; the player then concentrates on not starting the hands forward too early and maintaining as much bat speed as possible once the hands do come through.

Breaking balls are effective only to the extent that they disrupt a hitter's timing and are not often hit well. Therefore, a young batter should practice enough to become confident of regularly hitting these pitches. This makes breaking balls much less effective. And nothing affects a pitcher's confidence quite like having the breaking ball hit well. Consequently, the batter who has an effective strategy for dealing with such deliveries can surely be more successful personally while possibly improving the team's chances as well.

The Situation

Finally, game situations may require different strategies at the plate. For example, base runners sometimes may need to be advanced without bunting the ball. In such instances, the hitter usually tries to hit the ball to the right side of the field. Thus, a right-handed batter looks for a pitch on the outside part of the plate while a left-handed hitter waits for something to pull. At other times, a sacrifice fly may be all that is needed to win a game, so the batter anticipates a pitch up in the strike zone that can be driven to the outfield. Such relatively sophisticated skills require a great deal of practice; and as such, they should be attempted only by experienced players after much practice.

However, there are other strategies that are appropriate for even the youngest player to know and use. For example, when base runners are needed, the coach may expect the batter to take several pitches until a strike is called. Similarly, if a pitcher has walked two or three hitters in a row or a relief pitcher has just entered the game, the batter should plan to take a pitch or two. Such plays are common, and the coach should make certain the team members understand them.

Taking Pitches

At several points, the previous instructions suggested that the coach may expect players to "take" pitches—to not swing under any circumstances. This is an effective means of dealing with newly entered pitchers, pitchers having control problems, or the need to get base runners. Have batters act as though they are bunting, and taking a pitch also can force the defense to move or improve a base runner's chances of a steal. However, when deciding to give the "take" sign, the coach must consider more than these immediate circumstances.

The *level of competitiveness* is first among things to be considered. It is one thing to use the take sign in order to obtain a walk or to study a pitcher at the upper levels of youth competition, but quite another to have players take pitches when both they and the pitcher are just beginning their baseball experience. In the latter situation, many walks may result, but none of the players involved will get the experience they deserve. Thus, they will be less able to hit, pitch, or field when they do reach the upper levels of the sport. Or they may become so frustrated by the lack of action or success that they simply give up playing baseball. By being prepared to swing at every pitch, younger batters will learn the strike zone, will become able to adjust to different pitches and confidently manage situations in which they absolutely must make contact, like the run-and-hit or squeeze bunt.

In short, if taking pitches is to be part of the hitting strategy, then it should only occur at the very top levels of youth baseball. Further, the coach should use the take sign only as a component of some broader play—a steal, an effort to bring in the infielders, or a look at a new pitcher. In the long run, having young hitters take pitches to gain walks fails to benefit anyone.

The Run-and-Hit

The run-and-hit is a specialized play that few youth baseball players will be able to manage because of inadequate bat control. However, it bears mention because much is made of it in some baseball references. This play begins with a runner at first—or runners at first and second—breaking with the pitch. By starting early, the runners make the play look like a straight steal and thereby force the defenders to cover second and/or third. These actions leave much of the infield unprotected, and a batted ball will be likely to go through the infield. Consequently, the batter's responsibility is to get the bat on the ball, and the hitter must do everything possible to achieve this end. The run-and-hit play puts real pressure on the defense, and a well-executed run-and-hit can get a stalled offense moving. The main risk comes from the batter either missing the pitch or hitting a line drive that can be easily turned into a double play. Before deciding to use this play, the coach must consider these possibilities against the chances of getting a big inning started.

By referring to the play as the run-and-hit rather than the hit-and-run, emphasis is put on the base runners involved. These players initiate the action and lend much to the tactic's ultimate success. Thus, good base stealers are one key to success. Other considerations are:

- The pitcher's control—the run-and-hit is easier against an opponent known to throw strikes,
- The hitter's bat control—someone who makes

contact and avoids fly balls should be a good candidate for the run-and-hit.

Note: This play often appears in the form "hit and run." This form puts the emphasis on the batter's making contact as the runners, advancing at less than full speed, watch to see what happens. Both of these are very challenging for young athletes. It is better to use the play as a "run-and-hit." The runners concentrate on making the play look like a straight steal and the hitter focuses on making contact. The base runners need only check on the outcome as they approach the base—just as they would on a steal.

Conclusion

Hitters eventually should become able to use as many of these plays as they can absorb, but coaches must resist the temptation to load down youth athletes with adult-type strategies. Rather, sound, fundamental play should remain the primary concern. Practice correct hitting techniques. Learn the strike zone and the best pitches to hit. Concentrate at the plate, and put the ball in play—*hard*. These guidelines best serve the developing youth baseball player. This is not to say, however, that hitting strategy is unimportant. Rather, it should be seen as something that can make a good batter or team a bit more successful in certain situations and after adequate practice.

Bunting Strategies

Bunting is an essential batting skill that becomes increasingly important as the level of play becomes more sophisticated. Starting with simply being able to get the ball down, the youth baseball player learns to sacrifice and squeeze bunt, to execute the run-and-bunt, to bunt for a hit, and to slap bunt; there also are times when the batter may fake a bunt. Each of these tactics will be considered in turn. But first, some general thoughts on bunting as a strategy.

Bunting can be tried at any point during the game, but the goal of the bunt may limit the play's use. For example, a sacrifice, squeeze, or run-and-bunt should only be attempted with less than two outs. Bunting for a hit or slapping the ball may occur at any time, although coaches often use these as rally starters. Faking the bunt is done as part of some broader strategy—attempting a steal, bringing the infielders in closer or setting up the slap bunt. Good times to use the bunt are when the pitcher throws a high percentage of strikes or when the batter is ahead in the count—1-0, 2-0 or 2-1. Although the fake can be used throughout the count, bunts generally are not tried with two strikes on the batter because a fouled bunt then is considered a strike out. Finally, the player asked to use any of these tactics must have previously practiced the skill and should have reasonable running speed.

As with any strategic element of baseball, bunting is most successful when it surprises the opponents. Because this bit of unpredictability keeps them off-balance and gives the offense an edge, the coach should avoid falling into a pattern of bunting. Rather than sacrificing runners late in the game, try a run-and-bunt. Instead of squeezing a run across in the last inning, use the slap bunt as part of a safety squeeze. Have the game's first batter bunt for a hit. In short, keep the opposition guessing.

At the lower levels of play, the coach may find that the opponents are unable to defend against the bunt or that some team members are particularly good bunters. In such situations, the wise manager avoids the temptation to signal constantly for the bunt, because such a ploy limits the development and learning of players on both teams. Rather than relying on the bunt, the coach should consider it as but one component of a much more comprehensive offensive plan.

The Sacrifice

The name says it all. This offensive strategy gives up something—an out. The bunter, fully expecting to make an out at first base, gets the ball down to help any base runners advance. But because it uses one of the three outs per inning and does not directly score a run, the sacrifice is an inefficient offensive play. Consequently, the sacrifice bunt often is used in youth baseball only when scoring a single run is an absolute must, such as when the home team needs to tie the game in the last inning or two or when either team requires a run near the end of a game.

Note: As with many other strategies, the sacrifice bunt becomes more common as the level of play improves. The players become more capable of executing the play, and the games are generally lower scoring so a single run is more likely to make a difference. These points should be kept in mind by the coach planning to use this tactic.

The play generally begins with a runner at first and a reasonably competent bunter at the plate. Often even before the pitch, the batter assumes the squared around bunt position. The bunter, especially at the lower levels of play, evaluates the pitch and may choose not to bunt if the delivery is either high or well out of the strike zone. Once the decision to bunt has been made, the hitter tries to avoid popping the ball up while laying the bunt down in a position where the defender charging from first will have to field the ball. (This player typically is not in a position to make a play on the lead runner at second.) The runner, having plenty of time to reach second, need not break aggressively with the pitch but may extend the lead at about half speed. This gives the runner a chance to make sure the play is developing as planned and so avoid being doubled up if the batter pops up the ball.

If there are two runners on base, the sacrifice works essentially the same, but the person bunting should put the ball down the third base line. The opponent charging from third will have a difficult time fielding the ball and turning to throw to someone covering third base. However, if the defense is known to use the rotation play that sends the shortstop to third, the batter may try to bunt the ball towards the pitcher's throwing arm side. Generally the follow-through moves in the opposite direction, and the pitcher will be unable to cover this area defensively; the pitcher also may be in the way of a throw by another defender.

The Squeeze

With a runner at third and less than two outs, the coach may elect to call for a bunt. As with the sacrifice, this tactic is of most use in the final stages of a tied or one-run game, but the idea is a bit different. Called a "squeeze" bunt, the play has the batter bunting with the goal of providing enough time for the runner to cross the plate before a defensive play can be made. The play can be either a "suicide" or a "safety" squeeze.

The Suicide Squeeze

In the *suicide squeeze*, the runner breaks for the plate on the pitcher's delivery, and the batter *must* bunt the ball—no matter where it is thrown. If the hitter misses the ball, the base runner surely will be out, and thus the name— suicide squeeze. However, if the batter gets the bat on the ball, the runner almost certainly will score a key run but must expect to slide when approaching home plate. This is a very risky play; it must be practiced well in advance of its use. The batter has to be able to react to balls thrown anywhere, while being able to bunt them on the ground. And the runner must run hard toward a mass of players and a batted ball. Few hitters will have such skill, and not many potential runners will have the desire to make the play work. The coach must practice the play with the team well in advance of using it, so the coach knows which team members can perform the skills and the athletes realize what to expect.

The Safety Squeeze

Somewhat easier is the *safety squeeze*. Rather than breaking for the plate on the pitch, the runner extends the lead more aggressively than usual and watches the play at the plate. If the batter bunts the ball, then the runner sprints home; if not, the base runner quickly heads back to third. While putting the athlete at risk of being picked off at third, this tactic introduces a margin of safety in that the runner will not make a certain out if the ball is not bunted. However, the runner is farther from the plate when the ball is contacted, and a play at home almost certainly will result. The runner must be prepared to slide.

In either case, the batter should introduce a bit of deception by using the pivot bunting style and waiting to show it until after the pitch has been released. It is a bit more difficult to get the ball down this way, but the resulting squeeze play will be even more of a surprise. Consequently, potential bunters should work on this aspect of the play in practice.

Run-and-Bunt

With runners at first or first and second, an alternative tactic—the run-and-bunt—can be used. This play, beginning with the people on base moving, puts real pressure on the defense, and this in turn increases the chance of the bunter reaching base safely. Consequently the run-and-bunt represents a more aggressive and useful play than the sacrifice or squeeze bunts, and as such, it should be seriously considered by the youth baseball coach.

Note: As in the case of the run-and-hit, there is a difference in emphasis between the "run-and-bunt" and "the bunt-and-run." Again, the goal is to make the play more appropriate for younger athletes. The entire effort is designed to be more like stealing bases and bunting the ball, both of which should have been practiced in detail.

In the run-and-bunt, the base runners break with the pitch— not quite as hard as in an all-out steal, but quickly enough to force the defense into a "steal coverage." The runners continue moving until picking up the coach's instructions upon nearing the base. This allows them to concentrate on running, exactly as they would in a steal. Moreover, it puts them in position to take more than one base if the defense leaves a base unprotected.

As in the suicide squeeze, the hitter *must* bunt the ball, but the defense is to be pressured into throwing also. Therefore, the pivot style bunt may be the most successful. The bunt may be directed to any of several areas:

- the first base line, if a runner is at first
- the third base line, with runners at first and second
- the space between the pitcher and first base; or the space between pitcher and third, if the opponents use the rotation coverage.

The only bunt that will cause trouble is the pop-up, but a missed attempt or a pitch well out of the strike zone can also result in the runner being thrown out. These disadvantages need to be compared to the gains resulting from pressuring the defense to perform. As with the run- and-hit, the play gives the offense a chance to make a big inning out of a single base runner.

Because the batter must get the bat on the

ball, the run-and-bunt often works best when the pitcher has good control; good speed on the bases also helps. The hitter can turn this play into an attempt to get a hit by directing the bunt towards the areas vacated by the middle infielders as they move to cover the steal. Finally, the play can be used with runners at first and third; this often badly confuses the defense. In any case, the run-and-bunt is a more threatening play than the other forms of bunts and should be considered a basic tactic of youth baseball as soon as the athletes are reasonably skilled bunters.

Bunting for a Hit

This bit of strategy can be used to get a rally going when the team is behind and having a difficult time hitting the pitcher. Ideally, the player attempting this move has good speed, is a good bunter, but is not particularly likely to get a hit; the pitcher unknowingly cooperates by throwing strikes. If all these elements come together, the batter "reads" the defense while stepping to the plate or during the first pitch or two.

After checking the defense, the player decides which of two approaches to take.

1. If the defenders at first and third are playing well back of the base, the hitter tries to bunt the ball far enough down one of the baselines so that none of the defenders can make the play at first. This is a difficult maneuver, for the ball must be bunted hard enough so that neither the catcher nor the pitcher can easily field it but soft enough so that it does not reach the infielder quickly.
2. If the defenders at the corners appear to be in, expecting the bunt, the batter can still attempt to get a hit by either pushing or dragging the ball beyond their reach (see Chapter 6, "Bunting for a Hit"). Usually this play directs the ball toward the area between the mound and first base. If the ball is bunted hard enough in this area, it will get past these two defenders and force the opponent at second to make the play. Moreover, coverage at first presents a problem to the defense, and the play often turns into a race between the batter and one of the defenders.

The Slap Bunt

As previously mentioned, this is a seldom-used play in modern baseball, but it can be effective—especially if the batter using it has good bat control and is strong enough to drive the ball through the infield without using a full swing. While this strategy might be used whenever a bunt would seem appropriate, it is particularly effective for a player who has established a reputation of bunting for hits. Also, as with bunting for a hit, slapping the ball is a good way to start a rally.

The slap bunt begins with the hitter in the normal batting stance. As the pitch is released, the athlete pivots slightly and appears ready to bunt; this causes the infielders to move into bunt coverage. However, the offensive player draws the bat back and takes a half swing to punch the ball. This puts the defense at a disadvantage, and any number of positive things may happen. The defenders have little time to react to the ball and so may deflect or misplay it. The opponent closest to the ball's path may either freeze or duck out of the way. Finally, the slap may be hit well enough to go through the infield in one of the areas left unprotected by the opponent's movements. All these conditions work to the offensive player's benefit and increase the likelihood that the hitter will become a base runner.

The Fake Bunt

There are times when it is worthwhile for a batter to fake a bunt, but as with other such plays, the fake bunt must look like the real thing. It can be similar to a sacrifice or an attempt to bunt for a hit; it can be a square around or pivot bunt; but it must look realistic. The fake is best done when a bunt would seem logical to the defense. However, the hitter must remember that some other play is being established, so the batter need not worry about whether the pitch is called a ball or strike, for it is the continuation of the play that is important.

1. *Fake bunt to bring in infielders.*
    Faking the bunt on the initial pitch of a turn at bat generally brings the infielders in closer at the corners, and they often remain in for a pitch or two. If the batter subsequently takes a full swing, then these oppo-

nents will have much less time to react. Effectively, their range is cut down, and the hitter has a better chance of driving the ball through the infield.

2. *Fake bunt to assist a steal.*

The fake bunt can be used whenever the coach gives a base runner the steal sign. In this case, the squared around bunt is faked, and the position is held until after the catcher throws the ball. By so moving, the batter partially obstructs the catcher's view of both ball and target. This makes it more difficult to throw out the runner. (This is not interference, as the hitter is entitled both to attempt a bunt and to a legitimate position in the batter's box.)

3. *Fake bunt to precede a slap bunt.*

Finally, the bunt may be faked immediately prior to an attempt to slap hit. The fake comes on one pitch and the slap on the next. Again the goal is to bring the infielders closer, to get them thinking one thing and do another. Surprise and deception remain the keys to success.

Conclusion

Bunting is an essential part of baseball, especially at the upper levels. Every young player should have the opportunity to develop the various related techniques and use them in the appropriate circumstances. However, as with other strategies, bunting can be given more emphasis than it deserves. Instead of dominating the game, it is most effective when done well but not too often. The coach consequently must teach the skill to the players and give them enough practice to become proficient. However, the coach must also have a clear idea of both the athletes' abilities and when these skills can best be put to use. A well-executed bunt may bring in the winning run or start a big rally, but often bunts do not work out as planned. Double plays occur, the batter misses the ball and the base runner is thrown out, the lead runner is forced out, or a line drive results. The successful coach weighs the possibilities, makes certain that the right player is at the plate, and accepts the bunt's outcome. In this way, bunting is kept in perspective. It is an important bit of strategy that when properly used may affect the outcome of a game, but bunting should not become the centerpiece of play.

Nonstrategic Ways of Getting to First

Aside from hitting and bunting, several other occurrences can advance the batter to first. However, these do not involve strategy in the purest sense, for they generally are beyond the hitter's control. Nevertheless, such events should be considered, for they require a certain amount of planning and thought on the part of both coach and athletes.

Walks

Because they provide free base runners and may advance runners already on base, walks often start or extend rallies. However, walks should not be looked upon as gifts; rather, they should be seen as the result of practice and study. Very early on, baseball players need to learn the various strike zones (see "Hitting Strategy," "Strike Zones" earlier in this chapter) while developing the habit of swinging only at pitches within them. These bits of knowledge and skill allow the hitter to start helping the team by getting bases on balls. If the player develops enough bat control to foul off close pitches and becomes confident about doing so even with two strikes in the count, then the athlete becomes a real offensive asset to the team.

The skill of getting on base can be practiced but remains of limited effectiveness until the batter learns to study the opposing pitcher's choice of pitches and control. This final bit of understanding allows the offensive player to step to the plate with confidence in any situation. However, such study also reveals whether the current opponent is having trouble finding the strike zone. If this is the case or if the offense is having difficulty putting runners on base, the player may be pressed to use both skills and knowledge in an attempt to "work" the pitcher for a base on balls.

Similarly, the coach studies the opponent's pitcher to decide whether each hitter should take pitches until a strike is called. This ploy often works well late in the game, when the opponent has walked two or three batters in a row, or if the pitcher is showing signs of being tired. By using this tactic, the coach may help the batters get ahead in the count and increase their chances of walking.

Walks are somewhat beyond the control of the batter, as they involve the pitcher and umpire, as well. However, a skilled, experienced hitter can do much to improve the chances of getting a base on balls. This provides both player and coach with an extra element of strategy.

Batter Hit by Pitch

A batter hit by a pitch is awarded first base, but this is even less a tactical move than a walk. Nonetheless, it must be considered, if for no other reason than for safety.

In youth baseball, hitters are struck by pitches fairly often, but seldom because the pitcher intends to throw at them. Rather, most players get hit when the pitcher's control is faulty and they freeze in the batter's box. The coach, after helping the players learn to recognize when to get out of the way of a pitch, needs to teach players how to avoid being hit while minimizing the risk of injury if they are unable to move out of the way fast enough.

Generally, a player must begin by realizing the difference between the ball moving inside and one simply thrown toward the catcher. Using *tennis balls*, the coach teaches the difference by throwing various inside pitches toward the hitter, *who must be wearing a batting helmet*. Often the athlete recognizes inside pitches but fails to distinguish truly threatening ones. The coach can help by relating one way of telling when a ball is coming directly at the player: the ball may appear to be getting bigger but not necessarily moving. This, coupled with much practice, is probably the best way for an athlete to learn the difference among pitches. Having successfully learned this, the batter will be less likely to jump out of the way of pitches that simply are close.

Once knowing when to move, the player next must learn how to move out of the way. Faced with an inside pitch, the batter's first thought should be the protection of the most easily injured parts of the body—the front and head. This can best be accomplished by turning the front shoulder toward the catcher while bending at the waist. Thus, the more heavily muscled lower back and upper legs are pre-

sented to the pitch as the head drops below shoulder level. Any tendency to tuck the chin on the chest is minimized because this may expose the back of the head and neck to the ball; rather, the player keeps the neck firm (see Figure 9-1). After this first move, the player steps out of the batter's box with the back foot and crosses over with the front foot to move completely away from the ball (see Figure 9-2).

Note: A ball that hits the bat will be called a strike. Therefore, by learning to drop the hands to the waist while making the turn, the player will shield the bat with the body and so may avoid an inadvertent foul ball strike.

Most inside pitches will be between knee and shoulder height, and the previously described move will do; however, pitches near the head or feet present special problems. In the first case, the batter often initially freezes and so does not have time for the complete sequence of turn, bend and step; consequently, the player may only be able to turn the back and turn the bend into a fall to the ground. In the instance

Figure 9-1. Turning the back to a pitch likely to hit the batter.

Figure 9-2. Completing the move out of the way of an inside pitch.

of a very low pitch, the hitter often tries to avoid the ball by jumping, but the pitch may strike the ground and bounce up to hit the batter. Therefore, the athlete should still attempt to complete the turn, bend and step. (This is important, because the batter is still awarded first base even if hit by a pitch that has struck the ground; the rules require the batter to make an attempt to avoid the ball.)

As previously suggested, all of the moves to avoid being struck by a pitch must be practiced well in advance of their being needed. The coach or other adult starts this work by throwing tennis balls near a batter wearing a helmet. Gradually, the athlete will gain confidence in the ability to judge pitches and to move away from close ones. Then the coach may use slightly harder balls and repeat the cycle of learning. Finally the coach *may* decide to throw inside with easy pitches at close range. Such a sequence should adequately prepare the player for dealing with threatening pitches.

Catcher Interference

This situation is unique in being the only baseball play involving a choice. It begins with the batter's swing making contact with some part of the catcher—usually the mitt—and continues through the resulting action. This may be a swinging strike, a foul or fair ball, an out or a hit; but the play is allowed to completely unfold. The plate umpire then signals a dead ball and offers the hitter's coach a choice between the outcome of the play or an error on the catcher; this error awards the batter first base and advances any runners one base. Clearly the coach will have to weigh the alternatives, though the more advantageous choice is often clear.

Dropped Third Strike

With first base unoccupied, a strike out always must be completed. This can be done either by the catcher controlling the ball before it touches the ground or by someone at first base finishing the force out on the hitter. In other words, if the batter swings at and misses a third strike or if the umpire calls strike three, the catcher must hold the ball or throw it to first base to force the batter in the case of a dropped third strike. Occasionally, the ball is dropped, and the batter may reach base safely if prepared to run. Although the distances involved in baseball make this an uncommon occurrence, it happens just often enough that the coach should prepare the players for the possibility— especially because any base runners are free to advance on the play. Some youth coaches require every batter to run out third strikes hard; others use different techniques. But the athletes must be aware of the possibility of reaching first after striking out if they are to put the maximum pressure on the defense.

Errors

For the batter and base runners, errors are similar to missed third strikes in that both must be responded to quickly and aggressively. Practice, as with so many other plays, is key. The coach must constantly remind players that there really is no such thing as a routine play. Ground balls take strange bounces; fly balls fall in; fielders may drop throws. Thus, whenever the ball is in play, the batter and any base runners must be sprinting in an effort to go as many bases as possible. They cease attempting to advance only when the ball is near enough to present a risk or when a coach stops them.

Conclusion

Clearly, a number of possibilities are present with a batter at the plate. Some of these involve a great deal of strategy, while others include an element of chance. However, several important guidelines should be stressed.

1. The unexpected play often works best.
2. Both coach and athlete must practice tactic and strategy that they intend to use in a game.
3. When the ball is in play, runners have to be running hard for the next base.
4. Safety of teammates and opponents is a primary consideration.
5. Expect the unexpected.

Keeping these things in mind will enable the coach to develop an effective strategy of play. Being in command of these strategies gives the coach a measure of control which will allow the team to be successful.

STEALING BASES

Stealing bases advances runners without requiring the batter to hit or bunt the ball, but it involves an element of risk, for a player safely on base may be converted into an out. Often coaches and players believe that speed presents the sole means of minimizing the risk of having runners thrown out while attempting to steal bases, so they avoid using the running game. However, studying the opponents' battery, getting a good lead and timing attempts carefully are at least as important as speed to both individual and team success in base stealing. Skill in these areas allows a team to run the bases aggressively. While these factors are of primary concern, a number of others also must be weighed when deciding whether to run as a tactic. Some of these considerations involve personnel, some are environmental, and still others are situational, but in certain respects the decision to send base runners is philosophical.

Team Personnel

Aside from the particular base runners' abilities, the coach must consider those of the player at bat. If the batter is unlikely to be able to advance the runner, the coach can call for the steal; but if the hitter has good bat control and makes contact, a play such as the run-and-hit or a bunt may be used. However, if the batter draws a lot of walks, the steal may be put off in hopes of getting two players on base. Or, with a particularly good runner in position, the coach may decide to attempt the steal and so save the sacrifice until the runner can advance to third or score. Finally, the coach also should remember the batting order: The top of the order—skilled hitters with speed—should be more likely to drive in runners, so chancing the steal may not be as worthwhile as when the lower third of the order is coming to bat. Or, with a particularly good runner in position, the coach may decide to attempt the steal and so save the sacrifice until the runner can advance to third or score.

Field Environment

Field conditions add an element of chance, as well. A wet, muddy field effectively limits the runners' speed while making sliding a bit more risky. However, such conditions also make it harder for the catcher to throw, and the infielders have nearly as much difficulty as the runner in getting to the base. The coach may decide either to continue using the steal no matter what the conditions or to send players until one or more is thrown out. But the effect of weather and field conditions must be considered, for these factors slow down runners and increase the risk of injury.

Game Situation

The game situation—early or late, ahead or behind—as well as the number of outs also may influence the decision to steal bases. For example, some coaches feel reluctant to start runners unless it is early in the game and the team is no more than one run behind. However, this limits the effectiveness of the running game, while practically allowing the opponents to ignore certain aspects of defense at critical stages of the game. Other coaches are willing to call for the steal at any point during the game because they believe that this increases the pressure on the defense to perform. Still other coaches are somewhere between these extremes, in that they recognize such general rules as:

1. Do not cause the last out of an inning by getting the runner thrown out attempting to steal third.
2. Do not steal if the batter will then be walked intentionally.
3. Do not send runners with two outs or if more than two runs down.
4. With two outs and the lead-off hitter up, always send the runner.

Such situational considerations quickly fade into philosophical ones, and each coach will have to decide personally how much emphasis to put on base stealing and the running game.

Coaching Philosophy

Thus, coaches must consider how comfortable they feel with the consequent risk of runners being thrown out and with how the decision to run is made. Some coaches are at ease with the possibility of outs only after making the decision to run themselves and then giving the players a sign; others may feel comfortable with their players running more freely. However, as the athletes become more experienced, coaches should allow at least some of them to determine for themselves when to run (to the point that, at the top levels of play, a coach may only have a "don't run" sign). However, these coaches also will use signs to tell the remaining players to steal.

Within this context, the coach and team have three plays available to them: the straight, double and delayed steals.

Straight Steal

The simplest of steal plays, the straight steal usually focuses on second base; however, more and more often players are attempting to steal third. On a straight steal attempt, the runner takes the lead, reads the pitcher's motion, and sprints for the next base with the pitcher's move toward home. Speed is important, but knowing the pitcher is possibly of even more use. Espe-

cially easy to steal against is an opponent with an obvious pickoff move, weak skills in holding runners, a high leg kick, or poor control. At the upper levels of play, a breaking ball pitcher can be beaten more easily than one who throws mostly fastballs.

After reaching first, the coach and/or runner may wait until the second or third pitch before deciding to steal. The extra look gives everyone involved a final opportunity to gauge the pitcher's move. Additional observations on the straight steal appear in Chapter 7, Base Running.

Double Steals

Traditionally a play used with runners at first and third, the double steal offers a number of possibilities. Many of these are considered in Chapter 8, Defensive Strategies. But briefly put, most of the choices involve one of three general tactics:

1. a straight steal of second
2. a move toward second prior to the pitch in an effort to cause a balk or force a rundown play
3. a delayed steal of second

The first is detailed above, and the third play will be considered at length below. The second option requires further explanation.

The move toward second prior to the pitch is a trick play that depends upon the pitcher's actions. After looking over to hold the runner at first, the pitcher turns back to check third or deliver to the plate. With this move, the player breaks for second. Occasionally the defense may not even respond to the threat; but if they do, one of two actions occurs. The pitcher's attempt to turn and throw out the base stealer results in a balk call, which advances the runners a base and adds a ball to the batter's count. More often, the pitcher throws the ball to someone covering second, and the runner is caught in a rundown. This player is responsible for keeping the play going as long as possible, because the teammate at third is coached to break for home as soon as the run down begins.

Some coaches use this "sacrifice steal" as a set play when their team needs a run late in the game. If deciding to use the steal this way, one must instruct the team in the play's subtleties, as the goal is not a stolen base but a run. Thus, the runner from first may be expected to go at less than full speed, or the player may have to watch the defense closely in order to stop and move back toward first as soon as the ball gets to second. The intent is to draw a throw and trade an out for a run, almost as with a sacrifice bunt.

More recently, the double steal has come to be used with players at first and second. This play, usually done on the coach's signal and with a right-handed batter up, requires the lead runner to take a slightly longer than normal lead and to get a good jump on the pitcher. The teammate at first delays starting for second until it is clear that the steal has been attempted. (This eliminates the possibility of two athletes ending up on second base, if the lead runner has to return.) Although this double steal may be a bit more chancy, the play can be effective and, therefore, has become popular.

Delayed Steals

Although primarily directed at second, delays may be tried elsewhere. These efforts to steal bases come *after* the pitcher's delivery, so they are a bit "delayed" with respect to other attempts and so are appropriately named. The decision to try the delayed steal may be made by either coach or athlete; but in either case, it depends upon observations of the opponents. A catcher lobbing the ball back to the pitcher, a pitcher ignoring the runner after catching the ball, infielders unprepared to cover the base, all are clues to the possible success of a delayed steal. The more of these that occur, the less is there risk of an out.

To successfully complete a delayed steal, the runner takes a normal lead, but hesitates at the end. As the catcher releases the ball back to the pitcher, the player sprints for the next base. Often the player will slide in safely without a throw being made, even if the defense recognizes the delayed steal attempt. However, a certain element of risk remains, and some coaches are reluctant to use the delayed steal unless the game is close, the right runner is on base, and the defense appears completely distracted.

Conclusion

As suggested several times, aggressive running plays are risky, and the coach must make a conscious decision about how to use them. This is essentially a philosophical decision, but it has real consequences for how the team plays the game. An aggressive approach has been recommended throughout this chapter, for it can result in more runs scored and games won. However, this style's benefits spill over into other areas as well. Athletes find it exciting, and it often helps keep them mentally involved in the game. Coaches have an added strategy to exploit, are kept focused on the game, and so make fewer decisions from habit. The opposing team is kept off-balance, and the pitcher may be shaken. Finally, spectators enjoy the action surrounding base stealing. Much the same considerations apply to the taking of extra bases, whether on hits or defensive plays.

TAKING EXTRA BASES

Baseball's running game involves more than just base stealing. Taking the extra base on a hit, running on outfielders with erratic arms, tagging on fly balls at second—these are examples of pressuring the defense on the base paths.

The mechanics of taking the extra base were covered in Chapter 7, Base Running. However, success in picking up the extra base is an attitude as much as anything, and the effort begins with the coach's decision about the running game in general. Once deciding that the team will run whenever possible, the coach instills the idea through practice. With repetition, players come to expect two things each time the ball is on the ground in the outfield:

1. The hitter nearing first base plans to turn and try for second.
2. Any other runners hope to advance at least two bases.

Such an approach requires a high degree of trust and coordination between base coaches and athletes, because the players rely on the base coaches to watch play and stop the runners when necessary.

Knowledge of the opponents is a big part of the effort to advance further on hits. Again, both coaches and runners are involved, because all offensive players must have some knowledge of each outfielder's throwing ability. By studying these defenders, the base coaches will know who has the weakest throwing arm and who may throw out runners. Such information allows the coach confidently to send a runner home at one point, while stopping another in a seemingly similar circumstance. The athletes also can use such knowledge to improve their chances of scoring or advancing.

Besides taking advantage of outfielders' limitations, an aggressive offensive team can make use of some general guidelines for advancing runners on outfield plays.

- Defenders running to their glove side have a difficult time stopping and throwing; the runner should expect to go.
- Fielders catching fly balls with their backs to the infield seldom can keep runners from picking up at least one base; this may even apply to infielders taking shallow pop-ups. (Many young players do not realize that they may tag and advance on caught foul balls, so coaches should review this aspect of the rules while working on tagging up.)
- Most hits to right field should give the runners two bases.
- A runner at second may be able to tag up and advance on fly balls, especially ones in right-center or right field.

Somewhat similarly, players can be given basic rules for getting extra bases on infield plays. Of course, a player at first always must run on ground balls, and any other runners "forced" by this move must run as well. However, many other plays occur, and though things vary according to the infielders' depth of play, runners generally can advance as follows:

- With the defense back, players at second or third can go on most balls hit to the right side.
- Players at second or third should wait for the throw to first before advancing on ground balls to the left side; however, if the defense is back or if a run is needed, the coach may start a runner from third on "contact." (This means that the player sprints for home upon seeing the ball hit anywhere on the ground.)
- Runners always should check the next base

and consider advancing if it is unprotected—especially on bunts.
- Slowly hit ground balls should move up all runners.

Following these suggestions will make running an integral part of any team's game. However, the successful coach also will learn from experience how to further utilize their athletes' abilities.

PINCH HITTERS AND RUNNERS

Generally speaking, youth baseball games should give every player the chance to perform. This not only gives the athletes chances to use what they have learned in practice, it also motivates them to continue working and playing hard. However, not all athletes develop to the same level, and there are differences in ability that may affect playing time at the upper levels of competition. Consequently, there are starters and substitutes, and occasionally a starter may not have the skills required by the situation. For example, an excellent defensive shortstop may not be a particularly good bunter, or a right fielder may be a bit too slow getting to second in a double play situation. In these and similar cases, a pinch hitter or runner is appropriate.

Pinch Hitters

Batters have different skills. Some are good bunters; others regularly hit fly balls; some work pitchers for walks; and still others can hit to the right side to advance the runners. Thus, the play that is needed determines which hitter should be used, and the coach will have to know the personnel involved to make the right decision. Similarly, if the situation suggests that more than a pinch hitter may be necessary or if the move is made relatively early in the game, the best possible substitute may be saved for a more crucial point.

In any case, both the player being replaced and the pinch hitter should be told of the possible substitution as soon as possible. This allows the new batter to prepare mentally for the turn at bat and makes the switch go as smoothly as possible. However, the coach should wait to make the change until the opponents complete any strategy meetings and make any moves.

Pinch Runners

As with batters, runners sometimes do not have the skills necessary for a particular situation. Such situations usually arise late in the game when a run or two will make all the difference. Examples are as follows. With one out, a player safely reaches first and advances a teammate to third. However, the athlete at first does not have enough speed to steal second or avoid the double play. Or, with two outs, a runner reaches second but is likely too slow to score on a single. In these instances, using a pinch runner is a good move.

Conclusion

In youth baseball games, two rules generally apply to all substitutes:

1. The home plate umpire must be notified of all changes.
2. A starting player can reenter the game once after being replaced.

In other words, a replacement may be used and can remain in the game for an inning or two, and the starter still can go back in the game. The coach should keep this in mind and go over the possibility with the team.

Finally, the coach should prepare all the athletes for the possibility of being replaced. Whether a pinch hitter or runner or even a defensive change, all athletes involved deserve some warning. For the replaced player, this minimizes any possible distress with being taken out, while it gives the newly active athlete an opportunity to warm up. Handling personnel changes is an essential part of coaching, and one that becomes more important as the level of competition improves. The coach's success in this area has a great effect upon the team's performance.

SITUATIONAL PLAY

Describing the wide variety of situations that might arise in a baseball game is a difficult task. However, Supplements 9-1 a-e and 9-2 summarize some of the more common occur-

rences and indicates possible strategies: Supplements 9-1 a-e cover the desired reactions by base runners in various situations, and Supplement 9-2 deals with coaching strategies. The coach should have the players simulate the conditions outlined in Supplements 9-1 a-e until the athletes respond automatically. Further, the team must practice the skills required by the tactics included in Supplement 9-2, if they are to execute them properly. Recognizing that these supplements merely indicate options, the coach should choose among likely tactics after considering various factors. Among these are: the level of competition, the team's abilities and expectations, the skills of the players immediately involved, the opponents' defensive skills and strategies, the field conditions, and so forth. Consequently, while these materials provide some guidelines, the coach must still make the final decision about which play to use. Often the unexpected choice is the most effective.

BASE COACHING, SIGNS AND STRATEGY

An essential part of baseball are the base coaches and the signs they give, for these provide the means of implementing strategy. As the athletes become more experienced and their games become more competitive, coaching, signs and strategies gain in importance. People in coaching positions should know well the players' abilities and the overall strategy, because coaches must respond instantly to changing game situations. In this way, coaches save outs or help put runners in scoring position and they assist in pressuring the defense or save runs. But more importantly, coaches supply leadership, and they provide examples of good sportsmanship.

Base Coaching

If at all possible, adults should take the two base coaching positions. Young, relatively inexperienced athletes seldom either understand or communicate the strategy well enough to be effective coaches. Moreover, youngsters tend to be indecisive in giving signs, and they usually are tentative when instructing teammates. Finally, players often get caught up in watching the game and lose track of things. If only one adult is available, then the third base box is the place to be. In any case, the people in the coaching boxes need to be thoughtful and observant.

Coaches must know the game situation—outs, inning, score. They must keep track of the count on the batter, and they have to know all the possible signs. Coaches are responsible for watching the opposing pitcher for any moves that might indicate what pitch is being thrown, and they evaluate the fielders' ranges and throwing abilities. The first base coach in particular must study the pitcher's move to the bases. Coaches must know the general strategy to be used in common situations. Tag at second, go halfway on fly balls, take two bases on any hit to the outfield—these must be completely understood by the people in the coaching boxes. More specific responsibilities are as follows.

First Base

The batter and runner at first are the main concerns of the coach on the right side. Having hit the ball, any youth player will benefit from a first base coach yelling encouragement as the play develops. But more importantly, the coach helps focus the batter/runner's attention on what may happen next. The coach watches for errors and overthrows, for extra bases opportunities and for plays at other bases. The results have to be communicated—both verbally and physically. Spoken cues must be kept short, and they need to be loud. Thus, one or two word directions that are not easily mistaken for others are best. "Turn!", "Two!", "Stop!", "Go!", all are examples of effective spoken commands. These may be augmented by visual signs similar to those used at third base (see below). The most common signal is one indicating that the hitter should continue immediately on to second. Standing near the back corner of the box on the side closest to home and in clear view of the player, the coach points the right arm at second while repeatedly swinging the left in a full circle; this can be supported by a loud "Go!"

With a runner on first, the coach has added responsibility. First of all, the runner is reminded of the game situation and then told to check the third base coach for signs. A comment about the pitcher's pickoff move is in order, and some remark such as "Halfway on a fly ball" is also helpful. The coach also warns the athlete about being doubled off on a line drive with a statement like, "Make the line drives be through." (The usual response for youth players to any batted ball is to run. The coach must work with them to overcome this tendency, or else they will run themselves into any number of double plays. Unfortunately, this is counter to the idea of running aggressively, and the coach will have to spend much time in practice so every player knows how to react to line drives on the infield.)

The coach then takes a position in the box that will provide a good view of any pickoff play. If the defender is at the bag holding the runner close, the coach should be as near the base as the box allows (see Figure 9-3). This position gives the coach a good view of both opponents involved, and as soon as a pickoff is detected, the coach calls out "Back!" to signal the runner. However, if the defender at first is playing behind the runner, the coach moves to the side of the box closest to home (see Figure 9-4); and as soon as the opponent breaks for the base, the coach shouts "Back!"

Clearly the first base coach has a varied set of tasks to perform, and they must be done well. Whether adult or team member, the person filling this position must be completely involved in the game. The team's success may depend on it.

Third Base

If the coach at first base is important, then the person coaching at third is critical. This person is responsible for every player anywhere near second or beyond, so much of the job has to do with signaling to runners. To do this, the coach takes a position along the player's line of sight through third base. (If an opponent or umpire gets in the way, the coach *must* move to provide unobstructed signals.) A combination of arm motions and spoken commands should get the runners to the proper spots. These movements are fairly standard and straightforward; however, younger athletes will need to have them explained, and they will have to practice both finding and reacting to the coach's signs.

To stop a player at either second or third, the coach holds both hands up, palms toward

Figure 9-3. First base coaching position with a runner being held close.

Figure 9-4. First base coaching position used when the defender is playing behind the runner.

the runner (see Figure 9-5); something like "Stop!" or "Stay!" may be called out as well. The player is brought on to third base by extending the arms toward the athlete and making a pulling motion (see Figure 9-6) while yelling "Go!" or "Run!" To indicate that the athlete should slide at third, the coach makes a downward waving motion that ends with both hands pointed toward the base, much as a player would in starting a head-first slide (see Figure 9-7). If the play is especially close and no continuation is likely, the coach may even go down to the ground in making this move. Also, experienced teams may benefit from the coach directing the slide by pointing the hands to either side of the bag as needed.

The decision whether to send a runner on home must be made early enough that the athlete does not slow down or break stride nearing third. The coach should know the speed and aggressiveness of each player and use this knowledge in making the decision. If the runner is to be sent, the coach gets into a highly visible position—usually a bit up the line toward home

Figure 9-5. Stopping a runner.

Figure 9-6. Bringing a runner to third.

Figure 9-7. Signaling the runner to slide at third.

Figure 9-8. Signaling the runner to round third and continue to home.

but in line with runner's path to third. The coach points the right arm toward home and swings the left in a series of circles (see Figure 9-8).

Once the athlete reaches third, the coach's responsibilities are similar to those of the first base coach: keep the player informed of outs, watch for pickoffs, warn of line drives and so forth. However, the third base coach has two additional responsibilities:

1. The player always is told to lead off in foul territory,
2. The runner must be told whether to go on "contact."

The "On-deck" Hitter at Home

Though obviously not a base coach in the usual sense, the "on-deck" batter can make a real contribution at the more advanced levels of play. First, athletes in this role make the game safer for everyone involved if they retrieve the discarded bat whenever possible (see Figure 9-9). Secondly, teammates near the plate should watch the play develop so that they can signal

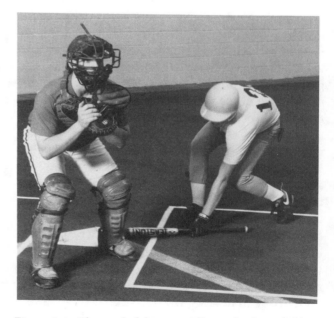

Figure 9-9. The on-deck hitter removing the discarded bat from the area of play.

for the runner to stand up or slide, much as the third base coach does (see Figure 9-10). Younger players should be taught to do the first as soon as possible, and by the time they are in their teen years, all baseball players should be able to help coach their teammates approaching the plate.

Signs

In addition to all the previously outlined responsibilities, the third base coach usually relays the signs to the batter and runners. These signals are a means of implementing strategic decisions, and they must be given quickly and efficiently; moreover, they must be clear and unmistakable. Because spoken instruction may be misunderstood or unheard, physical movements are often best, for they can be quite broadly drawn. However, like other elements of baseball, signs must be practiced and done with consideration.

Because players who need to see the signs may be 100 feet or more away, the movements involved should be simple and clearly discernible. Signs also should not involve movements likely to be made without thinking, such as touching glasses or tugging the cap. Usually signs are given as part of a sequence of moves

Figure 9-10. The on-deck hitter signaling for a slide by the runner coming home.

both meaningful and deceptive. Somewhere in this series, the coach shows the "indicator," which warns the players that the immediately following sign is "live." For example, if touching the chin is the indicator and wiping the hand across the stomach is the bunt, then these two motions performed in that order would call for the batter to bunt; but an intervening move or a different order would indicate something else. Clearly, both coach and players will benefit from practicing this form of communication.

Younger teams may use only bunt and steal signs, but older players should have more plays at their command. Therefore, experienced players may have quite a number of signs to learn. In either case, the coach should avoid hurrying through signs, so team members have time to read and interpret them. Further, the athletes also must learn how to take signs.

Typically, the batter steps out of the box and looks to the third base coach while *all* runners check for signs while tagging their base. The players watch the *entire* sequence of moves by the coach, so that signs are not given away by someone turning back to the plate or stepping off base too soon. A young player at bat may be instructed to acknowledge that a live sign has been seen with a simple nod of the head—but only after the coach finishes signing. Athletes also must have some means of indicating that the coach should run through the signs another time; players often hold out a finger while turning the hand in a circle to ask for a repeat of things.

Runners at second or third base often forget to look for signs. If the defender is playing back, the coach can talk directly to the player at third, but the runner at second may remain a problem. Although stressing that all runners must check for signs before each pitch, the coach must plan to make this part of base running drills—and still may need to remind players during games to check for signs when at second.

Finally, every player must realize that signs are important and that confusion leads to mistakes; consequently, if there is any misunderstanding about what to do, the athlete should ask for time to consult with the coach. (With time out and the two talking at such short distance, the coach asks the player to remove the helmet or else talks directly in the ear hole, because the helmet makes it difficult for the athlete to hear. In a final effort to avoid mistakes, the player may be asked to repeat the play.)

Each head coach will want to find what personally works best, but the following comments on possible signs are derived from several years experience in coaching younger athletes:

- Use an "indicator" to show that the next sign will be live, but avoid a habitual movement. Touching the chin with either hand is a good indicator.
- Help younger athletes by having some device for associating signs with plays. For example, indicate steals by using the shoulder ("S" in both words) and bunts by touching the belly ("B" in both). Thus, using either hand to touch the shoulder and then wiping across the upper chest might indicate a steal, while holding either hand to the shoulder calls for a delayed steal. Similarly, wiping either hand across the belly could denote a bunt, and holding either hand there communicates a fake bunt.
- With younger athletes, use a single bunt sign and treat all bunts as sacrifices or safety squeeze plays—the third base coach generally can communicate directly with the runner. However, older players need separate signs for bunting for a hit and the suicide; these can be shown by distinguishing between left and right hands to the belly and so increasing the number of possible signs to four.
- At least initially, show the run-and-bunt by using two indicators, each followed by a sign—the steal directed at the runner and the bunt for the batter. Both players must watch the complete series of signals; hitters should be out of the box and runners on the base.
- Once batters can execute the run-and-hit, consider assigning steals to the left hand at the shoulders while using a wipe across the shoulders with the right to indicate the run-and-hit.
- If the opponents appear to be stealing signs and a change seems advisable, alter the "indicator" but not the signs—especially with younger or inexperienced players. Consider changing indicators between games of double headers or before playing a team a second time; however, remember to tell the players about the new sign.
- Finally, have available some means of "wiping off" signs and starting over. The coach may show this by either of two signs: (1) running the hand down the upper leg, as though brushing dirt away, or (2) running the hand down the forearm, as if wiping off excess water. The player may ask for a new set of signs by holding the index finger horizontally in front of the body and making a circular motion.

Again, the number and complexity of signs is directly related to the athletes. The more experienced the team, the more strategies and signals they can be expected to use. Conversely, beginning players, who should concentrate on hitting the ball and running the bases, may not need any signs at all.

Conclusion

Close games occur at all levels of baseball, and good base coaching often is crucial to success—especially when the athletes are relatively inexperienced. Making strategic decisions, getting the runners safely to and around the bases, and communicating with players partially define the coaches' role. However, because coaching positions also should provide examples of sportsmanship, leadership, and team play, these roles are best taken by adults whenever possible. Moreover, it is best for the youngsters' development if there is little turnover among people filling these jobs. While youth teams often have difficulty realizing this level of adult involvement and support, they fully deserve it, and each baseball coach should continue to work toward this goal.

CONCLUDING COMMENTS

The length and complexity of this chapter suggest both the attraction and challenge of coaching youth baseball. On the one hand, it is easy to see how the strategy and thrill of competition draw adults into coaching. However, if they allow these considerations to dominate, these same adults will give little consideration to the reasons children commonly give for being part of a team: to have fun, to improve their skills and learn new ones, to experience competition, to get exercise, and to be with friends. Coaches must recognize these goals if young athletes are to get the most out of their experiences and remain part of the game. Clearly, coaching baseball—or any other youth sport— is more nearly an art than a science, no matter what might be inferred from reading this book.

ADDITIONAL READINGS

Editors of Sports Illustrated. (1960). *The Sports Illustrated Book of Baseball*. Philadelphia: J.B. Lippincott.

Weaver, E. with Pluto, T. (1984). *Weaver on Strategy*. New York: Macmillan.

Supplement 9-1a. Possible Responses by a Single Base Runner to Various Situations

Situation: Less than 2 outs, one runner on base

Event	At First	At Second	At Third
Passed Ball/Wild Pitch	Consider play; advance or return.	Consider play; advance or return.	Consider play; advance or return.
Ground Ball on Infield	Must advance to second.	Not forced to advance; evaluate and react to play. (Ground ball to left side, remain close; may advance on throw to first. Ground ball to right side, advance immediately.)	Not forced to advance; evaluate and react to the play. (Coach may decide to have player attempt to score on "contact." Otherwise, remain close and may go on throw to first from shortstop or third base. May advance on ball to right side.)
Line Drive on Infield	Return to first; advance if ball gets through (make sure ball goes through).	Return to second; advance if ball gets through.	Return to third; advance if ball gets through.
Pop-Up on Infield	Return to first; if missed must advance to second.	Return to second; if missed may move to third.	Return to third; if missed may score.
Fly Ball to Outfield	Go halfway to second; if caught, return to first; if missed, go to second and look to third base coach.	Two options: on a ball hit to the right fielder or one hit deep to the other positions, tag and look to advance; otherwise, go halfway and scores if missed.	Tag up and listen for coach's command to "GO!"
Foul Fly Ball	Tag up, look to advance if caught.	Tag up, look to advance if caught.	Tag up, listen for signal to "GO!"
Single to Outfield	Go to second and look at third base coach.	Go to third and look at third base coach.	Score.
Extra Base Hit	Advance at least to third but check coach as scoring is a possibility.	Score.	Score.

Supplement 9-1b. Possible Responses by Each Base Runner to Various Situations. Two Runners on Base at First and Second

Situation: Less than 2 outs, runners at First and Second

Event	At First	At Second
Passed Ball/Wild Pitch	Advance if lead runner goes.	Consider situation; advance or return as experience suggests.
Ground Ball on Infield	Must run.	Must run.
Line Drive on Infield	Return to base; look to advance only if ball goes through.	Return to base; advance only if ball goes through.
Pop-Up on Infield	Infield fly rule applies; check actions of lead runner if ball is dropped.	Infield fly rule applies; advance at own risk if ball is not caught.
Fly Ball to Outfield	Go halfway to second; return on catch; advance if ball drops. Check third base coach.	Either of two options apply: go halfway on balls, especially those to left field and center field, and advance or return as the fielder's actions dictate. Or, on balls hit to right field, tag up and look to advance.
Foul Fly Ball	Tag up, watch actions of lead runner.	Tag up; may attempt to advance, especially on plays well down the outfield lines or on ones that have the defender running hard with their back to the infield.
Single to Outfield	Advance; watch third base coach for help.	Look to score, but be prepared to stp at third if coach signals.
Extra Base Hit	Expect to advance at least to third. Check coach for possibility of scoring as lead can be lengthened with a runner at second.	Score.

Supplement 9-1c. Possible Responses by Each Base Runner to Various Situations. Two Runners on Base at First and Third

Situation: Less than 2 outs, runners at First and Third

Event	At First	At Third
Passed Ball/Wild Pitch	Advance unless ball is right with catcher.	Consider situation; advance or return as experience/speed allow.
Ground Ball on Infield	Must run.	May go on "contact," if coach has called that play. Otherwise, advance on balls to right side of infield and those to shortstop playing deep. Hold on ball to third and pitcher.
Line Drive on Infield	Return to base; advance once certain ball is through.	Return to base; advance once certain ball is through.
Pop-Up on Infield	Tag up; must advance if ball drops.	Tag up; may score if ball drops but defense must be in awkward position and home unprotected.
Fly Ball to Outfield	Play halfway; return or advance depending on outfield play.	Tag up and listen for "GO!"
Foul Fly Ball	Tag up; advance if play allows.	Tag up and listen for a call to "GO!" (The coach should have the runner attempt to score only if play is well down the line or the defender is moving away from the infield at the catch.)
Single to Outfield	Advance; watch third base coach.	Score.
Extra Base Hit	Advance at least to third; check coach and possible score.	Score.

Supplement 9-1d. Possible Responses by Each Base Runner to Various Situations. Two Runners on Base at Second and Third

Situation: Less than 2 outs, runners at Second and Third

Event	At Second	At Third
Passed Ball/Wild Pitch	Watch actions of lead runner; advance likely if runner at third goes.	Weigh situation; advance if experience/speed allow.
Ground Ball on Infield	Watch actions of lead runner; but avoid running into a play by the shortstop.	Score on balls to the right side and those hit deep to shortstop; hold on plays by third and pitcher.
Line Drive on Infield	Tag up; advance only after ball goes through.	Tag up; advance only after ball goes through infield.
Pop-Up on Infield	Tag up.	Tag up. If ball drops, score if plate is undefended.
Fly Ball to Outfield	Go halfway on balls to left field and center field. Tag up and advance on balls to right field.	Tag and listen for "GO!"
Foul Fly Ball	Tag up correctly and move part way to third if the lead runner tags. If the runner at third attempts to score, be prepared to advance, but only if the throw goes through to the plate.	Tag and score if play allows. (See previous comments on this situation.)
Single to Outfield	Score.	Score.
Extra Base Hit	Score.	Score.

Supplement 9-1e. Possible Responses by Each Base Runner to Various Situations. With the Bases Loaded

Situation: Less than 2 outs, bases loaded

Event	At First	At Second	At Third
Passed Ball/Wild Pitch	Watch runners in front; advance on break by runner at second.	Check actions of runner at third; advance on runner starting for home.	Consider situation; advance or return as experience/speed allow.
Ground Ball on Infield	Must go.	Must go.	Must go.
Line Drive on Infield	Tag up; advance once ball is through if runner at second goes.	Tag up; move up once ball is through.	Tag up; advance once ball is through infield.
Pop-Up on Infield	Infield fly rule applies. Must advance if ball drops; at risk of being put out.	Infield fly rule in force. Must move up if ball drops; at risk of being put out.	Infield fly rule in effect. Must run if ball drops; at risk of being put out.
Fly Ball to Outfield	Play halfway. Return or advance depending on outfield play.	Tag on balls to the right side; go halfway on balls to left field or center field.	Tag and listen for signal to "GO!"
Foul Fly Ball	Tag up. Advance if runners ahead move up.	Tag up. Go part way and then advance if a play is made at the plate.	Tag up. Listen for command to "GO!"
Single to Outfield	Advance; check coach at third for probable move to that base.	Score.	Score.
Extra base hit	Probably can score, as lead should be longer in bases loaded situation. However, check third base coach.	Score.	Score.

Supplement 9-2. Possible Strategies to Use in Different Situations.[1]

Situation	Middle Innings (3rd, 4th, 5th)	Late Innings (6th, 7th, Extra)
0 Outs		
No runners	Hit away	Hit away Bunt for a hit
Runner at 1 or 2	Steal Run and hit	Run and hit Run and bunt Bunt for a hit Sacrifice[2]
Runners at 1 and 2	Double steal Run and hit	Double steal Run and bunt Run and hit Sacrifice Bunt for a hit
Runners at 1 and 3	Steal/delayed steal (from first)	Steal/delayed steal (from first) Run (from first) and bunt Bunt for a hit Safety squeeze
Runner at 3[3]	Hit away	Hit away Bunt for a hit
Bases loaded	Hit away	Hit away
1 Out		
No runners	Hit away	Hit away Bunt for a hit
Runner at 1 or 2	Steal Run and hit	Run and hit Run and bunt Bunt for a hit Sacrifice[4]
Runners at 1 and 2	Double steal Run and hit	Double steal Run and bunt Run and hit Sacrifice Bunt for a hit
Runners at 1 and 3	Steal/delayed steal (from first)	Steal/delayed steal (from first) Run (from first) and bunt Bunt for a hit Sacrifice Safety squeeze Suicide squeeze[5]
Runner at 3	Hit away	Bunt for a hit Safety squeeze Suicide squeeze
Bases loaded	Hit away	Hit away Safety squeeze
2 Outs		
No runners	Hit away	Hit away Bunt for a hit
Runner at 1 or 2	Steal Run and hit	Run and hit Run and bunt Bunt for a hit
Runners at 1 and 2	Double steal Run and hit	Double steal Run and bunt Run and hit Bunt for a hit

Situation	Middle Innings (3rd, 4th, 5th)	Late Innings (6th, 7th, Extra)
Runners at 1 and 3	Steal/delayed steal (from first)	Steal/delayed steal (from first) Run (from first) and bunt Bunt for a hit
Runner at 3	Hit away	Hit away Bunt for a hit
Bases loaded	Hit away	Hit away

1 = First base
2 = Second base
3 = Third base

[1]These strategies are suggested with the idea that only one or two runs will make the difference in the game. With larger margins or earlier innings, the coach should give the players more opportunities to make their own decisions or should focus on hitting away and stealing.
[2]Sacrifice bunts are really effective only when they lead directly to the tying or go-ahead run. Otherwise, a more aggressive play is in order.
[3]Situations involving runners at second and third are not included as they can be played as though there were only a runner at third.
[4]With one out, sacrifice bunts should be used only if the batter is unlikely to advance the runner any other way.
[5]Suicide squeeze plays should be saved for game winning situations.

Section II
Rule Modifications
for Youth Baseball

10
Basic Baseball Rules With Modifications for Youth Players

Michael A. Clark, Ph.D.

QUESTIONS TO CONSIDER

- What modifications to the rules of baseball serve the developmental needs of youth players?
- What changes in the rules of baseball would promote greater safety, enjoyment, and fairness in competition?

INTRODUCTION

Baseball as a sport is played and enjoyed by millions of people the world over. What started out to be "the great American pastime" is now known and loved from Japan to Venezuela, from Canada to Australia, from Italy to Russia. There is even a variation of baseball in Finland, played by greatly modified rules, that maximizes offensive play. In the United States, individuals often begin playing when six or seven years old, play through their adolescent and young adult years, and are still able to join leagues for older athletes. These last opportunities go by many names, but they give people in their 60s or 70s an opportunity to keep in touch with the game they love. Young women have taken their place on baseball fields at various levels of amateur play, as well. And there are the numerous pick-up games played on weekends and at reunions everywhere. Rather than trying to deal

with all these variations, this chapter will focus on the rules that generally apply to baseball games played by boys and girls of school age.

The "official" rules of baseball are varied, as numerous governing bodies produce rule books describing the ins and outs of games they sanction. Among these are Major League Baseball, the American Baseball Congress, the National Collegiate Athletic Association, Little League of America, and on and on. In addition, many local agencies use workable variations that suit the needs of their particular populations. Thus, it would seem challenging to attempt to summarize the rules of play. Nevertheless, there is essential agreement on many points, for the spirit of American baseball has remained intact for quite some time. Noting this, it also is important to recognize that rules modifications often are appropriate. Although altering the game somewhat, these modifications remain true to the spirit of baseball, in addition to al-

227

lowing more young people to enjoy the game by

1. giving them the opportunity to develop the skills essential to the game
2. involving more players in each game
3. reducing the chance of injury
4. moving the game along quickly enough to hold everyone's attention

These modifications generally affect the following:

1. field size
2. pitching
3. base running
4. hitting/bunting
5. game length

RULE 1: DEFINITIONS

A glossary of terms used throughout this discussion of rules, as well as in the previous nine chapters dealing with skills and strategies, is to be found in Chapter 11. You may wish to take a moment and read some of those entries at this point, or at any time during the discussion when a word or phrase is unclear or confusing.

RULE 2: THE FIELD

Distance Between the Bases

At the upper levels of play, the bases are placed 90 feet apart. This distance is measured from the back corner of home plate to the outside back corners of first and third bases. From these points, the 90 feet is measured to the *center* of second base.

Pitching Distance

A distance of 60 feet 6 inches is measured along a straight line running from the back point of home plate to the middle of second base. This locates the center of the front edge of the pitcher's plate.

Fence Distance

Unlike other distances in baseball, the distance from home plate to the outfield fences

varies. Most rule books refer only to "recommended" distances, with 310 to 330 feet being most common for older players. These suggestions apply to the distances measured along the extensions of the first and third baselines, commonly called the foul lines. Typically, the distance to the fence increases as one moves from the foul lines to center field, thus the fence is not a simple arc.

See Figure 10-1 for an indication of these customary dimensions.

Other Common Dimensions

Figure 10-2 a-c and Table 10-2 shows such other common dimensions as:

1. the two boxes for batters
2. the catcher's box
3. the distance from home plate to the backstop
4. the circles for on-deck hitters
5. the two boxes for coaches
6. the first base runner's box
7. the pitcher's mound

Modifications for Youth Competition

Generally, each of the major distances is decreased in direct relation to the ages of the players involved. Common variations are sum-

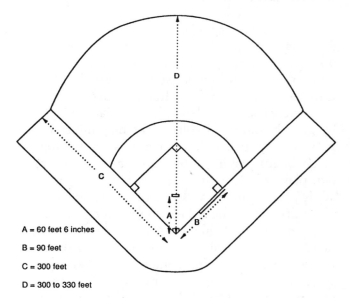

A = 60 feet 6 inches

B = 90 feet

C = 300 feet

D = 300 to 330 feet

Figure 10-1. Customary dimensions for a baseball field used by older youth.

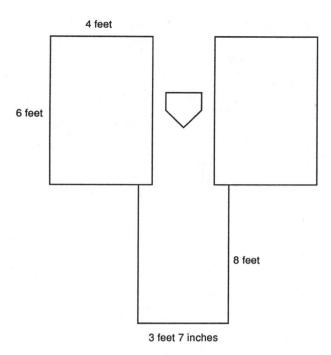

Figure 10-2a. Dimensions of the batters' and catcher's boxes.

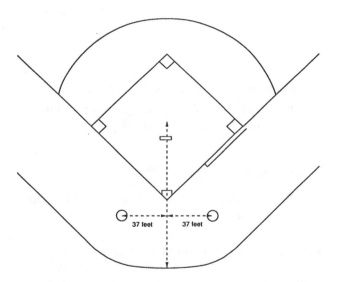

Figure 10-2b. Size and placement of the on-deck circles.

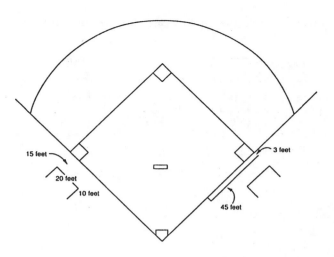

Figure 10-2c. Size and placement of the runner's and coaches' boxes.

RULE 3: EQUIPMENT

Bats

Although bats may be made of wood or non-wood materials, most today are made of aluminum. In any case, a bat must be marked "Official Baseball" to be legal for play. Bats for youth players generally vary from 24 to 36 inches in length and weigh from 20 to 31 ounces. (Bats may not weigh more than 5 units less than the length; thus a 33 inch bat must weigh at least 28 ounces.) Bats for younger players generally cannot exceed 2¼ inches in diameter while older players may use bats up to 2¾ inches across. Safety knobs are required on all bats. Material may be applied to the grip area; although tape or leather can be used for this purpose, a rubber sleeve is much more common.

Modifications for Youth Competition

As suggested Chapter 6, "Hitting and Bunting," the bat must "fit" the player. Younger players often use bats that are much too heavy; rather, they should find a bat that they can grip as in Figure 10-3 and hold comfortably. Table 10-3 includes some information that may be useful in helping coaches and players select the proper bat.

marized in Table 10-1. Some alterations also occur in other distances: size and location of the coaching boxes, the length of the runner's box, the size of the batting boxes and so on. Typical changes in minor dimensions are summarized in Table 10-2.

Table 10-1. Commonly found variations in dimensions of fields used at various levels of youth play.

Age Group (Years)	Fence Distances (Feet)			Distance Between Bases (Feet)	Pitching Distance (Feet)	Height of Mound (Inches)
	Foul line	Centerfield Min.	Max.			
5-6	125	200		50	38[1]	4
7-8	150	125	200	50	38[2]	4
6-7-8	200			60	46[3]	
9-10	175	150	225	60	44[4]	4
11-12	200	175	250	70	48	6
13-14	250	200	300	80	54	8
15-18	300	250	350	90	60.5	10

[1]Coach pitch or pitching machine set up; defensive player behind and to either side.
[2]Tee ball.
[3]Tee ball.
[4]Player pitch for ages 9 and up.

Warm-up Bats

Players often find it useful to prepare for their turns at bat by using a weighted warm-up bat. However, this must be a clearly marked, manufactured item. Any other weighted items are not to be used for warming up in the on-deck circle. Vanes may be attached to the bat for warming up.

Balls

Official-sized baseballs are used throughout youth play. These must weigh from 5 to 5¼ ounces while being 9 to 9¼ inches in circumference. Balls are made in two ways. Traditionally, they consist of yarn wrapped around a core of cork or rubber and covered with leather. In recent years, baseballs intended to decrease the likelihood of injury have been developed; these generally incorporate a solid, synthetic core.

Modifications for Youth Competition

Baseballs specifically designed to curtail injuries should be used for youth play.

Bases and the Pitcher's Plate

All ball games use the same size and shape for home plate, bases and pitcher's plate.

- *Home plate* is a five-sided piece of white rubber. The front edge is 17 inches long, while the parallel sides are 8½ inches each. The remaining two sides, which form the point and are placed along the base lines, are 12 inches each (see Figure 10-4). This white surface commonly is surrounded by a black, beveled edge that provides protection to a sliding player and is not considered part of the plate.
- *Bases* traditionally have been canvas bags filled with soft material. They are 15 inch squares from 3 to 5 inches thick, and provision is

Table 10-2. Typical variations in minor field dimensions.

(All dimensions are given in feet.)

a length of base line	b length of runner's box	c width of runner's box	d length of coaches' boxes	e width of coaches' boxes	f set back of coaches' boxes	g recommended distance to back stop
50	25	3	8	4	6	20
60	30	3	8	4	6	20 to 25
70	35	3	12	6	9	30
80	40	3	12	8	12	40
90	45	3	20	10	15	60

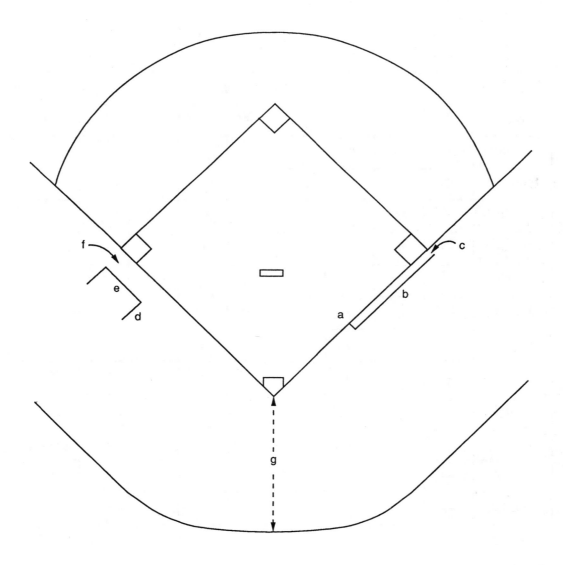

Figure 10-3. A player gripping a comfortably fitted bat.

Table 10-3. Selecting the right bat.

Player Weight	Batter's Height								
	3'-3'4"	3'5"-3'8"	3'9"-4'	4'1"-4'4"	4'5"-4'8"	4'9"-5'	5'1"-5'4"	5'5"-5'8"	5'9"-6'
Under 60 lbs.	26"	27"	28"	29"	29"	—	—	—	—
61-70	27"	27"	28"	29"	29"	30"	—	—	—
71-80	—	28"	28"	29"	30"	30"	31"	—	—
81-90	—	28"	29"	29"	30"	30"	31"	32"	—
91-100	—	28"	29"	30"	30"	31"	31"	32"	—
101-110	—	29"	29"	30"	30"	31"	31"	32"	—
111-120	—	29"	29"	30"	30"	31"	31"	32"	—
121-130	—	29"	30"	30"	30"	31"	32"	33"	33"
131-140	—	29"	30"	30"	31"	31"	32"	33"	34"
141-150	—	—	30"	30"	31"	31"	32"	33"	34"
151-160	—	—	30"	31"	31"	32"	32"	33"	34"
Over 160	—	—	—	31"	31"	32"	32"	33"	34"

Reprinted with permission by Hillerich & Bradsby Co., Louisville, Kentucky.

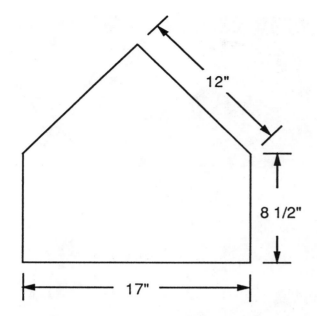

Figure 10-4. The dimensions of home plate.

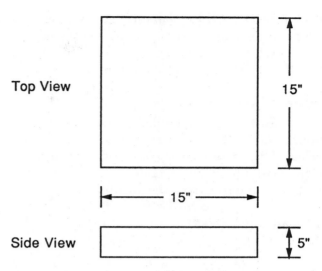

Figure 10-5. Dimensions of the bases used at first, second and third.

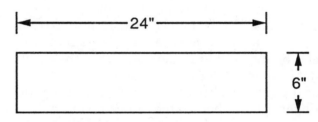

Figure 10-6. Dimensions of the pitcher's plate.

made for firmly attaching them to the ground (see Figure 10-5).

● *The pitcher's plate* is a rectangular piece of white rubber, 24 inches by 6 inches (see Figure 10-6).

Modifications for Youth Competition

Smaller Bases

In some instances, games for younger players make use of smaller bases and pitcher's plates. For example, bases are 14 inches square and no more than 2¼ inches thick, while the pitcher's plate is 18 inches by 4 inches.

Double-Wide Base

The double-wide first base represents another alteration to the rules for youth play. Constructed like other bases, this double base is 15 inches by 30 inches and the normal thickness (see Figure 10-7). Half white and half orange, the base is positioned at the usual distance with the white portion in fair territory and the orange outside the foul line. Offensive players are taught to use the orange part as they run out hits, and defensive players are expected to touch the white side to complete force outs. The double first base is intended to reduce injuries resulting from collisions during close plays at first base. After initially touching the orange side, offensive players make use of

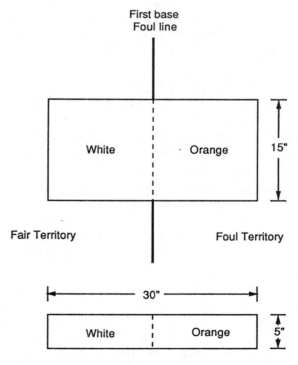

Figure 10-7. Dimensions and positioning of the double-wide first base.

the white half of the bag in retouching between pitches or on pickoff attempts; batted balls striking the white portion are in play, and those hitting the orange are in foul territory.

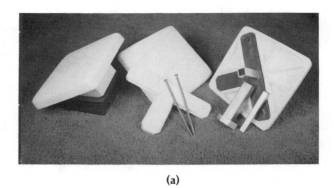

Progressive Release Bases

Another recommended modification for youth play is the use of so-called "progressive release" bases for second and third. Various designs exist, but all are intended to reduce injuries by coming free from the anchor if an athlete slides into the base with sufficient force. Figure 10-8 a-c illustrates two common types of such bases.

Gloves and Mitts

Gloves and mitts must meet size restrictions to be considered legal for play. Typically, gloves may not be longer than 12 inches from the bottom of the glove, across the palm, to the end of the second finger. Similarly, they may not be more than 8 inches wide—from the base of the thumb crotch to the outside of the little finger. The webbing area can be no more than 5¾ inches across (see Figure 10-9). The catcher generally is required to wear a catcher's mitt, although there are no specifications relating to size. The only other limitation affects the pitcher, whose glove must be one color and cannot be white or gray.

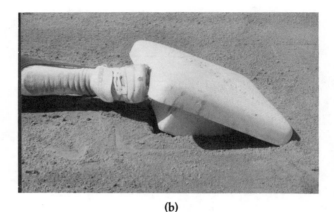

Modifications for Youth Competition

Gloves and mitts are very personal items that can last for quite a long time; therefore, care should be given to choosing one that fits properly. Often, young players end up with gloves that are much too large to be easily controlled, and as a consequence their skills fail to develop. Rather, it is better if they use smaller gloves that allow them to develop proper fundamental skills. Table 10-4 incorporates guidelines relating glove sizes to the ages of the players.

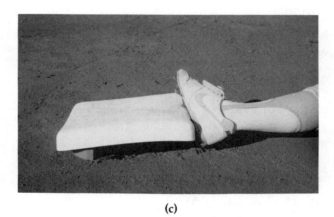

Figure 10-8. (a) This picture illustrates the two basic styles of progressive release bases. On the left is one having a large "plug" on the bottom which allows the entire base to come free when a sliding player hits it at a potentially injurious angle. Figure (b) shows this style in use. In the middle and on the right in (a) are two replacement bases which have a large "T" shaped piece mounted on the pegs typically used to hold bases in place. This "T" snaps into a matching opening in the bottom of the bag. If a sliding player hits this style of base in a dangerous manner, the base pops off the "T" as in (c).*

*Illustrations provided by and used with permission of Beacon Products Co.

Shoes

Shoes worn for baseball have canvas, plastic or leather uppers, and the soles are either smooth or have molded in cleats. These extensions may take a variety of patterns.

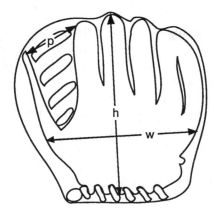

h = maximum height of glove (14 in.)

w = maximum width of glove (8 in.)

p = maximum dimension across top of pocket (5 3/4 in.)

Figure 10-9. Various limiting dimensions for gloves.

Modifications for Youth Competition

Metal spikes should not be worn in any youth play. Such shoes have been implicated in a variety of injuries. The runner wearing metal spikes may risk serious knee or ankle injury if the spikes catch while the player runs, pivots or slides, and other players may be badly cut by even accidental contact.

Catcher's Equipment

The catcher requires special protection because contact with pitches, batted balls, bats and base runners presents the possibility of injury. Essentially every set of baseball rules specifies full protection. Beginning at the top, this includes: a catcher's helmet and mask with a throat protector attached to the mask. A chest/body protector comes next. A male catcher wears an athletic supporter and protective cup. Shin guards—which should cover the upper part of the foot as well—complete the outfitting of a catcher. Neck collars and other protective wear are common as well, and even may be required by some organizations. Thus, the equipment mentioned represents the minimum protection for a catcher.

Modifications for Youth Competition

Any player warming up a pitcher should wear the helmet/mask/throat protector combi-

Table 10-4. Recommended glove/mitt sizes for youth baseball players.

Age Group (Years)	Maximum Length* (Inches)— Top of Second Finger to Bottom Edge of Palm	Maximum Width (Inches)— Width Across Palm
8 and under	9½	5¾
9-10	10¾	6½
11-14	12	7¼
15-18	14	8

*Measurement limitations do not apply to catcher's mitts. Also, gloves of the maximum length typically are used only at first base and in the outfield. Most infielders and pitchers prefer smaller gloves that allow the player to "find" the ball more quickly.

nation. However, it is recommended further that any athlete warming up a pitcher always wear the full complement of protective gear described under the heading "Catcher's Equipment."

Batting Helmets

Every hitter, base runner, on-deck batter, and non-adult coach must wear a helmet. Made of high-impact plastic and padded, these helmets have an extension that covers both ears and the lower rear of the head. Such helmets are approved by NOCSAE (National Operating Committee on Standards for Athletic Equipment) and are stamped with this seal of approval. Further, a warning label must be clearly visible on the outside of the helmet. Care should be given to the fitting of these helmets, and the players need instruction in how to wear them properly.

Younger players often end up with ill-fitting helmets, either by chance or choice; moreover, they compound the problem by wearing them incorrectly. Consequently, the coach is responsible for making certain that each player has a snugly fitting, approved helmet and that the player does not wear the helmet tipped back on the head. Especially for younger players, helmets with attached chin straps are an added safety feature.

RULE 4: PLAYERS AND SUBSTITUTES
Number of Players

Baseball is played with nine players on a team. Defensively they take positions at pitcher and catcher; first, second, and third bases; shortstop; and left, center and right fields. In play subject to most codified rules, a team must have all nine players to begin a game, and nine players must remain available to continue play. If at any time a team has less than this number, then they must forfeit the game.

Modifications for Youth Competition

Generally games played by children eight or younger add a tenth player to the lineup. This player, termed a "short" or "roving" fielder, takes a position in the outfield. Still younger players (those under seven) often play with rules that include three extra players, for a total of twelve defenders. One of these is the previously mentioned short fielder; the other two are positioned in the infield: one between the usual first and second base positions, and the other between the second base and shortstop spots. In either case, the team's batting order should include the entire roster of available players.

Reentry

Many organizations permit each player named in the starting lineup to be replaced and later reentered once. The player must reenter the game in the same position in the batting order. (Thus, if the shortstop is hitting sixth and is replaced by a substitute, then the shortstop may return later to the game only in the sixth spot in the order. However, the player may take a different defensive position.)

Modifications for Youth Competition

Most organizations require that all players have the opportunity to play at least two innings per game. Using the reentry rule makes this easier to accomplish.

Substitutions

Substitutes may be used for any player in the lineup. To be considered a legal substitute, the player cannot have previously entered the game as a substitute, and the home plate umpire must be notified of the change. The umpire informs the official scorer—in youth baseball this is usually the home team's scorer.

Designated Hitter

In an effort to involve as many athletes as possible rules governing youth baseball games generally allow the use of a *designated hitter* (shown by a DH in the lineup). Appearing only on offense, this player may replace any of the nine defensive players in the batting order. (*Note:* This is a modification of rules governing highly competitive situations where the designated hitter bats for the pitcher. The player for whom the designated hitter is substituted is also listed on the lineup card, with the defensive position shown. Typically, this player is listed at the end of the order, although the DH is shown in the desired spot in the batting order.)

The designated hitter's position is subject to the rules governing substitutions. Thus, pinch hitters or runners may be used for the player, and the starting DH may reenter the game once. However, two sorts of substitutions end the use of a designated hitter.

1. If the DH is replaced by any athlete—starter or substitute—for whom the designated hitter has been batting, the position of DH ends.
2. The role also ends if any player who has been the designated hitter takes a defensive position.

Further, the position of the DH in the batting order and the player for whom the designated hitter is substituted are "locked." Thus, any athletes involved in either role may only appear in the batting order where the DH originally appears, and no substitutions may change the batting order.

Summary

Table 10-5 summarizes the desirable modifications in youth baseball relating to players and substitutions.

RULE 5: THE GAME

Last at Bat

The home team has the advantage of batting last in each inning, unless specific rules state otherwise. If a home team is not designated, a coin toss supervised by the plate um-

Table 10-5. Recommended modifications relating to players and substitutions in youth baseball games.

Age Group (Years)	Number of Defenseive Players/Team	Number of Offensive Players/Team	Designated Hitter	Number of Innings/ Player	Re-entry
8 and under	10	Entire Roster	No	2 or More	Unrestricted
9-12	9	9	No	2 or More	Once per player
13-14	9	9	No	2 or More	Once per starter
15-18	9	9	Yes	No Restrictions	Once per starter

pire determines which team bats last. Batting alternates back and forth between visiting and home teams until the game is completed. The home team commonly does not use its turn at bat if it is winning when coming to bat in the last inning.

Number of Innings/Length of Game

Six or seven complete innings generally constitute a regulation youth baseball game. However, this may be shortened by one-half inning if the home team is leading after the visitors have batted in their final inning. Or if the home team starts the final turn at bat in a losing position or with the score tied, but scores enough runs to take the lead, then the game ends. If a game is tied after the designated number of full innings, extra innings are played until a winner is determined. If a game is ended before seven innings have been finished, it is considered a complete game if at least five full innings have been played or if the home team is ahead after 4½ innings. Games that are ended before completion are considered "suspended" and are resumed from the exact situation at a later date. Baseball rules generally do not recognize tie games; if a winner has not been determined before play stops, a suspended game usually is called.

Modifications for Youth Competition

For athletes ten and younger, regulation games should be five innings long. Also, players fourteen and younger should have their games subject to a time limit. This may be 2 hours for ballplayers 13 and 14 years old, and 1½ hours for those 12 and younger. This means that at the end of the time limit, any inning in progress is completed in its entirety, and the game then becomes official. (This also introduces the possibility of tie ball games. Additional modifications will have to be made to account for this.) Players 15 to 18 years old should have their games limited by the "10-run rule." This rule calls for the game to end when either team is 10 or more runs ahead after 5 complete innings, or if the home team has such a lead after at least 4½ innings.

The Winning Team

The team with the most runs when the game becomes official is the winner.

Scoring Runs

A player scores a run by properly touching each base in order—first, second, third and home—before the defensive team completes the third out of the inning. If the third out of an inning results from either a force out or the batter being put out before safely reaching first base, any runners crossing the plate before completion of the play are not counted. Similarly, if a base runner makes the third out of an inning, any subsequent runners crossing the plate are not credited with scoring. (For example, R1 is at second and R2 is on at first with two outs. B gets a hit, and both R1 and R2 cross the plate. However, R1 is called out for missing third base. R2's run does not count.)

Modifications for Youth Competition

The potential difference in runs scored in any inning should be limited for players 10 and younger. Any one of several rules may be used to accomplish this. A team may be allowed to score a maximum number of runs each inning; 5 or 8 runs are common limits. Only a limited number of players may bat each inning; 9 or 10 hitters usually are allowed. Or each team bats through its roster each inning no matter how many runs are scored.

Offensive Conferences

Each team is allowed one charged conference during their offensive inning. The coach initiates this process by asking the plate umpire for "time" and calling together the offensive player or players to be consulted. The umpire should not grant any subsequent delays for conferences during the team's remaining time at bat.

Summary

Table 10-6 summarizes the main modifications relating to games and innings played.

RULE 6: PITCHING

Taking the Sign

Pitching rules generally require the athlete to take time between pitches and begin each delivery by assuming a position on the mound as though taking signs from the catcher. Whether the full windup or the set position is used, the pitcher is required to do the following:

- The pivot foot must be in contact with the pitcher's plate.
- The ball may be in either the glove or the throwing hand.
- To change position, the pitcher first must move the pivot foot backward off the plate.

Further, if the pitch is to be legal:

- The pitcher may not make a "quick" pitch.
- The catcher must have both feet in the catcher's box when the pitch is thrown.

The Windup

To deliver a pitch from the full wind up position, the pitcher additionally *must*:

- not take more than two pumps or rotations of the arms
- not interrupt the delivery once motion begins
- once having positioned the feet for the windup, either deliver the pitch or step straight backwards off the plate

Further, the pitcher *may*:

- have the non-pivot foot in any position on or behind an imaginary line created by extending the front of the rubber
- step either forward or backward then forward with the non-pivot foot

Delivery from the Set Position

Besides following the general guidelines applied to pitching, the pitcher *must* do each of the following to legally deliver a pitch from the set position:

- take the sign with the pitching hand held at the side or behind the back
- have the non-pivot foot fully in front of the rubber
- move into the set position with a continuous motion
- come to a complete stop while having the ball in both hands
- stop with the hands below the chin and in front of the body

Further, the pitcher in the set position *may*:

- make one "stretch" move with the arms
- turn on the pivot foot or lift it to start a jump pickoff move

Table 10-6. Recommended modifications effecting games and innings played.

Age Group (Years)	Number of Innings/Game	Time Limit	10-Run Rule	Number of Batters/Inning
10 and under	5	Yes (1½ hrs.)	No	10 or Less
11-12	6	Yes (1½ hrs.)	No	No Restrictions
13-15	7	Yes (2 hrs.)	Yes	No Restrictions
15-18	7	No	Yes	No Restrictions

- step backward off the rubber with the pivot foot

Illegal Actions Taken by a Pitcher

The pitcher may not do any of the following:

- mar the ball by putting a substance—including spit—on it
- throw the pitch before the catcher takes a position in the catcher's box
- "quick" pitch
- have one or both feet on the dirt portion of the mound without having the ball in possession
- fail to throw a pitch within 20 seconds of receiving the ball or having "play" called
- take longer than one minute and eight pitches to warm up for the first inning of pitching
- take more than one minute and five throws to prepare for successive innings
- throw to anyone beside the catcher when a batter is in the box, unless the move is an attempt to pickoff a runner
- intentionally throw at a batter

Balks

With one or more opponents on base, a whole series of actions by the pitcher are considered balks, which result in all runners being awarded one base. *While touching the pitcher's plate, the pitcher balks by*:

- faking a throw to the plate or first base; however, fake throws may be made to either second or third base in an attempt to pick off runners
- dropping the ball and having it not cross a foul line
- not stepping toward a base with the non-pivot foot when either throwing or faking a throw
- either throwing or faking a throw to an unoccupied base
- making an illegal pitch
- not using a continuous delivery
- releasing the ball from one hand and then returning the hand to the ball without having made a play
- not making a pitch after the non-pivot foot

crosses behind the back edge of the plate, unless turning to throw to second

When not touching the rubber, the pitcher balks by:

- moving as though pitching
- being on the mound without the ball

Defensive Conferences

Each defensive team may call for "time" for purposes of discussing strategy. One conference per inning, up to a maximum of three such meetings, may be called. If more than these are taken, the pitcher must be replaced by a substitute who must throw to at least one batter or be in the position of pitcher until one out is achieved.

Modifications for Youth Competition

While many changes found in youth baseball games involve pitching, they do not represent modifications of these basic rules. Rather, they involve efforts to make the game safer and more enjoyable for everyone—while giving all players an opportunity to improve their skills. These are accomplished by not allowing players under the age of eleven to pitch. Children ten and under should play games involving tee ball, pitching machine, or coach pitch rules. These variations are summarized at the end of the chapter, although Table 10-7 outlines the common options.

Additionally, rules should limit the number of innings pitched to 4 per day with a minimum of 2 days of rest between appearances. A recommended variation of the "inning limit" to pitching is to restrict the number of pitches

Table 10-7. Recommended pitching changes for younger players.

Age Group (Years)	Type of Baseball Variation
8 and under	Tee Ball Only
9-10	1. Pitching Machine Ball or 2. Coach Pitch
11-12	1. Pitching Machine Ball or 2. Coach Pitch or 3. Regulation Baseball*
13-18	Regulation Baseball Only*

*Pitchers 15 years and younger should be limited to 50 pitches per game and have 2 days of rest between games. Pitchers who are 16 and older should have two days rest between games.

thrown to 50 in any game, with the accompanying requirement of two days rest between pitching assignments. Further, pitchers should not be allowed to throw breaking pitches—in other words, they should be limited to using the fastball and straight change—until they are physically mature enough to do so without risk of injury.

RULE 7: BATTING

Batting Order

Prior to the start of the game, the coach submits to the home plate umpire a lineup which lists the players in the order in which they will bat throughout the game. (This lineup also notes defensive positions and identifies the designated hitter.) Each athlete comes to bat in the order listed until the last batter named; once completing a turn at bat, the last player in the lineup is followed to the plate by the person listed first in the order. Play continues this way until the game is completed.

When a substitution is made, the new player bats in the position previously taken by the teammate being replaced. After the first inning of a game, the first batter in each inning is the athlete listed after the person batting last in the previous inning. (For example, in the fourth inning B5 makes the third out by popping up to the shortstop; B6 leads off in the fifth. Or B5 hits a ground ball that results in a runner being forced out at third; B6 starts the next inning.) However, if a batter does not have the chance to complete a turn at bat, then that player starts the next inning at bat, and the count reverts to no balls, no strikes. (For example, B2 is at bat; a runner, attempting to steal second, is thrown for the third out of the fifth inning. B2 starts the sixth inning.)

Batting Regulations

Once the home plate umpire signals for play to begin, a batter must have both feet in the batter's box. (The lines are considered part of the box, so a foot on a line qualifies as in the box.) The player may have either foot—or both, for that matter—off the ground when hitting the ball. However, the batter will be called out for hitting the ball with either foot completely outside the box or touching home plate.

Completing a Turn at Bat

Any of five actions may end a player's turn at bat:

- an out
- a walk
- the batter being hit by a pitch
- the batter being awarded first base as a result of interference
- a fairly hit ball

Strikes

The umpire signals a strike by raising the right hand and calling out, "Strike!" This occurs when any of the following happen:

- A pitch passes through the strike zone before hitting the ground.
- The batter swings at and entirely misses a pitch.
- The batter hits the ball which subsequently strikes something in foul territory, other than the ground, without first going beyond a base in fair territory.
- The batter takes more than 20 seconds to get ready to hit after the ball has been thrown back to the pitcher.
- The batter hits the ball, and it comes to rest in foul territory without passing a base in fair ground.
- With less than two strikes, the batter hits the ball which then strikes the batter still legally positioned in the batter's box.

Balls

The umpire signals a ball, with the left hand, when any of these things happen:

- The pitch is completely outside the strike zone, and the batter does not swing.
- The pitch bounces before crossing home plate, and the batter does not swing.
- The umpire calls an illegal pitch, quick pitch or illegal delivery; in some cases, the pitch may be delivered and the batter will have to avoid swinging.
- The pitcher takes extra warm-up pitches.

- The pitcher delays throwing the ball for more than 20 seconds after receiving it from the catcher.

Fair Ball

Fair/foul ball determinations cause a great deal of concern for players, coaches and umpires—especially because batted balls often curve or slice when hit near the line. Essentially, the decision of "fair" or "foul" is made depending on where the ball strikes the ground and whether it has gotten beyond first or third base. If the ball hits the ground and either stops in fair territory or goes beyond a base in fair territory, it is a fair ball. If the ball's initial contact is with anything other than the ground (an umpire, player, fence, bat, base, bench), the ball then has the same status—fair or foul—as the object struck.

A fairly batted ball may be indicated by the umpire's pointing inward toward the diamond. The umpire does not call out, "Fair," so players should assume that all batted balls are in play until they hear some other call. All the following qualify as fair balls:

- The ball comes to rest in fair territory between home plate and any of the bases.
- The ball bounces and then passes first or third base in fair territory.
- The ball initially touches the ground in fair territory past first or third base.
- The ball strikes either first or third base.
- The ball hits an umpire or player in fair ground.
- The ball hits or goes beyond the outfield fence in fair territory.

Foul Ball

The umpire signals that the ball is foul by pointing into foul territory and calling, "Foul," once the ball is no longer playable. In other words, the umpire waits to make the call until one of three things has occurred:

1. The ball is in foul ground and has stopped moving.
2. It has hit something other than the ground in foul territory.
3. It has passed first or third base without becoming fair.

Since the umpire does not make the call immediately, athletes should continue playing the ball.

Foul balls result from any of the following:

- The ball stops moving in foul territory between home and first or third bases.
- The ball bounces past either first or third base in foul ground.
- The ball first hits the ground in foul territory beyond first or third base.
- The ball hits an umpire, player or something other than the ground in foul territory without first having been determined to be a fair ball. (This means that a fair ball remains fair, even if it later rolls into foul ground. Thus, if a ball hits fair, passes third and slices into foul territory to hit the fence, the ball remains in play as a fair ball.)

Foul tips also can occur. These are batted balls that go directly to the catcher and are caught. The ball remains in play, and if it is the third strike, the batter is called out.

Outs

The umpire calls the player out, if the batter:

- takes a third strike caught by the catcher
- swings at and misses a third strike caught by the catcher
- swings at and misses a third strike and then is hit by the ball
- swings at and misses a third strike with a runner on first base and less than two outs (If there are two outs, the defensive team must complete the out. A defender does this by tagging the batter with the ball, touching first base while in possession of the ball, or by completing a force out on a base runner.)
- bunts the ball foul on a third strike
- hits or bunts a ground ball that is fielded and thrown to first base before the batter reaches the base
- hits or bunts a ground ball and a fielder touches the batter with the ball before first base is reached
- hits a fly ball that is caught
- hits a fly ball that a spectator keeps a defender from playing

- hits a fly ball that the umpire calls an "infield fly"
- hits the ball with either foot completely out of the batter's box
- hits the ball with either foot on home plate
- steps from one batter's box to the other while the pitcher is in position to pitch
- bats out of turn and the umpire becomes aware of the violation
- uses an altered or illegal bat
- interferes with any defensive player's attempt to either field or throw the ball
- with two outs, hinders the catcher trying to make a put out at home plate
- hits a foul fly and an offensive coach or player interferes with the defensive play
- hits a fair fly or line drive that is intentionally dropped by an infielder with less than two outs and at least first base occupied
- bunts or hits the ball and the ball hits the bat a second time after the batter leaves the batter's box
- has a teammate running bases who hinders a defender attempting to complete an obvious double play
- does not attempt to run on a dropped third strike, if there are two outs

Modifications for Youth Competition

The infield fly rule is inappropriate for players ten and younger. This rule applies in very specific circumstances: less than two outs have been recorded; runners are on first and second or on first, second and third; and the batter hits a fly ball likely to be played by an infielder. The rule requires the batter to be immediately declared out while runners are free to advance, at the risk of being put out. While this situation develops fairly often in games involving younger players, the play is not likely to result in a double play as it can when older athletes are involved. Moreover, calling the batter out often creates a great deal of confusion. Thus, younger children should complete the out as they would any other batted ball.

Players fourteen and younger should not be required to complete the strike out when the ball is not secured by the catcher. Rather, the batter should immediately be called out after a third strike—even if the catcher misplays

the ball. (However, runners should be free to advance on the error.)

Finally, the batter is to be discouraged from carelessly tossing away the bat. If this happens, the home plate umpire should warn the batter first. Subsequently, the batter should be subject to being called out for intentionally throwing the bat.

On-Deck Batter

The player waiting to hit after the batter currently at the plate is said to be "on deck." While preparing to bat, the athlete uses the on-deck circle closest to the team bench and may have two bats in the circle: a warm-up bat and the bat to be used for hitting. Normally, the player remains in the circle until the previous player completes the turn at bat; however, the on-deck hitter may move to the plate area to help coach a base runner trying to score. (This must be done without interfering with either the defensive player or umpire.)

Summary

Youth play should incorporate these modifications to the common batting rules:

1. Players 10 years old and younger should not be subject to the infield fly rule.
2. Athletes 14 years old and under should not have to complete the putout on a strike out.
3. All youth baseball players should be called out for endangering others by throwing bats. A warning is appropriate on the first violation.

See Table 10-8 for an outline of these changes.

RULE 8: BASE RUNNING

General Rules

As previously mentioned, runs are scored by a base runner safely touching each of the four bases in order. The runner must take a direct path from one base to the next and may not move more than 3 feet off this line to avoid being tagged out. However, the rules allow for the player's momentum causing bases to be overrun and turns to be made. Moreover, if a

Table 10-8. Recommended changes to batting rules.

Age Group (Years)	Infield Fly Rule	Third Strike Rule	Declared Out For Throwing a Bat
10 and under	No	No	Yes
11-14	Yes	No	Yes
15-18	Yes	Yes	Yes

base becomes loose during play, the runner does not have to attempt to touch it by running out of the typical path.

If needing to return to a previously held base, the athlete must retouch in reverse order any bases tagged during the play. (For example, a typical play might involve a runner from first moving on a long fly ball. The player breaks with the hit, touches second and is well around it when the ball is caught by an outfielder. In retreating to first base, the runner must first retouch second base.) Once safe at a base, the player may remain there until forced off it by a subsequent runner. However, because only one runner at a time may occupy a base, if two teammates end up on the same base, then the first player to occupy that base is awarded it and the second player is called out.

The Batter Becomes a Batter-Runner

The batter becomes a batter-runner and attempts to reach first base safely when any of the following occur:

- The ball is hit fairly.
- The batter takes or swings at a third strike (if the ball is caught, the batter is immediately out; otherwise the player may attempt to reach first).
- The batter is thrown a fourth ball and is walked.
- A pitched ball hits the batter, as long as the batter attempts to avoid the ball and does not swing at the pitch.
- The catcher, or other defensive player, interferes with the batter.

Bases Awarded to the Batter-Runner

The umpire may award a base to the batter-runner in certain cases. Besides the batter being walked, hit by a pitch or obstructed, situations involving awarded bases include:

- a teammate being hit by a batted ball while in fair territory and not on base
- a hit ball striking an umpire before a defender has an opportunity to make a play
- a batted ball touching a spectator
- a batted ball going through or wedging in a fence

Putting Out a Batter-Runner

In addition to the means given in Rule 7, a batter-runner is out whenever:

- a misplayed third strike ends with the batter-runner being tagged or with first base being touched by a defender having the ball before the batter-runner arrives
- running outside the marked runner's box along the first base line and interfering with a defensive player's effort to catch a thrown ball
- interfering with a defender's effort to field or throw the ball

Base Running Plays With the Runner Subject to Being Put Out

Under threat of being put out, a runner may attempt to advance to the next base in these instances:

- The ball is "live." (A "live" ball situation occurs whenever the ball is in possession of the pitcher and the umpire has signaled for play. This continues until the ball is declared "dead" or until "time" is called. Foul balls represent the most common "dead" ball situations. Basically, unless "time" or "dead ball" is called, players should assume that the ball is live and that they are subject to being put out.)
- The batter hits the ball into fair ground.
- A defensive player catches either a fair or foul fly ball.
- A "live" ball is thrown by a defender, is not caught, and remains in the field of play.

Modifications for Youth Competition

Youth baseball players twelve years old and younger should not be allowed to lead off until the ball has crossed the plate. Further, players ten years old and under should not be given the opportunity to steal bases or move up on wild pitches/passed balls, although they should lead off in accordance with the previous suggested modification. These changes relieve some pressures upon younger pitchers and catchers, so they can better concentrate on developing the skills basic to their positions.

Base Running Plays With the Runner Not Subject to Being Put Out

At times, runners are free to advance without being subject to put outs. These situations occur when:

- The pitcher balks.
- A play results in the batter being awarded one or more bases, and the runner is consequently forced to advance.
- The runner attempts to steal or is forced to run on a play involving obstruction of the batter.
- A fielder who does not have the ball interferes with the runner.
- A fielder without the ball fakes a tag play.
- A pitch or any other "live" ball is thrown out of play.
- A defensive player carries a "live" ball out of play.
- A fairly hit ball touches a spectator.
- A defender touches a fair ball with either an illegal glove or detached equipment.
- A fair ball goes over, under or through a field fence.
- A fair ball becomes wedged in a fence.
- A pitch lodges in a fence or equipment worn by the umpire or catcher.

Putting Out the Base Runner

The umpire signals with the right hand and calls, "Out" whenever a base runner does any of the following:

- runs more than 3 feet outside a direct line between bases in an attempt to avoid a tag or hinder a defensive player
- intentionally interferes with a "live" ball— either batted or thrown
- interferes with a defensive player attempting to either field or throw the ball
- is between bases when tagged with the ball
- fails to retouch the base before a fielder either tags the base or touches the player with the ball

- fails to touch a base or fails to retouch a base after a caught fly ball (The runner may be gotten out by the defense either tagging the runner or the base. However, if the defense does not make either of these plays, there is the possibility that the runner may be called out by the umpire or that an appeal may be made; the rules applied depend upon the sanctioning group.)
- makes a move to round first and attempt to reach second base and is tagged with the ball
- is forced to run but does not reach the next base before a defender either tags the runner with the ball or touches the succeeding base while holding the ball
- is hit by a fair ball before it passes an infielder other than the pitcher
- is hit by a fair ball before it passes through the infield untouched by any infielder other than the pitcher
- tries to score when the batter is charged with interference at home
- runs beyond a preceding runner who has not been called out
- circles the bases in the reverse direction to confuse the defense
- takes a position behind a base in order to get a running start
- fails to slide or attempt to avoid the defender either waiting to make a tag or completing a force out
- attempts to hurdle or maliciously run into a defensive player
- after touching a base, leaves the baseline and so gives up any effort to touch the next base
- gets physical assistance from a coach while the ball is in play
- otherwise reaches base safely as a result of a coach or teammate interfering with a thrown or batted ball or with a fielder attempting to make a play

Returning to a Base

Runners generally must return to touch bases previously occupied whenever a play results in a "dead" ball. Such plays include:

- "Time" being called
- an umpire inadvertently handling a live ball
- illegally batted balls

- balls hit a second time after the batter leaves the box
- plays resulting in an interference call
- interference by the plate umpire with the catcher's throw
- a walk or hit batter that does not result in the runner being forced to advance
- a defensive player failing to catch a foul fly
- an infielder intentionally dropping a line drive with less than two out and at least a runner at first

At other times, the runner may have to return and touch a base while the ball is "live." Generally, once having touched the base, the runner is free to attempt to advance. This applies:

- at or after a defender's catch of a fly ball, either foul or fair
- when the runner has missed a base
- when the batter-runner has rounded first in an attempt for second base

In these instances, the runner is subject to being put out, as described above. However, there is one particular instance in which the runner is free to return to the base without risk of being declared out:

- If the batter-runner either runs or slides beyond first and does not attempt to advance to second, then the player may return immediately to first safely.

Modifications for Youth Competition

Youth games should not involve appeal plays, although some rules books allow such requests of the umpires. Rather, the umpires should be allowed to call players out as soon as a base running infraction is noted.

Summary

Suggested modifications of rules involving base running as they apply to younger players relate to:

- leading off before the pitch crosses the plate
- stealing bases or advancing on wild pitches/passed balls
- using the appeal play

These modifications are summarized in Table 10-9.

Table 10-9. Recommended changes to base running rules.

Age Group (Years)	Lead Off With the Pitch	Steal or Advance On Wild Pitches/ Passed Balls	Appeal Play
10 and under	No	No	No
11-12	No	Yes	No
13-14	Yes	Yes	No
15-18	Yes	Yes	Yes

RULE 9: SCORING

Most rule books conclude with a description of how to score baseball games. Although not difficult, scoring is complicated, and to do the topic justice would require more space than seems reasonable to take here. Rather, the youth baseball coach should get a scorebook—one likely will be needed anyway—and study the description and sample usually included there.

BASEBALL VARIATIONS FOR YOUTH COMPETITION

Tee Ball

In tee ball, one of the defensive players takes the pitcher's position, but the ball is put in play by being hit from a tee. Other rules which apply specifically to tee ball are as follows:

1. The pitcher must be touching the pitcher's plate when the batter hits the ball. (Some rules require the defender acting as pitcher to actually make a pitching motion and still remain in contact with the pitching plate.) This is the typical rule for tee ball; however, research recently completed by the Institute for Youth Sports suggests that this places the pitcher too close to the hitter and so increases the risk of injury. Rather, it is recommended that a chalk line be marked 5 feet behind the pitcher's plate and that the pitcher be in contact with this chalk line when contact is made.
2. The home plate umpire stands behind the batter.
3. The catcher stands to the side of the um-

pire, on the side opposite the batter. Thus, the catcher is to the umpire's right for a right handed batter.

4. While a batter is hitting, the tee is positioned on home plate. (Tees with multiple positions may be considered so that the ball may actually be positioned at the front rather than the middle of the plate. This will allow for better hitting mechanics.)

5. The home plate umpire puts the ball on the batting tee.

6. Once the ball has been hit, the home plate umpire removes the tee. The umpire then replaces it after the defensive play is completed and before the next batter enters the batter's box.

7. Bunting is not permitted.

8. The ball must be hit at least 10 feet and land in fair territory, or it is called a foul ball. (There should be an arc with a radius of 10 feet marked as in Figure 10-10.)

9. Each batter is allowed three swings at the ball.

10. If a foul ball results from a third swing, then the batter continues to hit until the ball is batted into fair territory or missed completely.

11. Bats marked "Official Tee Ball" may be used.

12. The batting tee must be adjustable. Moreover, for safety, at least the upper 6 inches of the tee must be made of rubber tubing.

Pitching Machine Baseball

In pitching machine baseball, play begins with the ball being projected from a pitching machine.

1. A pitching machine is placed so that the ball exits over the pitcher's plate.

2. The offensive team's coach puts the ball into the machine.

3. The defender playing the pitcher's position is behind the pitching machine and to either side when the ball is being projected.

4. Bunting is not permitted.

5. A batted ball that strikes the pitching machine and bounces into foul territory before being touched by a player is a foul ball.

6. Similarly, a batted ball that strikes the pitching machine is a fair ball if it remains in fair ground or is touched by a player.

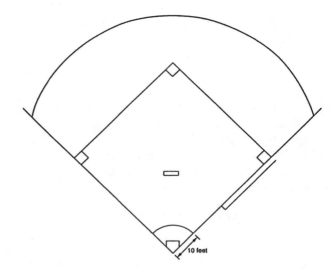

Figure 10-10. Arc used to determine when a batted ball is in play in tee ball.

7. A batted ball that lodges in the pitching machine is replayed.

8. Each batter is thrown five pitches.

9. A foul ball on the fifth pitch allows the hitter to continue at bat until either hitting the ball into fair territory or missing the pitch entirely.

10. The batter is not allowed to walk. Similarly, the batter is not allowed to advance to first if hit by the pitch.

Coach Pitch

This variation is similar to that of a machine pitching, but the offensive team's coach is responsible for delivering the ball. Specific rules are as follows.

1. The offensive team's coach is referred to as the "coach-pitcher" while the defensive player covering the mound is the "player-pitcher."

2. The coach-pitcher throws the ball from the pitcher's plate.

3. When the batter hits the ball, the player-pitcher is in a defensive position behind and to either side of the coach-pitcher.

4. Bunting is not permitted.

5. The coach-pitcher intentionally interfering with a batted ball causes the batter to be out and returns all base runners to their initial positions.

6. If the coach-pitcher accidentally interferes

with a batted ball or is hit by a batted ball, the pitch is replayed.

7. Each hitter gets five pitches.
8. A foul ball on the fifth pitch allows the hitter to continue at bat until either hitting the ball into fair territory or missing the pitch entirely.
9. The batter is not allowed to walk. Similarly, the batter is not allowed to advance to first if hit by the pitch.

2 Pitch

A common rule variation used in both machine and coach pitch games is called "2 pitch." Under this modification, the previously outlined rules apply until the hitter fails to put the ball in play on the first two swings. Then the batter is allowed to hit the ball from a batting tee.

3-2 Ball

"3-2 ball" means that the batter walks on the third ball and strikes out with the second strike. Rather than being a rules modification that benefits the developing youth player, this change seems to be intended to speed the game along. Instead of using a 3-2 count with older players, leagues should consider using the time limits previously suggested.

"No Ball" Game

This variation allows the pitcher some margin of error, as strikes accumulate but the count reverts to zero balls whenever a strike occurs. For example, if a batter has a count of 2-0 when the first strike is thrown, then the count on balls falls back to zero and the strike holds. Thus, the count becomes 0-1. This modification has several advantages; chief among them are:

• Pitchers can work on their deliveries with less worry about walking batters.

• Hitters are much more likely to swing at the ball than to take a number of pitches in hope of walking.
• The defense has an opportunity to play the ball on nearly every batter.

SUMMARY

This chapter provides a brief outline of the common rules used in baseball. A number of modifications have been suggested, as well. In general, the goal of these changes is to make baseball a safe and enjoyable activity for all who are involved. These variations maximize the opportunities for young players to develop their skills while making it possible for children of all skill levels to compete fairly. The various tables and figures summarize the main points of these modifications, and the coach may wish to review them occasionally. Further, when fair and enjoyable play is the goal, two more points are worth considering:

1. Coaches and administrators should develop and apply team selection criteria that produce teams of equal ability.
2. Coaches should discover and study any local variations that may differ from those included in this chapter.

REFERENCES

Kreutzer, P. & Kerley, P. (1990). *Little League's Official How-to-Play Baseball Book*. New York: Doubleday.
National Federation of State High School Associations. (1992). *Official High School Baseball Rules*. Kansas City, MO.

ADDITIONAL READINGS

Jacobs, G. & McCrory, J.R. (1990). *Baseball Rules in Pictures*. New York: Putnam.
Marazzi, R. (1980). *The Rules and Lore of Baseball*. New York: Stein and Day.
National Baseball Congress of America. (1992). *Official Baseball Annual: Rules, Teams, Photos*. Wichita, KS.
Pony Baseball, Inc. (1990). *Rules and Regulations: Pony Baseball/Softball*. Washington, PA.

11
A Glossary of Baseball Terms

Jill Elliott, M.S.
Michael A. Clark, Ph.D.

INTRODUCTION

This glossary contains a listing of terms and definitions common to the game of baseball. It is intended to familiarize coaches, parents and players with the vocabulary common to baseball and so allow them to better understand and enjoy the game known as "America's pastime." Further, having a common vocabulary will promote better communication with one another as they play, watch and enjoy the game. The terms are listed alphabetically and are accompanied by common variations of the defined term, when appropriate.

AB The abbreviation, usually found in scoring summaries, for *at bats*. (See below.)

Across-the-seams A variety of fastball. The pitcher grips the ball across one of the **U**s formed by the seams.

Ahead in the count The batter is ahead in the count when there are more balls than strikes and the count is not full (for example, 1-0, 3-1). The pitcher is ahead in the count when there are more strikes than balls (for example, 0-1, 1-2).

Altered bat An official baseball bat that has been changed in some manner. Most commonly, a metal bat has been dented. Or a wood bat may be drilled out at the large end and filled with some foreign material.

Appeal play An event in which an umpire may not make a ruling about an offensive violation until it has been properly reported by the defensive team. Appeal plays are not recommended for use in youth baseball. Some sanctioning bodies allow umpires to make "out" calls as soon as violations are noted.

Assist An assist is credited to a player who helps another player make a putout. For example, if a pitcher fields a ground ball and throws to the first baseperson in time to get the runner out, the pitcher gets the assist and the first baseperson gets the putout.

At bats Usually an official turn at bat. An official at bat occurs anytime a player bats and does not sacrifice, walk, or get hit by a pitch. Only official at bats are considered in the player's batting average.

Backhand On the throwing-hand side of a player. This may describe the position of a play, but more commonly it describes how the player positions the glove. To make a backhand play, the athlete crosses over the body with the glove hand and pronates the arm to play the ball. This causes the back of the glove to face the outfield.

Backup   Player assumes a position behind a play so that an overthrow or loose ball will be recovered more efficiently.

Backstop   The screen or fence behind home plate that is intended to keep foul balls, wild pitches and passed balls in play.

Bad hop   When the ball bounces in a direction other than what is expected. A bad hop is usually caused by uneven ground, a stone, or excessive spin on the ball.

Bag   See *base*.

Ball   A pitch that does not move through the strike zone and is not swung at by the batter, or a pitched ball that is not called a strike by the umpire.

Balk   An illegal move by the pitcher with a runner or runners on base. It results from either not coming to a set position or from making an improper pickoff move. Such moves commonly result from the pitcher either failing to step off the rubber before throwing to first, throwing to first after the kick leg passes behind the pivot leg, or not stepping toward first base when making a pickoff attempt.

Base   The canvas-covered bags placed at three corners of the infield.

Base coach   The people positioned in the coaching boxes near first and third bases, who are responsible for helping base runners while the team is on offense. Typically the third base coach also relays offensive signs to the batter.

Base hit   A batted ball meeting three criteria: it is not misplayed by a defender; it does not result in an out; and the batter reaches base safely.

Baseline   A synonym for *base path*. However, it also is used to describe the two lines, with extensions, drawn from home to first and third bases.

Base on balls   Also referred to as a walk. After the pitcher throws four balls to the batter during a turn at bat, the batter is awarded first base.

Base path   An area that encompasses 3 feet on both sides of the baseline.

Base runner   An offensive player who has reached first base safely and has not been declared out.

Batted ball   A ball that is struck—either inten- tionally or accidentally—by the bat and travels into either fair of foul terntory.

Batter   The offensive player at bat.

Batter/runner   A batter who has completed a turn at bat but has neither reached first base safely nor has been declared out.

Batter's box   A designated area in which the bat- ter must be positioned as the pitch is deliv- ered; the batter must be in the batter's box when the ball is contacted.

Battery   The pitcher, catcher combination.

Batting average   The average number of times a player reaches base as a result of a hit. A player's batting average is equal to the to- tal number of hits divided by the total offi- cial at bats.

Batting order   The order in which the offensive players take their turns at bat.

BB   The scoring abbreviation for a *base on balls*.

Behind in the count   The batter is behind in the count when there are more strikes than balls. The pitcher is behind in the count when there are more balls than strikes and the count is not full.

Bench   (1) The area set aside for players, sub- stitutes, coaches and other team personnel. (2) The players available as substitutes.

Big hop   A bounce taken by a ground ball that is a bit longer and comes up higher; thus, a defender can make the play more easily. Generally, the second bounce taken by a ground ball. Infielders often are told to "play it on the big hop."

Blooper   A short fly ball that drops between the infielders and outfielders—usually unin- tentional.

Bobble   When the ball is not fielded cleanly but there is still a chance it can be recovered for a putout.

Breaking pitch   Any pitch that has a definite curving path. It may be a curve or slider in youth play; however, at the upper levels pitchers may develop other breaking balls such as the screwball. All breaking balls result from how the ball spins as it moves through the air. Breaking balls generally are thrown at much lower speeds than the fastball.

Bull pen   An area near the field set aside for the purpose of warming up pitchers.

Bunt   A batted ball that is struck softly with

the bat and travels a short distance into the infield.

Call for the ball When a fielder communicates to other fielders that he or she is prepared to field the ball.

Catch An event in which a defensive player secures a batted or thrown ball in either the glove or bare hand.

Catcher's box The area in which a catcher must be positioned as the pitch is delivered.

Change-Up or **Change** An off-speed pitch thrown with the same motion as used to deliver a fastball. Usually the pitch does not break much; rather, its effectiveness lies in its looking like a fastball but being thrown significantly slower. Its delivery may be detected by the telltale three fingers that stick up, off the ball. This pitch also may be called a "straight change," a "circle change," or an "OK change." The latter two terms describe the same pitch: one that is thrown by gripping the ball with the thumb and forefinger making a circle around one of the **U**s of the ball.

Charged conference An event in which play is interrupted to enable a coach to meet with either a defensive or offensive player. These are limited to one per inning while on offense (additional requests will not be granted) and three per game on defense (additional conferences require that the pitcher be changed).

Charge the ball A direction given a defensive player; it asks that they move aggressively towards the ball to field it.

Check the runner If a runner is on base and does not have to advance on a batted ball, the fielder must check the runner's actions before finally deciding on the play to be made.

Choke up Moving the hands up (away from the knob) while holding the bat.

Coach May refer to either *base coaches* (see above) or to the person given ultimate responsibility for directing the team. (See also *coach's box*, below.)

Coach's box Either of the areas marked near first and third bases in which the base coach is to stand while play goes on.

Come set or **coming set** Describes the pause in the pitcher's motion that must occur be-

tween the windup and the pitch when runners are being held on base.

Contralateral throw The most advanced stage of motor development in which the thrower strides with the foot on the side opposite that of the throwing hand (for example, a right-handed thrower striding with the left foot).

Corners Players positioned at first and third bases are said to be "at the corners."

Corners of the plate The inside or outside portions of home plate.

Count The number of balls and strikes on the batter—stated as balls first, strikes second (for example, a 2-1 count means 2 balls, 1 strike).

Cover the base When a defensive player is at a base and ready for a play.

Crow hop A step taken, usually by an outfielder, preparatory to a throw. It involves the throwing-side foot stepping forward and behind the glove-side foot.

Crossover A step which causes a leg to "crossover" in front of the initial body position; it is taken with the foot on the side opposite the intended direction of motion. For example, a crossover to the left begins with the right leg being moved across the body toward the left.

Curve or **Curveball** A breaking pitch that curves dramatically. The most effective curve is thrown with the hand on top of the ball and downward pressure applied at release. This causes the ball to curve down and to the pitcher's glove side.

Dead ball A ball not in play. A number of plays may result in dead balls, but the most common are: illegal pitches; uncaught foul balls; balls that hit offensive players, coaches, umpires or spectators; and balls thrown, hit, or deflected out of play.

Dead ball area See *out of play area*.

Designated hitter An athlete, named in the starting lineup, who is assigned to bat for one of the defensive players.

Doubleheader Two games played in succession by the same teams; generally not recommended in youth play for athletes under the age of 16.

Double play Any play where two outs are made

in succession before the next batter has a turn at bat.

Double steal An offensive play involving two base runners, both of whom are attempting to steal a base.

Dugout See *bench*.

E The abbreviation used in scoring to show that an *error* has been made. It is followed by the defensive position number of the player making the error; for example, the notation "E-6" indicates an error on the shortstop.

Ejection An umpire's decision to have a player, coach or team representative removed from the field and/or bench area for engaging in unsportsmanlike behavior.

Error Anytime the batter is allowed to remain at bat and/or a base runner is allowed to stay on a base or advance to the next base(s) as a result of a defensive misplay.

Extra base hit Any hit where the batter safely reaches a base beyond first base without benefit of an error.

Extra bases Any bases beyond the one that the runner is immediately attempting to reach as the result of a play.

Extra inning or **extra innings** Additional inning or innings played to determine a winner in a tie ball game.

Fair ball Any legally batted ball on or within the foul lines. A ball that is initially foul and then, without being touched, rolls fair prior to first or third base is a fair ball. A ball that is initially fair and then rolls foul beyond first or third base is a fair ball.

Fair territory or **fair ground** That portion of the field which lies within and includes the first base line, third base line, back corner of home plate, and the outfield fence.

Fastball A hard, straight pitch; normally the first pitch learned and the one that should be worked on the most by youth players.

Fielder A member of the defensive team.

Fielder's choice A play in which the fielder chooses to put out a lead base runner rather than the batter running to first base. The batter/runner safe at first base does not get credit for a hit.

Fly ball A batted ball that travels up into the air.

Follow-through The movement of the body following the intended act of either hitting or throwing the ball. The follow-through allows the energy of the swing or throw to be safely dissipated.

Forehand The glove-hand side.

Force out or **force play** When a base runner is forced to advance on a batted ball because all of the previous bases are occupied. A fielder can put out the runner by touching the base.

Foul or **foul ball** Any batted ball that is touched outside the foul lines prior to first or third base or initially lands outside the foul lines beyond first or third base.

Foul line The line that extends from home plate to the outside edge of first base to the end of right field and the line that extends from home plate to the outside edge of third base to the end of left field. The foul lines help designate fair ground and are part of fair ground.

Foul tip A batted ball that travels straight back to the catcher and is secured by the catcher without its first touching the ground.

Full count When the count on the batter is 3 balls, 2 strikes.

Fungo hitting When a coach (or player) tosses the ball up and hits it as desired to give players practice fielding various types of batted balls.

Gap The area between the center fielder and right fielder and between the center fielder and left fielder. A ball hit through the gap is usually an extra base hit.

Glove-side: Foot, knee, shoulder, elbow On the same side of the body as the glove hand.

Go with the pitch To hit the ball in relation to the location of the pitch around the strike zone. A right handed batter would hit the inside pitch to the left side of the field, the center pitch to the center of the field, and the outside pitch to the right side of the field.

Ground ball A batted ball that strikes the ground.

H The scoring abbreviation for a *hit*.

Halfway Refers to the lead a runner on first or second base might take on a fly ball hit to the outfield. If the ball is hit fairly close to the runner's base, the runner actually goes less than halfway (for example, runner on first, fly ball to shallow right field). If the ball is hit a good distance from the base, the runner would go more than halfway (for example, runner on first, fly ball to deep left field). Going "halfway" allows the runner a greater chance to advance safely to the next base if the ball is dropped or to return safely to the initial base if the ball is caught.

HBP   The scoring abbreviation used to show that a batter has been hit by a pitch.

High set position   While pitching from the set or stretch position, a pitcher stops the motion of the hands near the chin.

Hit   A batted ball that allows the batter to reach first base safely without the benefit of an error and without a runner being put out.

Hitter   See *batter*.

Hole (in the hole)   An area of the field not easily covered by the defense. For example, a shortstop who fields a ball many steps to the right is said to have made the play "in the hole."

Home or *home plate*   The five-sided rubber base that is the pitcher's target. It determines the strike zone and must be touched by a base runner to score a run.

Home run   A legally batted ball that allows the batter to safely touch all four bases without the benefit of an error.

Home team   The team that hosts the baseball game and bats last each inning, unless already ahead at the end of visiting team's last turn at bat.

Hit by a pitch   If the batter is in the batter's box and is hit by a pitch, the batter is awarded first base.

Ipsilateral throw   A less advanced stage of motor development in which a thrower strides with the foot on the same side of the body as the throwing hand (for example, a right-handed thrower striding with the right foot).

Illegal bat   A bat that fails to meet the specifications of an official baseball bat, also a dented bat or one that may mar the ball.

Illegal player   A player who has entered the game without the home plate umpire being notified.

Ineligible player   A player who is not allowed to continue participating in the game. If an illegal player is discovered, that person is disqualified from play and becomes an ineligible player.

Infield   That portion of fair territory which is normally covered by the defenders at first, second, and third bases; the shortstop; pitcher; and catcher.

Infielders   May be used to describe any or all of the athletes responsible for defending the infield. However, the term more commonly is used to describe the shortstop and the three players covering the bases.

Infield fly rule   If there are runners on first and second OR first, second and third with less than 2 outs, and the batter hits a fly ball on the infield, the batter is declared out, even if the ball is misplayed. The runner should react as if the ball is caught. The runner must "tag up" but can choose to advance with the fielder's touch of the ball. If the fly ball rolls foul prior to first and third base and remains untouched, the infield fly rule is no longer in effect.

Inning: top/bottom   That portion of the game in which both teams are given the opportunity to participate for three outs on offense and three outs on defense. The top of the inning is the first half of the inning in which the visiting team bats. The bottom of the inning is the second half of the inning in which the home team bats.

Interference   Any act by an offensive player which hinders a defensive player's attempt to execute a play. Spectators and umpires may also be cited for interference with the ball. Catcher interference is called if the catcher's mitt is contacted by the bat as the batter executes a swing.

Intentional walk   A *base on balls* intentionally given a batter. It is a defensive strategy used to set up force plays or to keep a skillful batter from hitting. In many youth baseball games, the pitcher does not have to throw the four balls; rather, the pitcher or coach may notify the umpire that the batter is to be intentionally walked, and the umpire responds by awarding first base to the offensive player.

(Get a) Jump on the ball   An expression describ-

ing a player's quick response to a batted ball.

Lead, leadoff, or **leading off** (1) The movement, prior to the pitch, of a base runner into a position some distance away from the base. This may put the runner in position to steal a base or to get a quick start on a batted ball. (2) To be the first batter in an inning. The first batter in the batting order is also commonly called the "leadoff hitter."

Left on base When an offensive player reaches base safely but does not score before the half inning is over. If the bases are "loaded" and the batter strikes out for the third out, three runners are left on base.

Line drive A fly ball that is struck solidly and travels in a relatively straight line.

Live ball A ball that is in play. Players should assume that any ball on the field is a live ball until it is declared dead or not in play by an umpire.

Look the runner back/check the runner When a runner on base is not forced to advance, the defensive player attempts to determine the runner's intent by checking that player's response to the play. The intent of the runner determines whether the play is made on the runner or the batter-base runner. There almost always is enough time for a defender to check the runner and still complete the out at first base.

Mound The raised portion of the infield where the *pitcher's plate* is located. Also, the pitcher is said to "take the mound" at the beginning of an inning.

Moving fastball Describes a particularly well-thrown fastball. Such a pitch "moves," or breaks, even though it is not a breaking ball. Rather, its comparative speed is combined with different grips to cause the ball to move.

No hitter A game in which a team is not allowed a base hit.

Obstruction When a defensive player who is not attempting to field a ball or does not have possession of the ball interferes with the progress of a base runner.

Offensive team The team whose members are taking their turn at bat.

Off-speed pitch Any pitch other than a fastball.

It may be a breaking ball or a straight change.

On deck The offensive player next in order after the current batter is the on-deck batter. The on-deck batter generally warms up in a designated "on-deck circle."

Opposite field When a right-handed batter hits the ball to the right side of the field, the batter is said to have hit to the opposite field. The same is true for a left-handed batter who hits the ball to left field.

Out A play that keeps a runner from safely reaching a base. These may include *force outs*, caught fly balls, *strike outs*, *tag outs* and calls of *interference*.

Outfield That portion of *fair territory* which is normally covered by the left, center, and right fielders. These players are known collectively as "outfielders."

Out-of-play area The area beyond the boundaries of the playing area. When a baseball field is not enclosed by a fence, the out-of-play area should be indicated by a marked line extending from the backstop to the end of the outfield and parallel to the foul lines. However, in some cases the umpires may simply use an imaginary extension of the backstop.

Overhand A pitching delivery in which the throwing arm extends directly above the shoulder.

Overrun To run beyond a base. Runners can (and should) overrun first base but can be tagged out if they overrun second or third base. A player who overruns first base and then turns toward the field cannot be tagged out unless the umpire judges the runner has made a clear move to go on to second base.

Overslide Sliding beyond a base. Rules applied to oversliding are similar to those affecting *overrunning*. (Note that a batter/runner may slide into first base; however, this should be done only to avoid a tag play or a collision with the defensive player.)

Passed ball A pitch that is mishandled by the catcher and, as a result, allows a baserunner to advance.

Perfect game A complete game in which the pitcher has not allowed a base runner. There are no hits, no walks, and no errors.

Pick off   To tag out a runner who is leading off the base.

Pickoff move   Describes the pitcher's effort to pick off a base runner, usually at first base.

Pinch hitter   A substitute hitter; a player who has not yet been in the game who takes a turn hitting for a player who has been in the game.

Pinch runner   Similar to *pinch hitter* in that a player is used as a substitute for another. In this case, the substitute appears as a base runner.

Pitch   The ball delivered to the batter by the pitcher.

Pitcher   The defensive player assigned to throw pitches to the batter.

Pitcher's plate   The rubber rectangle that must be touched by the pitcher when throwing the ball.

Pitch out   To intentionally pitch the ball out of the *strike zone*. The pitch out is such that the catcher can easily catch the pitch and then throw to a base; yet the batter cannot hit the pitch.

Pivot foot   The foot used by the pitcher to push off the pitcher's plate when delivering a pitch (the right foot for a right-handed pitcher and the left foot for a left-handed thrower). The idea may be extended to other throws; in this case, the term is similar to *throwing-side foot*.

Plant the foot   To firmly place the foot on the ground so that a forceful push off the ground can occur.

Play or ***play ball***   The instruction given by the home plate umpire that begins or resumes action.

Pronation   In relation to throwing, when the lower arm rotates so that the palm of the hand faces down.

Pull hitter   A hitter who is consistently able to *pull the ball*.

Pull the ball   When a right-handed hitter hits the ball to the left side of the field, the hitter has pulled the ball. The same is true for a left-handed hitter who hits the ball to the right side of the field.

Put out   Describes the actual making of an out. The player who catches a fly ball or tags a runner or base is credited with a putout. Similarly, the catcher makes the putout on

a strike out. (A *strike out* may occur without a putout being recorded, if the catcher fails to catch the third strike and the batter/runner reaches base.)

Quick pitch   An illegal pitch obviously intended to take advantage of an unprepared batter.

R   The scoring abbreviation for the number of *runs* scored by a player or team.

Range   The amount of ground a fielder can successfully cover. The greater the fielder's range, the more effective the fielder.

RBI   The scoring abbreviation for *runs batted in*.

Relay   A second throw made on a defensive play. Usually made by an infielder who has caught a ball thrown in from the outfield.

Rubber   See *pitcher's plate*.

Run   The result of a runner legally advancing to and touching home plate. A run does not score if the player fails to touch the plate before the third out of the inning. Also, a run does not count even if the player touches home before the third out, if that out results from a *force play* or a caught fly ball.

Run down   A defensive play attempting to put out a runner trapped between bases.

Runs batted in   The batter is credited with a run batted in if a base runner scores as a result of the batter's hit, walk, sacrifice, or putout. Errors and double plays do not result in *RBIs*.

Sacrifice   (1) When a batter bunts the ball and is put out but the base runner advances; (2) when a batter hits a long fly ball that is caught but gives the base runner time to tag up and advance a base.

Safe   The umpire's decision that a player is entitled to the base being attempted.

Score   To touch home plate and make a *run*.

Set position   The position taken by the pitcher when runners are on base. The pitcher stands sideways on the mound with the glove-side shoulder pointed toward home plate.

Short hop   (1) A small, quick bounce of the ball. The first bounce of a ground ball is often a short hop. (2) To field the ball on such a bounce—a difficult defensive play.

Shut out   A game in which one of the teams does not score a run.

Sidearm   A throw made with the arm extending directly to the side. Sidearm throws tend to be less accurate but more quickly made; they may be the only means of getting the ball to a base in time for an out. Pitching with a sidearm motion should be discouraged because it may result in more strain being placed on the arm.

Slide An offensive play in which the runner initiates a controlled drop to the ground in an attempt to avoid contact with a defender or a tag. The forward momentum carries the athlete toward the base.

Slider A breaking pitch, thrown much like the curve, that breaks from side to side. It has more speed than a curve.

Soft hands Refers to "giving" with the force of the ball as it is being caught. A good fielder must have soft hands.

Squeeze play A bunt play used with a runner on third base. It may be a "safety squeeze," in which case the runner takes a slightly longer lead and advances once the ball is bunted. Or it may be a "suicide squeeze," in which case the runner sprints for home as soon as the pitcher releases the ball. On a suicide squeeze, the batter must make contact if at all possible, or the runner will be tagged out easily.

Steal, stealing, or **steal a base** (1) An attempt to advance to the next base during a pitch. (2) To safely advance to the next base without benefit of a hit, walk, error, or so forth.

Strawberry Another word for a burn acquired through excessive friction between the ground and the skin. A strawberry is a common sliding injury and merits treatment. Sliding pads or shorts may reduce the likelihood of such injury.

Stretch The movement of the arms made by a pitcher prior to coming set. Traditionally, this involved raising the arms over the head, so the term was descriptive; however, now many pitchers simply bring the arms from the waist to the high set position.

Stretch position See *set position*.

Strike A pitch that travels through the *strike zone* or a pitch that travels outside the strike zone and is swung at and missed by the batter.

Strike out The batter being charged with three strikes.

Strike zone An area over the plate that extends from a batter's arm pits to the knees.

Submarine Describes a throwing motion, used almost exclusively by pitchers, that drops the arm well below horizontal and may even require the athlete to bend to the throwing side.

Supination In relation to throwing, when the lower arm rotates so that the palm of the hand faces up. Forearm supination during the follow-through is an indication of an incorrect throwing arm motion.

Tag A play involving a fielder touching a base for an out. Any part of the body may be used, but the ball must be firmly held by the defender.

Tag out To get a runner, who is off a base, out by touching the runner with the ball while the ball is secured in the defender's hand(s). If the runner is tagged with the glove hand but the ball is in the bare hand, the runner is not out.

Tag up When a line drive or fly ball has been caught, the base runner must again touch the base before he or she can advance to the next base. The action of retouching the base is known as tagging up. If the ball is returned to the base or the runner is tagged out before the base is retouched, the runner is out. Once the runner has tagged up, he or she can advance to the next base as soon as the batted ball is touched by a fielder.

Tandem relay A relay in which the throw to the relay person is backed up by another player.

Throw A voluntary act by a defender that results in the ball being directed toward a target, usually a teammate. The ball may be thrown, tossed, handed, bounced or rolled. A throw is not the same as a pitch.

Throw down Generally refers to the catcher's throw to a player covering a base.

Throwing-side: foot, knee, hip On the same side of the body as the throwing arm.

Time or **time out** (1) A request, made to the umpire by either a coach or player, to interrupt play. (2) A stoppage of play called by an umpire. The ball is dead and no action may occur.

Three-quarter arm A style of throwing that has

the arm extended well above the shoulder— approximately halfway between sidearm and overhand. This is the throwing position most commonly used by players, including pitchers.

Triple play A very uncommon play in which three outs are recorded in rapid succession following a single turn at bat.

Unassisted When the same person that fields the ball makes the putout. A shortstop that fields a line drive and then immediately tags out a runner is said to have an unassisted double play.

Visiting team The team that bats first each inning.

Walk See *base on balls*.

Waste pitch A pitch intentionally pitched outside the *strike zone* so that the batter is tempted to swing. Because of the location of the pitch, if the batter does hit the pitch it is usually not a solid hit.

Wild pitch A pitch thrown so poorly that the catcher cannot control it and as a result, allows a base runner to advance.

Wind up or **full windup** (1) The position taken by the pitcher when no runners are on base. The pitcher faces the plate and has the pivot foot touching the rubber. (2) The motion, from this starting position, made by the pitcher prior to releasing the pitch.

Section III
Effective Coaching

12
Role of the Coach

Paul Vogel, Ph.D.

QUESTIONS TO CONSIDER

- What are the primary roles of a youth baseball coach?
- What benefits does baseball offer participants?
- What potential detriments can occur in the presence of inadequate adult leadership?
- What principal goals should a coach seek to achieve?

INTRODUCTION

For young people participating in a baseball program, the quality and subsequent benefits of their experience is determined largely by their coach. Strong leadership during practices, games, and special events encourages each young person to nurture and develop individual strengths physically, psychologically, and socially. Poor or weak leadership not only inhibits such growth, it actually undermines a youth's existing strengths in these areas.

While it's impossible to provide a totally beneficial experience, as a baseball coach it is your responsibility to ensure that the benefits gained by each youth far outweigh the detriments. To accomplish this, you must know what these benefits and detriments are, and you must set reasonable coaching goals.

Possible Benefits for Participants

The numerous benefits for youth include:

- developing appropriate skills
- developing physical fitness
- learning appropriate conditioning techniques that affect health and performance
- developing a realistic and positive self-image
- developing a lifetime pattern of regular physical activity
- developing a respect for rules as facilitators of safe and fair play
- obtaining enjoyment and recreation
- developing positive personal, social, and psychological skills (e.g., self-worth, self-discipline, team work, goal-setting, self-control)

Many players achieve significant benefits in at least some of these areas depending on the frequency, duration, and intensity of participation and the quality of coaching leadership.

Many significant benefits can be gained in youth baseball.

Possible Detriments for Participants

Players are likely to benefit from a baseball program when the coach sets appropriate objectives in the areas of skill, knowledge, fitness, and personal/social development. If, however, the coach sets inappropriate goals or teaches poorly, detriments may result.

To fully understand the value of a good coach, contrast the benefits listed previously with these possible detriments for the participant:

- developing inappropriate physical skills
- sustaining injury, illness, or loss of physical fitness
- learning incorrect rules and strategies of play
- learning incorrect conditioning techniques
- developing a negative or unrealistic self-image
- avoiding future participation in activity for self and others
- learning to misuse rules to gain unfair or unsafe advantages
- developing a fear of failure
- developing anti-social behaviors
- wasting time that could have been made available for other activities

When incorrect techniques and negative behaviors are learned by young athletes, the next coach must perform the difficult and time-consuming task of extinguishing these behaviors.

To maximize the benefits and minimize the detriments, you must understand your role as a baseball coach and provide quality leadership.

The benefits of participation relate directly to the quality of leadership.

GOALS FOR THE COACH

As a coach, it is important to:

1. effectively teach the individual techniques, rules, and strategies of the game in an orderly and enjoyable environment
2. appropriately challenge the cardiovascular and muscular systems of your players through active practice sessions and games
3. teach and model desirable personal, social, and psychological skills

Winning is also an important goal for the coach and participants but it is one you have little control over because winning is often contingent on outside factors (e.g., the skills of the

opposition, calls made by officials). If you concentrate on the three areas mentioned and become an effective leader, winning becomes a natural by-product.

The degree of success you attain in achieving these goals is determined by the extent to which you make appropriate choices and take correct actions in organizing and administering, teaching and leading, and protecting and caring.

Organization and Administration

Effective coaching relies heavily on good organization and administration. Organization involves clearly identifying the goals and objectives that must be attained if you are going to create a beneficial experience (with few detriments) for the participating youths. Steps necessary to organize the season so it can be efficiently administered include:

- identifying your primary purposes as a coach
- identifying goals for the season
- selecting and implementing the activities in practices and games that lead to achievement of the objectives
- evaluating the effects of your actions

Specific information, procedures, criteria, and examples necessary to effectively complete these steps are included in Chapter 14, Chapter 15, and Chapter 20.

Teaching and Leading

Teaching and leading are the core of coaching activity. Principles of effective instruction such as setting appropriate player expectations, using clear instructions, maintaining an orderly environment, maximizing the amount of practice time that is "on task," monitoring progress, and providing specific feedback are included in Chapter 15. This chapter gives you many insights into how you may effectively teach your players. Other important information for teaching and leading young athletes includes motivating your players, communicating effectively, maintaining discipline, and developing good personal and social skills. Coaching guidelines for each of these areas are included in the chapters that follow.

The only real control you have over winning and/or losing is the manner in which you plan and conduct your practices and supervise your games.

Because of the influence you have as "coach," your players will model the behaviors you exhibit. If you respond to competition (successes and failures), fair play, officials' calls, and/or spectators' comments with a positive and constructive attitude, your players are likely to imitate that positive behavior. If, however, you lose your temper, yell at officials, or bend and/or break rules to gain an unfair advantage, your players' actions are likely to become negative. When what you say differs from what you do, your players will be most strongly affected by what you do. Negative behavior by players can occur even if you tell them to "be good sports and to show respect to others" and then ignore this advice by acting in a contrary manner. In essence, "actions speak louder than words" and you must "practice what you preach" if you hope to positively influence your players' behavior.

Protecting and Caring

Although coaches often eliminate the potential for injury from their minds, it is important for them to (a) plan for injury prevention, (b) effectively deal with injuries when they occur, and (c) meet their legal responsibilities to act prudently. The information on legal liabilities in Chapter 21, and conditioning youth baseball players, nutrition for successful performance, and prevention, care, and rehabilitation of common baseball injuries in Chapters 22 through 26, provides the basis for prudent and effective action in these areas.

SUMMARY

Your primary purpose as a youth baseball coach is to maximize the benefits of participation in baseball while minimizing the detriments. To achieve this, you must organize, teach, model, and evaluate effectively. Your players learn not only from what you teach but from what you consciously or unconsciously do. You're a very significant person in the eyes of your players. They notice when you're organized and fair, are a good instructor, know the rules, are interested in them or in the win/loss record, know how to control your emotions, know how to present yourself, and treat others with respect. The choices you make and the actions you take determine how positive the experience is for them.

13
Working Effectively with Parents

Martha Ewing, Ph.D.
Deborah Feltz, Ph.D.
Eugene W. Brown, Ph.D.

QUESTIONS TO CONSIDER

- How can I obtain the information and help needed from parents to do a good job?
- What is my responsibility to the parents of the players on my team?
- How can I avoid the negative influence some parents have on a team or program?
- What are the responsibilities of the players and their parents to this program?

INTRODUCTION

Support and assistance from parents can be very helpful. Some parents, however, through lack of awareness, can weaken the effects of your coaching, and thus reduce the benefits baseball can provide to their children.

These negative influences can be minimized if you tell parents:

- how you perceive your role as the coach
- the purpose and objectives of the baseball program
- the responsibilities they and their children have in helping the team run smoothly

Some parents, through lack of awareness, can weaken the effects of your coaching.

The most effective way of communicating the purposes and needs of your program is through a parents' orientation meeting. A parents' orientation meeting can be used to:

- teach parents the rules and regulations of baseball so they understand the game
- provide details about the season
- provide a setting for collecting and distributing important information

At the parents' orientation meeting, you have the opportunity to ask for their assistance and discuss other items that are specific to the team. A meeting for parents is also an excellent way for them to get to know you and each other. A face-to-face meeting and a few short remarks go a long way toward uniting coaches and parents in a cooperative endeavor that benefits the players. Many potential problems can be eliminated by good communication that begins before the first practice.

CONTENT OF A PARENTS' ORIENTATION MEETING

Parents usually have a number of questions concerning their child's baseball program. With proper preparation and an outlined agenda, you should be able to answer most questions. A sample agenda is provided. This agenda can be supplemented with items you and/or the parents believe to be important.

Sample Agenda
Parents' Orientation Meeting

1. Introductions
2. Goals of the team and program
3. Understanding the sport of baseball
4. Dangers and risk of injury
5. Emergency procedures
6. Equipment needs
7. Athletes' responsibilities
8. Parents' responsibilities
9. Season schedule
10. Other

Each agenda item and its relationship to the baseball program is explained in the following paragraphs.

Introductions

Parents should be informed about who administers the baseball program. They should become acquainted with the coaches and the parents of the other players. As the coach, you should introduce yourself, briefly describing your background, coaching experience, and reasons for coaching.

The parents should also introduce themselves, identify where they live, and perhaps indicate how long their children have been involved in the program and the objectives that they have for their child's involvement in baseball. Learning who the other parents are makes it easier to establish working relationships for specific tasks and to initiate sharing of responsibilities (e.g., carpooling and bringing refreshments to games).

Finally, the purpose of the meeting should be explained to communicate important information about each agenda item. If handouts are available, they should be distributed at this time. We suggest that at least one handout, an agenda, be distributed to provide order to the meeting, a sense of organization on your part, and a place for parents to write notes.

Information about the players and their families should be collected (see Supplement

13-1). A team roster and telephone tree (see Supplement 13-2) could be compiled from the information collected, then typed and distributed to each of the families at another time.

Goals of the Team and Programs

The goals of the sponsoring organization, as well as your personal goals, should be presented. Parents then will be able to judge whether those goals are compatible with their beliefs regarding what is appropriate for their child. Goals that have been identified by young baseball players as most important are:

- to have fun
- to improve skills and learn new skills
- to be on a team and to make new friends
- to succeed or win

Most educators, pediatricians, sport psychologists, and parents consider these to be healthy goals that coaches should help young athletes achieve. Parents should be informed of the primary goals of the team and the amount of emphasis that will be placed on achieving these goals.

Parents should be informed of the primary goals of the team.

Other areas that should be addressed are your policies on eliminating players, the consequences of missing practices, and recognizing players through awards. You may be asked to answer many questions about how you will function as a coach. Some examples are:

- Will players be allowed to compete if they missed the last practice before a game?
- Will players be excluded from contests or taken off the team if they go on a two-week vacation?
- Will players receive trophies or other material rewards?
- How much emphasis will be placed on rewards?
- Are the rewards given only to good performers or are they given to all participants?

Chapter 16 discusses the issue of appropriate use of rewards. You may wish to comment on several points explained in Chapter 16 as you address this issue.

Understanding the Sport of Baseball

Many times spectators boo umpires, shout instructions to players, or contradict the coach because they do not know the rules or strategies of baseball. This is particularly true if the rules of play have been modified for younger age groups. Informing parents about basic rules, skills, and strategies may help those who are unfamiliar with baseball and will prevent some of this negative behavior.

The information may be presented in the form of a film, brief explanation, demonstration of techniques, and/or interpretations. In addition, parents could obtain copies of Handbook II — Rule Modifications for Youth Baseball — to learn more about the rules of the game. If you'd rather not use the meeting to cover this information, you could invite parents to attend selected practice sessions where a demonstration and/or explanation of positions, rules, and strategies will be presented to the team.

Dangers and Risk of Injury

Parents should be told what they can expect in terms of possible injuries their child may incur in baseball. As noted in Chapter 21, failure to inform parents of potential injuries is the most frequent basis for lawsuits involving coaches and players.

Tell them, for example, that generally the injuries are confined to sprains, bruises, and contusions, but that there is a possibility for broken bones, concussions, and catastrophic injuries. Supplement 13-3 provides information on sites of injuries in youth baseball. This information should be reviewed with parents. Let them know if a medical examination is required before their child's participation. If so, what forms or evidence of compliance is acceptable, to whom it must be provided, and when it is due.

Parents should be told what they can expect in terms of possible injuries in youth baseball.

Tell the parents what will be done to prevent injuries and assure them that the playing/practice area and equipment will be checked to help keep players safe and free from exposure to hazards.

Lastly, the program's policy of accident insurance should be described. Inform parents if the program maintains athletic accident coverage or whether parents are required to provide insurance coverage for injuries that happen during their child's athletic participation.

Emergency Procedures

Have the parents provide you with information and permission necessary for you to function during an emergency. The Athlete's Medical Information Form (Supplement 13-4) and Medical Release Form (Supplement 13-5) were designed for these purposes. You should have the parents complete these forms and keep them with you at all team functions. These forms will provide you with information to guide your actions in an emergency.

Equipment Needs

Explain what equipment the players need and where it can be purchased. Advice on the quality of particular brands and models and an indication of how much parents can expect to pay for specific items is also welcomed by the parents.

If an equipment swap is organized, tell them where and when it will be held. A handout describing proper equipment should be provided. Supplement 13-6 provides a list and guidelines for the selection of baseball equipment. This supplement could be reproduced and used as a handout to the parents for properly outfitting their child.

Athletes' Responsibilities

The "Bill of Rights for Young Athletes" (Martens and Seefeldt, 1979) reminds adults that the child's welfare must be placed above all other considerations. Children and their parents must realize, however, that along with rights, they must meet certain responsibilities. Young athletes must be responsible for:

- being on time at practices and games with all of their equipment
- cooperating with coaches and teammates
- putting forth the effort to condition their bodies and to learn the basic skills
- conducting themselves properly and living with the consequences of inappropriate behavior

These responsibilities should be discussed so parents may help reinforce them at home.

Parents' Responsibilities

Parents of young athletes must assume some responsibilities associated with their child's participation on the baseball team. This should be discussed at the parents' orientation meeting. Martens (1978) has identified a number of parental responsibilities. You may wish to cover all or a portion of the following responsibilities in the parents' orientation meeting.

- Parents should learn what their child expects from baseball.
- Parents should decide if their child is ready to compete and at what level.
- Parents should help their child understand the meaning of winning and losing.
- Parents are responsible for disciplining their child and ensuring that their child meets specific responsibilities for participating on the baseball team.
- Parents should not interfere with their child's coach and should conduct themselves in a proper manner at games.

Parents should also be sensitive to fulfill the commitment they and their child have made to the team. This often requires that parents displace other important tasks in order to get their child to practice on time, publicly support the coach, encourage players to give their best effort, reward players for desirable efforts, and participate in the social events of the team.

Children and their parents must assume certain responsibilities.

If called upon, parents should be willing to assist the coach to carry out some of the many tasks required to meet the needs of the team. If you, as the coach, can anticipate and identify tasks with which you will need assistance, these should be presented to the parents at the orientation meeting.

It is surprising how many parents will volunteer to help you if the tasks are well-defined. See Supplement 13-7 for a description of some qualifications required of assistants and some possible responsibilities. You may not be able to

anticipate all the tasks. However, by developing an expectation of shared cooperation at the orientation meeting, parents who are not initially called upon for assistance are more likely to provide help as the need arises.

One conflict that sometimes arises results from parents falsely assuming your responsibility as coach. They may attempt to direct the play of their child and/or others during practices and games. This type of action by a parent undermines your plans for the team. It may also create a conflict in the mind of the athlete as to which set of instructions to follow.

You must inform parents that their public comments should be limited to praise and applause and that you will be prepared to coach the team. There are many ways to coach young athletes and different strategies that can result in success. You should inform parents that, if they disagree with your coaching, you will be open to their suggestions when they are presented in private.

Season Schedule

Fewer telephone calls and memos will be needed later in the season if you prepare and distribute a schedule of events for the season at the orientation meeting. The most efficient way to provide parents with the entire season schedule is with a handout.

The schedule should inform the parents about the length of the season; the dates, sites, and times when practices and games will be held; lengths of practices and games; number of games; number of practices; and other events for the season. Maps and/or instructions about where team events will occur are often helpful.

GETTING PARENTS TO ATTEND AN ORIENTATION MEETING

After you have received your team roster and, if possible before the first practice, you should make arrangements to schedule a parents' orientation meeting. If you do not personally have sufficient space to accommodate the parents, a room in a neighborhood school usually can be scheduled free of charge for an orientation meeting.

Before scheduling the time and date for the meeting, the parents should be asked about the times that they could attend. This information, as well as items of parental concern for an agenda, can be obtained through a telephone conversation with the parents. Once the time and date have been determined, the parents should be notified about this information by telephone or brief letter.

If a letter is sent, the agenda for the meeting should be included. If possible, this notification should occur about two weeks before the meeting and should be followed by a courteous telephone reminder on the night before the meeting.

In your communication with the parents, you should stress the importance of the meeting and the need for each family to be represented at the meeting.

ORGANIZING THE PARENTS' ORIENTATION MEETING

If you are well-prepared and organized, conducting a parents' orientation meeting will be an enjoyable and useful event. Before this meeting, you should complete the agenda and write down key points you plan to communicate under each item. Next, assemble the handouts that will be distributed at the meeting. At the very least, the handouts should include an agenda for the parents to follow.

Other suggested handouts and forms for distributing and collecting information include: Information on common baseball injuries, medical examination form (if provided by your program), accident insurance form and information (if provided through your program), athletic medical information form, medical release form, description of proper equipment, list of team assistants and responsibilities, season schedule, telephone tree, and player and parent roster. The items in Supplements 13-1 through 13-7 are suitable for duplication (permission is granted) and could be distributed at the orientation meeting.

FOLLOW-UP ON THE PARENTS' ORIENTATION MEETING

After having conducted the parents' orientation meeting, you should contact the families who were unable to attend and briefly inform them about what was discussed. They should be given the handouts that were distributed at the meeting, and you should collect whatever information is needed from them. Once your records are completed, you may compile additional handouts (e.g., telephone tree).

Keep the lines of communication open between you and the parents.

No matter how many questions you answer at the parents' orientation meeting, it will not solve all of the problems. Thus, it is important to keep the lines of communication open. You should indicate your willingness to discuss any problems that were not discussed at the first meeting. This might be done with a telephone call or at a conference involving the coach and parent, or the coach, parent, and athlete. Immediately before or after a practice is often an appropriate time to discuss major issues with parents. You could even have another meeting for parents midway through the season to provide an update on the team's progress, to discuss any problems, or to listen to parent's comments. By inviting parents to talk with you, they will become a positive rather than negative influence on the players and the team.

SUMMARY

Parents can be an asset to your program, but some parents can have a negative influence on your program. Communicating to parents about how you perceive your role as the coach, the purpose of the baseball program, and the responsibilities that they and their children have to the baseball program can minimize these negative influences. The most effective way to communicate this information is through a parents' orientation meeting. The time and effort you put into developing a well-organized meeting will save you considerably more time and effort throughout the season.

In a parents' orientation meeting, you have the opportunity to explain to parents that they have responsibilities to you and the team, such as deciding if their child is ready to compete, having realistic expectations, disciplining, and not interfering with coaching or playing. Children's responsibilities of promptness, cooperation, commitment, and proper conduct can also be outlined for parents.

In addition, other agenda items can be discussed and information can be gathered at a parents' orientation meeting that may make your job run more smoothly throughout the season. Be sure to discuss such items as danger and risk of injury, equipment needs, emergency procedures, and the season schedule.

The agenda items outlined in this chapter may not cover all the issues you need to address with the parents of your players. Therefore, you must organize a specific meeting that meets the needs of your team.

REFERENCES

Martens, R. (1978). *Joys and sadness in children's sports.* Champaign, IL: Human Kinetics Publishers.

Martens, R. & Seefeldt, V. (Eds.). (1979). *Guidelines for children's sports.* Reston, VA: AAHPERD.

SUGGESTED READINGS

American College of Sports Medicine, American Orthopaedic Society for Sports Medicine & Sports Medicine Committee of the United States Tennis Association. (1982). *Sports injuries—An aid to prevention and treatment.* Coventry, CT: Bristol Myers Co.

Foley, J. (1980). *Questions parents should ask about youth sports programs.* East Lansing, MI: Institute for the Study of Youth Sports.

Jackson, D. & Pescar, S. (1981). *The young athletes' health handbook.* New York: Everest House.

Micheli, L.J. (1985). Preventing youth sports injuries. *Journal of Health, Physical Education, Recreation and Dance,* 76(6), 52-54.

Mirkin, G. & Marshall, H. (1978). *The sportsmedicine book.* Waltham, MA: Little Brown, & Co.

Supplement 13-1.

Team Roster Information

	Player's Name	Birth Date	Parents' Names	Address	Phone #'s Home/Work
1.		/ /	————	————	/
					/
2.		/ /	————	————	/
					/
3.		/ /	————	————	/
					/
4.		/ /	————	————	/
					/
5.		/ /	————	————	/
					/
6.		/ /	————	————	/
					/
7.		/ /	————	————	/
					/
8.		/ /	————	————	/
					/
9.		/ /	————	————	/
					/
10.		/ /	————	————	/
					/
11.		/ /	————	————	/
					/
12.		/ /	————	————	/
					/
13.		/ /	————	————	/
					/
14.		/ /	————	————	/
					/
15.		/ /	————	————	/
					/
16.		/ /	————	————	/
					/
17.		/ /	————	————	/
					/
18.		/ /	————	————	/
					/

Telephone Tree

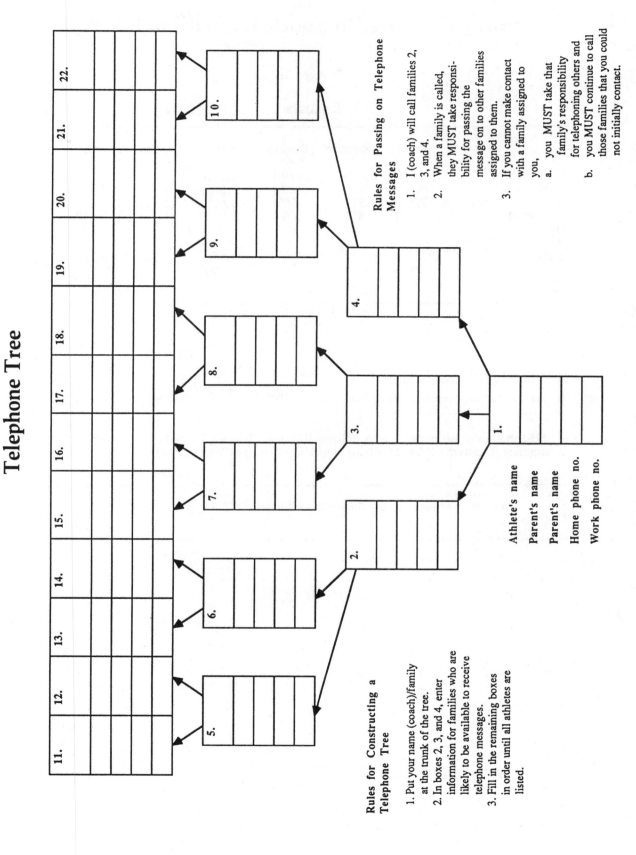

Rules for Constructing a Telephone Tree

1. Put your name (coach)/family at the trunk of the tree.
2. In boxes 2, 3, and 4, enter information for families who are likely to be available to receive telephone messages.
3. Fill in the remaining boxes in order until all athletes are listed.

Athlete's name
Parent's name
Parent's name
Home phone no.
Work phone no.

Rules for Passing on Telephone Messages

1. I (coach) will call families 2, 3, and 4.
2. When a family is called, they MUST take responsibility for passing the message on to other families assigned to them.
3. If you cannot make contact with a family assigned to you,
   a. you MUST take that family's responsibility for telephoning others and
   b. you MUST continue to call those families that you could not initially contact.

Sites of Injuries in Youth Softball and Baseball

Age Group[a]

	Total	0-4 Years		5-14 Years		15+ Years	
		Number	Percent	Number	Percent	Number	Percent
Head and Face	112,362	5,299	(87%)	48,306	(40%)	58,757	(19%)
Shoulder and Trunk	40,340	129	(2%)	7,509	(6%)	32,702	(10%)
Arms and Hands	137,799	317	(5%)	44,601	(37%)	92,881	(30%)
Legs and Feet	150,469	383	(6%)	21,034	(17%)	129,052	(41%)
Other	1,603	----	-------	200	-------	1,403	-------
Totals	442,573 (100%)	6,128 ----	(100%)	121,650 (28%)	(100%)	314,795 (71%)	(100%)

	Total All Ages	Age Group 5-14 Years
A. Medically attended injuries, 1980	1,236,800	359,400
B. Hospital emergency room-treated injuries, 1980	442,900	121,700

a   Distribution of Estimated Baseball/Softball-Related Injuries Treated in U.S. Hospital Emergency Rooms, by Body Part Injured and Age Group of Victim, 1980.

Source: National Electronic Injury Surveillance System, U.S. Consumer Product Safety Commission/EPHA

Athlete's Medical Information
(to be completed by parents/guardians and athlete)

Athlete's Name: _____ Athlete's Birthdate: _____

Parents' Names: _____ Date: _____

Address: _____

Phone No's.: (____)_____ (____)_____ (____)_____
  (Home)   (Work)   (Other)

Who to contact in case of emergency (if parents cannot be immediately contacted):

Name: _____ Relationship: _____

Home Phone No.: (____)_____ Work Phone No.: (____)_____

Name: _____ Relationship: _____

Home Phone No.: (____)_____ Work Phone No.: (____)_____

Hospital preference: _____ Emergency Phone No.: (____)_____

Doctor preference: _____ Office Phone No.: (____)_____

MEDICAL HISTORY

Part I. Complete the following:

	Date	Doctor	Doctor's Phone No.
1. Last tetanus shot?	_____		
2. Last dental examination?	_____	_____	_____
3. Last eye examination?	_____	_____	_____

Part II. Has your child or did your child have any of the following?

General Conditions:	Circle one		Circle one or both		Injuries:	Circle one		Circle one or both	
1. Fainting spells/dizziness	Yes	No	Past	Present	1. Toes	Yes	No	Past	Present
2. Headaches	Yes	No	Past	Present	2. Feet	Yes	No	Past	Present
3. Convulsions/epilepsy	Yes	No	Past	Present	3. Ankles	Yes	No	Past	Present
4. Asthma	Yes	No	Past	Present	4. Lower legs	Yes	No	Past	Present
5. High blood pressure	Yes	No	Past	Present	5. Knees	Yes	No	Past	Present
6. Kidney problems	Yes	No	Past	Present	6. Thighs	Yes	No	Past	Present
7. Intestinal disorder	Yes	No	Past	Present	7. Hips	Yes	No	Past	Present
8. Hernia	Yes	No	Past	Present	8. Lower back	Yes	No	Past	Present
9. Diabetes	Yes	No	Past	Present	9. Upper back	Yes	No	Past	Present
10. Heart disease/disorder	Yes	No	Past	Present	10. Ribs	Yes	No	Past	Present
11. Dental plate	Yes	No	Past	Present	11. Abdomen	Yes	No	Past	Present
12. Poor vision	Yes	No	Past	Present	12. Chest	Yes	No	Past	Present
13. Poor hearing	Yes	No	Past	Present	13. Neck	Yes	No	Past	Present
14. Skin disorder	Yes	No	Past	Present	14. Fingers	Yes	No	Past	Present
15. Allergies	Yes	No			15. Hands	Yes	No	Past	Present
Specify:_____			Past	Present	16. Wrists	Yes	No	Past	Present
_____			Past	Present	17. Forearms	Yes	No	Past	Present
16. Joint dislocation or					18. Elbows	Yes	No	Past	Present
separations	Yes	No			19. Upper arms	Yes	No	Past	Present
Specify:_____			Past	Present	20. Shoulders	Yes	No	Past	Present
_____			Past	Present	21. Head	Yes	No	Past	Present
17. Serious or significant ill-					22. Serious or significant in-				
nesses not included above	Yes	No			juries not included above	Yes	No		
Specify:_____			Past	Present	Specify: _____			Past	Present
_____			Past	Present	_____			Past	Present
18. Others:_____			Past	Present	23. Others: _____			Past	Present
_____			Past	Present	_____			Past	Present

Part III. Circle appropriate response to each question. For each "Yes" response, provide additional information.

	Circle one		Additional information

1. Is your child currently taking any medication? If yes, describe medication, amount, and reason for taking.   Yes   No   _____

2. Does your child have any allergic reactions to medication, bee stings, food, etc.? If yes, describe agents that cause adverse reactions and describe these reactions.   Yes   No   _____

3. Does your child wear any appliances (e.g., glasses, contact lenses, hearing aid, false teeth, braces, etc.)? If yes, describe appliances.   Yes   No   _____

4. Has your child had any surgical operations? If yes, indicate site, explain the reason for the surgery, and describe the level of success.   Yes   No   _____

5. Has a physician placed any restrictions on your child's present activities? If yes, describe restrictions.   Yes   No   _____

6. Does your child have any existing and/or past medical or emotional conditions that require special concern and attention by a sports coach? If yes, explain.   Yes   No   _____

7. Does your child have any deformities (e.g., abnormal curvature of the spine, heart problems, one kidney, blindness in one eye, one testicle, etc.)? If yes, describe.   Yes   No   _____

8. Is there a history of serious family illnesses (e.g., diabetes, bleeding disorders, heart attack before age 50, etc.)? If yes, describe illnesses.   Yes   No   _____

9. Has your child lost consciousness or sustained a concussion?   Yes   No   _____

10. Has your child experienced fainting spells or dizziness while exercising?   Yes   No   _____

Part IV. Has your child or did your child have any of the following personal habits?

Personal Habit	Circle one		Circle one or both		Indicate extent or amount
1. Smoking	Yes	No	Past	Present	_____
2. Smokeless tobacco	Yes	No	Past	Present	_____
3. Alcohol	Yes	No	Past	Present	_____
4. Recreational drugs (e.g., marijuana, cocaine, etc.)	Yes	No	Past	Present	_____
5. Steroids	Yes	No	Past	Present	_____
6. Others					
Specify: _____	Yes	No	Past	Present	_____
_____	Yes	No	Past	Present	_____
_____	Yes	No	Past	Present	_____

Part V. Please explain below any "Yes" responses in Parts II, III, and IV or any other concerns that have present implications for my coaching your child. Also, describe special first aid requirements, if appropriate. An additional sheet may be attached if necessary.

_____

_____

_____

_____

	Signature	Date
Athlete:	_____	_____
Parent or Guardian:	_____	_____
Parent or Guardian:	_____	_____

Supplement 13-5.

Medical Release Form

I hereby give permission for any and all medical attention necessary to be administered to my child in the event of an accident, injury, sickness, etc., under the direction of the people listed below until such time as I may be contacted. My child's name is _____.
This release is effective for the time during which my child is participating in the _____
_____ baseball program and any tournaments for the 19___/19___
season, including traveling to or from such tournaments. I also hereby assume the responsibility for payment of any such treatment.

PARENTS' OR GUARDIANS' NAMES: _____

HOME ADDRESS: _____
                    Street   City   State   Zip

                                      (_____)_____(W)
HOME PHONE: (_____)_____ (_____)_____(W)

INSURANCE COMPANY: _____

POLICY NUMBER: _____

FAMILY PHYSICIAN: _____

PHYSICIAN'S ADDRESS: _____ PHONE NO. (_____)_____

In case I cannot be reached, either of the following people is designated:

COACH'S NAME: _____ PHONE NO. (_____)_____

ASS'T. COACH OR OTHER: _____ PHONE NO. (_____)_____

SIGNATURE OF PARENT OR GUARDIAN _____

SUBSCRIBED AND SWORN BEFORE ME THIS _____ OF _____, 19 ____

SIGNATURE OF NOTARY PUBLIC _____

Supplement 13-6.

Guidelines for Selecting Baseball Equipment

- **Ball**

     There are a variety of baseballs available for purchase in sporting goods stores. The baseballs vary in size, weight, and material. Baseballs should be selected for their compatibility with the physical characteristics and needs of the youth player. Baseball-sized "Incrediballs" or RIF (Reduced Injury Factor) Level I balls are made of a softer material and are recommended for six to eight year old baseball players. The RIF ball or Incrediball will allow the beginning player to grip the ball more easily and play the game without fear of injury. The RIF and Incrediball are also recommended for any type of indoor use.

- **Bat**

     Bats are available in many different materials (e.g., wood, aluminum, graphite, and ceramic). The length and weight of the bat should be appropriate for the size and strength of the player. In general, a lighter bat is conducive to a faster swing speed.

- **Glove**

     The glove is an important piece of equipment for the youth baseball player. The glove should be large enough to enclose the ball yet not so large that the fielder cannot easily control it. The glove should be broken in in such a way that the thumb-side edge of the glove naturally closes to the small finger edge of the glove. If the thumb-side edge of the glove naturally closes to any other finger, the pocket will not effectively hold a baseball. Also, the glove should be flexible enough to allow the player to easily open the glove to the ball! Between games

or practices, a ball should be placed in the pocket of the glove to help maintain the glove's correct form.

- **Shoes**

     Baseball cleats are not a required piece of equipment and are not necessary for the young ages. Generally, a supportive basketball or tennis type of shoe will do. A basketball or tennis shoe will provide support for the starting, stopping, and change of direction moves required in baseball. However, as skills increase, cleats will add to the player's ability to maneuver on the field. Plastic or multi-purpose cleats are recommended. Metal spikes are not recommended.

- **Batting Helmets**

     All hitters, baserunners, and on-deck batters must wear a batting helmet. Helmets are often provided by the league or team. However, coaches, league officials, and parents should be sure all helmets are NOCSAE (National Operating Committee on Standards for Athletic Equipment) approved. Helmets should be checked periodically for wear of the inside padding or cracks in the helmet itself.

- **Catcher's Equipment**

     The catcher should wear a catching helmet with a face mask and throat protector, a body protector, and shin guards. The equipment must be adjusted to fit each player. When changing catchers, time must be taken to adjust the equipment to the new catcher. Also, extra face masks with throat protectors should be available for any player catching for a pitcher in the catching position — even if it is only practice!

• Clothing

Unless uniforms are provided, typical attire (T-shirts, shorts/sweats, athletic socks, and caps) will function well for youth baseball. Clothing should not inhibit movement or get in the way of the player. If the player is highly likely to slide during the course of a practice or game, long pants and/or knee pads will reduce the chance for injury.

Note: All equipment should be regulation baseball equipment (see Chapter 10, Baseball Rules).

Supplement 13-7.

Descriptions of Team Assistants and Their Responsibilities*

Assistant coach—aids the coach in all aspects of coaching the team during practices and games.

Team manager—keeps game statistics, completes line-up cards, and makes arrangements for practice sites and times; works approximately one hour per week.

Team treasurer—collects fees from players, identifies sponsors, maintains financial records; works approximately five hours at the beginning of the season and a few hours throughout the remainder of the season.

Team doctor/nurse/paramedic—establishes a plan to respond to possible emergencies for each practice and game site, prepares and updates a medical kit, assists the coach in responding to injured players by providing first aid, collects and organizes completed medical history forms and reviews these with the coach, maintains records of completed on-site injury reports and completes a summary of season injuries, delegates other parents to bring ice to games for initial care of certain injuries; works approximately five hours at the beginning of the season and approximately 1/2 hour per week throughout the remainder of the season. Note that only a certified medical doctor, trainer, nurse, or paramedic should assume some of these defined responsibilities. See Chapter 26, Prevention of Common Baseball Injuries, for more details.

Team social coordinator—plans team party and team social functions; works approximately five hours per season.

Team refreshments coordinator—contacts parents to assign them the shared expense and responsibilities of providing refreshments at all games (see Chapter 23, Nutrition for Successful Performance); works approximately two hours per week.

Team secretary—prepares and duplicates handouts, types, sends out mailings; works approximately 10 hours per season.

*Note that these are only suggestions for assistants and responsibilities. The way you organize your team may result in the need for different and/or additional assistants.

14
Planning for the Season

Paul Vogel, Ph.D.

QUESTIONS TO CONSIDER

- Why should planning for the entire season precede day-to-day planning?
- What steps should a coach follow when organizing for the season?
- What skills, knowledge, aspects of fitness, and personal social skills should be included as objectives for the season?
- How should the season be organized to be most effective from a coaching-learning point of view?

INTRODUCTION

Planning for the season involves two basic tasks. First, coaches must select the content that will be the focus of instruction during the season (objectives that involve physical skills, sport-related knowledge, fitness capacities, and personal/social skills). Second, these desired outcomes should be organized into a plan from which practices, games, and other events can be efficiently managed.

What follows provides reasons why season planning is useful and gives you steps necessary to develop a season's plan as well as examples of season objectives. Materials and examples are also provided at the end of this chapter for completing your season plan.

WHY PLAN?

Coaches agree that teaching the skills, rules, and strategies of baseball are among their primary responsibilities. Most coaches would also agree that improving the physical condi-

tion of the players, promoting enjoyment of the game, teaching good sportsmanship, and attempting to avoid physical and psychological injury are also outcomes they wish to achieve. Many coaches fail, however, to recognize the importance of planning to accomplish these goals.

Achievement of goals and objectives requires effective planning.

Organized practices are vital to maximizing the benefits of baseball. Disorganized practices often result in players failing to obtain desired skills, knowledge, fitness, and attitudes and often contribute to injuries and inappropriate skills. Organizing your season and planning your practices prior to going on the field can result in the following benefits:

- efficient use of limited practice time
- inclusion of season objectives that are most essential

- appropriate sequence of season objectives
- directing practice activities to the season's goals and objectives
- reduction of the time required for planning
- enhanced preparation of the team for competition
- improved ability to make day-to-day adjustments in practice objectives
- deterrent to lawsuits involving coaches' liability

DEVELOPING A SEASON PLAN

Use these three steps to develop a season plan:

1. Identify the goals and objectives of the season
2. Sequence the season objectives into the pre, early, mid, and late portions of the season
3. Identify practice objectives

The relationship of these three steps to fulfilling your role as the coach and to evaluating the outcomes you desire for your players is illustrated in Figure 14-1.

Identify Goals and Objectives for the Season

Your primary role as coach is to maximize the benefits for your players while minimizing

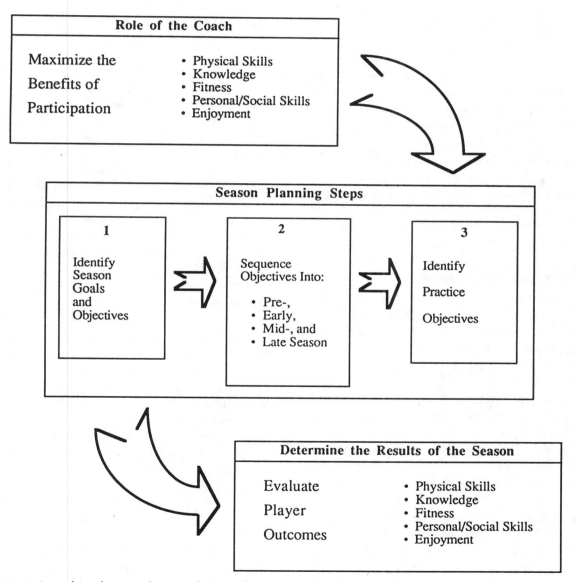

Figure 14-1. A coach's role as it relates to planning the season and evaluating the players.

the potential detrimental effects of participation. This alone provides the basis for identifying the specific goals and objectives for your coaching effort. You will affect your players either positively or negatively in each of the following areas:

- physical skills (fielding, batting, baserunning, infield play, outfield play, defensive strategies)
- knowledge (rules, tactics, training techniques, terminology, nutrition, safety)
- fitness (muscular strength, endurance, flexibility, aerobic fitness)
- personal/social skills (feelings about baseball, motivation, discipline, sportsmanship, other character traits)
- enjoyment (happy to attend practices, likes the coach and teammates)

By thinking of these five broad areas of player outcomes as goals, you are taking the initial step toward fulfilling your major role of "maximizing the benefits" of participation in baseball and "minimizing the potential detrimental effects of participation" by clearly specifying the objectives for the season.

Although the identification of goals is an important first step, it is the selection of specific objectives within each goal area that provides the direction necessary to organize the season and plan effective practices.

● Selecting Skill Objectives

Supplement 14-1 provides you with a list of objectives for each physical skill area. By reviewing the individual techniques listed, you can select objectives that are best for your players. To help with this task, appropriate objectives for players at three levels of play (beginning, ages 8-10; intermediate, ages 11-13, and advanced, ages 14 and over) are suggested. A detailed description of each of these individual techniques, including key elements and common errors in their performance, as well as progressions for teaching, can be found in Section 1. The key elements of performance are the bases for assessing players and for focusing your coaching efforts. This information should be reviewed if you do not have a good understanding of these individual techniques.

● Selecting Knowledge Objectives

Cognitive outcomes (e.g., knowledge of rules, strategies, and information related to physical conditioning) are important for your players. Rules pertaining to "violations," how to warm up and cool down, what to eat for a pre-game meal, and exercises to avoid are all important objectives because they can influence a player's performance. Objectives that include cognitive skills and tactics are listed in Supplement 14-2. You may wish to add to, delete from, or alter the objectives on this list as you determine those that are most appropriate for your team. By identifying these objectives, it's more likely they'll be taught at specific times during the season and at an appropriate level of understanding.

● Selecting Fitness Objectives

Generally, your primary concern for athletes in the 6-13 age range should be to develop physical skills, knowledge, and appropriate personal/social skills. This is not to suggest that conditioning is unimportant. It is, however, the studied opinion of many coaches and specialists in growth and development that the specific training designed to promote high levels of sport-related fitness should receive a lower priority at this age. For highly skilled baseball players 14 years of age and older, a gradually increasing emphasis should be placed on conditioning the muscular and energy production systems. Part of the reason for this recommendation is that when young athletes train for skilled performance, they also obtain conditioning stimuli that are sufficient to cause the body to adapt to the fitness demands associated with learning and performing baseball skills. As players become highly skilled, conditioning becomes a more important factor for enabling more frequent, more intense, and more enduring application of their abilities. Supplement 14-3 includes an overview of fitness objectives you may wish to include in your season plan for older players who are also highly skilled.

For younger players, fitness should be a by-product of learning the physical skills.

• Selecting Personal and Social Skill Objectives

A primary objective in the season plan should be to have all players feel increasingly better about their abilities as the season progresses. This should occur not only in the areas of physical skills, knowledge, and fitness, but should also include qualities such as persistence, self-control, tolerance, respect for authority, encouragement of teammates, concentration on the task, commitment to best efforts, and cooperation. Athletes need guidance (modeling, direction, encouragement, gentle rebuking, etc.) to develop such attributes. When achieved, these personal and social qualities contribute to performance in both athletic and non-athletic situations. Moreover, unlike opponents, officials, and/or the "breaks of the game," these qualities are within the control of individual players. The opportunity for individual control has been strongly linked to motivation, and motivation is strongly linked to performance.

Coaches are responsible for developing socially desirable skills in their players.

As a coach, perhaps your most important and lasting contribution is helping your players improve their feelings of self-worth and socially desirable skills. By focusing on controllable qualities such as "effort" versus uncontrollable "outcomes," which are often dependent on others (e.g., an official's call, a "lucky" bounce, the ability of another team), you have a unique opportunity to make a significant and lasting contribution to the personal character of your athletes.

Contributing to team membership is another worthy objective that coaches should set for every player. Athletes, especially those who engage in team sports such as baseball, must learn to overcome the natural tendency to blame others for a loss or even a bad performance. Players must be taught that their role is to play as well as they can and to think, do, and say those things that can help their teammates do the same. The team will only be as good as its weakest link. Often, an otherwise excellent team performs at a mediocre level due to the dissension created by "putting others down," making excuses, or transferring blame to others.

Coaches should reward effort when they review the accomplishments of the team.

Included in Supplement 14-4 is a listing of several personal and social skill objectives that you may want to incorporate into your season plan. The listing may be modified and made specific to your players.

Sequence Objectives Into Pre, Early, Mid, and Late Portions of the Season

Once you've identified season objectives for your team, they can be listed on the worksheet provided in Supplement 14-5. While the list may need to be revised as the season unfolds, the objectives should become the basis of your planning for the season.

Categorize the listed objectives into goals you want to achieve in the pre-, early-, mid-, and late-season (see Figure 14-2). Some objectives may be emphasized throughout the season, whereas others may be emphasized in only one division of the season. Photocopy Supplement 14-6 and use it to complete this step of your season plan.

Deciding what objectives should be achieved in the pre-, early-, mid-, and late-season is the basis for all subsequent planning.

• Pre-Season Objectives

If pre-season activity is possible, it can save you valuable practice time. Many of the objectives pertaining to knowledge of the rules and strategies and some of those involving conditioning can be all, or partially, achieved before formal practice even begins.

Objectives appropriate for the pre-season involve skills, knowledge, fitness capacities, or personal/social skills that can be achieved independently (all or in part) by the player in a safe and efficient manner before the initiation of formal practices. This could include learning the basic rules, violations and penalties, and strategies; obtaining appropriate equipment; and developing strength and aerobic fitness.

SEASON PLAN WORKSHEET

Coach: _____   Season: _____

Goal Areas	Objectives	Season Division			
		Pre	Early	Mid	Late
Physical Skills	Baserunning		X	X	
	Hitting		X	X	X
	Batting		X	X	
	Bunt: Square around		X	X	X
	Bunt: Drag		X	X	X
	Throwing		X	X	X
	Catching flys		X	X	X
	Fielding grounders		X	X	X
	Pitching		X	X	X
Knowledge	Rules of the Game				
	terms	X	X	X	
	scoring	X	X	X	
	substitution	X	X	X	
	Strategies				
	offensive			X	X
	defensive			X	X
Fitness	Flexibility				
	hip	X	X	X	X
	shoulder	X	X	X	X
	Cardiovascular	X	X	X	X
Personal/Social	Personal				
	best effort		X	X	X
	listening		X	X	X
	Social				
	cooperation		X	X	X
	fair play		X	X	X

Figure 14-2. An abbreviated example of a season plan for young baseball players.

● Early-Season Objectives

The early-season should be devoted to determining how well your players have mastered the fundamental and/or prerequisite objectives you have selected and to teaching, reteaching, or practicing those objectives. Objectives appropriate for the early-season should contain abilities that are prerequisite to attaining other identified objectives. For example, players must be able to field and ground before they can be expected to make a double play. This attention to the sequence of skills is particularly important for the inexperienced player, who should spend more time on learning skills typically placed in the early-season division. In addition to objectives associated with physical skills, early-season objectives should include logistical and organizational concerns, safety, strategy, discipline, fitness, socialization, rules of play, and team rules. These are all essential in preparing players for early-season games and to provide a foundation for the rest of the season.

● Mid-Season Objectives

Mid-season objectives should continue to focus on teaching individual techniques. However, a large share of practice time should be devoted to refining these techniques within the context of game-like drills and controlled scrimmages. Time should be spent combining individual techniques (e.g., batting the ball, then running to first), and integrating these techniques with game strategy. Many of the cognitive, fitness, and personal/social objectives established for the early-season should continue to be emphasized during the mid-season.

● Late-Season Objectives

Late-season objectives should be focused on the maintenance and refinement of the team's offensive and defensive play. A greater portion of practice time should be spent on "small-sided games," game-like drills, and controlled scrimmages. Practices should be organized so fitness levels are maintained and emphasis continues on cognitive and personal and social skills.

Generally, you should focus on single skills in the early-season, skill combinations in the mid-season, and combinations of both within systems of play in the later portion of the season. There are no hard and fast divisions among these three phases of the season (in fact, they should blend or overlap through good transitions). However, you should have them clearly in mind as you view the entire season in terms of what you wish to accomplish and the time in which it must be done.

Identify Practice Objectives

As you place objectives into season divisions and adjust the number of weeks assigned to each division, you will likely find that you have chosen to cover more than your available practice time allows. A good guide in such situations is to devote enough time to the cumulative instruction and practice of each objective so the majority of players are able to make significant improvements on most of the objectives included in the season plan. Merely exposing

your team to the individual techniques of the game, without spending sufficient time for them to be learned, results in frustration for you and the players. Your players must receive sufficient instruction, practice, and feedback to master the objectives at an appropriate level for use in a game situation. Accordingly, select, teach, and practice only the objectives that are essential to the game at your team's level of play. You can always add objectives to your plan as it is implemented, but you cannot recover time wasted on objectives that are not achieved or that are inappropriate for your players' level of development.

Select, teach, and practice the key objectives that are essential to your team.

Generally, the allotment of time to physical skill objectives should be based upon the following instructional sequence and distributed across several practices. You should allow time:

1. to introduce the objective—tell the players what you want them to learn and why it is important
2. for the players to try the individual techniques and for you to determine their levels of performance
3. for you to teach the key elements of the individual techniques and for players to practice these elements
4. for skill refinement and automation such that an individual technique can be used in game situations

The time allotment to fitness, cognitive, and personal/social objectives may not be as structured as the allotment for physical skill objectives. Fitness goals may be achieved along with practice of individual techniques in drills and scrimmages. Similarly, some cognitive, and personal/social objectives may be concomitantly attained during the practice of physical skills. However, some of these objectives may need practice time specifically devoted to them.

Integrating your chosen objectives into a season calendar (see Figure 14-3) will give you a master plan of everything you need to manage your coaching activities. The season calendar converts your plans to practice outlines. The daily entries on the calendar provide a guide

			SEASON PLANNING CALENDAR			
Coach __Goodbody__			Team __Falcons__			Month _____
S	**M**	**T**	**W**	**T**	**F**	**S**
	Coaches' education meeting 7:00-9:00 (High School)		Team rosters distributed, sign-up for practice times/fields 7:00-8:00 (Rec Office)			
		Parents' orientation meeting 7:00-8:30 (Elementary School Rm. 10)				
		Practice #1		*Practice #2*		*Practice #3*
		Practice #4		*Practice #5*		*Practice #6*
		Practice #7		*Practice #8*		

Figure 14-3. An example of a season planning calendar.

Figure 14-3 (continued)

Practice #1

05 Overview of practice
10 Team rules and regulations
05 Warm-up

Teach and evaluate:

15 Catching/throwing
10 Fielding ground balls (gbs)
15 Pitching (everyone)
20 Hitting
05 Cool-down
05 Handouts: team rules,
    practice and game schedule,
    rules of play

Practice #2

05 Overview of practice
10 Review rules of play
05 Warm-up (catching/throwing)*

Review and evaluate:

10 Baserunning (1B, EBH)
15 Outfield fly balls (fbs)/gbs

Practice:

10 Infield gb drills
15 Hitting drills
05 Cool-down/team talk
05 Cool-down/team talk
05 Handouts: Coaching hints
    for individual skills

Practice #3

05 Overview of practice
10 Review rules of play
10 Warm-up (catching/throwing)*

Teach and evaluate:

20 Position play: base
    coverage, position resp.

Practice:

15 Outfield fb/gb
20 Hitting*
05 Cool-down
10 Chalk talk: defensive
    strategies

Practice #4

05 Overview of practice
10 Warm-up (catching/throwing)

Teach and evaluate:

10 Baserunning: leadoffs
15 Position play: back ups*

Practice:

15 Position specific fielding
    (gb/fb)
20 Hitting drills
10 Baserunning (1B, EBH)
05 Cool-down
05 Defensive strategy review

Practice #5

05 Overview/questions
10 Warm-up (catching/throwing)*

Teach and evaluate:

15 Sliding
15 Bunting

Practice:

20 Hitting*
10 Infield/outfield gb drills
05 Cool-down
10 Chalk talk: offensive
    strategy

Practice #6

05 Overview/questions
15 Warm-up (catching/throwing)*

Teach and evaluate:

10 Relays/cutoff

Practice:

15 Position play (situations)
10 Bunting
15 Hitting drills
10 Baserunning
05 Cool-down
05 Review offensive strategy

Practice #7

05 Overview/questions
15 Warm-up (catching/throwing)*

Teach and evaluate:

10 Leads, stealing w/pitch*
10 Tag up, halfway w/fly ball

Practice:

10 Fielding gb drills
15 Fly balls w/relays
20 Hitting*
05 Cool-down

Practice #8

05 Overview/questions
15 Warm-up w/throwing*

Teach and evaluate:

10 Position play -- infield
    outfield priority

Practice:

15 Position play -- situations
    (include inf/of priority)
10 Bunting
20 Hitting
10 Baserunning
05 Cool-down

*Pitchers practice pitching
(i.e., before/after their turn to
hit). The pitcher must also
understand that to become a
highly skilled pitcher she/he
must also practice pitching
outside of team practices!

from which specific plans can be developed. Supplement 14-7 provides a blank reproducible worksheet that you can use to develop a master plan of practices.

The following list includes examples of entries that can be included on a calender:

- registration dates and deadlines
- date team roster is distributed
- sign-up date for practice time at available field
- dates and times for coaches' education meetings
- equipment distribution dates and times
- date and time for parents' orientation meeting
- dates and times for league meetings
- sequential numbers designating practices (e.g., #1 designates first practice)
- practice objectives and time allocations
- game days and times
- tournament dates
- dates and times for special events

The most important part of developing a season calendar is the decision you make about what objectives to include and how much practice time you devote to each objective on a practice-by-practice basis. Using your season plan worksheet, select an appropriate number of objectives listed under "early-season" that you wish to include in your first practice and enter them in the space labeled "practice #1" on your season calendar. This process should be repeated for your second, third, and subsequent practices through the early, mid-, and late-season divisions.

The two most important decisions in planning the season are deciding what objectives to teach and how much time you should spend teaching them.

You will spend less total time planning for your season and practice if you use the approach suggested here than if the task is done practice-by-practice throughout the season. This process will also help you verify which skills you believe are most important as you run out of available practice time and are forced to either exclude objectives from your plan or find other ways to achieve them outside of the normal practice time. In addition to the good feeling and confidence that comes with completing a season calendar, you will have developed the base necessary to systematically change your plans as unexpected events develop. More importantly, you will know before the mid- to late-portions of the season whether in your initial plan you assigned too much or too little time to some of your early-season objectives. A completed plan that's been implemented and refined is also an invaluable resource for next year's coaching assignment or as a guide for new coaches coming into the program.

SUMMARY

Your role as a coach can be best filled through the leadership and instruction you provide in practice and game situations. Clearly, those coaches who are most effective in helping their players acquire the necessary physical skills, knowledge, fitness, and personal/social skills are those who have clear objectives and who organize to achieve them. Organization of the season by selecting and then teaching objectives in a proper order, and for an appropriate amount of time, is a major step toward helping players acquire the benefits of baseball.

Skills and Abilities of Baseball

FUNDAMENTAL MOTOR SKILL	SUGGESTED EMPHASIS				
	6 yrs.	7-8 yrs.	9-10 yrs.	11-13 yrs.	14 yrs. and up
Defensive Skills					
Catching	X	X	X	X	X
Throwing	X	X	X	X	X
Speed throwing				X	X
Fielding					
Direct ground balls	X	X	X	X	X
Crow hop			X	X	X
Charging ground balls			X	X	X
Forehand/backhand					X
Fly balls: direct			X	X	X
Fly balls: overhead					X
Pitching (non-game situation)	X	X	X		
Pitching (game situation)				X	X
Position Play					
General (play/learn each position equally)	X	X	X		
Specialization				X	X
Base coverage			X	X	X
Back ups			X	X	X
Position responsibilities	X	X	X	X	X
Situations					
General (easiest out)	X	X			
Specific (lead runner, bunt defense, etc.)			X	X	X
Offensive Skills					
Hitting					
T-ball	X	X			
Coaches pitch/machine pitch			X		
Player pitch				X	X
Bunting					
Square around				X	X
Pivot					X
Bunt for a hit					X
Slap hit					X
Baserunning					
Through first	X	X	X	X	X
Extra bases		X	X	X	X
Leading off					
Option 1			X	X	
Option 2					X
Tagging up (fly ball)	X	X	X	X	X
Halfway/tag (base specific)					X
Stealing					X
Sliding					
Bent leg		X	X	X	X
Pop-up					X
Head first					X

FUNDAMENTAL MOTOR SKILL	SUGGESTED EMPHASIS				
	6 yrs.	7-8 yrs.	9-10 yrs.	11-13 yrs.	14 yrs. and up
Offensive Strategy					
Bunt				X	X
Bunt/run				X	X
Bunt for a hit					X
Slap hit					X
Steal					X
Hit and run				X	X
Take					X
Defensive Strategy					
Cutoff					X
Relays				X	X
Rundowns					X
First and third (double steal)					X
Pickoffs					X

Supplement 14-2.

Knowledge Objectives*

LEVEL OF PLAYER APPROXIMATE AGE	SUGGESTED EMPHASIS		
	Elem. School Beginner 6-10 yrs.	Middle School Intermediate 11-13 yrs.	High School Advanced 14 yrs. and up
Rules of the Game			
the playing field	X	X	
the start of play	X		
method of scoring	X		
unlimited substitutions		X	X
pitching	X	X	
baserunning	X	X	X
fair balls/foul balls	X	X	
outs—tag, force.	X	X	
out of play area			X
infield fly			X
Prevention of Injuries			
equipment and apparel	X	X	X
field conditions	X	X	X
structural hazards	X	X	X
environmental hazards.	X	X	X
use of appropriate techniques	X	X	X
contraindicated exercises	X	X	X
overuse injuries	X	X	X
Conditioning			
energy production system			X
muscular system			X
principles of training			X
methods of conditioning			X
warm-up/cool-down procedures.	X	X	X
Nutrition			
proper diet	X	X	X
vitamins and minerals	X	X	X
water intake	X	X	X
ergogenic aids	X	X	X
steroids	X	X	X
meal patterns	X	X	X
weight control	X	X	X
Baseball Terminology	X	X	X

Other Knowledge Objectives

*Note that these knowledge objectives must be taught. It should not be assumed that young athletes will have learned these just by playing baseball.

Fitness Objectives*

	SUGGESTED EMPHASIS		
	Elem. School	Middle School	High School
LEVEL OF PLAYER	Beginner	Intermediate	Advanced
APPROXIMATE AGE	6-10 yrs.	11-13 yrs.	14 yrs. and up

Energy Production

aerobic capacity			X
anaerobic capacity			X
aerobic/anaerobic capacity			X

Muscular Fitness (strength, endurance, and power)

neck			X
shoulder			X
upper arm			X
lower arm			X
wrist			X
abdominal			X
hip/spine			X
low back			X
groin			X
upper leg			X
lower leg			X
ankle			X

Muscular Flexibility

neck			X
shoulder			X
trunk			X
hip			X
ankle			X

Other Fitness Objectives

*Note that progress is made in many of these objectives at the beginning and intermediate levels of play. This development should occur concomitantly through carefully planned practice sessions designed to enhance physical skills. The "Xs" in this chart suggest that coaches should not plan "fitness only" drills for their team until the players have reached approximately 14 years of age and are at the advanced level of play.

Personal and Social Objectives

	SUGGESTED EMPHASIS		
LEVEL OF PLAYER	Elem. School Beginner	Middle School Intermediate	High School Advanced
APPROXIMATE AGE	6-10 yrs.	11-13 yrs.	14 yrs. and up

Personal

best effort	X	X	X
initiative	X	X	X
persistence	X	X	X
responsibility	X	X	X
self-discipline	X	X	X
following directions	X	X	X
listening	X	X	X

Social

respect for authority	X	X	X
leadership	X	X	X
respect for others	X	X	X
fair play	X	X	X
cooperation	X	X	X
appropriate winning behavior	X	X	X
appropriate losing behavior	X	X	X
tact	X	X	X
encouragement of teammates	X	X	X
respect for rules	X	X	X
sport-related etiquette	X	X	X
respect for property	X	X	X

Other Objectives

Supplement 14-5.

SEASON PLAN WORKSHEET					
Coach: _____		Season: _____			

Goal Areas	Objectives	Season Division			
		Pre	Early	Mid	Late
Physical Skills	Catching fundamentals				
	Throwing fundamentals				
	Speed throwing				
	Fielding				
	ground balls/fly balls				
	position techniques				
	Pitching				
	Hitting				
	Bunting				
	Baserunning				
Knowledge	Rules of the game				
	baserunning/scoring				
	tagging up (ground balls/fly balls				
	force outs/tag outs				
	foul ball/out of play ball				
	Strategies				
	offensive				
	defensive				
Fitness	Flexibility				
	leg, hip, shoulder, etc.				
	Strength				
	leg, shoulder, abdominal, arm				
	Cardiovascular: general				
	Speed: sprint work				
Personal/Social	Personal				
	effort				
	listening				
	Social				
	cooperation				
	fair play				
	positive communication				
	(inter-player)				

SEASON PLAN WORKSHEET

Coach: _____   Season: _____

Goal Areas	Objectives	Season Division			
		Pre	Early	Mid	Late

Supplement 14-7.

SEASON PLANNING CALENDAR						
Coach _____ Team _____ Month _____						
S	**M**	**T**	**W**	**T**	**F**	**S**

15
Planning Effective Instruction

Paul Vogel, Ph.D.
Eugene W. Brown, Ph.D.

QUESTIONS TO CONSIDER

- What four steps can coaches use to systematically instruct their players?
- What guidelines for instruction should be applied to ensure effective instruction?
- What are the features of an effective practice plan?
- What are the characteristics of a good drill?

INTRODUCTION

Effective instruction is the foundation of successful coaching. This is particularly true when you are coaching players in the six- to 16-year-old age range. Successful results in competition are directly related to the quality of instruction that players have received during practices. Effective instruction requires:

- clear communication of "what" is to be learned (objectives which represent skills, rules, strategies, and/or personal/social skills)
- continual evaluation of players' performance status on the objectives selected
- use of a systematic method of instruction
- application of guidelines for effective instruction
- evaluation and alteration of instruction in accordance with the degree to which players obtain the desired objectives

CLEARLY COMMUNICATING THE CONTENT TO BE LEARNED

The results (or outcomes) of effective instruction can be grouped into three areas.

1. Physical—individual techniques and conditioning
2. Mental—rules, strategies, positional responsibilities
3. Social—personal and social skills

Clearly stated objectives are a prerequisite to effective instruction.

To provide effective instruction, you must identify the teaching objectives for each of these three areas. Players do not learn skills merely through exposure and practice. Rather, they must have specific feedback revealing what they are doing correctly and, equally as important,

293

what they are doing incorrectly. Specific feedback cannot be communicated to your players unless the skill to be learned and its key elements of performance are clearly specified and understood by the coach. By using the suggestions and procedures outlined in Chapter 14, you can be confident that the objectives you include are appropriate for your players. Application of the steps explained in Chapter 14 also results in a systematic plan (pre-season to late-season) for covering the objectives you select. This type of season plan provides a solid base from which effective instruction can occur.

CONTINUALLY EVALUATING THE PERFORMANCE OF PLAYERS

As a coach, it's important to evaluate your players' ability based on the objectives you have selected. Their current status on these objectives determines the instructional needs of the team. The evaluation should include physical, mental, and social content because deficiencies in any one of these areas may preclude successful participation in the sport. For example, the highly skilled baseball player who lacks motivation may be a liability rather than an asset to the team because of the poor example set for teammates. Also, knowledgeable players who understand the rules and strategies of offense and defense but who lack the skills and fitness to perform as team members must also be evaluated and taught to improve their deficiencies.

To conduct effective practices, continually assess players' needs.

The physical, mental, and attitudinal abilities of players who are new to the program or team are usually unknown. And even when accurate records are available from the previous season, considerable changes normally occur in the abilities of returning players. The result is you know very little about many of your players. Accordingly, you may have to spend more time evaluating players' abilities at the beginning of the season. However, evaluations must also occur, skill by skill, practice by practice, throughout the entire season. As their needs change, so should your instructional emphasis.

Assessment of Physical Needs

Performance Assessment

Assess physical skills by carefully observing your players while they participate in individual and small group drills, scrimmages, and/or games. Descriptions of individual techniques, their key elements, and common errors of performance are found in Section 1. You must have this information to properly evaluate your players.

In addition to knowledge about how individual techniques of baseball are performed, the following visual evaluation guidelines help you make accurate observations and assessments regarding physical performance.

- Select a proper observational distance
- Observe the performance from different angles
- Observe activities in a setting that is not distracting
- Select an observational setting that has a vertical and/or horizontal reference line
- Observe a skilled reference model
- Observe slower moving body parts first
- Observe separate key elements of complicated skills
- Observe the timing of performance components
- Look for unnecessary movements
- Observe the full range of motion

Fitness Assessment

Evaluating the fitness of your players requires two levels of assessment; namely, the aerobic and anaerobic energy systems. Precise physiological abilities are difficult to determine because they often require sophisticated measurement apparatus, take a lot of time, and the results are often confounded by players' skills and experience. Due to these complexities, your assessment of fitness should be at a more practical level. For the most part, you should compare individual players with their teammates on the characteristics of energy and muscular system fitness that are explained in Chapter 22. When skill, size, and maturity levels are judged to be similar between players and one is more (or less) fit than the others on a given attribute, you can assume a differential on that attribute. You can then instruct the underdeveloped player on how to make changes. Similarly, when a player cannot keep up with teammates on a series of drills that require either maximum effort or longer, sustained effort, it is prudent to assume that one or both of the energy systems is inadequately trained.

Assessment of Cognitive Needs

Knowledge of strategy, rules, positional responsibilities, and set plays can be evaluated during drills, scrimmages, and games by noting the response of your players to situations that require a decision prior to action. By clearly communicating what you want the players to know in certain circumstances, and then asking questions and observing how they react, you can learn what they know and what skills and knowledge they can appropriately apply.

Assessment of Personal/Social Needs

An assessment of social needs, though subjective, is not difficult. Informally converse with your players and observe their interactions with other team members during practices, games, and informal gatherings to determine what needs exist. Strengthening the personal/social weaknesses of your players, however, may be more difficult than enhancing their performance of individual physical techniques and their knowledge about the game.

As skilled performance is contingent on learning the key elements of each skill, the modification of a negative or interfering attitude requires you to correctly analyze the underlying problem. Ask yourself, the parents, or the player why the behavior in question is occurring. This may require some probing. Often the problem is not related to baseball. The fact that you care enough about the individual player to invest some time and energy may be all that is needed to reverse or eliminate a negative quality that could become a burden for the individual and the team. Based upon the information obtained, generate a specific strategy for modifying the behavior. The information in Chapters 16 through 20 will help you identify strategies for dealing with important personal/social skills.

Evaluating the status of players in the physical, mental, and attitudinal areas of performance is necessary in order to obtain insight about how to conduct practices that match your players' needs. Whether your players are performing at low, moderate, or high levels, they can all improve with good instruction.

USING A SYSTEMATIC MODEL FOR INSTRUCTION

Although there are many ways to instruct young baseball players, the following approach has proven both easy to use and effective in teaching and/or refining skills.

1. Get the attention of the players by establishing credibility
2. Communicate precisely what needs to be learned
3. Provide for practice and feedback
4. Evaluate results and take appropriate action

Step 1: Establish Credibility

Players must direct their attention to the coach before instruction can occur. To encourage this, arrange the players so that each one can clearly see your actions and hear your instructions. Choose where you stand in relation to the players so that you avoid competing with other distractions. Often it's a good strategy to have the players seated or kneeling on the ground in front of you as you begin.

Immediately establish the precedent that when you speak, important information is being communicated. Point out that the team cannot maximize its practice opportunity when several people are talking at once.

Establish and maintain the precedent that when you speak, important information is being communicated.

As you begin your instruction, establish the need for competence on a particular physical skill or ability by relating it to some phase of successful team and/or individual play. An excellent way to gain your players' attention and motivate them to want to learn individual techniques is to mention how a local, regional, or national level player or team has mastered the skill and has used it to great advantage. The objective of your introductory comments is to establish the idea that mastery of this skill is very important to individual and team play and that the key elements of its execution are achievable.

The next, and perhaps even more important, task is to clearly establish in the minds of the players that they need to improve their abilities on this skill. This can be accomplished with the following steps:

1. Briefly describe the new skill and then let them try it several times in a quick paced drill.
2. Carefully observe their performance and identify their strengths and weaknesses (use the key elements of the skill as a basis for your observations).
3. Call them back together and report your observations.

This approach allows you to point out weaknesses in performance on one or more key elements that are common to many, if not all, of the players. Using this approach enhances your credibility and motivates the players to listen to and follow your instructions. Also, your subsequent teaching can be specifically matched to the needs (weaknesses) you observed. Of course, if in observing you determine that your players have already achieved the desired skill level, then you should shift your focus to another skill. This might mean moving on to the next phase of your practice plan.

Step 2: Communicate Precisely What Needs To Be Learned

When you and your players know their status (strengths and weaknesses of their performance) on a particular skill, you have created an environment for teaching and learning. Because individuals learn most efficiently when they focus on one aspect of a skill at a time, it's important to precisely communicate the one key element you want an individual, pair, group, or team to concentrate on. Demonstrate the key element, and explain it, so that all players know exactly what they're trying to achieve.

Individuals learn most effectively by focusing their practice efforts on one clearly understood element of skilled performance.

When your players are at two or three different levels of ability, you may want to establish two or three instructional groups. This can be accomplished using the following three divisions:

1. Early Learning—focus on learning the key elements of the skill in a controlled situation
2. Intermediate Learning—focus on coordination of all key elements in common situations
3. Later Learning—automatic use of the skill in game-like conditions

Step 3: Provide for Practice and Feedback

Organize your practice time and activities to provide players with:

1. as many repetitions (trials) as possible within the allotted time (minimize standing in lines); and
2. specific, immediate, and positive feedback on what they did correctly and then on what they can do to improve. Follow this instruction with some form of encouragement to continue the learning effort.

Repetitions and feedback are essential to players' achievement and are therefore fundamental to effective coaching. You can expect a direct relationship between the gains in players' performances and the degree to which you find ways to maximize these two dimensions of instruction. John Wooden, UCLA basketball coach of fame, was found to provide over 2,000 acts of teaching during 30 total hours of practice, of which 75 percent pertained directly to skill instruction. This converts to more than one incidence of feedback for every minute of coaching activity!

Repeated trials and specific feedback on what was right, followed by what can be improved and an encouraging "try again," produces results.

Feedback can be dramatically increased by using volunteers and/or the players themselves as instructional aids. When instruction is focused on one key element of performance and the important aspects of performing the skill have been effectively communicated to the players, they are often as good, and sometimes better, at seeing discrepancies in a partner's performance as some adults. Thus, working in pairs or small groups can be very effective in increasing both the number of trials and the amount of feedback that individuals get within a given amount of practice time. Also, by providing feedback, players are improving their mental understanding of how the skill should be performed.

Step 4: Evaluate Results and Take Appropriate Action

Evaluation of players' performances must occur on a continuing basis during practices and games. This is the only valid means to answer the question, "Are the players achieving the skills?" If they are, you have two appropriate actions to take:

1. Enjoy it. You're making an important contribution to your players.
2. Consider how you can be even more efficient. How can you get the same results in less time or how can more be achieved within the same time allotment?

If the players are not achieving the instructional objectives, it's important to ask why. Although it is possible that you have players who are very inept at learning, this is seldom the case. First assume that you are using inappropriate instructional techniques or that you simply did not provide enough instructional time. Go through the instructional factors related to effective planning, motivating, communicating, and discipline in this section, and conditioning in Section 4, to determine which of the guidelines or steps were missed and/or inappropriately implemented. Then alter your subsequent practices accordingly. Steps for how to complete this type of evaluation are described in more detail in Chapter 20. Continuous trial, error, and revisions usually result in improved coaching effectiveness, which then translates into increased achievement by the players. In those instances where you cannot determine what to alter, seek help from a fellow coach whose teams are consistently strong in the physical skills that are causing difficulty for your play-

ers. This is an excellent way to obtain some good ideas for altering your approach.

APPLYING GUIDELINES FOR EFFECTIVE INSTRUCTION

As you provide for practice and feedback to your players (step 3), you may wish to use some of the guidelines for instruction that have been found by recent research to be effective in improving student learning. Nine guidelines for effective instruction are named below and described in more detail in Supplement 15-1.

1. Set realistic expectations
2. Structure instruction
3. Establish an orderly environment
4. Group your players according to ability
5. Maximize on-task time
6. Maximize the success rate
7. Monitor progress
8. Ask questions
9. Promote a sense of control

PLANNING EFFECTIVE PRACTICES

If practices are to be effective, they must be directed at helping players meet the objectives defined in the season plan. Objectives are best achieved by using appropriate instructional methods. Instruction is both formal (planned) and informal (not planned) and can occur during practices, games, and special events. Virtually any time players are in your presence, there is potential for teaching and learning.

All coaches, even those who are highly knowledgeable and experienced, are more effective teachers when they organize and plan their instruction. This does not mean that unplanned instruction should not be used to assist your players in learning more about baseball. In fact, unplanned events that occur often present ideal opportunities to teach important skills. By capitalizing on temporary but intense player interest and motivation, a skilled coach can turn an unplanned event into an excellent learning opportunity. For example, an opponent's offense may prove so effective during a game that your defensive players become highly motivated to learn the tactics necessary to stop such an attack. Often these "teachable moments" are unused by all but the most perceptive coaches.

Features of an Effective Practice

Scheduled practice sessions usually constitute the largest portion of contact between you and your players. Each practice session requires you select both the content of instruction and its method of presentation. To do this effectively and efficiently, each of your practice plans should:

- be based upon previous planning and seasonal organization (see Chapter 14)
- list the objectives that will be the focus of instruction for that practice
- show the amount of time allotted to each objective during the practice
- identify the activities (instructional, drill, or scrimmage) that will be used to teach or practice the objectives
- identify equipment and/or special organizational needs
- apply the guidelines for effective instruction (included in Supplement 15-1)

An effective practice combines the seasonal plan, assessment of your players' abilities, instruction, and an evaluation of practice results. The evaluation portion should be retained even if it means changing future practices to meet the needs of players that may have been unanticipated. The features of an effective practice plan are outlined in Table 15-1. Not all of the features are appropriate for every practice you conduct. There should be a good reason, however, before you decide not to include each feature.

Format and Inclusions in a Practice Plan

Several ingredients that should be included in a practice plan are: the date and/or practice number; the objectives and key points, drills and/or activities; amount of practice time devoted to each objective; equipment needs; and a place for evaluation. The date and/or practice number are helpful to maintain organizational efficiency. The objectives are the reason for conducting the practice and, therefore, must be clearly in mind prior to selecting the activities, drills, games, or scrimmage situations you believe will develop player competence. The key points of each objective you desire to have your players achieve must be clearly in mind. It also

Table 15-1. Features of an effective practice.

Features	Coaching Activity
Practice overview	Inform the team about the contents and objectives of the practices (e.g. important new skills, positional play, new drills) to motivate and mentally prepare them for the upcoming activity.
Warm-up	Physically prepare the team for each practice by having them engage in light to moderate aerobic activity sufficient to produce slight sweating. Follow this by specific stretching activities.
Individual skills and drills	Review and practice objectives previously covered.
Small group skills and drills	Introduce and teach new objectives.
Team skills and drills	Incorporate the individual and small group drills into drills involving the entire team.
Cool-down	At the end of each practice, use activities of moderate to light intensity followed by stretching to reduce potential soreness and maintain flexibility.
Team talk	Review key points of the practice, listen to player communications, make announcements, and distribute handouts.

helps to have the key points written prominently on your plan or notes. Supplement 15-2 provides an example plan written to cover the objectives of Practice 5 listed on the season calendar in Chapter 14. In order to communicate the essential features of a practice plan to many readers, this example contains far more narrative than is necessary for most coaches. You need to record only information that will be needed at some later date. Accordingly, phrases, symbols, key words, and other personalized communications will substitute for the more extensive narrative included in the example. A full-sized copy of the practice plan form that you may reproduce is included in Supplement 15-3.

Practice Time

Allotting time for each objective during practices is a difficult but important task for the coach. Sufficient practice time results in the majority of your players making significant improvement on each objective. Although these changes may not be noticeable in a single session, they must occur over the season. Assigning too little time may result in players' exposure to individual techniques but often in little change in performance. Keep in mind, however, that practice time must be distributed across several objectives (and/or drills or activities within the practice of a single objective) to keep players' interests high. This is particularly true for younger players who tend to have short attention spans and thus need frequent changes in drills or activities.

Instructional Activities

The selection and implementation of instructional activities, drills, or games should constitute most of each practice session. Players' achievements are directly related to your choices and actions in these important areas. Instructional activities should be conducted in accordance with the guidelines presented in Supplement 15-1. Because most practices are composed largely of drills you should follow the same guidelines in Supplement 15-1, and develop your drills to include these important features:

- have a meaningful name
- require a relatively short explanation
- provide an excellent context for mastering an objective
- match skill, knowledge, or fitness requirements of baseball
- keep the players' "on-task time" high
- are easily modified to accommodate skilled and unskilled players
- provide opportunity for skill analysis and feedback to players

Drills should be written on file cards or paper. It's also helpful to organize drills according to objective, group size (individual, small group, team), inning (offensive and defensive), and position (shortstop, catcher, right field). When you find a good drill, classify it and add it to your collection. A format for collecting drill information is provided in reproducible form in Supplement 15-4.

Equipment Needs

The equipment needed to conduct a drill or activity should be recorded on the practice plan. It's frustrating and ineffective to discover after you've explained and set up an activity or drill that the necessary equipment is missing. Therefore, after you've planned all the activities for your practice, review them and list the essential equipment needed.

Evaluation

The evaluation/comment portion of the practice plan can be used to highlight ways to alter the practice to accommodate players at unexpected skill levels, or to note changes to be made to improve the plan. It also provides a place for announcements or other information that needs to be communicated to your players.

SUMMARY

Effective instruction is the foundation of successful coaching. It requires practices that include clear communication of what is to be learned, a continuous evaluation of players' performance on the objectives of the practices, a systematic method of instruction, and the use of guidelines for instruction that have been associated with player achievement.

Systematic instruction includes: (a) establishing credibility; (b) providing precise communication of what needs to be learned; (c) providing many practice trials and specific, immediate, and positive feedback; and (d) evaluating the achievement of your players. Use of the guidelines for effective instruction (realistic expectations, structured instruction, order, grouping, maximizing time, success, monitoring, and providing a sense of control) in combination with systematic instruction maximizes the results of your coaching effort.

Guidelines for Effective Instruction

QUESTIONS TO CONSIDER

- What are the nine guidelines for effective instruction?
- How can setting realistic expectations for your players influence their achievement?
- How can you coach players of different ability levels on the same team?
- When players are attempting to learn new things, what success rate motivates them to want to continue to achieve?

Introduction

This supplement provides an overview of nine guidelines for effective instruction. As you plan your practices, this list should be reviewed to help maximize your coaching effectiveness. The nine guidelines are:

1. Set realistic expectations
2. Structure instruction
3. Establish an orderly environment
4. Group your players according to ability
5. Maximize on-task time
6. Maximize the success rate
7. Monitor progress
8. Ask questions
9. Promote a sense of self-control

1. *Set Realistic Expectations*

The expectations coaches communicate to their players can create a climate for learning that will positively influence player achievement (Rutter et al. 1979). Clear, but attainable, objectives for performance and expenditure of effort for all players on your team will facilitate achievement. As stated in a recent review (Fisher et al. 1980), the reasons associated with this occurrence may be related to the following ideas.

In comparison to athletes for whom coaches hold high expectations for performance, the athletes perceived to be low performers are:

- more often positioned farther away from the coach
- treated as groups, not individuals
- smiled at less
- receive less eye contact from the coach
- called on less to answer questions

- have their answers responded to less frequently
- praised more often for marginal and inadequate responses
- praised less frequently for successful responses
- interrupted more often

Players tend to achieve in accordance with the coaches' expectations.

Coaches and former athletes will be able to understand how even a few of the above responses could reduce motivation and achievement. It is saddening that many capable children are inappropriately labeled as non-achievers on the basis of delayed maturity, poor prior experience, inadequate body size, body composition, and/or many other factors which mask their true ability. Yet, if expectations are low, achievement is likely to be low.

There are at least two important messages in this guideline:

- Expect that, as the coach, you're going to significantly improve the skills, fitness, knowledge of rules and strategies, and attitude of every one of your players during the course of the season.
- Set realistic goals for your players. Make a commitment to help each player achieve those individual goals, and expect improvement.

2. *Structure Instruction*

Your players' achievement is strongly linked to clear communication of the intended outcomes of instruction (objectives), why the goals and objectives are important (essential or prerequisite skills), and what to do to achieve outcomes (instructional directions) (Bruner 1981 and Fisher et al. 1980). Effective instruction is based upon the systematic organization of the content to be taught. The critical steps to take are as follows:

- Select the essential skills, fitness capacities, knowledge of rules and strategies, and personal/social skills from the many options available
- Clearly identify the elements of acceptable performance for each objective that you include in your plans
- Organize and conduct your practices to maximize the opportunity your players have to acquire the objectives by using the effective teaching practices contained in this chapter

3. *Establish an Orderly Environment*

High achievement is related to the following elements (Fisher 1978):

- an orderly, safe, business-like environment with clear expectations
- player accountability for effort and achievement
- rewards for achievement of expectations

Where such conditions are missing, achievement is low.

The following coaching actions will lessen behavioral problems that interfere with learning and, at the same time, promote pride and responsibility in team membership.

- Maintain orderly and disciplined practices
- Maintain clear and reasonable rules that are fairly and consistently enforced

Caution: strong, over-controlling actions can backfire. Over-control causes frustration and anxiety while under-control leads to lack of achievement. The best of circumstances is a relaxed, enjoyable but business-like environment. The ability to balance these two opposing forces to maximize achievement and enjoyment by keeping both in perspective may be one of your most difficult tasks.

4. *Group Your Players*

Decisions about the size and composition of groups for various learning tasks are complex, but nonetheless related to achievement (Webb 1980). Typically, in groups of mixed ability, the player with average ability suffers a loss in achievement, while the player with low ability does slightly better. The critical condition for grouping to be effective is to have players practicing at the skill levels needed to advance their playing ability. Typically, this involves groups of similar ability being appropriately challenged. Although this can be difficult to achieve, most effective coaches design practices that maximize a type of individualized instruction.

Your team will have individuals at many levels of ability. While this situation presents a seemingly impossible grouping task, there are some good solutions to this problem:

- When a skill, rule, or strategy is being taught that all your athletes need to know, use a single group for instruction
- As you identify differences in your players' abilities, divide the team and place players of similar ability in small groups when working on these tasks
- When a skill, rule, or strategy is being practiced where individual athletes are at several levels of ability (initial, intermediate, or later learning levels), establish learning stations that focus on specific outcomes to meet each groups' needs.

The placement of players into smaller groups for learning the various physical skills, rules, and strategies must be independently decided for each skill, rule, or strategy. A player who is placed at a high level group for practicing individual techniques for batting and baserunning should not necessarily be placed in a high level group for fielding ground balls or fly balls. It is important that the following conditions be established at each learning station:

- order is established and maintained (an assistant may be necessary)
- tasks that are to be mastered at each station must be clearly understood
- many opportunities must be provided at each station
- a means for giving immediate, specific, and positive feedback must be established.

5. *Maximize On-Task Time*

Reports of research that document the amount of time that athletes are active in the learning process, rather than standing in lines or watching others perform, reveal that actual "engaged" learning time during practices is regularly less than 50 percent of the total practice time, and often falls to five or 10 percent for individual athletes. Such procedures waste much of a limited amount of practice time. There are several actions you can take as a coach to maximize the use of available time.

- Reduce the number of athletes who are waiting in line by using more subgroups in your drills.
- Secure sufficient supplies and equipment so that players do not have to wait for a turn when these supplies and equipment are essential to practice activities.
- Reduce the transition time between drills by preplanning practices to minimize reformulation of groups and equipment set-up time.
- Use instructional grouping practices that have players practicing skills at their appropriate performance level.
- Clearly outline and/or diagram each portion of practice and communicate as much of that information as possible before going on the field.
- Complete as many pre and post warm-up/cool down activities outside of the time scheduled on the field.
- Recruit assistants (parents or older players) to help you with instructional stations under your supervision.

Remember: saving ten minutes a day across 14 weeks of two practices per week equals 280 minutes of instructional time for each player. Time gained by effective organization is available for practicing other portions of the game.

6. *Maximize the Success Rate*

The relationship among successful experiences, achievement, and motivation to learn is very strong (Fisher 1978 and Rosenshine 1983.) The basic message in this research is to ask players to attempt new learning that yields 70% to 90% successful experiences. This level of success motivates them to want to continue to achieve. There are two major implications of the finding:

- Reduce each technique, rule, or strategy into

achievable sub-skills and focus instruction on those sub-skills
- Provide feedback to the players such that, on most occasions, something that they did is rewarded, followed by specific instructions about what needs more work, and ending with an encouraging "Try again!"

7. *Monitor Progress*

If you organize your practice to allow athletes to work at several stations in accordance with their current abilities and needs, it follows that players often will work independently or in small groups. When players are left to work on their own, they typically spend less time engaged in the activities for which they are responsible. When coaches are actively moving about, monitoring progress, and providing individual and small group instructional feedback, players make greater gains (Fisher 1978). Within this context, you can provide much corrective feedback, contingent praise, and emotionally neutral criticism (not personal attacks or sarcasm) for inappropriate behavior. These actions have a positive influence on both achievement and attitude.

8. *Ask Questions*

Asking questions also relates to player achievement (Brophy 1976). Questions must, however, promote participation or establish, reinforce, and reveal factual data associated with physical skills, rules, or strategies. Use of this teaching technique seems to work best when there is a pause of three or more seconds before you ask for a response, at which time the players are cued to think about the answer (Rowe 1974).

9. *Promote a Sense of Control*

Your players should feel that they have some control over their own destiny if they are to reach their potential as baseball players. This sense of control can be developed by:

- organizing your instruction to result in many successful experiences (i.e., opportunities to provide positive feedback)
- teaching your players that everyone learns at different rates and to use effort and their

own continuous progress as their primary guides (avoid comparing their skill levels with those of other players)

- encouraging individual players to put forth their best effort (reward best efforts with positive comments, pats on the back, thumbs up signs, or encouraging signals)

In these ways, players quickly learn that the harder they work and the more they try, the more skillful they will become. At the same time, you'll be eliminating the natural feeling of inferiority or inability that grows in the presence of feedback which is limited to pointing out errors. Although some players develop in almost any practice situation, many potentially excellent players will not continue in an environment where they feel there is no possibility of gaining the coach's approval.

Summary

The information in this supplement provides a base from which effective practices can be developed and implemented. Not all coaches can claim that they use all of these guidelines throughout all of their practice sessions. All coaches should, however, seek to use more of these techniques more frequently as they plan and implement their practices.

REFERENCES

Brophy, J.E., & Evertson, C. (1976). *Learning from teaching: A developmental perspective.* Boston, MA: Allyn and Bacon.

Bruner, J. (1981, August). On instructability. Paper presented at the meeting of the American Psychological Association, Los Angeles, CA.

Fisher, C.W. et al. (1978). Teaching behaviors, academic learning time and student achievement. Final report of Phase III-B, Beginning teacher evaluation study, technical report. San Francisco, CA: Far West Laboratory for Educational Research and Development.

Fisher, C.W. et al. (1980). Teaching behaviors, academic learning time and student achievement: An overview. In C. Denham and A. Lieberman (Eds.), *Time to learn.* Washington, D.C.: U.S. Department of Education, National Institute of Education.

Rosenshine, B.V. (1983). Teaching functions in instructional programs. *The Elementary School Journal, 83,* 335-352.

Rowe, M.B. (1974). Wait time and rewards as instructional variables: Their influence on language, logic, and fate control. Part one, Wait time. *Journal of Research in Science Teaching, 11,* 81-94.

Rutter, M. et al. (1979). *Fifteen thousand hours.* Cambridge, MA: Harvard University Press.

Webb, N.M. (1980). A process-outcome analysis of learning in group and individual settings. *Educational Psychologist, 15,* 69-83.

Supplement 15-2.

Sample Practice Plan

Eugene W. Brown, Ph.D.

QUESTIONS TO CONSIDER

- How should coaches determine the amount of detail to be included in their practice plans?
- How is a practice plan related to a season planning calendar?
- What are the features of an effective practice?
- How can practice plans help a coach to achieve objectives previously listed for the team?

Introduction

This supplement contains a sample practice plan for baseball. It is presented as an example of what might be included in a well-organized practice of intermediate level youth players (10 to 13 years of age) conducted by a highly organized coach. This practice plan represents the fifth of eight practices before the first game. Its outline is derived from the procedures outlined in the season planning calendar presented in Chapter 15, Planning for the Season.

Organization and Content of the Sample Practice Plan

Note that a considerable amount of detail is included in the sample plan. This is provided to make it easier to understand the nature of the activities included in the practice. When you prepare a plan for your own use, the level of detail can be substantially reduced. If you're a seasoned coach, you may only need the names of the drills, key coaching points, and a few diagrams. However, most inexperienced coaches will need more detail.

Note that this sample practice plan contains all of the features of an effective practice that are presented in Table 15-1 of this chapter. These features have also been checked at the bottom of the first page of the sample practice plan.

Objectives

The objectives of the sample practice plan should be taken directly from the objectives previously listed by the coach in a season planning calendar in Chapter 15. These objectives may need to be modified slightly because of what the coach was able to cover in previous practices and what the coach has learned from assessing the abilities of the players in previous practices.

Overview of Practice Activities

The overview of practice activities should last only a minute or less. The coach only needs to simply state what is planned for the practice. This helps to mentally prepare and organize the players for the practice. The overview gets the players to "think baseball" again. Therefore, a good time to respond to players' questions is immediately after the overview.

Warm-up & Stretching

The baseball-specific warm-ups included in this sample practice plan consist of two light aerobic activities. These activities are used to increase the breathing rate, heart rate, and muscle temperature to exercise levels. They also help to reacquaint the athletes to their practice environments and prepare the muscles and joints for stretching activities which follow.

The six stretching activities were selected to maintain flexibility in several muscle groups and joints of the body. On average, approximately 45 seconds can be spent on each of the eight activities included in this phase of the practice. Thus, it is assumed that the players are familiar with each of the eight activities and can quickly change from one to the next. If any of these stretches needs to be taught to the players, more time will be needed for the warm-up session or some activities will need to be excluded.

Review & Practice Set Plays

The coach must be ambitious and highly organized in order to coordinate six activities in the one hour and thirty minutes that are allotted for the practice. The only way this could be achieved is for the players to have received handouts on these set plays at a previous practice and to have been encouraged to read and study these set plays before the current practice. Key points of the practice should be briefly reviewed on a portable chalkboard before having the players begin the practice.

Note that practice for the hitting drill and the infield/outfield ground balls drill are grouped together at the end of this phase of the sample practice plan. These are organized in this manner because both of them require players to use all of the practice area.

Individual Skill Techniques

The drills selected and the manner in which they are conducted should challenge the players to achieve higher levels of performance of individual skills. Selection and conduct should be based upon what the coach has learned from observing the players in previous practices and an understanding of the direction players must proceed to achieve future goals.

While the players are engaged in the practice of individual techniques, the coach should be active in observing performances, providing individual and immediate feedback to the players, and developing ideas about what to include in future practices to improve their level of performance.

Note that in addition to sliding, bunting, and hitting, players should be alerted to other aspects of play that are integral parts of these drills. These aspects include use of these skills in various offensive and defensive situations and communicating. Also, if the drills run at a brisk pace, the players may concomitantly enhance their fitness level. The potential for simultaneous enhancement of individual techniques, tactical knowledge, and fitness of players within the same practice activities is an example of economical training.

Hitting Stations

Twenty minutes has been allotted for a variety of hitting experiences in this practice plan. From the players' perspectives, hitting is often the highlight of the practice. Alerting your players at the beginning of the practice (Overview of Practice Activities) that you have scheduled hitting near the end of practice encourages them to participate in other phases of the practice in an efficient manner. It should be noted, however, that hitting drills are not just a reward for a team that pays attention during the practice. Building competition and dynamic activities into hitting drills is an excellent lead-up to full-scale competition. A knowledgeable coach can use small group drills and controlled scrimmages to teach players offensive and defensive tactics, as well as the transition of individual techniques into the skills of play.

Cool Down

In this sample practice plan the same activities are used in the cool down as were planned for the warm-up and stretching for the beginning of the practice. The cool down activities could differ from the warm-up activities. The important aspect of the cool down activities, however, is that they involve the body parts exercised during the practice. This helps clear out waste products built up in the muscle, reduce the pooling of blood in the extremities, reduce the potential for soreness in the muscles, and prevent the loss of flexibility that may accompany intense muscular exercise.

Note that, in an attempt to save time, simple information can be given to the players while they're engaged in their cool-down activities.

Equipment

After coaches plan their practice, they should review each activity to determine what equipment will be needed to carry out the practice. A written list, included on the practice plan, is helpful when coaches are in a hurry to get to practice on time.

Evaluation

The evaluation of the practice should be completed after the practice and before planning the next practice. This evaluation should address (a) the appropriateness of the organization and content of the practice, (b) the success of the coaching methods used, and (c) the degree to which planned objectives (physical skills, tactics, personal/social skills, and fitness) were achieved. This type of evaluation is helpful in improving your coaching methods and in directing future practices to meet the needs of your players.

Summary

The sample practice plan and overview of its organization and content are presented in this supplement to provide guidance and insight to coaches for planning their own practice plans. It is not presented to be directly used by coaches because each team is unique in its needs at any point in time during the season. Therefore, coaches should plan each practice session to meet the specific needs of their players.

PRACTICE PLAN

OBJECTIVES: *Review & practice sliding and bunting; practice hitting, fielding ground balls by infielders and outfielders; discuss offensive strategy*

DATE: *June 18*

#: 5

TIME	COACHING ACTIVITIES (name, description, diagram, key points)
5 min.	*Overview of Practice Activities:* (1) *teach sliding and bunting techniques* (2) *individual hitting and fielding ground balls* (3) *offensive strategy*
10 min.	*Warm-up:* (1) *Jog 2 times around the bases* (2) *Throwing and catching: including pitching* *Stretching:* (1) *calf-stretch* (2) *seated straddle* (3) *kneeling quad stretch* (4) *trunk and hip stretch* (5) *arm circles* (6) *shoulder stretch*

EQUIPMENT: *One baseball per 2 players, bats, bases, portable chalkboard, chalk, eraser, whistle, clipboard, and batting helmets.*

NOTE: Features of an effective practice include: √ practice overview; √ warm-up; √ individual skills and drills; √ small group skills and drills; √ team skills and drills; √ cool-down; √ team talk. (Check the features included in this practice plan.)

EVALUATION: _____

PRACTICE PLAN CONTINUED

TIME	COACHING ACTIVITIES (name, description, diagram, key points)
15 min.	**Teach Sliding** (Key points: bent left leg; hands in air; chin on chest; shoulders parallel to ground) **Finding Your Sliding Leg Drill** (a) Move to grassy area (b) "Inverted" crab position **Sliding Progression Drill** (a) Learn "Figure 4" straight-in slide (b) Wet grass -- start with 3 steps and slide (c) Add more steps prior to take-off
15 min.	**Teach Bunting** (Key points: Square around; grip; catch ball on bat) **Practice Bunting Position** (a) Correct position -- square around bunt (b) Bat height (c) Bend knees for pitches of various heights (d) Bat movement

PRACTICE PLAN CONTINUED

TIME	COACHING ACTIVITIES (name, description, diagram, key points)
	Soft Toss Bunting Drill
	(a) Feeder tosses ball to bunters
	(b) Bunter focuses on giving with the pitch with both arms
20 min.	*Hitting Stations*
	(a) Practice hitting off tee into backstop (tennis balls) from behind backstop
	(b) Shadow swings (on-deck circle)
	(c) Pitching machine (live balls) or coach pitching
	(d) Hip Rotation Drill
	(Key points: Weight transfer -- hit against front foot; eyes on ball; arm and wrist action (bent to straight))
10 min.	*Infield/Outfield Ground Ball Drills*
	(a) Diamond Drill (straight to fielder)
	(b) Glove side; throwing side (3rd and 4th lines)
	(Key points: correct technique; ball hit / rolled to specific location)

PRACTICE PLAN CONTINUED

TIME	COACHING ACTIVITIES (name, description, diagram, key points)

5 min.	*Cool-down*
	
	 (a) Slow jog around bases
	
	 (b) Stretching
	     (1) Shoulder stretch
	     (2) Calf stretch
	     (3) Trunk and hip stretch

10 min.	*Chalk Talk: Offensive Strategy* (Have players put on warm-up jacket or sweatshirt) (a) Sacrifice bunt (b) Characteristics of Number One hitter (c) Hitting in relation to the count

Supplement 15-3.

	PRACTICE PLAN	

OBJECTIVES: _____ DATE: _____
_____ #: _____
_____
_____
_____

TIME	COACHING ACTIVITIES (name, description, diagram, key points)

EQUIPMENT: _____
_____

NOTE: Features of an effective practice include: ___ practice overview; ___ warm-up; ___ individual skills and drills; ___ small group skills and drills; ___ team skills and drills; ___ cool down; ___ team talk. (Check the features included in this practice plan.)

EVALUATION: _____
_____

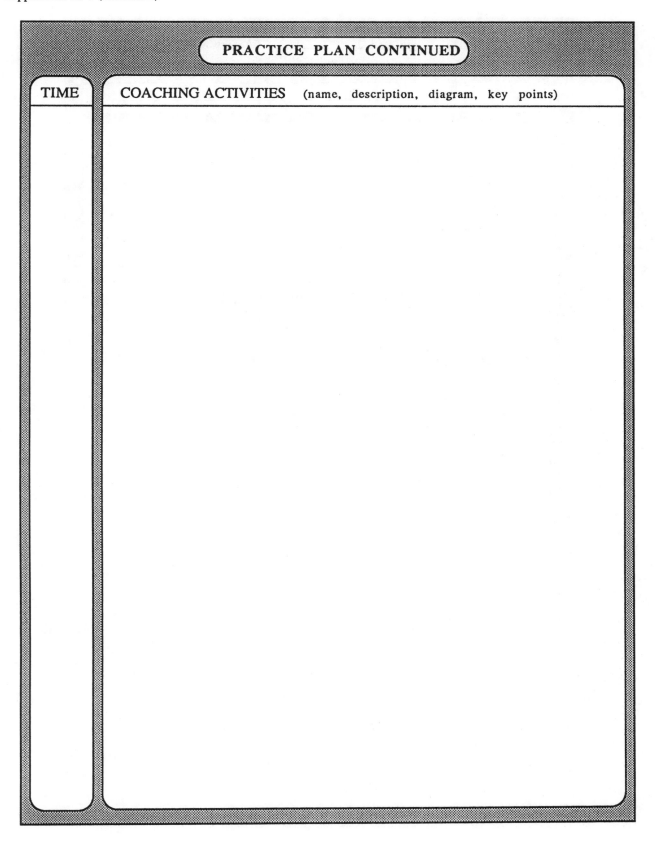

PRACTICE PLAN CONTINUED

TIME	COACHING ACTIVITIES (name, description, diagram, key points)

Supplement 15-4.

DRILL NAME: _____ CLASSIFICATION(S): _____

SOURCE: _____ _____

OBJECTIVES: _____

FACILITIES AND EQUIPMENT: _____ _____

DIAGRAM: DIRECTIONS:

COMMENTS: _____
_____
_____

16
Motivating Your Players

Martha Ewing, Ph.D.
Deborah Feltz, Ph.D.

QUESTIONS TO CONSIDER

- Why do children play baseball?
- What techniques can you use to minimize the number of "dropouts" from your team?
- What are the four elements of "positive" coaching?
- What can you do to help your players set realistic goals for themselves?

INTRODUCTION

The key to understanding your athletes' motivation is to understand each of their needs. As a coach, you play an important role in determining whether an athlete's needs are fulfilled. Previous research indicates that motivation will be high and young athletes will persist in a sport if their needs are met by that sport. But what are those needs and why do children desire to participate in sports?

WHY YOUNG ATHLETES PARTICIPATE IN BASEBALL

In order to help your players maintain or improve their motivation in baseball, you must understand why they participate and why some of them stop participating. Based on interviews with young athletes who participated in a variety of sports, the following reasons for playing were identified and are listed in the order of their importance.

1. To have fun
2. To improve skills and learn new ones
3. For thrills and excitement
4. To be with friends or make new friends
5. To succeed or win

While these research findings provide some insight as to why most children play baseball, they are only general guidelines. The best information available to you is to learn from the athletes on your team why they are participating in the baseball program.

To improve your players' motivation, you must know why they participate in baseball.

WHY YOUNG ATHLETES DROP OUT OF BASEBALL

Knowing why some youngsters stop playing baseball can help you find ways to encourage them to continue playing. From a survey of 1,773 young athletes (Youth Sports Institute

1977) who dropped out of baseball and other sports, we learned that the reason for dropping out was that they did not achieve the goals they set when they initially enrolled to play.

This is not surprising if you consider that their reasons for getting involved in sports represent goals that can only be achieved through participation. When these goals are not being met, withdrawal occurs. Some of the reasons most often cited for dropping out of sports are discussed in the following paragraphs.

Other Interests

Children are often very good at assessing their relative ability in various activities. They may "shop around" and participate in several sports and other activities before deciding which ones provide them the greatest chance of being successful.

Dropping baseball to achieve in other activities such as music, soccer, swimming, dance, and scouting is acceptable. When children tell you or their parents that they want to pursue other activities, they should be encouraged to do so but welcomed to return to baseball later if they desire.

Work

Many children who would like to participate in baseball discontinue because their help is needed at home or they desire to obtain a job. If it is possible, practices and games should be arranged at times that allow all individuals to stay involved. Attempt to find a creative alternative so that having a job does not preclude participation in baseball. Although much can be learned from work, the lessons that can be learned in sport are also valuable.

Another compelling reason for sports participation during childhood is that this experience may be a prerequisite for successful performance in later years. However, children who find that they must discontinue their participation should be assured that they may return to baseball at a later time.

No Longer Interested

For many children, playing baseball is a prestigious achievement. However, once they get involved, some may determine that baseball is not as glamorous as it first appeared. Although these children may have enjoyed their sport experience, they may decide that other interests are more important and/or enjoyable.

Children with interests in other activities should not be forced by parents or pressured by coaches and peers to continue participation in a baseball program. Doing so often transforms a normally well-behaved child into one who becomes a discipline problem. Parents and coaches should give children a chance to explore other activities and return to baseball if they so decide.

Not Enough Playing Time

Children sign up for baseball because they anticipate the enjoyment and skill development that will result from their involvement. Many young athletes who cited "not playing enough" as a reason for dropping out were telling coaches that they needed more playing time to achieve their goal. These children are not usually asking to be starters or even to play the majority of the time. However, to be told indirectly that they aren't good enough to play during a game can be devastating to a child's feelings of self-worth. Coaches of young athletes need to ensure that a fair and equitable pattern of play occurs both during practices and games.

Skills Were Not Improving

Young athletes want to learn skills and see themselves improving in those skills. Coaches need to recognize that each athlete is different in his/her skill level. Instruction should be designed to help each athlete on the team improve in performance abilities.

It is important to show athletes how they have improved. Too often, young athletes compare their skills to the skills of other athletes rather than their own past performances. This type of comparison is destructive to the self-esteem of unskilled players. Players of all ability levels should be taught to evaluate their performance based on the progress they are making.

Young athletes expect to see improvement in their skills if they are to remain in baseball.

Did Not Like the Coach

This reason for dropping out may be another way for athletes to tell coaches that they were not playing enough and their skills were not improving. In a study of youth sport participants, the athletes who did not like the coach said they did not like being yelled at, thought the coaches played only their favorite players, and did not think the coaches were fair.

To be effective, coaches must treat young athletes with the same respect that coaches expect from the athletes. It is not necessary or effective to yell at athletes to communicate with them. Avoid all sarcastic and degrading comments. Use a positive approach to create an enjoyable and motivating environment for players to learn and have fun playing the game.

HOW TO HELP MOTIVATE YOUR PLAYERS

Athletes are most highly motivated when they obtain what they seek from their participation in sport. Therefore, motivational techniques that you select should be based on the reasons athletes have for joining the team. The following strategies may help you improve your players' motivation.

Know Why Your Athletes Are Participating

Young athletes differ in their personalities, needs, interests, and objectives for playing baseball. You must, therefore, get to know your athletes as individuals to determine why they participate. One way to accomplish this is through a team meeting at the start of the season.

Ask your players why they are participating and what their personal objectives are for the season. They may be asked this question before, during, and after practices and special events or whenever you have a chance to talk one-on-one with your players.

Help Your Athletes Improve Skills and Learn New Skills

Skill improvement is a very important reason for joining a baseball team. Therefore, practice sessions should focus on skill development, with regular opportunities for players to mea-

sure their progress. In addition, you can help athletes set performance goals that are appropriate for them. For example, as young players first learn to field the ball, they should practice fielding a thrown ball with a slower pace at first. More advanced players should be encouraged to practice fielding batted balls that travel at a greater speed, and involve moving laterally and charging the ball. As players improve, they can understand and measure their progress both in practice and in game situations.

Make Practices and Games Enjoyable

As indicated by various studies, young athletes want to have fun. This means they want to play; they do not want to sit on the bench or stand in long lines waiting their turn at a drill. One of the best ways to ensure that practices are enjoyable is to use short, snappy drills that result in all players being involved most of the time. You can also keep your players' interest by incorporating new and challenging drills. Your players may even be able to invent useful drills of their own.

Having a chance to display their skills during a game is an excellent motivator of young athletes.

In games, too, all players can be involved, even if they are sitting on the bench. Team members can be watching the individuals who are playing similar positions to learn from their good techniques or their mistakes. They can also watch for strategies used by the other team. Most importantly, however, they should all have a chance to play in every game. The knowledge that they will have a chance to display their skills during the course of the contest is a primary source of motivation before and after the experience. Players who sit on the bench, unable to test their skills in a game, are not likely to have fun.

Allow Players to be with Their Friends and Make New Friends

Many athletes view their baseball participation as a chance to be with their friends while doing something they enjoy. Allowing your players to have fun with their friends does not mean your practices have to be disruptive. You can encourage an esprit de corps within the team. Social activities, such as a midseason pizza party, require more time on your part but may foster rewarding friendships among players and coaches.

Remember, many of your players' friends may be on opposing teams. Encourage athletes to continue their friendships with players on opposing teams and even develop new friendships with opponents.

Help Players Understand the Meaning of Success

Children learn at an early age to equate winning with success and losing with failure. If athletes win a game, they feel good or worthy. If they lose, they feel incompetent or unworthy. This attitude toward winning can be discouraging to players, unless they are always winning. One of your most important roles, therefore, is to help your players keep winning in perspective. One way to accomplish this is to help your players understand that winning a game is not always under their control. For example, after losing a game, you may explain the loss to your team: "We hit the ball well today, but their team played very good defense, so we didn't get as many runs as we expected."

Your players also need to know that, although striving to win is an important objective in baseball, being successful in baseball also means making personal improvements and striving to do one's best. This attitude can be developed by:

- encouraging maximum effort during practices and games
- rewarding effort
- helping players set important but realistic goals that they can attain and thus feel successful when they are achieved

In helping your players understand the meaning of success, it is also important not to punish them when they fail, particularly if they gave a maximum effort.

Your coaching approach is the factor with the greatest influence on player motivation.

Use the Positive Approach to Coaching

Probably the most important factor that influences your players' motivation is the approach you take in coaching. There are many different styles or approaches used by coaches, but most fall into either of two categories: the negative approach and the positive approach.

• Negative Approach

The negative approach is the most visible model of coaching. The negative approach, demonstrated by some professional, college, and even high school coaches, is often highlighted in the media. This approach is one in which the coach focuses on performance errors and uses fear, hate, and/or anger to motivate players.

The negative approach doesn't work very well with young athletes. Constant criticism, sarcasm, and yelling often frustrate young athletes, deteriorate their self-confidence, and decrease their motivation. Remember that young athletes are just beginning to develop their skills, and they have fragile self-concepts.

Focus on correct aspects of performance and use liberal amounts of praise and encouragement.

• Positive Approach

The positive approach, in contrast, is one where the coach focuses on the correct aspects of performance and uses plenty of encouragement and praise for the tasks that players perform correctly. When errors occur, a coach who uses the positive approach corrects mistakes with constructive criticism.

A positive, supportive approach is essential when coaching young athletes if high levels of motivation are to be maintained. Key principles for implementing a positive approach to coaching are listed and explained in the following paragraphs.

Key Principles for Implementing a Positive Approach to Coaching (Smoll & Smith 1979)

• Be liberal with rewards and encouragement.

The most effective way to influence positive behavior and increase motivation is through the frequent use of encouraging statements and rewards. The single most important difference between coaches whom young athletes respect most and those they respect least is the frequency with which coaches reward them for desirable behaviors.

The most important rewards you can give are free. They include a pat on the back, a smile, applause, verbal praise, or a friendly nod. The greater your use of encouraging statements and rewards, the more your players will be motivated.

- **Give rewards and encouragement sincerely.**

For rewards to be beneficial, they must be given sincerely. It will mean little to your players to tell them they played well if, in fact, they played poorly. This does not mean that you should not give them positive feedback about their performance when they make mistakes. You can point out their errors and at the same time praise them for the plays they performed well. It is important to be positive but also honest.

- **Reward effort and correct technique, not just results.**

It is easy to praise a player who just got a hit, but it is less natural to praise a player who tried hard but struck out. Sometimes, too, we forget to reward correct technique when it does not result in scoring runs. It is important, however, to reward players' efforts and the use of correct technique if you want this behavior to continue. A hit to the outfield that is caught by a defensive player who makes a spectacular catch should be recognized as if it was a hit. Occasionally, spend a few extra minutes with the lesser skilled players, before or after practice, to help them learn the correct techniques. This extra attention and caring will greatly increase their motivation to keep trying.

- **Have realistic expectations.**

Base your rewards and encouragement on realistic expectations. Encouraging your baseball players to strive for major league standards, without the feelings of success associated with achieving the many levels of performance leading to such standards, will probably make them feel as though they have failed. It is much easier for you to give honest rewards when you have realistic expectations about your players' abilities.

Help Players Set Goals

Young athletes learn from parents and coaches that success is equated with winning and failure is equated with losing. Adopting this view of success and failure confuses the players. Let's take, for example, the play of Tim and Rick, members of the winning and losing teams, respectively.

Both boys played about half of the game. Tim's unsporting conduct was noticed quickly by the umpire. After the third inning, the umpire cautioned him about his unnecessary rough play. Earlier in that inning, he pushed an opponent who was attempting to round second base. Rick on the other hand, masterfully used his practiced skills to assist his teammates in scoring and scored his first run of the season. However, since Tim was a member of the winning team, he was able to "laugh-off" his behavior and revel in the success of his team. On the other hand, Rick felt that his efforts were insignificant and worthless and joined his teammates in the disappointment of a 7-3 loss.

As adults, we recognize the inaccuracy of these perceptions. But, our actions at the end of a contest may tell our players that a winning score is what really matters.

Equating success with winning and failure with losing results in mixed messages to the athlete.

Athletes need a way to compare their current performances with their past performances to determine whether they are successful. This can be accomplished through goal setting. You as a coach can help each of your athletes establish individual goals. By doing this, each athlete can regain control over personal success or failure. In addition to removing the mixed messages, remind your players that there are some factors that are out of their control that may determine the outcome of a game. For example, the person your athlete is batting against may be pitching the best game of his/her career. Although your athlete is playing very well, there is just no hitting the opposing player. Or, due to injury or illness, a player is forced to play an unfamiliar position. These examples highlight the need to establish goals for personal improvement that are consistent with the objective of winning, but not entirely dependent on their achievement, to maintain player motivation. There are several guidelines for goal setting that can markedly help performance.

Guidelines for Goal Setting

- ### Success should be possible for everyone on the team.

When implementing a goal setting program, each athlete must experience some success. In other words, each athlete should perform at a level that demands a best effort for the existing conditions. Help each athlete realize that effort equals success by focusing rewards on such efforts.

- ### Goals under practice conditions should be increasingly more challenging and goals during competition should be more realistic.

When you set up drills to work on hitting or fielding, help your players set goals for practice that will challenge each of them to exceed a previous effort. For example, when practicing hitting, you may ask your "star" to hit seven out of 10 pitches in practice, while another player may be challenged with four out of 10. You should not expect the same level of performance in a game because neither you nor the players control all the factors. With this approach, motivation at practice is increased and players have a realistic chance of experiencing self-worth in a game.

- ### Goals should be flexible.

If goal setting is to be effective, goals must be evaluated frequently and adjusted depending on the athlete's success ratio. If an athlete is achieving the set goal, raise the goal to provide a greater challenge and motivation. If the goal is too difficult and the athlete is feeling frustration or failure, the goal should be lowered rather than have the athlete continue to experience failure. Having to lower the level of a goal may also be frustrating. Therefore, it is important to be as accurate as possible when initially setting goals for individual players.

- ### Set individual goals rather than team goals.

In general, team goals should not be made. This is because team goals are not under anyone's control, and they are often unrealistic. It is too difficult to assess accurately how a team will progress through a season. Will your team improve faster than other teams, at the same pace, or be a latecomer? If you set winning a certain number of games (e.g., eight of 10 games) as a goal and the team loses their first three games, you cannot achieve the goal even by winning the remaining seven games. This will only cause greater discouragement among team members. Work on individual improvement through goal setting, and let the team's improvement reflect the individual's improvement.

Goal setting can be very effective in improving a player's performance, confidence, and self-worth. To be effective, however, you must know your players well enough to know when they are setting goals that are challenging, controllable, and realistic. In addition, goals must be adjusted to ensure feelings of self-worth.

DEALING WITH COMPETITIVE STRESS

Some coaches believe the best way to motivate a team for competition is to get them "psyched-up" before the game. With young athletes, however, getting psyched-up is not usually the problem; rather, the problem for them is getting "psyched-out."

Competitive stress in young athletes can originate from many sources—the athlete, the teammates, the coach, and the parents. When young athletes were asked what caused them to worry, among the most frequently given answers were:

1. Improving their performance
2. Participating in championship games
3. Performing up to their level of ability
4. What their coach and parents would think or say

Thus, young baseball players are most likely to be worried about performance failure. This worry about failure may increase players' anxieties, which, in turn, may cause poor performance, and eventually may decrease motivation. Figure 16-1 illustrates this cycle.

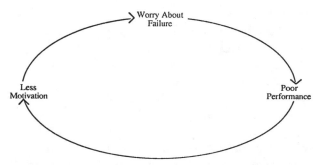

Figure 16-1. A cyclic representation of performance failure.

A good way to help your players avoid the effects of competitive stress is to reduce their fear of failure. This can be achieved by encouraging them to enjoy the game and to do their best. When your players lose or make a mistake, do not express displeasure; rather, correct their mistakes in a positive way by using the following sequence:

1. Start with a compliment. Find some aspect of the performance that was correct.
2. Tell the player what was wrong and how to correct it.
3. Give another positive statement such as, "Everyone makes mistakes. Keep working at it and you will get it."

This approach allows players to keep practicing their skills without the fear of making a mistake. The following guidelines may be helpful in preventing competitive stress.

Guidelines for Preventing Competitive Stress

- Set realistic goals.
- Use the positive approach when correcting mistakes.
- Eliminate the type of "pep talks" that communicate overemphasis on the game and the outcome.

APPROPRIATE USE OF TEAM TROPHIES, MEDALS, AND OTHER AWARDS*

Anyone who has ever attended a post-season baseball team party is aware that pre-

*Much of the material presented in this section has been adapted from Gould (1980).

senting trophies and awards is a common practice. Young athletes may receive any number of external awards, ranging from small ribbons to large trophies. However, whether it is appropriate to give children these awards is a controversial issue.

The advocates of awards such as medals, trophies, ribbons, certificates, and jackets indicate that they increase the children's desire and motivation to participate. Critics, in contrast, suggest that giving rewards to young athletes for activities in which they are already interested turns play into work and decreases their desire to participate. What is the answer: Awards or no awards?

While the advocates and critics of this issue would have us view it as a simple one, researchers have found that no simple answer exists. The purpose of this section is to provide you with information on how and in what situations external rewards influence young athletes' self-motivation to participate in sports.

Understanding Rewards

An activity is defined as intrinsically motivating if an individual engages in that activity for personal interest and enjoyment, rather than for external reasons such as receiving a trophy, money, or publicity. In essence, young athletes are intrinsically motivated when they play for the sake of playing. Until recently, coaches assumed that if external rewards are given for activities that are already intrinsically motivating, the result will be a further increase in intrinsic motivation.

However, research has shown that this is not always the case. The presentation of extrinsic rewards for an already self-motivated activity may result in reduced intrinsic motivation. The following adapted story (Casady 1974) illustrates how rewards can undermine intrinsic motivation.

An old man lived next to an open field that was a perfect location for the neighborhood children's "pick-up" baseball games. Every afternoon the children would come to the field, choose sides, and engage in a noisy game. Finally, the noise became too much for the old man, so he decided to put an end to the games. However, being a wise old man who did not want to stir up trouble in the neighborhood, he changed the children's behavior in a subtle way.

The old man told the children that he liked to hear them play, but because of his failing hearing, he had trouble doing so. He then told the children that if they would play and create enough noise so he could hear them, he would give each of them a quarter.

The children gladly obliged. After the game, the old man paid the children and asked if they could return the next day. They agreed, and once again they created a great deal of noise during the game. However, this time the old man said he was running short of money and could only pay them 20 cents each. This still satisfied the children. However, when he told them that he would be able to pay only 5 cents on the third day, the children became angry and indicated that they would not come back. They felt that it was not worth the effort to make so much noise for only 5 cents apiece.

In this example, giving an external reward (money) for an already intrinsically motivating activity (playing baseball and making noise) resulted in decreased intrinsic motivation in the children. Hence, when the rewards were removed, the amount of participation decreased.

An increasing number of individuals have suggested that this phenomenon also occurs in organized youth sports. In many programs, young athletes are presented with a substantial number of external awards (trophies, jackets, ribbons, etc.) for participating in an already desirable activity. Critics of external awards feel that giving these rewards decreases the youngsters' intrinsic motivation and when the rewards are no longer available, they no longer participate. Thus, external rewards may be one cause of discontinued participation in baseball.

Effects of Intrinsic Awards

There are two aspects of every reward that can influence a young athlete's intrinsic motivation (Deci 1975). These are:

1. the controlling aspect of the reward
2. the informational aspect of the reward

• Controlling Aspects of Rewards

Extrinsic rewards can decrease intrinsic motivation when they cause players to perceive that their reasons for participation have shifted from their own internal control to factors outside (or external to) themselves. This was illustrated clearly in the story of the old man and the children. The children's reasons for playing shifted from internal factors (fun and self-interest) to external factors (money). Then, when the rewards were diminished, they no longer wanted to play. In essence, the children were no longer participating for the fun of it but were participating solely for the reward. If young baseball players are made to feel that their primary reason for participating is to receive a trophy or a medal to please their parents, their intrinsic motivation will probably decrease.

• Informational Aspects of Rewards

External rewards can also communicate information to individuals about their competence and self-worth. If the reward provides information that causes an increase in a child's feelings of personal worth and competence, it will increase intrinsic motivation. If it provides no information about self-worth or competence or reduces these feelings about oneself, it will decrease intrinsic motivation.

Seek to elevate feelings of self-worth in the awards you give.

A "Most Improved Player" award is a good example of how material rewards can enhance motivation. This award usually tells the player that he/she has worked hard and learned a lot. This award would probably increase intrinsic motivation. Constant failure and negative feedback, however, would decrease a young player's feelings of competence and self-worth and, in turn, would decrease intrinsic motivation. Consequently, you must help children establish realistic goals. When rewards are given, they should be based upon some known criteria (performance, effort, etc.). This helps to ensure that rewards provide the recipients with information to increase feelings of self-worth and competence.

• Informational Versus Controlling Aspects of Rewards

Because most rewards in children's athletics are based upon performance, thus conveying information about the recipient's self-worth, giving external rewards should never undermine intrinsic motivation. However, this may not always be true. Even though external rewards may convey information about a child's sense of personal competence, the child may perceive the controlling aspect as being more important than the information conveyed (Halliwell 1978). Thus, instead of increasing the young athletes' intrinsic motivation, the extrinsic rewards undermine children's interest in sports by causing them to perceive their involvement as a means to an end. They are pawns being "controlled" by the pursuit of winning the reward.

Practical Implications

Extrinsic rewards have the potential to either increase or decrease intrinsic motivation. Two key factors determine which will occur:

1. If children perceive their baseball involvement as being controlled primarily by the reward (e.g., they are participating only to win the trophy or to please Mom or Dad), intrinsic motivation will decrease. In contrast, if children feel they are controlling their involvement (playing because they want to), then intrinsic motivation will increase.
2. If the reward provides information that increases the young players' feelings of self-worth and competence, intrinsic motivation will increase. If, however, the reward provides no information at all or decreases a person's feelings of competence or self-worth, then intrinsic motivation will decrease.

These findings have important implications for you as the coach. Be very careful about using extrinsic rewards! These rewards should be relatively inexpensive and not used to "control" or "coerce" children into participation in already desirable activities. Moreover, because you play such a vital role in determining how children perceive rewards, you must keep winning in perspective and stress the non-tangible values of participation in baseball (fun and personal improvement) as opposed to participating solely for the victory or the reward.

The frequent use of inexpensive or "free" rewards will increase player motivation.

One way to increase intrinsic motivation is to give your players more responsibility (more internal control) for decision making and for rule making (Halliwell 1978). This could be done by getting input from your athletes about making team rules or letting them help organize practices. Younger players could be selected to lead a drill or favorite warm-up exercise and given some playing time at positions they desire. Older, more experienced players could help conduct practices and make actual game decisions (allowing players to call some plays without interference, for example).

Intrinsic motivation can also be increased by ensuring that when external rewards are given, they provide information that increases your players' feelings of self-worth and competence. The easiest way to accomplish this is to have realistic expectations of the players. Not all children will have a winning season or place first in the tournament. However, some realistic goals can be set with each athlete in terms of improved personal skills, playing time, etc., and the players can be rewarded for achieving their goals. This could be accomplished through the use of "Unsung Hero" and/or "Most Improved Player" awards.

These "official" rewards are not nearly as important, however, as the simple ones that you can give regularly. Remember, some of the most powerful rewards are free (pat on the back, friendly nod, or verbal praise). These rewards should be frequently used to acknowledge each athlete's contribution to the team, personal improvement, or achievement of a personal goal.

Finally, remember that the rewards must be given for a reason that has meaning to your players. Rewards not given sincerely (not based upon some criteria of success) may actually decrease intrinsic motivation. Therefore, coaches must set realistic, attainable goals and reward children when they attain those goals.

SUMMARY

Children play baseball because they want to improve their skills, have fun, be with friends, and be successful. Children who drop out of baseball typically do so because one or more of their goals was not met. You can maximize your players' desire to participate, and help prevent them from dropping out, by getting to know them as individuals.

Learn why they are participating. Focus on skill development in practice sessions and make sure the practices are enjoyable. Allow time for friendships to develop by creating a cordial environment both on and off the field. Help players understand the meaning of success and have them set realistic goals.

Using a positive approach to coaching is the most effective way to improve players' performance. Positive coaching also makes playing and coaching more enjoyable. Be sure to reward effort and correct techniques in addition to the results that meet your expectations.

Having realistic expectations of players' performances will provide more opportunities to give rewards. However, when players make mistakes, use the positive approach to correcting errors. The positive approach involves issuing a compliment, correcting the error, and then finishing with another positive statement. Using a positive approach and helping players reach their goals are effective ways to motivate your players toward maximum performance.

Extrinsic rewards have the potential to either increase or decrease intrinsic motivation.

Extrinsic rewards are most effective when they are kept in perspective, are inexpensive, and are used to reflect improvements in personal competence. The non-tangible values of participation in baseball should be stressed, as opposed to participating only for winning or for the reward.

REFERENCES

Casady, M. (1974). The tricky business of giving rewards. *Psychology Today*, 8(4): 52.

Deci, E.L. (1975). *Intrinsic motivation.* New York: Plenum.

Gould, D. (1980). *Motivating young athletes.* East Lansing, MI: Institute for the Study of Youth Sports.

Halliwell, W. (1978). Intrinsic motivation in sport. In W.F. Straub (Ed.), *Sport psychology: An analysis of athlete behavior.* Ithaca, NY: Movement Publications.

Smoll, F.L. & Smith, R.E. (1979). *Improving relationship skills in youth sport coaches.* East Lansing, MI: Institute for the Study of Youth Sports.

Youth Sports Institute (1977). *Joint legislative study on youth sports program, phase II.* East Lansing, MI: Institute for the Study of Youth Sports.

SUGGESTED READINGS

Orlick, T. (1980). *In pursuit of excellence.* Ottawa, Ontario: Coaching Association of Canada.

Singer, R.N. (1984). *Sustaining motivation in sport.* Tallahassee, FL: Sport Consultants International, Inc.

Smoll, F.L., & Smith, R.E. (1979). *Improving relationship skills in youth sports coaches.* East Lansing, MI: Institute for the Study of Youth Sports.

17
Communicating With Your Players

Martha Ewing, Ph.D.
Deborah Feltz, Ph.D.

QUESTIONS TO CONSIDER

- How can you send clear messages to your players?
- What is the positive approach to communication?
- What are the characteristics of a good listener?
- How can good communication skills improve your ability to coach?

INTRODUCTION

The most important skill in coaching is the ability to communicate with your players. It is critical to effectively carry out your roles of leader, teacher, motivator, and organizer. Effective communication not only involves skill in sending messages but skill in interpreting the messages that come from your players and their parents.

SENDING CLEAR MESSAGES

Any means you use to convey your ideas, feelings, instructions, and/or attitudes to others involves communication. Thus, when communicating with your players, your messages may contain verbal as well as nonverbal information. Nonverbal messages can be transmitted through facial expressions such as smiling, or through gestures and body movements.

When you send messages to your players, you may, without thinking, send unintentional nonverbal information as well as your intentional verbal message. If your nonverbal message conflicts with what you say, your message will probably be confusing. For example, when you tell your players that they have done a good job and let your shoulders slump and heave a heavy sigh, don't be surprised if your players are less receptive to your next attempt at praise.

Another example of mixed messages occurs when you tell your players they should never question umpires' calls and then you denounce an umpire's decision. If the need should arise to question an umpire's call, you should ask the umpire for clarification in a professional manner.

Using a Positive Approach to Communicate

Communication is more effective when you use the positive approach. The positive approach to communication between you and your athletes involves establishing:

- mutual trust
- respect
- confidence
- cooperation

Essential Factors in Sending Clear Messages

• Getting and Keeping Attention

Getting and keeping your athletes' attention can be accomplished by making eye contact with them; avoid potential distractions but be enthusiastic, and emphasize the importance of what you have to say. For example, when you want to instruct your players on a new skill, organize them so everything you do is visible to them. Be sure that they are not facing any distractions, such as children playing at the other end of the field. It is also helpful to use a story, illustration, or event that will highlight the importance or focus attention on the instruction that is to follow.

• Using Simple and Direct Language

Reduce your comments to contain only the specific information the player needs to know. For example, when a player makes a mistake in a fielding drill, make sure your feedback is simple, focuses on one error at a time, and contains only information that the player can use to correct the mistake. Keep information simple and specific.

The positive approach to communication is an essential element of good coaching.

• Checking With Your Athletes

Make certain that your players understand what you are saying. Question them so you will know if they understood the key points of your message. For example, let's say you are trying to explain how to run a double play drill. After showing them the drill, you can save time and frustration by asking your players before they practice the drill where they should position themselves, what base should the ball be thrown to first, and where they should make the next play. If your athletes cannot answer these questions, they will not be able to participate effectively in the drill.

• Being Consistent

Make sure your actions match your words. When a discrepancy occurs between what you say and what you do, players are affected most by what you do. "Actions speak louder than words." You need to practice what you preach if you wish to effectively communicate with your players and avoid the loss of credibility that comes with inconsistent behaviors.

• Using Verbal and Nonverbal Communication

Your athletes are more likely to understand and remember what you have said when they can see it and hear it at the same time. Using the previous example, simultaneously demonstrating the double play drill while explaining the key points will result in clearer instructions.

BEING A GOOD LISTENER

Remember, too, that you must be a good listener to be an effective communicator. Communication is a two-way street. Being receptive to your players' ideas and concerns is important to them and informational to you.

Part of good coaching involves listening to your players.

By listening to what your athletes say and asking them how they feel about a point, you can determine how well they are learning. Their input provides you the opportunity to teach what they do not understand.

Essential Factors in Good Listening Skills

• Listening Positively

Players want the chance to be heard and to express themselves. You can encourage this by using affirmative head nods and occasional one- to three-word comments (e.g., "I understand.") while you're listening. The quickest way to cut off communication channels is by giving "no" responses or negative head nods.

• Listening Objectively

Avoid prematurely judging the content of a message. Sincerely consider what your players have to say. They may have good ideas! A good listener creates a warm, non-judgmental atmosphere so players will be encouraged to talk and ask questions.

• Listening With Interest

Being a good listener means being attentive and truly interested in what your players have to say. Look and listen with concern. Listen to what is being said and how it is being said. Establish good eye contact and make sure your body also reflects your interest in your player's message. Be receptive to comments that are critical of you or your coaching. Criticism is the most difficult communication to accept, but it is often the most helpful in improving our behavior.

● **Checking for Clarity**

If you are uncertain of what your athletes are communicating to you, ask them what they mean. This will help to avoid misinterpretation.

Being receptive to your players' thoughts and comments is important to them, and it also provides you with essential information.

SUMMARY

The ability to communicate with your players is critical in your role as a coach. It is a skill that involves two major aspects: speaking and listening. Coaches who are effective communicators get and keep the attention of their players, send clear and simple messages, and check to make sure their message is consistent with their actions. They also have good listening skills, which involve listening positively, helpfully, objectively, and with concern.

SUGGESTED READING

Martens, R. (1987). *Coaches guide to sport psychology*. Champaign, IL: Human Kinetics.

18
Maintaining Discipline

Martha Ewing, Ph.D.
Deborah Feltz, Ph.D.

QUESTIONS TO CONSIDER

- What is the best way to prevent misbehavior?
- Should players be involved in establishing team rules?
- How should team rules be enforced?
- What are the key points of an effective plan for handling misconduct?

INTRODUCTION

Coaches often react to their athletes' misbehaviors by yelling, lecturing, or using threats. These verbal techniques are used because we often do not know what else to do to regain control. Many discipline problems could be avoided, however, if coaches anticipated misbehavior and developed policies to deal with them.

Harsh comments may prevent misbehavior, but they often create a hostile, negative environment that reduces learning and motivation.

PLAN FOR SOUND DISCIPLINE

Although threats and lectures may prevent misbehavior in the short term, they create a hostile, negative atmosphere. Typically, their effectiveness is short-lived. Hostility between a coach and team members neither promotes a positive environment in which it is fun to learn

the game of baseball nor motivates the players to accept the coach's instructions.

Sound discipline involves a two-step plan that must be in place before the misbehaviors occur. These steps are: (1) define team rules, and (2) enforce team rules.

Athletes want clearly defined limits and structure for how they should behave. You can accomplish this without showing anger, lecturing, or threatening. As the coach, it is your responsibility to have a systematic plan for maintaining discipline before your season gets under way. If you have taken the time to establish rules of conduct, you will be in a position to react in a reasonable manner when children misbehave.

Athletes want clearly defined limits and structure for how they should behave.

Define Team Rules

The first step in developing a plan to maintain discipline is to identify what you consider to be desirable and undesirable conduct. This list can then be used to establish relevant team rules. A list of potential behaviors to consider when identifying team rules is included in Table 18-1.

Your players (especially if you are coaching individuals who are 10 years of age or older) should be involved in establishing the rules for the team. Research has shown that players are more willing to live by rules when they have had a voice in formulating them (Seefeldt et al. 1981). This can be done at a team meeting, early in the season. The following introduction has been suggested (Smoll & Smith 1979) to establish rules with players:

> *"I think rules and regulations are an important part of the game because the game happens to be governed by rules and regulations. Our team rules ought to be something we can agree upon. I have a set of rules that I feel are important. But we all have to follow them, so you ought to think about what you want. They should be your rules, too."*

Rules of conduct must be defined in clear and specific terms. For instance, a team rule that players must "show good sportsmanship" in their games is not a very clear and specific rule. What, exactly, is showing good sportsmanship? Does it mean obeying all the rules, calling one's own errors, or respecting officials' decisions? The Youth Sports Institute has adopted a code of sportsmanship which defines sportsmanship in more specific terms (Seefeldt et al. 1981). This code has been reprinted in Table 18-2. You

may wish to use some of the items listed as you formulate your team rules.

Players are more willing to live by rules when they have had a voice in formulating them.

Remember, you are a part of the team and you should live by the same rules. You should demonstrate the proper behaviors so the children will have a standard to copy. As a coach, you must also emphasize that behaviors of coaches as seen on television (such as screaming, throwing bats out of the dugout and belittling and embarrassing players) are also examples of undesirable conduct!

Enforce Team Rules

Not only are rules needed to maintain discipline, but these rules must be enforced so reoccurrences are less likely. Rules are enforced through rewards and penalties. Players should be rewarded when they abide by the rules and penalized when they break the rules. The next step, therefore, in developing a plan to maintain discipline, is to determine the rewards and penalties for each rule. Your players should be asked for suggestions at this point because they will receive the benefits or consequences of the decisions. When determining rewards and penalties for the behaviors, the most effective approach is to use rewards that are meaningful to your players and appropriate to the situation. Withdrawal of rewards should be used for misconduct. A list of potential rewards and penal-

Table 18-1. Examples of desirable and undesirable behavior to consider when making team rules.

Desirable Behavior	Undesirable Behavior
Making every effort to attend all practices and games except when excused for justifiable reasons	Missing practices and games without legitimate reasons
Being on time for practices and games	Being late or absent from practices and games
Attending to instructions	Talking while the coach is giving instructions
Concentrating on drills	Not attending to demonstrations during drills
Treating opponents and teammates with respect	Pushing, fighting, and/or using abusive language with opponents and teammates
Giving positive encouragement to teammates	Making negative comments about teammates
Bringing required equipment or uniform to practices and games	Forgetting to bring required equipment or uniform to games and practices
Reporting injuries promptly	Waiting till after the team roster is set to report an injury
Helping to pick up equipment after practices	Leaving equipment out for others to pick up

Table 18-2. Youth sportsmanship code.

Area of Concern	Sportsmanlike Behavior	Unsportsmanlike Behavior
Behavior toward officials	No ejections	Arguing with officials
	When questioning officials, do so in the appropriate manner (e.g., lodge an official protest, have only designated individuals such as a captain address officials)	Swearing at officials
	Treat officials with respect and dignity at all times	Ejections
	Thank officials after game	
Behavior toward opponents	Treat all opponents with respect and dignity at all times	Arguing with opponents
	Talk to opponents after the game	Making sarcastic remarks about opponents
		Making aggressive actions toward opponents
Behavior toward teammates	Give only constructive criticism and positive encouragement	Making negative comments or sarcastic remarks
		Swearing at or arguing with teammates
Behavior toward spectators	No talking	Arguing with spectators
		Making negative remarks/swearing at spectators
Behavior toward coach	Share likes and dislikes with the coach as soon as possible	
Rule acceptance and infraction	Obey all league rules	Intentionally violating league rules
		Taking advantage of loopholes in rules (e.g., everyone must play, so coach tells unskilled players to be ill on important game days)

ties that can be used in baseball is given in Table 18-3.

The best way to motivate players to behave in an acceptable manner is to reward them for good behavior. When appropriate behavior is demonstrated, comment accordingly or be ready to use nonverbal interactions such as smiling or applauding. Some examples are:

- "We only had five errors in that game, that's the fewest we ever had. Way to be!"
- "I know you are all very disappointed in losing this game. I was real proud of the way you congratulated and praised the other team after the game."
- "Do you realize that for our first five practices everyone was dressed and ready to play at 3 o'clock, our starting time? That helped make the practice go better. Keep it up! Let's see if we can make it a tradition!"

Table 18-3. Examples of rewards and penalties that can be used in baseball.

Rewards	Penalties
Being a starter	Being taken out of a game
Playing a desired position	Not being allowed to start
Leading an exercise or part of it	Sitting out during practice: • until ready to respond properly • a specific number of minutes • rest of practice or sent home early
Praise from you • in team meeting • to media • to parents • to individual	Dismissed from drills: • for half of practice • next practice • next week • rest of season
Decals	Informing parents about misbehavior
Medals	
Certificates	

Penalties are only effective when they are meaningful to the players. Examples of ineffective penalties include showing anger, giving a player an embarrassing lecture, shouting at the player, or assigning a physical activity (e.g., running laps or doing push-ups). These penalties are ineffective because they leave no room for positive interactions between you and your players. Avoid using physical activity as a form of punishment; the benefits of baseball, such as learning skills and improving cardiovascular fitness, are gained through activity. Players should not associate these types of beneficial activities with punishment.

Rewards and penalties that are meaningful to your players and appropriate to the situation are most effective.

Sometimes it is more effective to ignore inappropriate behavior if the infractions are relatively minor. Continually scolding players for minor pranks or "horseplay" can become counterproductive. If team deportment is a constant problem, the coach must ask, "Why?" Misbehavior may be the players' way of telling the coach that they need attention or that they do not have enough to do. Coaches should check to see if the players are spending a lot of time standing in lines while waiting a turn to practice. Try to keep your players productively involved so they don't have time for inappropriate behavior. This is accomplished through well-designed practice plans. A lack of meaningful baseball activity in your practices could lead to counterproductive or disruptive behavior.

Misbehavior may be the players' way of telling the coach that they need attention or do not have enough to do.

When the rules for proper conduct have been outlined and the rewards and penalties have been determined, they must then be stated clearly so the players will understand them. Your players must understand the consequences for breaking the rules and the rewards for abiding by the rules. Violators should explain their actions to the coach and apologize to their teammates. You must also follow through, consistently and impartially, with your application of rewards for desirable conduct and penalties for misconduct.

Nothing destroys a plan for discipline more quickly than its inconsistent application. Rules must apply to all players equally and in all situations. Thus, if your team is in a championship game and your star player violates a rule that requires that he or she not be allowed to start, the rule must still be enforced. If not, you are communicating to your players that the rules are not to be taken seriously, especially when the game is at stake.

It is impossible to predetermine all rules that may ultimately be important during the season. However, by initiating several rules early in the season, a standard of expected behavior will be established. Positive and negative behaviors that are not covered by the rules can still be judged relative to these established standards and appropriate rewards or punishment can be given.

Key Points to An Effective Discipline Plan

- Specify desirable and undesirable conduct clearly in terms of rules.
- Involve players in establishing the team rules.
- Determine rewards and penalties for rules that are meaningful to players and allow for positive interaction between you and your players.
- Apply rewards and penalties consistently and impartially.

SUMMARY

Although threats, lectures, or yelling may deter misbehavior in the short term, the negative atmosphere that results reduces long-term coaching effectiveness. A more positive approach to handling misbehavior is to prevent it by establishing, with player input, clear team rules and enforcement policies. Use fair and consistent enforcement of the rules primarily through rewarding correct behaviors rather than penalizing wrong behaviors.

REFERENCES

Seefeldt, V. et al. (1981). *A winning philosophy for youth sports programs.* East Lansing, MI: Institute for the Study of Youth Sports.
Smoll, F., & Smith, R.E. (1979). *Improving relationship skills in youth sport coaches.* East Lansing, MI: Institute for the Study of Youth Sports.

19
Developing Good Personal and Social Skills

Annelies Knoppers, Ph.D.

QUESTIONS TO CONSIDER

- Which personal and social skills should youth baseball coaches attempt to foster?
- Why are personal and social skills important?
- How can a coach bolster the self-esteem of athletes?
- How important is fun in youth sports?
- What can a coach do to ensure that sport participation is an enjoyable experience for athletes?
- What strategies can be used to help young athletes develop positive interpersonal skills?
- What is sportsmanship and how can it be taught?

INTRODUCTION

Youth sport experiences can play, and often do play, a crucial role in the development of personal and social skills of children. The learning of these skills is different from that of physical skills in the following ways:

- Athletes will learn something about these skills whether or not we plan for such learning. If we do not plan for this learning, however, it is possible that the sport experience will be a negative one for some of the athletes. If we do plan, then it is more likely that the sports experience will be positive. Obviously then, this is different than the learning of physical skills. If you don't teach your players to do a specific sport skill, they will not learn anything about these skills. In contrast, at every practice and game, players are learning something about the personal and social skills regardless of planning.

- You as the coach continually model these skills. You may never have to model certain physical skills, but personal and social skills always show.

- The learning of these skills is also different from learning physical skills in that you cannot design many drills for the personal and social skills. These skills are a part of every drill and experience.

Coaches, therefore, can have an influence on children that goes well beyond the sport setting. The extent of this influence is increased when:

- the coach and athletes work together over a long period of time

- the athletes are participating in sport because they want to
- the coach is respected and liked by the athletes

Research has also shown that many parents want their children to participate in sports so their daughters and sons can develop personal and social skills through their sport experiences. Thus, coaches can and should work on the development of these skills in athletes.

The basic skills on which a beginning coach should focus are: self-esteem, fun in sport, interpersonal skills, and sportsmanship. Although self-esteem and interpersonal skills are not solely developed through sport, sport experiences can play a crucial role in the enhancement of these skills. In contrast, having fun in sport and showing sportsmanlike behavior are elements specific to the sport setting. Therefore, the coach is often held responsible for their development.

Regardless of the type of personal and social skills emphasized, the more coaches are liked and respected by the athletes and the more they work to create a positive atmosphere, the more likely it is they will influence the development of those skills in their players. The development of these skills is also likely to be enhanced when there is respect for teammates, opponents, officials, the spirit and letter of the rules, and the sport. Consequently, coaches who are very critical when athletes practice and compete, who are angry after a game or after errors, or who will do anything for a win, should change their ways or get out of coaching. Coaches who are unhappy or angry with athletes who make mistakes or lose contests retard the development of personal and social skills.

PERSONAL AND SOCIAL SKILLS

Self-Esteem

Self-esteem is the extent to which an individual is satisfied with oneself, both generally and in specific situations. The level of your athletes' self-esteem will affect their performance, relationships with others, behavior, enjoyment, and motivation. Thus, self-esteem plays a large part in the lives of your athletes as well as in your own life.

All of the players on your team will have feelings about themselves and their ability to do the things you ask of them. Those feelings were developed through experience. They will tend to behave in a way that reflects how they feel about themselves, making that behavior a self-fulfilling prophecy.

The level of self-esteem in young athletes influences their performance level.

Examples

If Sam feels clumsy when playing the shortstop position, he is likely to mishandle the ball when fielding, which reinforces for him that he is clumsy.

If adults or kids always laugh at Susan's batting technique, then she may be very self-conscious about batting and tend to strike out.

A combination of a sense of failure and the derisive or negative comments from others can, therefore, lower self-esteem. Luckily, the level of self-esteem is not something that is fixed forever. It can be changed, not overnight nor with a few comments, but over a period of time with a great deal of encouragement. Consequently, enhancing levels of self-esteem requires consistent and daily planning by a coach. Positive changes in the self-esteem of players come about through the implementation of a coaching philosophy that places a priority on this change. Mere participation in sport will not automatically enhance Susan's self-esteem; her coach must plan for experiences and develop strategies that promote self-esteem.

- **Show Acceptance of Each Athlete**

Showing acceptance of each athlete means you must take a personal interest in each of your players regardless of their ability, size, shape, or personality. You need to be sensitive to individual differences and respect those differences. Coaches have to accept their athletes as they are. This does not mean that you have to accept or condone all their behaviors and actions. It means you should still show an interest in Tom even though he seems to whine a lot. You can talk to him about his whining, but you still should give him the same amount of attention as the other players, praise him for good behavior, encourage his effort, chat with him about his non-sport life, and compliment him when he does not whine.

You also can show your acceptance of each player by demonstrating an interest in them as people, not just as athletes. Show an interest in their school life and their family as well as in the things they like and dislike. Take the time to make each athlete feel special as both a player and a person. All athletes should know that without them the team would not be such a great place to be.

● **React Positively to Mistakes**

In practice, be patient. Don't get upset with errors. Instead, focus on the part of the skill that was correctly performed and on the effort made by the player. Give positive suggestions for error correction. Helpful hints on how to do so are given in Chapter 16. Often in games, it is best to let mistakes go by without comment; simply praise the effort and the part of the skill that was performed correctly.

Kids usually know when they make mistakes and do not need an adult to point them out publicly. A coach who constantly corrects errors publicly not only embarrasses the players but may also be giving them too much information. Ask them privately if they know why the error occurred. If they know, then no correction needs to be given. Encourage them also to ask for help when they need it: "Coach, why did I miss the ball?" This type of question encourages self-responsibility and ensures that an athlete is ready to respond to your helpful suggestions.

● **Encourage Athletes**

Encouragement plays a vital role in building self-esteem. Coaches can never encourage their athletes enough. Athletes benefit most from coaches who are encouraging. Also, athletes who have supportive coaches tend to like sports more and are more likely to develop a positive self-image in sports. Encouragement is especially crucial for athletes who have low self-esteem, who have difficulty mastering a skill, who make crucial errors in a game, who are not highly skilled, and who are "loners." Encouragement conveys to athletes that the coach is on their side, especially if that encouragement is individualized.

Appropriate Times for Encouragement

● when a skill performance is partially correct
● when things aren't going well (the more discouraging the situation, the more encouragement is needed)
● right after a mistake; focus on the effort, not the error
● when any effort is made to do a difficult task
● after each game and practice; do not let players leave feeling upset or worthless

How to Give Encouragement

In general, give encouragement by publicly naming the athlete so that recognition is directly received for the effort. If an athlete is struggling with something personal, then encourage the athlete privately.

● Publicly acknowledge each athlete's effort and skill as they occur
● Recognize each athlete as they come off the field in either a verbal way: "Good hustle in going for that ball, Joan!" or in a nonverbal way: a smile, pat on the back, or wink
● Praise players who encourage each other
● Monitor your behavior or have someone else observe a practice or game
● Be sincere; make the encouragement both meaningful and specific

Examples

After a player fails to catch a ball, instead of saying "Nice try, John!" say "Way to get in position, John! Good hustle!"

After a player fell, instead of saying "I'm sorry you fell, Sue!" say "Way to get back up on your feet so quickly, Sue! I like your determination!"

Before a game, instead of saying "Play well in this game, OK?" say "I want all of you to try to do a little better than you did in the last game. I know you can do it!"

Additional Tips for Enhancing Self-Esteem

● Credit every player with the win
● Applaud physical skills (or parts of them) that were performed correctly
● Praise the use of appropriate social skills and effort
● Be more concerned that each player gets a

substantial amount of playing time than whether or not the team wins

- Give special and more attention in practices and games to nonstarters
- Give athletes responsibilities; ask for help in setting up team rules and in creating new drills
- Never call athletes by degrading names; poke fun at their physiques, abilities, or gender; or use ethnic, racial, or gender stereotypes or slurs

Examples

Instead of saying (in a derogatory manner), "John runs like a girl!" say "John needs to improve his running."

Instead of saying (in a derogatory manner), "You played like a bunch of sissies!" say "We're going to have to work on being a bit quicker and more assertive!"

Instead of saying, "Paul really looks funny the way he runs to first base!" say "Of all the kids on this team, Paul seems to show the most determination in getting to the base. Good for him!"

FUN IN SPORT

One of the main reasons why youngsters participate in sport is to have fun. Conversely, if they do not enjoy being on the team, players are more likely to drop out. Fun, therefore, is a crucial element in participation. Even though fun occurs spontaneously in sport, each coach should plan carefully to ensure that each athlete is enjoying the sport experience. The following ideas, when put into practice, increase the likelihood that the athletes and you will enjoy the team experience.

A primary reason young athletes participate in sports is to have fun.

- Conduct well-organized practices. Plan so all of the players have the maximum amount of physical activity that is feasible in conjunction with your objectives for a practice. Try to eliminate standing in line and waiting for turns as much as possible. If you have a large group, use the station method to keep all the players busy (see Chapter 14).

- Select drills that are suitable for the skill level of the players.
- Create enjoyable ways of learning skills; use innovative drills and games for practicing fundamental skills; and ask the players for suggestions and innovations.
- Watch the players' faces; if you see smiles and hear laughter, your players are enjoying practice!
- Project fun yourself; tolerate some silliness; avoid sarcasm; and be enthusiastic!
- Use games or drills that end when each person has won or has performed a skill correctly a specific number of times.
- Give positive reinforcement.
- Encourage athletes to praise, compliment, and encourage each other; do not allow them to criticize each other nor use degrading nicknames.
- Make sure athletes regularly change partners in drills.
- Allow each child to learn and play at least two positions, if possible, and to play a lot in every game.
- Keep the atmosphere light; don't be afraid to laugh and to gently joke.
- Smile; show that you enjoy being at practice or at the games. Say, "I really enjoyed this practice!" or "This is fun!"
- Take time to make each athlete feel very special. "The team could not function as well as it does without YOU!"

INTERPERSONAL SKILLS

Since sport involves teammates, opponents, officials, and coaches, it can be a great place to develop good interpersonal, or people, skills. Sport, however, can also be a place where athletes learn poor interpersonal skills. The type of skills that the athletes learn depends on the coach. If you, for example, praise Deb because she encouraged Donna, then you are reinforcing a positive interpersonal skill and creating a cooperative environment. If you say nothing when you hear Mike call one of the Hispanics on the team Chico, then you are reinforcing a racial slur and an inequitable climate. Just as youngsters need to be taught the proper technique for hitting a bunt, they also need to be taught how to relate to others in a way that bolsters self-esteem and sensitivity.

● The Coach as Model

If you want your athletes to develop good people skills, you must consistently model the skills you wish them to develop. If you explain to them that they are not to yell and scream at each other and yet you yell and scream at them, you are giving a conflicting message: "Do as I say, not as I do." Similarly, if you state that your athletes may never criticize each other because it shows lack of respect and yet you criticize officials, you are sending a mixed message.

The greater the inconsistencies in your messages (that is, between what you say and what you do), the less likely that the players will develop good people skills. When you send mixed messages, players are likely to ignore what you say and imitate your behavior. Thus they will yell, scream, and criticize if you yell, scream, and criticize. As part of practice and game plans, therefore, you should give serious thought to the type of behaviors you wish your athletes to show to each other, opponents, officials, and coaches.

The overriding principle that should guide your planning and behavior is to show respect and sensitivity to all others without exception.

What does respectful behavior look like? According to Griffin and Placek, a player who shows respect for others:

- follows rules
- accepts umpire's calls without arguing
- compliments good play of others including that of opponents
- congratulates the winner
- plays safely
- says "my fault" if it was
- accepts instruction
- will hold back rather than physically hurt someone
- questions coach and officials respectfully

Players show sensitivity to the feelings of others when they:

- pair up with different teammates each time

- cheer teammates on, especially those who are struggling
- help and encourage less skilled teammates
- stand up for those who are belittled or mocked by others
- are willing to sit out sometimes so others can play
- feel OK about changing some rules so others can play or to make the competition more even
- refrain from using abusive names, stereotypic slurs, and from mocking others

The above behaviors are those you must model, teach, discuss, and encourage to enhance the people skills of your players. When you "catch" your players using these skills, praise them! Praise as frequently, if not more, the use of these skills as you would praise correct physical performance.

However, modeling, teaching, discussing, and encouraging these behaviors is not enough. You must also intervene when players use poor interpersonal skills. If you see such actions and ignore them, you are giving consent and approval.

When should you intervene? Griffin and Placek suggest that you should act when a player:

- criticizes teammates' play
- yells at umpires
- pushes, shoves, or trips teammates or opponents
- throws their glove
- gloats and rubs it in when the team wins
- baits opponents, e.g., "you're no good"
- bosses other players
- will hurt someone just to win
- makes fun of teammates because of their shape, skill, gender, race, or ethnic origin
- calls others names, like "wimp," "stupid," "klutz," etc.
- blames mistakes on others
- complains to umpires
- shares a position unwillingly
- ignores less skilled players
- complains about less skilled players
- gets into verbal or physical fights
- uses racial, ethnic, or gender slurs

Obviously, the lists of desirable and undesirable behaviors could be much longer. Their overall theme suggests that everyone should show respect and sensitivity to all people. This includes coaches, officials, teammates, and opponents. Coaches should be firmly committed to this *people principle* and should try to express it in their coaching.

• Tips for Enhancing People Skills

- Explain the people principle and establish a few basic rules as examples of the principle (e.g., praise and encourage each other).
- Discuss how you feel when you are encouraged and when you are hassled. Ask them how they feel.
- Praise behavior that exemplifies the people principle.
- Work to eliminate stereotypic grouping of players for drills; don't let players group themselves by race, gender, or skill level. They should rotate so all will have a chance to work with everyone else.
- Call the entire team's attention to an undesirable behavior the first time it occurs and explain or ask why that behavior does not fit the people principle.
- Talk to the team about the use of racial jokes and slurs such as calling a Native American "Chief," an Asian American "Kung Foo," and an Hispanic "Taco," and the derogatory use of gender stereotypes such as "sissies," "playing/throwing like a girl," and "wimp." Explain how these behaviors convey disrespect and insensitivity and cannot be tolerated. Remember, too, that often these verbalizations by players echo those they have heard used by adults.
- Assign drill partners on irrelevant characteristics such as birthday month, color of shirt, number of siblings, etc.
- Stress the "one for all and all for one" concept.
- Monitor your own behavior.

SPORTSMANSHIP

Sportsmanship is a familiar term that is difficult to define precisely. When we talk about sportsmanship, we usually are referring to the behavior of coaches, athletes, and spectators in the competitive game setting, especially in stressful situations. Thus, it is easier to give examples of sportsmanlike and unsportsmanlike be-

haviors than to define sportsmanship. For some examples, see Table 18-2 in Chapter 18.

• Displaying Sportsmanship

Treatment of Opponents

Sportsmanlike behaviors

- At the end of the game, athletes shake hands sincerely with their opponents and talk with them for a while.
- An opponent falls and Joan helps her back on her feet.
- John forgets his game shoes and the opposing team lends him a pair.
- A team brings orange slices and shares them with their opponents.
- After the game, a coach praises the play of both teams.

Unsportsmanlike behaviors

- Joan stomps away in disgust after her team loses.
- An athlete verbally hassles an opponent, saying "You dummy! We're going to run right over you!"
- A player swears after the opponents score.
- After a player on the Stars is tripped by an opposing player, the Stars players decide they have to "get physical" too.

Treatment of Officials

Sportsmanlike behaviors

- The Stars coach saw a Blazers player touch the baseball in fair territory before it rolled out of bounds. When the hit is ruled a foul ball, because the official thought the ball was not touched by a player on the Stars, the Stars coach says nothing.
- The only Stars player who asks the official to explain a call is the captain. When other Stars players have a question, they ask the captain to speak for them.
- When the captain or coach speaks to an official, they do so in a respectful and courteous manner.

Unsportsmanlike behaviors

- The coach of the Stars throws the clipboard into the fence after an umpire calls a runner attempting to steal second safe on a close play.

- When an official makes two calls in a row against the Blazers, the coach yells "Homer!"

Reaction to Rules

Sportsmanlike behaviors

- Since league rules permit only one practice per week, the coach of the Tigers holds only one practice and schedules no "secret" practices.
- One league requires that all its players play an equal amount of time. Although some coaches ask lesser skilled players to "be sick" on important game days, the coach of the Panthers continually stresses that all players are expected and needed for every game.

Unsportsmanlike behaviors

- The players on the Eagles are taught by their coach how they can break the rules without being detected.
- In order to get play stopped, the coach of the Falcons tells an athlete to fake an injury.
- Sue elbows Joan whenever the official is not looking in their direction.

• Creating a Positive Climate

Because one of the goals of youth sports is to teach sportsmanship, a coach should know in which situations unsportsmanlike actions are most likely to occur. Often these situations are under the control of the coach and by changing them, the likelihood of unsportsmanlike behavior occurring decreases.

Situations when unsportsmanlike behavior is most likely to occur are those in which coaches, parents, and athletes view:

- competition as war rather than as a cooperative, competitive game;
- opponents as enemies rather than as children playing a game;
- abusive language towards opponents and officials as "part of the game" rather than as disrespectful and intolerant behavior;
- errors by officials as proof that they favor the other team rather than as evidence that officials make mistakes, too;
- winning as the only important part of the game rather than as being only a part of the game; and
- every game as serious business rather than as a playful, fun-filled, and skillful endeavor.

Obviously then, a coach can decrease the likelihood of the occurrence of unsportsmanlike behavior by viewing youth sport as a playful, competitive, cooperative activity in which athletes strive to be skillful and to win and yet know that neither winning nor perfect performance are required. This type of attitude creates a positive climate and tends to enhance sportsmanship.

• Teaching Sportsmanship

Stress-filled situations are the second type of condition under which unsportsmanlike behaviors tend to occur. These situations are created by the game rather than by the coach. As a coach, therefore, you must teach the athletes how they should behave in these situations. Sportsmanship can be taught.

Role Modeling

Often the behavior of athletes in a stress-filled situation reflects that of their coach. If you stay calm, cool and collected when the score is tied in the championship game, so will your players. To do so, however, you need to keep the game in perspective which you can do by answering "no" to the following questions:

- Will the outcome of the game matter a month from now?
- Will it shake up the world if our team wins or loses today?
- Is winning more important than playing well and having fun?

Once you begin to answer "yes" to these questions, the game has become so important to you that you will be more likely to snap at the players and argue with the officials. Perhaps then you should ask yourself whether you should stay in youth sport.

On the other hand, if you can answer "no" to the above questions, you are probably approaching the game from a healthy perspective and are more likely to stay calm, cool, and collected and exhibit good sportsmanlike behavior.

Using the People Principle

If children are to behave in a sportsmanlike manner, they must be told specifically what is expected of them and must be praised for doing so. The "people principle" that was described in an earlier section requires all to show respect and sensitivity to others.

The people principle is the basic guideline for sportsmanlike behavior.

Use Praise

When athletes follow the "people principle," they should be praised.

Examples

Sally helps her opponent back up to her feet. Coach immediately says "Way to be, Sally!"

You know Johnny thinks the umpire made a mistake, but Johnny says nothing. You immediately say, "Way to stay cool, Johnny!"

Eliminate Unsportsmanlike Behaviors

Ideally, when an athlete behaves in an unsportsmanlike way, you should say something immediately, and if possible, pull the child aside. Firmly indicate:

- that the behavior was inappropriate
- how it violates the people principle
- that you expect everyone to follow this principle
- that the athlete will be in trouble if the behavior is repeated
- that you know the athlete will try hard not to do it again

If the behavior is repeated, remind the athlete of the previous discussion and give an appropriate penalty. For examples of penalties see Chapter 18.

If athletes are to develop sportsmanship, you must not tolerate any unsportsmanlike actions. Sometimes it is easy to ignore a youngster's outburst because you feel the same frustration. By ignoring it, however, you are sending the message that at times such behavior is acceptable. Consequently, athletes will not acquire a clear sense of sportsmanship.

Discuss Sportsmanship

Young athletes need to have time to discuss sportsmanship because it is so difficult to define precisely. Team meetings before or after a practice provide a good opportunity for discussion. The following tips should help you facilitate such a discussion:

- Ask opening questions such as "Who can give an example of sportsmanlike behavior? Unsportsmanlike behavior? Why is one wrong and not the other?"
- Read the examples from this section of both types of behaviors and ask the athletes to label them as sportsmanlike and unsportsmanlike. Ask them to explain their reasoning.
- Encourage role playing. "What would it be like to be an umpire who is trying to do what's best and to have a coach or players yelling at you?"
- Discuss the relationship between the importance attached to winning and sportsmanship.
- Point out examples from college and professional sports. Ask the players to classify the behaviors and to give a rationale.

During these discussions, refrain from lecturing. Think of yourself as a facilitator who attempts to encourage discussion and an exploration of the "people principle."

The extent to which your athletes display or react to sportsmanlike or unsportsmanlike behavior will determine the frequency with which you should hold such discussions at practice. To reinforce these discussions, you should point out examples of both types of behaviors at the brief team meeting after some game. Publicly praise each player who acted in a sportsmanlike manner and remind those who acted otherwise of your expectations. Remember also to continually examine your own behaviors to ensure that you are demonstrating the type of actions in which you want your players to engage.

SUMMARY

The extent to which athletes develop personal and social skills through the sport experience depends a great deal on you. Just as physical skills cannot be mastered without planned and directed practice, neither can personal and social skills be developed without specific strategies and guidelines. If a coach does not plan such strategies nor set guidelines for the development of these skills, then the sports experience may be a negative one for the athletes. They may lose self-esteem, develop a dislike for sport participation, and drop out. Conversely, those athletes who feel good about themselves, their teammates, and the sports experience are more likely to stay in sport. Thus a coach has a responsibility to develop these skills.

REFERENCES

Berlage, G. (1982). Are children's competitive team sports socializing agents for corporate America? In A. Dunleavy et al. (Eds.), *Studies in the sociology of sport*. Fort Worth, TX: Texas Christian University Press.

Coakley, J. (1986). *Sport in society* (3rd ed.). St. Louis, MO: Times/Mirror Mosby.

Griffin, P., & Placek, J. (1983). *Fair play in the gym: Race and sex equity in physical education*. Amherst, MA: University of Massachusetts.

SUGGESTED READINGS

Martens, R. (Ed.). (1978). *Joy and sadness in children's sports*. Champaign, IL: Human Kinetics.

National Coaching Certification Program (NCCP I). (1979). *Coaching theory, level one*. Ottawa, Ontario: Coaching Association of Canada.

National Coaching Certification Program (NCCP II). (1979). *Coaching theory, level two*. Ottawa, Ontario: Coaching Association of Canada.

Orlick, T., & Botterill, C. (1975). *Every kid can win*. Chicago: Nelson Hall.

Tutko, T., & Burns, W. (1976). *Winning is everything and other American myths*. New York: Macmillan, Inc.

Yablonsky, L., & Brower, J.J. (1979). *The little league game*. New York: Times Books.

20
Evaluating Coaching Effectiveness

Paul Vogel, Ph.D.

QUESTIONS TO CONSIDER

- Why evaluate coaching effectiveness?
- What should be evaluated?
- Who should evaluate it?
- What steps can be used to conduct an evaluation?

INTRODUCTION

No individual can coach with 100 percent effectiveness. While beginning coaches who have had no formal coaching education programs, sport-specific clinics, or prior coaching experience are particularly susceptible to using ineffective techniques, experienced professionals have their weaknesses as well. To determine where both strengths and weaknesses exist, beginning as well as experienced coaches should conduct systematic evaluations of their effectiveness.

All coaches can significantly improve their coaching effectiveness by completing an evaluation and then acting on the results.

At least two evaluation questions should be asked:

1. Was the coaching effective in achieving its purpose?
2. What changes can be made to improve the quality of coaching?

The evaluation described herein provides a relatively simple procedure for estimating the effects of your coaching efforts. It will also help you identify ways to improve your techniques.

WHAT SHOULD BE EVALUATED?

Evaluation should be based on more than whether or not you're a good person, worked the team hard, or even had a winning season. The important issue is whether or not you met the objectives identified for your players at the beginning of the season (see Chapter 14), including technique, knowledge, tactics, fitness, and personal/social skills. The worksheet in Figure 20-1 (also included in reproducible form in Supplement 20-1) provides an example of how to evaluate the objectives identified as important.

Coaching effectiveness should be judged by the degree to which players meet their objectives.

For a discussion on how to use Supplement 20-1, see "Step 2: Collect the Evaluation Data."

⌐ALUATE?

...y, you should evaluate your own effectiveness. To ensure a broader and more objective evaluation, however, you should have others participate in the evaluation. For example, by using the worksheet illustrated in Figure 20-1, you might rate the majority of your players as achieving one or more objectives in the areas of sport skills, knowledge, tactics, fitness, and personal/social skills. Another person, however, may feel that what you thought was appropriate was in fact an inappropriate technique, an incorrect interpretation of a rule, an improper tactic, a contraindicated exercise, or an improper attitude. Obtaining such information requires courage on your part but it often yields important information to help you improve your coaching effectiveness.

Self-evaluation is a valuable means for improving your coaching effectiveness.

To obtain the most useful second party information, use individuals who meet the following three criteria:

1. They are familiar with your coaching actions.
2. They know the progress of your players.
3. They are individuals whose judgment you respect.

A person fulfilling these criteria could be an assistant coach, parent, official, league supervisor, other coach, local expert, or even one or more of your players.

The evaluation form illustrated in Supplement 20-2 provides another way to obtain information relative to coaching effectiveness as perceived by others. This form can be used for individual players (one form per player) or for the team as a whole (one form for the entire team). The purpose of the form is to obtain information that will reveal areas of low ratings. Follow-up can be completed in a debriefing session with the rater to determine the reasons for low ratings and to identify what can be done to strengthen the ratings. Debriefing sessions with this type of focus have proven to be highly effective in identifying ways to improve programs and procedures.

WHAT STEPS CAN BE USED TO CONDUCT AN EVALUATION?

Four steps can be used to complete an evaluation of your coaching effectiveness. These are:

1. Identify the objectives
2. Collect evaluation data
3. Analyze the evaluation data to identify reasons why some coaching actions were ineffective
4. Implement the needed changes

Step 1: Identify Objectives

The form illustrated in Supplement 20-1 can be used to identify the objectives you have for your players. Simply list the specific sport skills, knowledges, tactics, fitness abilities, and personal-social skills that you intend to develop in your players. Completion of this step clearly identifies what you believe is most important for your players to master and it provides a basis for later evaluation.

A prerequisite to conducting an evaluation of coaching effectiveness is to clearly identify the objectives that you want your players to achieve.

Once the objectives are identified, the remaining evaluation steps can be completed. This step also provides a good opportunity for you to obtain information from others regarding the appropriateness of your season's objectives for the age and experience level of your players.

Let your players know what the objectives are. Research shows that when players know what they need to learn, they are more likely to improve.

Step 2: Collect the Evaluation Data

The primary source of evaluative data should be your self-evaluation of the results of all or various parts of the season. However, assessments by others, combined with self-assessment, are more valuable than self-evaluation alone. Both approaches are recommended.

COACH'S EVALUATION OF PLAYERS' OUTCOMES

Coach _Joe Smith_   Season _Summer_   Date _August 15, 1992_

CATEGORIES	SEASON OBJECTIVES	Todd	Randy	Jon	Clay	Doug	Tim	Brandon	Keith	Lee	Rick	Darron	Marty	Roger	Paul				Total (% yes) / Other notes
	EVALUATION QUESTION: Did significant, positive results occur on the objectives included in the performance areas listed below?																		
	Baseball skills																		
	Hitting	Y	N	Y	Y	Y	N	Y	N	N	Y	Y	Y	N	Y				64
	Bunting	N	N	Y	Y	Y	Y	N	Y	N	Y	N	N	Y	Y				82
	Fielding	Y	Y	Y	Y	Y	Y	Y	Y	Y	N	N	Y	N	Y				79
	Throwing	Y	Y	N	N	Y	Y	Y	N	Y	Y	Y	Y	Y	N				71
	Pitching	N	Y	Y	Y	N	N	Y	Y	N	Y	Y	N	Y	Y				64
	Catching	N	Y	Y	Y	N	Y	N	Y	Y	Y	N	Y	N	Y				71
	Position play	N	Y	Y	N	Y	Y	N	Y	Y	N	Y	Y	N	Y				64
	Offensive strat.	Y	Y	Y	N	Y	Y	Y	Y	N	Y	N	Y	Y	N				71
	Defensive strat.																		
	Lead runner	Y	Y	Y	N	N	Y	Y	N	Y	Y	N	Y	Y	Y				71
	Throw to cut	N	Y	Y	Y	Y	N	Y	Y	Y	N	Y	N	Y	Y				71
	Conditioning	Y	Y	Y	Y	Y	Y	N	Y	Y	N	Y	Y	Y	Y				86
	Personal skills																		
	Cooperative	Y	Y	N	Y	Y	Y	Y	Y	N	Y	Y	Y	Y	Y				86
	Support team	Y	Y	Y	Y	Y	Y	Y	Y	Y	Y	N	N	Y	Y				86
	Resp. officials	Y	Y	Y	Y	Y	Y	Y	Y	Y	Y	Y	Y	Y	Y				100
	Good sports.	Y	Y	Y	Y	N	Y	Y	Y	Y	Y	Y	N	Y	Y				86
Total (% yes)		73	87	87	73	73	80	73	80	67	73	60	67	73	87				

EVALUATIVE RESPONSES: Record your assessment of player outcomes for each objective by answering the evaluative questions with a "Y" ("YES") or "N" ("NO") response.

Figure 20-1. An example of a coach's evaluation of players' outcomes.

● Completing the Coach's Assessment of Player Performance

After you have identified objectives and entered them in the first column of the "Coach's Evaluation of Players' Outcomes" form, enter the names of your players in the spaces on the top of the form. Next, respond either Y (Yes) or N (No) to the question, "Did significant improvements occur?" as it relates to each season objective for each player.

Your decision to enter a Y or N in each space requires you to define one or more standards. For example, all of your players may have improved on a particular season objective but you may feel that several of those players did not achieve enough to receive a Y. However, an N may also seem inappropriate. To resolve this difficulty, clarify the amount of player achievement for each objective that you are willing to accept as evidence of a significant positive improvement. There is no exact method of determining how much gain is enough; therefore, you need to rely on your own estimates of these standards. The procedures suggested on the following pages of this chapter allow for correction of erroneous judgments. It is also possible to use a scale to further divide the response options: 0 = none, 1 = very little, 2 = little, 3 = some, 4 = large, and 5 = very large. Given ratings of this type, you may establish 4 and/or 5 ratings as large enough to be categorized as a Y and ratings of 3 or less as an N.

It is important to remember that players who begin the season at low levels of performance on various objectives have the potential for more improvement than players who are near mastery. Players who begin the season at high levels of performance often deserve Y rather than N for relatively small gains.

Injury, loss of fitness, or development of inappropriate sport skills, knowledge, tactics, or personal/social skills are detrimental effects that can occur and should be identified. In this situation the appropriate entry is an N circled to distinguish it from small or slight gains.

You must decide if your players achieved significant gains on the outcomes you intended to teach.

Completion of the coach's evaluation form will reveal your perception of the degree to which your players achieved important objectives. By looking at one objective across all players as well as one player across all objectives, patterns of your coaching effectiveness will emerge. (This is explained in more detail in Step 3.)

● Obtaining Information from Selected Other Persons

To obtain information from others about your coaching effectiveness, use the form in Supplement 20-2. Remember, the form can be used for individual players or for an entire team. Note that the estimates of performance are relative to other players of similar age and gender participating in the same league. When using the form to rate individual players, ask the evaluator to simply place a check in the appropriate column (top 25 percent, mid 50 percent or bottom 25 percent) for each performance area. When using the form to rate the entire team, estimate the number of players judged to be in each column.

Ratings of players' performance at the end of the season (or other evaluation period) are not very useful without knowing your players' performance levels at the beginning of the season. Changes in performance levels are the best indicators of your coaching effectiveness. To determine change in players' performance, it is necessary to estimate performance before and after coaching occurred. Pre- and post-ratings may be difficult to obtain, however, because of the time it requires of your raters.

A good alternative is to have the evaluators record pre and post ratings at the end of the evaluation period. For example, if three of your players were perceived to be in the top 25 percent of their peers at the beginning of the season and seven players were perceived to be in that performance category at the end of the season, the net gain in performance would be 4. Your desire may be to have all of your players move into the top 25 percent category during the course of the season. Such a desire is, however, probably unrealistic. Having 50 percent of your players move from one performance level to the next would be an excellent achievement.

It would be nice to look at your evaluations of player performance and the evaluations of their performance by others and see only Y responses or ratings in the top 25 percent. Such a set of responses, however, would not be helpful for improving your coaching effectiveness. An excessive number of high ratings probably signals the use of a relaxed set of standards.

All coaches vary in their ability to change behavior across stated outcome areas and across various individual players on a team. The incidences where individual players do not attain high ratings on various objectives are most useful to reveal principles of coaching effectiveness that are being violated. Accordingly, use standards for your self-ratings (or for the ratings by others) that result in no more than 80 percent of the responses being Y on the "Coach's Evaluation of Player Outcomes" or moving from one category of performance to another when rated by others. As you will see in Step 3, ratings that are more evenly distributed among the response options are the most helpful for determining how your effectiveness may be improved.

Use of the form "Evaluation of Player/Team Performance Relative to Others" (Supplement 20-2) provides you with an estimate of changes in player performance as viewed by other persons whose judgment you respect. The relatively broad performance areas upon which the evaluation is based does not, however, provide enough detailed information to fully interpret the data obtained. Simply stated, more information is needed. Additional information can be obtained by using the technique of debriefing.

A debriefing session, based upon the information included in the completed evaluation form, provides a good agenda for discussing potential changes in your coaching procedures with the person who completed the evaluation. The debriefing should include these elements:

- Thank the individual for completing the evaluation form and agreeing to discuss its implications.
- Indicate that the purpose of the debriefing session is to identify both strengths and weaknesses, but that emphasis should be focused on weaknesses, and how they may be improved.
- Proceed through the outcome areas and their corresponding ratings, seeking to understand

why each area resulted in large or small gains. For example, if a disproportionate number of the players were rated low relative to their peers on defensive skills, and there were very small gains from the beginning to the end of the evaluation period, you need more information. Attempt to determine what defensive skills were weak and what might be changed to strengthen them in the coming season.

- In your discussion, probe for the things you can do (or avoid doing) that may produce better results. Make a special attempt to identify the reasons why a suggested alternative may produce better results.
- Take careful notes during the discussion. Record the alternative ideas that have good supporting rationales and how they might be implemented.

The information collected in this way is invaluable for helping to identify good ideas for increasing your ability to help players achieve future season objectives.

Coaching strengths are pleasing to hear, but identified weaknesses are more helpful for improving effectiveness.

Step 3: Analyze the Data

The first step necessary to analyze the information collected on the "Coach's Evaluation of Players' Outcomes" form is to total the number of Y responses entered for each player across all season objectives.

From a coaching improvement viewpoint, it is necessary to have a mixture of Y and N responses across both the objectives and players. It is important that no more than 80 percent of your ratings be Y responses. No more than 80 percent of the players can be listed as showing improvement from one performance level to another in their pre/post estimates. It may be necessary to "force" the appropriate number of Y and N responses to meet this requirement.

When you have met the criteria of no more than 80 percent positive answers, divide the number of Y responses by the total number of objectives and enter the percent of Y responses in the row labeled "Total" for each player. Similarly sum the number of Y responses across players for each objective and enter the percent of Y responses in the column labeled "Total" for each season objective.

The pattern of Y and N responses that emerges from "forced ratings" can be very helpful in identifying the season's objectives and/or the kinds of players for which your coaching is most or least effective. By looking at the characteristics of the players who obtained the highest ratings versus those that achieved the lowest ratings, you may obtain good insight into things you can change to be more effective with certain kinds of players. This same type of comparison provides similar insight into how to be more effective in teaching certain objectives.

The real benefits of this kind of analysis come with evaluating the reasons why no or few players received Y responses. Answers to these "Why?" questions reveal changes you can make to improve your coaching effectiveness.

To help you determine why you were (or were not) successful with your coaching in certain player performance areas, a "Checklist of Effective Coaching Actions" was developed (Supplement 20-3). It provides a number of items you can rate that may help you identify ways to increase your coaching effectiveness. For example, if several of your players made insufficient progress in the bunting technique, you could review the checklist to help determine coaching actions you used (or did not use) that may be related to insufficient gains, fitness, or qualities of character. As you identify coaching actions that may have detracted from player improvement, note these and then alter your subsequent coaching actions accordingly.

● **Interpreting Unmet Expectations**

The above suggestions provide a systematic method for you to identify ways to improve your coaching ability. There are, however, other ways to interpret lack of achievement. The first and foremost (and nearly always incorrect) is to blame lack of performance on lack of talent or lack of player interest.

Be sure to consider all possibilities for self improvement before accepting other reasons for unmet expectations.

Effective coaches can improve the ability of their players, even those with only average abilities. The most helpful approach you can use to improve your coaching effectiveness is to assume that when the performances of your players do not meet your expectations, the solutions to the problem will be found in your coaching actions. This assumption may prove to be wrong, but you must be absolutely sure that you have considered all possibilities for self-improvement before accepting other reasons for unmet expectations.

If you determine that insufficient players' achievement is not likely to be due to ineffective coaching, it is possible that the expectations you hold for your players is unrealistic. Remember, motivation is enhanced when players perceive that they are improving. Expectations that are too high can have a negative effect on motivation and improvement. Reasonable expectations divided into achievable and sequential steps will result in appropriate standards of performance.

Allotment of insufficient time for teaching and learning the objectives selected for the season can also result in poor players' achievement, even when performance expectations and other coaching actions are appropriate. Players must have sufficient time to attempt a task, make errors, obtain feedback, refine their attempts, and habituate the intended actions before it is reasonable to expect them to demonstrate those actions in competition. Attempting to cover too many objectives within limited practice time is a major cause of insufficient achievement.

If the changes identified to improve coaching effectiveness are not implemented, evaluation is a waste of time.

Step 4: Act on the Needed Changes

The primary reason for conducting an evaluation of your coaching effectiveness is to learn what can be done to improve the achievement levels of your players. Identifying the changes that will lead to improvements, however, is a waste of time if those changes are not implemented. Improvements can occur in planning, instruction, motivation, communication, knowledge of the game, and evaluation. Regardless of your level of expertise, by systematically evaluating your coaching actions, you can find ways to become more effective and more efficient.

SUMMARY

By systematically evaluating players' performance on the intended outcomes of the season, you can estimate the effectiveness of your coaching actions. Limited achievement of players in some performance areas can signal a need to change some coaching actions. Use of the forms and procedures outlined in this chapter will reveal changes you can make to improve your coaching effectiveness. By taking action on the changes that are identified, you can make significant steps toward becoming a more effective and efficient coach.

Supplement 20-1.

Coach's Evaluation of Player Outcomes

Coach _____ Season _____ Date _____

CATEGORIES	EVALUATION QUESTION:	Did significant, positive results occur on the objectives included in the performance areas listed below?															
	SEASON OBJECTIVES	R O S T E R														Total (% yes)	
																	Other notes
	Total (% yes)																

EVALUATIVE RESPONSES:	Record your assessment of player outcomes for each objective by answering the evaluative questions with a "Y" ("YES") or "N" ("NO") response.

Evaluation of Player/Team Performance Relative to Others

Evaluator _____   Player/Team _____   Season _____

EVALUATION QUESTION:	In comparison with other players in this league, how does the player (or team) listed above perform in the areas listed below?					
PERFORMANCE AREAS	**PLAYER OR TEAM PERFORMANCE LEVELS**					
	SEASON START			**SEASON END**		**COMMENTS**
	TOP 25%	MID 50%	BOTTOM 25%	TOP 25%	MID 50%	BOTTOM 25%	

INDIVIDUAL EVALUATION:

For each performance area indicate, by placing a check in the top, mid, or bottom column, the start and end of the season performance level of the player.

TEAM EVALUATION:

For each performance area estimate the number of players (% or actual numbers) in the top, mid, or bottom performance levels at the start and end of the season.

Checklist of Effective Coaching Actions[1]

Introduction

This checklist can be used to identify coaching actions that may be related to player achievement (or lack of achievement) of desired outcomes. It, therefore, serves as an aid to identify the reason(s) why a player(s) did not achieve one or more of your expected outcomes. To use the checklist in this way, read the items in each content category (i.e., coaching role, organization, effective instruction) and ask yourself the question, "Could the coaching actions (or inactions) implied by this item have contributed to the unmet expectation?" Answer the question by responding with a 'Yes' or 'No.' If you wish to rate the degree to which your actions (inactions) were consistent with the guidelines implied by the items, use the 5 point rating scale described below. Items which result in "No" or low ratings suggest that you are in discord with effective coaching practices. The process of seeking answers to specific concerns identified by your reaction to checklist items is an excellent way to obtain information most likely to help you become more effective as a coach.

Directions

Rate the degree to which you incorporate each of the following items into your coaching activities. Check "Yes" or "No" or use the following 5 point scale where: 1 = Strongly Disagree, 2 = Disagree, 3 = Neutral, 4 = Agree, 5 = Strongly Agree.

Item	Rating							
	Disagree						Agree	

Coaching Role

1. My primary purpose for coaching was to maximize the benefits of participation for <u>all</u> of the players.   (NO)   1   2   3   4   5   (YES)

2. The beneficial (individual techniques, knowledge, tactics, fitness, attitudes) and detrimental (time, money, injury, etc.) aspects of participation were constantly in mind during planning and coaching times.   (NO)   1   2   3   4   5   (YES)

3. I communicated through actions and words that I expected each player to succeed in improving his/her level of play.   (NO)   1   2   3   4   5   (YES)

Organization

4. I completed a plan for the season to guide the conduct of my practices.   (NO)   1   2   3   4   5   (YES)

[1] Modified from: Vogel, P.G. (1987). Post season evaluation: What did we accomplish? In V.D. Seefeldt (ed.) *Handbook for youth sport coaches*. Reston, VA: American Alliance for Health, Physical Education, Recreation and Dance.

5. Performance expectations set for the players were realistic and attainable.   (NO) 1 2 3 4 5 (YES)

6. I conscientiously decided which objectives must be emphasized in the pre-, early, mid-, and late season.   (NO) 1 2 3 4 5 (YES)

7. Objectives for developing my practices were drawn from those identified and sequenced from pre- to late season.   (NO) 1 2 3 4 5 (YES)

8. The amount of total practice time allocated to each season objective was sufficient.   (NO) 1 2 3 4 5 (YES)

9. My practices would be characterized by others as orderly, safe, businesslike, and enjoyable.   (NO) 1 2 3 4 5 (YES)

10. Objectives were broken down as necessary to allow players to achieve them in several small steps.   (NO) 1 2 3 4 5 (YES)

Knowledge of the Sport

11. I am familiar with the rationale for each season objective selected and clearly communicated to my players its purpose and described how it is to be executed.   (NO) 1 2 3 4 5 (YES)

12. I was able to identify the key elements of performance necessary for achievement of each season objective.   (NO) 1 2 3 4 5 (YES)

Effective Instruction

13. I clearly communicated (by word and/or example) the key elements to be learned for each objective included in a practice.   (NO) 1 2 3 4 5 (YES)

14. Practice on an objective was initiated with a rationale for why the objective is important.   (NO) 1 2 3 4 5 (YES)

15. Instruction did not continue without players' attention.   (NO) 1 2 3 4 5 (YES)

16. Practice on an objective provided each player with many practice trials and with specific and positive feedback.   (NO) 1 2 3 4 5 (YES)

17. During practice, I regularly grouped the players in accordance with their different practice needs on the season's objectives.   (NO) 1 2 3 4 5 (YES)

18. I used questions to determine if the players understood the objectives and instruction.   (NO) 1 2 3 4 5 (YES)

19. The players sensed a feeling of control over their own learning which resulted from my emphasis on clearly identifying what they needed to learn and then encouraging maximum effort.   (NO) 1 2 3 4 5 (YES)

20. My practices were pre-planned and clearly associated the use of learning activities, drills, and games with the season objectives.   (NO) 1 2 3 4 5 (YES)

21. I evaluated my practices and incorporated appropriate changes for subsequent practices.   (NO) 1 2 3 4 5 (YES)

Motivation

22. My practices and games resulted in the players achieving many of their goals for participation.   (NO) 1 2 3 4 5 (YES)

23. I taught the players how to realistically define success in terms of effort and self-improvement.   (NO) 1 2 3 4 5 (YES)

24. An expert would agree, upon observing my practices, that I use a positive, rather than negative, coaching approach.   (NO) 1 2 3 4 5 (YES)

Communication

25. There was no conflict between the verbal and non-verbal messages I communicated to my players.   (NO) 1 2 3 4 5 (YES)

26. I facilitated communication with the players by being a good listener.   (NO) 1 2 3 4 5 (YES)

27. Accepted behaviors (and consequences of misbehavior) were communicated to players at the beginning of the season.   (NO) 1 2 3 4 5 (YES)

28. Players were involved in developing or confirming team rules.   (NO) 1 2 3 4 5 (YES)

29. Enforcement of team rules was consistent for all players throughout the season.   (NO) 1 2 3 4 5 (YES)

Involvement with Parents

30. Parents of the players were a positive, rather than negative, influence on player's achievement of the season objectives.   (NO)   1   2   3   4   5   (YES)

31. I communicated to the parents my responsibilities and the responsibilities of parents and players to the team.   (NO)   1   2   3   4   5   (YES)

Conditioning

32. The intensity, duration, and frequency of the physical conditioning I used was appropriate for the age of the players.   (NO)   1   2   3   4   5   (YES)

33. I routinely used a systematic warm-up and cool-down prior to and after practices and games.   (NO)   1   2   3   4   5   (YES)

34. The physical conditioning aspects of my practices appropriately simulated the requirements of the sport.   (NO)   1   2   3   4   5   (YES)

Injury Prevention

35. I followed all recommended safety procedures for the use of equipment and facilities.   (NO)   1   2   3   4   5   (YES)

36. I did not use any contraindicated exercises in my practices.   (NO)   1   2   3   4   5   (YES)

Care of Common Injuries

37. I established and followed appropriate emergency procedures and simple first aid as needed.   (NO)   1   2   3   4   5   (YES)

38. I had a well stocked first aid kit at each practice and game, including players' medical history information and medical release forms.   (NO)   1   2   3   4   5   (YES)

Rehabilitation of Injuries

39. None of the players experienced a recurrence of an injury that could be attributed to inappropriate rehabilitation.   (NO)   1   2   3   4   5   (YES)

Evaluation

40. I completed an evaluation of player improvement on the season objectives.

    (NO)   1   2   3   4   5   (YES)

41. I identified the coaching actions (or inactions) that appeared most closely related to unmet player expectations.

    (NO)   1   2   3   4   5   (YES)

42. I made the changes in coaching action needed to improve my coaching effectiveness.

    (NO)   1   2   3   4   5   (YES)

21
Legal Liabilities

Bernard Patrick Maloy, J.D., M.S.A.
Vern Seefeldt, Ph.D.

QUESTIONS TO CONSIDER

- In terms of legal liability, what are the coaching duties?
- Against which risks to their players are coaches responsible for taking reasonable precautions?
- Do children who participate in youth sports assume the risk of their own injuries?
- What influence does the age and maturity of the athletes have upon the coach?
- Do coaches' legal responsibilities to their players extend beyond the field of play?
- Are coaches responsible for informing players, parents, and guardians about the risks and hazards inherent in sports?
- What legal responsibilities do coaches have to their players when coaches delegate duties to assistants?

INTRODUCTION

It is inevitable that the role of a coach is expanded beyond that of mere instructor or supervisor when it comes to working with youth sports. Because coaches are the most visible administrators to players, parents, and officials, they are expected to handle anything from correcting player rosters to picking up equipment on the field, from assuaging parents' feelings to arranging transportation for players. While these duties may tax the limits of a coach's patience, they remain very important areas of responsibility.

LEGAL DUTIES

Coaches are subject to certain terms of legal responsibility. However, it would be wrong to assume these legal duties were created by the courts to be imposed on the coaching profession. They are time-honored, recognized obligations inherent in the coaching profession. Thus, they should be termed coaching responsibilities (see Chapter 12). These are responsibilities expected of a coach regardless of pay and regardless of whether the coaching is performed for a school, a religious organization, or a youth sports association.

WHERE DOES COACHING RESPONSIBILITY BEGIN?

The primary responsibility of coaches is to know their players. In that regard it is always important to remember that young athletes are children first, athletes second. The degree of responsibility that coaches owe their teams is measured by the age and maturity of their players. The younger and more immature a player, the more responsibility a coach bears in regard to the instruction, supervision, and safety of that child (see Chapter 26). Additionally, the coach is expected to be aware of any physical or mental handicap that a player may have and must know how to recognize emergency symptoms requiring medical attention (see Chapter 24). A coach in youth sports must always bear in mind that:

- Nine-year-olds participating in organized sport activities for the first time require more instruction and attention than teenagers with playing experience
- A 10-year-old child should not be expected to behave, on or off the playing field, differently than other 10-year-old children
- All children with special needs or handicaps must be identified
- A plan for the emergency treatment of children with special needs and those who sustain injuries should be devised

As will be discussed, coaches do not have to guarantee the safety of their young players. However, they are responsible for taking reasonable precautions against all foreseeable risks that threaten their players. Coaches must realize that those precautions are not measured by what they thought was reasonable, but rather by what was reasonable according to the age and maturity of their players.

Do You Know How to Coach?

The volunteer coach is the backbone of many organized youth activities. Nevertheless, despite good intentions, some degrees of qualifications and certification are necessary for responsible coaching. Therefore, in addition to personal athletic experience and background, coaches should attend programs and seminars on the development of athletic skills, youth motivation, and emergency medical treatment. A coach's responsibility begins with an understanding of current methods of conditioning (Chapter 22), skill development (Section 2), and injury prevention and care (Chapters 24-26).

Coaches have certain responsibilities that they may not transfer to assistant coaches, parents, or league officials.

In many cases, a youth sports league or association offers classes, materials, or advice on skill development and injury prevention and care. Generally, those associations require some certification or recommendation regarding coaching background, skills, and experience before an applicant is permitted to coach youth sports. Coaches must avail themselves of instructional programs or other information helpful for coaching youth sports. In other words, coaches are responsible for their own incompetencies. A youth sports coach should create a competency checklist:

- Does the youth sports association certify its coaches?
- Does the association require coaches to attend coaching clinics and emergency medical programs?
- Do you know how to identify the necessary individual athletic skills based on size, weight, and age?
- Do you know of any agencies that help identify those skills?
- What steps should you take to become certified in first aid treatment?

Knowledge of your coaching incompetencies is the first step toward seeking a corrective solution.

Coaches must be able to recognize their limitations. Acknowledging that skills, youth motivation, and medical treatment may be different today than when you played is the first step toward becoming a responsible coach.

Where Do Your Coaching Duties Lie?

As noted, youth sports coaches are many things to their teams, parents and guardians, and supporters. Coaching responsibilities extend to areas beyond the baseball field. The responsibilities require the same effort and devotion and may include:

- league or team fund-raising activities
- assisting during registration periods
- talking to interested players and their parents about the league and its athletic and social goals
- providing or planning team transportation to and from practices and games
- attending league or association meetings

- buying, selecting, or maintaining equipment
- maintaining locker rooms and playing areas
- supervising players during pre-practice and post-practice periods

What Misconceptions Do Many Coaches Have?

There are two common misconceptions regarding youth sports. The first is that children participating generally assume the risk of their own injury; the second, that the role of the coach is severely limited by legal liability.

The legal defense of assumption of risk as it applies to sports is very specific. An athlete assumes the risk of injury from dangers inherent to the sport itself. In other words, it is recognized that injuries occur, especially in sports such as baseball (e.g., the collision of two players at a base, the injury of a baserunner resulting from a fielder's attempt to field the ball).

Many risks confronting athletes are not inherent to the sport, however; rather, they're the result of improper instruction, supervision, or equipment (e.g., protective equipment or pads that are defective or have been poorly fit, lack of instruction in athletic skills).

The interpretation of *assumption of risk* is complicated when it is applied to youth sports because young athletes require careful supervision regarding their own welfare. The concept that young athletes must assume the responsibility for their injuries sustained in practices or games must be contrasted with whether or not the coach or other adult supervisors were negligent in their instruction and supervision of the activity. In such a comparison it is unlikely that responsibility for *assumption of risk* will serve as a viable excuse.

When an injury occurs in youth sports, the coach's responsibility is considered a much greater factor than the assumption of risk by the player.

Fortunately, most coaches inherently understand the limitations involved in *assumption of risk*. The motivation for many youth coaches is the involvement of their own children in sports. And, like most parents, those coaches accept injury as a natural risk of the sport, but they will not tolerate an injury resulting from lack of proper skill development or poor equipment.

Youth sport coaches should concern themselves less with whether adhering to these responsibilities is good legal protection, and more with the thought that their actions represent the standards expected of youth sport coaches. Actually, the areas of expertise legally required of coaches can serve as measures of qualification and certification. Youth sport leagues and conferences realize that coaches must adhere to legal principles of liability not merely to protect the league and the coach from costly litigation but also to ensure that children continue to participate in athletics. It's very doubtful that parents would continue to support youth sports if it were plagued by poor coaching, lack of supervision, or poor medical treatment procedures. In short, these imposed responsibilities are good business practices for youth sports.

COACHING RESPONSIBILITIES

As a youth baseball coach you have many responsibilities beyond teaching your players to throw, field, and bat a baseball. Your coaching responsibilities are: providing proper instruction, providing reasonable supervision, warning of hazards and risks, providing competent personnel, preventing and caring for injuries, providing safe equipment, and selecting participants. Each of these responsibilities are discussed in subsequent sections.

Providing Proper Instruction

A coach must teach the physical skills and mental discipline or attitude required to play baseball (see Sections 1, 2, and 3). You must enhance the development of those skills while reducing the chance of injury. Specifically, volunteer coaches, who represent that they can teach the sport or activity, must be aware of the rules of safety and know how to teach the proper methods of conditioning. For example, when young players are injured, coaches should be prepared to competently assess whether:

- the conditioning or skill drills are realistic for players of young or immature years
- video, film, or written materials, in addition to on-the-field instruction, would improve instructional techniques

- the players are taught the correct way to wear equipment
- all the players, starters and substitutes, have been given the same amount of time, instruction, and practice on the correct methods of play, conditioning, and the rules
- conditioning techniques and skill drills are current
- coaching methods are accurately evaluated by the league
- parental comments and concerns have been integrated into the coaching instruction
- provision has been made in coaching instruction for learning-disabled and mentally or emotionally handicapped children who participate
- criticism or comments regarding coaching instruction are met with a positive response

The foregoing list consists of some expectations a parent or guardian has of a coach. While those expectations impact heavily on liability, they more accurately serve as guidelines by which youth sports coaches can evaluate their instruction. Again, a youth sports coach must remember that the age and immaturity of the players are key factors to instructional techniques. The coach must be sensitive to the outside environment in which a young player lives, as well as the sports environment created by the coach. Only then can you ensure a youngster the full benefit of your instruction (see Chapter 12).

Providing Reasonable Supervision

A coach is responsible for the reasonable supervision of the players. There is little question that this responsibility starts on the field of play during all practices and games. Again, the scope of this responsibility depends on the age and maturity of the players. The younger the player, the greater the degree of responsibility a coach must take for the player's safe supervision.

In youth sports, a coach's supervisory responsibility may extend to times and places other than the field. In some instances, this may include managing parents or guardians and supporters as well as the players and assistant coaches. A coach's checklist of potential supervisory functions should question:

- Is there a supervisor available for a reasonable time before and after practice?
- Have parents or guardians advised who will pick up their children after practices and games?
- Who is assigned to remain with the players until all have been called for, according to instructions provided by parents or guardians?
- How are parents or guardians notified of practice and game times, dates, and places?
- Who is responsible for player transportation to and from games?
- Are substitute players supervised off the field during games?
- Are players allowed off the field during practice for bathroom or other personal comforts? If so, how are those players supervised?

Many youth sports leagues or associations have a rule that coaches are responsible for the behavior of team parents, guardians, and fans. Such a rule becomes very important in those instances where parents believe their child has been slighted on the field during play, or off the field from lack of play. Coaches should recognize that their conduct can incite parents, guardians, and supporters. A coach must ask:

- Have team and league rules regarding parental involvement, the rules of play, and rules regarding team participation been communicated to parents and guardians?
- Do parents and guardians know my coaching philosophy and team goals?
- Have the team and parents and guardians been notified that only the coach is permitted to discuss a decision with a referee?

The coach's role in supervision of the baseball field can be eased by holding a parents' orientation meeting at the start of the season (see Chapter 13). The parents have a right to know what to expect of the coach. Also, the meeting prepares parents to become actively involved with other parents in stopping any unruly conduct. Again, the supervisory responsibility starts with coaches who conduct themselves in the spirit of good sportsmanship. It also includes a coach's support of game officials in order to defuse angry parents, guardians, supporters, or players.

Warning About Hazards and Risks

A coach is responsible for informing players, parents, and guardians about the risks and hazards inherent to baseball. Obviously, it's not expected that coaches will dissuade parents and guardians from permitting their youngsters to participate. By the same token, a coach's experience and knowledge helps to assure parents and guardians that the greatest care possible will be taken for the well-being of their children.

The age and maturity of the players play a major role in the degree of risk from playing baseball. Older, more experienced children may face a greater risk of injury from baseball simply due to the more sophisticated style of play. However, those children and their parents or guardians already should be fairly well-versed in the risks of baseball. Therefore, they don't need the same information and assurances as parents and guardians whose children are younger and have never participated.

The coach must inform athletes and parents of the potential dangers inherent in playing youth baseball.

The youth league or association may provide information regarding sports hazards, but the responsibility to warn parents and athletes remains a very important coaching duty (see Chapter 26). Therefore, a coach would be well-served to provide parents, guardians, and players with as much information and materials as possible regarding baseball at registration, as well as during the season. The coach must be prepared to instruct or advise:

- how many injuries his or her teams with similar age and experience have suffered, and what types of injuries occurred
- what types of equipment, clothing, or shoes are not recommended or permitted for play
- how equipment should properly fit
- what written, video, or audio materials are available that will instruct parents and guardians about the sport and its risks
- what style, conduct, or manner of play is to be avoided due to the likelihood of injury to the player or an opponent
- whether the field and facilities have been inspected for hazards and determined to be safe for play

Hosting a parents' orientation meeting prior to the first game is an excellent way to describe your role in the prevention and care of their children's injuries.

Providing Competent Personnel

We've already examined the coach's responsibility to provide quality instruction. Also, we have examined many of the attendant roles and duties that coaches must provide with that instruction. In many cases, the sheer numbers of players and responsibilities demand that a coach have some assistance. It is not unusual for a coach to delegate some of those coaching or supervisory duties to assistant coaches or parents (see Supplement 13-7). However, the coach must ensure that the people who are assisting are competent. Obviously, having a responsible coach is of little value if the players are subject to the directions of incompetent assistants. Therefore, in a coach's absence, an assistant coach or aide must be able to provide the same responsible instruction and supervision as the players and parents expect from the head coach. It is wise, then, for a coach to learn:

- whether the league or association certifies assistant coaches
- what policies the league or association has regarding the use of parents for supervision, transportation, or instruction
- whether assistant coaches have any hidden past regarding child abuse, or other conduct that constitutes a threat to children
- whether there is any reason to suspect an assistant's or aide's coaching competency
- whether teenagers may be qualified as assistants with coaching and supervisory duties

It is a coach's responsibility to determine whether assistant coaches and team aides are qualified to step into the coach's shoes.

Preventing and Caring for Injuries

There are few areas that demand as much attention as the prevention and care of injuries (see Chapters 24, 25, and 26). It is not uncommon to find youth sports programs conducting baseball practices without qualified medical personnel or knowledgeable athletic trainers readily available. In those instances, the first attendant to an injured player is usually the coach or teammates. The coach's responsibility is to recognize when immediate medical treatment is required and to ensure that assistant coaches and teammates do not attempt to touch, move, or help the injured player. Obviously, the care of injuries can be a very confusing task.

Many problems in the initial care of athletic injuries might be solved if coaches were required to qualify as emergency medical technicians, or to have some type of comparable training in first aid and health care. In the absence of those qualifications, however, coaches must use their best discretion, based on experience. Obviously, those deficiencies are compounded in youth sports where most of the coaches are volunteers.

In addition to recognizing when emergency medical help is needed, a coach must be able to recognize symptoms of ongoing problems. If a player has a disease, diabetes for instance, the coach has the responsibility for checking with the player's parents about medication, learning how to recognize the symptoms of shock or deficiency, and what type of emergency treatment to request.

A coach must also be aware of the effects a conditioning program may have on players (see Chapter 22). For instance, if practices are conducted during hot weather, a coach should provide ample water (see Chapter 23), change the time of practice to early morning or late afternoon, learn the symptoms of heat stroke or exhaustion, and learn how to provide for immediate care (see Chapter 24).

It's impossible to categorize all the areas of concern for injuries that a coach may face. However, there are precautions that you can take to ensure that your responsibilities have been reasonably met:

- Attend league-sponsored programs dealing with athletic injuries
- Check with local health authorities, local hospitals, and coaching associations to learn about the availability of emergency medical care
- Implement a plan for the immediate notification of parents or guardians in case their child is seriously injured
- Do not attempt unfamiliar care without emergency medical competency or ability

- Identify players with specific medical handicaps before the season and prepare reasonable emergency plans in case of sudden illness
- Do not permit players who have suffered injuries requiring medical attention to play or participate until their return to practice and competition has been approved by a physician
- Notify parents or guardians of any minor injuries occurring to, or complaints by, their children

It is wise to document the circumstances of a serious injury (see Chapter 24). In many cases, a written report shows that coaches have reasonably met their responsibility. Such a report is also helpful to medical personnel in the subsequent treatment of an injury. The documentation should include:

- a record of all facts surrounding the injury including who, when, and where the injury occurred and the injured player's responses
- a list and description of the equipment involved, if any
- a list of those who witnessed the injury
- a record of actions taken in response to the injury prior to the arrival of medical personnel

When completed, provide copies of the injury report to the attending physician, the medical response personnel, and the league or association. Be sure to keep a copy for your own files.

Providing Equipment

A coach must take reasonable care to provide the team with proper and safe equipment (see Supplement 9-6). You should know the various types and brands of equipment, master the proper maintenance procedures, and learn to outfit players properly and safely. Generally, you are not responsible for equipment defects unless you're directly involved in the manufacture of equipment. However, you are expected to know whether or not the proper equipment is being used, or if it is defective, and to ensure that defective equipment is not distributed to players. A coach must take reasonable care to:

- select or recommend the proper equipment for the sport

- select or recommend specific types of equipment for specific uses
- properly fit players
- verify that old equipment has been properly reconditioned or recertified for use
- disallow players who are not properly equipped and dressed to participate in practices or games
- have knowledge of league or association rules regarding proper dress and equipment
- instruct players and parents on the proper maintenance of sports equipment in their possession
- utilize a written inventory for reporting and tracking the repair of damaged equipment
- become aware of manufacturers' recommendations and warnings

Selecting Participants

A baseball coach is obligated to protect the health and safety of players during practices and games. The potential for injuries to occur in baseball is reduced when players are matched according to size, age, and playing experience. Injuries that occur when players are mismatched in terms of body size and playing experience are more likely to be viewed as the result of irresponsible teaching and supervision rather than as an inherent risk of playing baseball.

Coaches should protect players by following these guidelines:

- Never permit an injured athlete to compete in practices and games
- Never allow athletes who are out of condition to participate in drills, scrimmages, or games
- Never place players in drills, scrimmages, or games in which there is the potential for mismatches in physical conditioning, chronological age, and/or skill level.

SUMMARY

A youth sports coach cannot guarantee a child's safety. Legally, a coach is responsible for reasonably foreseeing risks and hazards to the players.

For example, if a youth sports group uses a field that has permanent benches installed near the foul lines, or if the field is full of holes or broken glass, a coach should recognize the foreseeable risks to players and supervise, instruct, and/or warn of those dangers.

Some consider this foreseeability factor as a legal precept. However, it is predicated on knowledge and experience of baseball. Therefore, its true application is not in legal theory but in the real world of sports.

The curricular objectives for youth sports coaches are defined in the following reference: *Guidelines for Coaching Education: Youth Sports*, National Association for Sport and Physical Education, 1986. The Guidelines identify the competencies that coaches of young athletes should possess or acquire. The competencies are listed under five categories of content within the general title of "Scientific Bases of Coaching." An outline of the content follows:

Curricular Objectives for Youth Sport Coaches

Scientific Bases of Coaching

A. *Medical-Legal Aspects of Coaching*

Every young athlete should be provided a safe and healthful environment in which to participate. The coach should have basic knowledge and skills in the prevention of athletic injuries, and basic knowledge of first aid.

Every Youth Sports Coach Should:

1. Demonstrate knowledge and skill in the prevention and care of injuries generally associated with participation in athletics.
2. Be able to plan and coordinate procedures for the emergency care of athletes.
3. Be knowledgeable about the legal responsibilities of coaching, including insurance coverage for the coach and athlete.
4. Recognize and insist on safe playing conditions and the proper use of protective equipment.
5. Be able to provide young athletes with basic information about injury prevention, injury reporting, and sources of medical care.

B. *Training and Conditioning of Young Athletes*

Every youth sport athlete should receive appropriate physical conditioning for sports participation. The coach should use acceptable procedures in their training and conditioning programs.

Every Youth Sports Coach Should:

1. Be able to demonstrate the basic knowledges and techniques in the training and conditioning of athletes.
2. Recognize the developmental capabilities of young athletes and adjust training and conditioning programs to meet these capabilities.
3. Know the effects of the environmental conditions (e.g., heat, cold, humidity, air quality) on young athletes and adjust practice and games accordingly.
4. Be able to recognize the various indications of over-training, which may result in injury and/or staleness in athletes, and be able to modify programs to overcome these consequences.

C. Psychological Aspects of Coaching

A positive social and emotional environment should be created for young athletes. The coach should recognize and understand the developmental nature of the young athlete's motivation for sport competition and adjust his/her expectations accordingly.

Every Youth Sports Coach Should:

1. Subscribe to a philosophy that emphasizes the personal growth of individuals by encouraging and rewarding achievement of personal goals and demonstration of effort, as opposed to overemphasis on winning.
2. Demonstrate appropriate behavior of young athletes by maintaining emotional control and demonstrating respect to athletes, officials, and fellow coaches.
3. Demonstrate effective communication skills such as those needed to provide appropriate feedback, use a positive approach, motivate athletes, and demonstrate proper listening skills.
4. Emphasize and encourage discussion of matters concerning the display of sportsmanship in competitive and noncompetitive situations.
5. Be sufficiently familiar with the principles of motivation, including goal setting and reinforcement, in order to apply them in constructive ways.
6. Be able to structure practice and competitive situations to reduce undue stress, and/or to

teach young athletes how to reduce any undue stress they experience related to performance.

D. Growth, Development, and Learning of Youth Athletes

Youth athletes should have positive learning experiences. The coach should have a knowledge of basic learning principles and consider the influence of developmental level on the athlete's performance.

Every Youth Sports Coach Should:

1. Recognize the physical and cognitive changes that occur as children develop and how these changes influence their ability to learn sports skills.
2. Concentrate on the development of fundamental motor and cognitive skills that lead to improvement of specific sports skills.
3. Understand the physical and cognitive differences manifested by early and late maturers.

E. Techniques of Coaching Young Athletes

Every young athlete should have the opportunity to participate regularly in a sport of his/her choosing. The coach should provide guidance for successful learning and performance of specific sport techniques, based on the maturity level or proficiency of the athlete.

Every Youth Sports Coach Should:

1. Know the key elements of sport principles and technical skills and the various teaching styles that can be used to introduce and refine them.
2. Recognize that young athletes learn at different rates and accommodate these differences by flexibility in teaching styles.
3. Be able to organize and conduct practices throughout the season in order to provide maximal learning.
4. Be able to select appropriate skills and drills, and analyze errors in performance.
5. Be able to provide challenging but safe and successful experiences for young athletes by making appropriate modifications during participation.
6. Understand why rules and equipment should be modified for children's sports.

Implementation

These guidelines are considered the minimum levels toward which youth sport coaching education programs should strive. To cover the topics of Sections A to D requires at least three hours of clinic time plus additional home study. Another three hours should be devoted to the techniques of coaching session.

Presentations developed for the scientific bases of coaching (Sections A to D) should be as sport specific as possible. The frequent use of audiovisual aids such as videotapes, films, overheads, and slides is helpful. Presentations should be short, with numerous practical examples as well as opportunities for practical exercises and questions. Having materials (books, pamphlets, self study exams, etc.) available for the coaches to study either prior to or following the clinic is essential for adequate coverage of the topics.

For additional information about youth sport coaching education materials and organizations, write the Youth Sports Coalition Steering Committee, 1900 Association Drive, Reston, VA 22091.

REFERENCES

Berry, R., & Wong, G. (1986). *Law and business of the sports industries.* (Vol. II, pp. 227-302, 320-341). Dover, MA: Auburn House.

Clement, A. (1988). *Law in sport and physical activity.* (pp. 27-61). Indianapolis, IN: Benchmark Press.

Maloy, B. (1988). *Law in sports: Liability cases in management and administration.* Indianapolis, IN: Benchmark Press.

National Association for Sport and Physical Education. (1986) Guidelines for Coaching Education: Youth Sports, Reston, VA.

Responsibility is also Part of the Game. 13 *Trial,* 22-25, January, 1977.

Schubert, G. et al (1986). *Sports law.* (pp. 220-231). St. Paul, MN: West Publishing Co.

Seefeldt, V. (1985). Legal liability. In P. Vogel & K. Blase (Eds.), *AHAUS associate coaches manual: Fundamentals of coaching youth ice hockey.* (pp. 167-174). East Lansing, MI: Institute for the Study of Youth Sports.

Wong, G. (1988). *Essentials of amateur sports law.* (pp. 336-350). Dover, MA: Auburn House Publishing Co.

Section IV
Training and Conditioning the Youth Baseball Player

22
Conditioning Youth Baseball Players

Jean Foley, Ph.D.
Paul Vogel, Ph.D.
Eugene W. Brown, Ph.D.
Karen Garchow, M.A.

QUESTIONS TO CONSIDER

- What are the energy production systems and how important are they to performance in baseball?
- What are muscular strength, power, endurance, and flexibility and how important are they to performance in baseball?
- What are the five principles of training that should be used when conditioning youth baseball players?
- What are interval training, circuit training, and weight training and how can they be used to enhance the conditioning of your athletes?

INTRODUCTION

Aerobics, anaerobics, strength, power, and endurance are some of the many terms that may lend confusion to your understanding of sport conditioning. The goals of this chapter are to provide you with an understanding of the basic principles of conditioning and how these principles apply to baseball. The information will provide you with a more detailed understanding of the process involved in conditioning so that you can appropriately integrate these concepts into your coaching.

Sport conditioning is the participation in physical activity, intended to enhance the energy production and muscular systems of the body, which may supplement and improve the performance of learned sport skills in future play.

ENERGY PRODUCTION SYSTEMS

Anyone who has played or watched baseball knows that much energy is required to participate in the game. Sport scientists have discovered that the body can produce energy for physical activity by two different systems—

the aerobic system and the anaerobic system. Muscle cells, which use the energy, can only store enough reserves for a few seconds of all-out exercise. When this immediate energy supply is used up, new energy is generated by one of these two energy "refill" systems.

Aerobic System

The aerobic system is sometimes called the "endurance" system. In this system, food, the body's fuel, is converted into energy in the presence of oxygen. The aerobic system functions during long-duration, low-intensity exercise. This type of activity allows the body plenty of time to react effectively to the energy needs of the working muscle.

The aerobic system is very efficient because it converts fuel into energy with relatively little waste and produces little unnecessary heat. The aerobic system can function for extended periods of time because it can produce energy from fats, carbohydrates, and protein.

Protein is not a major source of energy for exercise except in cases of extreme starvation.

Carbohydrates are stored in a limited supply in the muscles and liver, and can be used for both aerobic and anaerobic work.

Fats can be used only by the aerobic system. The virtually unlimited supply of this fuel, stored as adipose tissue or fat, is the basis for the long-term functioning of the aerobic system.

In baseball, conditioning the aerobic system is a necessary base for energy system conditioning. The reasons for this are twofold:

1. Baseball has an endurance component.

The baseball player with a well-conditioned aerobic system is not as susceptible to fatigue toward the end of a game. The delayed onset of fatigue in an aerobically fit athlete can also be a factor in determining how much high quality work can be accomplished during lengthy practice sessions and games.

2. The body learns to "spare" carbohydrates.

As the aerobic system is trained, the body learns to use more fat for fuel and to conserve carbohydrates for high-intensity (anaerobic) activities.

Anaerobic System

High-speed or sprint-type activities require a refilling of the muscle cells' energy supplies at a faster rate than is possible by the aerobic system. In this situation, energy production switches over to a special, faster operating system that converts carbohydrates into energy without using oxygen. This system is called anaerobic, meaning "without oxygen." As with any emergency procedure, there are trade-offs that must be made. In order to gain the advantage of quicker replenishment of energy supplies, the anaerobic system suffers two limitations:

1. Reduced energy yield.

For each sugar (carbohydrate) unit consumed, the anaerobic system can produce only three basic energy units. On the other hand, the aerobic system can produce 39 energy units from each sugar unit. Therefore, the aerobic system yields 13 times more energy (per fuel unit utilized) than the anaerobic system.

2. Lactic-acid build-up.

The anaerobic system produces a byproduct called lactic acid that is not produced by the aerobic system. This chemical quickly builds up in fast-working muscles, causing temporary fatigue, discomfort, and impaired performance. The only way the body can get rid of lactic acid is to slow down and use the aerobic system to convert the lactic acid into usable fuel.

The anaerobic system can produce energy at high speed for about 30 to 90 seconds or at a moderate speed for about 90 seconds to three minutes before the body is forced to slow down so it can switch to the aerobic system. After a recovery period, the anaerobic system can be turned on again to give another short burst of high-speed work. This alternating of sprint work and recovery periods can be continued only until the body's stores of carbohydrates are used up or until the lactic acid removal system can no longer keep up with the rate of anaerobic work.

The energy production system responds to anaerobic training in three major ways:

1. By learning to tolerate larger amounts of lactic acid

The body physiologically adapts to tolerate larger amounts of lactic acid. Therefore, high-intensity work can be maintained for longer periods of time.

2. By reducing the recovery period

The body adapts by reducing the recovery time required before the anaerobic system can be used again.

3. By increasing the rate at which the anaerobic system can operate

Training adaptations increase the speed at which the system can produce energy.

A summary of the two energy production systems is presented in Figure 22-1.

USE OF THE ENERGY SYSTEMS IN BASEBALL

Now that the basic principles of the energy production systems have been presented, let's look at the sport of baseball and determine where its requirements fit on the energy scale from aerobic to anaerobic. In analyzing the relative importance of the two energy systems in baseball, the main concept to keep in mind is that performance time and effort determine the extent to which the aerobic, anaerobic, or both systems are called upon.

Baseball generally can be considered a sport that places a relatively high demand on the anaerobic system and a moderate demand on the aerobic system. The anaerobic system is used during high-intensity work such as sprinting

Energy Production Systems	Characteristics
Aerobic	• produces energy from fuel with oxygen • can use fats, carbohydrates, or protein for fuel • high energy yield per fuel unit • no lactic acid produced • slow rate of energy production
Anaerobic	• produces energy from fuel without oxygen • can only use carbohydrates for fuel • low energy yield per fuel unit • produces lactic acid as a byproduct • fast rate of energy production

Figure 22-1. Energy production summary.

around the bases. The aerobic system is used during recovery between the short bursts of activity and during longer periods of low-intensity work. Thus, it is important to condition both of these energy systems to be prepared best for the various demands of baseball.

MUSCULAR SYSTEM

In addition to requiring energy, baseball calls upon the muscles to produce forces for various activities. Throwing the ball requires upper body strength while exploding from the batter's box requires powerful legs.

Muscles can produce force only by shortening or contracting. All muscle forces, therefore, are pulling forces and not pushing forces. For example, if you forcefully bend (flex) your knee, the muscles in the back of the thigh (hamstrings) are active. On the other hand, forcefully straightening (extension) the knee results in contraction of the muscles in the front of the thigh (quadriceps). Almost all muscles in the body operate in this paired fashion. As one muscle (or muscle group) shortens to pull a body part in a particular direction, the paired muscle (or muscle group) relaxes and allows the movement to take place. To cause movement in the opposite direction, the muscles simply reverse their roles. If it is desirable to hold a body part in a fixed position, both muscles in the pair exert force to stabilize the joint.

When planning to condition the muscular system for baseball, several factors need to be addressed. In addition to the "muscle pair" concept, the components of muscular power, endurance, and flexibility; age and ability level of the players; and the specific muscular needs for participation in baseball must be carefully considered. These factors are covered in the sections that follow.

Muscular Power

The force that a muscle can apply is called muscular strength. In baseball, many of the movements not only require large muscular forces, but these forces must be exerted during short periods of time. This concept of rate of application of muscular force is called muscular power.

Muscular Endurance

Power is the high-intensity component of muscular conditioning. There is also a low-intensity aspect, the muscular endurance component. Muscular endurance refers to the ability of a muscle to exert a sub-maximal force for a prolonged period of time.

Scientists have shown that there are actually different types of muscle fibers within a muscle. Some of these fibers, called fast-twitch or white fibers, are used primarily for brief, powerful muscular movements. Other fibers, called slow-twitch or red fibers, are mainly used for longer, low-intensity movements. As with the aerobic and anaerobic energy systems, the power and endurance components of the muscular system require different types of conditioning.

Flexibility

Flexibility refers to the range of motion of a joint or the range through which the muscle groups can move the bones of a joint without causing injury.

Stretching exercises, used as part of a conditioning program to maintain or increase flexibility, are often ignored by coaches and athletes. However, flexibility exercises are an important component of a baseball conditioning program. They may reduce the occurrence of certain injuries and enhance the performance of certain techniques.

• Reducing injury potential

When muscles are worked hard, there is a temporary breakdown in their tissue. This breakdown is quickly repaired, but the muscle fibers become shortened unless they are stretched. A shortened, inflexible muscle on one side of the joint won't be able to readily stretch when its muscle pair on the opposite side of the joint fully contracts. The result may be a muscle tear (strain) or damage to the connective tissues of the joint (sprain). Flexibility exercises may reduce the occurrence of these types of injuries.

• Enhancing performance

Lack of flexibility may inhibit or prevent the performance of certain techniques. For example, limited trunk flexibility may retard a player's ability to make a long infield throw. This is only one of the many examples of the influence of flexibility on performance.

USE OF THE MUSCULAR SYSTEM IN BASEBALL

Picture again a typical game of baseball. How would you rate the three muscular factors of power, endurance, and flexibility in terms of their importance to successful performance? (See Figure 22-2.) Clearly, most of the actions in baseball can be characterized as powerful movements. Along with powerful, high-force actions comes a high risk of injury, so flexibility should also be a high priority in conditioning for baseball. Finally, for the same reasons aerobic fitness is necessary in conditioning the energy systems for baseball, a muscular endurance base is required by the repetitive nature of the movements (such as throwing).

Five Principles of Training

Now that we have examined conditioning, we can turn to the problem of how to develop programs to promote the kind of conditioning needed for baseball.

You should now have a basic knowledge of the underlying concepts of conditioning. The contrasts between the aerobic and anaerobic ends of the energy production continuum have been described. Three critical aspects of the muscular system continuum (power, endurance, and flexibility) have been explained. Both the energy production systems and the muscular system have been analyzed in relation to their specific applications to baseball. Now we come to the practical application of this information. How can you as a coach use the discoveries of the sport scientists to develop better baseball players?

The following five principles of training should be used as guidelines for conditioning both the energy production and muscular systems.

1. Warm-Up/Cool-Down

Before beginning a training session or game, use jogging, calisthenics, baseball-specific exercises, and stretching to prepare the body for more strenuous activity. A program for accom-

Where should the various positions in baseball be placed?

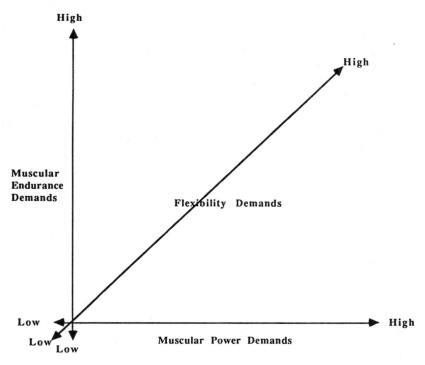

Figure 22-2. Graph showing the continuum of the muscular system demands.

plishing this goal, as well as cooling down the body after strenuous exercise, is outlined in Supplement 22-1. Warm-up activities increase the breathing rate, heart rate, and muscle temperature to exercise levels. Warm-up also causes cartilage pads in the joints to absorb fluids, thereby increasing their shock-absorbing capabilities. It is a period in which the athlete becomes more aware of his/her surroundings (the dugout, field, bleachers, etc.) and gradually reacquainted with the demands of more vigorous activity to follow. Providing the opportunity for your athletes to become aware of their surroundings and sensitive to the demands of the sport are important factors in reducing the potential for injury.

Proper warm-up can thus improve performance and reduce the likelihood of injury to the athlete. Note that the warm-up should not be used as a conditioning period. Having your players exercise too hard during warm-ups defeats the purpose of this period and may cause, rather than prevent, injuries. Stretching exercises are appropriate after a warm-up.

As the age of the athlete group increases, a greater amount of time is needed to warm-up for exercises. Seven-year-olds may only need five minutes to warm up, whereas 18-year-olds may need as much as 10 to 15 minutes of warm-up exercises. It is, however, important to include a warm-up interval before practices and games even with the youngest athletes because this proper approach to training is more likely to persist as they grow older.

After a workout session or game, the body should be cooled down. This process should include light, aerobic activity (e.g., jogging) to help the body clear out any remaining lactic acid from the muscles and to reduce the pooling of blood in the extremities. This will reduce soreness and speed the recovery process in preparation for the next day's activities. The cool-down should also be followed by stretching exercises, as emphasized earlier, to help maintain flexibility.

2. Overload

In order to cause a change to take place in the energy production and muscular systems, a stress must be applied to these systems. Repeatedly demanding more than usual of a bodily system causes the system to respond by changing to a state in which it can more easily handle that stress. Overload does not mean placing an impossibly heavy work load on the system, but rather, asking the system to work harder than it is normally accustomed to doing, without reaching a work load at which injury may occur.

Regulation of the overload is the basis of all conditioning programs.

There are five factors that can be manipulated to produce an exercise overload within a workout:

● *Load*

This is the resistance to muscular force. It can be the body, a body part, or any object, such as a weight, which is to be moved. Systematic variation of resistance (load) can be used to create an exercise overload to enhance the development of muscular strength.

● *Repetitions*

This is the number of times muscular force is applied in moving a load. Conditioning of the aerobic energy-production system and enhanced muscular endurance result from progressively increasing the number of repetitions of muscular contraction.

● *Duration*

This is the length of time muscular force is applied in performing a set (bout) of repetitions. Similar to a systematic increase in repetitions, increasing duration of exercise can be used to enhance the aerobic energy-production system and muscular endurance.

● *Frequency*

The rate of exercise (number of repetitions for a given time unit) is the frequency. As frequency increases, exercises shift from having a conditioning effect on the aerobic energy-production system and muscular endurance to having a conditioning effect on the anaerobic energy-production system and muscular power.

● *Rest*

The recovery interval between bouts of exercise, during which a muscle or muscle group is

moderately inactive to inactive, is the rest period.* Note that rest for the anaerobic system also may occur when the frequency of exercise is reduced so the demands of the exercise are placed upon the aerobic system.

3. Progression

The overload principle must be applied in progressive stages. Conditioning must start with an exercise intensity the body can handle, allowing time for recovery from the physical stress before progressing to an increased work level. Overloading your athletes too rapidly or failing to allow sufficient time for them to recover between workouts can cause injury or illness rather than enhance their fitness.

A good example to keep in mind is the method by which muscles get stronger. A training overload actually causes a temporary breakdown of the muscle fibers, which are then repaired to an even stronger state. If the muscles are overloaded again before the repair period is over, the result may be further damage instead of adaptation. Coaches should be familiar with the signs of overtraining as outlined in Chapter 21 and should monitor their athletes closely to make sure they are progressing at a rate their bodies can handle.

4. Specificity

In order to activate the energy production systems, the muscular system must also be activated. Even though this relationship exists, it is important to carefully consider the desired nature of conditioning when selecting physical activity to achieve these goals.

Physical exercises have specific conditioning effects. Stretching the hip joints will have little, if any, influence on increasing the power of the muscles that move these joints. Exercises to strengthen the calf muscles will not increase the strength of the stomach muscles. Similarly, a well-conditioned gymnast is not likely to possess the type of fitness required for baseball. Thus, when planning a conditioning program, it is important to first assess the demands of baseball on your players in order to select exercises

---

*Longer rests are required for short, high-intensity exercise bouts. Shorter rests are required for long, low-intensity exercise bouts.

and manipulate the overload factors to help condition your players to meet these specific demands.

The specific components of the energy and muscular systems can be conditioned by application of the following general guidelines to overload these systems. However, these guidelines must be applied in conditioning the energy and muscular systems associated with the specific demands of baseball.

Training the Energy Production Systems

- Aerobic system—use endurance activities involving moderate exercise intensity of large body segments or the whole body. Some examples include jogging around the bases or to the outfield fence.
- Anaerobic system—use "sprint" type activities involving very intense exercise of large body segments or the whole body. In contrast to aerobic training, in anaerobic training the distance is reduced and intensity or effort increased.

Training the Muscular System

- Power—use exercises, by specific muscle groups, involving the rapid application of relatively large forces and few repetitions.
- Endurance—use exercises, by specific muscle groups, involving the application of relatively small forces and many repetitions.
- Flexibility—use slow and sustained (six to 30 seconds) stretching of specific muscle groups to the point of slight discomfort. Don't bounce!

5. Reversibility

It is not enough to plan and carry out a developmental conditioning program. Once an athlete's body attains a certain fitness level, a maintenance program is necessary to prevent the conditioning benefits from being lost.

Studies on athletes have shown that even starting players will experience a decrease in fitness level during the competitive season unless provisions are made to maintain conditioning throughout the season. The maintenance program does not have to be as frequent or as intense as the build-up program, but without a minimal program of this type, the hard-earned fitness will gradually be lost.

METHODS FOR CONDITIONING

Regulation of the exercise overload is the basis for all conditioning programs. As previously stated, this can be accomplished by manipulating the factors of load, repetition, duration, frequency, and rest. There are three distinct training methods that can be used to effectively manipulate these factors to enhance conditioning. These methods are *interval training, circuit training,* and *weight training.*

1. Interval Training

This type of training was first used in training runners. Interval training, however, has been used in many sports, including baseball. Interval training involves a period of vigorous exercise followed by a recovery period. It functions by using aerobic and anaerobic activities to condition the energy production systems. By gradually increasing the duration, intensity, and number of exercise bouts and by decreasing the rest interval between bouts, an overload can be achieved.

Interval training can be adapted to baseball by alternating bouts of intense practice on basic skills, such as throwing or base stealing, with recovery periods. In fact, a series of practice sessions can be structured with an interval training basis. The first session would consist of relatively low-intensity exercises of short duration with relatively long rest intervals; whereas, in subsequent practice sessions, the exercise intensity and duration would be increased and the number and duration of rest intervals would be decreased. It should be noted that in interval training, rest periods can be used for rest, water breaks, strategy sessions, team organization, and light aerobic activity.

The specific conditioning components enhanced by an interval training program depend upon the nature of the exercises included in the program. A systematic interval training program can improve the energy production systems (aerobic and anaerobic) as well as the strength and endurance of specific muscle groups that are exercised. A year-round interval training program for highly skilled and motivated players who are 14 years of age or older is included in Supplement 22-2.

2. Circuit Training

This type of training involves participation in a variety of activities in rapid succession. These activities are conducted at various locations (stations) around the basketball court. The team is divided so that an equal number of players are at each station. When the circuit begins, all players attempt to perform their best at the tasks assigned to each station within a set time. Successive stations should differ in the demand they place on the body. For example, an intense arm exercise should not be followed by a throwing/pitching drill. Recovery occurs as the groups rotate, within a specified time interval, to the next station and as subsequent stations differ in their demands upon the body.

In circuit training an exercise overload is produced by:

- increasing the number of stations in the circuit
- increasing the number of repetitions or work intensity at one or more stations
- increasing the time for exercise at each station
- increasing the number of times the circuit is completed
- decreasing the recovery period between stations

The variety of activities that can be included in a circuit provides the opportunity to be flexible in creating different and specific exercise overloads as well as simultaneously enhancing skill. Supplement 22-3 contains an example of a baseball training circuit and recording form, which can be photocopied as is, as well as a blank form upon which you can implement your own training circuit to meet the specific needs of your players.

3. Weight Training

This type of training involves the lifting of weights to produce an exercise overload. In weight training, a variety of sub-maximal lifts are performed to produce increased strength, power, and endurance in the specific muscle groups that are exercised. In general, weight training involves applying the "Five Principles of Training" to produce increases in muscular strength.

Following the "Five Principles of Training,"

the first part of a weight training routine is the warm-up and stretching program. The weight resistance is the overload, which is increased in a progression as the athlete's workout record indicates gains in strength. Analysis of the strength requirements of baseball (specificity) has resulted in the list of exercises outlined in Table 22-5s. The cool-down and post-lifting stretching routine decreases muscle soreness and prevents loss of flexibility. Finally, once strength gains are achieved, the maintenance program must be used to avoid reversal of strength increases acquired during the developmental program.

In weight training, an exercise overload can be produced by varying the:

- exercise load
- number of repetitions per set
- frequency of exercise during each set
- number of sets
- length of rest interval between exercise sets

The exercise load determines the number of repetitions of an exercise an athlete can perform during each set. Generally, no fewer than eight repetitions per set of each exercise are recommended when attempting to increase muscular strength for baseball. However, if increased muscular endurance is the goal of a particular weight training exercise, (a) the load should be decreased to permit a much greater number of repetitions, (b) the number of sets should be increased to three or more, and (c) the rest intervals between sets should be decreased. On the other hand, if increase in muscular power is the goal, this can be achieved by rapidly and repeatedly lifting a relatively heavy load eight to 12 repetitions per set.

It should be noted that it is possible to train some muscle groups to increase power and others to increase endurance. The degree to which either component increases depends upon the specific nature of the overload condition.

Several factors should be carefully considered before engaging your players in a weight training program. These factors include:

- ### Age of the athletes

A weight training program for baseball is not recommended for players under 14 years of age.

- **Level of interest**

  A weight training program is not an essential element for participants in a recreational league. However, a weight training program can be beneficial to highly skilled players who are interested in participating in a very competitive league.

- **Availability of facilities and equipment**

  Sites and equipment for weight training may not be accessible. Before encouraging your athletes to participate in a weight training program, some investigation of availability is needed.

- **Availability of qualified adults**

  Before encouraging your players to participate in a particular weight training program, a qualified adult must be available to supervise the weight room and to provide instruction in proper spotting and performance techniques for each of the suggested exercises.

  Because of the great variety of weight training equipment and the availability of many books and guides to weight training, only general guidelines are presented here. A suggested program of weight training exercises appropriate for the highly skilled baseball player who is 14 years of age or older is included in Supplement 22-2. These exercises can be done using either free weights or weight machines. The guidelines given cover training schedules and how to fit a weight training program into the overall plan of the season. Specific techniques and explanations of weight training exercises can be found in manuals available in most local bookstores. Some references are listed in Supplement 22-2.

ECONOMICAL TRAINING

The relative importance of conditioning for baseball must be put into perspective with the importance of meeting the cognitive, psychosocial, strategy, and sport techniques needs of your players. As a baseball coach, you must address all of these needs, to varying degrees, during practices and games. However, because of the limited amount of time available to meet the needs of your players, whenever possible, you should plan activities that simultaneously meet

needs in more than one area. This approach is referred to as economical training. If practice sessions are carefully planned, it is possible to devise activities that simultaneously meet needs in more than one area. For example, the intensity, duration, and structure of a bunting drill could be organized to enhance components of conditioning and strategy, as well as techniques of fielding.

It is easier to get 14-year-olds in condition to play than it is to make up for the years in which they were not taught the techniques of the game.

The concept of economical training is presented here because many coaches erroneously set aside blocks of time within their practices for conditioning-only activities. Push-ups, sit-ups, sprints, and distance running are typical of what is included in these conditioning-only blocks of time. With youth players who have not achieved a high level of mastery of the techniques of the game, conditioning-only activities are not recommended. Practice time needs to be spent on learning the techniques and strategies of the game of baseball, with conditioning an accompanying outcome as the result of planned economical training. As players develop a higher level of mastery of the techniques of baseball, conditioning-only activities could be included in practices. However, they should be made as closely related to baseball as possible.

SUMMARY

In this chapter you have learned how the energy and muscular systems work, how they are used in baseball, and how to condition these systems. Although separate conditioning-only workouts were not recommended for the under-14 age group, guidelines were given for incorporating the principles of training into the regular practices for the double purpose of skill improvement and enhanced conditioning (economical training). Athletes begin to require and benefit from supplementary programs for conditioning the energy and muscular systems around the age of 14. Examples of such programs have been provided, with guidelines for varying the training at different points in the year. Suggested schedules and workout routines to guide this training are provided in the supplements.

A basic knowledge of the scientific principles of physical conditioning will help you design effective practices and training sessions. It will also help you communicate to your athletes the importance of each type of conditioning activity you use. Conveying this understanding to your players will not only make them more knowledgeable, but will also help them develop good lifelong habits and attitudes towards exercise and fitness.

SUGGESTED READINGS

Fox, E.L. (1979). *Sports physiology*. Philadelphia: W.B. Saunders.

Lamb, D.R. (1984). *Physiology of exercise* (2nd ed.). New York: Macmillan.

Sharkey, B. (1984). *Physiology of fitness* (2nd ed.). Champaign, IL: Human Kinetics Publishers.

Stone, W.V., & Knoll, W.K. (1978). *Sports conditioning and weight training*. Boston: Allyn and Bacon.

Supplement 22-1.
Warm-Up, Cool-Down, and Stretching Activities for Baseball

Introduction

The players' preparation for each practice and game should begin with a warm-up session and should be followed by a cool-down period. Warm-up and cool-down activities should be conducted at light to moderate intensities and should be followed by stretching exercises.

Warm-Up

Warm-up activities should be performed to increase the breathing rate, heart rate, and muscle temperature to exercise levels. These are done to prepare the body for the demands of subsequent strenuous activities. Additionally, warm-ups enhance the players' awareness for their surroundings. Warm-ups can also be used as a valuable introduction in setting the tone of the players' attitude toward the activity to follow. Warm-ups for sport should involve the regions of the body upon which more intense exercise demands will be placed during training for and participation in the sport. Thus, with baseball, virtually all regions of the body should be prepared. The following categories included some examples of warm-ups that can be used for baseball.

Light Aerobic/General Warm-Ups

- Jogging
- Jogging in place

Light Aerobic/Baseball-Specific Warm-ups

- Jogging the bases
- Playing catch with a partner

Body Region-Specific Warm-ups

- Shoulder circles—With arms horizontal and to the side of the body, small circular rotations of the arms are made. These circles are gradually increased. This pattern is then repeated; however, the arms are rotated in the opposite direction.
- Trunk circles—While standing with the feet shoulder-width apart and the hands on the hips, the trunk is moved in a circular manner. (Note: Avoid an excessive arch of the lower back by keeping the head in an upright position.)

Stretching

Stretching should be performed by slowly and gently extending each muscle group and joint to the point of slight discomfort. This position should be held for 6 to 30 seconds. The stretch should then be released and repeated in the same manner two or more times. Bouncing or fast, jerky movements are inappropriate in that they activate the muscles' stretch reflex mechanism and, therefore, limit rather than enhance flexibility.

Stretching exercises, used as part of a baseball conditioning program to maintain or increase flexibility, may reduce the occurrence of certain injuries, such as muscle strains and joint sprains, and may enhance performance of certain techniques. Because baseball involves virtually all major muscle groups and joints of the body, a variety of flexibility exercises, targeted at these regions, should be a part of each pre- and post-practice and game. The following flexibility exercises are some examples that are appropriate for baseball.

- Calf stretch—With the legs straddled in a forward-backward alignment, the knee of the back leg is bent while the entire sole of the back foot maintains contact with the ground. By switching the position of the feet, the other calf is stretched.
- Kneeling quad stretch—From a kneeling position, the hip is pressed forward. By switching the positions of the legs, the other quadriceps muscle and hip joint are stretched. Note that this exercise also stretches the trunk.
- Seated straddle (groin stretch)—From a seated position with the legs straddled, the trunk is moved forward. The head should be kept upright to reduce pressure on the lower back.
- Butterfly (groin stretch)—In a seated position place the soles of the feet together with the knees bent no more than 90 degrees. Grasp the ankles with the hands and apply pressure with the elbows to the inside of the legs to rotate the legs outward. Keep the back straight with the head in an upright position.
- Trunk and hip stretch—From lying flat on the back (a *supine* position), both arms are placed 90 degrees from the trunk. The head is turned toward one of the outstretched arms while bringing the opposite leg (90 degrees from the trunk) over the midline of the body and toward the ground. This exercise should be performed on both sides.
- Shoulder stretch—Bend the elbow and position the arm behind the head. The hand of the opposite arm grasps the bent elbow and slowly pulls it toward the midline of the trunk. To stretch the other shoulder, the roles of the arms are switched.
- Shoulder stretch—Stand with your side to the fence and extend your arm and grasp the fence as far behind you as possible to feel stretch of the pectoral muscles (across the front of the chest). To stretch the other shoulder, the roles of the arms are switched.
- Shoulder stretch—Extend one arm straight ahead at shoulder height. Use opposite arm to hook extended arm between the elbow and shoulder and pull to stretch the muscles across upper back. Switch the role of the arms to stretch the other shoulder and arm.

Cool-Down

The importance of cooling down has not received sufficient emphasis among coaches of young athletes. Cool-down sessions are infrequently used to end a practice session and are rarely used following a game. A cool-down period helps to:

- clear out lactic acid accumulated in the muscles
- reduce the pooling of blood in the extremities
- prevent the loss of flexibility that may accompany intense muscular exercise

Like the warm-up, cool-down activities should include movements similar to those included in the practice or game. Thus, the warm-up and stretching activities, previously listed, are appropriate for the cool-down. Have your athletes perform the cool-down exercises first, then the stretching activities.

Supplement 22-2.
Year-Round Conditioning Program

Introduction

This supplement contains information on a year-round conditioning program. It is directed at conditioning the energy production system, through a program of interval training, and the muscular system, through a weight training program. This year-round program is appropriate for the highly motivated player who is 14 years of age or older. It is for players who have chosen to concentrate on baseball and wish to maximize their performance through enhanced conditioning on a year-round basis. This program is NOT for beginning players and/or players below the age of 14 years who would derive greater benefit by devoting their time to learning and perfecting the techniques of baseball.

Interval Training Program

Interval training is a method for developing the anaerobic energy-production system while maintaining and/or enhancing a previously established base of aerobic fitness. This type of training uses alternating periods of short-duration, high-intensity anaerobic ("sprint" type) exercises with longer periods of moderate- to low-intensity aerobic exercises.

The training outlines provided in this supplement can be used with different modes of exercise, depending on individual preference and the availability of equipment and facilities. Swimming, jogging and running, and/or bicycling are modes of exercise suggested for interval training in baseball. Specific distances are not indicated in this supplement because of the variety of exercises possible and because of variations in individual fitness. All players should, however, maintain a record of distances covered on individual forms provided in this supplement so their progress can be assessed. Distance records can be kept in yards, meters, miles, kilometers, blocks, or laps.

An important concept to keep in mind when planning an interval training program is that the program should progress to a point where it places a similar aerobic and anaerobic demand

on the athlete as that of a hard-played game of baseball. This type of work load in an interval training program conditions the athletes to the demands they will be confronted with during competition. Regulation of the duration and intensity of exercise, as well as the rest intervals, are the components of an interval training program that can be manipulated to achieve the desired exercise levels.

The interval training program included in this supplement is divided into five phases. These phases are briefly described and followed by forms that can be used by athletes to keep records of their progress.

- Pre-season Aerobic/Anaerobic Transition Program—This four-week program is used to prepare athletes for high intensity anaerobic conditioning after they have developed a good aerobic fitness base (see Table 22-1s).
- Pre-season Anaerobic Developmental Interval-Training Program—This is an eight-week program to be started 10 weeks before the first game. The program should be preceded by anaerobic training and the four-week Aerobic/Anaerobic Transition Program (see Table 22-2s).
- In-Season Anaerobic Maintenance Program—This program should be completed twice a week starting two weeks before the first game and continuing through the end of the season (see Table 22-3s).
- Post-Season Aerobic Program—This program involves rhythmical, low intensity aerobic activities such as swimming, jogging, running, and bicycling for three days per week to enhance aerobic fitness (see Table 22-4s).
- Post-Season Anaerobic Maintenance Program—This program should be done once a week to maintain anaerobic fitness levels during the aerobic phase of off-season conditioning (see Table 22-4s).

Weight Training Program

Weight training for baseball should focus on the development of muscular power, or the ability to quickly exert large muscular force.

The load should be lifted explosively, then returned to the starting position slowly. Generally, the larger muscle groups should be exercised first. Also, the same muscle groups should not be exercised in succession. Table 22-5s contains weight-lifting exercises that can be used to meet the specific requirements of baseball. They are arranged in an appropriate order.

Since the weight training exercises listed can be done using a variety of equipment, details of technique and an explanation of procedures for each exercise will not be given here. Many good guides for weight training are available in local bookstores. A few examples of such guides that contain explanations of correct technique and details for each specific exercise are:

- *Sports Conditioning and Weight Training* by William J. Stone and William A. Kroll (Allyn & Bacon, 1978). This book is designed to offer sound, systematic training programs for those who wish to apply strength and conditioning techniques to specific sports.
- *Strength Training by the Experts* by Daniel P. Riley (2nd edition, Leisure Press, 1982). This book covers a variety of lifting equipment, including free weights, Universal equipment, and Nautilus equipment, and explains which muscle groups are used in each exercise.
- *Weightlifting for Beginners* by Bill Reynolds (Contemporary Books, 1982). This book is designed primarily for free weights and at-home weightlifting.

Year-round conditioning for muscular power can be divided into three parts: pre-season (developmental), in-season (maintenance), and post-season (developmental). Pre-season and post-season workouts have improvement in muscular power as their goals. In-season workouts are done less frequently and should be used to maintain the muscular fitness developed during the off-season.

Pre-Season Weight Training

Athletes new to weight training should start a developmental program at least three months before the first competition. Overloaded muscles require about 48 hours to repair and recover sufficiently, so a lifting schedule of three days per week with a minimum of one day off between workouts will give best results.

For the first one to two weeks, the athlete should do one exercise eight to 12 times (repetitions), then move on to the next exercise until each exercise in the weight training program has been covered. This series of repetitions of each exercise is called a set.

The appropriate weight load or resistance is a load the athlete can lift properly a minimum of eight times, but is not so light that it can be lifted more than 12 times. Some experimenting with weight loads will be necessary to determine correct starting weights for each exercise. Once these weight loads are determined, they should be recorded on the "Weight Training Program Checklist" included in this supplement (see Table 22-6s).

During this first phase of the weight training program (two weeks), the athlete should master the proper lifting technique and work through the initial muscle soreness that accompanies learning the correct weight loads. After this initial phase, the work can be increased to two sets while maintaining the initial weight levels for eight to 12 repetitions per exercise. Two sets of the same exercise are completed before the next exercise is done. This second phase also lasts two weeks.

In the third phase, three full sets are done during each workout. Three full sets of eight to 12 repetitions on an exercise are completed, then the next exercise is done. This phase should last for eight or more weeks and should end about two weeks before the first competition. It is during this third phase that weight levels are adjusted upward as strength increases. This information is summarized in Table 22-7s.

When 12 repetitions of a given exercise have been completed for each of the three sets for two successive workouts, the weight load for that exercise can be increased to the next level for the following workout. The athlete should be able to do a minimum of eight repetitions for each of the three sets at the new weight level. If this is not possible, a smaller weight increase is indicated.

In-Season Weight Training

Strength improvement is the goal of the preseason weight training developmental program. Maintenance of the increased strength is

Table 22-1s. Pre-Season Aerobic/Anaerobic Transition Program

(To be started 14 weeks before the first game)

Name_____

The information at the top of each week's schedule specifies a suggested duration and intensity of the workout for that week. Space is provided for a coach or player to write an alternate workout for each week. The frequency of workouts is three per week, on an every-other-day basis. Each workout should be preceded and followed by stretching exercises. Work intensity is specified in terms of percentage of effort as follows:

LM	= Light to Moderate	**50% of maximum** effort*
H	= Hard	**80% of maximum** effort
S	= Sprint	**100% of maximum** effort

For example, **3x(2:H,2:LM)** means do three sets of (two minutes at 80% of effort followed by two minutes at 50% of effort). For each workout completed, record the **date** and the **total distance covered.**

Preseason Aerobic/Anaerobic Transition Program				
WEEK		**Day 1**	**Day 2**	**Day 3**
1	[9:LM,3x(2:H,2:LM),9:LM]	alternate workout: [		]
	Date:			
	Distance:			
2	[7:LM,4x(2:H,2:LM),7:LM]	alternate workout: [		]
	Date:			
	Distance:			
3	[5:LM,5x(2:H,2:LM),5:LM]	alternate workout: [		]
	Date:			
	Distance:			
4	[3:LM,6x(2:H,2:LM),3:LM]	alternate workout: [		]
	Date:			
	Distance:			
TOTAL TIME FOR EACH WORKOUT = 30 MINUTES				

*If the intensity of the hard and sprint portions of the exercise intervals cannot be maintained, the athlete should reduce the intensity of the light to moderate intervals.

Table 22-2s. Pre-Season Anaerobic Developmental Interval Training Program

(To be started 10 weeks before the first game)

Name⎯⎯⎯⎯⎯⎯⎯⎯⎯⎯⎯⎯⎯⎯⎯⎯⎯⎯⎯⎯⎯⎯

The information at the top of each week's schedule specifies a suggested duration and intensity of the workout for that week. Space is provided for a coach or player to write an alternate workout for each week. The frequency of workouts is three per week, on an every-other-day basis. Each workout should be preceded and followed by stretching exercises. Work intensity is specified in terms of percentage of effort as follows:

LM	= Light to Moderate	**50% of maximum** effort*	
H	= Hard	**80% of maximum** effort	
S	= Sprint	**100% of maximum** effort	

For example, **4x(:20S,2:LM)** means do four sets of (20 seconds at maximum effort followed by two minutes at 50% of effort). For each workout completed, record the **date** and the **total distance covered**.

Preseason Anaerobic Developmental Interval Training Program			
WEEK	**Day 1**	**Day 2**	**Day 3**
1	[4:LM,2x(1:H,2:LM),4x(:20S,:40LM),4:LM]		
	alternate workout: [		]
	Date/Distance		
2	[4:LM,2x(1:H,2:LM),5x(:20S,:40LM),4:LM]		
	alternate workout: [		]
	Date/Distance		
3	[4:LM,2x(1:H,2:LM),6x(:20S,:40LM),4:LM]		
	alternate workout: [		]
	Date/Distance		
4	[4:LM,2x(1:H,2:LM),7x(:20S,:40LM),4:LM]		
	alternate workout: [		]
	Date/Distance		
5	[4:LM,3x(1:H,2:LM),8x(:20S,:40LM),4:LM]		
	alternate workout: [		]
	Date/Distance		
6	[4:LM,3x(1:H,2:LM),9x(:20S,:40LM),4:LM]		
	alternate workout: [		]
	Date/Distance		
7	[4:LM,3x(1:H,2:LM),6x(:10S,:20LM),2:LM,6x(:10S,:20LM),4:LM]		
	alternate workout: [		]
	Date/Distance		
8	[4:LM,3x(1:H,2:LM),8x(:10S,:20LM),2:LM,8x(:10S,:20LM),4:LM]		
	alternate workout: [		]
	Date/Distance		

*If the intensity of the hard and sprint portions of the exercise intervals cannot be maintained, the athlete should reduce the intensity of the light to moderate intervals.

Table 22-3s. In-Season Anaerobic Maintenance Program

(To be started two weeks before the first game)

Name_____

A suggested workout is provided at the top of the In-Season Aerobic Maintenance Program form. Space is provided for the coach or player to write an alternate workout. The frequency of workouts is one per week. Workouts should be completed at the end of a practice but not on a day before a game. Each workout should be preceded and followed by stretching exercises. Intensity is specified in terms of percentage of effort as follows:

LM	= Light to Moderate	50% of maximum effort*
H	= Hard	80% of maximum effort
S	= Sprint	100% of maximum effort

For example, **3x(2:H,2:LM)** means do three sets of (two minutes at 80% of effort followed by two minutes at 50% of effort). For each workout completed, record the **date** and the **total distance covered.**

<table>
<tr><td colspan="7" align="center">In-Season Anaerobic Maintenance Program</td></tr>
<tr><td colspan="7">[2:LM,2x(1:H,2:LM),2x(:20S,:40LM),8x(:10S,:20LM),4:LM]</td></tr>
<tr><td colspan="7">alternate
workout: [   ]</td></tr>
<tr><td colspan="2" rowspan="2" align="center">MONTH</td><td colspan="5" align="center">WEEK</td></tr>
<tr><td align="center">1</td><td align="center">2</td><td align="center">3</td><td align="center">4</td><td align="center">5</td></tr>
<tr><td rowspan="2">1</td><td>Date:</td><td></td><td></td><td></td><td></td><td></td></tr>
<tr><td>Distance:</td><td></td><td></td><td></td><td></td><td></td></tr>
<tr><td rowspan="2">2</td><td>Date:</td><td></td><td></td><td></td><td></td><td></td></tr>
<tr><td>Distance:</td><td></td><td></td><td></td><td></td><td></td></tr>
<tr><td rowspan="2">3</td><td>Date:</td><td></td><td></td><td></td><td></td><td></td></tr>
<tr><td>Distance:</td><td></td><td></td><td></td><td></td><td></td></tr>
<tr><td rowspan="2">4</td><td>Date:</td><td></td><td></td><td></td><td></td><td></td></tr>
<tr><td>Distance:</td><td></td><td></td><td></td><td></td><td></td></tr>
<tr><td rowspan="2">5</td><td>Date:</td><td></td><td></td><td></td><td></td><td></td></tr>
<tr><td>Distance:</td><td></td><td></td><td></td><td></td><td></td></tr>
</table>

*If the intensity of the hard and sprint portions of the exercise intervals cannot be maintained, the athlete should reduce the intensity of the light to moderate intervals.

Table 22-4s. Post-Season Aerobic and Anaerobic Program

(To be started two to four weeks after the last game)

AEROBIC PROGRAM

Aerobic capabilities should be developed during the post-season to provide the base for building the more intense anaerobic work capacity required for top performance during the season. Aerobic work combined with muscular strength/power work on alternate days is a good variation from the typical season routine. In the post-season time period, the development of aerobic capacity and muscular strength/power become primary, rather than secondary, objectives.

Begin three days of aerobic activity (dribbling, jogging and running, bicycling, or other rhythmical, low intensity, long duration activities) alternated with three days of weight training. Progress up to 40 minutes of continuous aerobic activity and then work on increasing the speed or intensity at which the 40 minutes of work is done. Each workout should be preceded and followed by stretching exercises. Record the date and workout time on the "Year-Round Conditioning Checklist" in the portion of the checklist devoted to post-season.

ANAEROBIC MAINTENANCE PROGRAM

A suggested workout is provided at the top of the Post-Season Anaerobic Maintenance Program form. Space is also provided for the coach or player to write an alternate workout. The post-season anaerobic maintenance program should be done once a week. It should not be completed on the same day as an aerobic workout. Each workout should be preceded and followed by stretching exercises. Intensity is specified in terms of percentage of effort as follows:

LM	= Light to Moderate	50% of maximum effort*
H	= Hard	80% of maximum effort
S	= Sprint	100% of maximum effort

For example, **4x(:20S,:40LM)** means do four sets of (20 seconds at maximum effort followed by 40 seconds at 50% of effort). For each workout completed, record the **date** and the **total distance covered**.

Post-Season Anaerobic Maintenance Program					
[4:LM,2x(1:H,2:LM),4x(:20S,:40LM),4x(:20S,:40LM),4:LM]					
alternate workout: [　　　　　　　　　　　　　　　　　　　　　　　　　　　　]					
MONTH		WEEK				
		1	2	3	4	5
1	Date:					
	Distance:					
2	Date:					
	Distance:					
3	Date:					
	Distance:					
4	Date:					
	Distance:					

---

*If the intensity of the hard and sprint portions of the exercise intervals cannot be maintained, the athlete should reduce the intensity of the light to moderate intervals.

Table 22-5s. Conditioning activities for baseball players.

Order	Exercise	Comment
1	Squat lift	The angle at the back of the knee should not be allowed to become less than 90 degrees. An upright position of the head should be maintained, and the back should be kept as close to vertical as possible throughout the lift. Trained spotters must be used. If using free weights, wrap a towel or foam pad around the center of the bar to lessen the discomfort of the bar across the back of the neck.
2	Bench press	Trained spotters must be used.
3	Bent knee sit-ups	A weight can be held high on the chest and/or the sit-up can be done on an incline to increase resistance. The feet should be held down by a partner or restraining structure.
4	Finger flexion	Grip strength exercises can be done with a spring hand gripper.
5	Hip abduction	This exercise can be done on a specially designed weight machine or by having a partner provide resistance. Both legs should be exercised. (Note! Communication is necessary as to how much force is necessary. Over resistance may injure muscles and ligaments.)
6	Bent over row	The head should be supported, and the back should be in a horizontal position.
7	Hip abduction	This exercise can be done on a specially designed weight machine or by having a partner provide resistance. Both legs should be exercised. (Note! Communication is necessary as to how much force is necessary. Over resistance may injure muscles and ligaments.)
8	Toe rise	If using free weights, wrap a towel or foam pad around the bar to lessen the discomfort of the bar across the back of the neck. Trained spotters must be used. A block of wood can be used under the toes to increase the range through which the muscles must exert force in lifting the body.
9	Arm curl	A rocking motion of the body should not be used to aid the arms in lifting the resistance.
10	Knee flexion	
11	Lat pull-down	Keep the hips extended and do not use hip flexion to aid in the pull-down motion.
12	Back hyperextension	A partner or restraining structure is needed to hold the legs down.
13	Knee extension	
14	Reverse forearm curl	

Table 22-6s. Weight Training Program Checklist

Name _____

INSTRUCTIONS:

- Record the weight load only when there is a change in load.
- Record the number of repetitions for each set (example: 12/10/10)
- Increase the weight load when you have done 12 repetitions for each of three sets for two consecutive workouts.
- Use a smaller load increase if you cannot do a minimum of eight repetitions per set at a new load.

Date		Squat lift	Bench press	Bent knee sit-up	Finger flexion	Hip abduction	Bent over row	Hip adduction	Toe rise	Arm curl	Knee flexion	Lat pull-down	Back hyperextension	Knee extension	Reverse forearm curl		
	WT.																
	REPS.	/ /	/ /	/ /	/ /	/ /	/ /	/ /	/ /	/ /	/ /	/ /	/ /	/ /	/ /	/ /	/ /
	WT.																
	REPS.	/ /	/ /				/ /		/ /	/ /	/ /	/ /	/ /	/ /	/ /	/ /	/ /
	WT.																
	REPS.	/ /	/ /		/ /	/ /	/ /	/ /	/ /	/ /	/ /	/ /	/ /	/ /	/ /	/ /	/ /
	WT.																
	REPS.	/ /	/ /														
	WT.																
	REPS.	/ /	/ /	/ /	/ /	/ /	/ /	/ /	/ /	/ /	/ /	/ /	/ /	/ /	/ /	/ /	/ /
	WT.																
	REPS.	/ /	/ /	/ /	/ /	/ /	/ /	/ /	/ /	/ /	/ /	/ /	/ /	/ /	/ /	/ /	/ /
	WT.																
	REPS.	/ /	/ /	/ /	/ /	/ /	/ /	/ /	/ /	/ /	/ /	/ /	/ /	/ /	/ /	/ /	/ /
	WT.																
	REPS.	/ /	/ /	/ /	/ /	/ /	/ /	/ /	/ /	/ /	/ /	/ /	/ /	/ /	/ /	/ /	/ /
	WT.																
	REPS.	/ /	/ /	/ /	/ /	/ /	/ /	/ /	/ /	/ /	/ /	/ /	/ /	/ /	/ /	/ /	/ /
	WT.																
	REPS.	/ /	/ /	/ /	/ /	/ /	/ /	/ /	/ /	/ /	/ /	/ /	/ /	/ /	/ /	/ /	/ /
	WT.																
	REPS.	/ /	/ /	/ /	/ /	/ /	/ /	/ /	/ /	/ /	/ /	/ /	/ /	/ /	/ /	/ /	/ /
	WT.																
	REPS.	/ /	/ /	/ /	/ /	/ /	/ /	/ /	/ /	/ /	/ /	/ /	/ /	/ /	/ /	/ /	/ /
	WT.																
	REPS.	/ /	/ /	/ /	/ /	/ /	/ /	/ /	/ /	/ /	/ /	/ /	/ /	/ /	/ /	/ /	/ /
	WT.																
	REPS.	/ /	/ /	/ /	/ /	/ /	/ /	/ /	/ /	/ /	/ /	/ /	/ /	/ /	/ /	/ /	/ /
	WT.																
	REPS.	/ /	/ /	/ /	/ /	/ /	/ /	/ /	/ /	/ /	/ /	/ /	/ /	/ /	/ /	/ /	/ /
	WT.																
	REPS.	/ /	/ /	/ /	/ /	/ /	/ /	/ /	/ /	/ /	/ /	/ /	/ /	/ /	/ /	/ /	/ /
	WT.																
	REPS.	/ /	/ /	/ /	/ /	/ /	/ /	/ /	/ /	/ /	/ /	/ /	/ /	/ /	/ /	/ /	/ /
	WT.																
	REPS.	/ /	/ /	/ /	/ /	/ /	/ /	/ /	/ /	/ /	/ /	/ /	/ /	/ /	/ /	/ /	/ /
	WT.																
	REPS.	/ /	/ /	/ /	/ /	/ /	/ /	/ /	/ /	/ /	/ /	/ /	/ /	/ /	/ /	/ /	/ /

Table 22-7s. Pre-season developmental weight training program.

Phase	Duration	Reps	Sets	Days/Week	Comments
1	2 weeks	8-12	1	3	Maintain starting resistance level.
2	2 weeks	8-12	2	3	Maintain starting resistance level.
3	8 or more weeks	8-12	3	3	Increase resistance levels as strength gains are made.

accomplished by a scaled-down in-season weight training program that should begin about two weeks before the first game. If weight training is done only during the preseason period, the strength gains will gradually be lost as the season progresses. Research has shown that a weight training maintenance program of one to two workouts per week will prevent the reversal of strength gains. Performance will not be hampered by in-season weight training if three general rules are followed:

- Lifting should be limited to once or twice a week, with two to three days between weight training workouts.
- Do not schedule weight training workouts for the day before or the day of a game.
- Maintain the resistance at the last load level where 12 repetitions for all three sets could be done. Do not increase weight loads during in-season workouts. Use pre- and post-season periods for strength improvement with strength maintenance as the goal of the in-season workouts.

The workout program itself remains the same as in Phase 3 of the developmental program. The same series of exercises is followed, with eight to 12 repetitions per exercise, for a total of three sets. As long as the athlete lifts at least once every four days and does not increase the weight load, there should be no muscle soreness or undue fatigue that will interfere with performance during games.

Post-Season Weight Training

Once the competitive season is over, players can again focus on achievement of higher strength levels. A post-season break from training of at least two weeks can be followed by a return to the program outlined in Phase 3 of the preseason developmental program (see Table 22-2s). Three-set workouts, three times per week, can be continued throughout the off-season months. The "Weight Training Program Checklist" can be used to determine when weight loads should be increased. After the first year in which players build up gradually through the one-set and two-set phases during the preseason developmental program, Phase 1 and 2 should not be needed.

Year-Round Conditioning Program

The year-round conditioning program contains two components. They are: (a) an interval training program for conditioning the aerobic and anaerobic energy-production systems, and (b) a weight training program for conditioning the muscular system (see Tables 22-8s through 22-10s). These components are integrated into a year-round conditioning program (see Table 22-11s).

Table 22-8s. Year-Round Conditioning Checklist

Name _____

(Mark the date of each completed workout in the box.)

PRESEASON

WEEK	AEROBIC/ANAEROBIC TRANSITION PROGRAM AND WEIGHT TRAINING PROGRAM (Phases 1 and 2 or 3)					
	TRANSITION WORKOUT	WEIGHT TRAINING	TRANSITION WORKOUT	WEIGHT TRAINING	TRANSITION WORKOUT	WEIGHT TRAINING
1						
2						
3						
4						

PRESEASON

WEEK	DEVELOPMENTAL INTERVAL TRAINING PROGRAM AND WEIGHT TRAINING PROGRAM (Phase 3)					
	INTERVAL TRAINING	WEIGHT TRAINING	INTERVAL TRAINING	WEIGHT TRAINING	INTERVAL TRAINING	WEIGHT TRAINING
5						
6						
7						
8						
9						
10						
11						
12						

(After 12th week, begin **in-season maintenance programs** (intervals once per week, weights one to two times per week)

Table 22-9s. Year-Round Conditioning Checklist

Name _____

IN-SEASON MAINTENANCE PROGRAMS

Place a check in the box corresponding to the month and week for each time you complete the interval and weight workout.

WEEK

MONTH	1		2		3		4		5	
	Wts.	Interval	Wts.	Interval	Wts.	Interval	Wts.	Interval	Wts.	Interval
1										
2										
3										
4										
5										
6										

Table 22-10s. Post-Season Conditioning Checklist

Name _____

Mark the date of each workout in the corresponding box. For aerobic workouts, record the distance covered and the total time of the workout.

WEEK	Aerobic	Weights	Aerobic	Weights	Aerobic	Weights	Anaerobic Maintenance
1							
2							
3							
4							
5							
6							

Table 22-10s (continued)

POST-SEASON CONDITIONING CHECKLIST

WEEK	Aerobic	Weights	Aerobic	Weights	Aerobic	Weights	Anaerobic Maintenance
7							
8							
9							
10							
11							
12							
13							
14							
15							
16							
17							
18							
19							
20							
21							
22							
23							
24							
25							
26							
27							
28							
29							
30							

Table 22-11s. Overview of year-round conditioning program.

Time	Interval Training Activity for Conditioning the Energy Production System*	Weight Training Activity for Conditioning the Muscular System**
Pre-season (start 14 weeks prior to first game)	Complete the Pre-season Aerobic/Anaerobic Transition program (four weeks).	New lifters complete the Pre-season Weight Training Program by beginning with four weeks of introductory weight training (Phase 1 and 2) and then starting the Post-Season Weight Training Program (Phase 3).
	Complete the Pre-season Anaerobic Developmental Interval Training Program (eight weeks).	Continuing lifters complete the Post-Season Weight Training Program.
In-Season (two weeks prior to first game until last game)	Participate in interval training as part of regularly scheduled practices. Complete the In-Season Anaerobic Maintenance Program.	Complete the In-Season Weight Training Maintenance Program.
Post-Season (two to four weeks after last game until 14 weeks before first game of next season)	Complete three days/week of aerobic activity (swimming, jogging and running, or bicycling). Complete the Post-Season Anaerobic Maintenance Program.	Complete the Post-Season Weight Training Program.

*Note that all conditioning sessions should be preceded by warm-up and stretching and followed by cool-down and stretching (see Supplement 22-1).

**Descriptions of these activities are included in this supplement.

Supplement 22-3.
Circuit Training Program

Introduction

This supplement contains an example of a baseball training circuit and recording form (see Table 22-12s). These forms can be photocopied and duplicated on the front and back of a 5 x 8" card. Also included in this supplement is a blank form (see Table 22-13s) upon which you can write your own training circuit to meet the specific needs of your players.

Using a Training Circuit

A training circuit can be implemented one to three times per week during the season. The number of times per week you have your players engage in a training circuit should vary according to the number of games scheduled for a given week, the physical demands of an in-season interval training and weight training program, and other activities included in your practice. You should not have your players perform a circuit the day before or the day of a game.

The requirements for performance and scoring each station need to be thoroughly explained to the players. Players need to be informed that the correct performance of each station is as important as the number of repetitions. After all the players understand each of the items in the complete circuit, you may have them perform a partial circuit of four or five stations and then increase the number of stations by one on subsequent days until all stations of the training circuit are performed.

The prescribed time for exercise and for the rest interval, during which the players write their scores on their recording forms and rotate from one station to the next, should be controlled to create an exercise overload. The first day the team performs the entire circuit, 30 seconds of exercise and 20 seconds rest between each station might be appropriate. This results in an eight-station circuit that can be completed in 6 minutes and 20 seconds. Gradually the exercise interval should increase and the rest interval should decrease. You will need to judge what is the appropriate exercise/rest interval ratio for your players.

Table 22-12s. Example of a ten-station baseball training circuit and recording form on two sides of a 5 x 8" card.

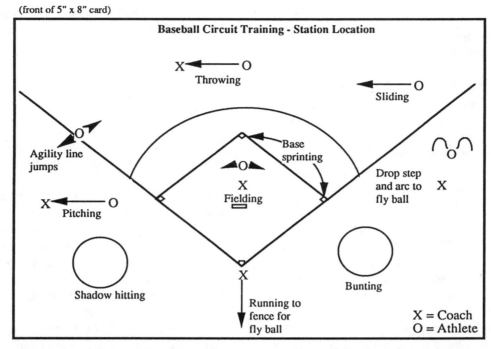

(front of 5" x 8" card)

Baseball Circuit Training - Station Location

Throwing

Sliding

Agility line jumps

Base sprinting

Drop step and arc to fly ball

Pitching

Fielding

Shadow hitting

Bunting

Running to fence for fly ball

X = Coach
O = Athlete

10 Stations

1. Shadow hitting
2. Pitching
3. Agility line jumps
4. Throwing
5. Sliding
6. Drop step and arc to fly ball
7. Base sprinting
8. Fielding
9. Bunting
10. Running to fence for fly ball

(back of 5" x 8" card)

Baseball Circuit Training - Recording Form

Name:																	
Date (mo./day)																	
Exercise/Rest interval (seconds)																	
STATIONS	**Performance Scores**																
Shadow hitting																	
Pitching																	
Agility line jumps																	
Throwing																	
Sliding																	
Drop step and arc to fly ball																	
Base sprinting																	
Fielding																	
Bunting																	
Running to fence for fly ball																	

Table 22-12s. (continued)

Station	Description	Equipment
Shadow hitting	See drill	1 bat
Pitching	Player works on pitching technique Coach serves as catcher. Stress concentration and proper mechanics.	1 ball, portable plate
Agility line jumping	Player begins with both feet on one side of the foul line. The player jumps rapidly and continuously from one side of the line to the other. Stress quick footwork.	foul line
Throwing	Player throws bigger ball to coach. Distance thrown is varied by the coach depending on arm strength of player. Stress proper mechanics. *Variation:* speed throwing	one 12 in. or 16 in. softball
Sliding	Player starts in foul territory, runs toward base, and slides when 8 to 12 ft. from base. Stress proper technique. *Variation:* slide to inside and outside of bag; head first slide	1 movable base 15 ft. from foul line
Drop step and arc to fly ball	Player is positioned 40 to 60 ft. from coach who throws fly balls to right and left of player. Stress drop step and arc to get proper position for catching a fly ball.	1 baseball
Base sprinting	Start at first base and sprint to second. Start at second and sprint to first. Stress quick start with imaginary pitch and rounding second. Stress proper running mechanics. Time each sprint.	2 movable bases
Fielding	Player faces coach who is 10 ft. away. Coach rolls balls directly to player, to player's right, to player's left. Stress proper mechanics and footwork. Continue as quickly as possible.	1 baseball
Bunting	Player starts in hitting position and moves to bunt position, executes bunt, drops bat, and takes crossover step and two additional steps to first base. Repeat as many times as possible in allotted time. Stress proper mechanics.	1 bat
Running to fence for fly ball	Player starts at home plate and visualizes a fly ball going to the fence. Player drop steps and runs to fence feeling for fence while keeping eye on ball. Repeat as many times as possible in allotted time.	portable plate

Table 22-13s. Recording form to photocopy and complete.

(front of 5" x 8" card)

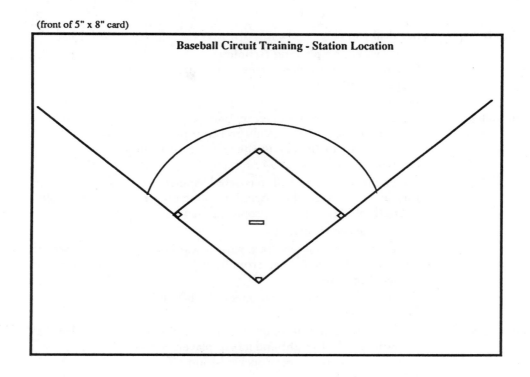

Baseball Circuit Training - Station Location

(back of 5" x 8" card)

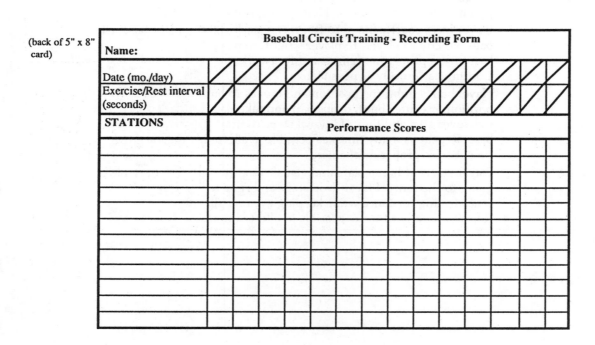

	Baseball Circuit Training - Recording Form																
Name:																	
Date (mo./day)																	
Exercise/Rest interval (seconds)																	
STATIONS	**Performance Scores**																

23
Nutrition for Successful Performance

Elaina Jurecki, R.D., M.S.
Glenna DeJong, M.S., M.A.

QUESTIONS TO CONSIDER

- What is a proper diet for young baseball players?
- Do young athletes need protein, vitamin, and mineral supplements?
- Should there by any restriction on the amount of water consumed before, during, and after games and practices?
- Should salt tablets be provided for the players during practices and games?
- Are ergogenic aids important in improving baseball performance?
- When should a pre-game meal be eaten and what should it contain?

INTRODUCTION

All children have the same nutritional needs, but young athletes use more energy and, therefore, need to consume more calories. Good performance does not just happen; it requires training sessions to improve techniques, increase endurance, and develop game strategies. Good nutrition is another important factor that affects an athlete's performance, but it is less frequently understood and practiced. Studies have shown that good overall eating habits are more beneficial to the athlete than taking vitamin or protein supplements or eating special foods at a pre-competition meal.

Food consists of all the solid or liquid materials we ingest by mouth, except drugs. Breads, meats, vegetables, and fruits, as well as beverages—even water—are considered food, because they contain essential nutrients for the body. These nutrients include carbohydrates, protein (amino acids), fats, vitamins, salts (electrolytes), minerals, trace elements, and water. Water constitutes more than half the body's weight and provides the medium within which other nutrients are delivered to different body parts to perform their important functions.

What impact could you have on your athletes' diets? How can you influence what your athletes eat when you do not cook their meals? When you meet with the team's parents during an orientation meeting, explain to them how good nutrition can aid their children's performance. This information can be reinforced by giving your athletes similar nutritional advice. Frequently, your athletes will listen more closely to your advice than that of their parents and use the tips you suggest on improving their diets because they believe these tips will also improve their performance.

PROPER DIET

A good diet is one that provides adequate energy (calories), proteins, carbohydrates, fats, vitamins, minerals, and water in the amounts needed by the body in order to perform its normal daily functions. A variety of foods needs to be eaten to provide the 40 plus nutrients essential for good health. This can be achieved by eating the specified number of servings from each of the four food groups (see Table 23-1).

Calories

Calories are the energy content of food used to satisfy the needs of the body so it can properly function. Energy obtained from food is temporarily stored as glycogen in the liver and muscle, as fat in various deposit sites, and as protein in muscle and other places although protein is used as an energy source only during extreme situations. Foods vary in calorie and nutrient content. Foods to avoid are those that are high in calories and low in nutrient content. Foods that are high in sugar (candy, cakes, soda pop, cookies) or fat (fried foods, chips, salad dressings, pastries, butter) supply "empty calories," meaning they do not contribute to the essential nutrients discussed earlier but do contribute many calories. These foods should be used with discretion.

The energy cost of physical activity, or amount of calories burned, depends upon (a) the intensity of the physical activity, and (b) the length of time of exertion. A young baseball player, about 120 pounds in body weight, burns approximately 240 calories per hour of practice. During a game or training session, ranging from 45 to 90 minutes, your players burn up to 25 percent more energy than they do on a day in which they don't practice. Hence, heavy training may require an additional 180 to 360 calories per day intake to compensate for the calories burned during the activity.

An average adolescent burns differing amounts of calories during the various activities listed in Table 23-2.

When your players reach exhaustion, most of their bodies' energy stores are depleted and their blood sugar decreases, causing fatigue. This situation is remedied with appropriate rest and calorie ingestion—preferably from carbohydrate sources since these foods can replenish energy stores more efficiently.

Carbohydrates

Carbohydrates are a group of chemical substances which include sugars and starches. They are available in many foods. As stated previously, carbohydrates can be stored as liver and muscle glycogen or can be found in the blood as glucose. During moderate to high intensity exercise, carbohydrates supply the majority of the energy needed in the body (see "Energy Production Systems" in Chapter 18). However, the carbohydrate storage capacity of the body is limited and can be greatly decreased by skipping

Table 23-1. Recommended daily intake of each of the four food groups.

Dairy Products	3-4 servings (milk, cheese, yogurt) to provide calcium, phosphorus, vitamin D, protein, and energy.	1 serving = 1 cup of milk or 2 oz. of cheese
Protein Products	2 servings (meat, fish, poultry, or vegetable protein foods such as beans and whole grains) to provide amino acids, B vitamins, iron, essential fatty acids, energy, and more.	1 serving = 2 to 3 oz. of meat
Fruits and Vegetables	4 servings (oranges, apples, pears, broccoli, carrots, green beans) to provide vitamin A and C, and electrolytes.	1 serving = 1/2 cup of vegetables or fruit
Grain Products	4 servings (bread, cereal, pasta, rice) to provide B vitamins and protein.	1 serving = 1 slice bread or 1 cup of cereal, pasta, or rice.

Table 23-2. Caloric expenditure during various activities.

Activity	Calories/ minute*	Activity	Calories/ minute
Sleeping	0.9	Basketball	5-7
Sitting, normally	1.0	Calisthenics	4
Standing, normally	1.2	Running (10 mph)	16
Sitting in class	1.4	Baseball	3-4
Walking indoors	2.5	Soccer (game)	6-8

*Based on an average adolescent, 120 lbs. Add 10 percent for each 15 lbs. over 120, subtract 10 percent for each 15 lbs. under 120.

meals or with exercise. Since carbohydrates can be digested easily and quickly, they are the most readily available sources of food energy for storage energy replacement.

A diet high in carbohydrate (55-60 percent of total caloric intake) helps maintain adequate stores in the body. Most of the dietary carbohydrates should come from complex carbohydrate sources such as pasta, rice, fruits, and kidney beans. Refined sugars found in candy, cookies, and syrup should be avoided.

Carbohydrates are easily digested and are the most readily available source of food energy.

Fat

Fat is the most concentrated source of energy. It contains twice as much energy (calories) per unit weight as either carbohydrate or protein. Fats have many important functions in the body including carrying vitamins A, D, E, and K to perform their necessary functions, building blood vessels and body linings, and providing a concentrated store of energy (calories).

During mild to moderate exercise, fats are an important energy source along with carbohydrates (see Energy Production Systems section in Chapter 22). The storage capacity for fat is much greater than that for carbohydrate and only in extreme cases are fat stores depleted. Therefore, dietary intake of fat should be 30 percent or less of total caloric intake since replenishment isn't normally necessary. In fact, high levels of fat in the diet have been implicated in diseases such as coronary artery disease and cancer.

Foods high in fat content are digested at a slower rate than foods high in carbohydrates or protein. If players have high fat meals (ham-

burger, fries, pizza, etc.) before their game, chances are good that such meals will not empty completely from their stomachs for three to five hours, and this may adversely affect their play. Foods having a high concentration of fat include butter, margarine, vegetable oils, peanut butter, mayonnaise, nuts, chocolate, fried foods, chips, and cream products.

Figure 23-1 lists the percent of fat from a variety of food sources.

Protein

Proteins are important as structural components of all body tissues (e.g. muscle, skin, brain, etc.), regulators of metabolism (e.g. hormones and enzymes), and as an energy source during starvation and exercise although its contribution is minor as compared to fats and carbohydrates (see Energy Production Systems section in Chapter 22). Amino acids are the "building blocks" which comprise all proteins. Of the twenty amino acids necessary for protein synthesis in the body, eleven can be manufactured in the body and are considered nonessential amino acids. The other nine are considered essential amino acids as they must be supplied in the diet. In a balanced diet, 12-15 percent of the total caloric intake should come from protein.

Foods from animal sources (e.g., meat, fish, poultry, eggs, milk, and cheese) provide the body with all of the essential amino acids. Vegetable foods (dried peas, beans, nuts, cereals, breads, and pastas) are also important sources of protein, but most vegetables are lacking in certain essential amino acids. Therefore, a combination of foods from animal and vegetable sources assures meeting the body's requirement for essential amino acids, as well as other nutrients.

Because of an increased rate of muscular growth, athletes have a *slightly* larger protein requirement than non-athletes. Studies on the dietary habits of athletes show that this increased requirement can be easily met by the athlete's normal diet; no protein supplement is necessary. During training, at most, an additional nine grams of protein (which can be provided by one cup of milk or two ounces of meat or cheese) is sufficient to meet increased demands. In fact, too much protein can place undo stress on the body.

Food Items

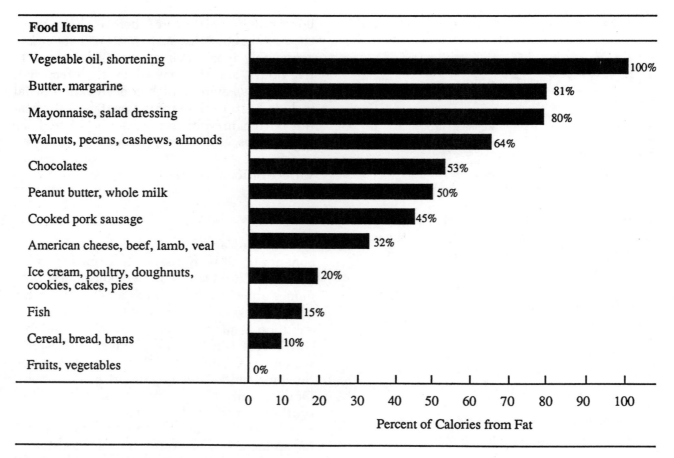

Food Items	Percent of Calories from Fat
Vegetable oil, shortening	100%
Butter, margarine	81%
Mayonnaise, salad dressing	80%
Walnuts, pecans, cashews, almonds	64%
Chocolates	53%
Peanut butter, whole milk	50%
Cooked pork sausage	45%
American cheese, beef, lamb, veal	32%
Ice cream, poultry, doughnuts, cookies, cakes, pies	20%
Fish	15%
Cereal, bread, brans	10%
Fruits, vegetables	0%

Figure 23-1. Percentage of calories from fat when ingested from specified food items.

Eating a high-protein diet could lead to dehydration of the body, which could actually decrease athletic performance.

Excessive amounts of ingested protein—greater than the body's needs—are converted into body fat. The waste products from this conversion must be excreted by the kidneys, placing a greater strain on these organs. Water also is excreted with the protein-waste products in the urine. Thus, eating a high-protein diet could lead to dehydration of the body, which could actually decrease athletic performance.

It is a myth that building muscle requires a high-protein diet featuring large quantities of meat. Another myth is that a steak dinner eaten before an athletic event will help team members improve their performance. This type of meal may actually work against them if consumed less than three or four hours before playing time. These meals, as well as any high protein meal, are also usually high in fat. Players cannot digest this type of meal as easily as a high-carbohydrate meal and may suffer from cramps and/or feel weighted down and sluggish.

Vitamins and Minerals

Vitamins and minerals are found in varying quantities in many different kinds of foods, from a slice of bread to a piece of liver. Vitamins and minerals are nutrients required by the body in very small amounts for a larger number of body functions. They do not contain calories or give the body energy. When an athlete feels "run down," *this is usually not caused by a vitamin deficiency.*

We need vitamins and minerals in only minute quantities. Requirements of most vitamins and minerals are in milligram (1/1000 gram) amounts. These substances taken in excess of the body's need will either be stored in the body or excreted in the urine. The extra amounts will not provide more energy or enhance performance; however, they can be toxic or interfere with normal metabolism.

Vitamin and mineral supplementation is not necessary for the athlete who consumes a balanced diet. However, in certain sports such as wrestling, bodybuilding, and ballet, where weight loss through starvation is achieved, the athlete may not be obtaining adequate amounts solely due to the diminished caloric intake. Therefore, in situations where the athlete's diet is not balanced or caloric intake is low, supplementation may be advised. A much better approach, however, would be to encourage proper eating habits.

Vitamins and minerals do not supply energy; high levels of vitamins and minerals can hinder the athlete's performance.

Some vitamin and mineral supplements contain 10 or more times the Recommended Daily Allowance (RDA), which is sometimes just below the level of toxicity. If vitamin and mineral supplements are used, a single daily multi-vitamin/mineral tablet, that provides 100 percent of the RDA or less for each nutrient is preferable to therapeutic level supplements providing greater than 100 percent of the RDA. The RDAs of vitamins and minerals are listed in Table 23-3.

Water

Water plays a vital role in the health and performance of an athlete. Your baseball players may lose more than two percent of their body weight due to dehydration from playing a game on a hot day or during a long workout. A player's performance significantly deteriorates after dehydration of more than two percent of his/her body weight. Drinking plenty of water is necessary for baseball players who are physically active in hot, humid weather (see Figure 23-2).

Physical exercise increases the amount of heat produced in the body. If sufficient water is not available for cooling of the body through perspiration, the body temperature may exceed safe limits. The individual will become tired more rapidly and in severe cases, heat exhaustion and heat stroke may result (see Chapter 24). A temperature/humidity guide for fluid and practice time is included in Table 23-4.

Maintenance of adequate body water levels is necessary to help prevent heat illness.

Feeling thirsty is not an adequate indication that the body needs water. In fact, by the time athletes feel thirsty, they already may have reached a dangerous level of body water depletion. It takes several hours to regain water balance once water loss has occurred. There is no physiological reason for restricting water intake before, during, or after athletic contests and practices. Players should drink eight to 16 ounces of water 30 minutes before the game and eight ounces every 20 minutes during the game.

Athletes should be encouraged to drink water before, during, and after each game and practice session.

Salts and Electrolytes

Another common myth is that salt (sodium) tablets and electrolyte solutions (solutions containing the elements sodium, potassium, and chloride) are needed by the athlete. These are not only unnecessary but can be harmful.

Salt tablets are irritating to the stomach and intestine and can increase the danger of dehydration by causing diarrhea when taken before a practice or game. Although the body needs to replace both water and sodium, the need for water is more critical.

Table 23-3. Recommended daily dietary allowances.*

Age (Years)	Children 7-10	Males 11-14	Females 11-14
Weight (pounds)	62	99	101
Height (inches)	52	62	62
Energy (calories)	2,400	2,700	2,200
range of calories	1,650-3,300	2,000-3,700	1,500-3,000
Protein (grams)	34	45	46
Vitamin A (mg RE)	700	1,000	1,000
Vitamin C (mg)	45	50	50
Calcium (mg)	800	1,200	1,200
Iron (mg)	10	18	18

*Adapted from Food and Nutrition Board, National Academy of Sciences—National Research Council, Revised, 1980.

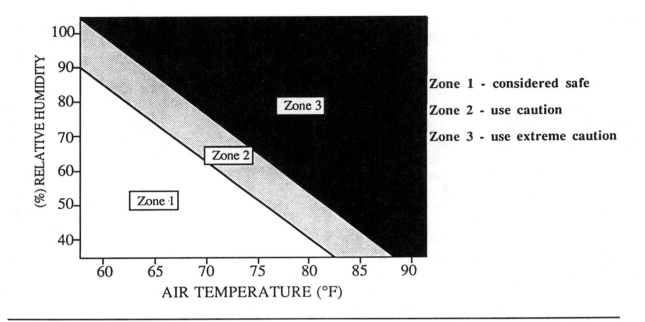

Figure 23-2. Guide for preventing heat illnesses associated with participation in physical activities under various conditions of temperatures and humidity.

Table 23-4. Temperature/humidity guide for taking precautionary action during baseball practices and games.

Temperature	Precautions to Take
Under 60° (F)	No precaution is necessary.
61-65° (F)	Encourage all players to take fluids. Make sure water is available at all times.
66-70° (F)	Take water breaks every 30-45 minutes of playing or practice time.
71-75° (F)	Provide rest periods with water breaks every 30-45 minutes of playing time—depending on the intensity of exercise. Substitute players during the game, so all may receive appropriate rest and fluids.
76° (F) and up	Practice during coolest part of the day. Schedule frequent rest breaks. Force water intake.
	Tell players to wear light, loose clothing that allows free circulation of air. Remove outer clothing when it gets wet because wet clothing reduces evaporation, thus hindering one of the body's cooling mechanisms.
	Move to the shade if possible.
	Drink water before, during, and after practice sessions and competition.
Relative humidity greater than 90%	Similar precautions should be taken as those listed for 76° (F) and up.

Some coaches provide 0.2 percent salt solutions (drinking water containing small amounts of salt) during an athletic event, but research has shown that plain water is just as effective. The body needs water immediately to replace the water lost during a game or practice, but any sodium lost can easily be replaced by eating salted foods after the event. Most Americans get more sodium than they need from salt already in their diet; therefore, excessive salting of food is unnecessary and not recommended.

The best replacement fluid is water.

ERGOGENIC AIDS

Ergogenic is derived from the Greek words ergon meaning work and gennan meaning to produce. In sports, ergogenic aids are agents thought to increase potential for work output. Various mechanical, psychological, physiological, nutritional, and pharmacological aids exist which purportedly improve performance. This discussion will focus on nutritional and pharmacological aids.

Nutritional Aids

Ergogenic foods are those substances that claim to "give you more energy," "improve your performance," and/or "enhance your endurance." There is no scientific evidence supporting any of these claims. Most of these foods and dietary practices are harmless to the athlete. The only danger these foods pose occurs when they replace necessary foods that the athlete needs for normal bodily functions. Some examples of these foods are bee pollen, pangamic acid, honey, lecithin, wheat germ oil, phosphates, alkaline salts (e.g., sodium bicarbonate, tomato juice, or organic juice), and gelatin.

Inform your athletes that these substances do not improve performance contrary to advertiser's claims. Encourage them to eat healthy diets and explain that this is the key to improving their performance.

Pharmacological Aids

• Steroids

Anabolic steroids (Dianabol, Anavar, Winstrol, etc.) have structures similar to the male sex hormone, testosterone. They are referred to as anabolic because, under certain circumstances, they promote tissue-building via increases in muscle mass and decreases in muscle breakdown. This effect is most evident in males when great increases in muscle mass and strength are seen at puberty. A 20-fold magnification in circulating testosterone levels accompanies these increases at this time. However, muscle mass and/or strength gains following steroid administration on already sexually mature subjects are questionable or at best show only moderate improvements.

In addition to their anabolic effects, steroids used in athletics also have androgenic or masculinizing effects. Males and females both may experience increased facial and body hair, baldness, voice deepening, and aggressiveness while using these drugs. Anabolic steroids also produce many reversible and irreversible side effects that are of great concern to the medical community as described in Table 23-5.

Steroid abuse is a major problem in athletics today even at the junior high and high school levels despite cases of well-known athletes who have been negatively affected by such abuse. In the 1983 Pan American games, seven of the 19 athletes tested were disqualified for steroid use and many more withdrew from competition to prevent detection. Ben Johnson, the great Canadian sprinter, had his gold medal rescinded at the 1988 Olympic games following discovery of steroid abuse. Not only is steroid use unethical, it is dangerous. Your athletes should be informed of the dangerous and potentially fatal effects of steroid usage. The risk of infertility, liver damage, immune dysfunction, and aggressive behavior far outweighs any possible advantages of taking steroids.

• Amphetamines

The use of pep pills or amphetamines is on the rise in athletics. These drug compounds cause reactions similar to adrenaline in that they increase heart rate, blood pressure, metabolism, breathing rate, and blood sugar levels. They may also cause headaches, dizziness, confusion, and sometimes insomnia, all of which could actually be detrimental to good physical performance. In fact, research suggests that amphetamines have little or no positive effect on exercise performance. Urge your athletes to stay clear of amphetamines as evidence for their potential detriment far exceeds any known benefits.

The best prescription for increased strength and improved performance is hard practice, plenty of rest, a good diet, healthy eating habits, and plenty of fluids.

• Caffeine

A stimulant commonly found in coffee, tea, cola, and chocolate is caffeine. Its ingestion has been found to improve physical performance in such long duration events as cycling and running. Therefore, its use may be warranted in endurance events and if used should be consumed one hour prior to the event. However, caffeine may cause headache, insomnia, and/or irritability in persons who normally avoid this drug. These people should avoid caffeine as these symptoms may be detrimental to performance. Don't rely on caffeine as a miracle performance drug, as it is not! Sensible training and proper diet are the best prescriptions that can't be beat for improving performance.

MEAL PATTERNS

Preadolescents and adolescents should eat at least three meals daily. Nutritional snacks

Table 23-5. Harmful effects of anabolic steroids.*

Body System	Reversible Effects	Irreversible Effects
Cardiovascular (heart/blood vessels)	High blood pressure, changes in blood fats, predisposing to heart disease, sticky platelets	Abnormal heart muscle, heart disease, stroke, heart attack
Skeletal	Minor changes in height	Early closure of the growth plates, making you shorter than you would be otherwise
Muscular	Increased water in muscle	Abnormal muscle cells, tendon rupture
Reproductive—male	Shrunken testicles, decreased sperm production, breast development, increased size of the prostate gland	Cancer of the prostate, increased breast development, abnormal testicles
Reproductive—female	Decreased breast size, increased body hair (facial also), menstrual problems	Increased size of clitoris, deepening voice, baldness, use during pregnancy may cause fetal deformity or death
Liver	Increased leakage of liver enzymes, abnormal growth of liver cells, turning "yellow" from backup of bile in liver	Cancer of liver, blood-filled sacs in liver
Endocrine (hormones)	Too much insulin secreted, decreased thyroxine, decreases hormone secretion from pituitary gland in brain	Do not know which effects are permanent
Skin	Acne, increased facial hair	Severe acne, baldness
Mental Attitude	Irritability, aggressiveness, mood swings, problems getting along with people, change in sex drive	Relationships with people damaged, possible personality changes
Immune	Decreased functioning of the immune cells and antibody formation	Serious infections, cancer

*This table comes from a paper entitled "What the High School Athletes, Coaches and Parents Should Know About Anabolic-Androgenic Steroids." This paper is available upon request from the Michigan State University Sports Medicine Clinic, Clinical Center, East Lansing, MI 48824.

may be added to the regular breakfast-lunch-dinner pattern if extra calories are needed. Most active athletes tend to skip meals, grab quick-fix meals, or depend on fast food restaurants and vending machines for meals on the run. This practice could lead to diets low in vitamins and minerals and high in fat and sodium. For example, a meal consisting of a hamburger, fries, and soda would provide 571 calories or approximately one-fourth of the energy requirement of a 15 to 18-year-old athlete, but less than one-tenth of the other nutritional requirements. Nutritional foods with good ratios of nutrients to calories are listed in Table 23-6. To maximize performance during periods of intense daily training, an athlete should consume approximately 500 grams (2000 Kcal) of carbohydrates per day.

Pre-Game Meal

One of the biggest concerns of athletes and coaches is what the team members should eat for the pre-game meal. Unfortunately, there are no foods that contain any special, magical properties that can improve your baseball players' performances if eaten before the game. Performance during an event or workout is dependent more on food consumed hours, days, or even weeks before the event. The most important consideration should be to select foods that can be digested easily, tolerated well, and liked by the players.

Pre-game stress causes an athlete's stomach and intestine to be less active. Minor food intake is recommended before vigorous exercise to delay exhaustion, but should be eaten two or three hours before the competition to give the stomach and intestines sufficient time to empty. Meals eaten before a practice session should be given the same general consideration as the pre-game meal, except there is no need to compensate for nervous stress.

Carbohydrates leave the stomach earlier and are digested more readily than either fats or protein. Foods that are easily digested include cereals, bread, spaghetti, macaroni, rice, potatoes (baked, not fried), and fruits. Examples of

Table 23-6. Contributions of nutritional snacks.

Food	Amount	Calories	% Recommended Daily Allowance			
			Vit A	Vit C	Calcium	Iron
Fresh orange	1 med. size	65	8	150	7	5
Orange juice	1 cup	110	14	200	3	5
Peanut butter	1 tablespoon	95	—	—	0.5	3
2% Milk	1 cup	120	14	4	37	1
Cheese and crackers	1 oz. cheese, 4 crackers	175	9	—	27	7
Carrot sticks	8 or 1 carrot	30	70	13	3	5
Ice cream	1 cup	270	15	2	22	1
Fruit-flavored yogurt	1 cup	230	14	2	43	2
Raisins	1/4 cup pressed	120	—	—	56	15
Applesauce	1/2 cup	115	1	3	—	7
Banana	1 med.	100	6	27	—	7
Ready-to-eat cereal	1 ounce	110	29	27	—	36

high-fat foods which should be avoided include cake, peanut butter, nuts, luncheon-type meats, gravy, yellow cheese, butter, and ice cream. Gas-forming foods (e.g., cabbage, cucumbers, cauliflower, and beans) and foods high in fiber and roughage (e.g., whole wheat bread, bran cereal, and raw vegetables) may cause discomfort to the player if eaten the day of competition.

Those athletes who have difficulty digesting solid foods before competition may prefer a liquid meal. These products should not be confused with instant powdered meals or "instant breakfasts," which have too much fat, protein, and electrolytes to be eaten before athletic contests. Liquid meals have the following advantages: (a) they leave the intestine rapidly, (b) they provide substantial calories, and (c) they are more convenient than preparing a solid meal. However, liquid meals do not provide any greater benefits for improving performances than do easily digested, well-tolerated meals.

Lunch should be eaten about three hours prior to afternoon practices or games. Possible choices for lunch include: spaghetti with tomato sauce; sandwich of white bread with a thin spread; chicken noodle or vegetable soup; low-fat yogurt or cottage cheese; fresh or canned fruits and fruit juices; crackers with white cheese or cheese spread; low-fat milk; baked potato sprinkled with white cheese and bacon bits (not real bacon but the soybean-flavored brand); or pizza—heavy on the tomato sauce and light on the cheese. If the team has an early morning practice or game, (8:00 a.m.) athletes should eat breakfast about 5:00 a.m. to ensure plenty of time to digest their meal before playing time. If they do not wish to eat breakfast that early, they could eat a lighter meal (e.g., liquid meals or juice and a piece of white toast with jelly—no butter or margarine) an hour before playing time. However, eating the larger meal two or three hours before playing time would delay feelings of fatigue and hunger and would be recommended when the team has to play in a baseball tournament lasting more than four hours. Possible selections for breakfast would include: cereal with low fat milk, pancakes, French toast, fruit juice, oatmeal or cream of wheat, white toast with jelly or cinnamon sugar, soft- or hard-boiled eggs, and fresh or canned fruit.

Pre-game meal:
- *Eat carbohydrate-rich foods*
- *Avoid fatty foods*
- *Avoid gas-forming and high-fiber foods*
- *Eat three or four hours before the game*
- *Drink plenty of fluids hourly*
- *Avoid concentrated sweets*

Candy bars are not a good source of quick energy and will not help your players perform better. A candy bar eaten right before the game may give your athletes a sudden burst of energy, but this energy boost is only temporary. The body over-compensates for the increase in blood sugar that results from eating a simple sugar (such as candy), causing feelings of tiredness and hunger. Your athletes will be full of energy for only a short time, then they will become sluggish and weak. Therefore, candies and anything high in sugar should be avoided especially just prior to activity.

Nutritional Support During Competition

Prolonged activity such as tournament play requires significant fluid and energy replacement throughout the day. Water is the most important replacement, but performance and endurance may be enhanced with proper carbohydrate replacement.

In a study of elite soccer players (Williams 1983), muscle glycogen (carbohydrate) stores were assessed after a 90-minute soccer match. The groups of players that drank one liter of a 7 percent sugar solution during the game had 63 percent more glycogen in their muscles than the group that drank plain water. In other words, the group that drank the sugar solution had much more "reserve" energy stores.

A 7 percent carbohydrate solution easily can be made by dissolving 70 grams (4.5 tablespoons) of glucose (sugar) in one quart (32 ounces) of water. Athletes should drink about 8 ounces of this mixture every 30 minutes during a game to maintain normal blood glucose levels. Many commercial carbohydrate replacement "sport drinks" are available with similar concentrations.

WEIGHT CONTROL

Each of your baseball players is different in height and build and, therefore, they have different ideal body weights. Rather than suggesting that your players weigh a specific number of pounds, you should work at improving their skill and physical fitness.

Weight Loss

Athletes who have too much fat will tend to be slower and tire more easily. For those individuals, some weight loss could improve their performance. In order to lose weight, energy output must exceed energy intake. Because of this, the more active athletes have an easier time losing weight than their less active peers.

One pound of fat has the energy equivalent of approximately 3,500 calories. Reducing food intake by 500 calories per day will result in a loss of about one pound per week. Increasing

the athlete's activity or training may also result in extra weight loss. Because fat cannot be lost at a rate faster than one or two pounds per week, weight loss greater than this amount could result in loss of body protein and not body fat. Hence, crash diets are not recommended because loss of valuable body protein (muscle mass) can occur.

Sauna baths, cathartics, and diuretics are methods used to lose weight by dehydration. These methods are not recommended because body fluids, not body fat are lost which reduces strength and endurance. The key to losing weight is to begin months before the season starts, follow a healthy diet, avoid high-calorie foods, eat three balanced meals, and increase activity level.

Important points to consider when attempting to lose weight:
- *Start early*
- *Lose at a slow pace*
- *Lose fat, not fluid or muscle*
- *Avoid excessive weight loss, especially during growing periods*
- *Avoid use of saunas, diuretics, or cathartics*

Weight Gain

The goal for athletes trying to gain weight is to add more muscle, rather than fat. Eating an extra 500 calories per day should result in gaining one pound of muscle per week. This increase in caloric intake must be accompanied with intensive exercise, at a level that is slightly less than full exertion. A good way to add those extra calories is by adding a daily snack such as dried fruit, nuts, peanut butter sandwich, juice, milk shake, or oatmeal-raisin cookies. Trying to gain weight at a faster rate will result only in more body fat in the wrong places, rather than muscle in the right places.

Important points to consider when attempting to gain weight:
- *Start early*
- *Gain at a slow pace*
- *Eat nutritious foods, and not foods high in fat content*

As a coach, you can give your players some tips on how to gain or lose weight properly—eating the right foods and gaining/losing weight at the proper pace. Encourage your players to eat a healthy diet because they should naturally achieve their ideal body weight by eating balanced meals and exercising. Most of your athletes will still be growing and will require additional calories to meet the demands of their growing bodies.

If you have athletes who are excessively over- or underweight, you may tactfully approach their parents and suggest that they seek medical attention for their child.

At the ideal body weight, the athlete performs best.

Many teenagers eat a lot of junk foods—high in calories and low in nutrients—but the motivated athletes would prefer foods high in nutrients if they realize that these foods could help them in performing their best.

SUMMARY

Your group of baseball players are motivated individuals who want to improve their performances to become a successful team. As their coach, you can provide them with the necessary information on how they can play their best. Providing your team with the nutritional advice presented in this chapter will as-sist them in obtaining maximum performance through eating a healthy diet and avoiding unsafe habits.

REFERENCES

Ivy, J.L. (1988). Muscle glycogen storage after different amounts of carbohydrate ingestion. *Journal of Applied Physiology, 65,* 2018-2023.
Ivy, J.L. (1988). Muscle glycogen synthesis after exercise: Effect of time on carbohydrate ingestion. *Journal of Applied Physiology, 64,* 1480-1485.
Mathews, D., & Fox, E. (1976). *The physiological bases of physical education and athletics.* Philadelphia: W.B. Saunders.
Williams, M.H. (1983). *Ergogenic aids in sports.* Champaign, IL: Human Kinetics.

SUGGESTED READINGS

American College of Sports Medicine. (1987). Position stand on the use of anabolic-androgenic steroids in sports. *Medicine and Science in Sports and Exercise,* 19(5), 534-539.
Clark, N. (1981). *The athlete's kitchen: A nutrition guide and cookbook.* Boston: CBI Publishing.
Darden, E. (1976) *Nutrition and athletic performance.* Pasadena, CA: The Athletic Press.
Food and Nutrition Board: Recommended dietary allowances. Rev. Ed., 1980. Washington, D.C.: National Academy of Sciences.
Higdon, H. (1978). *The complete diet guide for runners and other athletes.* Mountain View, CA: World Publications.
Katch, F.I., & McArdle, W.D. (1977). *Nutrition, weight control, and exercise.* Boston: Houghton Mifflin.
McArdle, W.D., Katch, F.I., & Katch, V.L. (1986). *Exercise physiology: Energy, nutrition, and human performance.* Philadelphia, PA: Lea & Febiger.
National Association for Sport and Physical Education. (1984). *Nutrition for sport success.* Reston, VA: American Alliance for Health, Physical Education, Recreation and Dance.
Smith, N.J. (1976) *Food for sport.* Palo Alto, CA: Bull Publishing.
Williams, E.R., & Caliendo, M.A. (1984) *Nutrition, principle issues, and application.* New York, NY: McGraw-Hill.
Williams, M.H. (1983) *Nutrition for fitness and sport.* Dubuque, Iowa: Wm. C. Brown.

24
Care of Common Baseball Injuries

Eugene W. Brown, Ph.D.
Rich Kimball, M.A.
Wade Lillegard, M.D.

QUESTIONS TO CONSIDER

- Can you identify and provide first aid for the different medical conditions commonly associated with baseball?
- What items belong in a well-stocked first aid kit?
- What procedures should you follow when an injury occurs?
- What information should you have about your players in case they become injured?

INTRODUCTION

Tom rounds third base and heads for home on a single to right field. He is going full speed and arrives at the plate at the same time that a perfect throw arrives from the right fielder. A violent collision occurs leaving Tom motionless on the field. The umpire, sensing the likelihood of an injury, immediately signals the coach onto the field to tend to Tom.

Watching from the bench, the first, and normal, reaction of a coach is to be frightened by the possible outcome of this violent collision. The sinking feeling in the stomach and the "Oh, no!" message sent out by the brain when Tom went down have been felt by most coaches at some point in their careers.

If this, or some similar situation confronted you, what would you do? Are you prepared to act appropriately? As a coach of a youth baseball team, it is your obligation to be able to deal with such an emergency. Before your first practice, you should:

- obtain medical information on your players
- establish emergency procedures
- prepare to provide first aid

You must not rely on the likelihood that a serious injury will not occur to the players on your team as an excuse for not being prepared to handle an emergency situation!

MEDICAL INFORMATION

The completed Athlete's Medical Information (see Supplement 24-1) and Medical Release (see Supplement 24-2) forms must be in your possession whenever your players are under your supervision. Hopefully, the need to use this information will never arise. But, if any injury does occur, the information on these forms will help you and qualified medical personnel respond quickly to an emergency.

EMERGENCY PROCEDURES

As the coach of an injured player, you are responsible for the actions taken until the player is placed in the care of competent medical personnel, parents, or guardians. Parents and players expect you to know how to proceed.

It is fortunate that life threatening situations rarely occur in youth sports. However, as a coach you must not rely on the likelihood that a serious injury will not occur to your athletes as an excuse for not being prepared to handle a medical emergency.

Prior to the first practice, completed Athlete's Medical Information forms (see Supplement 24-1) and Medical Release forms (see Supplement 24-2) for all athletes must be in possession of the coach.

Athlete's Medical Information

The Athlete's Medical Information form provides essential information about whom to contact during the emergency as well as a comprehensive overview of past and current medical conditions that may have implications for coaching and/or emergency care.

Medical Release

The Medical Release form is a mechanism by which parents and guardians can give permission to the coach and/or someone else to seek medical attention for their child. If the parents or guardians of an injured athlete cannot be contacted, this signed and notarized form is an essential element in the process of providing emergency medical attention.

On-Site Injury Report

Another essential medical form is the On-Site Injury Report form (see Supplement 24-3). This information may be very important if any legal problems develop in connection with an injury.

Emergency Plan

The final form that the coach must have is the Emergency Plan form (see Figure 24-1). This form provides guidance for handling an emergency. The Emergency Plan form provides directions to a number of people in helping them to carry out their assigned responsibilities in an emergency. One completed form is needed for each of these individuals. The form also contains space for inserting site-specific emergency information. The following paragraphs will describe the procedures associated with the Emergency Plan form.

Before the first practice, a number of responsible individuals must be assigned roles to carry out in an emergency. These roles are: coach, attending to an injured athlete, attending to the uninjured athletes, calling for emergency medical assistance, and flagging down the emergency vehicle. Note that when a medical emergency occurs, all assignments must be simultaneously activated.

For most agency sponsored and for many school sponsored sports, a physician or athletic trainer are not present to assist the coach in handling the medical aspects of an emergency. Thus, after taking charge of the situation and alerting individuals with assigned tasks, the coach is likely to be the person to attend to the injured athlete. The steps in attending to the injured athlete are presented in Figure 24-1 under section B. In order to provide emergency care, knowledge and skill in cardiopulmonary resuscitation (CPR), controlling bleeding, attending to heat stroke, attending to shock, and use of an allergic reaction kit are essential. This knowledge is briefly reviewed here. However, this knowledge and skill should be obtained through Red Cross courses offered in most communities.

When emergency medical personnel arrive, responsibility for the injured athlete should be transferred to these professionals. The Medical Release should be presented to the emergency medical personnel. If the parents or guardians are not available, the person designated on the Medical Release form (usually the coach) must accompany the injured athlete to the medical center.

If the coach is attending the injured ath-

Emergency Plan Form*

Essential Items:

1. Well-stocked first aid kit
2. Medical forms for each athlete (Athlete's Medical Information, Athlete's Medical Information Summary, and Medical Release)
3. On-Site Injury Report form

PROCEDURES

A. COACH

1. Take charge of situation
2. Alert previously assigned people to their tasks

B. _____ / _____
(Name and alternate person in charge of injured athlete; likely the coach or assistant coach.)
1. Calm and assure athlete.
2. If possible, determine nature and extent of injury.
3. If possible, privately report nature and extent of injury to person calling for emergency medical assistance.
4. If athlete is unconscious or a spinal injury is suspected, do not move the athlete.
5. Provide appropriate emergency care if warranted.
   a. ABC's (open Airways, restore Breathing, and restore Circulation)
   b. Control bleeding by direct pressure.
   c. For heat stroke, immediately cool body by cold sponging, immersion in

C. _____ / _____
(Name and alternate person in charge of uninjured athletes.)
1. Direct uninjured athletes to safe area within voice and vision of coach.
2. Have a plan in place to divert the attention of uninjured athletes from the emergency situation.
3. Use accepted procedure to dismiss athletes from practice/competition.

D. _____ / _____
(Name and alternate person responsible for phoning for emergency medical assistance.)
1. Get coins from first aid kit if needed for phone call.
2. Location of nearest phone by site of activity:
   Site   Location
   _____ _____
   _____ _____
   _____ _____
3. Emergency phone number by site of activity:
   Site   Phone No.
   _____ _____
   _____ _____
4. Report the nature of the injury and calmly respond to questions.

E. _____ / _____
(Name and alternate person responsible for flagging down emergency vehicle.)
1. Go to designated location to flag down emergency vehicle.
   Site   Location
   _____ _____
   _____ _____
   _____ _____
   Note that the site and location information corresponds to D.6. If no phone is within reasonable distance from the activity site, flag person should go to location where a vehicle can be flagged down.
2. Direct emergency medical personnel to injured athlete.

Figure 24-1. Emergency plan form.

cold water, and cold packs.

d. For shock, have athlete lie down, calm athlete, elevate feet unless head injury, control athlete's temperature, loosen tight fitting clothing, and control pain or bleeding if necessary.

e. For allergic reaction, use ana-kit if available.

6. Transfer care to emergency medical personnel. (Note that the Medical Release Form and one individual whose name appears on the form must accompany athletes to medical center unless parents or guardians are available.)

7. Provide Athlete's Medical Information Summary to emergency medical personnel.

---

5. Directions to sites:

Site   Directions

_____
_____
_____
_____
_____

6. Location of flag person by site:

Site   Location

_____
_____
_____

7. Remain on the phone until the other person hangs up.

8. Return to person attending to injured athlete and privately report status of emergency medical assistance.

A. COACH, cont.

3. Use the information on the Roster Summary of Contacts in an Emergency to phone the injured athlete's parents (guardians) or their designees.

4. Complete the On-Site Injury Report form.

---

*A minimum of 4 completed copies of this form is needed; one for each of the individuals with assigned tasks. Make sure that information is included on all practice and competition sites.

Providing Emergency Care

Many emergency situations can be appropriately handled if you remember the ABC's of emergency care, as advocated by the American Red Cross.[1]

A = Airway
B = Breathing
C = Circulation

Remembering the ABC's will remind you of how to proceed in a life-threatening situation.

It is beyond the scope of this chapter to provide the complete information necessary to handle all emergencies. To familiarize you with what is involved and to encourage you to obtain appropriate first aid and CPR (cardiopulmonary resuscitation) instruction, the ABC's and bleeding are briefly outlined. More complete information on artificial respiration is available through your local chapter of the American Red Cross.

The ABC's

* Open the Airway

    Always check the airway to make sure it is free of any items that may impede breathing. In baseball anything in the mouth—gum, sunflower or pumpkin seeds, or candy—can obstruct the airway and should be removed immediately. The primary method advocated for opening the airway is the jaw thrust or chin lift method. The Red Cross provides materials and training for developing this skill.

* Restore Breathing

    Once the airway is open, check to see if the player is breathing. Is the chest moving up and down? Are there sounds of breathing? Can you feel exhaled air at the mouth or nostrils? If breathing is not taking place, begin artificial respiration. The procedures taught by the Red Cross are the standard to follow when attempting to restore breathing.

* Restore Circulation

    If the heart has stopped beating, circulation should be restored via CPR. Cardiopulmonary resuscitation is a valuable skill to learn and maintain because you are coaching a sport in which the temporary interruption of cardiopulmonary function could occur. The techniques of CPR are beyond the scope of this manual. You are encouraged to attend one of the many American Red Cross CPR courses that are regularly offered in nearly every local community that sponsors youth baseball.

Bleeding

If the player is bleeding profusely, you must still follow the ABC's. Stopping the bleeding will serve no benefit if the injured player cannot breathe.

Extensive bleeding should be controlled by applying direct pressure over the wound for 10 to 20 minutes without checking the wound. You should use latex gloves to do this. (See "Precautions for Preventing the Transmission of Blood-Borne Pathogens.") A sterile pad is preferred, but in an emergency, use whatever is available: a towel, a shirt, your hands, etc. The use of a tourniquet is ill-advised and should only be employed when one accepts the fact that its use may be trading the loss of a limb to save a life.

Figure 24-2. Providing emergency care.

lete, the uninjured athletes should be directed to a safe area within voice and vision of the coach. The responsibilities assigned to the person in charge of the uninjured athletes is presented in Figure 24-1 under section C. A "rainy day" practice plan could have been prepared and available for an emergency or an accepted procedure for dismissing the uninjured athletes could be used.

Under section D of Figure 24-1, the responsibilities of the individual assigned to call for emergency medical assistance are presented. This section also includes space for entering site-specific information for the location of the nearest telephone, emergency telephone number, directions to the injured athlete, and the location of the flag person. If known, the person calling for assistance should report the nature of the injury to the receptionist. After the call for assistance, this individual should privately report the status of emergency medical assistance to the person attending the injured athlete.

Whether or not someone is needed to flag down and direct the emergency vehicle will depend on the site of the team's activities. The procedures for the flag person are described in Figure 24-1 under section E. In rare situations, where there is no telephone near the site of the injury, the flag person will be responsible for securing emergency medical assistance.

After the injured player is released to emergency medical personnel, the coach should complete the On-Site Injury Report form. Also, if the injured athlete's parents or guardians are unaware of the emergency situation, information on the Athlete's Medical Information form should be used to contact them.

Rehearsing emergency care procedures can be invaluable.

PROVIDE FIRST AID

Aids for Proper Care

If the injury is less serious and does not require assistance from trained medical personnel, you may be able to move the player from the field to the bench area and begin appropriate care. Two important aids to properly care for an injured player include a first aid kit and ice.

- ### First Aid Kit

A well-stocked first aid kit does not have to be large but it should contain the basic items that may be needed for appropriate care. This checklist provides a guide for including commonly used supplies. You may wish to add to and subtract from the kit on the basis of your experience and/or local policies or guidelines.

A good rule of thumb for coaches is, "If you can't care for the problems by using the supplies in a well-stocked first aid kit, then it is too big a problem for you to handle." You should be able to handle bruises, small cuts, strains, and sprains. When more serious injuries such as fractures, dislocations, back, or neck injuries occur, call for professional medical assistance.

- ### Ice

Having access to ice is unique to every local setting. Thus, every coach may have to arrange for its provision in a different way. Ice, however, is very important to proper, immediate care of many minor injuries and should, therefore, be readily available. Many coaches may decide to carry a cooler containing small bags of crushed ice.

Precautions for Preventing the Transmission of Blood-Borne Pathogens (BBP's)

It is generally agreed among experts that the likelihood of transmission of blood-borne pathogens—such as the human immunodeficiency virus (HIV) and hepatitis B—through athletics is extremely low. In fact, to date the only case of rumored transmission of HIV in athletics—that of an Italian soccer player—has been dismissed. Even though transmission of BBP's is unlikely in athletics, coaches should exercise precautions by

- removing from play athletes who have bloody wounds and
- personally avoiding direct contact with blood and other fluids likely to contain blood.

First Aid Kit and Contents

First aid kit—durable plastic ("fishing tackle" type) kit with shelves and various size partitions.

Penlight
Tape measure
Blanket, light weight foil
Scissors
Pocket knife
Airway
Bulb suction syringe
Sling, medium
Cervical collar, medium
Elastic wraps (2", 3", 4", and 5")
Tweezers
Stethoscope (NE*)

Ana-kit**
Eye stream 30 ml.

Athletes' Medical Information
    forms or Athletes' Medical
    Information Summary
    forms***
Medical Release forms***
Emergency Plan forms
On-Site Emergency Report
    forms

Plastic bags (qt., 1/2 gal., and gal. sizes)
Garbage bag labeled "biohazardous materials"
PR microshield—clear mouth barrier
Germ filter masks
Tongue blades—regular, sterile
Sterile latex gloves, size 8
Betadine swabs
Alcohol preps
Gauze bandage (1" x 126')
Cling bandage (3" x 5 yds.)
Plastic bandages (3/4")
Flexible bandages (3/4")
Gauze sponge (4" x 4" x 8 ply)
Non-stick pads, sterile (2" x 3")
Eye pads, small and large
Hard candy
Gauze pads (4" x 4" and 2" x 2")
Disinfectant
Moleskin
Safety pins
Soap
Sun screen
Petroleum jelly
Insect repellant
Liquid bleach containing hypochlorite (3 oz.)
Plastic bottle (1 qt.) for mixing 10:1 water to
    bleach solution

---

*   (NE)—non-essential
**   Requires prescription
*** Required for all members of the team

Figure 24-3. First aid kit and contents.

Removing an Athlete from Competition

If an athlete sustains a wound in which blood or exudate are present, bleeding must be stopped and open skin lesions must be covered completely before permitting the athlete to return to competition.

Avoiding Direct Contact with Blood and Bodily Fluids Containing Blood

Latex gloves should be worn when tending to an injury in which blood or fluids containing blood are present. If the hands and skin become contaminated, they should be washed immediately after removing the gloves.

Disposable contamined materials should be placed in a biohazard container. This may be a plastic trash bag that is clearly labeled as containing biohazardous materials and that can be sealed.

Contaminated structures, equipment and instruments must be cleaned with a freshly mixed bleach solution. (This contains one part bleach and ten parts water.) Clothing that becomes contaminated must be removed, placed in an appropriately labeled container, and later washed at 160° F. (71° C.) with detergent for 30 minutes.

If mouth-to-mouth resuscitation is performed, a mouth shield should be worn.

Care of Minor Injuries

• R.I.C.E.

Unless you are also a physician, you should not attempt to care for anything except minor injuries (for example, bruises, bumps, sprains). Many minor injuries can be cared for by using the R.I.C.E. formula.

Most minor injuries can benefit from using the R.I.C.E. formula for care.

When following the R.I.C.E. formula, ice should be kept on the injured area for 15 minutes and taken off for 20 minutes. While ice is being applied, a towel should be placed between the ice and the skin, and compression should not be used at the same time. Repeat this procedure three to four times. Icing should continue three times per day for the first 72 hours following the injury. After three days, extended care is necessary if the injury has not healed. At this time, options for care include:

- stretching and strengthening exercises
- contrast treatments
- visiting a doctor for further diagnosis

• Contrast Treatments

If the injured area is still swollen after 72 hours and the pain is subsiding, contrast treatments will help. Use the following procedure:

1. Place the injured area in an ice bath or cover with an ice bag for one minute.
2. After using the ice, place the injured area in

R.I.C.E. Formula

The R.I.C.E. formula for care of minor injuries involves the following steps:

R = Rest: Keep the player out of action.

I = Ice: Apply ice to the injured area.

C = Compression: Wrap an elastic bandage around the injured area and then around the ice bag to hold the bag in place. (Using the elastic wrap or a layer of towel between the ice bag and skin will minimize the chance of injury from ice therapy.) The bandage should not be so tight as to cut off blood flow to the injured area.

E = Elevation: Let gravity drain the excess fluid.

Figure 24-4. R.I.C.E. formula.

warm water (100 degrees - 110 degrees) for
three minutes.

3. Continue this rotation for five to seven bouts
   of ice and four to six bouts of heat.
4. Always end with the ice treatment.

Contrast treatments should be followed for
the next three to five days. If swelling or pain
still persists after several days of contrast treatments, the player should be sent to a physician
for further tests. Chapter 25 deals with the rehabilitation of injuries. Read it carefully, because
proper care is actually a form of rehabilitation.

COMMON MEDICAL PROBLEMS IN BASEBALL

Information about 24 common medical conditions that may occur in baseball is presented
in this section. The information about each condition includes: (1) a definition, (2) common
symptoms, (3) immediate on-field care, and
(4) guidelines for returning the player to action.
In cases of abrasions, blisters, dental injuries,
eye injuries, open fractures, lascerations, nose
bleeds, and puncture wounds, review the section titled "Precations for Preventing the Transmission of Blood-Borne Pathogens."

Abrasion

Definition:
- superficial skin wound caused by scraping

Symptoms:
- minor bleeding
- redness
- burning sensation

Care:
- Cleanse the area with soap and water.
- Control the bleeding.
- Cover the area with sterile dressing.
- Monitor over several days for signs of infec-
  tion.

Return to Action:
- after providing immediate care
- after abrasion is covered completely

Back or Neck Injury

Definition:
- any injury to the back or neck area that
  causes the athlete to become immobile or
  unconscious

Symptoms:
- pain and tenderness over the spine
- numbness
- weakness or heaviness in limbs
- tingling feeling in extremities

Care:
- Make sure the athlete is breathing.
- Call for medical assistance.
- Do not move the neck or back.

Return to Action:
- with permission of a physician

Blisters

Definition:
- localized collection of fluid in the outer portion of the skin

Symptoms:
- redness
- inflammation
- oozing of fluid
- discomfort

Care:
- Put disinfectant on the area.
- Cut a hole in a stack of several gauze pads to
  be used as a doughnut surrounding the blister.
- Cover the area with a Band-aid.
- Alter the cause of the problem when possible (e.g., proper size and/or shape of the baseball shoes).

Return to Action:
- immediately, unless pain is severe
- after blister is covered completely

Contusion

Definition:
- a bruise; an injury in which the skin is not
  broken

Symptoms:
- tenderness around the injury
- swelling
- localized pain

Care:
- Apply the R.I.C.E. formula for first 3 days.
- Use contrast treatments for days 4-8.
- Restrict activity.
- Provide padding when returning the athlete to activity.

Return to Action:
- when there is complete absence of pain and full range of motion is restored

Cramps

Definition:
- involuntary and forceful contraction of a muscle; muscle spasm

Symptoms:
- localized pain in contracting muscle

Care:
- Slowly stretch the muscle.
- Massage the muscle.

Return to Action:
- when pain is gone and full range of motion is restored

Dental Injury

Definition:
- any injury to mouth or teeth

Symptoms:
- pain
- bleeding
- loss of tooth (partial or total)

Care:
- Clear the airway where necessary.
- Stop the bleeding with direct pressure.
- Make sure excess blood does not clog the airway.
- Save any teeth that were knocked free; store them in the athlete's own mouth or a moist, sterile cloth.

- Do not rub or clean tooth that has been knocked out.
- Transport athlete to a hospital or dentist.

Return to Action:
- when the pain is gone (usually within two to three days)
- with permission of a dentist or physician

Dislocation

Definition:
- loss of normal anatomical alignment of a joint

Symptoms:
- complaints of joint slipping in and out (subluxation)
- joint out of line
- pain at the joint

Care:
- mild
  —Treat as a sprain (i.e., R.I.C.E.).
  —Obtain medical care.
- severe
  —Immobilize before moving.
  —This type of injury must be treated by a physician.
  —Obtain medical care. Do not attempt to put joint back into place.
  —Use the R.I.C.E. formula.

Return to Action:
- with permission of a physician

Eye Injury—Contusion

Definition:
- direct blow to the eye and region surrounding the eye by a blunt object

Symptoms:
- pain
- redness of eye
- watery eye

Care:
- Have the athlete lie down with his/her eyes closed.
- Place a folded cloth, soaked in cold water, gently on the eye.

- Seek medical attention if injury is assessed as severe.

Return to Action:
- for minor injury, player may return to action after symptoms clear
- for severe injury, with permission of a physician

Eye Injury—Foreign Object

Definition:
- object between eyelid and eyeball

Symptoms:
- pain
- redness of eye
- watery eye
- inability to keep eye open

Care:
- Do not rub the eye.
- Allow tears to form in eye.
- Carefully try to remove loose object with sterile cotton swab.
- If object is embedded in the eye, have the player close both eyes, loosely cover both eyes with sterile dressing, and bring the athlete to an emergency room or ophthalmologist.

Return to Action:
- for minor injury, athlete may return to action after symptoms clear
- for severe injury, with permission of a physician

Fainting

Definition:
- dizziness and loss of consciousness that may be caused by an injury, exhaustion, heat illness, emotional stress, or lack of oxygen

Symptoms:
- dizziness
- cold, clammy skin
- pale
- seeing "spots" before one's eyes
- weak, rapid pulse

Care:
- Have the athlete lie down and elevate his/her feet or have the player sit with his/her head between the knees.

Return to Action:
- with permission of a physician

Fracture

Definition:
- a crack or complete break in a bone [A simple fracture is a broken bone, but with unbroken skin. An open fracture is a broken bone that also breaks the skin.]

Symptoms:
- pain at fracture site
- tenderness, swelling
- deformity or unnatural position
- loss of function in injured area
- open wound, bleeding (open fracture)

*(**Note:** A simple fracture may not be evident immediately. If localized pain persists, obtain medical assistance.)*

Care:
- Stabilize injured bone by using splints, slings, or bandages.
- Do not attempt to straighten an injured part when immobilizing it.
- If skin is broken (open fracture), keep the open wound clean by covering it with the cleanest available cloth.
- Check for shock and treat if necessary.

Return to Action:
- with permission of a physician

Head Injury—Conscious

Definition:
- any injury that causes the athlete to be unable to respond in a coherent fashion to known facts (name, date, etc.)

Symptoms:
- dizziness
- pupils unequal in size and/or non-responsive to light and dark
- disoriented
- unsure of name, date, or activity
- unsteady movement of eyeballs when trying to follow a finger moving in front of eyes

- same symptoms as noted for back or neck injury may be present

Care:
- If above symptoms are present, player may be moved carefully when dizziness disappears. Athletes with head injuries should be removed from further practice or competition that day and should be carefully observed for a minimum of 24 hours.
- Obtain medical assistance.

Return to Action:
- with permission of a physician

Head Injury—Unconscious

Definition:
- any injury in which the athlete is unable to respond to external stimuli by verbal or visual means

Symptoms:
- Athlete is unconscious
- cuts or bruises around the head may be evident

Care:
- **ANY TIME AN ATHLETE IS UNCONSCIOUS, ASSUME AN INJURY TO THE SPINAL CORD OR BRAIN.**
- If necessary, clear the airway keeping the athlete's neck straight.
- Do not move the athlete.
- Call for medical assistance.

Return to Action:
- with permission of a physician

Heat Exhaustion

Definition:
- heat disorder that may lead to heat stroke

Symptoms:
- fatigue
- profuse sweating
- chills
- throbbing pressure in the head
- nausea
- normal body temperature
- pale and clammy skin

- muscle cramps
- rapid, weak pulse

Care:
- Remove the player from heat and sun.
- Provide plenty of water.
- Rest the athlete in a supine position with feet elevated about 12 inches.
- Loosen or remove the athlete's clothing.
- Fan athlete.
- Drape wet towels over athlete.

Return to Action:
- next day if symptoms are no longer present

Heat Stroke

Definition:
- heat disorder that is life-threatening

Symptoms:
- extremely high body temperature
- hot, red, and dry skin
- rapid and strong pulse
- confusion
- labored respiration
- fainting
- convulsions

Care:
- Immediately call for medical assistance.
- Immediately cool body by cold sponging, immersion in cool water, and cold packs.

Return to Action:
- with permission of a physician

Lacerations

Definition:
- a tearing or cutting of the skin

Symptoms:
- bleeding
- swelling

Care:
- Elevate area.
- Direct pressure with gauze (if available) to the wound for four or five minutes usually will stop bleeding.
- Continue to add gauze if blood soaks through.
- Clean the wound with disinfectant.

- Use the R.I.C.E. formula.
- If stitches are required, send to a doctor within six hours.

Return to Action:

- as soon as pain is gone, if the wound can be protected from further injury
- after laceration is completely covered
- with permission of a physician, if stitches are required

Loss of Wind

Definition:

- a forceful blow to mid-abdomen area that causes inability to breathe

Symptoms:

- rapid, shallow breathing
- gasping for breath

Care:

- Check athlete to determine if other injuries exist.
- Place athlete in a supine position.
- Calm the athlete in order to foster slower breathing.

Return to Action:

- after five minutes of rest to regain composure and breathing has returned to normal rate

Nose Bleed

Definition:

- bleeding from the nose

Symptoms:

- bleeding
- swelling
- pain
- deformity of nose

Care:

- Calm the athlete.
- Get the athlete into a sitting position.
- Pinch the nostrils together with fingers while the athlete breathes through the mouth.
- If bleeding cannot be controlled, call for medical assistance.

Return to Action:

- minor nosebleed—if no deformity and no impairment to breathing, pack nose with gauze before athlete continues competition—when bleeding has stopped for several minutes
- serious nosebleed—no more competition that day; doctor's permission if a fracture has occurred

Plantar Fasciitis

Definition:

- inflammation of the connective tissue (fascia) that runs from the heel to the toes

Symptoms:

- arch and heel pain
- sharp pain ("stone bruise") near heel
- gradual onset of pain, that may be tolerated for weeks
- morning pain may be more severe
- pain may decrease throughout day

Care:

- Rest the foot.
- Stretch the Achilles tendon before exercise.
- Use shoes with firm heel counter, good heel cushion, and arch support.
- Use of a heel lift may reduce shock to the foot and decrease the pain.
- Use adhesive strapping to support the arch.

Return to Action:

- when pain is gone

Puncture Wound

Definition:

- any hole made by the piercing of a pointed instrument

Symptoms:

- breakage of the skin
- minor bleeding, possibly none
- tender around wound

Care:

- Cleanse the area with soap and water.
- Control the bleeding.
- Cover the area with sterile dressing.
- Consult physician about the need for a tetanus shot.

- Monitor over several days for signs of infection.

Return to Action:
- with permission of a physician

Shin Splints

Definition:
- a general term for any pain located in the front or side of the lower leg

Symptoms:
- pain over the shin bone (tibia)
- shin may be tender to the touch
- pain and aching around shin during and after activity

Care:
- Rest the lower leg.
- Avoid activities involving a jarring action of the lower leg.
- Avoid activities which use musculature of the front of the lower leg.
- Use the R.I.C.E. formula.
- Avoid possible causes of injury (for example, poor shoes, sudden change in activity, incorrect running mechanics, over training).
- See trainer or physician for appropriate taping and/or arch supports.

Return to Action:
- when pain is gone

(Note: Mild pain may be tolerated. However, if post activity pain is pronounced, the athlete should continue the R.I.C.E. process and refrain from running types of activity.)

Shock

Definition:
- adverse reaction of the body to physical or psychological trauma

Symptoms:
- pale skin
- cold, clammy skin
- dizziness and disorientation
- nausea
- faint feeling
- bluish lips and nails

Care:
- Have the athlete lie down.
- Calm the athlete.
- Elevate the feet, unless it is a head injury.
- Send for emergency help.
- Control the athlete's temperature.
- Loosen tight-fitting clothing.
- Control the pain or bleeding if necessary.

Return to Action:
- with permission of a physician

Sprain

Definition:
- a stretching or a partial or complete tear of the ligaments surrounding a joint

Symptoms:
- pain at the joint
- pain aggravated by motion at the joint
- tenderness and swelling
- looseness at the joint

Care:
- Immobilize at time of injury if pain is severe.
- Use the R.I.C.E. formula.
- Send the player to a physician.

Return to Action:
- when pain and swelling are gone
- when full range of motion is reestablished
- when strength and stability are within 95 percent of the non-injured limb throughout range of motion
- when light formal activity is possible with no favoring of the injury
- when formal activity can be resumed with moderate to full intensity with no favoring of the injury

Strain

Definition:
- stretching or tearing of the muscle or tendons that attach the muscle to the bone (commonly referred to as a "muscle pull")

Symptoms:
- localized pain brought on by stretching or contracting the muscle in question
- unequal strength between limbs

Care:
- Use the R.I.C.E. formula.
- Use contrast treatments for days 4-8.

Return to Action:
- when the athlete can stretch the injured segment as far as the non-injured segment
- when strength is equal to opposite segment
- when the athlete can perform basic baseball tasks without favoring the injury

(Note: Depending on the severity of the strain, it may take from one day to more than two weeks for an athlete to return to action.)

MAINTAINING APPROPRIATE RECORDS

The immediate care you provide to an injured athlete is important to limit the extent of the injury and to set the stage for appropriate rehabilitation. However, immediate care is not the end of prudent action when an injury occurs. Two additional brief but valuable tasks should be completed. The first of these is to fill out an On-Site Injury Report Form (see Supplement 24-3) and the second is to log the injury on the Summary of Season Injuries Form (see Supplement 24-4).

On-Site Injury Report Form

It is important for you to maintain a record of the injuries that occur to your players. This information may be helpful to guide delayed care or medical treatment and may be very important if any legal problems develop in connection with the injury. Supplement 24-3 includes a standard form that will help guide the recording of pertinent information relative to each injury. You should check on legal requirements in your state to determine how long these records should be kept (is usually at least several years following an injury).

Summary of Season Injuries Form

Supplement 24-4 lists each of the common medical conditions that occur in baseball and also provides a space for you to record when each type of injury occurred. At the end of the season, you should total the incidences of each injury type to see if there is any trend to the kind of injuries your team has suffered. If a trend exists, evaluate your training methods in all areas of practices and games. Try to alter drills or circumstances that may be causing injuries. Review Chapter 26, "Prevention of Common Baseball Injuries," for techniques that may help you prevent injuries. Perhaps your practice routine ignores or overemphasizes some area of stretching or conditioning. Decide on a course of action that may be implemented for next season, and write your thoughts in the space provided or note the appropriate changes you wish to make on your season or practice plans.

SUMMARY

This chapter attempts to acquaint you with various injuries associated with baseball and how you should be prepared to deal with these injuries. If you have prepared your first aid kit, brought along the medical records, and familiarized yourself with the different types of injuries, you should be able to handle whatever situation arises. Follow the steps that are outlined for you, and remember—you are not a doctor. If you are in doubt about how to proceed, use the coins in your first aid kit and call for professional medical help. Do not make decisions about treatments if you are not qualified to make them.

Remember, react quickly and with confidence. Most injuries will be minor and the injured players will need only a little reassurance before they can be moved to the bench area. Injuries cannot be completely avoided in baseball. Therefore, you must prepare yourself to deal with whatever happens in a calm, responsible manner.

REFERENCES

American Red Cross. (1981). *Cardiopulmonary resuscitation.* Washington, D.C.: American Red Cross.

Tanner, S.M., & Harvey, J.S. (1988). How we manage plantar fasciitis. *The Physician and Sportsmedicine, 16*(8), 39-40, 42, 44, 47.

Whitesel, J., & Newell, S.G. (1980). Modified low-dye strapping. *The Physician and Sportsmedicine, 8*(9), 129-131.

SUGGESTED READINGS

American Academy of Pediatrics. (1991). American Academy of Pediatrics policy statement—Human immunodeficiency virus [acquired immunodeficiency syndrome (AIDS) virus] in the athletic setting. *AAP News, 6,* 18.

American College of Sports Medicine, American Orthopaedic Society for Sports Medicine & Sports Medicine Committee of the United States Tennis Association. (1982). *Sports injuries— An aid to prevention and treatment.* Coventry, CT: Bristol-Myers Co.

Centers for Disease Control. (1988). Universal precautions for prevention of transmission of human immunodeficiency virus, hepatitis B virus, and other blood-borne pathogens in health-care settings. *MMWR, 37*(24), 337-382, 387-388.

Hackworth, C. et al. (1982). *Prevention, recognition, and care of common sports injuries.* Kalamazoo, MI: SWM Systems, Inc.

Hamel, R. (1992). AIDS: Assessing the risk among athletes. *The Physician and Sportsmedicine, 20*(2), 139-140, 142, 145-146.

Izumi, H. (1991). AIDS and athletic trainers: Recommendations for athletic training programs. *Athletic Training, 26,* 358-360, 362-363.

Jackson, D., & Pescar, S. (1981). *The young athlete's health handbook.* New York, NY: Everest House.

Lyons, B. (1992). Blood-borne pathogens in the health care of the athlete. *The First Aider, 62*(1), 1-2.

Oren, M.L. (1992). HIV infection and AIDS: Education is our best defense. *Spotlight on Youth Sports, 15*(3), 1-2, 5-6.

Risser, W.L. (1992). HIV makes caution necessary in sports settings. *The Physician and Sportsmedicine, 20*(5), 190.

Rosenberg, S.N. (1985). *The Johnson & Johnson first aid book.* New York: Warner Books, Inc.

Athlete's Medical Information

(to be completed by parents/guardians and athlete)

Athlete's Name: _____ Athlete's Birthdate: _____

Parents' Names: _____ Date: _____

Address: _____

Phone No's.: (____)_____ (____)_____ (____)_____
(Home)   (Work)   (Other)

Who to contact in case of emergency (if parents cannot be immediately contacted):

Name: _____ Relationship: _____

Home Phone No.: (____)_____ Work Phone No.: (____)_____

Name: _____ Relationship: _____

Home Phone No.: (____)_____ Work Phone No.: (____)_____

Hospital preference: _____ Emergency Phone No.: (____)_____

Doctor preference: _____ Office Phone No.: (____)_____

MEDICAL HISTORY

Part I.   Complete the following:

	Date	Doctor	Doctor's Phone No.
1. Last tetanus shot?	_____		
2. Last dental examination?	_____	_____	_____
3. Last eye examination?	_____	_____	_____

Part II.   Has your child or did your child have any of the following?

General Conditions:	Circle one		Circle one or both		Injuries:	Circle one		Circle one or both	
1. Fainting spells/dizziness	Yes	No	Past	Present	1. Toes	Yes	No	Past	Present
2. Headaches	Yes	No	Past	Present	2. Feet	Yes	No	Past	Present
3. Convulsions/epilepsy	Yes	No	Past	Present	3. Ankles	Yes	No	Past	Present
4. Asthma	Yes	No	Past	Present	4. Lower legs	Yes	No	Past	Present
5. High blood pressure	Yes	No	Past	Present	5. Knees	Yes	No	Past	Present
6. Kidney problems	Yes	No	Past	Present	6. Thighs	Yes	No	Past	Present
7. Intestinal disorder	Yes	No	Past	Present	7. Hips	Yes	No	Past	Present
8. Hernia	Yes	No	Past	Present	8. Lower back	Yes	No	Past	Present
9. Diabetes	Yes	No	Past	Present	9. Upper back	Yes	No	Past	Present
10. Heart disease/disorder	Yes	No	Past	Present	10. Ribs	Yes	No	Past	Present
11. Dental plate	Yes	No	Past	Present	11. Abdomen	Yes	No	Past	Present
12. Poor vision	Yes	No	Past	Present	12. Chest	Yes	No	Past	Present
13. Poor hearing	Yes	No	Past	Present	13. Neck	Yes	No	Past	Present
14. Skin disorder	Yes	No	Past	Present	14. Fingers	Yes	No	Past	Present
15. Allergies	Yes	No			15. Hands	Yes	No	Past	Present
Specify:_____			Past	Present	16. Wrists	Yes	No	Past	Present
_____			Past	Present	17. Forearms	Yes	No	Past	Present
16. Joint dislocation or					18. Elbows	Yes	No	Past	Present
separations	Yes	No			19. Upper arms	Yes	No	Past	Present
Specify:_____			Past	Present	20. Shoulders	Yes	No	Past	Present
_____			Past	Present	21. Head	Yes	No	Past	Present
17. Serious or significant ill-					22. Serious or significant in-				
nesses not included above	Yes	No			juries not included above	Yes	No		
Specify:_____			Past	Present	Specify: _____			Past	Present
_____			Past	Present				Past	Present
18. Others:_____			Past	Present	23. Others: _____			Past	Present
_____			Past	Present	_____			Past	Present

Part III. Circle appropriate response to each question. For each "Yes" response, provide additional information.

	Circle one	Additional information

1. Is your child currently taking any medication? If yes,   Yes   No   _____
    describe medication, amount, and reason for taking.

2. Does your child have any allergic reactions to medica-   Yes   No   _____
    tion, bee stings, food, etc.? If yes, describe agents that
    cause adverse reactions and describe these reactions.

3. Does your child wear any appliances (e.g., glasses,   Yes   No   _____
    contact lenses, hearing aid, false teeth, braces, etc.)?
    If yes, describe appliances.

4. Has your child had any surgical operations?   Yes   No   _____
    If yes, indicate site, explain the reason for the surgery,
    and describe the level of success.

5. Has a physician placed any restrictions on your child's   Yes   No   _____
    present activities? If yes, describe restrictions.

6. Does your child have any existing and/or past medical   Yes   No   _____
    or emotional conditions that require special concern
    and attention by a sports coach? If yes, explain.

7. Does your child have any deformities (e.g., abnormal   Yes   No   _____
    curvature of the spine, heart problems, one kidney,
    blindness in one eye, one testicle, etc.)? If yes, describe.

8. Is there a history of serious family illnesses (e.g.,   Yes   No   _____
    diabetes, bleeding disorders, heart attack before age 50,
    etc.)? If yes, describe illnesses.

9. Has your child lost consciousness or sustained a   Yes   No   _____
    concussion?

10. Has your child experienced fainting spells or   Yes   No   _____
    dizziness while exercising?

Part IV. Has your child or did your child have any of the following personal habits?

Personal Habit	Circle one		Circle one or both		Indicate extent or amount
1. Smoking	Yes	No	Past	Present	_____
2. Smokeless tobacco	Yes	No	Past	Present	_____
3. Alcohol	Yes	No	Past	Present	_____
4. Recreational drugs (e.g., marijuana, cocaine, etc.)	Yes	No	Past	Present	_____
5. Steroids	Yes	No	Past	Present	_____
6. Others					
Specify: _____	Yes	No	Past	Present	_____
_____	Yes	No	Past	Present	_____
_____	Yes	No	Past	Present	_____

Part V. Please explain below any "Yes" responses in Parts II, III, and IV or any other concerns that have present implications for my coaching your child. Also, describe special first aid requirements, if appropriate. An additional sheet may be attached if necessary.

_____

_____

_____

_____

_____

_____

_____

Medical Release Form

I hereby give permission for any and all medical attention necessary to be administered to my child in the event of an accident, injury, sickness, etc., under the direction of the people listed below until such time as I may be contacted. My child's name is _____.
This release is effective for the time during which my child is participating in the _____
_____ baseball program and any tournaments for the 19____/ 19____
season, including traveling to or from such tournaments. I also hereby assume the responsibility for payment of any such treatment.

PARENTS' OR GUARDIANS' NAMES: _____

HOME ADDRESS: _____
                           Street   City   State   Zip

                                         (____)_____(W)

HOME PHONE: (____)_____ (____)_____(W)

INSURANCE COMPANY: _____

POLICY NUMBER: _____

FAMILY PHYSICIAN: _____

PHYSICIAN'S ADDRESS: _____ PHONE NO. (____)_____

In case I cannot be reached, either of the following people is designated:

COACH'S NAME: _____ PHONE NO. (____)_____

ASS'T. COACH OR OTHER: _____ PHONE NO. (____)_____

SIGNATURE OF PARENT OR GUARDIAN _____

SUBSCRIBED AND SWORN BEFORE ME THIS _____ OF _____, 19 ____

SIGNATURE OF NOTARY PUBLIC _____

Supplement 24-3.

On-Site Injury Report Form

Name _____ Date of injury ____/____/____
         (Injured Player)   mo   day   yr

Address _____
         (Street)   (City, State)   (Zip)

Telephone _____
         (Home)   (Other)

Nature and extent of injury: _____

_____

How did the injury occur? _____

_____

Describe first aid given, including name(s) of attendee(s): _____

_____

Disposition: to hospital   to home   to physician

Other _____

_____

Was protective equipment worn?   _____ Yes   _____ No

Explanation: _____

_____

Condition of the playing surface _____

_____

Names and addresses of witnesses:

Name	Street	City	State	Tel.
Name	Street	City	State	Tel.
Name	Street	City	State	Tel.

Other comments: _____

_____

Signed	Date	Title-Position

Summary of Season Injuries Form

Injury Type	First 4 Weeks	Middle Weeks	Last 4 Weeks	Total
1. Abrasion				
2. Back or Neck Injury				
3. Blisters				
4. Contusion				
5. Cramps				
6. Dental Injury				
7. Dislocation				
8. Eye Injury—Cintusion				
9. Eye Injury—Foreign Object				
10. Fainting				
11. Fracture				
12. Head Injury Conscious				
13. Head Injury Unconscious				
14. Heat Exhaustion				
15. Heat Stroke				
16. Lacerations				
17. Loss of Wind				
18. Nose Bleed				
19. Plantar Fascitis				
20. Puncture Wound				
21. Shin Splints				
22. Shock				
23. Sprain				
24. Strain				
25. Others:				

Do you see a trend?   YES   NO

Steps to take to reduce injuries next season:

(1) _____

(2) _____

(3) _____

SUMMARY OF SEASON INJURIES

(4) _____

(5) _____

(6) _____

(7) _____

(8) _____

(9) _____

(10) _____

(11) _____

(12) _____

(13) _____

(14) _____

(15) _____

(16) _____

(17) _____

(18) _____

(19) _____

(20) _____

(21) _____

(22) _____

(23) _____

(24) _____

(25) _____

(26) _____

(27) _____

(28) _____

(29) _____

(30) _____

(31) _____

(32) _____

(33) _____

(34) _____

25
Rehabilitation of Common Baseball Injuries

Rich Kimball, M.A.
Eugene W. Brown, Ph.D.
Marjorie Albohm, A.T., C.

QUESTIONS TO CONSIDER

- What are the important components of a rehabilitation program?
- How can a coach tell when athletes are trying to "come back" too fast?
- Is it necessary to obtain permission from parents and a physician before returning an injured athlete to competition?
- Following an injury, what determines if an activity is too stressful?

INTRODUCTION

Decisions about the rehabilitation of injuries and reentry into competition must be made according to a flexible set of guidelines; not hard and fast rules. Every individual on your team and each injury is unique. Therefore, rehabilitation techniques and reentry criteria will differ for each injured player.

GENERAL PROCEDURES

Most injuries suffered by your athletes will not be treated by a physician. Therefore, you, the athlete, and the athlete's parents will determine when the athlete returns to action.

Athletes, coaches, and parents realize that missing practices will reduce the athlete's ability to help the team. Pressure is often exerted on the coach to return injured athletes to ac-

tion before they are fully recovered, especially if they are the stars of the team. If an athlete has been treated by a physician for an injury, written clearance by both the physician and the parents should be obtained before permitting the athlete to return to practices and games. Also, clarification as to any limitations on participation should be obtained from the physician.

Chances of an injury recurring are greatly increased if an athlete returns too soon. The following five criteria should be met, in order, before allowing an injured athlete back into full physical activity:

1. absence of pain
2. full range of motion at the injured area
3. normal strength and size at the injured area
4. normal speed and agility
5. normal level of fitness

If a physician is not overseeing an injured athlete's rehabilitation, the task of rehabilitation will probably fall upon the coach. Flexibility exercises, to help regain normal range of motion, and resistive exercises, to help regain normal strength, form the basis of a rehabilitation program. Presence of pain during movement is the key to determining if the activity is too stressful. The onset of pain means too much is being attempted too soon. When athletes can handle flexibility exercises, then resistive exercises may be added to the program. The principles of training included in Chapter 22 should guide all phases of the rehabilitation program.

Absence of Pain

Most injuries are accompanied by pain, although the pain is not always evident immediately when the injury occurs. Usually, the pain disappears quickly if the injury is a bruise, or a minor sprain or strain. For more serious injuries such as dislocations or fractures, the pain may remain for days or weeks. Once the pain is gone, the athlete can start the stretching portion of a rehabilitation program.

The main goal of a rehabilitation program is to reestablish range of motion, strength, power, and muscular endurance at the site of the injury. As long as athletes remain free of pain, they should proceed with their program. If pain recurs, they should eliminate pain-producing movements until they are pain-free again.

The chance of an injury recurring is greatly increased if an athlete returns to action too soon.

Full Range of Motion

Injuries generally reduce the range of motion around a joint. The more severe the injury, the greater the reduction in range of motion, particularly when the injured area has been immobilized. As soon as they are able to move an injured area without pain, athletes should be encouraged to progressively increase the range of movement until a normal range is achieved. For example, if the athlete has strained a groin muscle, a fairly common injury early in the season, the muscle should be stretched as much as possible without causing pain. Initially, the movement may be slight if the injury was

severe. With stretching, the full range of motion will eventually return. When the athlete can move the injured joint through its normal range, strengthening exercises should begin.

Normal Strength and Size

After a body part has been immobilized (by cast, splint wrap, or disuse), muscles become smaller and weaker than they were before the injury. Just because a cast is removed and the injuries have "healed" does not mean that athletes are ready to practice or play at full speed. Loss of muscle mass means a loss of strength. Letting athletes resume a normal practice schedule before their strength has returned to pre-injury levels could lead to re-injury. Strengthening the injured area should be done conservatively. If weights are used, start with light weights and perform the exercise through the entire range of motion. If the exercise causes pain, then lighter weights should be used. To determine when full strength and size has been regained, compare the injured area to the non-injured area on the opposite side of the body. When both areas are of equal size and strength, then the athletes may progress to the next phase of recovery.

Your goal is to have the athletes regain full strength through the entire range of motion before allowing them to return to competition.

Normal Speed and Agility

When an athlete returns to practice, incorporate progressively greater levels of intensity of activity. You should be careful to gradually challenge the previously injured body part. In your observation of injured athletes, try to detect any favoring of an injured part or inability to smoothly perform a skill at increasing intensities. When athletes can move at pre-injury speed and agility, they are almost ready to play.

The main goal of a rehabilitation program is to reestablish range of motion, strength, power, and muscular endurance to the injured area.

Normal Level of Fitness

Every extended layoff reduces the level of muscular fitness. While recovering, the athlete may be able to exercise other body parts without affecting the injured area. For example, someone with a sprained ankle may not be able to run, but he/she may be able to swim. Someone with a broken wrist may be able to do a variety of lower body activities such as jog or run the bases. Cautiously encourage this type of activity, because it helps to maintain portions of the athlete's pre-injury levels of fitness. Athletes who have missed long periods of time due to an injury should practice for several days after meeting the previous criteria before being allowed to compete. Their cardiovascular and muscular systems need time to adjust to the demands of the game. The longer the layoff, the more conditioning work the athlete will need.

SUMMARY

When the pain is gone, and the range of motion, strength, agility, and conditioning are back to normal, your athlete is ready to reenter practice and competition. The entire process may have taken two days for a bruise to 12 or more weeks for a fracture. In either case, if you have followed the general guidelines of this chapter, you know you have acted in the best long-term interest of the athlete. Participation is important, but only if participation is achieved with a healthy body. Resist the pressure and temptation to rush athletes into a game before they are ready. Your patience will be rewarded in the games to come.

26
Prevention of Common Baseball Injuries

Glenna DeJong, M.S., M.A.
Rich Kimball, M.A.
Eugene W. Brown, Ph.D.
Wade Lillegard, M.D.
Cathy Lirgg, A.T., C.

QUESTIONS TO CONSIDER

- What constitutes proper equipment and attire for injury prevention in baseball?
- How can the facilities be made safer for baseball?
- What effect can warm-ups, cool-downs, and conditioning have on preventing injuries?
- What role does teaching players safety, appropriate baseball techniques, and proper drills have in injury prevention?
- What injury prevention techniques can be implemented over the course of a season?

INTRODUCTION

The number of injuries occurring in baseball can be reduced greatly by ensuring a safe environment and insisting on proper equipment and apparel. The following guidelines, aimed at preventing injuries, can make baseball a safer game for your athletes.

As a youth baseball coach, you are responsible for doing everything reasonable to provide participants the opportunity to compete in an environment that is healthy and safe.

INJURY PREVENTION TECHNIQUES
Equipment and Apparel

A properly equipped and attired baseball player is less likely to be injured. Turf shoes or rubber-spiked shoes should be worn to increase traction and reduce chances of slipping. Running or tennis shoes are not built for the playing surface of baseball fields and should be avoided. A catcher needs special equipment which includes a face mask, chest protector, and shin guards. All of this equipment should fit properly and be in good repair or chances of injury may increase rather than decrease.

Especially important for baseball players is a well-fitting batter's helmet. The helmet should fit snugly and not fall over the batter's eyes, obstructing vision. Preferably, the helmet should extend over the ears for added protection. To prevent face injuries, many teams are purchasing guards that fit over the front of the helmet. Use of these guards is highly recommended.

Garments should be loose enough to allow freedom of movement. If a player must wear glasses, safety lenses or glass guards should also be required. In addition, shin guards are recommended.

Parents should be informed during a pre-season parents' orientation meeting about appropriate equipment and apparel for their children. They should be made aware that: (a) if eyeglasses are essential for their child to play, they should be safety glasses worn with a safety strap; (b) their child's shoes should fit properly and have the appropriate soles; (c) jewelry is not appropriate at practices or games; and (d) gum chewing is prohibited.

At the start of the first practice, you should reinforce what you told the parents about appropriate equipment and apparel and determine if:

- all players are properly attired
- optional equipment (e.g., eyeglasses, shin guards) fits properly

This type of inspection should be carried out regularly.

Playing Areas

Inspection of a practice or game field for safety hazards is the responsibility of the adults in charge. For practices, the coach is responsible for the safety of all facilities. For games, both the officials and coaches are responsible. Therefore, you or your assistant must inspect the field before permitting your players to participate in practices and games. Whoever is responsible for inspecting the field should arrive approximately 10 minutes before the players to carry out the inspection.

If a safety hazard is present, it must be avoided by either relocating, rescheduling, restricting the activity, or removing the hazard.

There are three categories of safety hazards associated with playing areas. These are field conditions, structural hazards, and environmental hazards. Safety hazards that are not easily rectified must be reported to the league and/or program administrators. If corrections are not made quickly, you should resubmit your concerns in writing. Do not play in areas that you consider hazardous to your athletes!

- **Field Conditions**

Inspect the surface condition of the playing field for potential hazards. Holes in the ground, rocks, broken glass, or trash are dangerous in addition to detracting from the skill of playing the game. Remove or rectify these potential dangerous conditions before allowing your athletes to begin activity.

- **Structural Hazards**

The baseball field should be free of obstacles too close to the playing area. Bleachers, water fountains, and spectators should be well behind the boundary lines. In addition, chain-link fences and backstops should be securely fastened.

- **Environmental Hazards**

No matter how important a practice or game may seem to be, it is not worth the risk of an injury or a fatality due to environmental hazards. Extreme weather conditions, such as high winds, hail, lightning, high temperatures, humidity, cold, snow, and rain need to be cautiously evaluated as potential safety hazards. Insufficient light is another environmental condition that could be hazardous.

Activity should not be permitted to continue under the threat of lightning or any other environmental hazard.

Management of Practices and Games

Every physical activity that occurs during practices and games has some potential to result in an injury. Fortunately, in baseball, most practice and game activities do not result in an injury if properly executed. In addition to having an influence over the equipment, apparel, and facilities in reducing the risk of injuries, you have a major influence over the physical activities of your players during practices and games. There are several steps you can take to properly manage the physical activities to reduce the rate and severity of injuries. These steps include:

• Teaching Safety to Players

Whenever appropriate, inform your players about the potential risks of injury associated with performing certain baseball activities, and methods for avoiding injury. For example, teach correct catching techniques so that injuries are not sustained by incorrectly placing the hands when catching the ball.

The key to teaching safety to your players is to prudently interject safety tips in your instruction whenever appropriate.

• Warming Up

A warm-up at the beginning of your team's practices and before games provides several important benefits. If the field is not immediately available for your team's use, warm-ups (i.e., stretching exercises) can start in the locker room. Specific warm-up suggestions are included in Chapter 22 under "Warm-Up, Cool-Down," and "Stretching Activities for Baseball." When warm-ups and stretching are completed, the skill-oriented drills on your practice plan or the formal drills before the game may begin. A warm-up period:

- increases the breathing rate, heart rate, and muscle temperature to exercise levels
- reduces the risks of muscle pulls and strains
- increases the shock-absorbing capabilities of the joints
- prepares players mentally for practices and games

• Teaching Appropriate Techniques

The instructions you provide during practices on how to execute the skills of baseball have an influence on the risks of injuries to your players as well as to their opponents. Teach your players the proper ways to perform baseball techniques, and avoid any temptation to teach how to intentionally harm opponents.

First, an improper technique often results in a greater chance of injury to the performer than does the correct execution. Acceptable techniques in sports usually evolve with safety as a concern.

Second, techniques involving intentional harm should never be taught or condoned. Coaches who promote an atmosphere in which intentional violent acts are acceptable should be eliminated from the youth baseball program. You should promote fair and safe play in practices and games with strict enforcement of the rules. Encourage skill as the primary factor in determining the outcome of the game.

• Selecting Proper Drills

Drills that you select or design for your practices and the ways in which they are carried out have an influence on the risks of injuries for your players. Drills should be selected and designed with safety as a primary feature. Before implementing a new drill into your practice, several safety questions should be considered.

- Is the drill appropriate for the level of maturation of the players?
- Are the players sufficiently skilled to comply with the requirements of the drill?
- Are the players sufficiently conditioned to handle the stress of participation in the drill?
- Are other, less risky drills available to achieve the same practice results?
- Can the drill be modified to make it less risky and yet achieve the desired training result?

• Conditioning

High-intensity work is part of the game of baseball. How well your players can handle fatigue determines how well they perform during the latter part of a game. Is there, however, any relationship between fatigue and injury? The following sequence of events (Figure 26-1) draws an association linking fatigue with an increased potential for injury.

In addition to improving performance, every conditioning program should be designed to minimize fatigue and the potential for injury. Being "in shape" can postpone fatigue and its detrimental effects. By progressively intensifying your practices throughout the season, you can produce a conditioning effect that can be an important deterrent to injury (see Chapter 22.)

Athlete becomes fatigued

↓

Skilled performance is reduced

↓

Concentration becomes difficult

↓

Reactions slow down

↓

Judgment becomes impaired

↓

Faulty decisions are made

↓

Injuries may result

Figure 26-1. How fatigue is linked to an increased potential for injuries.

Coaches must also be aware that older players who engage in intense, frequent practices and games may need time off as the season wears on. It is possible to overtrain, and predispose to, rather than prevent, injuries. Injuries caused by overtraining have grown to represent an increased portion of reported sports injuries. Some telltale signs of overtraining include:

- elevated resting heart rate
- poor performance
- loss of enthusiasm
- depression
- higher incidence of injury
- longer time to recover from injury

Antidotes to overtraining include time off from practice, shorter practices, alternating intense practices with lighter workouts, or any combination of these suggestions. Overtraining is not usually a problem when players are practicing two or three times a week, unless they are also: (a) playing two or more games per week, (b) playing on more than one baseball team, or (c) playing on a different sport team during the same season.

- **Avoiding Contraindicated Exercises**

Over the past several years, researchers and physicians have identified a list of exercises that are commonly used by coaches but are potentially harmful to the body. These are called contraindicated exercises. This information has been slow in reaching coaches and their players. Table 26-1 contains a list of these exercises and how contraindicated exercises can be modified to eliminate their undesirable characteristics. Also included in Table 26-1 are substitute baseball exercises that accomplish the same purpose in a safer manner.

- **Cooling Down**

There are few feelings more uncomfortable than finishing a vigorous workout, sitting down for a while, then trying to walk. Muscles in the body tighten during periods of inactivity following hard work.

To minimize the stiffness that usually follows a workout, and the soreness the following day, take time to adequately cool down at the end of practice. A gradual reduction of activity (the reverse of the warm-up procedure) facilitates the dissipation of waste products associated with muscular activity. Letting the body cool off gradually may not prevent injuries, but the players may experience less discomfort and be better able to function at high levels during the next workout (see Chapter 22, "Warm-up, Cool Down," and "Stretching Activities for Baseball.")

SUMMARY

This chapter focused on three areas in which you can exert an influence to reduce the potential number and severity of injuries in baseball. The first area involves your insistence that your players wear appropriate apparel and protective equipment. Avoiding safety hazards associated with the playing areas (field conditions, structural hazards, and environmental hazards) is the second area. Management of practices and games is the third area. Proper management includes teaching your players safety, appropriate baseball techniques, and proper drills; and proper direction also means conducting practices that include warming up, conditioning, and cooling down exercises but exclude known contraindicated exercises. Safety and injury prevention should be primary factors to consider in whatever plans you make

Table 26-1. Contraindicated exercises and alternatives.

This table contains an outline of information on contraindicated exercises associated with the knee and spine. Safer alternative exercises that achieve the same objectives as the sample contraindicated exercises are provided.

I. PROBLEM AREA: KNEE JOINT

A. Problem Activity—Hyperflexion (over flexion)

Contraindicated Activities	Intended Purposes of Activities	Safer Alternatives
1. Hurdler's stretch 	Stretch the hamstring (back of thigh)	Seated straight leg stretch  Standing bent knee thigh pull  Lying hamstring stretch 
2. Deep knee bend	To develop quadriceps (front of thigh), hamstrings, gluteal (buttocks), and back muscles	Half squat or half knee bend 

A. Problem Activity—Hyperflexion (over flexion)

Contraindicated Activities	Intended Purposes of Activities	Safer Alternatives

3. Lunge

Wall sit

4. Landing from jumps

5. Deep squat lift

6. Squat thrust

I. PROBLEM AREA: KNEE JOINT (continued)

A. Problem Activity—Hyperflexion (over flexion)

Contraindicated Activities	Intended Purposes of Activities	Safer Alternatives
7. Lying quad stretch (back lying position from hurdler's stretch)	Stretch quadricep muscles	Kneeling thigh stretch

8. Double leg lying quad stretch

9. Standing one leg quad stretch

B. Problem Activity—Hyperextension (over extension)

Contraindicated Activities	Intended Purposes of Activities	Safer Alternatives
10. Standing toe touch	Stretch the hamstring muscles	Seated straight leg stretch

I. PROBLEM AREA: KNEE JOINT (continued)

B. Problem Activity—Hyperextension (over extension)

Contraindicated Activities	Intended Purposes of Activities	Safer Alternatives
11. One leg standing hamstring stretch		Standing bent knee thigh pull

Lying hamstring stretch

C. Problem Activity—Twisting or forcing knee joint into unnatural position

Contraindicated Activities	Intended Purposes of Activities	Safer Alternatives
12. Hurdler's stretch—see Contraindicated Activity 1.		
13. Standing one leg quad stretch	Stretch quadricep muscles	Seated straight leg stretch

I. PROBLEM AREA: KNEE JOINT (continued)

C. Problem Activity—Twisting or forcing knee joint into unnatural position

Contraindicated Activities	Intended Purposes of Activities	Safer Alternatives

14. Hero

Standing bent knee thigh pull

Lying hamstring stretch

15. Standing straddle groin stretch

Stretch inner thigh (groin) muscles

Seated straddle groin stretch

Butterfly

Lying groin stretch

Elevated legs straddle groin stretch

II. PROBLEM AREA: SPINE

A. Problem Activity—Forceful hyperflexion of cervical (neck) region

Contraindicated Activities	Intended Purposes of Activities	Safer Alternatives

16. Yoga plough

Stretch back and neck muscles

Standing bent knee thigh pull

17. Shoulder stand

Alternate yoga plough (Note that when lifting legs from the floor to assume this position, the knees should initially be bent.)

Supine tuck

Half neck circle

438   YOUTH BASEBALL: A COMPLETE HANDBOOK

II. PROBLEM AREA: SPINE (continued)

B. Problem Activity—Hyperextension of the spine

Contraindicated Activities	Intended Purposes of Activities	Safer Alternatives
18. Wrestler's bridge	Stretch neck muscles	Half neck circle

19. Full neck circle

20. Partner neck stretch

21. Donkey kick	Stretch abdominal muscles	Kneeling thigh stretch

22. Full waist circle   Reduced waist circle

II. PROBLEM AREA: SPINE (continued)

B. Problem Activity—Hyperextension of the spine

Contraindicated Activities	Intended Purposes of Activities	Safer Alternatives
23. Back bend 		
24. Back arching abdominal stretch 		
25. Donkey kick (see Contraindicated Activity 21)	Strengthen gluteal muscles	Half squat or half knee bend 

C. Problem Activity—Excessive lumbar curve or hyperextension of the low back

Contraindicated Activities	Intended Purposes of Activities	Safer Alternatives
26. Straight leg sit-ups 	Strengthen abdominal muscles	Bent knee sit-up 
27. Double leg lifts 		Reversed sit-up 

for your baseball team. You will be more than compensated for the extra time and effort required to implement the suggestions found in this chapter by the comfort of knowing that you have done as much as you can to assure that your players will have a safe season.

REFERENCES

Rutherford, G., Miles, R., Brown, V., & MacDonald, B. (1981). *Overview of sports related injuries to persons 5-14 years of age.* Washington, DC: U.S.Consumer Product Safety Commission.

Seidel, B.L.et al. (1980). *Sport Skills.* Dubuque, IA: W.C. Brown.

SUGGESTED READINGS

American College of Sports Medicine, American Orthopaedic Society for Sports Medicine & Sports Medicine Committee of the United States Tennis Association (1982). *Sports injuries—an aid to prevention and treatment.* Coventry, CT: Bristol-Myers Co.

Jackson, D., & Pescar, S. (1981). *The young athletes health handbook.* Everest House.

Lane, S. (1990). Severe ankle sprains. *The Physician and Sportsmedicine,* 18, 43-51.

Micheli, L.J. (1985). Preventing youth sports injuries. *Journal of Health, Physical Education, Recreation and Dance,* 76(6), 52-54.

Mirkin, G., & Marshall, H. (1978). *The sportsmedicine book.* Little, Brown, & Co.

Ross Laboratories. (1987). *Nutrition and hydration in basketball: how they affect your performance.* Columbus, OH: Ross Laboratories.

Appendix

DEFENSIVE AND OFFENSIVE DRILLS

The following pages contain: (1) a drill matrix indicating which drills are appropriate for a variety of skill levels and various positions within those skill levels; and (2) a description and illustration of each drill.

BASEBALL DRILL MATRIX

KEY: P-pitcher, C-catcher, 1-first base, 2-second base, 3-third base, S-shortstop, O-outfield, H-hitting, B-bunting, BR-baserunning

| | | SKILL LEVEL | |
DEFENSIVE DRILLS	Beginning 6-10 yrs.	Intermediate 11-13 yrs.	Advanced 14 and over
Catching, Throwing Infield Drills			
Mirror Throwing	P C 1 2 3 S O	P C 1 2 3 S O	
Taped ball throwing	P C 1 2 3 S O	P C 1 2 3 S O	P C 1 2 3 S O
Long toss drill	P C 1 2 3 S O	P C 1 2 3 S O	P C 1 2 3 S O
Hot potato drill	P C 1 2 3 S O	P C 1 2 3 S O	P C 1 2 3 S O
Pick-up drill	P C 1 2 3 S	P C 1 2 3 S	P C 1 2 3 S
Continuous ground balls	P C 1 2 3 S O	P C 1 2 3 S O	P C 1 2 3 S O
Short hop drill	P C 1 2 3 S O	P C 1 2 3 S O	P C 1 2 3 S O
Over the head	1 2 3 S O	1 2 3 S O	1 2 3 S O
Pop fly with return throws	1 2 3 S O	1 2 3 S O	1 2 3 S O
Diamond drill	1 2 3 S	1 2 3 S	1 2 3 S
Infielder's range drill	1 2 3 S	1 2 3 S	1 2 3 S
Outfield Drills			
Fly ball tennis drill	P C 1 2 3 S O	P C 1 2 3 S O	P C 1 2 3 S O
Quarterback drill		P C 1 2 3 S O	P C 1 2 3 S O
Outfielder drop step/crossover drill		O	O
Zig Zag	O	O	O
Outfield pickup drill	O	O	O
Outfield fence drill		O	O
Shoestring catch drill		P C 1 2 3 S O	P C 1 2 3 S O
Sun fly ball drill		P C 1 2 3 S O	P C 1 2 3 S O
Outfield game-saver drill		O	O

BASEBALL DRILL MATRIX (continued)

KEY: P-pitcher, C-catcher, 1-first base, 2-second base, 3-third base, S-shortstop, O-outfield, H-hitting, B-bunting, BR-baserunning

| | SKILL LEVEL | | |
DEFENSIVE DRILLS	Beginning 6-10 yrs.	Intermediate 11-13 yrs.	Advanced 14 and over
Position Drills			
Pitcher's fielding drill	P	P	P
Pitcher covering home plate drill	P	P	P
Pitcher's quick throw			P
Pitcher covering first base	BR P C 1	BR P C 1	BR P C 1
Leading, steals, and pickoffs		BR P C 1 2 3 S	BR P C 1 2 3 S
Catcher's bunt drill	C	C	C
Catcher's pop-up drill	C	C	C
Catcher's down-up drill	C	C	C
Catcher's no-mitt blocking drill	C	C	C
Passed ball/wild pitch 3 in 1 drill	P C	P C	P C
First base one-handed drill		1	1
First base scoop drill		1	1
Shortstop/second double play drill	2 S	2 S	2 S
Third base slow roller drill		3	3
Infield reaction drill	C 1 2 3 S	C 1 2 3 S	C 1 2 3 S
Unassisted, force out double play drill	P C 1 2 3 S O	P C 1 2 3 S O	P C 1 2 3 S O
Infield priority drill	P C 1 2 3 S	P C 1 2 3 S	P C 1 2 3 S
Infield/Outfield priority drill	P C 1 2 3 S O	P C 1 2 3 S O	P C 1 2 3 S O
Outfield priority drill	O	O	O
Relay drill	P C 1 2 3 S O	P C 1 2 3 S O	P C 1 2 3 S O
Basic relay drill	P C 1 2 3 S O	P C 1 2 3 S O	P C 1 2 3 S O
Look the runner back	BR P C 1 2 3 S	BR P C 1 2 3 S	BR P C 1 2 3 A

OFFENSIVE DRILLS

	Beginning 6-10 yrs.	Intermediate 11-13 yrs.	Advanced 14 and over
Hitting			
Mirror hitting	H	H	H
Shadow drill	H	H	H
Hip rotation drill	H	H	H
Batting tee drill	H	H	H
Soft toss hitting drill	H	H	H
Power swing drill		H	H
Pepper game drill		H P C 1 2 3 S O	H P C 1 2 3 S O
Bunting			
Soft toss bunting drill		B	B
Bunting with gloves		B	B
Target bunting drill		B	B
Bunt and slap drill		B	B

BASEBALL DRILL MATRIX (continued)

KEY: P-pitcher, C-catcher, 1-first base, 2-second base, 3-third base, S-shortstop, O-outfield, H-hitting, B-bunting, BR-baserunning

| | | SKILL LEVEL | |
DEFENSIVE DRILLS	Beginning 6-10 yrs.	Intermediate 11-13 yrs.	Advanced 14 and over
Baserunning			
General baserunning drill	BR	BR	BR
Rounding first base drill	BR	BR	BR
Leadoff and react drill	BR	BR	BR
Leadoff/get a jump at first base drill	BR	BR	BR
Leading off and reacting at other bases drill	BR	BR	BR
Tag up drill	BR	BR	BR
Finding your sliding leg drill	BR	BR	BR
Sliding progression	BR	BR	BR
Relay sliding	BR	BR	BR
Rundown drill	BR P C 1 2 3 S O	BR P C 1 2 3 S O	BR P C 1 2 3 S O

BASEBALL DRILLS

Name: Mirror Throwing

Objective: To work on throwing skills alone.

Suggested For: Beginning and intermediate levels.

Description: Players face a large mirror and watch themselves as they perform throwing motions. They should focus on one element at a time: shoulder turn, arm pronation, follow through, and so forth.

Key Points:

- Athletes need to understand proper throwing mechanics before working on this. However, this drill will allow them to improve their throwing at home as they watch themselves.

Common Errors:

- Failing to take full motions.

- Failing to follow through on all attempts.

Modifications:

- Athletes can use a rolled-up pair of socks to approximate a ball.

Name: Taped Ball Throwing (see Figure A-1a and b)

Objective: To practice throwing with proper spin on the ball.

Suggested For: All skill levels.

Description: This drill emphasizes correct grip and ball rotation for the overhand throw. A single strip of black electrical tape is applied around and across the wide seams of the ball. When the ball is thrown in a correct overhand fashion, a solid stripe appears on the ball. The stripe provides visual feedback to the thrower and indicates whether the ball is spinning correctly. To execute the drill, players form two parallel lines and throw the ball back and forth to each other emphasizing proper grip and rotation.

Key Points:
- This drill may be used as a throwing warm-up.
- The ball should be gripped with 2 to 4 fingers across the wide seams so that the black strip of tape is between the fingers. The thumb is opposite the fingers.
- The force production phase of the throw should not be sacrificed for spin. The two should occur together.

- The absence of the solid stripe on the ball in flight is an indication of a mechanical flaw in the throwing motion.

Common Errors:
- Gripping the ball improperly.
- Throwing sidearm or three-quarter arm rather than overhand.

Modifications:
- More experienced players can perform this drill "hot potato" fashion.
- Proper spin can be achieved initially by moving players close together and using the wrist only.

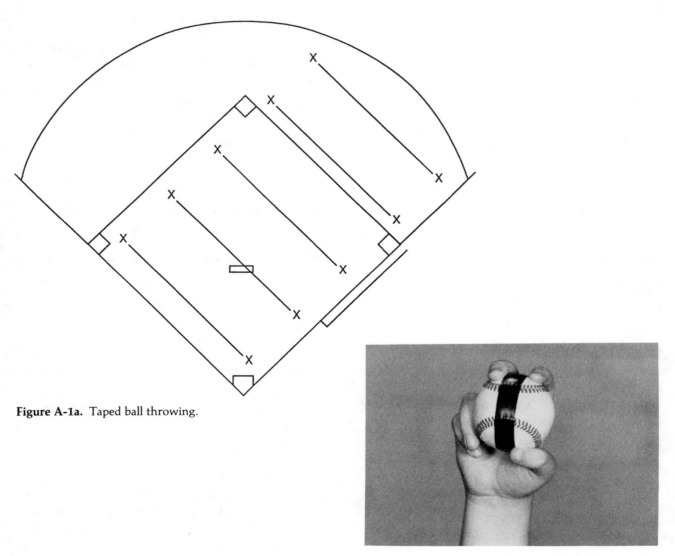

Figure A-1a. Taped ball throwing.

Figure A-1b. An athlete properly gripping a taped ball.

Name: Long Toss Drill (see Figure A-2)

Objective: To strengthen and improve the accuracy of players' throwing arms.

Suggested For: Players of all skill levels.

Description: Partners play catch at a routine distance and gradually increase the distance of the throw. The final distance is determined by the skill level. The throws should be challenging but not unrealistic. Players continue to play catch for about 10 successful throws and catches.

Key Points:

- Players should be thoroughly stretched before throwing long.
- Players must concentrate on throwing with correct form.

- All throws should reach the target in the air or on one bounce.

Common Errors:

- Throwing three-quarter arm or sidearm rather than overhand.
- Incomplete joint sequence (that is, arm-only throws) which may be indicated by little or no follow-through.
- Excessive arc on the ball in an attempt to increase distance. Throws should be low and hard.

Modifications:

- The drill can be done individually by throwing down a foul line to home plate. The player gradually moves back on successive days. The player goes down the foul line with a bag of balls and uses home plate as a throwing target.

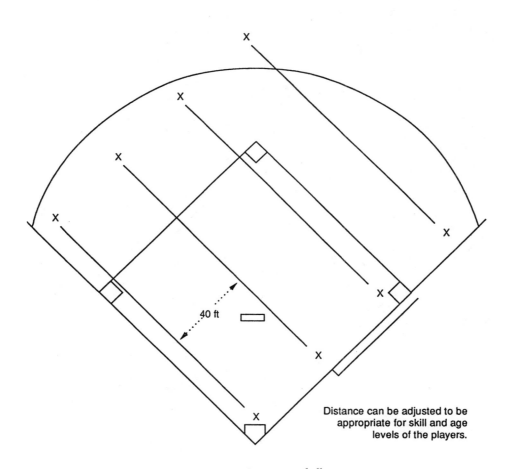

Figure A-2. Long toss drill.

Name: Hot Potato Drill (see Figure A-3)

Objective: To practice receiving and throwing a ball quickly and accurately.

Suggested For: All players proficient in catching and throwing.

Description: Players are in pairs, 70 to 90 feet apart. The drill begins on a command from the coach, and each pair tries to make as many successful catches and throws as possible in a given period of time. Every time this drill is repeated, the pair should try to beat their previous total. Players can progress up to 1½ minutes of continuous catching and throwing.

Key Points:
- Throws should be chest high.
- The "receiver" should raise both hands as a target for the thrower.
- To catch throws that are off target, players should move their feet while the ball is in flight in order to be correctly positioned for an efficient return.
- Wild or missed throws should be chased promptly with the chaser returning to the original position before returning the ball.

Common Errors:
- Lacking concentration.
- Catching the ball one-handed, slowing down the ball transfer to the throwing hand.
- Slowing the return efficiency, by reaching for an inaccurate throw rather than moving the feet.
- Not moving back to the starting position after the throw.

Modifications·
- Move less skilled players closer together and eliminate the time element. Focus on correct technique.
- Use tennis balls without gloves to reinforce the use of two hands.
- Space more advanced players farther apart in order to build arm strength.

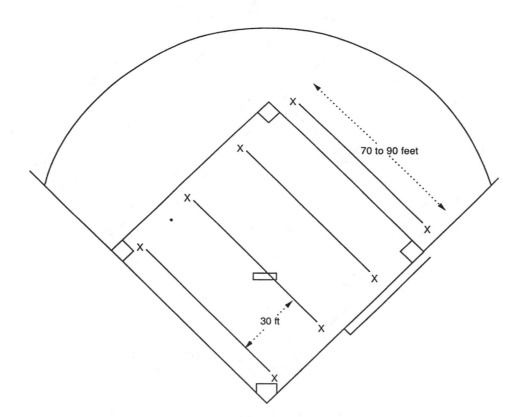

Figure A-3. Hot potato drill.

Name: Pick-Up Drill (see Figure A-4)

Objective: To improve endurance and to practice staying low when fielding ground balls.

Suggested For: All skill levels.

Description: Players are in pairs, about 6 feet apart. Player A has a ball and Player B assumes a fielding position, with or without a glove. Player A rolls the ball about 5 feet to one side of Player B who shuffles into position, fields the ball, and tosses it back. The ball is then rolled 5 feet to the other side of Player B. This continues until Player B has 20 to 25 rollers. The players then switch roles.

Key Points:
- Each pair should be given enough space so as not to interfere with other pairs.
- The fielder receives the ball with two hands out in front of the body, watching the ball all of the way into the glove.
- Throughout the drill, the fielder must stay low. Form should not be sacrificed in order to increase the speed of performance.
- The pace of the drill is adjusted to challenge the fielder.

Common Errors:
- The feeder bounces the ball rather than rolling it.
- The feeder rolls the ball too slow, too fast, or too wide. This causes the drill to break down.
- The feeder does not challenge the fielder.
- The fielder does not work to get in front of the ball.

Modifications:
- The drill can be done with two balls to quicken the pace.
- Increase the number of repetitions as players become more proficient.

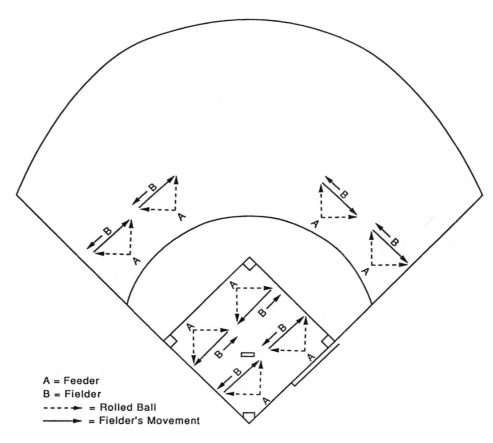

A = Feeder
B = Fielder
- - - - ▶ = Rolled Ball
───── ▶ = Fielder's Movement

Figure A-4. Pick-up drill.

Name: Continuous Ground Balls (see Figure A-5)

Objective: To have players in continuous motion fielding ground balls on both the back hand and forehand side.

Suggested For: Players of all skill levels.

Description: Three players form a line 15 to 20 feet on the infield side of one of the base lines, for example, between first and second. The remaining players line up at one of the bases, while a coach stands near each of the two bases involved. The coach near the line of players has a ball and, on the signal "Go," tosses it to the nearest infield person. At the same time, the first player in line starts running toward the other base. The person with the ball rolls a ground ball toward the running fielder who must pick it up, throw to the next person in the infield group, and continue to the next base. The second person on the infield rolls another ground ball; the fielder makes another play and throws to the third person on the infield. This third player rolls another ground ball which is fielded and handed to the coach at the base. The coach tosses the ball to the nearest infield person, and the running fielder starts back. The sequence repeats until all players have gone through at least three times in each direction.

Key Points:
- Use good mechanics when fielding the ball.
- Use the backhand when necessary.
- Make good snap throws or sidearm throws.

Common Errors:
- Running at less than full speed.
- Failing to look the ball into the glove.
- Making poor backhand pick-ups.

Modifications:
- Always adjust throws to the speed of players.

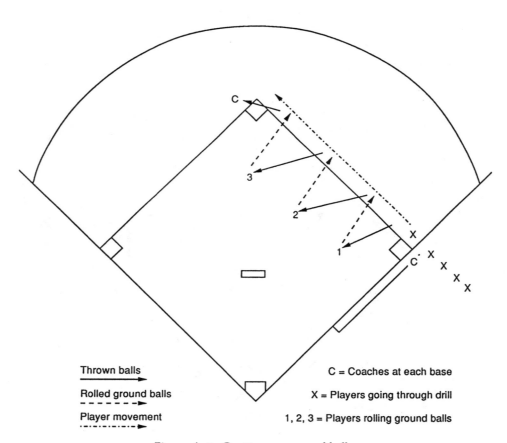

Thrown balls ⟶

Rolled ground balls - - - - ▶

Player movement -·-·-·-·- ▶

C = Coaches at each base

X = Players going through drill

1, 2, 3 = Players rolling ground balls

Figure A-5. Continuous ground balls.

Name: Short Hop Drill (see Figure A-6)

Objective: To practice fielding balls that bounce sharply in front of the fielder.

Suggested For: Players of all skill levels.

Description: Players are in pairs, 15 to 20 feet apart. Player A bounces the ball about 2 feet in front of Player B. The short hop is fielded by absorbing the ball with both hands and drawing it up toward the body. The ball is then bounced back to Player A who fields the ball in the same fashion. The drill continues until a specific number of short hops are successfully fielded.

Key Points:

- Fielders must begin with the hands low and the feet apart.
- Fielders must execute the drill with "game intensity."
- Fielders must absorb the ball with both hands.

Common Errors:

- Fielders raise the glove up before moving it back down to attempt the catch.
- Fielders raise their head and lose sight of the ball.
- The ball is bounced too far away or too close to the fielder and does not result in a short hop.

Modifications:

- Make short hop throws to the backhand and forehand sides.
- Make the location of the short hop random.
- Use tennis balls or rag balls to ensure safety.
- Decrease the distance between fielders to sharpen reflexes.

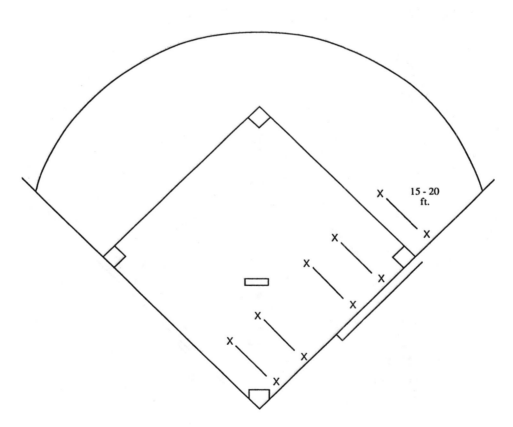

Figure A-6. Short hop drill.

Name: Over the Head (see Figure A-7)

Objective: To help defensive players—especially outfielders—become confident about playing the ball over the shoulder or after they have lost sight of it. This is also a good pre-game or warm-up drill.

Suggested For: .Players of all skill levels.

Description: This drill requires each player to have a ball. The players form a line facing a coach standing 50 to 60 feet away. Each athlete makes a good throw to the coach and sprints by the coach, coming as close as possible to the coach. After the player passes by, the coach leads the running athlete with a throw that should land well in front of the player. The player must try to locate the ball while running and catch it. After catching the ball, the player continues on until 50 or 60 feet from the coach and stops. The next player starts as soon as the coach turns back around. After each player goes through the drill in one direction, the players turn and start back the other way.

Key Points:
- Run hard and on the balls of the feet.
- Once passing the coach, run with the hands extended in front. The glove should be open and facing up.
- Find the ball and focus on it as quickly as possible.

Common Errors:
- Running with the head down; running at less than full speed.
- Stopping to look for the ball.
- Failing to look the ball into the glove.

Modifications:
- Shorten distances for younger players.

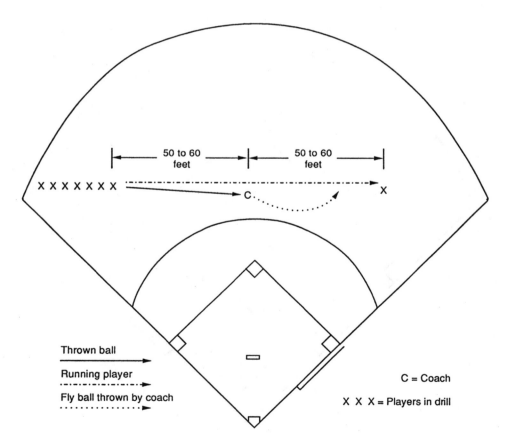

Figure A-7. Over the head.

Name: Pop Fly With Return Throws (see Figure A-8)

Objective: To help fielders become confident in finding the ball and making good return throws.

Suggested For: Players of all skill levels.

Description: Each player stands in line beside the coach, who has a supply of balls. The first player in line moves into position 10 to 15 feet in front of the coach with the back to the coach. With the shout of "Go," the player starts running away from the coach who throws a pop fly. After throwing the fly, the coach calls out its position: "left," "right," "in," or "back." The player turns, finds the ball, and makes the catch. The player makes a quick return throw to the coach and sprints to the back of the line.

Key Points:

- Run hard and on the balls of the feet.
- Concentrate on locating the ball and making a quick return throw.
- The coach's throws should be catchable.

Common Errors:

- Running at less than full speed.
- Failing to look in the direction called upon turning.
- Failing to look the ball into the glove.

Modifications:

- Always adjust throws to the speed of players.

Name: Diamond Drill (see Figure A-9)

Objective: To provide players with more ground ball fielding opportunities in a given period of time.

Suggested For: Infielders of all skill levels.

Description: Infielders are stationed at each infield position (1B, 2B, 3B, SS). Two players

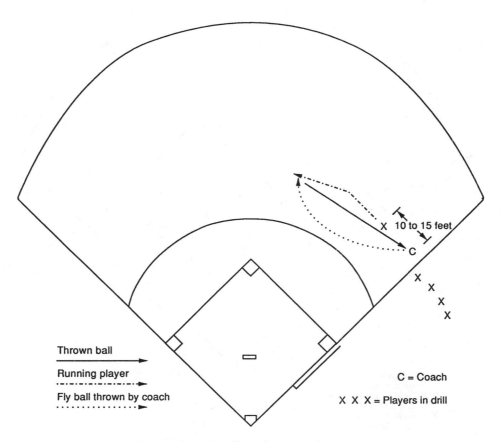

Figure A-8. Pop fly with return throws.

from each group hit ground balls and catch return throws. Players at each position field a ball that is hit to them and return to the end of the line. All four groups work simultaneously. After 10 ground balls per group, a different player hits, the hitter becomes the catcher and the catcher returns to the field.

Key Elements:

- Fielders must use correct fielding technique and move quickly to field the ball.
- Activity in this drill must be constant!
- For safety reasons, all ground balls should be hit to a specific location (that is, "right," "left," "straight on") to eliminate the chance of two fielders colliding.

Common Errors:

- The ball is hit outside of the fielding area, and the activity is stopped until the ball is retrieved.

- The hitters do not control the direction of the hit.

Modifications:

- If players are not skilled fungo hitters, throw or roll the ground balls.

Name: Infielders' Range Drill (see Figure A-10)

Objective: To help infielders improve their range—especially to the backhand side.

Suggested For: Infielders of all skill levels.

Description: This drill requires infielders to take their basic defensive stance and then execute a pivot, crossover and extension of the glove to both the forehand and backhand sides. The coach notes each player's range and places two easily seen markers approximately 6 inches

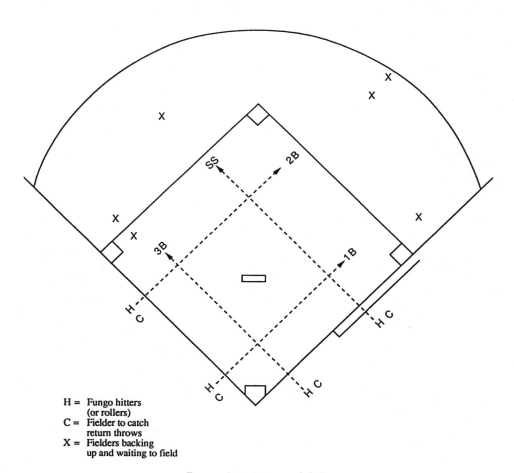

H = Fungo hitters (or rollers)
C = Fielder to catch return throws
X = Fielders backing up and waiting to field

Figure A-9. Diamond drill.

further to each side. (Various markers can be used: Safety cones, half gallon milk jugs with sand in the bottom, or unused gloves will work.) A coach throws ground balls to either side of the infielder, and the infielder makes a crossover step to play the ball. Once fielding the ball, the athlete rolls it to one side and resumes the defensive position. The coach repeats then throws another ball.

Key Points:

- The step to the ball involves a pivot and a crossover step.
- Balls to the backhand side must be played with the glove in the backhand position.
- The player must return to the middle of the area and take a good defensive stance before playing the next ball.

Common Errors:

- Failing to execute a crossover step.

- Not getting into a good position between ground balls.
- Not looking the ball into the glove—especially on the backhand side.
- Failing to get the glove into the backhand position.

Modifications:

- The coach throwing the ball adjusts the speed of the ground balls with respect to the distance to the player; the closer the infielder is, the slower the balls should be rolled.
- The distance between cones can be adjusted in consideration of the defender's range; an older, quicker player may need the markers half a step rather than 6 inches further to the side.
- The coach should hit balls to older, experienced players.
- Goals may be set for each player: So many balls to be fielded cleanly or a certain number of attempts in a specified time.

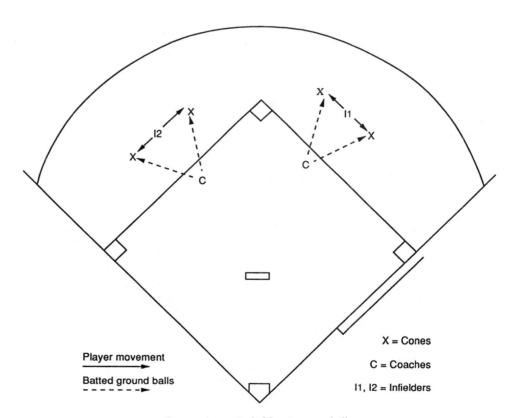

Figure A-10. Infielders' range drill.

Name: Fly Ball Tennis Drill (see Figure A-11)

Objective: To practice judging fly balls without fear or risk of injury.

Suggested For: All skill levels.

Description: Using a tennis racket and a tennis ball, the coach hits a fly ball to a fielder. The fielder correctly catches the ball, makes a return throw to the coach and moves to the end of the line. The height of the fly ball and the distance between the fielder and the coach should be based on the skill of the fielder.

Key Points:

- Be sure the fielder assumes the correct ready position before hitting the ball.
- Keep lines small in order to reduce waiting time.
- Keep the lines moving in order to decrease opportunities for distraction.

Common Errors:

- Lines are (1) too close to the fielder, resulting in a dangerous situation; (2) too long; and (3) too slow, resulting in a loss of interest.
- The height and distance of the fly ball is not proportional to the skill of the fielder, and the fielder (1) cannot make the catch or, (2) is not challenged by the fly ball and loses interest in the drill.

Modifications:

- Because tennis balls are being used, fielders can do this with or without gloves. Both ways are recommended: without a glove reinforces two hands and eye contact, and with a glove teaches glove control.
- Fielders form two lines 30 to 60 feet apart. One fielder calls for the ball ("mine") and the other fielder moves into a backup position.
- Fielders practice catching fly balls on the run, focusing on running on the balls of their feet in order to maintain a steady focus on the ball.
- Fielders set up in regular defensive positions, and fly balls can be hit between infielders and outfielders. The fielders must work on fielding technique, as well as communication.

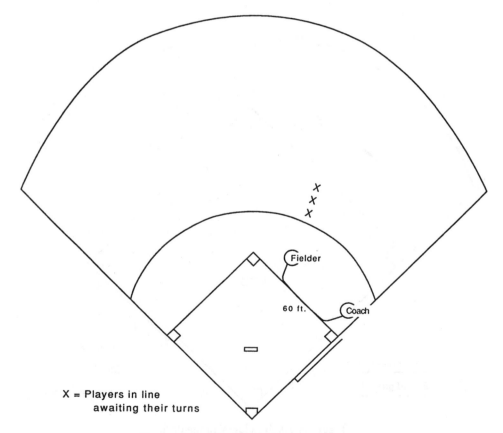

X = Players in line awaiting their turns

Figure A-11. Fly ball fielders tennis drill.

Name: Quarterback Drill (see Figure A-12)

Objective: To enhance conditioning and agility and to practice catching fly balls on the run.

Suggested For: Intermediate and advanced skill levels.

Description: Players line up on the right field foul line, about 10 feet beyond the infield dirt. The coach stands about 20 feet behind second base, facing the players. The first player in line runs toward the coach and tosses him/her a ball. The player continues to run past the coach, sprinting toward the left field foul line. When the player is half the distance to the foul line, the coach yells, "RIGHT" or "LEFT." The player cuts in the designated direction, the coach throws the ball to "lead" the player and the player catches the ball. When the ball is thrown, the next player in line runs toward the coach. When each player has had a turn, the drill is repeated in the opposite direction.

Key Points:
- Before doing this drill, the players must be stretched and warmed up.
- The coach's toss should be challenging but realistic.
- Players must sprint on the balls of the feet.

Common Errors:
- The player fails to sprint for the ball or gives up too early.
- The player does not run on the balls of the feet and the ball is not clearly seen.

Modifications:
- The number of repetitions may be increased or decreased depending on the physical condition of the players.
- The coach can roll ground balls as the player passes. The player must get to the ball before it stops rolling.

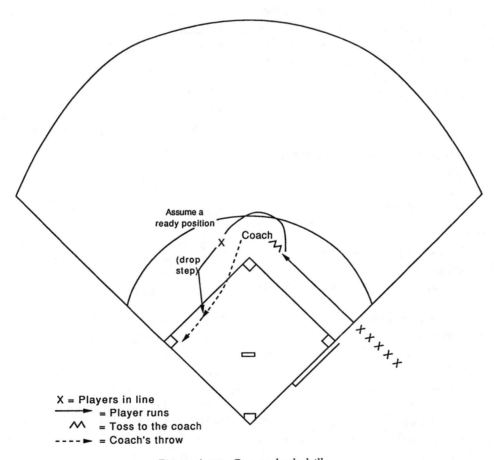

Figure A-12. Quarterback drill.

Name: Outfielder Drop Step/Crossover Drill

Objective: To have outfielders practice getting an efficient jump on deep fly balls.

Suggested For: Intermediate and advanced outfielders.

Description: Outfielders are spread about 5 yards apart. The coach faces the group and on command, the outfielders demonstrate the drop step/crossover step in the direction of the command (that is, "deep right," "deep left," "straight back"). Once the players consistently execute the correct form, a ball is used and the players perform one at a time. The first player assumes the ready position, the coach gives a command, the player executes the drop step/crossover and moves in the direction of the ball. The coach leads the player with a long fly ball.

Key Points:

- From the ready position, the outfielder uses an initial drop step/crossover and sprints to the ball.
- Whenever possible, the outfielder moves behind the ball and catches it with two hands on the throwing side of the body, so that the body's momentum is moving toward the coach.
- The fielders run to the ball on the balls of the feet.

Common Errors:

- Starting in an incorrect ready position trying to anticipate the direction of movement.
- Misjudging the ball.
- Using incorrect footwork.

Modifications:

- Coaches stress moving behind the ball with more advanced players.
- As skill improves, coaches can hit challenging fly balls.
- Infielders can use this drill to practice moving back on pop ups.

Name: Zig Zag (see Figure A-13)

Objective: Outfielders learn to pick up the ball with both hands and make a good throw with either a crow hop or pivot throw.

Suggested For: Players of all skill levels.

Description: Outfielders form a line facing two staggered rows of three balls each. The balls are 20 to 25 feet apart, and the lines are 30 feet apart. On a signal, the outfielder runs to the nearest ball, uses both hands to pick it up and throws to a player or coach in cutoff position. The player then sprints to pick up the first ball in the opposite line, repeats the sequence, and goes for the second ball in the original line. The player continues alternating between lines of balls until all six balls have been retrieved and thrown.

Key Points:

- Sprint from one ball to the next.
- Concentrate on using both hands to pick up the ball.
- Make good throws to the person in cutoff position.

Common Errors:

- Running tentatively.
- Not using two hands to pick up the ball.
- Failing to look at the ball while picking it up.
- Not using good mechanics in throwing: failing to point the glove-side shoulder to the target; making no crow hop.

Modifications:

- Always adjust distances between balls to the age/experience of the players.

Name: Outfield Pick-Up Drill (see Figure A-14)

Objective: To increase the conditioning level and the range of outfielders.

Suggested For: All skill levels.

Description: Minimum requirements include a hitter, a catcher, and an outfielder. The hitter hits a ground ball about 60 to 90 feet to one side of the outfielder. The outfielder sprints, correctly fields the ball, and throws it to the catcher. The outfielder runs back to the initial position and the hitter hits a ground ball 60 to 90 feet to the other side. After three ground balls to each side, the fielders change roles.

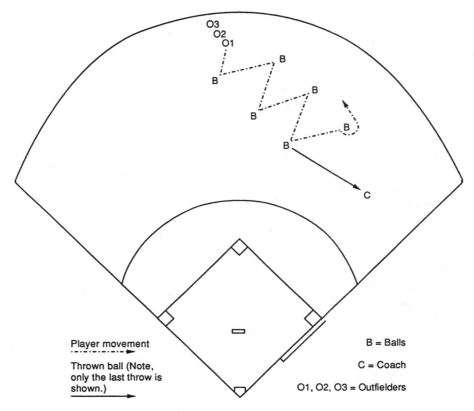

Player movement ----→

Thrown ball (Note, only the last throw is shown.) ——→

B = Balls

C = Coach

O1, O2, O3 = Outfielders

Figure A-13. Zig zag.

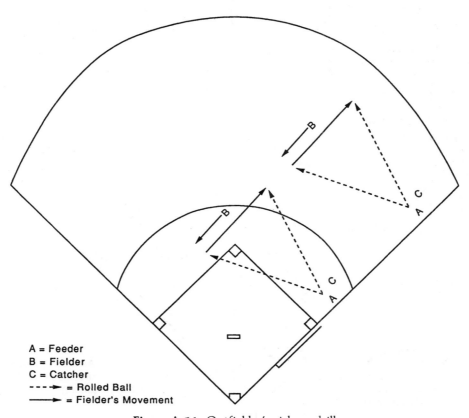

A = Feeder
B = Fielder
C = Catcher
---→ = Rolled Ball
——→ = Fielder's Movement

Figure A-14. Outfielder's pick-up drill.

Key Points:

- The fielder must take a proper angle to the ball, and the ball should be fielded along the midline of the body. Forehand or backhand is used as a last resort!
- The ground ball should challenge the outfielder.
- Extra balls should be available to the hitter in the event of a ball being overthrown or missed.
- The catcher may move toward the fielder or a relay person may be used to eliminate long throws.

Common Errors:

- The hitter does not give enough time is given between ground balls, and the outfielder sacrifices technique for speed. This results in missed ground balls and poor throws.
- The fielder jogs rather than sprints to field the ball.
- The fielder attempts to make the throw off

balance, increasing the strain on the throwing arm.

Modifications:

- Increase the number of repetitions as the players become more conditioned.
- Mix ground balls with fly balls for more advanced players.
- Have the outfielder field the ball and attempt to knock a ball off of a batting tee placed at least 30 feet in front of the catcher.

Name: Outfield Fence Drill (see Figure A-15)

Objective: To practice moving to and catching fly balls in front of an outfield fence.

Suggested For: Intermediate and advanced outfielders.

Description: Outfielders form a line about 15 feet in front of an outfield fence. The coach hits or throws a fly ball that lands a few feet in

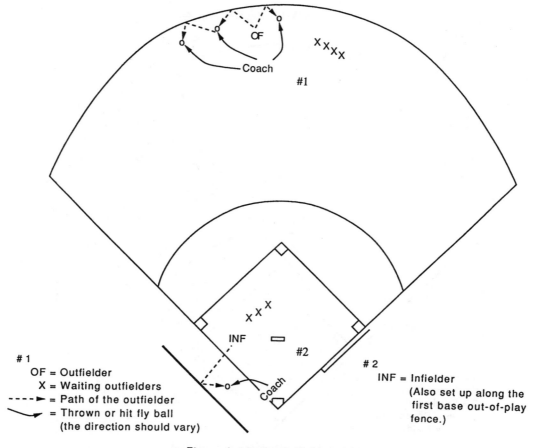

Figure A-15. Outfield fence drill.

front of the fence. The outfielder runs back, finds the fence by extending the throwing arm and moves to the ball in order to make the catch. The fielder uses the throwing arm on the fence to facilitate jumping on balls hit over the fence.

Key Points:
- The outfielder uses an initial drop step with the ball-side foot and crosses over with the other foot.
- The outfielder catches the ball with two hands, moving away from the fence.
- The outfielder must be aware of the distance to the fence prior to the "hit."

Common Errors:
- Back peddling instead of sprinting.
- Being unaware of the distance to the fence.

Modifications:
- As a lead-up drill, players can execute the correct technique without a ball: Move back, find the fence, and "make the catch."

- Skilled players may attempt to catch balls thrown closer to the fence in order to practice making difficult catches.
- Infielders can practice catching fly balls next to the fences or out-of-play lines.

Name: Shoestring Catch Drill (see Figure A-16)

Objective: To practice catching sinking line drives or short fly balls and to help condition the players.

Suggested For: Intermediate and advanced skill levels.

Description: Players are divided into groups of six to eight. Half of each group acts as "tossers," the other half as "catchers." The groups begin 90 feet apart facing each other. The first catcher sprints toward the first tosser. When the catcher is about halfway to the tosser, the tosser throws a short fly ball and the catcher attempts a catch on the "shoestrings." Once the toss is

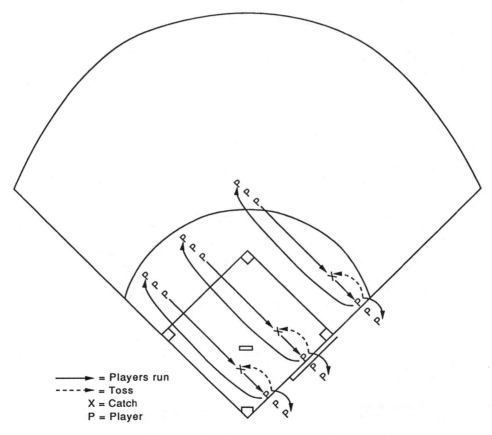

= Players run
- - - ► = Toss
X = Catch
P = Player

Figure A-16. Shoestring catch drill.

made, the tosser sprints to the end of the catching line. Once the catch is made, the catcher continues to sprint toward the tossing line, hands the ball to the next tosser and moves to the end of the tossing line. Players continue until each player has been the catcher five to ten times.

Key Points:

- The toss is the key to this drill. It must be challenging but realistic.
- If the ball cannot be caught in the air, the fielder must field it on the short hop and keep it in front of the body. The ball should not get by the fielder.
- Players in both groups must sprint hard. Any missed ball must be recovered quickly.
- Players must move to opposite lines without interfering with other players.

Common Errors:

- Lacking intensity and concentration.
- Jogging rather than sprinting.

- Sprinting heel to toe causing a "jarred" perception of the ball.
- Raising the head on a possible short hop.

Modifications:

- Groups of four to six players increase the conditioning benefits.
- Low line drives can be tossed as an alternative to short fly balls. The ball can also be tossed to either side.
- The players can form a line, and the coach can fungo hit or toss the ball. The players charge the ball, throw to the catcher, and move to the end of the line.

Name: Sun Fly Ball Drill (see Figure A-17)

Objective: To practice fielding fly balls in the sun.

Suggested For: Intermediate and advanced players.

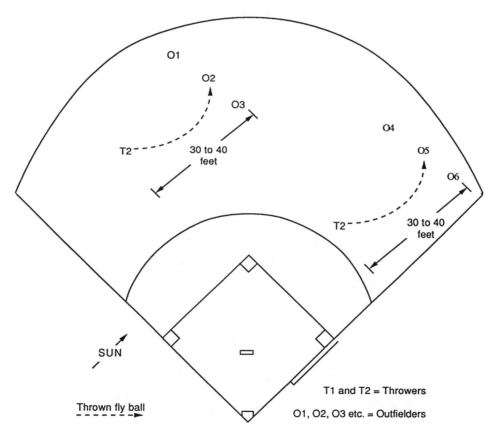

Figure A-17. Sun fly ball drill.

Description: Players work in groups of three or four. One player is the thrower and stands with the sun behind her or his back. The other fielders stand 30 to 40 feet from the thrower and face the sun. The thrower launches a fly ball and the fielders use their gloves to shade their eyes. The fielder in the best position calls for the ball and makes the catch.

Key Elements:

- The fielders use the glove to shield out the sun.
- As the ball nears the fielder, the throwing hand raises to make a two-handed catch.
- The fielders must call for the ball in order to make the catch.

Common Errors:

- Failing to correctly shade the eyes with the glove.
- Attempting to make the catch after losing sight of the ball in the sun.

Modifications:

- Tennis balls can be used in order to ensure safety.
- More advanced players may have fly balls thrown at all angles and depths in order to simulate game conditions.

Name: Outfield Game-Saver Drill (see Figure A-18)

Objective: To give outfielders practice in fielding and throwing with the winning run in scoring position.

Suggested For: Intermediate and advanced players.

Description: Base runners take a normal lead at second base and the coach hits a hard ground ball to an outfielder. On the hit, the runner attempts to score while the outfielder charges the ball and attempts to throw the runner out

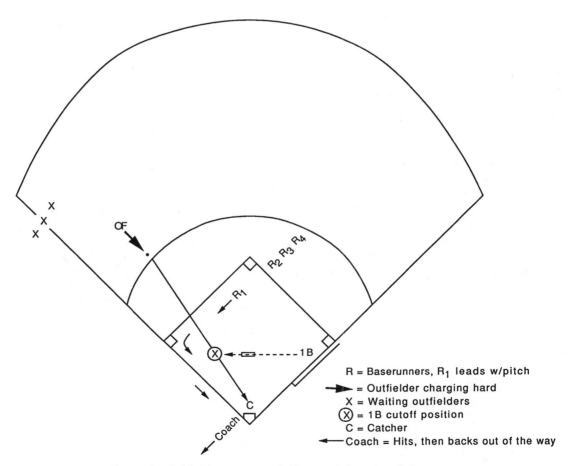

R = Baserunners, R₁ leads w/pitch
➤ = Outfielder charging hard
X = Waiting outfielders
Ⓧ = 1B cutoff position
C = Catcher
◄— Coach = Hits, then backs out of the way

Figure A-18. Outfielders' game-saver fielding and throwing drill.

at home plate. The catcher calls for the throw, receives the ball and tags the non-sliding runner. The coach hits another ball to another outfielder and the drill continues.

Key Points:

- The outfielder must charge the ball.
- The outfielder must field ball on the glove side of the body as the glove-side foot hits the ground.
- The outfielder must throw overhand and throw "through" the cutoff person.

Common Errors:

- Failing to charge the ball.
- Taking too many steps to throw after fielding the ball.
- Raising the head before the ball is secured.

Modifications:

- Initially, outfielders may execute this drill without base runners in order to focus on proper technique.

Name: Pitcher's Fielding Drill (see Figure A-19)

Objective: To improve pitchers' fielding ability and to teach throwing locations for various situations.

Suggested For: All skill levels.

Description: A pitcher throws a ball to a catcher. The coach hits or rolls another ball on the ground to the pitcher. First, the pitcher fields a ground ball and throws to first base. Second, the pitcher fields a bunt and throws to first base. The process is repeated with the pitcher throwing going to 2B, 3B, and to home plate. When the series is completed, a new pitcher repeats the drill.

Key Points:

- The pitcher must be sure the ball is secured before making the throw.
- The pitcher must sprint to the ball.
- The pitcher must field the ball with two hands.

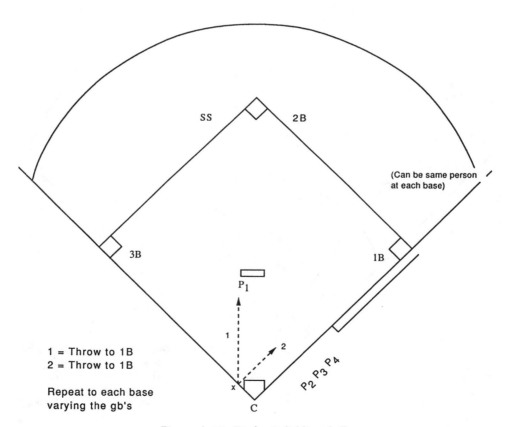

Figure A-19. Pitcher's fielding drill.

- After the ball has been fielded, the pitcher must step toward the target and throw to the target.

Common Errors:

- Letting the anticipation of a ground ball detract from the pitching motion.
- Attempting to throw to a base off-balance; moving away from the target as the ball is thrown, or throwing off of the wrong foot.
- Raising the head before the ball has been fielded.

Modifications:

- The coach calls the situation prior to the pitch (for example, R1, less than two outs). The pitcher must throw to the correct base.
- R1 and defenders at shortstop, second base, and first base can be used to practice talking to middle infielders and attempting the double play.
- An entire infield can be used: the ball is hit or bunted after the pitch, P, C, 1B, 3B must

call for the ball and react to the catcher's call.
- Base runners can be added: the catcher must make the correct call, fielders call for the ball, field it, and react to the catcher's call.
- Two pitchers can practice throwing to 1B or 3B simultaneously by using another catcher at second base and using third base as a first base.

Name: Pitcher's Covering Home Plate Drill (see Figure A-20)

Objective: To practice covering home plate on a wild pitch or passed ball, with a runner on third base.

Suggested For: All skill levels.

Description: A catcher is placed at various locations along the backstop. A pitcher charges the plate after executing a pitching motion. The catcher tosses a ball to the pitcher, who then applies a tag to an imaginary runner.

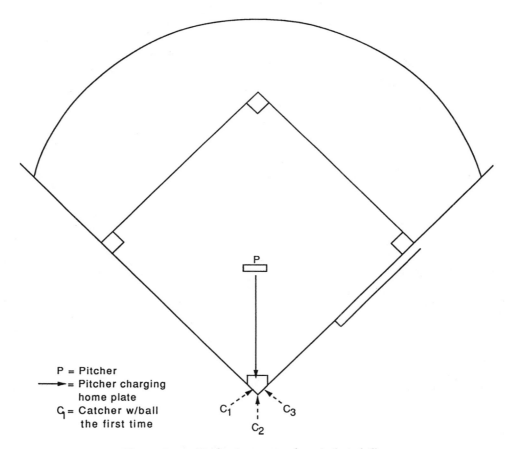

Figure A-20. Pitcher's covering home plate drill.

Key Points:

- The pitcher must sprint to home plate, holding the glove high in order to give the catcher a target.
- To improve reaction time, the pitcher should expect a bad throw from the catcher.
- The pitcher must practice making the correct tag on throws from all areas of the backstop.
- After the tag, the pitcher should look for plays at other bases.

Common Errors:

- The pitcher jogs to the plate.
- The pitcher tries to tag the runner before catching the ball.
- The pitcher sets up in the runner's path.

Modifications:

- Base runners can be added to the drill to create game-like situations.
- See Passed Ball/Wild Pitch 3-in-1 Drill.

Name: Pitcher's Quick Throw (see Figure A-21)

Objective: To enhance the pitching motion and to increase pitching endurance.

Suggested For: Advanced pitchers only.

Description: Two pitchers pitch to each other at regulation distance. Pitcher A assumes the normal pitching position, and pitcher B presents a target. Pitcher A pitches the ball to pitcher B's target. Pitcher B repeats the process. The ball is pitched as many times as possible within a given time limit, up to one minute. The pitchers concentrate on correct pitching mechanics as they throw fastballs and straight changes. (Fastballs should be no more than three-quarter speed or so.)

Key Points:

- The pitchers must be completely warmed up prior to beginning this drill.

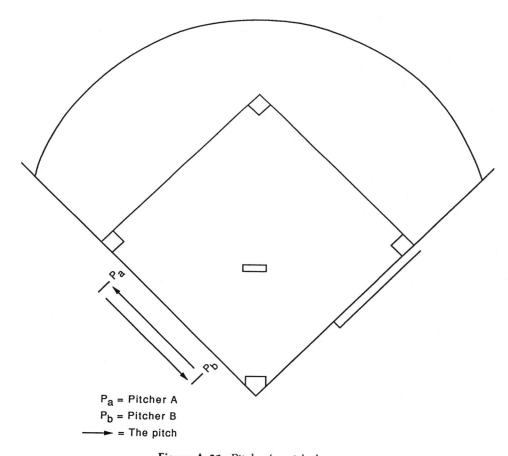

P_a = Pitcher A
P_b = Pitcher B
——→ = The pitch

Figure A-21. Pitcher's quick throw.

- Correct pitching form is essential with each pitch.
- Pitchers should throw hard with each pitch.
- For safety reasons, the area behind the pitchers should be kept clear.

Common Errors:
- Pitchers tense up in an attempt to increase speed.
- Pitchers do not concentrate on the target.
- Pitchers do not move back to their starting position following the pitch.
- Pitchers do not take time to adequately set and deliver the pitch.

Modifications:
- Pitchers can set goals such as the number of strikes per minute.
- Each pitcher can throw to a catcher who immediately returns the ball to the pitcher.
- Younger pitchers can throw successive pitches with quality (mechanical) goals rather than quantity goals.

Name: Pitcher Covering First Base (see Figure A-22)

Objective: To give pitchers the opportunity to practice covering first base both with and without other runners on base.

Suggested For: All skill levels.

Description: Pitcher, catcher and first base take their positions as a coach, with bat and ball, stands on the third base side of the plate. (Additional pitchers can line up behind the mound to await their turns.) The pitcher delivers a ball, and as the ball is thrown, the coach hits a second ball to the player at first base. The pitcher sprints for a spot 10 to 15 feet in front of first then turns to run parallel to the line. The defender at first should get the ball—chest high—to the pitcher approximately 3 feet in front of the base. (1) If no other runners are on, the pitcher touches first with the right foot and pushes off to the infield side of the base to avoid the runner. (2) If a runner is on base, the

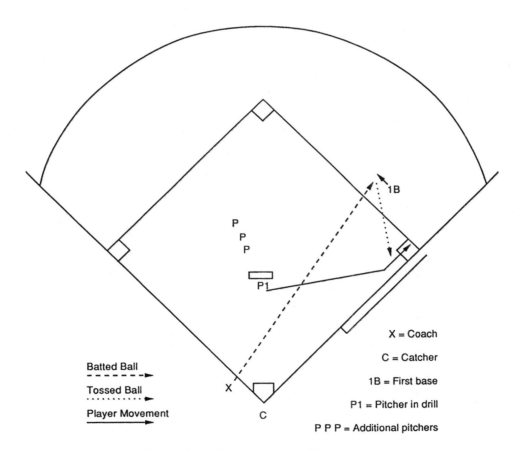

Figure A-22. Pitcher covering first base.

pitcher's action depends upon the throwing arm. A right-handed pitcher touches base, continues another stride, plants the right foot, and pivots back to the target. A left-handed pitcher touches base, plants the left foot, and pivots to the target.

Key Points:

- Pitchers: Break on contact and run the correct path to the base. Move to the infield and make the pivot as efficiently as possible.
- Catchers: Observe any runners and communicate their actions to the pitcher.
- First base: Get the ball to the pitcher well in front of the base and aim for the pitcher's chest.

Common Errors:

- Pitcher: Breaking too slowly for the base, does not look the ball into the glove, misses base, fails to pivot to find runner.
- Catcher: Watches play rather than runners.
- First base: Tosses the ball to the pitcher too late.

Modifications:

- A runner may be put on second base to simulate game conditions.
- A player may run from home to first also.

Name: Leading, Steals, and Pickoffs (see Figure A-23)

Objective: To combine base running practice with opportunities for infielders, pitchers and catchers to work on pickoff plays.

Suggested For: All skill levels, as appropriate.

Description: Pitcher, catcher and complete infield take their positions. Remaining players, with helmets, line up in foul territory near first base. The first athlete takes a lead off first base as the pitcher works from the set position. The runner attempts to steal as the pitcher, catcher and infielders try pickoff plays and work on steal coverages. Runners should attempt to go on each pitch. The same procedure should be

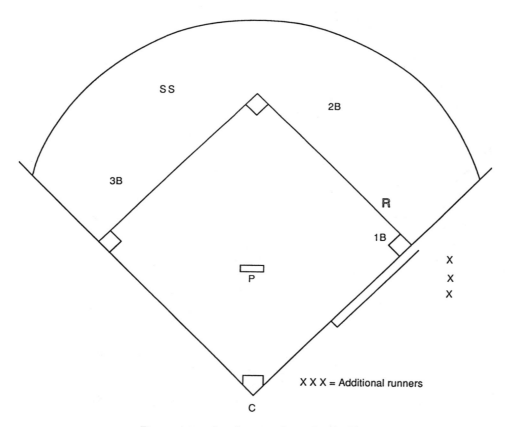

Figure A-23. Leading, steals, and pickoffs.

used at second and third bases. Players should also be rotated so that everyone runs and all infielders and battery players get adequate practice.

Key Points:

- Pitchers: Use quick moves that are not balks.
- Catchers: Work on jump pivots as needed.
- Infielders: Use proper coverages. (See Chapter 4, Position Play.)
- Runners: Slide at every base.

Common Errors:

- Runners: Going at less than game speed.
- Pitchers: Balks, using low set position.
- Catchers: Releasing ball too slowly.
- Middle infielders: Not communicating on base coverage.

Modifications:

- Runners may be placed at first and second to create double steal situations.
- Runners may be placed at first and third.

Name: Catcher's Bunt Drill (see Figure A-24)

Objective: To practice staying low while fielding bunts, and to facilitate throwing to the correct base.

Suggested For: Catchers of all skill levels.

Description: A catcher charges a ball that is rolled 5 to 10 feet in front of him or her, fields the ball, and pretends to throw to a base. The catcher rolls the ball again in another direction and repeats the process. All catchers repeat the drill down the first base line and back.

Key Elements:

- Catchers must stay low when charging the ball.
- Catchers must field the ball with two hands.
- Catchers must crow hop and shift the weight into the throw.

Common Errors:

- Picking up the ball with the bare hand only or scooping the ball with the glove only.

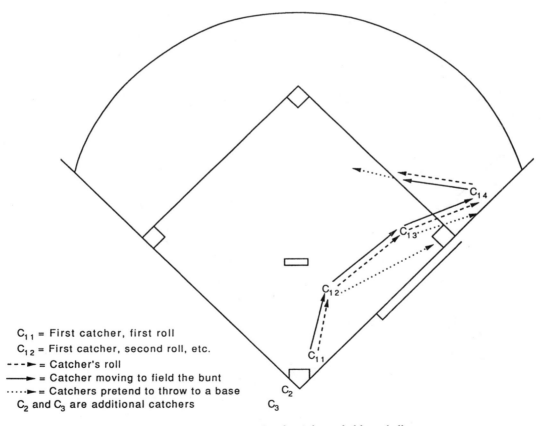

C_{11} = First catcher, first roll
C_{12} = First catcher, second roll, etc.
- - -► = Catcher's roll
——► = Catcher moving to field the bunt
······► = Catchers pretend to throw to a base
C_2 and C_3 are additional catchers

Figure A-24. Catcher's bunt fielding drill.

- Standing up and moving to field the ball.
- Throwing the ball with the glove-side foot pointing away from the target.

Modifications:

- The drill can be done in the gym or on the perimeter of the infield for conditioning purposes.
- The coach can stand next to the catcher and roll a "bunt."
- The coach can add base runners that the catcher must "throw out."
- The coach can mix in popups. The catcher can practice catching the popup and throwing to a base to complete a double play.

Name: Catcher's Pop-Up Drill (see Figure A-25)

Objective: To practice reacting to and catching the infield drift of popups. *Note:* Popups that stay in play around the plate almost always fol-

low a circular path: The ball starts moving up and out toward the infield. It then curves back toward the backstop as it reaches maximum height, but as the ball starts falling, it tails back toward the infield.

Suggested For: All skill levels.

Description: The catcher assumes the "crouch" position behind the plate. The coach hits or throws a popup in the home plate area. The catcher must locate the ball, call for it, throw the mask away from the vicinity of the descending ball, and make the catch.

Key Points:

- The catcher's back is to the infield when catching most popups.
- In judging the popup, the catcher must take into account the wind's strength and direction as well as the popup's height.
- The catcher must wait until the flight of the ball is determined before discarding the mask.

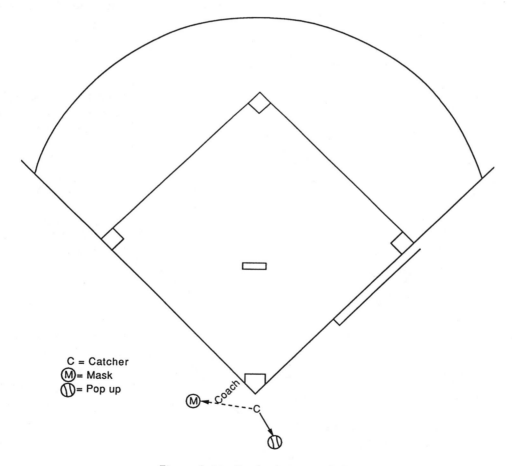

Figure A-25. Catcher's pop-up drill.

Common Errors:

- Discarding the mask too soon, before the catcher finds the ball.
- Catching the ball with the hands low.
- Facing the infield, the ball may "tail" away from the catcher forcing the player to lower the hands to make the catch.

Modifications:

- The height of the popups can be varied. As the catcher becomes more skilled, the popups can be hit higher.
- The coach can hit the popups with a tennis racket for better control.
- The catcher can keep her or his head down then look up after the ball is hit, locate the ball, and move to make the catch.

Name: Catcher's Down-Up Drill

Objective: To get the catcher from the receiving position, to the two-knee blocking position, and back to her/his feet as quickly as possible.

Suggested For: Catchers of all skill levels.

Description: Catchers in full equipment assume the correct receiving position. On a command from the coach, the catchers drop to both knees as if blocking a pitch in the dirt then hop back to the receiving position in one motion. The drill is repeated in sequences of four every ten seconds.

Key Points:

- Catchers must execute proper position and technique.
- Catchers should use equipment, especially shin guards.
- Catchers should do each "down-up" as quickly as possible.

Common Errors:

- Sacrificing correct technique for speed.
- Losing balance when the knees are not dropped simultaneously.
- Failing to fully return to the receiving position.

Modifications:

- Repetitions can be progressively increased (as

in, 20 to 25 repetitions in 30 seconds for conditioning purposes).
- The coach or another player can throw the ball in the dirt for the catcher to block.
- The catcher can scramble after the blocked ball, field it, and "fake" a throw.

Name: Catcher's No-Mitt Blocking Drill (see Figure A-26a, b and c)

Objective: To practice moving the entire body in front of pitches in the dirt.

Suggested For: Catchers of all skill levels.

Description: In full gear, the catcher assumes the receiving position, with both hands behind the back. The coach or another catcher throws balls in the dirt in front of and to the sides of the catcher. The catcher concentrates on quickly dropping to the knees and getting into a position to block the ball. For safety reasons, the catcher should move blocked balls out of the way of the next throw.

Key Points:

- The focus is on correct technique with EVERY repetition: (1) The catcher must quickly shift and drop to the knees in order to get the body in front of the ball; (2) the catcher must roll the shoulders forward in order to keep the ball in front of the body.

Common Errors:

- Pitching the ball before the catcher is ready.
- Using improper technique due to fatigue.

Modifications:

- Use tennis balls instead of baseballs to eliminate any fear of injury.
- For advanced catchers, throw different pitches to teach adjustments for bounces with different spins.
- Allow the catcher to block with her or his mitt, recover quickly and retrieve to throw.
- Have the pitcher vary the speed and placement of the pitch.
- Encourage many correct repetitions to build endurance.

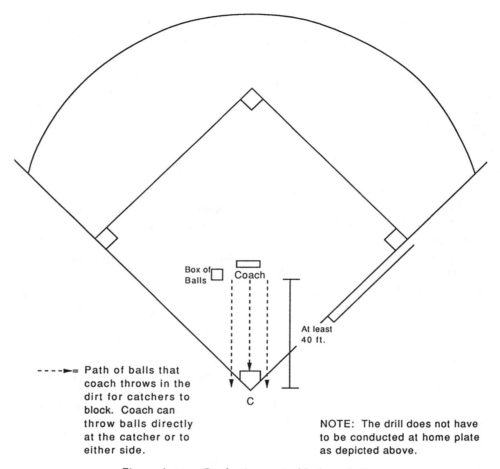

Box of Balls

Coach

At least 40 ft.

- - - - ▶ = Path of balls that coach throws in the dirt for catchers to block. Coach can throw balls directly at the catcher or to either side.

C

NOTE: The drill does not have to be conducted at home plate as depicted above.

Figure A-26a. Catcher's no-mitt blocking drill.

Figure A-26b. Catcher in position to start no-mitt blocking drill.

Figure A-26c. Catcher blocking ball.

Name: Passed Ball/Wild Pitch 3-in-1 Drill (see Figure A-27)

Objective: This drill is designed to develop (1) communication between pitchers and catchers on passed balls or wild pitches with runners on base; (2) catchers' technique in retrieving the ball; and (3) pitchers' technique in covering the plate.

Suggested For: Intermediate and advanced players.

Description: The pitcher executes an imaginary pitch and the coach rolls a ball to a variety of locations behind the catcher. The pitcher, while running toward the ball, points to it and calls out the direction in which the ball is rolling ("1," "3," or "back" tells the catcher 1st base side, 3rd base side, or straight behind). The catcher correctly fields and throws the ball to the pitcher covering the plate. The pitcher correctly receives the ball and tags an imaginary runner.

Key Points:

- The pitcher must yell the direction of the ball, as well as point to the ball.

- The catcher may remove the mask and must quickly move to the ball, and the pitcher must immediately cover home plate.
- The throw to the pitcher should be made with a compact snap throw.
- The pitcher must provide a target on the first base side of the plate, catch the throw, and make the tag.

Common Errors:

- The pitcher and catcher move slowly.
- The catcher does not field the ball with the throwing side to the backstop.
- The catcher does not "show" the ball; rather he or she hides it in the mitt or with the body prior to the throw.
- The pitcher tries to tag the runner before the ball has been caught.

Modifications:

- Another player may roll the ball behind the catcher.
- Each drill may be done separately.
- The pitcher may pitch the ball in the dirt.
- The coach may add base runners to the drill (but do not encourage them to slide).

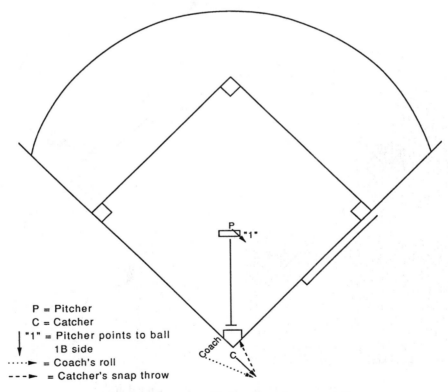

P = Pitcher
C = Catcher
"1" = Pitcher points to ball 1B side
••••► = Coach's roll
---► = Catcher's snap throw

Figure A-27. Passed ball/wild pitch 3-in-1 drill.

Name: First Base One-Handed Drill (see Figure A-28)

Objective: To help the first baseperson gain confidence and competence in using one hand to stretch for the ball.

Suggested For: Players of intermediate and advanced skill levels.

Description: Players work in groups of two; players within each group are spaced 60 to 90 feet apart. Players stretch with the glove-hand to receive a thrown ball, while keeping the throwing hand in their back pocket. Throws should vary from side to side, and from high to low.

Key Elements:

- The first baseperson should always stretch to the ball.
- When catching the ball, the glove-side arm should be slightly flexed in order to absorb the force of the ball.
- The first baseperson should not jump in order to catch the ball unless absolutely necessary. If a jump is necessary, the first baseperson should propel the body upward with the glove-side leg and land on the throwing-side foot.

Common Errors:

- Failing to stretch for the ball.
- Stretching too soon, before the throw is made.
- Incorrectly positioning the foot on the base as the ball is caught.

Modifications:

- As players become adept at the drill, they can keep their hand out of the pocket but still catch the ball one-handed.
- The coach may also throw balls to the first baseperson.

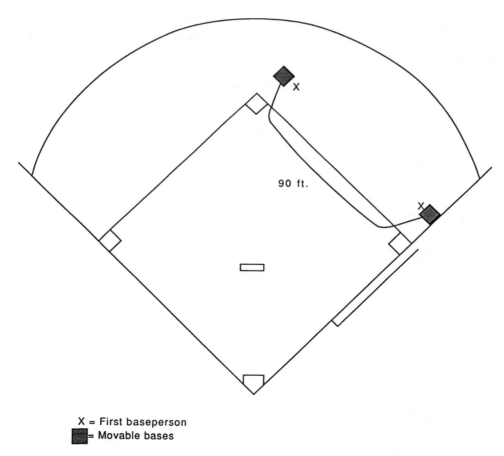

X = First baseperson
▨ = Movable bases

Figure A-28. First baseperson's one-handed drill.

Name: First Base Scoop Drill (see Figure A-29)

Objective: To facilitate fielding throws in the dirt.

Suggested For: Intermediate and advanced players.

Description: Players throw a baseball back and forth so that all throws bounce in the dirt. Players should practice stretching to the ball and fielding it on the short hop.

Key Points:
- The glove should be open and low to the ground. The arm and hands should absorb the force of the throw.
- The eyes follow the ball into the glove.

Common Errors:
- Raising the head and losing sight of the ball.
- Stretching before the throw has been made.
- Standing upright with the glove well above the ground.

Modifications:
- Infielders can throw the ball in the dirt to the first baseperson during regular infield practice.
- Other infielders involved in force plays can also participate in the drill.
- The first baseperson can wear a catcher's mask and shin guards to eliminate the fear of fielding balls in the dirt.
- Less-skilled players can use tennis balls.

Name: Shortstop, Second Base Double Play Drill (see Figure A-30)

Objective: To practice and enhance the 6-4-3 and 4-6-3 double play.

Suggested For: All skill levels.

Description: A "roller" rolls a ground ball to the shortstop or second baseperson. The player

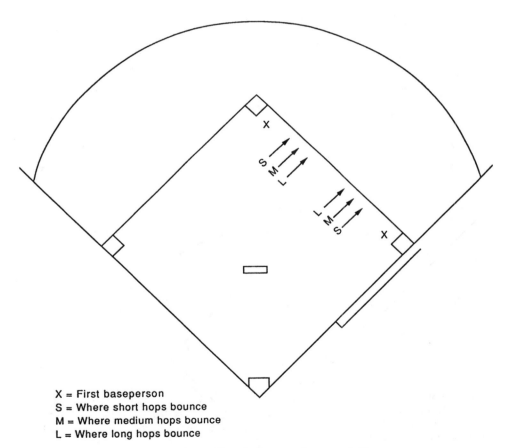

X = First baseperson
S = Where short hops bounce
M = Where medium hops bounce
L = Where long hops bounce

Figure A-29. First baseperson's scoop drill.

not receiving the ground ball covers second base, receives the throw from the fielder, and completes the double play by throwing the ball to first base.

Key Points:
- The ball should be rolled so that the shortstop and second baseperson can practice receiving throws from different areas of the infield.
- The ball must be fielded cleanly and thrown chest high to the person covering the base.
- The fielders must insure that they complete the force out at second base before throwing the ball to first base.
- The fielders should concentrate on receiving and throwing the ball correctly.

Common Errors:
- The shortstop or second baseperson tries to throw the ball before making the catch.
- The shortstop or second baseperson moves

into the runner's path in order to make the throw to first base.
- The first baseperson does not stretch to make the catch.

Modifications:
- This drill can be set up on the infield with two groups of infielders performing simultaneously. One group is stationed at second base, throwing to first base, while the other group is stationed at home plate and throwing to third base. The rollers are positioned at the front and back of the pitcher's mound (see Figure A-30).
- The fielders can position themselves at their regular infield positions while the coach fungo hits ground balls.
- Base runners may be added to provide an players with understanding of the time required to complete a double play.
- The coach may time the double play execution, with the goal of decreasing the time of execution.

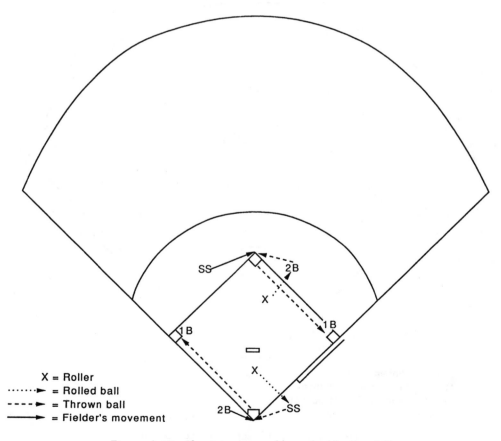

Figure A-30. Shortstop, second base double play drill.

Name: Third Base Slow Roller Drill (see Figure A-31)

Objective: To practice charging and fielding slow rolling ground balls.

Suggested For: Advanced-level third basepersons.

Description: The coach or another player rolls a slow grounder toward third base. The third baseperson charges the ball and fields it. In a continuous motion, she or he throws the ball to first base.

Key Points:

- The player must use two hands.
- The fielder must charge the ball hard.
- Ideally, fielding and throwing the ball should occur in one smooth continuous motion—with or without a crow hop.

Common Errors:

- The player does not charge the ball as quickly as possible.

- The head raises up before the ball is fielded.
- Players attempt to throw while off-balance.

Modifications:

- Players performing this drill for the first time may run through the play in slow motion, focusing on each component individually.
- Balls may be lined up from the third base line out toward the pitcher's plate, and one at a time, players charge, field, and throw the stationary ball.

Name: Infield Reaction Drill (see Figure A-32)

Objective: To help infielders learn to respond quickly to situations, pick the ball up cleanly, and make good throws.

Suggested For: Infielders—including catchers—of all skill levels.

Description: Infielders, along with the catcher, take their positions, and the coach stands to the

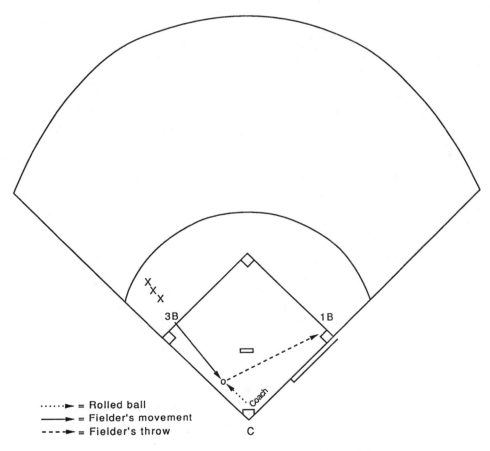

······▶ = Rolled ball
——▶ = Fielder's movement
- - -▶ = Fielder's throw

Figure A-31. Third baseperson's slow roller drill.

third base side of home. Two or three balls are placed some 5 to 7 feet in front of the players. The coach calls out a play to be made: for example, shortstop to second, third to first, or catcher to first. The first Named player fields the ball and throws to the second player covering the assigned base. (Shortstop covers second base.) The player receiving the throw finishes the play by returning the ball to the coach. Play continues until the coach has all the baseballs. Action should be continuous, but the athletes should be back in their starting positions before the next call is made.

Key Points:

- Field the ball with both the hands and the feet properly positioned.
- Use good mechanics in throwing.

Common Errors:

- Going at less than game speed through the drill.
- Failing to look the ball into the glove.

- Using poor body position.
- Not using two hands to get the ball.
- Making poor throws.

Modifications:

- Adjust speed of play calls to players' ability. Place balls farther away as players' range improves.

Name: Unassisted Force Out Double Play Drill (see Figure A-33)

Objective: To learn to recognize a potential unassisted force out double play opportunity and to practice the skills necessary to execute the play.

Suggested For: All skill levels.

Description: Standing at home plate, the coach indicates the situation and hits a ground ball to an infielder. The infielder must field the ball, tag the base, and throw to first base. For exam-

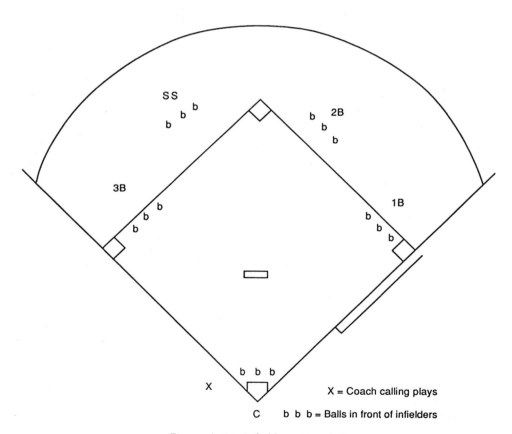

Figure A-32. Infield reaction drill.

ple: the coach says "runners on 1 and 2, less than two outs." The coach then hits a ground ball to third base. The third baseperson fields the ball, tags third base, and throws to first base.

Key Points:

- The fielder must first concentrate on fielding the ball.
- The fielder must be aware of her or his position in relation to the base and take the shortest path to the base.
- The throwing-side foot should touch the base so the player may execute an immediate throw to first base.
- The fielder must understand and recognize the situation.

Common Errors:

- The thrower moves away from the first base target after tagging the base, resulting in an off-balance throw.

- The fielder does not communicate to the other fielders that he or she will make the play unassisted.
- The fielder is distracted by the base runner and does not watch the ball all the way into the glove.

Modifications:

- Base runners can be added to make the situation more realistic.
- For intermediate and advanced players, pop-ups and line drives may be mixed in with ground balls to make the situations more complex.

Name: Infield Priority Drill (see Figure A-34)

Objective: To learn, reinforce and promote communication among infielders.

Suggested For: All skill levels.

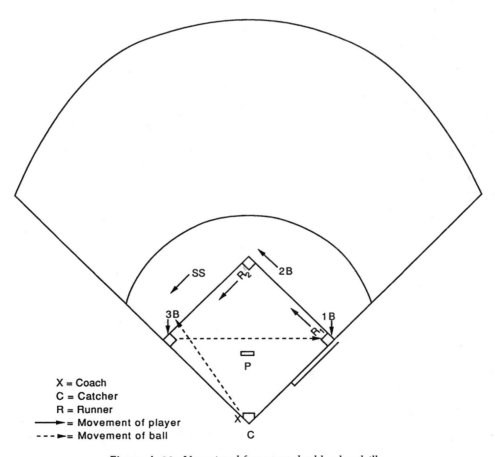

X = Coach
C = Catcher
R = Runner
———► = Movement of player
- - -► = Movement of ball

Figure A-33. Unassisted force out double play drill.

Description: The coach hits or throws pop ups to the infield. When the ball is in the air, the player who thinks she or he has the best chance to catch it yells "Mine!" If two or more players call for the ball, the player with priority will make the catch. After several attempts, players alternate or switch positions.

Key Points:
- Players should call for the ball loudly!
- The player with priority should repeat the call several times in order to ensure being heard.
- Priority players should call off another player only if she or he has an equal or better chance of making the catch (for example, the shortstop would not call anyone off on a popup near the first base line).
- The coach should give appropriate feedback.

Common Errors:
- Failing to call for a ball before attempting to catch it.

- Calling for the ball too late. Other players may not have time to react and yield.
- Two players calling for the ball simultaneously and one not giving way to the infielder with priority.

Modifications:
- Tennis balls may be used with less skilled players.
- The coach may vary the difficulty of the pop ups according to skill level.
- Instead of hitting or throwing a pop up, the coach throws a flat object on the ground (such as a Frisbee®) and the infielders move and call to stand on the object according to position priority.

Name: Infield/Outfield Priority Drill (see Figure A-35)

Objective: To learn, promote and reinforce communication between infielders and outfielders.

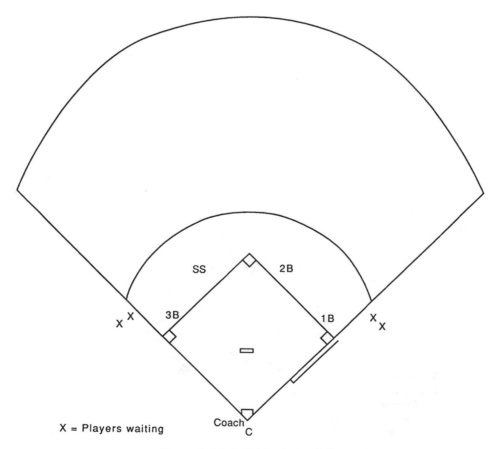

X = Players waiting

Figure A-34. Infield priority drill.

Suggested For: Intermediate and advanced skill levels.

Description: The coach hits or throws pop ups between the infield and outfield. The fielder who thinks she or he has a chance to catch the ball yells "Mine!" If an infielder and outfielder call for the ball at the same time, the outfielder has priority to make the catch, and the infielder moves out of the way.

Key Points:

- All players involved must be assertive.
- Balls should be called for loudly and repeatedly.
- If called off by an outfielder, the infielder must yield to her or him. The outfielder has priority over infielders, and the center fielder has priority over all fielders.

Common Errors:

- Communicating poorly or not at all.
- Expecting someone else to catch the ball.

Modifications:

- Tennis balls may be used for less-skilled players. The primary emphasis is on calling for the ball and priorities. Catching skills should be stressed in more specific drills.
- For more advanced players, the coach can increase the difficulty of the popups.

Name: Outfield Priority Drill (see Figure A-36)

Objective: To promote and facilitate communication and backup skills among outfielders.

Suggested For: Intermediate and advanced players.

Description: The coach hits or throws a ground ball between two outfielders. The outfielder with the best position yells "Mine!" and fields the ball while the other outfielder backs up the play. If both fielders call for the ball, the center fielder has priority.

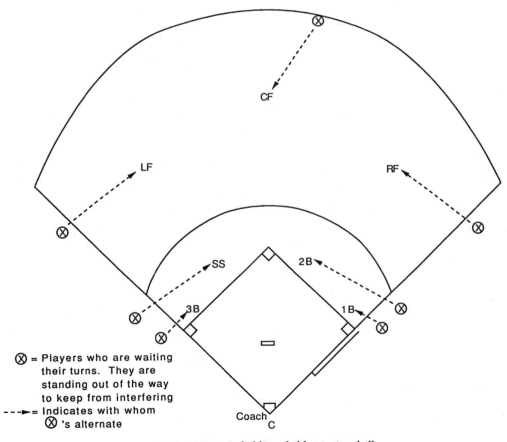

Figure A-35. Infield/outfield priority drill.

Key Elements:

- The outfielder must call for the ball loudly!
- The center fielder has priority over the other two outfielders.
- Outfielders must assume their roles quickly.
- The non-fielding outfielder backs up the play.

Common Errors:

- Failing to yield to the center fielder when both fielders call for the ball.
- Failing to back up the play.
- Fielders not "taking charge" and immediately calling for the ball, especially the center fielder.

Modifications:

- The drill can also be done with two lines of outfielders, with one line being the designated center fielder.
- For less experienced players, the coach may make the ball easier to field so that the outfielders may focus on priorities, calling for the ball, and backing up the play.

Name: Relay Relay (see Figure A-37)

Objective: To help players learn, practice and improve relay throws.

Suggested For: Intermediate and advanced skill levels.

Description: This drill is a race to see which row of players can most quickly get the ball from one end of the row to the other, and back again. A ball is placed on the ground beside the players at the same end of each of the rows. The coach says "Go," and the first player in each row picks the ball up and throws it to the next player. The throws continue until the ball travels to the end of the row and back again. The first row to finish is the "winner."

Key Points:

- The receiver keeps the arms up, makes the catch, and turns to throw.
- Throws should be chest high.

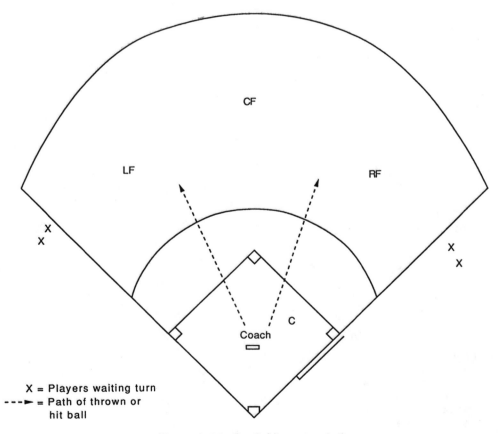

X = Players waiting turn
---►= Path of thrown or hit ball

Figure A-36. Outfield priority drill.

Common Errors:

- The player receiving the ball does not hold his or her arms up as a target.
- The player catching the ball does not step toward the target as the ball is caught.
- The thrower overthrows the target.

Modifications:

- For more advanced players, the distance between the players in each row may be increased.
- As players become more proficient at this drill, each row may be rearranged so that players are staggered to the left and right of each other.
- For lower-skilled players, each group may be timed, with the goal of decreasing the time needed to complete the drill.

Name: Basic Relay Drill (see Figure A-38)

Objective: To introduce the basic relay and provide practice for enhancing relay throws.

Suggested For: All skill levels.

Description: Players are divided into equal groups of three or more. Players are arranged in lines across the field with about 60 feet between each line. Players within a line are spaced 90 to 100 feet apart with outfielders at the outfield end of the line and second base players and shortstops next in line. Balls are placed an equal distance beyond each outfielder. On the coaches signal, the outfielders sprint to the ball. A fielder lines up the "relay" players in order to maintain a straight line between all the players involved in the play. The relay person correctly receives the outfielder's throw and throws it to the appropriate fielder to complete the play.

Key Points:

- The fielder must provide loud, verbal commands.
- The relay person keeps the arms up and provides instruction to the outfielder (such as, "hit me").

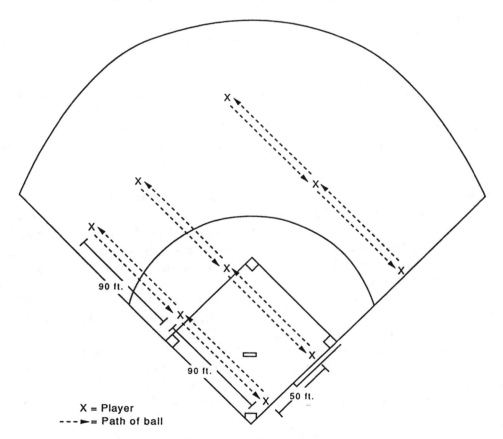

90 ft.

90 ft.

50 ft.

X = Player
- - - ►= Path of ball

Figure A-37. Relay drill.

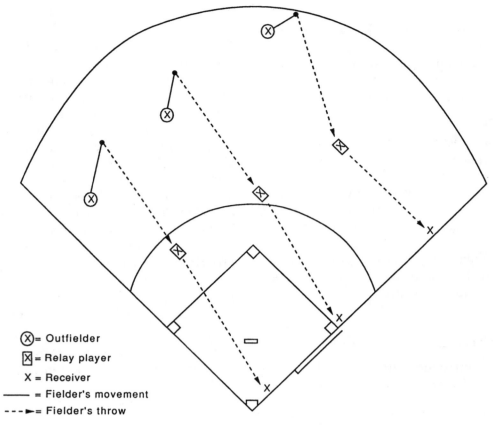

Figure A-38. Basic relay drill.

- = Outfielder
- = Relay player
- = Receiver
- = Fielder's movement
- = Fielder's throw

- The relay person turns to the glove side to relay the throw.
- The relay person should move to catch all throws in the air. A ball that bounces is harder to field.

Common Errors:
- The relay person looks to throw the ball before it is caught.
- The outfielder overthrows the relay person.
- The relay person makes a poor throw.
- Players fail to communicate.

Modifications:
- The distance between players may be increased or decreased according to the strength and accuracy of the fielders' throwing arms.
- Highly skilled players may compete with other groups. The first line to complete the relay is the "winner."
- The ball may be relayed from one end of the line to the other and back again.

Name: Look the Runner Back (see Figure A-39)

Objective: To combine work for infielders on holding runners after ground balls with possible rundown plays.

Suggested For: All skill levels.

Description: Pitcher, catcher and complete infield take their positions. Remaining players, with helmets, are divided into two groups: One runs from third base, the other from behind the plate. The coach hits ground balls and the runner behind the plate sprints for first. The infielders are playing in to cut off the run (see Chapter 8, Defensive Strategies). They look the runner at third back and complete the force out at first. Once the throw to first is made, the runner at third is free to try to score. The defender at first should be aware of this possibility and attempt to either throw the runner out at the plate or initiate a run down. Players

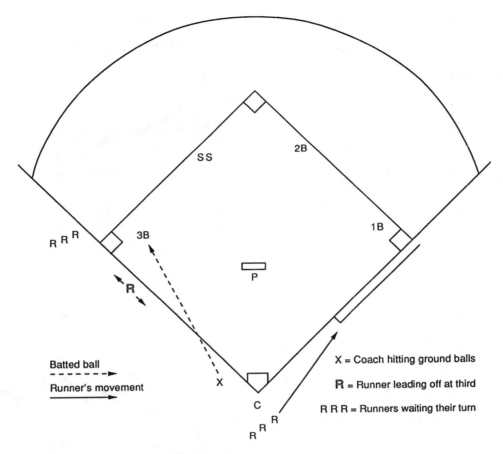

SS

2B

3B

1B

P

R R R

R

Batted ball
- - - - - →

Runner's movement
————→

X

C

R
R R

X = Coach hitting ground balls

R = Runner leading off at third

R R R = Runners waiting their turn

Figure A-39. Look the runner back.

should rotate so that all run and every infielder, pitcher and catcher has practice.

Key Points:

- Infielders: Take a good look at the runner, but do not wait too long before throwing.
- Catchers: Observe the runner at third and communicate with the player covering first.
- First base: Make sure of the out, but be prepared to throw home.
- Runners: Slide.

Common Errors:

- Runners: Going at less than game speed.
- Fielders: Not looking at runner.
- Catchers: Watching play rather than runner at third.
- First base: In response to runner from third, coming off bag before completing out.

Modifications:

- Use infielders only at third and first to simulate other than game saving situations.

Name: Mirror Hitting

Objective: To make hitters become aware of their own mechanics.

Suggested For: All skill levels.

Description: Hitters face a large mirror and watch themselves as they swing. They should focus on one aspect of the swing at a time: level swing, eyes, head movement, opening of the hips, and so forth.

Key Points:

- Athletes need to understand the mechanics of a sound swing first. Then they can watch themselves develop these.

Common Errors:

- Failing to take complete swings.

Name: Shadow Drill

Objective: To reinforce correct weight transfer when swinging a bat.

Suggested For: Players of all skill levels.

Description: The hitter assumes the hitting ready position with the sun or a bright light at his or her back. Another player places a ball on the shadow cast by the hitter's head. The batter swings the bat, holds the follow through and checks the shadow. If the ball is still on the head shadow, no weight transfer took place. If the ball is not on the head shadow, the other player places another ball on the new shadow to show how much the head moved forward and, subsequently, how much weight transfer occurred.

Key Points:
- The shadow must be clear!
- The batter's swing must be as if hitting a pitch.
- The weight shifts against the front foot rather than over the front foot.

Common Errors:
- Moving the weight over the front foot, thus moving the head.
- Swinging "easy" in order to keep the head still.
- Overstriding, causing the head to lower.

Modifications:
- If the hitter cannot keep the weight from shifting forward, a heavy rubber cord around the waist can be used to keep the midline steady. The hitter should focus on the difference between "moving forward" and "moving against."

Name: Hip Rotation Drill (see Figure A-40a, b and c)

Objective: To promote correct stride and hip rotation for hitting. This drill can also be used as a warm-up technique in the on-deck circle.

Suggested For: All skill levels.

Description: A bat is placed behind the player's back and is held parallel to the ground by the elbow joints of each arm. The hitter assumes the hitting ready position and strides with the front foot. The weight shifts "against" the front foot as the hips quickly rotate forward.

Figure A-40a. Player in stance at beginning of hip rotation drill.

Figure A-40b. Starting the stride.

Key Points:
- The stride is about 6 to 8 inches, and the front foot is pointed about 45 degrees on a line from the pitcher to home plate.
- The weight shifts "against" the front leg and the front leg pushes forcefully against the ground in order to rotate the hips forward.
- At the end of the movement, the "belt buckle" should point toward the pitcher.

Figure A-40c. Player with hips fully rotated.

Common Errors:

- Overstriding.
- Shifting the weight over the front foot rather than against the front foot.
- Rotating forward by leading with the shoulders. This increases the friction between the bat and the arms and the arms may become sore.

Modifications:

- Advanced players can kneel on the back knee in order to execute the drill. This will reduce the effect of front knee extension but will help the player keep the weight from moving over the front leg.

Name: Batting Tee Drill (see Figure A-41)

Objective: To supplement the regular batting practice and to work on hitting mechanics.

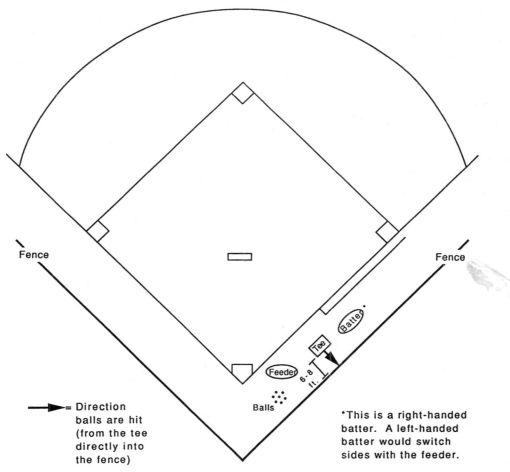

Fence

Fence

Batter*

Tee

Feeder

6-8 ft.

Balls

→ = Direction balls are hit (from the tee directly into the fence)

*This is a right-handed batter. A left-handed batter would switch sides with the feeder.

Figure A-41. Batting tee drill.

Suggested For: All skill levels.

Description: The batting tee is positioned 6 to 8 feet from a fence or net and away from any rigid support poles. Batters attempt to hit line drives into the fence. Batters can (1) work individually and focus on specific hitting mechanics, one item at a time, or (2) work in pairs and focus on reinforcing a correct swing by doing a specific number of repetitions. When working in pairs, the non-hitter places balls on the tee until all balls have been hit.

Key Points:
- Any type of ball can be used to hit off the tee. Used baseballs, baseballs, or flat tennis balls are good to use for this drill.
- Each tee station should have balls equal to the number of balls to hit.
- When working in pairs, the player placing the ball on the tee must remain clear of the batter.

Common Errors:
- Hitters are too close to the tee and cannot fully extend their arms at contact.

- Players are even with the tee and cannot properly rotate their hips prior to contact.
- Practicing an incorrect swing reinforces that incorrect swing. It is important that the batter have a correct swing before practicing it on the tees.

Modifications:
- Less skilled players may execute this drill using a larger ball. The larger ball will provide a greater chance of success.
- Highly skilled players can adjust the height and location of the tee in order to practice the swing required to hit pitches in various locations.
- The tee can be placed at home plate with the batter hitting to a defense. The batter practices hitting while the defense practices situation play.

Name: Soft Toss Hitting Drill (see Figure A-42a and b)

Objective: To isolate and enhance components of the swing. Also to provide variety for batting practice.

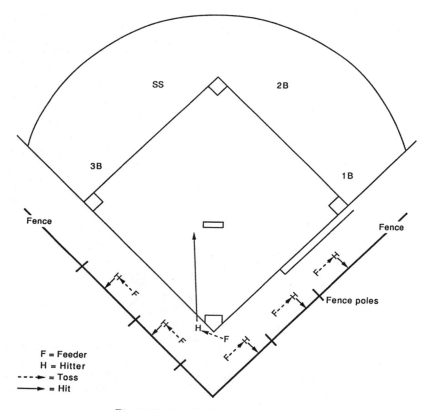

Figure A-42a. Soft toss hitting drill.

Suggested For: All skill levels.

Description: Players work in groups of two, one being the hitter the other being the "feeder." The feeder kneels opposite the hitting side of home plate with a bucket of balls and tosses the ball underhand in the strike zone. The hitter attempts to hit line drives. Balls can be hit into an open field or into a net or fence. For safety reasons, groups must be spread out and clear of hitting into rigid fence poles.

Key Points:

- The feeder must toss the ball in front of the hitter.
- The feeder should limit the arc and speed of the toss.
- The hitter should concentrate on a specific component of hitting or on hitting hard line drives.
- The hitter should focus on hitting one toss at a time.

Common Errors:

- The tosses are unhittable (thrown at the hitter).
- Timing of the toss is too slow or too fast.
- The hitter shifts the weight over the front foot.
- The hitter drops his or her hands and swings up at the ball.

Modifications:

- The toss can be placed in a variety of locations for more experienced players.
- The hitter can hit to a defense so that batted balls are used as fielding practice for the fielders.
- The type and size of ball can vary: tennis balls, baseballs, plastic golf balls, and so on.
- The hitting implement can vary: dowel rod, broom stick handle, tee ball bat, and so on.

Caution: This soft toss hitting drill presents the possibility of eye injury—especially if soft plastic or tennis balls are used. If the coach decides to incorporate this drill into practices, eye protection must be made MANDATORY for all participants. The tosser may be placed behind a protective screen or alternatively may wear a catcher's mask or safety goggles; the

Figure A-42b. Players in position for soft toss hitting. Note eye protection in use and distance involved.

hitter should wear goggles. Study the illustration carefully and see how these athletes have been protected against the possibility of injury.

Name: Power Swing Drill (see Figure A-43a and b)

Objective: To increase hitting power and strength.

Suggested For: Intermediate and advanced hitters.

Description: Starting in a correct batting stance, the batter takes a full swing with a weighted bat. After completing the follow-through phase, the batter returns the bat to the original position and repeats the swing. Initially, the batter may do 1 set of 10 repetitions. The number of sets may gradually increase as strength increases (for example, 3 sets of 10).

Note: Homemade weighted bats *should not* be used. Attachments such as vanes and doughnuts are available, but rules governing their use must be followed. Younger players should do this drill with their regular bat only.

Key Points:

- The batter focuses on "feeling" and maintaining a correct swing. If the swing cannot be repeated 10 times correctly, reduce the number of repetitions or the weight on the bat.
- The eyes focus on a fixed object throughout the swing in order to promote correct head position.
- The batter executes the swing at full speed.

Figure A-43a. Player at beginning of power swing drill.

Figure A-43b. Completion of the power swing.

Common Errors:
- The batter begins to return the bat for the next swing before completing the follow through.
- The bat is too heavy, and the batter cannot execute a correct swing.
- The batter does not concentrate, resulting in "lazy," incorrect repetitions.

Modifications:
- Younger batters should execute this drill with their regular bat.
- This drill can be executed in shoulder deep water with a regular bat in order to obtain constant resistance.

Name: Pepper Game Drill (see Figure A-44)

Objective: To enhance hand-eye coordination and agility necessary to perform fielding and batting drills.

Suggested For: Intermediate and advanced skill levels.

Description: Players work in groups of three or four. One player is the batter and the other players are fielders. A fielder throws a ball to the batter and the batter hits the ball on the ground to any of the fielders in the group, using a half swing. The fielder fields the ground ball and quickly lobs it back to the batter. After 10 to 15 swings, the batter and one fielder trade positions.

Key Points:
- The batter takes a half swing.
- The batter should attempt to hit the ball to each fielder.
- Fielders must work on quickly fielding and throwing the ball.
- Extra balls should be kept nearby in order to replace missed balls.

Common Errors:
- The batter lacks intensity and concentration.
- The batter swings too hard, endangering the fielders.
- Fielders shift their weight to their heels when fielding ground balls.

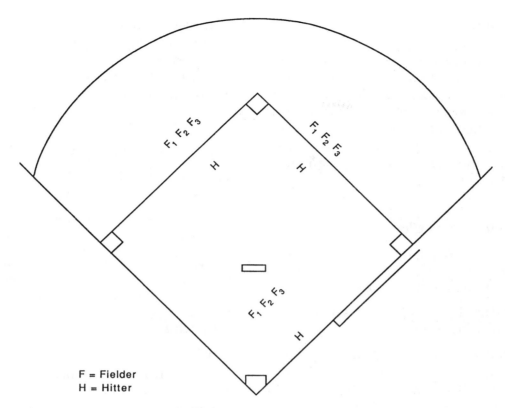

F = Fielder
H = Hitter

Figure A-44. Pepper game drill.

Modifications:

- For more advanced players, decrease the number of players in each group and/or move the fielders closer to the batter.
- For lower skilled players, use rag balls to ensure safety.
- Move more advanced players to "the end of the line" with a bad throw or a fielding error.
- Introduce competition between groups by counting the number of hits in a given time.

Name: Soft Toss Bunting Drill

Objective: To practice "giving" with both arms while executing a sacrifice bunt.

Suggested For: Beginning, intermediate, and advanced bunters.

Description: Players work in groups of two; one player is the bunter, and the other player is the tosser. The tosser stands about 10 feet in front of the bunter and tosses the ball to the bunter. The bunter, already squared to the tosser, absorbs the force of the toss by giving equally with both arms. Because of the "slow" speed of the toss, if the toss is executed correctly the ball will drop directly to the ground. After 7 to 10 bunts the players switch roles.

Key Elements:

- The batter holds the bat with the barrel near the top of the strike zone and higher than the handle; the arms are extended.
- The eyes follow the center of the ball to the center of the bat.
- Both arms give equally to absorb the force of the toss and drop the ball directly to the ground.

Common Errors:

- The bunter gives with one arm only, usually the arm near the top of the bat.
- The bunter attempts to bunt tosses that are not in the strike zone. If the bat is held at the top of the strike zone, anything above the bat is a ball.
- The bunter starts with the arms flexed, then extends the arms to the ball and "pushes" it back to the tosser.

Modifications:

- The batter starts in the hitting ready position then squares around or pivots to the bunting position. Once in the bunting position, the tosser tosses the ball.
- The tosser moves to 20 feet in front of the bunter and the bunter practices the bunt for a hit. *Note:* In this situation, the players should wear eye protection as in the regular soft toss drill.

Name: Bunting With Gloves

Objective: This drill is meant to improve the confidence of beginning bunters or players who are having trouble with bunting skills.

Suggested For: Beginning bunters and players having trouble bunting.

Description: As each batter steps into the box, they have a glove on the "wrong" hand: A right-handed batter wears a glove normally worn by a left-handed thrower and a left-handed hitter uses a glove worn by a right-handed thrower. As the delivery is made, the batter squares as though to bunt and catches the ball. After building confidence with this action, the athlete steps in with the glove and bat: The lower, bare hand grips the bat as in a regular bunt, but the barrel of the bat is cradled in the glove's pocket. Again pitches are thrown and the batter concentrates on catching the ball on the bat. *Note:* As in any batting drill, helmets should be worn by all players.

Key Points:

- The glove is moved only as the bat should be: in or out, up or down. It is not extended to meet the ball.
- Bunting is catching the ball on the bat.

Common Errors:

- Extending the arms to meet the ball.
- Not using the knees to move.

Modifications:

- As an introduction to bunting or as practice in moving into bunting position, have the players not use a bat and simply catch the ball in the glove.
- Use this drill to reinforce bunting skills at

the beginning of seasons for older players or when opposing pitchers come up with new deliveries.

- Use this drill to teach the timing involved in squeeze plays.

Name: Target Bunting Drill (see Figure A-45)

Objective: To improve bunting accuracy and consistency.

Suggested For: Intermediate and advanced bunters.

Description: A target is placed on each baseline, approximately 10 feet from the plate and 3 feet inside the baseline. Wearing a helmet, a bunter squares or pivots and attempts to bunt the pitch as close to the target as possible.

Key Points:

- The pitcher should throw strikes consistently.
- The bunter should be selective and bunt only strikes.
- The bunter should work on timing the square or pivot.
- The bunter should use proper bunting technique.

Common Errors:

- Bunting pitches that are not strikes.
- Dropping the bat away from the eyes.
- Pushing the ball rather than "catching" the ball with the bat.

Modifications:

- More experienced players can alternate sacrifice bunts and bunts for hits.
- Players can be placed into groups (such as infielders vs. outfielders) and groups can compete for accuracy points.

Name: Bunt and Slap Drill (see Figure A-46)

Objective: To practice the various types of bunts and the slap against a live defense. Also, to practice defensive reactions to bunt situations.

Suggested For: Intermediate and advanced skill levels.

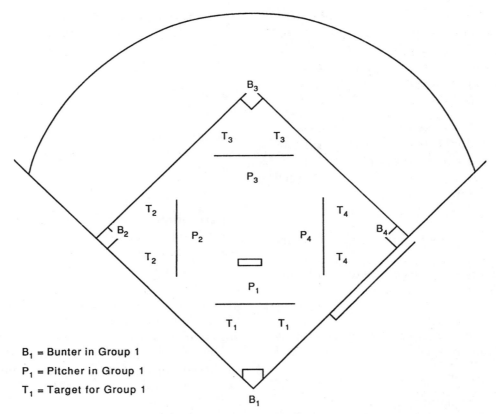

B₁ = Bunter in Group 1
P₁ = Pitcher in Group 1
T₁ = Target for Group 1

Figure A-45. Target bunting drill.

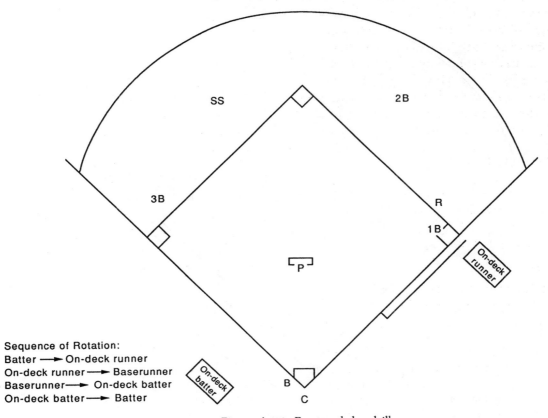

Sequence of Rotation:
Batter ⟶ On-deck runner
On-deck runner ⟶ Baserunner
Baserunner ⟶ On-deck batter
On-deck batter ⟶ Batter

Figure A-46. Bunt and slap drill.

Description: A batter decides before entering the batter's box whether to execute (a) a bunt, or (b) a slap. As a pitcher prepares to pitch, the batter squares around to bunt. If the pitch is in the strike zone, the batter executes the play.

Key Points:
- Pitchers should throw consistent strikes.
- Players must duplicate the intensity and concentration of a game situation.
- The batter can wait for the ball to approach the plate and bunt for a hit.

Common Errors:
- The batter attempts to bunt pitches that are not strikes.
- The batter does not decide before entering the batter's box which bunt to execute.

Modifications:
- For more advanced players, pitchers can throw a variety of pitches (curves, change-ups, and so forth).
- The coach can give signs to the batter, simulating a game situation.
- The coach can act as the pitcher.

- Advanced players may use pickoff plays in order to keep the base runners "honest."

Name: General Base Running Drill (see Figure A-47a-d)

Objective: To have players practice touching and rounding bases correctly. Also to condition players.

Suggested For: All skill levels.

Description: Players line up behind home plate. The first player in line assumes the hitting ready position in the batter's box and pretends to swing and hit a pitch. The player runs hard to first base as if trying to beat out an infield ground ball. As the first player touches first base, the next player swings and runs, and so on. After passing first base, the runners slow down, turn toward the foul line, and walk back to the end of the line. The next time through, each player will react as if hitting a single to the outfield. In successive rounds, each runner will "hit" a double and then a triple.

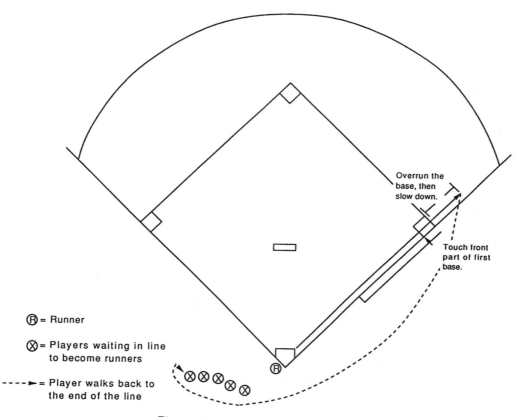

Figure A-47a. Running out an infield grounder.

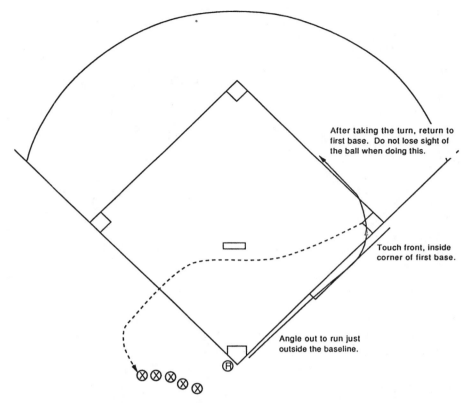

Figure A-47b. Running out a single to the outfield.

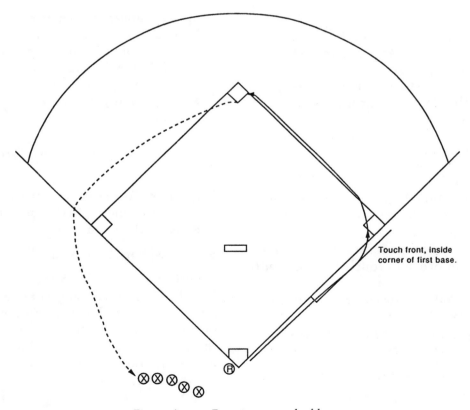

Figure A-47c. Running out a double.

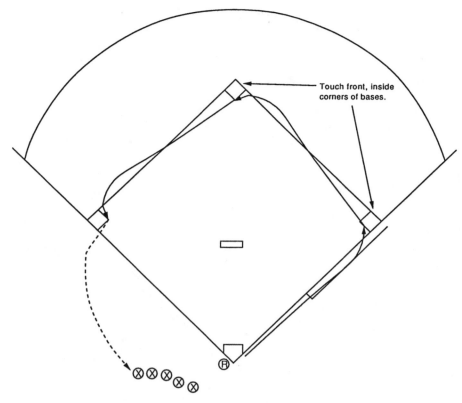

Figure A-47d. Running out a triple.

Key Elements:

- The run to first base is in foul territory.
- The bases are touched with the left foot, without slowing down.
- The runners should slow down gradually and return to the line without interfering with other runners.
- Base runners must use correct technique and simulate game speed!

Common Errors:

- Not allowing enough time between runners; the faster runners have to slow down or pass the slower runners.
- Slowing as the base is approached or taking small steps in order to touch the base with the left foot.
- Not running at full speed or running with the head down.
- Not concentrating on making changes when technique is incorrect.

Modifications:

- For less experienced players, the coach can walk the players through each step of the drill to familiarize them with the proper steps.
- More advanced players can do several repetitions for conditioning purposes.
- Traffic cones can be used as markers to direct the players in where to look, when to arc, and what path to take.

Name: Rounding First Base Drill (see Figure A-48)

Objective: To teach players the proper techniques for rounding first base. Also to emphasize taking the extra base whenever possible.

Suggested For: Players of all skill levels.

Description: This drill requires fielders at 1B, 2B, 3B, SS, one OF, and runners lined up behind home plate. The first runner assumes the hitting ready position in the batter's box. The coach hits a hard ground ball to the outfielder, who either fields the ball or purposely misplays it. When the ball is hit, the runner runs to first base and rounds the base. As the base is rounded, the runner locates the ball and reacts ac-

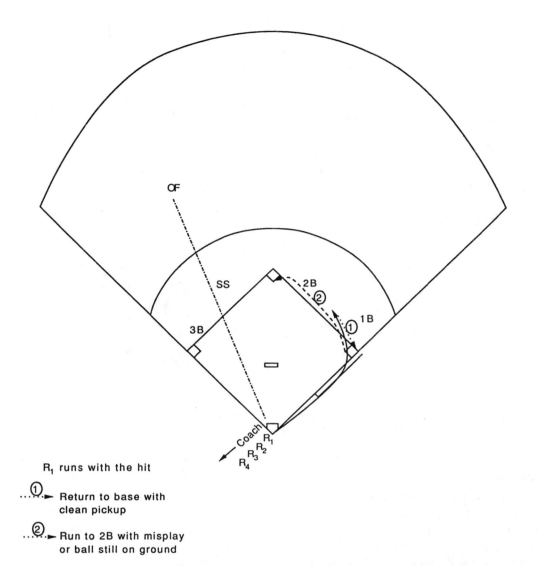

R₁ runs with the hit

① → Return to base with clean pickup

② → Run to 2B with misplay or ball still on ground

Figure A-48. Rounding first base drill.

cordingly. The runner should always expect a misplay! The second baseperson and shortstop work on the relay in the event the outfielder misses the ball.

Key Points:

- The initial step to first base is a crossover step.
- On the third step, the runner looks to locate the ball and begins an arc in order to round the base.
- Upon rounding the base, the runner must focus on the fielding action of the outfielder, always anticipating an error.

Common Errors:

- Running with the head down.

- Turning too wide after first base has been touched.
- Assuming the fielder will field the ball and not advancing on a misplayed ball.

Modifications:

- A full team can be put on the field to simulate game conditions.

Name: Lead Off and React Drill (see Figure A-49

Objective: To practice taking a good lead and reacting to batted balls or the catcher's actions.

Suggested For: All skill levels.

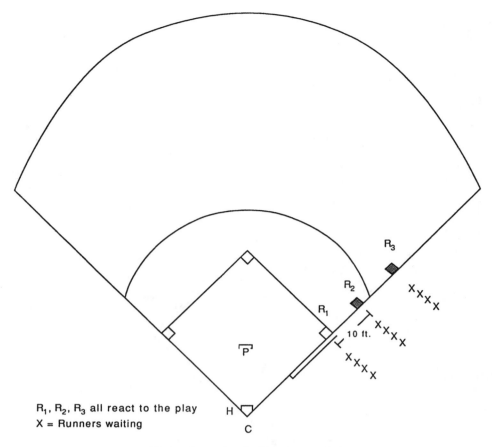

R₁, R₂, R₃ all react to the play
X = Runners waiting

Figure A-49. Lead off and react drill.

Description: This drill requires a pitcher, catcher, batter, and base runners with helmets. Base runners line up in foul ground behind first base or behind any of several extra bases spaced 10 feet or so apart down the first base line. With the pitcher working from the set position, the runners take a lead and on the pitch get their secondary lead. The hitter may (1) swing at the ball, (2) take the pitch, or (3) swing and miss. Runners break aggressively for second on ground balls or pitches that get away from the catcher. Infield fly balls send runners back to first, while fly balls to the outfield cause the runners to extend their lead halfway to second. Runners return to first if the batter swings and misses or takes the pitch. Once the runners react to a situation that gets them to second, they sprint to the end of their line and are replaced by the next person.

Key Points:
- Runners must focus on the action and react quickly and aggressively to whatever happens.
- They should anticipate advancing to second on every pitch.
- Pivots and crossover steps should be used when moving to a base.
- Each athlete should use the drill to learn their limits and so ensure correct reactions in games.

Common Errors:
- Runners go through the motions and lack intensity.
- Drill does not contain enough variety of action—ground balls, popups, fly balls, passed ball, wild pitches, blocked balls, and so on.
- Players do not use crossover steps in making a move to a base.

- Runners focus on the base and so lose sight of the ball.

Modifications:

- Tennis balls or rag balls can be used to do this drill indoors.
- Middle infielders may be added to the drill so that base runners may attempt steals.
- Someone can cover first so pickoffs can be practiced.
- A coach can be positioned in the box at third and steal signs can be given.

Name: Leading Off/Getting a Jump at First Base Drill (see Figure A-50)

Objective: To practice taking leads, reading situations, and getting a jump to steal second base.

Suggested For: All skill levels.

Description: This drill requires a pitcher, catcher, and a defender at first base plus runners with helmets. The base runners form a line in foul ground behind first base. One at a time, runners practice leading off first toward second. The pitcher works from the set position and may throw home or try a pick off move: If the pitcher throws home, the runner pivots on the right foot, takes a crossover step toward second, and returns to a squared up position facing home as the ball gets to the plate. (This is the "secondary" lead so essential to good, aggressive base running.) If the pitcher throws to first, the runner pivots on the left foot and gets back to first. If back in safely, the runner knows to extend the lead a bit; if tagged out, the runner shortens the lead. In any case, each runner learns the maximum lead to be taken. Once accomplishing this, the runner attempts to steal second. After making the steal attempt, the runner sprints to the end of the line and another player moves into position.

Key Points:

- The runner must concentrate on the pitcher's delivery.
- The runners should use pivots and crossover in going toward either base.

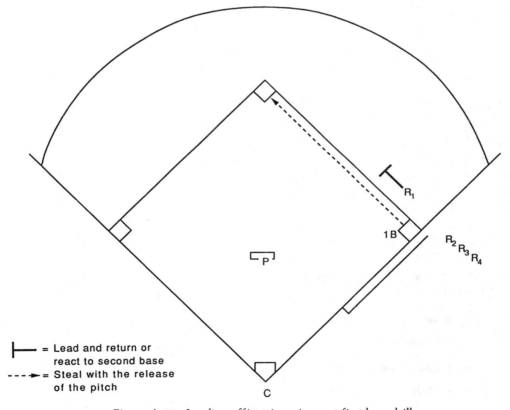

┣━ = Lead and return or react to second base
---▶ = Steal with the release of the pitch

Figure A-50. Leading off/getting a jump at first base drill.

Common Errors:

- Lack of concentration and intensity.
- Failing to react quickly to situations.
- Failing to use crossover steps in either getting the secondary lead or returning to first.
- Failing to get a good jump off of the base.

Modifications:

- Catcher may try pickoff throws.
- Coach may give steal signs from third base box.
- Players may practice delayed steals.
- Experienced players may work on diving back to the base.
- The drill may incorporate extra, temporary bases along the first base foul line and additional runners placed at them.

Name: Leading Off and Reacting at Other Bases Drill (see Figure A-51)

Objective: To practice taking a good lead and reacting aggressively to game situations at second and third bases.

Suggested For: All skill levels.

Description: This drill requires a pitcher, a catcher, a hitter, base runners with helmets at second and third, and a third base coach. (*Note:* For safety reasons, additional players waiting to run should line up in foul ground beyond first base.) The pitcher may use the full windup or work from the set position. The runners take leads on the pitch and establish their secondary leads. At second, the runner can take a longer lead and should be 4 to 6 feet behind the base line; at third, the runner takes a walking lead in foul ground The batter may (1) swing at the ball; (2) take the pitch; or (3) swing and miss. Runners break hard for the next base on batted ground balls or on pitches that get away from the catcher. Infield fly balls send runners back, while fly balls to the outfield cause them to tag up. (A runner at third always tags up and waits for the coach to call "Go." A player at second may tag up on balls hit to center or right field and watch the play develop; however, fly balls hit to left probably should cause the runner to advance halfway to third.) Runners return

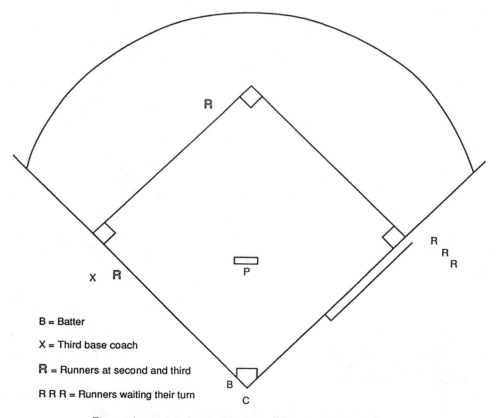

B = Batter

X = Third base coach

R = Runners at second and third

R R R = Runners waiting their turn

Figure A-51. Leading off and reacting at other bases drill.

to their bases if the batter takes the pitch or swings and misses. Once reacting to a situation and scoring, the runner from third sprints to the end of the line. Usually the runner from second advances as well, but if not the athlete moves up and is replaced by another.

Key Points:

- As in the drill done at first base, players focus on action and react aggressively, anticipate moving up on every pitch, and learn their limitations.

Common Errors:

- Lack of concentration and intensity.
- Failing to react quickly to situations.
- Failing to use crossover steps in either getting the secondary lead or returning to first.
- Failing to get a good jump off of the base.

Modifications:

- Use tennis or rag balls indoors.
- Add infielders to the drill so that the pitcher and catcher can practice pickoff plays and the infielders can work on coverages.

Name: Tag Up Drill (see Figure A-52)

Objective: To teach runners at third base to take a proper lead, to return to the base on a fly ball, and to break for home plate when the coach shouts, "Go!".

Suggested For: All skill levels.

Description: Two additional third bases are placed in foul territory in line with the original base. Three runners take their leads, and a coach or player acting as a coach takes position outside the last base. The coach hits a fly ball to the outfield. The runners tag up, face home, and on the command "Go!" all break for home.

Key Points:

- Lead off should be in foul territory.
- Players should not watch the catch. Rather they retouch the base by putting one foot firmly against the front edge of the bag and are prepared to push off aggressively on the command to "Go!"
- Runners must run at full speed.

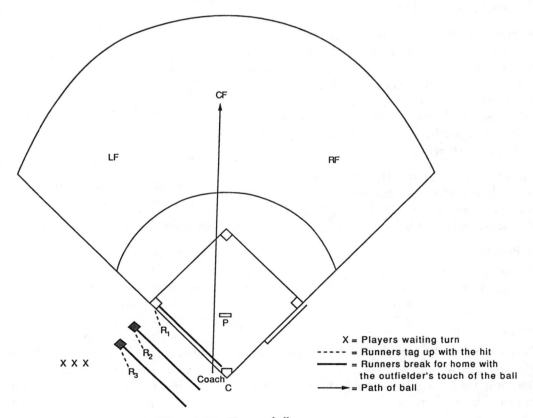

Figure A-52. Tag up drill.

Common Errors:

- Runners do not concentrate.
- Runners stand and watch outfield ball.
- Runners do not react at full speed.
- Runners lead off in fair territory, resulting in an out if hit by a batted ball.
- Runners leave the base too soon.
- Runners return to base, touch it, and run. They do not wait for the coach's signal.

Modifications:

- This drill can be done during batting practice with the runner reacting to a "real" batter.
- An indoor drill can be done with a coach using tennis balls to throw the fly balls.
- Outfielders can practice catching a fly ball and throwing it in one motion. The catcher can practice catching the outfield throw and tagging a runner.

Name: Finding Your Sliding Leg (see Figure A-53a and b)

Objective: To teach and reinforce correct sliding technique.

Suggested For: All skill levels.

Description: Players spread out in the practice area and support their body with their hands and feet, belly facing skyward. On a command from the coach, the players tuck one leg and settle to the ground. The leg that instinctively bends is generally the leg that bends when sliding. If either leg is comfortable, a bent left leg should be reinforced.

Caution: Do not allow the athletes to bridge or arch their backs, as these are contraindicated positions. See Chapter 26, Prevention of Injuries, Table 26-1, Activities 18 and 23.

Key Points:

- "Inverted" crab position should have chest parallel to the ground.
- The "straight" leg extends to the base.

Common Errors:

- Not snapping the bent leg under and kicking the straight leg out.
- Moving up to a sitting position as the leg tucks. Players should keep their head and shoulders back.

Figure A-53a. Three players ready to find their sliding leg.

Figure A-53b. Players showing the leg on which they likely will slide.

Modifications:

- Everyone sits on the ground with the legs extended. The players bend one leg under, then the other. The position that feels most comfortable should be used for sliding.

Name: Sliding Progression

Objective: To understand and learn the "figure 4" straight-in slide.

Suggested For: All Players.

Description: Once players know their sliding leg, they line up in a sliding area. The first player takes three steps and drops onto a sliding mat, bending the take-off leg and extending the other leg. The chin stays down and the hands move up. As the player progresses, more steps are added prior to the take-off. Eventually the players run the regulation distance to the base at full speed and slide on a sliding surface (cardboard; plastic tarp sprayed with silicone lubricant; or other smooth, slippery surface).

Key Elements:

- The hands are in the air rather than on the ground.
- The chin is on the chest.
- The runner should lean back on contact with the ground.

Common Errors:

- Taking too many steps too soon.
- Sitting up in the slide and jamming the knee into the ground.

Modifications:

- The runners can slide on a plastic sheet covered with water or on wet grass.
- The runners can wear football pants for added protection during the learning process.

Name: Relay Sliding (see Figure A-54)

Objective: To maximize the number of sliding repetitions and provide conditioning, while stressing the point that players should expect to slide at every base.

Suggested For: Players with intermediate sliding skills: those already able to slide.

Description: Athletes line up on the outfield side of first, facing second. On the coach's signal, the first player in line sprints for second base. Upon nearing the base, the athlete slides, touches the base, and gets up. The player immediately turns and returns to first. Again the runner slides when getting to the base. Once the first player in line touches the base, the second athlete takes off. The relay continues until everyone has gone through.

Key Points:

- Always expect to slide.
- Use correct mechanics in sliding.
- Slide too early rather than slide too near the bag.

Common Errors:

- Injuries result from sliding too late. Decide to slide early and do not change the decision.
- Player leaves too early on the relay "exchange."

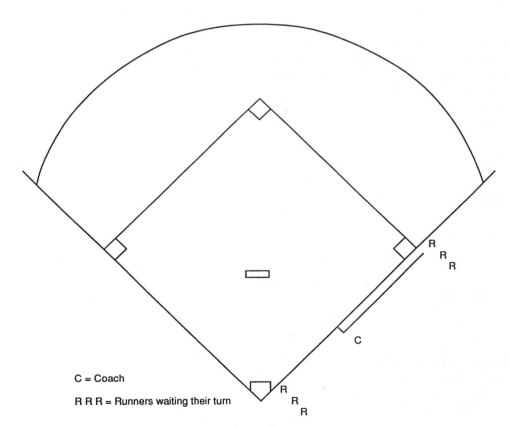

C = Coach

R R R = Runners waiting their turn

Figure A-54. Relay sliding competition.

- Player uses poor slide mechanics.

Modifications:

- Specific slides can be assigned: such as the figure-4 for less skilled athletes and fade away slides for those with more experience.
- A maximum time limit can be established: Everybody must complete in 2½ minutes.
- By using the set up shown in Figure A-54, the drill can be turned into a relay competition. Besides allowing more repetitions, this introduces an element of fun into practice.

Name: Rundown Drill (see Figure A-55)

Objective: To introduce and reinforce the fundamentals of a run down situation.

Suggested For: Intermediate and advanced players.

Description: Players work in groups of five on a pair of regulation bases. Two players are pri-

mary fielders, two are backup fielders, and one is the runner. Primary Player A starts with the ball visibly held high, calls the side of the baseline, and chases the runner toward the opposite base. If the runner cannot be tagged, primary Player B in front of the other base yells, "NOW!" in a timely manner. Player A snaps the ball to Player B who moves to the throw and immediately tags the runner. If the runner cannot be immediately tagged, Player B chases the runner back, Player A moves to become a backup player, and backup player 1 becomes a primary player.

Key Elements:

- The runner must wear a helmet.
- The action should take place at full speed with the runner trying to prolong the run down by avoiding the tag.
- The fielders must be positioned on the same side of the baseline, and the chaser must make the ball visible to the receiver.
- The receiver calls for the ball and moves into the throw.

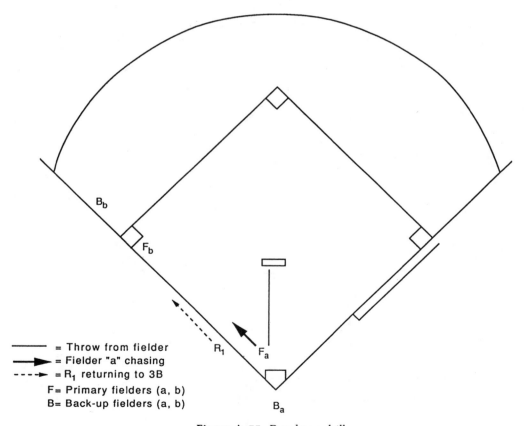

	= Throw from fielder
	= Fielder "a" chasing
	= R₁ returning to 3B
F=	Primary fielders (a, b)
B=	Back-up fielders (a, b)

Figure A-55. Rundown drill.

Common Errors:

- The players make too many throws; the receiver calls for the ball too soon and gives the runner time to change direction.
- The fielders are on opposite sides of the baseline causing the throw to cross the runner's path.
- The chaser hides the ball in the glove, and the receiver cannot see it. This wastes valuable time as the ball is moved into throwing position.

Modifications:

- Tennis balls can be used for less experienced players.
- A full infield and runner at third can be used. The coach hits a ground ball, and the runner on third breaks for home as the "batter" runs to first base. The defense runs down the player breaking from third and prevents the batter from reaching second base.
- Less experienced players can initially be walked through the rundown.

Index